ECONOMICS for BUSINESS

Pearson
Education

We work with leading authors to develop the
strongest educational materials in economics,
bringing cutting-edge thinking and best learning
practice to a global market.

Under a range of well-known imprints, including
Financial Times Prentice Hall, we craft high quality
print and electronic publications which help
readers to understand and apply their content,
whether studying or at work.

To find out more about the complete range of our
publishing please visit us on the World Wide Web at:
www.pearsoneduc.com

ECONOMICS for BUSINESS

Competition, Macro-stability and Globalisation

Dermot McAleese

Trinity College Dublin

FINANCIAL TIMES
Prentice Hall

An imprint of Pearson Education

Harlow, England · London · New York · Reading, Massachusetts · San Francisco · Toronto · Don Mills, Ontario · Sydney
Tokyo · Singapore · Hong Kong · Seoul · Taipei · Cape Town · Madrid · Mexico City · Amsterdam · Munich · Paris · Milan

Pearson Education Limited
Edinburgh Gate
Harlow
Essex CM20 2JE
England

and Associated Companies throughout the world

Visit us on the World Wide Web at:
http://www.pearsoneduc.com

First published under the Prentice Hall Europe imprint 1997
Second edition 2001

© Pearson Education Limited 2001

ISBN 0 273 64622 2

British Library Cataloguing-in-Publication Data
A catalogue record for this book is available from the British Library

Library of Congress Cataloging-in-Publication Data
McAleese, Dermot.
    Economics for business: competition, macro-stability, and globalisation /
Dermot McAleese. – 2nd ed.
        p.cm.
    Includes bibliographical references and index.
    ISBN 0-273-64622-2 (alk. paper)
    1. Managerial economics. I. Title

    HD30.22.M29 2001
    330'.024'658–dc21   00-068103

10 9 8 7 6 5 4 3 2
06 05 04 03 02

Typeset by 4
Printed and bound in Great Britain by Henry Ling Ltd., at the Dorset Press,
Dorchester, Dorset

BRIEF CONTENTS

CONTENTS

Part III The global economy

PREFACE to second edition

This second edition updates tables and data, improves presentation and introduces new material to cover recent developments in the world economy. Among many changes, the analysis of privatisation and regulation has been extended, account has been taken of the establishment of the euro and the European Central Bank; and a new chapter on labour migration has been added.

My sincere thanks to Ruth Gill (Trinity College Dublin) and Dominic Burke (School of Business, Institute of Technology, Carlow) who provided the bulk of the research work in preparing new material, updating tables and making suggestions for improvement. Suzanne O'Neill (Trinity College Dublin) generously provided economics and computing expertise throughout the period of revision as well as acting as a marvellous sounding board for new ideas.

Professor Jacob Kol (Erasmus University, Rotterdam) provided intellectual stimulus and made numerous detailed suggestions for which I am profoundly grateful. Professors David Barrows and Farrokh Zandi (Schulich School of Business, York University, Toronto) wrote a penetrating critique of the macro section of the book, which I have taken as guide in revising Part II and some of Part III. Dr Ciara Whelan (University College Dublin) helped to revise Box 6.2. Dr Andrew Somerville (Trinity College Dublin) and Moore McDowell (University College Dublin) permitted me to draw on recent research to update Boxes 4.1 and 20.3 respectively. I am indebted to Dr John Gallivan for incisive comments on Chapters 9 and 10 and to Professors Ian Jackson (The Business School, Staffordshire University) and Robert Alexander (University of Otago, New Zealand) for suggestions and encouragement. Dr Nagendra Chowdary and Mr Rajesh Tharyan (IIS Institute of Management, Kochi) pointed out errors in the text and helped to improve the questions and exercises. I am indebted to the publisher's three anonymous referees for specific advice on the second edition.

Participants in MBA and executive courses in Trinity College and in different parts of the world have been enormously helpful in drawing my attention to mistakes and ambiguities. I have gratefully incorporated their suggestions into this revised text. I am deeply grateful to them all and ask their pardon for not naming them individually.

Finally, I wish to thank Paula Harris and Paula Parish at Pearson Education for encouragement and support at every stage of this second edition, and Jasmina Behan (Trinity College, Dublin) for her expert assistance with corrections and proof reading.

Dermot McAleese
Trinity College, Dublin, August 2000
www.tcd.ie/economics/staff/dermot_mcaleese.htm

PREFACE to first edition

Economics is an integral part of the curriculum for graduate and undergraduate business programmes. Most MBA courses contain several economics modules, as do professional courses in banking, insurance, actuarial science and information technology. *Economics for Business* has been written to provide a considered, comprehensive, yet accessible introduction to economics to accompany such courses. It is designed as a self-contained unit. No previous background in economics is assumed. This book is addressed to the many individuals both inside and outside the classroom who want to understand the workings of a modern economy. It describes and analyses the external economic environment for business.

Although there are many good introductory economics texts, I have found that none quite matches the needs of the many MBA and 'economics for business' modules that I have taught over the past twenty years. The standard economics text is over-inclusive in some respects – for example, in the treatment of consumer choice theory. But it is not comprehensive enough in other respects – for example, in explaining interest rates or the determinants of exchange rates, which are central issues in a business-oriented economics course. Also, some texts tend to talk down to students in a way that is alienating to mature students with years of work experience. I suspect I am not the only lecturer in these circumstances who has had to rely on a mixture of extracts from textbooks, own notes and readings from diverse sources. Apart from being inconvenient, this expedient makes it difficult for students to get a proper overview of economics. As a result, the class derives less benefit from studying the subject than they should. (And the study of economics can and should be a pleasurable as well as an instructive experience; its description as 'the dismal science' is thoroughly undeserved.) Also, the lack of a single textbook means that colleagues providing related courses find it hard to ascertain exactly what material I have covered. This problem becomes particularly acute when, as is the case in business programmes, one's colleagues come from different disciplines.

Hence my motivation to write this book. By being specially tailored for a business-oriented audience, I hope that it will make the economics module in a business or professional programme a more instructive and enjoyable experience for students and lecturers alike.

What this book offers

The book examines economics from a *business perspective*. We focus on concepts and information which are helpful in understanding economic performance and policy. The book is especially concerned with the interaction between business and practical economic problems. We pay attention to points of overlap and contrast between economics and other business subjects such as accountancy, strategic management and marketing.

Economic textbooks cover subjects that currently concern economists. They provide a snapshot of where economics is, without enquiring too much about whether this is a useful place to be. *Economics for Business* is *selective*. Subjects are included because they throw light on issues relevant to business. Business has to operate in an economic environment that has become vastly more competitive, more open in terms of foreign trade, investment and capital markets, and where government support to business has become more targeted and results-oriented.

Within this context, the book aims to provide a *comprehensive overview* of the three branches of economics essential to business: the economics of the market system and competition, macroeconomics, and international trade and exchange rates. Managerial economics textbooks cover microeconomic aspects, and some textbooks address macroeconomic issues from a business point of view. This book covers both micro- and macro-topics. Most important of all, it extends the analysis to take account of the increased openness and globalisation of the economy. This means addressing trade liberalisation, economic integration and exchange rates, subjects on which every business reader needs to be well informed.

The style is non-technical and down to earth. We rely on words and diagrams to convey the message, and avoid equations. For students with a technical background who wish to probe deeper into the subject, there are references to more advanced literature at the end of each chapter.

This book gives an insight into the *origin of contemporary economic ideas*. Economic ideas do not spring from the air. They are inspired by particular economic and social events and perspectives. Further, economic ideas change. They are not set down in tablets of stone. Particular attention is given to changing ideas about competition and the market system, the need for a stable macro-economic framework and the benefits of a global trade system.

Many business people believe that *economic forecasting* is a core competence of economics. Economists are probably better at economic prediction than anyone else, but their record of economic forecasting has been unimpressive. This book provides an insight into the economic analysis underlying economic forecasts so that the reader can evaluate these forecasts and understand how they are formulated.

Some people find economics an infuriatingly elusive subject. Business readers often start by expecting much more precision from the subject than it can honestly provide. The questions are simple:

- How does the market system work?
- How do firms maximise profits in an open market? What should their pricing strategy be?
- What role should government play in a modern economy?

- What determines interest rates?
- What role do central banks play in the economy?
- How can we moderate business fluctuations?
- What is the balance of payments, and why is it important?
- Why do exchange rates fluctuate so much?
- What can be done to speed up economic growth?

The answers are complex – usually of the 'it all depends' type – because the issues are complex. Economics is not a body of laws, but is rather a way of thinking. Only ideologues claim otherwise. Students appreciate this. In my experience, they are not afraid of complexity and do not want facile answers. They would like to know enough economic theory to make their own assessment of economic policies, without having to go through long disquisitions about the finer points of the subject. This book strikes a *balance between the theory and practice of economics*.

What the reader should learn

Having read this book, the reader should have acquired an understanding of:

1. How the economy functions, how resources are allocated and how income distribution is determined.
2. The analytical basis of economic policy decisions and economic forecasts.
3. The role of government in the economy, both at the sectoral and firm level and at the broader macroeconomic level.
4. The linkages between economics and other subjects on a business programme.
5. The basic vocabulary of economics and its intellectual origins.

To check their understanding, readers should study the Questions for Discussion and Exercises at the conclusion of each chapter. This can be done individually or in groups.

Plan of the book

Our starting point is a discussion of economic policies (Chapter 1) and the causes of economic growth (Chapter 2). The latter topic is often omitted from business economics courses which is a pity, given the practical, as well as academic, importance of growth. This chapter sketches arguments, concepts and points of view, which are elaborated later in the book.

Following the introductory chapters, Part I provides an analysis of competition and the market system, with discussion of the role of markets, determinants of demand and supply, the role of the firm and how its pricing and output decisions are made, the effects of competition and privatisation on economic performance and the reasons why government intervenes in the economy. This part helps us understand why economic policy has become more focused on using the market system to achieve objectives.

Part II provides an overview of modern macroeconomics. It explains why price stability and budgetary restraint are important policy objectives, how these objectives can best be achieved and how the resulting policy decisions affect business. Interest rates, the central bank and fiscal policy enter into consideration here. We explain why rising public debt is a major source of concern to business in many countries. Unemployment and business fluctuations are also discussed.

Part III examines the role of foreign trade, the increasing globalisation of investment, the expansion of capital flows (reflected in the growth of derivatives trading) and labour migration. The balance of payments and exchange rates are discussed. Special attention is given to proposals for Economic and Monetary Union (EMU) in Europe, which, will have major implications for business.

Appreciation

This book is written by a single author, but many people have helped to bring it to its present stage. An author of a textbook must rely on criticism and conversation if mistakes are to be avoided. 'It is astonishing what foolish things one can temporarily believe if one thinks too long alone,' as Keynes remarked in the Preface to the *General Theory*, 'particularly in economics where it is often impossible to bring one's ideas to a conclusive test either formal or experimental.' I owe a great deal to colleagues in the economics department and business school at Trinity College Dublin, and elsewhere, and to interactions and conversations with business people in Ireland and abroad.

I am particularly grateful to Professor Alan Matthews (Trinity College Dublin) and Dr Suman Modwel (MIB, Paris), who commented on Part III; to Professor Kieran Kennedy (Economic and Social Research Institute, Dublin) who reviewed Part II; Dr Francis O'Toole read most of the chapters in Part I and saved me from numerous errors, as well as directing me to useful literature. John Martin (OECD) commented with great perception on draft chapters and allowed me to draw upon his prodigious wealth of knowledge of economic theory and policy. Professor John Bristow gave generous advice on the subjects of fiscal policy and on the role of government intervention. Paul Coughlan, Director of the Trinity MBA programme and Lucas Professor of Industrial Management, gave me the benefit of his erudition in drafting Chapter 5. Professor W. (Billy) Kingston made helpful suggestions for improving Chapter 7 and advised me of the relevance of the Schumpeterian approach to modern business. Dr Paul Walsh provided valuable comments on the chapter on unemployment. I also had helpful conversations with Dr Andrew Burke (now of the University of St. Andrews), John Fahey, Anne Keegan, Professor Antoin Murphy, Dr P. Waldron and Eric Strobl. I have drawn inspiration from exchange of views on economic issues over many years with Dr Sean Barrett and Professor John O'Hagan.

Dr John Gallivan kindly provided valuable feedback on several chapters, allowing me to draw on his extensive expertise as a petroleum consultant.

Special thanks are due to Dr Marius Brulhart (Trinity College Dublin) who was involved in the book literally from day one, and who commented in depth on practically the entire manuscript. He was a resourceful, searching and yet ever-encouraging critic and helped to the point of virtual co-authorship in drafting several chapters.

I also owe thanks to a changing roster of students who sacrificed their summer vacation to assist with this book: Michelle Boylan, Gareth Davis, Caoimhe Donnelly, Patricia Dowling, Fiona Hayes and Muireann Kelliher. Mary O'Donnell read a number of chapters and redrafted others. Ciara Whelan kindly supplied material for Chapter 6. Cathy Lennon, Orla Sheehan and Maura Walsh provided encouragement and support at every stage of the project, for which I am most grateful. The assistance of Oorla Gallagher, Brian Corduff, Sylvia Charmant, Paolo Figini, Justin Spain, Lisa Weston and David Unger is also acknowledged.

This book has grown out of lectures to various graduate courses, executive seminars and undergraduate programmes in Trinity College Dublin, the Irish Management Institute, the graduate school of the International Business (MIB) programme at the Ecole Nationale des Ponts et Chaussées, Paris, and associate courses in Cujo, Argentina and Cochin, India. The enthusiasm, commitment and probing questions of the participants in these courses have been a source of inspiration to me for many years.

The staff at Prentice Hall, in particular acquisitions editor, Tony Johnston, and production editor, Jill Birch, and her team, including the anonymous readers, were unfailingly helpful and a source of many improvements. Finally my thanks to Camilla for her extensive editorial advice and support, and to Emma and Susannah for their patience.

Dermot McAleese
Trinity College, Dublin, 1995

ACKNOWLEDGEMENTS

We are grateful to the following for permission to reproduce copyright material:

Figure 3.2 from Smith, S. (1986) *Britain's Shadow Economy* (Oxford, Clarendon Press), reproduced by permission of Oxford University Press; Table 4.2 from Falvey, R.E. and Gemmell, R. 'Are services income-elastic? Some new evidence', *Review of Income and Wealth*, University of Nottingham, September 1996; Case Study 5.1 from P. Milgrom and J. Roberts, 'Applying the MR rule within a vertically integrated firm', *Economics, Organisation and Management* (Prentice Hall Inc, Upper Saddle River, NJ, 1992); Tables 6.3, 6.4 and 6.6 from *The European Observatory for SMEs Fifth Annual Report* (1997), reproduced by permission of EIM Small Business Research and Consultancy, Zoetermeer, The Netherlands; Box 6.3 from Whelan, C. and Walsh, P.P., 'Loss-leading and price intervention: welfare outcomes in a second best world', *The International Review of Law and Economics*, 19 (3), 1999; extracts used in Case Study 6.1 and Box 7.2 from *The Economist* (various dates); Box 10.1 from Gray, A. (1995) *EU Structural Funds and Other Public Investments: A guide to evaluation methods* (Dublin, Gill & Macmillan); Figure 12.2 from Barro, J. and Grilli, V. (1994) *European Macroeconomics* (Macmillan Press), reproduced with permission of Palgrave; Figure 17.4 from Porter, M. (1990) *The Competitive Advantage of Nations* (adapted with the permission of The Free Press, a Division of Simon & Schuster, Inc. © 1990, 1998 Michael E. Porter); Box 17.5 from Blinder, A.S. (1989) *Macroeconomics Under Debate* (Hemel Hempstead, Harvester Wheatsheaf), originally published in *American Economic Review*, May 1998; Table 18.3 from Dunning, J.H. (1993) *The Globalisation of Business* (London, Routledge); Box 20.4 from Krugman, S. (1994) *The Age of Diminished Expectations* (Cambridge, Mass, MIT Press); Figure 22.3 from 'Dollar hits record low as Japan and US fail to halt slide', © *Financial Times*, 4 April, 1995.

Whilst every effort has been made to trace the owners of copyright material, in a few cases this has proved impossible and we take this opportunity to offer our apologies to any copyright holders whose rights we have unwittingly infringed.

Chapter 1

THE ECONOMIC POLICY CONSENSUS

Introduction

Economic policies throughout the world have converged around three basic principles:

1. There is increasing emphasis on *using market mechanisms* to achieve objectives rather than supplanting them with state intervention.

2. Macroeconomic policy is now oriented more to ensuring *a stable economic framework* rather than achieving proactive counter-cyclical targets or national plan growth rates and investment targets.

3. National policies have become *more outward-looking*, as evidenced by the successful completion of the Uruguay Round, the steadily increasing membership of the World Trade Organisation (WTO), the relaxation of controls on capital mobility and the globally more benign stance towards foreign investment.

The new policy consensus has evolved not because the principles of economics have changed, but because over time we have learned more about the inferences that can be drawn from them. Accompanying this consensus are new policy priorities, which are having a major impact on global standards of living, income distribution and lifestyles.

The global reach of the new economic consensus is its most remarkable characteristic. In Europe and North America, the key turning points were the policy reforms of Prime Minister Thatcher and President Reagan in the first half of the 1980s. New Zealand and Australia developed even more radical pro-market policies. In South America, dramatic policy initiatives were taken in Chile during the 1980s, and Chile's example was followed by Bolivia, Mexico, Colombia, Argentina and Brazil. In Asia, India embraced a reform package in the early 1990s which focused on a more intensive use of market incentives in domestic labour and product markets, openness to trade and foreign investment, and fiscal stability. China too has become more conscious of the need to use market mechanisms. Throughout Eastern Europe and the former Soviet Union, policy-makers have turned away from economic planning and price controls, and are searching for ways of making their markets function more efficiently, through privatisation programmes, market flexibility measures, competition policy and more enterprise-friendly tax regimes.

These policy changes are having a profound effect on the business environment. In this chapter we present a brief sketch of what the new economic consensus is, why it has evolved and what its likely future impact will be on the economy.

1.1 The new economic policy consensus

Competition and the market system

The first pillar of the new consensus concerns the role of the market system and competition in ensuring that the economy operates effectively. One manifestation of the new policy is the movement towards 'smaller' government. The share of government spending in Gross National Product (GNP) in most industrial countries lies in the range 40–50 per cent, apart from Japan and the United States (US) where it is under 40 per cent. Prior to the First World War, government spending was typically below 20 per cent of GNP. Governments with high spending ratios began to query if they were getting value for money and concluded that they were not. They responded by introducing programmes of privatisation and deregulation, two hallmarks of the new policy orientation. Also, the public sector was subjected to market-type disciplines through tendering, charging for public services, contracting out of services and extension of managerial accountability to government departments. Market mechanisms are being used in preference to regulation as a way of achieving policy objectives. For example, instead of prohibiting pollution by rules, environmental policy applies the 'polluter pays' principle, whereby polluters are taxed according to the amount of pollution they create. The price mechanism replaces legal and administrative hassle as the means of achieving the desired reduction in pollution.

As we shall see, markets perform efficiently only if there is competition. In many countries, competition law is being strengthened and its range of application extended to hitherto protected sectors in telecommunications, transport, energy and postal services. Tendering for public contracts has become open to foreign as well as to domestic firms. Trade unions also have found their monopoly power challenged. There is an emphasis on labour market flexibility as being the way to solve the unemployment problem. Capital markets too have been affected by the new thinking. The markets have been liberalised and long-established distortions between different types of financial institutions are being removed.

Policy-makers have also become more conscious of the distortionary effects of the tax system on the behaviour of economic 'agents' in their role as buyers and sellers, savers and investors, employers and employees. High marginal tax rates tend to blunt economic incentives, as well as being complicated and unfair. Greater tax uniformity and tax 'neutrality' between different types of economic activity have become important fiscal objectives in many countries. Enterprise is being subjected to fewer regulations and lower tax rates. The buzz-word is 'enterprise-friendly environment'. But business beware! Enterprise-friendly does

Box 1.1

The new consensus

1. Competition and the market system

- Pro-competition policies
- Labour market flexibility
- Privatisation
- De-regulation
- Enterprise-friendly environment

2. Macro-stability

- Price stability (independent central bank, 'hard' exchange rate)
- Budget balance
- Control of government spending

3. Globalisation of business

- Free trade
- Foreign investment
- Liberalisation of capital
- Labour mobility

not mean friendly to all enterprises. The new environment is decidedly *un*friendly to state enterprises that were once sheltered from private sector competition and to national enterprises exposed to competition from low-cost competitors. 'Friendly' has to be interpreted in a Darwinian sense.

Macroeconomic stability

In macroeconomic policy there has also been a marked shift in orientation. During the 1990s, many countries identified price stability as a key objective. Central banks were given the responsibility for keeping inflation at bay and legislation was enacted in many countries to ensure that the monetary authorities have the degree of independence from political control needed to carry out their remit. Some smaller countries have tied their currencies to larger, low-inflation currencies as a way of maintaining price stability. Argentina has chosen to align the peso to the US dollar, for example, and many European countries have tied their exchange rate to the euro for this reason.

Together with prioritising inflation, another key element in a macro-stability package is a commitment to low budget deficits. Fiscal policy in the 1990s in Europe, for example, was dominated by the Maastricht criteria – conditions which countries must satisfy as a condition of membership of the single currency. One of these criteria stipulates that government borrowing should not exceed 3 per cent of a country's national output, a limit that continues to be imposed on those countries that participate in the euro. Many countries outside Western Europe embarked on stabilisation and structural adjustment programmes which incorporated fiscal 'balance' (i.e. low budget deficits and declining debt relative to national output) as a key objective. Even the Scandinavian countries, once regarded as enthusiastic practitioners of counter-cyclical policies, became converts to a more cautious and conservative use of fiscal instruments. The spectre of ageing populations and unfunded entitlement programmes have combined to make governments more concerned about the future viability of public finances.

The objective of macro-stability cannot be divorced from the problem of unemployment. A central tenet of the new consensus is that better control of government finances will stimulate private investment and help to reduce unemployment. Reduction in public spending creates space for tax reductions. Tax reductions reduce disincentives to work and to hire employees. In addition, low inflation helps employees reach more rational decisions about pay. Macro-stability is an effective means of achieving sustained growth.

Global trade in goods, services and factors of production

The liberalisation of international transactions is the third pillar of the new policy consensus. The catchword *globalisation* has been coined to describe this process. Having tried import-substitution policies, many countries concluded that they are of limited value and that openness was a superior policy. Since the 1980s, a virtual revolution in trade policy has taken place, as one country after another liberalised its trade regime. Over 130 countries have signed up to membership of the World Trade Organisation. Developing countries are now active participants in the movement towards a more liberal world trading system. Although having a per capita income only 10 per cent that of the United States, Mexico voluntarily concluded a free trade area agreement with the United States and Canada.

Likewise, the Central European countries have concluded free trade agreements with the European Union (EU). Turkey's low per capita income has not prevented it from forming a customs union with the EU. Although wedded for many decades to the idea of self-sufficiency, China has applied for membership of the WTO and has indicated its readiness to abide by the liberal trade rules of that organisation. In the early 1990s, India too abandoned its *dirigiste* policies and replaced them with trade liberalisation and a more open door policy to foreign investment. Further liberalisation of international transactions has been effected through regional integration initiatives in Asia, Latin America and, more tentatively, in Africa. Most countries have abandoned the idea of development through intensive cultivation of the domestic market and have replaced it with the ambition of penetrating foreign markets and of achieving growth through exports.

The three elements of the new policy package are interdependent. The logic of the package was described by Professor Jeffrey Sachs in the context of Poland's stabilisation plan in the late 1980s:

> The basic goal was to move from a situation of extreme shortages and hyperinflation to one of supply-and-demand balance and stable prices. For this, Poland needed tight macroeconomic policies with the decontrol of prices. To have a working price system, Poland needed competition. To have competition it needed free international trade. ... To have free trade it needed not only low tariffs, but the convertibility of currency. To have convertibility of currency at a stable exchange rate, it needed monetary discipline and a realistic exchange rate.[1]

This logic underpinned the 1990 Balcerowitz Plan, which guided Poland's successful, if by no means painless, transformation from socialism to capitalism during the 1990s. The changed perception of what makes economies prosperous has influenced economic policy in a way and to a degree which has had momentous consequences for firms, individuals and the state itself.

1.2 Why policy has changed

Economic policy changes in response to the perceived failure of past policies. Up to the 1970s, it seemed that Russia and the other socialist economies were performing well – even outpacing many Western countries. At the same time, activist government policies were thought to have been instrumental in setting many industrial countries on a more stable and rapid growth path than ever before. That perception changed after the oil price increases and the resultant slowdown in growth. The first reason for the change in policy, therefore, was the deterioration in the industrial countries' economic performance.

Second, the socialist model lost prestige. The poor record of achievement of the socialist countries gradually became apparent. Even benign versions of socialism, such as the justly admired social market economy of Scandinavia, began to run into difficulties.

Third, the economic success of East Asia contrasted with the economic decline of Africa and Latin America. While the reasons for the former's success continue to be debated, and the currency crisis of 1997–98 removed some of the gloss on the region's 'success', the key factor in Asia's superior performance was the adoption of more liberal economic policies. For many developing countries wedded to an interventionist policy regime, the 1980s was a 'lost decade' – 'lost' because zero or even negative growth per person was achieved in that period. Reviewing the many conflicting explanations for India's 'dismal' economic performance since the 1960s, Professor Balusubramanyam concluded:

> The interventionist economic regime, with import substitution and self-sufficiency as its objectives, is largely responsible for India's poor economic performance.[2]

Fourth, developments in economic theory showed how even the best-intentioned government intervention tended to create distortions in the system, which could be even more damaging than the faults in the private sector market it was designed to correct. This is called the problem of 'government failure'.

---

1 Jeffrey Sachs, *Poland's Jump to the Market Economy* (Cambridge, MA: MIT Press, 1993), p. 54.
2 V.N. Balusubramanyam, 'India's trade policy review', *The World Economy* (special issue 1995), p. 80.

Furthermore, new ways of measuring the gains from foreign trade revealed the important benefits to be derived from economies of scale and competition. The potential benefits of fiscal consolidation on growth were also found to be greater than once expected. Generally, countries that placed higher priority on market incentives, macro-stability and freer trade performed better.

Practical experience and theoretical developments therefore conjoined to induce governments to undertake a radical review of their economic policies. Out of this review, which extended over two decades, came the economic policy programmes now being adopted in more and more countries in both the developed and the developing worlds.

1.3 Implications for the future

This change in policy regime will have, and is having, major implications for the business environment and living standards. Its long-term effects are as yet a matter of speculation. For firms, it will mean widening opportunities, but less safety, as the domestic market becomes more exposed to competition. For employees, it will mean higher productivity and higher salaries for those able to adjust to the new system. Advocates of the new policy regime claim that economies adopting it will grow faster as a result.

Alongside this, there may be less job security. Governments will be smaller and safety nets less generous and less encompassing. Within developed countries, there may well be a widening gap between rich and poor; something that is evident in the most advanced market economies in the reform league, such as the UK and the US. The new policy regime will force the labour market to be more flexible and, in the process, will remove some of the major causes of unemployment in Europe. At a global level, trade and capital flows are likely to bring about continuing shifts in global economic power. China and India, with a combined population of 2 billion, appear to be well placed to benefit from the changing economic environment. Radical reforms implemented in Latin America and elsewhere during the past decade are already having a profound impact on the way their ecomomies are performing.

The new policy consensus involves losers as well as gainers. The gainers are likely to be far more numerous than the losers but this does not rule out the possibility of temporary backlashes such as witnessed at the Seattle trade conference in December 1999 and, before that, during the Asian curreny crisis 1997–98. Alongside this, there will be ongoing debate about the precise con-stellation of new consensus policies to adopt. The contest between the European labour market model (with its emphasis on job security, decent holidays and partnership) and the US model (emphasising low taxes, labour mobility) will feature prominently in this debate. Policy reform is based on ideas both about the causes of growth and the link between economic growth an economic policy. It is precisely the existence of such a link that makes economics an important subject for a business-oriented reader, and that makes the study of the principles on which economic policy is based an essential element in any business studies programme.

1.4 Will the consensus last?

The new consensus consists of an integrated and coherent set of policies that promise to engender better economic perfomance than the policies of the past. A vast amount of research has been devoted to measuring the impact of the new policy menu on economic performance. The results of this research suggest that the impact, to date, is generally positive. Free trade and globalisation has generated more jobs and higher incomes than protection and inward-looking policies. Countries that restrained inflation and controlled goverment spending have tended to perform better than average. Emphasis on competition and the market system paid dividends in terms of more efficient enterprises and more effective achievement of government objectives.

Economic policies, however, are means to an end and not sacrosanct in themselves. The new consensus will last only so long as it delivers on its promise. Clearly it has done much for the developed countries of Western Europe and North America. (The case of New Zealand, an early and radical proponent of new consensus policies, where economic growth remains sluggish and where social cohesion has been damaged by excessive income disparities, is, however, a worrying exception.) A key issue will be the capacity of the new consensus policies to provide convincing outcomes for developing countries. These countries comprise some eighty per cent of the world population. Most of them have changed policy orientation but still await a level of payback that the general public will find convincing. India and Morocco are two cases in point. The 'right' things appear to have been done but their inhabitants remain poor and growth is modest relative to aspirations. Among developing countries, while there is acceptance that the old policies were ineffective, there is continuing scepticism about whether the new policies will produce any markedly better outcome. To ensure that this scepticism is proved unjustified will require (a) concentration on the correct sequencing of new consensus policies, (b) attention to income distribution, (c) acceptance that economic reforms must be applied consistently and take time to bear fruit, and (d) international cooperation and increased aid.

Threats to the new consensus have come and gone during the 1990s. A succession of financial crises in Mexico, East Asia, Russia and Brazil, cast doubt on the benefits of one element in the packages – free capital mobility – as well as underlining the vulnerability of open, competitive economies to changes in 'market sentiment'. To date, most economies have managed to survive these traumas. The advent of a financial crisis occurring at the heart of the Western economy, leading to a stock market collapse, would be more serious. Were it to be combined with simultaneous problems in the form of oil price increases and general economic downturns, the attractions of globalisation, competition and price stability could easily pall. This does not necessarily imply a reversion to the failed economic policies of yore but rather a move towards a more moderated and circumspect approach to the implementation of the new consensus among the unconverted, and less enthusiasm for deepening global integration in the West. In the event of the market being seen to fail either because of its inability to provide solid advances for the poor or because of the abuse of wealth and monopoly power against weaker sections of the community, a return towards more pervasive state intervention could not be ruled out. We must hope, however, that the mistakes of the past arising from excessive use of government will not be repeated.

✔ Summary

1. A new policy consensus has swept through the global economy. Its three principles centre on the importance of competition and market incentives, macroeconomic stability and global integration. The more enthusiastic advocates of the new policies include such geographically and culturally diverse nations as Argentina, Australia, Chile, the Czech Republic, Malaysia, New Zealand and Singapore. In Western Europe, the UK has been a leader, but its example is being followed with varying degrees of enthusiasm by mainland Europe. Since Ronald Reagan's term of office, the US has espoused and promulgated the new economic doctrines.

2. The new economic policy regime has important implications for business. It has tended to bring lower taxes and a more supportive, pro-business and pro-entrepreneurial climate. On the negative side, from the point of view of the individual firm, it has also meant greater exposure to domestic and foreign competition, and less security. Individuals, too, have had to adjust to a more cut-throat economic climate, with substantial rewards for the successful and less comfort for the unsuccessful. There is some evidence that the change in policy has stimulated faster growth, but it is too early to be certain. But policy-makers around the world are increasingly convinced that the new policy regime, based on textbook economic principles, offers the best prospect of prosperity.

❓ Questions for discussion

1. Outline the three pillars of the new economic consensus. Show how policy changes along new consensus lines can lead to better economic performance.

2. A feature of the modern economy is the growing share of the services sector in national production (e.g. financial services, recreation, information technology and communication). Discuss how the services sector has been affected by the three main elements of the new policy consensus in terms of the exposure of services to more domestic competition and market forces, to greater openness to foreign competition and a context of low inflation.

3. Is the new economic policy consensus likely to last? What factors might tend to undermine it?

☞ Exercises

1. Outline the contemporary economic policy stance in a country such as the UK and indicate how closely it approximates the prescriptions of the new policy consensus.

2. How does economic policy change impact on business? Why should a student of business take a course on economics?

3. List four questions about the economy and economic policy that you would like to have answered in an introductory course on economics such as this.

📖 Further reading

A landmark study of the case for an open trading system was the *World Bank Development Report* (Washington, DC: World Bank, 1987). Robert Skidelsky's *The World after Communism* (London: Macmillan, 1995) offers an accessible, brief advocacy of the potential benefits of a free market regime. The intellectual high priest of the free market is F.A. Hayek, a prolific author and Nobel prize-winner; *The Fatal Conceit: The errors of socialism* (London: Routledge, 1989) gives the flavour of his work. David Henderson's *The Changing Fortunes of Economic Liberalism* (London: Institute of Economic Affairs, 1999) puts the new consensus into historical focus and assesses its durability. A brief, idiosyncratic and thought-provoking account of globalisation is provided by Daniel Cohen, *The Wealth of the World and the Poverty of Nations* (Cambridge, MA: MIT Press, 1998).

Chapter 2

WHAT MAKES NATIONS GROW?

Introduction

Before making a business decision in a foreign country, we usually ask about that country's 'rate of growth'. Fast economic growth means an expanding domestic market and higher living standards, and is associated with a changing and dynamic business environment. Slow or zero growth is perceived as stagnation and is not attractive to business. Confronted with the record of a slow-growing economy, we naturally ask what has gone wrong. From a business perspective, the cause of economic growth is an important subject.

Economic growth is desired for many different reasons. Affluent countries see faster growth as a way of maintaining their superior living standards. Governments of poor countries see faster economic growth as a means of catching up with the prosperity of the affluent countries. Faster growth makes it easier to reduce unemployment, to mitigate poverty, to improve education and health services, and to provide material well-being. There are, of course, negative aspects of growth, such as environmental degradation, the breakdown of community life and destruction of rural values. Since the Industrial Revolution in the late eighteenth century, economic growth has had its critics, some of the most trenchant of whom have been economists. The tradition of scepticism, verging on hostility, towards growth remains active to this day. Despite all this, business and governments evidently believe that the positive effects of growth outweigh its negative effects, and both groups continue to accord it a high priority.

Chapter outline

1. The main statistical facts about economic growth.
2. The contribution of growth theories to the understanding of these facts and the political and institutional framework required for successful growth performance.
3. The relationship between economic growth and human welfare.
4. Current thinking on the economic policies most likely to encourage growth.

2.1 Trends in economic growth

Economic growth is measured by Gross National Product (GNP). GNP is a universally used measure of the value of goods and services produced in a country. GNP divided by total population, or GNP per capita, is the economic indicator most commonly used to measure the standard of living in a country. When we say economic growth, we refer to growth in GNP measured in real terms, i.e. abstracting from the effects of price increases. Growth data are compiled according to detailed, internationally agreed conventions.

GNP comparisons over time give a rough indication of how much better-off we have become. Table 2.1 compares GNP per capita in year 2000 with its level in 1900 and 1950 for several countries. To ensure comparability, goods and services produced in those years are valued in US dollars at year 2000 prices. The figures show that the value of GNP per person varies enormously between countries. For example, official statistics indicate that Japan's output per person is almost 23 times higher than India's and two and a half times higher than Mexico's. The UK is not regarded as a high performer in the growth league, yet the table shows that output per person has quadrupled since 1900.

Studies of economic growth, based on data such as that in Table 2.1, reveal certain general patterns which can be summarised in a number of *'stylised' facts*.

First, *economic growth was the norm rather than the exception during the twentieth century*. Despite two world wars, major increases in national output per person have been recorded in the industrial countries. The period since 1950 has seen a prodigious increase in living standards. Between 1950 and 2000 national output

Table 2.1 GNP per person for selected countries at constant 2000 US $

	1900	1950	2000
Belgium	5039	7382	25216
Denmark	4912	11064	25391
Finland	2774	7070	22305
France	2689	4942	24205
Germany	3718	5986	22391
Italy	2947	5097	21650
Japan	1993	3287	23640
Netherlands	4825	7991	23401
Sweden	3793	9977	21084
UK	5184	7729	21883
US	5336	12274	31942
India	659	626	1951
South Korea	904	928	13500
Argentina	2865	5162	10199
Mexico	116	2011	9021

Source: Computed from Angus Maddison, *The World Economy in the Twentieth Century* (Paris: OECD, 1989) and the International Monetary Fund, *World Economic Outlook*, May 1999. Purchasing power parties have been used for the developing countries (see Chapter 11 for definition).

Table 2.2 Share of world output, trade and population 1998 (% share)

	Output	Trade	Population
United States	21.7	17.0	4.6
European Union	23.0	20.3	6.3
Japan	8.7	9.7	2.2
Top three	53.4	47.0	13.1
Rest of world	46.6	53.0	86.9
Total	100	100	100

Source: European Economy (Brussels, no. 66, 1998); WTO, 1999.

per capita rose by an annual average of 6 per cent in Japan, 3.7 per cent in Germany, 3.1 per cent in France, 2.4 per cent in the UK and 1.9 per cent in the US. These growth rates may appear unspectacular, but if sustained long enough they can bring about huge improvements in output per person. For example, a 3 per cent growth rate will lead to a doubling of output every 23 years.

Second, *countries that were relatively well-off in 1900 have tended to stay well-off.* However, some significant changes in ranking have occurred:

- the UK slipped from being one of the world's richest countries in 1900 to 22nd place in the league,
- Japan, a relatively poor country in 1900, has risen to being one of the most affluent,
- Argentina, once among the wealthiest countries, suffered a serious decline in its relative position since the start of the twentieth century.

As Table 2.2 shows, the three most affluent areas of the world – the US, EU and Japan, accounting for only 13 per cent of world population of 6 billion – generate 53 per cent of world GNP.

Third, *the developing countries have achieved significant improvements in living standards since the 1950s.* Life expectancy has increased by about 50 per cent; the proportion of children attending school has risen from less than one half to more than three-quarters; and average GNP per person has doubled, albeit from an extremely low initial level.

Fourth, *the problem of acute poverty continues to persist.* One billion people, most of them living in Sub-Saharan Africa and Asia, are still struggling to survive on about $1 per day.[1] Furthermore, the economic progress of the majority of developing countries has not been smooth. Income per capita in India actually fell between 1929 and 1950. During the 1990s, many African and former socialist countries experienced negative growth rates (Table 2.3). Thus, while growth is the predominant feature of the world economy, it has not been a universal experience.

Fifth, *dramatic changes have occurred in the distribution of economic activity among the developing countries since the 1960s.* Asian countries have grown at an extraordinarily fast pace, starting with Japan, followed by Korea, Taiwan,

---

1 World Bank, *Global Economic Prospects and the Developing Countries* (World Bank: Washington DC, 1999) p. 33.

Table 2.3 **How growth rates differ 1965–98**

	Total Real GNP 1965–98 (% p.a.)	Real GNP per head 1965–98 (% p.a.)	Population 1998 (millions)
Low income ($760 or less) countries (63)	5.9	3.7	3536
Middle income countries (75)	3.7	1.9	1474
High income ($9,361 or more) countries (35)	3.0	2.3	886
East Asia	7.5	5.7	1817
South Asia	4.9	2.7	1305
Latin America	3.5	1.3	502
Sub-Saharan Africa	2.6	−0.3	627
World	3.2	1.4	5897

Source: World Bank, *World Development Indicators 2000.*

Singapore and Hong Kong, and then succeeded by a later generation which includes China, Malaysia and Thailand, among others. China, with a population of 1200 million, has recorded an astonishing annual rate of growth of almost 9 per cent per person since the early 1980s (although this figure may not be entirely reliable).

Sixth, *resource-rich countries have experienced mixed fortunes.* Being 'rich' in terms of natural resources does not guarantee prosperity. One reason is that the prices of many primary commodities, such as cocoa, coffee, sugar, groundnuts and minerals, have been on a declining trend for some decades now. Oil prices shot up to unprecedented levels in the late 1970s, but fell back in real terms to their pre-1973 levels in the 1990s, before recovering again in the late 1990s. Many countries dependent on primary exports have suffered a decline in their export prices relative to import prices, thus reducing these countries' purchasing power and level of income. Apart from this price (or terms of trade) effect, *human* resources – meaning a skilled and motivated workforce – have been found to be a more significant source of economic prosperity than an endowment of *natural* resources.

Seventh, *over the five years 1989–94, the countries of the former Soviet Union suffered a cumulative fall in real output of over 40 per cent* (Table 2.4). The fall in measured GNP may exaggerate the decline in consumer living standards, because GNP included goods such as military hardware which provided little direct benefit to the average consumer. Moreover, the official GNP statistics take no account of informal market activities, which were booming during this period. Yet the fall in real living standards was appreciable and, for many individuals in these countries, traumatic. The experience of the *economies in transition*, as they are called, shows that countries can be well endowed with both natural and human resources, and yet perform poorly because of unstable and inadequate institutional structures and a history of poor economic management. Some of these countries showed signs of recovery in the late 1990s, such as Poland, Estonia and the Slovak Republic, while Slovenia has recorded positive growth since 1993. But resumption of growth in Russia and the Ukraine remained an elusive goal at the turn of the century.

Table 2.4 GDP growth rates in former socialist countries

	1989–94	1995–99
	Decline and recovery...	
Estonia	−6.6	5.1
Latvia	−8.3	3.2
Lithuania	−6.6	4.2
Albania	−2.7	5.4
Czech Rep.	−1.3	1.8
Hungary	−2.6	3.1
Poland	−1.1	5.7
Slovak Rep.	−3.8	5.2
Slovenia	−2.8	3.9
	Decline and fall...	
Russia	−6.8	−1.9
Ukraine	−10.3	−5.9
Bulgaria	−5.0	−1.6
Romania	−4.9	−1.4

Source: European Bank for Reconstruction and Development, *Transition Report 1999*.

2.2 Growth theories

Theories of economic growth seek to identify the *long-term* determinants of growth. In this section we provide a bird's-eye, non-technical view of how economists explain growth and what policies they recommend on the basis of their analyses. Some concepts introduced here will be explained in more detail in later chapters.

Imagine an economy which produces only two goods, X and Y. Suppose we set up a list of combinations of X and Y that could be produced if the resources of the economy were fully and most effectively deployed. The *production frontier* traces the various combinations of X and Y derived in this way (Figure 2.1). An *efficient* economic system is one that operates on the production frontier (see Box 2.1). This ensures *productive* efficiency. *Allocative* efficiency is also very important. It ensures that there is no feasible redistribution of income which would permit one person to be better-off without anyone else being worse-off. We shall see later that the market system helps an economy achieve an efficient outcome. Efficiency, in turn, speeds up economic growth.

Economic growth can be characterised as an outward shift in the production frontier, represented by the move from TT to T^1T^1 in Figure 2.1. This outward movement is desired because of the expanded range of options it provides society. Economic growth is regarded as a 'good thing', in so far as it enables the consumers in the economy to enjoy:

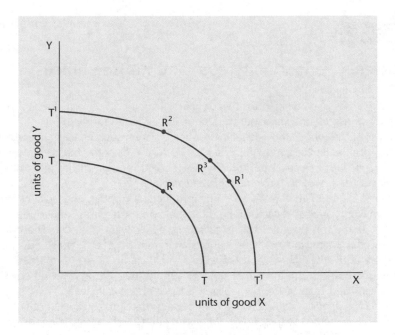

Figure 2.1 The production frontier

- more of X and the same amount of Y – at a point such as R^1.
- more of Y and the same amount of X – at a point such as R^2.
- more of both X and Y – at a point such as R^3.
- any other desired combination of X and Y on the expanded frontier.

Growth extends the range of consumption possibilities, and people choose between these different possibilities through the market system, supplemented by government intervention. Growth provides the means to enjoy more of all goods, including leisure. Economic development in industrial countries has enabled people to have more goods and services while working fewer hours.

The production frontier can be shifted outwards by two forces: first, increases in the *quantity* of productive factors; and second, improvements in the *productivity* of these factors. Since we are primarily concerned with growth per person rather than total growth, it is common to abstract from the increase in growth which is attributable solely to the increase in the population. Growth in living standards, or GNP per person, therefore, depends on (1) the *amount* of productive factors at each person's disposal (the more machinery and the more hectares of land at the disposal of an employee, the more will be produced per employee), (2) the *productivity* of these factors of production (better machinery, improved seeds and fertilisers and more advanced technology improve productivity), and (3) the skill and motivation of the workforce. We shall discuss these three elements in turn.

Box 2.1

Efficiency, opportunity cost and no free lunch

Economics has been defined as the science of scarcity. Its view of the world is one where people's wants are unlimited, but the resources needed to satisfy them are limited. Provided society is at the production possibility frontier, where resources are fully employed, more of good X implies less of good Y. In order to produce more of X, scarce resources have to be transferred from industry Y to industry X. Hence the origin of the well-known maxim: *in economics there is no such thing as a free lunch*.

Again, assuming that we are on the production frontier, the cost of producing one additional unit of good X can be defined as the amount of good Y that has to be given up in order to make this possible. This is called *the opportunity cost of X*. The opportunity cost concept has many practical applications. It reminds us that 'free' education, or 'free' transport and other 'free' goods offered by politicians, convey a misleading impression. Nothing is costless. The resources used to supply these 'free' government services could have been used to produce, say, automobiles or holidays instead.

An *efficient* economy is one which (1) operates on its production frontier, at a point such as P in the figure below (*productive efficiency*); and (2) allocates the goods produced at the frontier in an efficient way (*allocative efficiency*).

Productive efficiency: At any point below the production frontier, society could have more of both X and Y by moving from its present position to a point closer to the production frontier. By definition, point U is not an efficient position. At that point, some productive resources are either being used inefficiently or, worse, not being used at all. Here free lunches are a possibility. If the market system is performing as it should, such situations will be rare and short-lived. Price incentives should move the economy from U to a point on the frontier such as P, where the economy has more of both X and Y than at U. Analysis of the role of prices and market structures shows how an economy reaches its production possibility frontier and stays there.

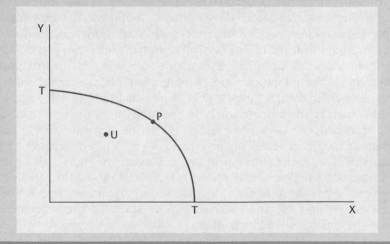

Box 2.1 continued

So much for productive efficiency, which has to do with getting from points like U to the production frontier. The second criterion for economic efficiency, *allocative efficiency*, requires that the goods produced at P are allocated in an optimal way between consumers. Allocative efficiency is achieved when there is no feasible redistribution of the fixed bundle of goods P which would make one person better-off without leaving anyone else worse-off. At this stage, an economy is said to have achieved *Pareto efficiency*. Not least of the attractions of a free market system is that, subject to certain assumptions, it can lead to a Pareto-efficient outcome, i.e. productive and allocative efficiency.

The productive capacity of a nation can be put to many uses. An interesting example of this is the case of the US during the Second World War. In 1939 the armed forces of the US were extremely weak. The army had more horses than tanks. The air corps and navy possessed only 1600 aircraft in total (mostly ancient biplanes), while Germany manufactured 8295 modern military aircraft in that year alone. However, the US had the world's largest industrial production capacity and was easily able to turn this to rearmament. By 1941, it was producing military aircraft at the rate of 26,277 a year. This illustrates how rapidly GNP can be switched from consumer goods to the production of the military hardware needed to win a war.

But what makes the production frontier shift outwards? This question lies at the heart of economics. It constituted the central theme of Adam Smith's masterpiece, *An Inquiry into the Nature and Causes of the Wealth of Nations* (1776). This chapter gives an overview of current thinking on the growth debate.

Source: US war data from R. Overy and A. Wheatcroft, *The Road to War* (London: Macmillan, 1989), pp. 258–97, 317–21.

Quantity of inputs

Quantity of productive factors (in economic jargon, 'factors of production') refers to inputs such as the physical infrastructure (roads, ports, railways, telecoms), plant and machinery (factories, machinery, tractors) and natural resources. As the quantity of inputs increases, so too does the volume of final output. The production function measures the relationship between inputs and output (Box 2.2).

Just as investment plays a key role in explaining the growth of firms, the share of investment in a country's GDP is linked closely to economic growth. A country that invested more than another would be expected, everything else being equal, to grow faster. There are some outstanding cases to support this hypothesis. Japan's average investment: GDP ratio since 1960 has exceeded the investment ratio in the EU and the US by more than 10 percentage points (31 per cent as against 22 per cent and 18 per cent respectively) and, not surprisingly, Japan's growth rate of 6 per cent up to the 1990s was twice the rate of most industrial countries (Table 2.5). Within Europe, the faster growing countries, such as Spain, Italy and Germany, invested more than the slower growing countries, such as the UK. Following India's setting of a 7 per cent GDP growth target for the decade to

Box 2.2

Production functions and economic growth

A country's output depends on its resources or productive inputs, and on the techniques it employs for transforming these inputs into outputs. The relationship between inputs and outputs is known as a *production function*. It is a technical, engineering-type relationship, which we use to conceptualise the diverse and complex influences which determine economic growth. A simple production function might be described as:

$$y = a.\mathrm{f}(k)$$

where: y = output per person
k = capital per person
a = residual factor, including technology.

This relationship indicates the maximum amount of output per person (y) that society can produce for any given input of capital per person (k) and technology and other production inputs (a). This residual is also called *total factor productivity*.

It is possible to specify the production function in detail and to derive estimates of the effect of changes in each of these inputs on the level of output. By accumulating capital, a country can move to a higher output level per person along its production function. The greater the amount of capital available per person, the greater is output per person. The same result can be achieved by raising the productivity of this capital. Machines can be operated more efficiently, break down less often and economise on raw material inputs. The faster the pace of technological progress, the faster the increase in output – for a given capital stock, greater technological awareness allows greater amounts of output to be produced.

Estimates of production functions suggest that increases in capital per person do indeed contribute to higher output, but what really matters is the residual factor, representing the technology and other influences. Between one third and one half of growth in major industrial countries since 1950 falls into this unexplained 'residual' category.

Source: N. Crofts and G. Tonioli (eds), *Economic Growth in Europe since 1945* (Cambridge: Cambridge University Press, 1996).

2007 in 1997, the IMF concluded that this would require an investment ratio of at least 30 per cent (*Finance and Development*, June 1997).[2]

The observed connection between investment and growth led many to believe that growth in the developing countries was mainly constrained by insufficient investment reflecting low savings and poverty. Multi-annual development plans explored ways of raising the savings ratio and allocating investment to sectors where productivity was highest. According to this way of thinking, foreign aid could make a vital contribution by supplying the additional capital input needed for sustained growth.

2 Martin Mühleisen, 'Improving India's saving performance', *Finance and Development* (June 1997), pp. 38–41.

Table 2.5 Investment and growth

	Investment/GDP ratios			Investment/GDP ratios		
	European Union	US	Japan	European Union	US	Japan
1961–70	23.4	18.1	32.2	4.8	4.2	10.1
1971–80	23.0	19.1	32.7	3.0	3.2	4.4
1981–90	20.4	18.3	29.1	2.4	2.9	4.0
1991–2000	19.0	16.0	29.0	2.0	2.5	1.4

Source: *European Economy* (Brussels: no. 16, 1999).

But how to explain Japan's high investment rate in the 1990s (29 per cent) being accompanied by GDP growth of only 1.4 per cent? Clearly, the level of investment is only one of many determinants of growth. What is called the *growth accounting approach* examines the contribution of other factors in the growth process.[3] Studies have examined historical trends in a country's productive resources, disaggregated in comprehensive detail, and have tracked the association between these inputs and the subsequent growth of output. This research has underlined the importance of total factor productivity and of the *quality* of the labour force as independent determinants of economic performance.

Total factor productivity

Total factor productivity typically accounts for between one-third and one-half of total GNP growth in industrial countries. It is derived as a residual, after allowing for capital investment and labour force growth, and reflects the influence of factors which improve productivity but which are not amenable to exact measurement. There are many candidates for inclusion in this residual category:

- advances in technology,
- redistribution of resources from lower to higher productivity sectors,
- terms of trade,
- institutions and political stability,
- quality of the labour force (human skills and motivation),
- better business organisation,
- economic policy.

Low growth in total factor productivity has been identified as the primary culprit for the comparative decline of the UK economy. During the boom years 1950–73, UK TFP growth was 1.27 per cent per year compared with 3.02 per cent in France and 3.50 per cent in West Germany.

---

3 This approach stemmed from an investigation by Edward Dennison into the sources of growth in the US. Dennison and his followers later extended the research to international comparisons of growth experience. See E.F. Dennison, *Why Growth Rates Differ* (Washington, DC: Brookings Institution, 1967). More recent accounting estimates are reviewed in A. Maddison, *Dynamic Forces in Capitalist Development* (Oxford: Oxford University Press, 1991).

The link between *advances in technology* and economic growth involves three separate steps. First, there is invention – the scientific discovery – which often originates from pure research, not necessarily motivated by commercial factors. Second, the invention needs to be applied to the production of a good or service. Innovation refers to this application. This may involve a more efficient method of producing an existing good (e.g. quality control methods for an automobile) or production of an entirely new product (e.g. the video recorder). The third step is diffusion of the innovation to other industries and other economies. Countries in the early stages of economic development typically focus on this last step. Because it is cheaper to adopt new technologies that have been brought to commercial level by others than to have to discover them from scratch, poorer countries mostly borrow, imitate and adapt technology from the more advanced economies. But technological progress does not descend like manna from heaven.[4] It is costly to develop and costly to acquire. The process of technology acquisition and diffusion requires large infusions of machinery and skilled manpower. For this reason, there tends to be a close association between technological advance and investment in human and physical capital – another example of dynamic interdependence between different inputs in the growth process.

Advances in technology are not directly observable, but are measured by proxy variables such as the numbers of registered patents or the amount of spending on R&D. A country's 'system of national innovation' is seen as a critical component of economic growth. The amount of commercially oriented research undertaken in a country can contribute to the discovery and adoption of new products and new ways of producing them. But such research does not take place by accident. It needs to be nurtured by an environment that encourages innovation. The education system must provide the key personnel in terms of technological competence and motivation. Fiscal incentives also have a part to play. If these are missing, spending on research and development will fail to translate into effective innovation – as, many would say, happened in Britain through much of the postwar period.

Studies of innovation show that technological advance has a tendency to feed on itself. Innovation can be a self-perpetuating process. As more of it is carried out, a pool of skilled labour and managerial competence accumulates which reduces unit costs. It may become independently profitable and require fewer government incentives. Economic growth can be path-dependent. *Endogenous growth theories* focus on these self-reinforcing interactions between technology, human skills and economies of scale.[5]

The different influences on total factor productivity vary in importance from country to country and from one time-period to another. For example, one major source of productivity growth derives from the *transfer of the labour force from low-productivity agriculture to high-productivity industry*. In the decades immediately after the Second World War, this contributed significantly to Europe's high growth rates.

---

4 There are some exceptions such as the application of DDT or antibiotics and penicillin: very cheap to acquire and requiring little skill to apply.

5 See P.M. Romer, 'The origins of endogenous growth', *Journal of Economic Perspectives* VIII (I) (1994); R.E. Lucas, 'On the mechanics of economic development', *Journal of Monetary Economics* (July 1988).

The same forces are at work in boosting the growth rates of developing countries. As the proportion of the workforce in agriculture diminishes, the scope for exploiting these gains contracts, and the opportunity for really fast growth diminishes proportionately. However, opportunities for continuing productivity gains remain. Even within the manufacturing sector, productivity can grow because of movement from low-productivity to high-productivity activities. Further productivity gains are yielded by the transfer of resources from manufacturing to high-tech services. Continuing innovation, and readiness to shift to activities with the highest returns, is a characteristic of successful market economies.

Developments in a country's *terms of trade* can have a major impact on growth. The terms of trade are defined as the ratio of changes in a country's export prices to import prices. Small trade-dependent countries are more sensitive to terms of trade changes than larger countries. Developing economies dependent on just a few commodity exports are particularly vulnerable. A decline in the terms of trade of 10 percentage points over a decade reduces economic growth by 0.8 percentage points annually in that decade.[6] Since 1980, real commodity prices have declined by 45 per cent. Countries in Sub-Saharan Africa have been badly hit both by declines in export prices and by the extreme volatility of these prices. Ghana's terms of trade, dominated by cocoa, fell by over 30 per cent during this period. The post-1973 oil price increases vastly enhanced the incomes of oil-producing countries, but they had a profoundly negative and lasting impact on oil-consuming countries.

Economic growth takes place in a particular *political and institutional context*. This background can have an important bearing on productivity and growth. For example, political stability, in the sense of stable democratic government, by offering protection against arbitrary removal of property rights and confiscation of savings, is conducive to investment. Unstable political systems generate uncertainty about the future, encourage capital outflow and discourage business investment. At the same time as political stability encourages growth, so economic growth can encourage political stability. It is a chicken-and-egg problem to decide which comes first. Moreover, political stability cannot be identified with democracy in a cut-and-dried manner. Singapore developed successfully under a regime much closer to benevolent dictatorship than to democracy in a Western sense. Some dictatorships can be successful in laying the foundations of growth, such as Chile during the 1980s; others have been associated with disastrous performance, such as Romania and Zaïre (Congo) since the 1970s. Political stability, therefore, has to be combined with consistent and rational economic policies. In high-growth countries, the viability and credibility of growth-oriented economic policy has been reinforced by strong popular support for such policy. This support has been engendered by the widespread diffusion of the fruits of growth through society.

---

6 William Easterly and Lance Pritchett, 'The determinants of economic success: Luck and policy', *Finance and Development* (December 1993), p. 40.

Quality of the labour force

High investment and high productivity are hard to envisage without high-quality people. To produce high-quality people, however, requires investment. Every business knows this, but it has taken time for the message to be appreciated fully in economic policy. One problem is that investment in people may take decades to bear fruit and its effects are hard to measure, whereas investment in physical capital – such as a bridge or a fertiliser plant – leads to a highly visible and measurable result in a much shorter time.[7] It was not easy to get over the message that investment in education is just as 'real' and as 'profitable' from a national point of view as any other type of investment. *Human capital* refers to the development of human skills and motivation through investment in education, training and experience. Educated, skilled workers are generally more productive than uneducated, unskilled workers. High-productivity industries in the biotechnology and information sectors require a skilled and educated workforce. Simple measures of human capital such as the level of secondary school enrolment have been found to be strongly correlated with subsequent economic growth. Labour productivity growth in East Asia, three to six times the developing country average, has been credited to major investments in workers' skills. The return on investment in women's education seems to be especially high, through its effects on the health and education of the next generation, and by reducing family size.

A better-educated workforce must also be motivated. Overmanning, demarcation and poor industrial relations can retard growth just as surely as lack of physical investment. The reason why some countries have been better able to motivate their workforce than others has been much debated. One important lesson of Europe's experience has been the need to achieve a balance between the redistribution of income for social reasons and the preservation of incentives. The search by pressure groups in the developed countries to obtain a higher share of total GNP has led to the rise of what Mancur Olson has called 'distributional coalitions'.[8] Efforts by trade unions, professional groups and trade associations to increase their share of national income involve a zero-sum exercise. One group's gain is another's loss. According to Olson, the Allies performed relatively poorly after the Second World War because their distributional coalitions were left intact and even strengthened, while Germany and Japan, having lost the war, found that their distributional coalitions were discredited and destroyed. This opened the way for a better institutional framework which encouraged the workforce to abandon the old adversarial relationship with management and concentrate on building up a competitive economy instead. These ideas also help to explain why some countries seem to make little constructive use of favourable terms of trade 'windfalls'. Too much effort is devoted to working out how the windfall should be distributed. In extreme circumstances, the windfall may even damage a country's

---

7 The proposition that educating a workforce improves its productivity dates back to Adam Smith. The modern concept of human capital is due primarily to the work of T.W. Schultz, 'Investing in human capital', *American Economic Review* (1961), pp. 1–17.

8 M. Olson, *The Rise and Decline of Nations* (New Haven, CT: Yale University Press, 1982).

long-run growth as squabbles over income distribution lead to a deterioration in saving and excessive government spending. Tornell and Lane refer to this as the *voracity effect.*[9] Economists have become increasingly conscious of the importance of good *governance* as a determinant of economic prosperity.

The list of determinants of growth can be extended indefinitely. Business organisation and culture, the work ethic, religion and even climate have at one time or another been adduced to explain it. In the practical context of trying to improve economic performance, we have to try to identify which of the many determinants of growth are acting as a binding constraint on faster growth in a particular situation and how these constraints can be most effectively prioritised by economic policy.

Population growth and living standards

The link between between population growth and economic development is a highly contentious topic. While every additional worker adds to potential output, the crucial question is how population growth will affect not just total GDP, but GDP per person. Take, for example, a country such as Nigeria with an annual population growth of 3%. *Output growth of 3% is needed simply to prevent living standards from falling.* To generate and support that output growth in turn necessitates a high level of investment. To obtain sufficient growth to achieve an increase in living standards means that investment must be even higher still. The mathematics of generating a growth rate high enough to outstrip the growth in population has attracted attention since the writings of Thomas Malthus in the eighteenth century.

Many argue that growth in population can depress income per person. An expanding population of young people and large family-size reduces national saving and consequently limits the volume of investment. Simultaneously, a burgeoning population puts pressure on a country's infrastructure. In other words, *the rate of growth of population may interact negatively with the growth of other inputs.* As a result of this interdependence, a vicious circle of economic decline can be generated. By the same line of reasoning, lower population growth may facilitate economic growth by creating a virtuous circle of high investment leading to higher growth, which generates more saving, more investment and so on.

Affluent households tend to have smaller families than poor households and, in the same way, developed countries have lower population growth than poor countries. World Bank figures for population growth since 1980 show that higher income countries had population growth of 0.6% p.a., while low income populations have been increasing by 2% annually. But are affluent countries better-off because they have low population growth, or is their population growth low because they are affluent? There is no definitive answer to this question. Two general points, however, can be made. First, many governments in the developing world have concluded that population growth has damaged their efforts to raise living standards and, for this reason, official support has been given to family

---

9 A. Tornell and P.R. Lane, 'The voracity effect', *American Economic Review* (March 1999).

planning.[10] The governments of two of the world's most populous countries, China and India, have been persuaded of the case for lower population growth and support measures to encourage smaller family size. In this they have the backing of international organisations such as the United Nations and the World Bank. Second, while Western governments are concerned about the lack of population growth and the associated problem of caring for a rising proportion of elderly people, none of them has espoused a deliberate policy of population expansion as a way out of the difficulty.

2.3 Human welfare and sustainable growth

> The Gross National Product does not allow for the health of our children, the quality of their education or the joy of their play. It does not include the beauty of our poetry or the strength of our marriages; the intelligence of our public debate or the integrity of our public officials. It measures neither our wisdom nor our learning, neither our compassion nor our devotion to our country; it measures everything, in short, except that which makes life worthwhile. (Robert F. Kennedy, quoted in *Finance and Development*, December 1993, p. 20)

So far we have discussed economic growth as if it were the sole objective of economic policy. Growth is taken to be desirable because it enlarges the range of consumption possibilities available to society.

It is well known that GNP is an inadequate indicator of human welfare. There is no evidence that people in countries with high GNP are 'happier' or spiritually better than those in poorer countries. GNP leaves out of the account many of the things that make for the good life; and some items are included in GNP that have an ambiguous effect on welfare (e.g. resources devoted to crime prevention are treated as part of GNP, but some would regard them as an input). Three specific criticisms of GNP have been made on this account. First, that it puts no value on leisure and the household economy. Second, that it ignores income distribution. Third, that it takes no account of resource depletion and degradation of the environment.

Leisure and the household economy

Suppose that a person takes a second job. This makes large inroads into leisure time. GNP includes all the output generated by the second job but totally ignores the welfare cost of the loss of leisure. Human welfare has presumably increased as a result of this decision – otherwise the second job would not have been taken – but the net increase in welfare will be much less than the GNP indicates. The individual is likely to be more harassed and to have less time for the family.

GNP includes only transactions that involve a monetary exchange. Housework done by members of a household, being unpaid, is not recorded in GNP. As members of the household enter the workforce and household tasks, such as repair, maintenance, and care of children, are passed over to paid professionals,

---

10 'Population Growth and Economic Development', UN Cairo Conference, 1994.

GNP rises. Yet all that is happening is that functions are being shifted from the traditional realm of the household and the community to the monetised economy. Welfare has presumably increased, since the decision to work outside the home was taken voluntarily. But the increase in GNP will grossly exaggerate the increase in welfare.

Income distribution

GNP per person, being an arithmetic average of total output divided by total population, reveals no information about the distribution of resources within a society. It could rise even though the majority of the population may be worse-off. For example, if the income of the most affluent one-third of a population rose by 50 billion dollars, and the income of the poorest two-thirds fell by a total 30 billion dollars, GNP would increase. But does it necessarily follow that society as a whole is better-off?

Some argue that the long-run sustainability of growth depends on income being shared on an equitable basis. One reason is that successful policy-making requires change, and change involves implementing measures that harm certain vested interests. A social consensus is required in order to push through such measures. This consensus can only be achieved if the majority of people believe that they have a stake in the economy and will benefit from its growth and prosperity.

For example, at the start of the century many Latin American nations enjoyed high per capita incomes under policy regimes which were favourable to free enterprise and the market system. However, income disparities were great and the power of vested interests was correspondingly strong. These interest-groups resisted change and the next eighty years saw relative economic decline, as inward-looking, protectionist policies were adopted. A more liberal market regime might have benefited the majority of people but the free market regime had given them little and they saw no reason to defend it even if the alternative protectionist regime may have made matters even worse. By contrast, in East Asia, governments succeeded in moderating income disparities (without undermining incentives). The result was a social consensus behind growth-oriented policies. In addition to strong economic growth performance, East Asian countries have made what the IMF described as 'outstanding progress' in reducing absolute and relative poverty.[11] Notwithstanding the setback of the 1997–98 currency crisis, most of these countries have succeeded in cultivating a strong market system and incentives to enterprise, while simultaneously achieving widely spread prosperity.

GNP and the environment

Conventional GNP measures do not deal satisfactorily with *environmental and ecological factors*. Higher GNP has implications for the environment on several levels which fail to be recorded in the statistics. Two aspects in particular merit attention: (1) higher levels of pollution, and (2) depletion of natural resources.

---

11 IMF, *World Economic Outlook* (May 1993), p. 54.

Higher levels of pollution can arise because higher levels of production imply more waste, including carbon dioxide emissions and other chemical waste.[12] These pollutants should be deducted from a measure of welfare. Also, by a perverse quirk, the cost of moderating the adverse effects of pollution is often included in GNP as an output (service provided) instead of as an input (a production cost to society). For example, the medical attention given to a radiation victim will be recorded in the national accounts as a positive entry instead of as a 'negative input' occasioned by the radiation exposure. Likewise, the introduction of catalytic converters in cars or a new waste water treatment plant adds to GNP, though arguably these activities are merely defensive protection measures.

Second, the *depletion of non-renewable resources* such as oil and coal is not accounted for in GNP calculations. Nor is account taken of the usage of resources such as rainforests, fishery stocks, etc., which are in danger of being consumed faster than the replacement rate. Other examples include soil erosion in Sub-Saharan Africa and the decline in animal and vegetable output caused by pollution of the water supply.[13] We shall discuss these issues further in Chapter 9.

GNP and human development indicators

In evaluating a country's growth, account should be taken of the quality of the lifestyle enjoyed by the population. We need to measure the quality as well as the quantity of economic growth. Imagine two countries. One has a lower GNP per person than the other, but has a healthier, more literate, more democratic and less crime-ridden society. In this instance, GNP is an inaccurate measure of the relative welfare of the two countries. In an effort to develop a more comprehensive socioeconomic measure, the United Nations has published a series of Human Development Indicators, which provide information on these issues. It is possible to compute a human development index consisting of a weighted average of data on GNP per person, income distribution, life expectancy and education attainment of the population (Box 2.3).

As one would expect, the new index involved some changes in ranking. The 1999 Report, for example, indicates a Human Development Index (HDI) ranking higher than the GDP ranking for Canada, France and the UK, and a deterioration for Singapore and South Africa. By adding to the list of indicators, and measuring them in different ways, more radical alterations in ranking can be computed. There is ample scope for further experimentation and analysis along these lines.

Yet, the limitations of GNP as a measure of welfare must not be exaggerated. For

---

12 A useful example in this context is the destruction of mountain forests in Europe. Huge forests have perished because of Slovak heavy industries and the condition of Alpine forests is worsening yearly. In Switzerland the annual scientific report on the state of forests has been attracting front-page media attention since the mid-1980s. Acid rain in the Alps is blamed mainly on emissions from road traffic. This is the bad side of growth. The good side is that technological advances include the catalytic converter, which significantly reduces harmful emissions from cars.

13 In response to these problems, the United Nations has developed a set of 'satellite' accounts, attached to the national accounts, which incorporate adjustments for the problems mentioned above. Because of the lack of precision of these 'green' accounts, they accompany, rather than replace, the orthodox accounts.

Box 2.3

The human development index

In 1990, the United Nations developed the Human Development Index (HDI) as an alternative measure of the relative socioeconomic progress of nations. It did so in response to criticisms of GNP as a measure of welfare. The HDI is a composite index, incorporating three basic components of human development, *life expectancy at birth*, *knowledge* and *standard of living*. Life expectancy at birth is the number of years a person is expected to live at birth based on law of averages computed by demographers; knowledge is measured by a combination of adult literacy and mean years of schooling; standard of living is estimated by real income per capita adjusted for the local cost of living.

2000 HDI ranking – selected countries

	HDI value	HDI rank	GDP per capita rank
Industrial countries			
Canada	0.935	1	9
US	0.929	3	3
Sweden	0.926	6	27
Netherlands	0.925	8	19
Japan	0.924	9	14
UK	0.918	10	22
France	0.917	12	17
Switzerland*	0.915	13	7
Germany	0.911	14	20
Denmark*	0.911	15	11
Italy	0.903	19	24
Hungary	0.817	43	49
Poland	0.810	44	83
Developing countries			
Singapore*	0.881	24	5
South Korea	0.854	31	55
Argentina	0.887	35	64
Mexico	0.784	55	71
Malaysia	0.772	61	79
Romania	0.770	64	109
Brazil	0.747	74	88
China	0.706	99	129
South Africa*	0.697	103	79
Indonesia	0.670	109	141
India	0.563	128	163
Zambia	0.420	153	195
Uganda	0.409	158	185

*Denotes that the HDI ranking is worse than the GNP\capita ranking.

Box 2.3 continued

These indicators are combined in the HDI which is expressed as a value between 0 and 1. The ranking by HDI is often compared with GDP per capita.

The figures show a positive correlation between the HDI and GNP per capita rankings but it breaks down in many cases. Countries with an HDI rank ahead of its GNP rank are taking a more balanced approach to economic development. Recent experience suggests that, in the long run, such an approach will translate into faster GNP growth too.

The single HDI value for each country is a national average which can conceal inequalities at a regional and sectoral level. Work continues on constructing separate HDIs by gender, income group, geographical region, race or ethnic group, for example. Separate HDIs would reveal a more detailed profile of living experiences in each country. Some countries have attempted to estimate disaggregated HDIs but availability of data is a pervasive problem.

Source: *Human Development Report 2000* (Oxford: Oxford University Press).

all its defects, a higher output per person gives society the *capacity* to achieve a better quality of life. Also, there is a strong positive correlation between GNP growth and some important empirical measures of the quality of life. Countries with higher GNP tend to be healthier and better educated than those with lower GNP. They also tend to be better policed and are more secure in a financial and physical sense. Central New York is safer than central Lima, Manila or Mogadishu. Affluent Tokyo is one of the safest cities in the world. While many forms of recorded crime in the industrial world have increased since 1945, prosperity has resulted in a reduction in civil disorder. During the nineteenth century, crime rates fell as the cities industrialised.[14]

Global convergence?

Income distribution is a source of concern at international as well as at national level. One question often asked is whether poorer countries are catching up with the richer countries. The statistics, as we have seen, show rather mixed results. In favour of the convergence hypothesis is the average 3 per cent yearly increase of GNP per person in low-income countries during the period 1980–2000, a figure considerably in excess of the 2.2 per cent achieved by high-income countries during the same period. Against this, one could argue that, excluding China and India, income per capita of the average developing country has risen by only 0.1 per cent annually and conclude with the World Bank,

> while some poorer countries are catching up with the richer ones, just as many have failed to narrow the gap, and some are losing ground. *Overall divergence, not convergence, has been the rule.* (The World Bank, *World Development Report*, 1995, p. 54; emphasis added)

---

14 J.J. Tobias, *Crime and Police in England, 1700–1900* (Dublin: Gill and Macmillan, 1979).

Do rich countries, because they are rich, grow faster than poorer countries? Endogenous growth theories give reasons for believing that, once ahead, the more developed countries – the first-movers – will tend to stay ahead. This accords with the empirical fact that the list of industrial countries has remained fairly stable since the start of the twentieth century. Another reason for divergence is that poorer countries find it more difficult to invest as much relatively as richer countries. Yet many individual countries and regions, despite their low initial starting point, have managed to catch up on the richer countries. Indeed, one could argue that the lower a country's income, the greater is its potential to outpace the growth of the richer countries, because of the technological spillovers from rich to poor countries. Poor countries can 'piggy-back' on the findings of expensive research undertaken and exploited in the better-off countries. World Bank forecasts up to the year 2008 predict annual growth per capita of 6 per cent in East Asia and 4 per cent in South Asia as compared with just over 2 per cent in high-income countries.

The catching-up controversy cannot be resolved by theory. Ultimately, it is an empirical question. One much cited empirical study estimated that the gap in income per person between a typical poor and a typical rich country diminishes at roughly 2 per cent per year.[15] This suggests that convergence will eventually dominate, albeit at a gradual rate (Box 2.4). Perhaps the most significant advance of recent research is the finding that poor countries will converge only under certain conditions. The *conditional convergence* literature stresses the importance of openness (globalisation), education (social capability to adapt to new technologies) and governance.

2.4 Policy prescriptions for growth

Economic growth is the result of the confluence of many different forces, both economic and non-economic. There is no single recipe for economic success. But a review of our knowledge to date suggests certain broad guidelines (Box 2.5).

First, we are now more conscious than in the past of the need to operate the economic system in an efficient way. Economic policy must be directed towards sustained growth: in formal terms, moving the 'production frontier' outwards. But we have learned that one way of achieving such outward shifts is to ensure that the economy is operating on the frontier in the first place. In the past, it was assumed that market inefficiencies were an acceptable price to pay for faster growth. Experience has shown that this supposed trade-off is illusory. The former socialist countries allocated a large portion of their resources to raising aggregate investment but, by neglecting the efficiency of individual investment and consumption decisions, the investment yielded a poor return in living standards. By and large, countries which emphasise economic efficiency also succeed in achieving the most rapid outward shifts in their production frontier.

---

15 R. Barro and X. Sala y Martin, 'Convergence across states and regions', *Brookings Papers on Economic Activity* 1 (1991); and *Economic Growth* (New York: McGraw-Hill, 1995).

Box 2.4

The arithmetic of growth

Just how slowly the catching-up process of economic growth works may be illustrated by a simple arithmetical example.

Consider country A growing at a rate of 3 per cent per annum, in contrast to poorer country B growing at the faster rate of 6 per cent per annum. The initial income of A is $26,000, while that of B is $6000. Despite Country B's faster growth rate, it will be 25 years before it reaches today's income level of country A. Moreover, since A's income is increasing each year, the absolute gap in income between the two economies increases for the first 29 years. It will take 53 years before income per head in country B finally exceeds that in country A.

Growth Rate	Country A	Country B	Absloute Income Gap
Year 1	26,000	6,000	20,000
Year 10	33,924	10,137	23,787
Year 20	45,591	18,154	27,438
Year 28	**57,754**	**28,934**	**28,819**
Year 29	59,486	30,670	28,816
Year 30	61,271	32,510	28,760
Year 40	82,343	58,221	24,122
Year 50	110,662	104,260	6,402
Year 53	**120,923**	**124,181**	**−3,258**
Year 54	124,551	131,632	−7,081

Yet, the cumulative effects of compound growth rates over the long term must not be neglected. Even small changes in the growth rate may have major cumulative effects. At a 3 per cent growth rate, GNP doubles in size every 25 years but, at a 4 per cent growth rate, doubling would occur in just under 18 years.

Second, as a consequence of the above, there is greater understanding of the need for government intervention to complement rather than replace market forces. Unless policy interventions are market-conforming, high investment and other prerequisites for growth will not be attained. (Hence the adage: getting prices right may not be the end of economic development; getting them wrong certainly is.) There is enhanced awareness of the importance of education, of a stable and transparent institutional framework, competition policy, labour market policy and basic infrastructure, for which the government has a major responsibility. The information revolution has spawned a new set of 'brainpower' industries – computers, electronics, biotechnology, robotics – which rely heavily on skilled labour. Countries that have adjusted their education systems to these new realities have grown fastest and will continue to prosper.

Box 2.5

Lessons from East Asia

The East Asian Miracle: Economic Growth and Public Policy, the product of a World Bank research team, published in 1993, stimulated widespread debate on the components of economic policy that underpinned the spectacular performance of the East Asian countries. From the mid-1960s to 1997 these countries registered an average yearly growth in GNP per person in excess of 5 per cent. Their export performance was particularly impressive, raising their share of world exports of manufactures from 9 per cent in 1965 to 21 per cent in 1990. Not only did these countries grow rapidly, they were also successful in sharing the fruits of growth, achieving low and declining inequality of income.

The World Bank report found that there was little that could be described as 'miraculous' about the economic performance, even though the chances of such a concentration of growth, assuming it were randomly distributed worldwide, were just one in 10,000. *Fundamentally sound development policy was the major ingredient in achieving rapid growth*, the report observed. Although each country pursued a diverse mix of policies with varying degrees of intervention, they all shared a commitment to getting the economic policy fundamentals right.

The report commented extensively on the role of government intervention in this growth process. Previous World Bank studies had tended to focus on the negative aspects of government interventions. State efforts to subsidise interest rates or to protect key industries or to encourage farming were severely criticised. By contrast, the 1993 study concluded that a combination of sound fundamentals and selective interventions was crucial to East Asia's success. Specifically, their governments focused on:

■ managing monetary and fiscal policy to ensure low inflation and a competitive exchange rate;
■ concentrating public investment in education on primary and secondary level schooling;
■ fostering effective and secure financial systems to encourage savings and investment;
■ limiting import protection so that domestic prices are close to international prices;
■ supporting agriculture by assisting the adoption of 'green revolution' technologies and investing in rural infrastructure;
■ encouraging exports.

	Population (millions) 1998	GDP per person (US$ PPP) 1998	Real GDP Growth Rate		Exports/GDP 1998
			1991–1997	1998–2000	
Indonesia	203.7	288	7.4	−2.4	53.9
Malaysia	22.2	7,450	8.6	−1.6	114.4
Thailand	61.1	6,633	6.7	−0.6	58.9
Singapore	3.2	27,545	8.4	2.1	152.5
Hong Kong	6.7	21,960	5.3	−1.1	125.1
Korea	46.4	12,471	7.2	0.4	48.7
China	1238.0	3,285	11.2	7.0	19.1

Source: International Monetary Fund, *World Economic Outlook*, May 1999; World Bank, *World Development Indicators Database*, 1999.

Box 2.5 continued

The countries comprised Japan, the four 'Tigers' (Hong Kong, Korea, Singapore, Taiwan) and three newly industrialised economies, Indonesia, Malaysia and Thailand.

Sources: The World Bank Atlas 1999 (World Bank, Washington, DC); J. Page, 'The East Asian miracle: Building a basis for growth', *Finance and Development* (March 1994); Helen Hughes, 'Why have East Asian countries led economic development?', *Economic Record* (March 1995); B. Aghveli, 'The Asian crisis: Causes and remedies', *Finance and Development* (June 1999). For a contrarian view, blaming the crisis on premature capital liberalisation and counterproductive IMF policies, see Joseph Stiglitz, 'What I learned at the world economic crisis', *The New Republic* (17 April 2000).

The third lesson is that poor macroeconomic management significantly impairs growth and that outward-oriented policies have positive effects on economic performance. Countries, like firms, need to focus on becoming internationally competitive. Attack in this sense may be the best defence, as well as being the most effective way of protecting one's domestic market from foreign competition.

Fourth, the economic environment needs to encourage and mobilise individual effort in a socially productive way. Countries with a poor economic growth record do not necessarily lack entrepreneurship. Rather, they lack the right type of entrepreneurship. Entrepreneurial effort needs to be allocated towards productive activities and away from unproductive, 'rent-seeking' activities. Rent-seeking refers to entrepreneurial behaviour which improves the welfare of some individuals or groups at the expense of the welfare of some other individuals or groups. Robert Reich, US Secretary of Labor in the Clinton administration, criticised the amount of human resources devoted to 'paper entrepreneurialism', i.e. 'creative' accounting, tax avoidance, financial management and litigation.[16] These activities mostly rearrange the distribution of wealth from one section of the population to another. Much has been made of the statistic that in the United States there is one lawyer for every 400 citizens, by comparison with one lawyer for every 10,000 in Japan. This difference in the allocation of talents can be attributed to national character and culture, but often it represents the rational response of individuals to the economic incentives existing in the respective societies.

2.5 Conclusions

For most of the nineteenth and twentieth centuries, formal economic analysis has focused on the problem of investment. Accumulation of capital was seen as the key to faster growth. The nineteenth-century economist worried about whether profits would remain sufficiently high to provide enough incentives to investment. Added to Malthusian concerns about growing population, this led some of the best-known nineteenth-century economists to pessimistic

---

16 Robert B. Reich, *The Next American Frontier* (New York: Penguin Books, 1983).

conclusions about the possibility of sustained growth. Hence the label of economics as 'the dismal science'.

Later models continued to lay stress on capital accumulation but added a crucial variable, technical progress, envisaged as a built-in propensity to innovate. Growth per person in this perspective was determined by (1) the level of saving and investment, and (2) technical progress which affected the productivity of that investment. What governs the *amount* of investment was still seen as the crucial element in the growth process. This way of thinking encouraged what now appears an overoptimistic and naive belief that if only investment could be raised to a sufficiently high level, growth would automatically follow. Governments formulated economic plans in which state investment projects figured prominently and, in the case of developing countries, into which foreign aid was integrated. The government was to some extent regarded as an investor of last resort, in the event of the private sector not investing as much as was warranted. Ways of thinking about growth had a very practical impact. They underpinned the era of economic planning and multi-year investment programmes, which flourished in the 1950s and 1960s.

Since then, the emphasis has shifted dramatically from concern about the *amount* of investment to *quality* of investment and to a deeper understanding of the importance of the 'knowledge economy' as well as investment activities. This change of perspective was prompted by the fact that economic planning had outlived its usefulness. Investment, if badly allocated, will yield poor results and eventually prove unsustainable. The gradual seizing-up of the socialist economies and the failure of planning regimes in developing countries encouraged the search for new and more effective approaches to development. Out of this came the revival of liberal economics.

Experience suggests that economic policy matters a great deal. While not reverting to complete *laissez-faire*, the new orthodoxy sets more critical and demanding criteria for government intervention. More than the free operation of market forces is necessary to guarantee everybody a better life. But market-oriented policies can help us on the way. And, for certain, a thorough understanding of the working of market forces is necessary for an understanding of today's business and economic environment.

In the industrial countries, postwar growth has been attributed to high investment, advancing levels of education, trade liberalisation and social consensus. The slowdown in growth since the 1970s has been blamed on excessive government spending, lax policies towards inflation and (in Europe) over-regulation of the labour market.

In developing countries, the main feature of the postwar era is the sharp contrast in performance between different sets of countries over different time-periods. In the 1950s and early 1960s, the prevailing expectations were optimistic with regard to the growth prospects of Africa and Latin America, and pessimistic with regard to Asia. Asian countries, it was feared, would run up against a Malthusian 'trap', with population growth outpacing the limited availability of land and other natural resources. As it transpired, these fears have proved unwarranted. Asia's growth has been sustained, notwithstanding the 1997–98 currency crisis. The factors underlying East Asia's growth have been much analysed – success always attracts would-be emulators – and have been found to be very diverse. The priority given to education, high investment rates in both the private and public sectors, efficient deployment of the labour force and involvement in international trade seem to have combined, albeit in different ways in each country, to give Asian countries a strong competitive position. The fortunes of South Asia and Latin America are also changing for the better. Their improved prospects have been associated with the implementation of a comprehensive package of 'new consensus' economic reforms.

The central conclusion of modern growth theory is that consistent market-oriented policies, political stability and efficient institutions are essential to growth. Icelandic economist Professor Thorvaldur Glyfason expresses this view forcefully in his recent textbook on growth theory:

> The main point of this book is that, with appropriate economic policies and institutions, rapid economic growth is achievable almost anywhere (*Principles of Economic Growth*, Oxford: Oxford University Press, 1999, p. 15).

One is tempted to add – even in a small, remote island with as inhospitable a climate as Iceland's! *To grow or not to grow*, he asserts, *is in large measure a matter of choice*. Economic growth takes place in the first instance because of a myriad of decisions made by individual firms. Decisions on where, when and what to invest, how much to spend on R&D, the development of a new product or a new process, collectively constitute the driving forces of growth. These decisions are strongly influenced by expected profitability. Fast-growing economies are likely to be those where rewards and incentives are closely associated to activities that encourage productive entrepreneurial activity.

✔ Summary

1. Economic growth measures the increase in a country's material prosperity. Sustained growth is a primary target of economic policy.

2. Most countries have experienced average annual growth of between 2 per cent and 4 per cent during the past forty years. Growth at 3 per cent sustained over twenty-three years results in a doubling of income. Some areas have performed much better than average, notably the high-performing economies of East Asia, but a number of countries in Sub-Saharan Africa have suffered an absolute decline in living standards. Economic growth is the norm, but it cannot be taken for granted.

3. The growth process is stimulated and sustained by increases in supplies of factors of production. Traditionally, emphasis was placed on physical investment and on the necessity of ensuring that capital stock grew faster than the number of people. Recent empirical studies have drawn attention to the overwhelming importance of productivity growth, in particular total factor productivity.

4. Among the ultimate causes of higher productivity growth are technological advance, quality of education, reallocation of resources from low-productivity to high-productivity sectors, political stability and business incentives. Recent growth theories stress the mutually reinforcing nature of the growth process. Thus, fast growth helps an economy achieve technological advance, which in turn speeds up growth even more. Economic policy also plays a vital part. Its objective is to ensure that optimum use is made of society's resources and that there are strong incentives to improve national productivity. Under certain assumptions, it can be shown that the free market system leads to a more efficient outcome than any other system.

5. The connection between income distribution and economic performance has proved difficult to quantify. Curiously, better-off societies often tend to be more egalitarian than poorer countries. Use of market incentives is not inconsistent with an even income distribution. The nature of the growth–equity trade-off is still a controversial subject and the precise direction of causality is not clear. To be sure, a country does not become rich just by redistributing income from poor to rich. But, as a result of becoming rich, it can afford to redistribute income. Neglect of equity can damage growth prospects: too much emphasis on it damages efficiency.

6. Economic growth has implications for the environment, as well as for income distribution, which impact on its usefulness as an indicator of human welfare. Standard growth measures such as average annual GNP per person are far from being perfect indicators of welfare, but they are the best available.

7. There is no magic formula for economic growth, but three lessons have been learned which have important implications for the business environment. First, the economic system must be allowed to operate in an efficient way. Second, government must intervene in the economy but, in so doing, it should seek to complement, rather than to supplant, market forces. Third, the macroeconomic management of an economy and its foreign trade policies can be an important influence for good or ill on its growth performance.

? Questions for discussion

1. What are the main points of similarity and difference between the determinants of the growth of a firm and the growth of an economy?

2. In judging an economy's growth performance, distinctions must be kept in mind between:
   (a) quantity and quality of growth;
   (b) the benefits of growth and the costs of growth;
   (c) the short and the long run.
   Discuss growth performance with respect to each of these headings.

3. An article in *Atlantic Monthly* (October 1995) commented on the discordance between booming GNP figures for the US economy and an electorate which felt

insecure and worse-off than before. The article explained this paradox of 'gloomy voters in good times' by the inadequacies of GNP as a measure of welfare and criticised GNP because it 'treats leisure time and time with family the way it treats air and water: as having no value at all. When the need for a second job cuts the time available for family and community, the GDP records this loss as an economic gain.' Do you agree with this criticism?

4. Effective economic policies lead to faster economic growth not only by creating a business environment conducive to investment, but also by increasing the amount of growth pay-off per unit of investment. Discuss the policy measures which would be effective in raising a country's total factor productivity.

5. It is often said that technological progress is the key to economic progress. Explain how advances in technology affect growth. What other factors are important?

6. How 'exportable' is the Asian experience to regions such as Sub-Saharan Africa?

Exercises

1. Find out the level of GDP of any country you have a special interest in. Examine its rate of increase during the past decade. Compare its growth with that of the country groups in the chapter tables. What features would you identify as critical in explaining this growth? How might you test whether your views are correct?

2. You are asked to prepare a business report on an Asian economy. In evaluating its prospects for future growth, what variables would you consider most important, and why?

3. Between 1960 and 1990, Korea and Zambia had the same ratio of investment to GDP. Yet Korea's GDP grew by 9 per cent per year, while Zambia's grew by just 1 per cent. What factors would you consider in trying to explain this difference in performance?

4. Two economies, Lilliput and Oz, exist beside each other. Last year Lilliput experienced an annual growth rate of 8 per cent in GDP, while Oz experienced annual growth of 5 per cent. 'The citizens of Lilliput are clearly better-off than the citizens of Oz', claimed a local journal. Explain what further information you would require before accepting this assessment as valid.

5. An executive marries his housekeeper, who continues to work in the home after marriage. Explain what happens to GDP.

6. India's per capita GNP was $2060 in 1998 (PPP basis). Assuming a growth rate of 3 per cent per person was sustained, how many years will it take India to reach average GDP level in the industrial countries of $23,420? Suppose industrial countries continue to grow at 2 per cent, how long before India catches up with the industrial countries? Comment on the plausibility of these projections.

📖 Further reading

Information on the growth performance of developed economies and up-to-date estimates and forecasts are provided by the OECD (Paris), by the European Commission (Brussels) and by research institutes such as the UK's *National Institute of Economic Review*. *The World Development Report* of the World Bank is an authoritative source of data on developing countries. The World Bank's publications provide regular reviews and assessments of growth performance and constraints. The causes of economic growth have occupied the attention of economists since the foundation of the subject and are the subject of continuing analysis and controversy. T. Gylfason offers a concise and non-technical overview of recent growth theory in *Principles of Economic Growth* (Oxford: Oxford University Press, 1999). Jeffrey Sachs of Harvard has written extensively on the empirical determinants of growth. See J. Sachs and A. Warner, 'Economic reform and the process of global integration', *Brookings Papers on Economic Activity* 1 (1995). One of the more controversial topics has been the negative aspects of economic growth, on which both E.J. Mishan, *The Costs of Economic Growth* (Harmondsworth: Penguin Books, 1967) and Fred Hirsch, *The Social Limits to Growth* (London: Routledge, 1977) are standard and highly engaging references.

Appendix 2.1: The economics of the new economy

The 'new economy' refers to a range of new industries and activities, mostly in information technology (IT) and biotechnology, that have grown at breakneck speed during the past decade, have generated vast fortunes on the stock market and have revolutionised the way work is done in many sectors of the economy. The new economy has been fed by a once- or twice-in-a-century surge in technology that has boosted productivity-enhancing and cost-reducing investment and raised long-term economic growth. The Internet is an example of the rapidity of change. It had fewer than 3 million users worldwide in 1991 and its application to e-commerce was non-existent. Ten years later, an estimated 250 million users accessed the Internet and about one quarter of them made purchases online from electronic sites, worth approximately $110 billion. At present this amounts to well under 5 per cent of total business-to-business (B2B) and business-to-consumer (B2C) transactions, but the potential for e-commerce growth beyond this figure is enormous. By 2003, estimates of worldwide e-commerce range from $1,200 billion to $4,600 billion. Computer-related spillovers, increasing returns in the production and use of computers, and network effects are fundamentally changing the US economy (Jorgenson and Stiroh, 1999).

Initially some believed that IT-related advances in technology were part of a continuum of change: capable of generating productivity improvements, but not at a rate that was any different from the past. The 'new economy' was seen more as a phenomenom affecting trends in the stock market than trend growth in the real economy. By the turn of the millennium, however, the consensus had shifted to the view that the IT revolution has made an important contribution to trend change in both labour productivity and total factor productivity and that these have translated into an increase of 0.5 percentage point in trend GNP growth.

To date the US has been the laboratory test case. It is the world's largest producer and consumer of high-tech products. According to World Bank figures, the US has

459 personal computers per 1000 people compared with only 263 in the UK, 305 in Germany (Table A2.1). Comparisons between e-commerce transactions and other indicators of IT use, such as availability of Internet hosts, show the US to be vastly more developed than most other countries. However, this superiority has been slow to translate into higher US productivity growth. The expected surge became evident only since the mid 1990s, when labour productivity began to grow at 3 per cent annually, double the rate of previous decades. Some sightings of a similar acceleration have been observed in the UK; and euro-optimists expected this to pass through to other member states in the EU that had invested heavily in IT. IT raises productivity in several ways: capital-deepening via investment in high-tech activities; total factor productivity increases in these activities; and spillover effects on 'old economy' activities as new technology is applied to them.

The new economy has important indirect effects on the economy. First, high-tech industries have a strong appetite for skilled computer-literature labour, while at the same time diminishing the relative demand for unskilled employees. This tends to raise the renumeration of the skilled and better-paid employees relative to the unskilled. US Department of Labor statistics show the real weekly earnings of graduates have risen by 15 per cent compared with a 12 per cent fall in pay for those who left education after high school. In Europe the trend is much less pronounced, partly because it is less advanced in IT investment and partly also because the supply of skilled labour has been increased through investment in education (supply and demand analysis is outlined in Chapter 3). The new economy requires, and stimulates, massive investment in education.

The advance in technology also has implications for competition. This effect applies especially to activities where 'new' economies of scale and scope (network economies) apply. Robert Metcalfe, founder of 3Com, the network vendor, argued that in a network the value of intercommunication among particpants increases with the square of the number of participants, while the costs increase only linearly. Metcalfe's law applies especially to electronic marketplaces and helps to explain why many new economy industries such as software (Microsoft) and media (Time Warner), tend to be dominated by a few firms. (Economies of scale and monopoly are discussed in Chapters 5 and 6 below.) At the same time, IT tends to enhance competition in activities where small firms can benefit from access to data and information sources that formerly were limited to the better off. It falls to the competition authorities to weigh the balance between these opposing forces in specific cases.

New economy activities have raised measurement problems for GNP statisticians. IT products have fallen dramatically in price. The price of PCs fell by an annual average of 24 per cent during the 1990s. The acquisition price of IT equipment for investment fell 16 per cent during the same period. Statistical problems arise when it comes to assessing the price equivalent of dramatic improvements in quality, as in the case of PCs and Intel chips. The US authorities estimate these effects in a different way to the EU statisticians. For this reason, a Bundesbank report published in 2000 revealed that EU growth would be half a percentage point higher if US statistical methodology was applied to EU GNP calculation.

Table A2.1 Access to new technology

	Mobile phones per 1000 people	Personal computers per 1000 people	Internet hosts per 10,000 people
United States	256	459	1508
United Kingdom	252	263	271
Germany	170	305	174
France	188	208	111
Italy	355	173	68
Argentina	78	44	28
Morocco	4	3	0.3
Brazil	47	30	18
China	19	9	0.5
India	1	3	0.2

Source: World Bank, *World Development Indicators* 2000. Figures relate to 1998.

How will new tech developments affect poorer countries? Optimists argue that latecomers enjoy the luxury of being able to 'catch up' without incurring all the development costs that richer countries have had to pay in bringing the product to market. A business in India, for example, can avail of the Internet to access the same information that is available to citizens of the richest countries. New, 'weightless' goods and services have caused the 'death of distance' that gives remote and marginalised peoples a better opportunity of boarding the high-tech bandwagon. On the other hand, economies of scale often tend to benefit first movers, through exploitation of network economies of scope, and thus to reinforce the income gains of the richer countries. Research indicates that on balance the positive effects on developing countries outweigh the negative effects subject to one proviso: that developing countries ensure basic levels of education and skills that enable their people to utilise and understand the new technologies being imported from the industrial countries.

Sources: 'E-commerce: Impacts and Policy Challenges', OECD *Economic Outlook*, June 2000; C. Leabetter, *Living on Thin Air* (London: Viking Penguin Books, 1999); 'The New Economy', *The Economist* 23 September 2000; D. Jorgenson and K. Stiroh, 'Information Technology and Growth', *American Economic Review*, May 1999.

Part I

THE MARKET SYSTEM AND COMPETITION

Introduction to Part I

How does the market system function? We begin (in Chapter 3) with an overview of forces of demand and supply, and show how these interact to determine prices. Prices in a free market act as a signalling device. A rise in the price of a product indicates that this product has become scarcer. The price increase signals to consumers the need to purchase less, by seeking cheaper substitutes for instance, and it signals to business the need for more supply. Consideration is given to the institutional background required if the free market system is to operate efficiently. In long-established market economies this background tends to be taken for granted, but the experience of the newly liberalised economies of Europe showed the importance of an adequate institutional framework of law, custom and behaviour.

Next (Chapter 4) we study the determinants of demand. Students of marketing will find many points of similarity and contrast between the marketing and the economics approach to this issue. The meaning and usefulness of the concept of elasticity of demand and its relevance to the firm's pricing decision is explained.

This is followed by chapters detailing the determinants of supply and the response of the individual firm to changes in the economic environment. We study the firm's cost structure, paying particular attention to economies of scale and scope (Chapter 5), and also to the extent of competition in the market (Chapter 6). As competition intensifies, goods tend to become cheaper and businesses tend to be managed more efficiently. The assumptions underlying the economic case for competition and the market mechanism are analysed.

Under conditions of competition companies make profits, but in equilibrium these will be just sufficient to service the capital invested in its assets and to keep the firm in business. Competition from new entrants makes it impossible to earn any more than this. Thus a company can only make 'real' money when there is imperfect competition. A firm will strive to move away from the 'ideal', perfectly competitive market. It can build up a degree of monopoly power by a number of strategies: product differentiation, innovation, creation of a patent or brand name.

There is a tension between the imperative of exploiting economies of scale on the one hand and keeping large numbers in the industry in order to preserve competition on the other. In some industries, the cost of developing new products has become so large that small independent producers have been driven out of the market. Scale economies have led to the absorption of many formerly independent firms into much larger entities. The cost of developing new products is driving many firms to seek out new forms of organisation. Multinationals have found it possible to compete fiercely with each other in some markets, while agreeing cooperative sales and distribution arrangements in other markets.

The marketplace needs to be policed. Fair trading rules have to be enforced in order to protect the consumer. They are also needed to protect many firms which are vulnerable to unfair and unscrupulous competition from financially powerful rivals. For this reason, most countries have established institutions to enforce competition. Where monopoly cannot be avoided, public intervention is also needed to regulate the monopolist's behaviour. These issues are discussed in Chapter 7. Also, we analyse the privatisation programmes, which have been such a distinctive feature of the economic scene for the last two decades of the twentieth century.

Although there is a strong movement towards smaller government, public intervention can and does contribute significantly to the market system. Business complains of taxes, as does everyone else, but knows that some level of taxation is essential if the fabric of society, and the market system itself, is to be preserved. The question is less one of whether government intervention is *needed*, as what type and how much government intervention is *optimal* (Chapter 8).

Economic policies relating to the environment have a serious impact on many firms. Chapter 9 examines the relevance of the economic concepts developed in this section to this topical and important issue.

Finally, we outline (Chapter 10) how simple demand and supply analysis can be used to explain the determination of pay at plant level and industry level, and also to illuminate the nature of a firm's investment decisions.

Microeconomics, as the type of economics used in this section is called, provides useful and practical insights for business. The material in this section is not designed to teach the reader an easy way of becoming either an economist or an entrepreneur. But it will help budding entrepreneurs – and those who in the future will advise and assist them – to understand the market system and to participate in the ongoing task of improving it.

Chapter 3

THE MARKET SYSTEM IN ACTION

Introduction

The free market comprises a series of interconnected markets. These markets are assumed to be highly competitive and to operate free of government interference. This is an initial simplifying assumption, which will be relaxed in later chapters. In reality, many markets are subject to monopolistic influences, and government intervention in the market system is a feature of even the most enthusiastically capitalist society. Indeed, in some circumstances, such intervention can be shown to be a necessary condition for achieving economic efficiency. Additionally, we assume a stable institutional framework of law and order within which market transactions can be conducted in an orderly and predictable way.

What is a market? There are many types of market, but the one we start with is a *perfectly competitive market*. It has the following characteristics:

- Large numbers of sellers and buyers, each acting independently and exerting no individual monopolistic power.
- Full information – everyone knows what the going price is and can evaluate the quality of the good or service being produced.
- Consumers aim to maximise utility (i.e. personal satisfaction) and firms aim to maximise profits.
- Prices are flexible in all markets.

Given these conditions, the market system fulfils the function of allocating resources between different uses and among different people. It acts as an equilibrating mechanism between supply and demand. Prices act as *signals*; and the price system is the coordinating mechanism which ensures that markets 'clear', i.e. that supply equals demand in each market.

The operation of the price system is by no means obvious. The fact that a free market system works at all may be considered, if one stops to think about it, as somewhat miraculous. Millions of individual decisions are taken daily in a market economy by producers and consumers. These decisions are independent and uncoordinated. Yet, by and large, goods and services are available in the shops to meet consumer demands as they arise. The market system is the mechanism which brings this about in an automatic and efficient manner.

Chapter outline

1. Description of the overall market system.

2. The functioning of prices in the context of a single market.

3. What causes demand and supply to change, how the price system responds to such changes, and the effect of taxes, subsidies and price limits on market quantities and prices.

4. The role of traders and middlemen in the system.

5. The efficiency of free market competition.

6. The social and institutional conditions necessary for the market system to operate smoothly.

3.1 The market system

The market system can be sketched by reference to three major markets – the product market, the labour market and the capital market – and two primary sets of participants: firms and households (see Figure 3.1). The *product market* comprises the markets for individual goods and services; the *labour market* involves the buying and selling of labour; and the *capital market* deals with the lending and borrowing of capital. Each market involves the participation of *firms* and *households*. Thus, households sell their labour to firms; and, with the salaries so earned, they buy goods and services from firms. Firms produce goods and services by hiring labour and capital from households (and other firms). Households and firms also interact on the capital market. If individuals choose not to spend all their income, their savings are channelled to firms by intermediaries such as banks and pension funds. If they choose to spend more than their income, loans will be supplied by the same intermediaries. The lines in Figure 3.1 run both ways. However, the savings arrow from households to firms is thicker than the reverse arrow from firms to households in recognition of the fact that the corporate sector is the key investor and borrower in an economy. Households are generally net suppliers of funds to firms.

This is a much simplified conceptualisation of the market system as we know it in the real world, but it is sufficient to illustrate the strong interconnections between markets. Households need to sell their labour to firms in order to be able to buy goods. Unless households spend their incomes on purchases of goods and services, there will not be any demand for their labour. Or, to take another example, if firms do not invest, there will be no demand for household savings: savings are useful only in so far as there is an investor somewhere ready and willing to use them for investment. Clearly, a mechanism must exist to bring these disparate and independent decisions into equilibrium. A sustained disequilibrium in one part of this closely interconnected market system can have serious repercussions on other parts of the system. The market system is, in other words, a general equilibrium system. If anything goes wrong with the market mechanism, an economy could run into serious trouble.

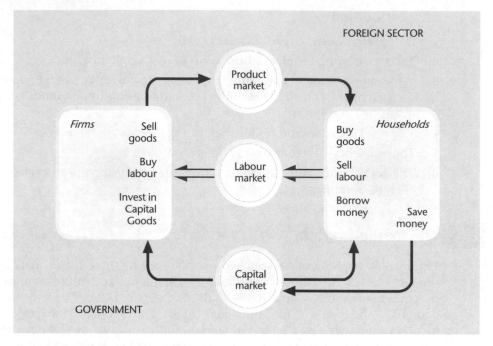

Figure 3.1 The market system

Two other market participants must be considered – the *foreign sector* and the *government sector*. Firms do not have to sell their entire output to domestic consumers. They also have the option of exporting. Likewise, households can import goods and services instead of buying the output of domestic firms. Imports, exports and the foreign trade market are an integral part of an analysis of the market system. Factors of production such as capital and labour can also be traded internationally. The rise in global capital mobility, especially between developed countries, has meant that the domestic economy is no longer restricted to domestic savings for its supply of investment funds. The foreign sector has been growing rapidly in relative importance during the postwar period.

The government is also an important participant in the market. Government spending amounts to about 40 per cent of total national expenditure in industrial countries generally and exceeds 50 per cent in a number of European countries. Sweden's ratio is 60 per cent (and it exceeded 70 per cent in 1993). Even in an economy as free market-oriented as the US, the government's share of total spending ratio is 30 per cent (2000). The spending ratio, however, gives only a rough impression of the extent of government influence in the market system. Public intervention takes many forms in addition to government spending. Official regulations impinge on all areas of economic life – planning requirements for new buildings, health and safety regulations, environmental restrictions, for example. State-owned commercial companies are another vehicle of government influence not reflected in the spending : GDP ratio.

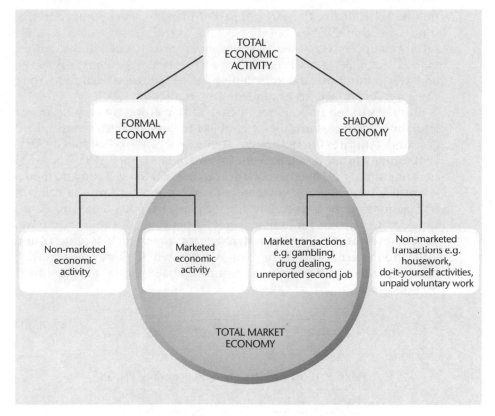

Figure 3.2 Total economic activity and the market economy

Source: S. Smith, *Britain's Shadow Economy*, 1986, Oxford, Clarendon Press.

Economics is primarily about the market economy. The market economy includes all those goods and services that are sold on the market at a price determined by supply and demand. In the market economy, price plays the key role in determining production and allocation of output. The market economy, however, is not coterminous with total economic activity.

This point is illustrated in Figure 3.2. Total economic activity is divided into two components: the *formal economy*, the activities of which are measured and recorded in national economic statistics; and the *shadow economy*, the activities of which largely escape classification and measurement. The market economy extends over a large section of both these economies, but it does not include all their activities. Thus, in the shadow economy, unpaid housework, do-it-yourself repairs, and the activities of voluntary organisations are useful and important activities, but they are not part of the market economy. Housework includes childcare, cooking, cleaning, household repairs and decorations. Voluntary activities include activities such as mountain rescue, the lifeboat services, and unpaid administration of clubs, churches and agencies for the elderly and the handicapped. The distinctive features of these activities are that their output is not marketed (hence they are not part of the market economy) and that they are not recorded in GDP (hence they belong to the shadow economy). By contrast, several components of the shadow economy are included in the definition of the market sector. Black market activities such as double-jobbing, casual service work and the production and distribution of illegal goods fall into the marketed category. A conspicuous example is drug trafficking.

Estimates of the importance of the shadow economy vary between countries and, for obvious reasons, they are subject to large margins of error. Underground economy estimates for 1997 range from 30 per cent of GDP for Greece and 27 per cent for Italy to a low of 8 per cent for Switzerland (Table 3.1). These figures show how important the shadow economy can be even for well run and modestly-taxed countries. Where central government is weak and corrupt, the value of 'hidden' transactions can be expected to rise. Schneider reports figures of 62 per cent for Georgia, 39 per cent for Romania and 54 per cent for the Ukraine. Equally hair-raising estimates have been derived for many developing countries. The underground economy in the US was estimated at 11 per cent of GDP in 1992, comprising $585 billion of legal income and $88 billion of illegal income[1] (Box 3.1).

Table 3.1 **Size of the shadow economy (% GNP)**

Country	1990	1997
Austria	5	9
Belgium	20	22
Canada	14	15
Denmark	11	18
Germany	12	15
Greece	27	30
France	9	15
Ireland	12	16
Italy	23	27
Netherlands	14	14
Norway	15	19
Spain	21	23
Sweden	16	19
Switzerland	7	8
UK	10	13
USA	7	9

Source: F. Schneider, 'The shadow economies of Western Europe', Economic Affairs, September 1997.

---

1 These figures are reported in R. Mirus, R.S. Smith and V. Karoleff, 'Canada's underground economy revisited: Update and critique', *Canadian Public Policy* (September 1994).

Box 3.1

The shadow economy

The 'shadow', 'underground' or 'black' economy is a feature of most economies. It is part of the market economy because it involves marketed transactions freely entered into by third parties. Shadow market activities are motivated sometimes by the desire to evade legal restrictions (for example, illegal gambling, drug dealing), sometimes by the desire to evade tax or avoid loss of state payments (for example, part-time work by the unemployed, casual earnings, unreported rental income, tips, baby-sitters' earnings, sales of home-grown produce, 'skimming' cash receipts by shopkeepers). Sometimes the two motivations coexist. For example, smuggling can be a way of simultaneously evading the law and the tax authorities.

The key characteristic of the shadow economy is that its activities are not officially reported. The question is often asked: to what extent are GDP estimates distorted by this omission?

How to measure?

By its nature, measurement of the shadow economy is difficult and uncertain. Estimation of the shadow economy has been described as a 'scientific passion for knowing the unknown' (Schneider and Enste 1999, p. 4). Most methods rely on indirect procedures.

Monetary aggregates method

Market activities in the shadow economy involve cash transactions since payment in cash is the safest and surest way of keeping them unrecorded. Hence, the larger the shadow economy, the greater the use of currency relative to bank deposits. Data on the currency/deposit ratio can be used to estimate the value of the shadow economy.

Income expenditure discrepancy

Shadow economy incomes must be spent. Often, the effect of such spending is to create a divergence between spending and income measures of GNP. Divergences between reported spending and reported income can be used as an indicator of shadow economy activity.

Special investigations

These can be based on household surveys, special labour market surveys and tax audits. They are undertaken from time to time by the statistical authorities.

How large relative to official GNP?

Estimates of the shadow economy based on monetary aggregates frequently amount to as high as 30 per cent of official GNP, while the income expenditure estimates reveal something of the order of 2–15 per cent for most countries. There are wide variations among countries and, more worryingly, between different methods of estimation. To some extent this is an ineradicable problem because of the nature of the activity being measured.

Box 3.1 continued

Causes

The main factors contributing to the black economy are:

1. high taxes and a perceived lack of 'fairness' of the tax system,
2. high burden of regulation,
3. high unemployment combined with high unemployment compensation,
4. onerous employment regulations,
5. cultural and personal behaviour characteristics.

Cures

First, the most effective cure is to reduce tax rates and to make them simpler to comply with. Many countries are seeking to achieve this without detriment to overall tax revenue by measures to 'broaden' the tax base. This reduces the rewards of tax evasion.

Second, regulation and legal restrictions can be made less onerous and more focused. Small businesses are particularly affected by many employee protection and other regulations which involve high compliance costs. A better system would diminish the often high degree of tacit public support for black economy activities.

Third, a higher degree of compliance can be enforced by better internal monitoring and by international cooperation among tax authorities.

Sources: F. Schneider, 'The shadow economies of western Europe', *Economic Affairs* (September 1997); F. Schneider and D. Enste, 'Shadow economies around the world – size, causes and consequences', CESifo Working Paper no. 196 (September 1999).

These figures show how important the shadow economy can be even for well run and modestly-taxed countries. Where central government is weak and corrupt, the value of 'hidden' transactions can be expected to rise. Schneider reports figures of 62 per cent for Georgia, 39 per cent for Romania and 54 per cent for the Ukraine. Equally hair-rising estimates have been derived for many developing countries.

Most of the formal economy consists of marketed activity. But there is one major exception. The government provides many services which are not sold on the market. There is no market for defence, for example. Government does not offer to sell the services of its soldiers to the highest bidder! Likewise the judiciary and the police are not included in the market economy. In the EU, about 22 per cent of the workforce in the formal economy is employed in producing non-marketed services.[2]

Despite these qualifications, the major proportion of economic activity is marketed. GDP, however, is not a fully accurate measure of the market economy. It is too small in so far as it excludes illegal and unreported transactions in the shadow economy, and too large in so far as it includes non-marketed services. But it may be taken as a reasonable approximation in many industrial countries.

The non-marketed sector makes an important contribution to society's welfare. That some activities are not marketed means it is difficult to value them, not that

---

2 *Panorama of EU Industry* (Brussels: European Commission, 1997).

they are without value. Yet a crucial strength of the marketed sector, as a way of providing goods and services, is that its activities are kept under competitive scrutiny and subjected repeatedly to the test of the marketplace. Producers of a good or service usually think highly of the product they provide and believe that it is good for, and will please, the consumer. The market subjects this perception to an acid test. It provides an instant poll of whether the consumer agrees or disagrees with the provider's assessment. The verdict of the market is impersonal, decisive and measurable. It is conveyed to the producer through the price mechanism.

3.2 The role of prices

Price is determined by demand and supply. If demand exceeds supply, price tends to rise. If supply exceeds demand, price tends to fall. This description of the role of price is familiar to most people. It can be illustrated by a simple example. Consider the demand for rice and the supply of rice, and how changes in the price of rice bring supply and demand into equilibrium.

The first step is to draw a demand curve. This shows how much rice will be demanded at each price level. We make the reasonable assumption that the relationship is negative. As rice becomes cheaper, it becomes more affordable and people consume more of it. As price falls, demand rises. The corollary also holds: as rice becomes dearer, quantity demanded falls. This is termed the law of demand. The demand curve in Figure 3.3 illustrates this point. As we *move along the demand curve, we refer to a rise or a fall in demand.*

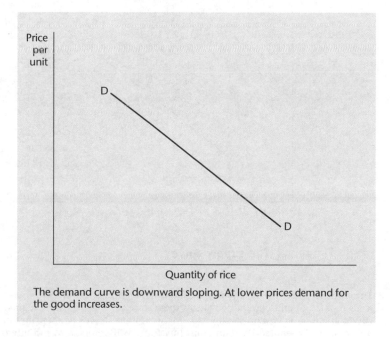

The demand curve is downward sloping. At lower prices demand for the good increases.

Figure 3.3 The demand curve

The next step is to construct a supply curve. This indicates the amount supplied by firms at each price level. We assume that the curve is upward-sloping: that is, the supply of rice increases as price rises, and falls as price declines. A higher price enhances the profitability of rice production and makes it economical for producers to offer overtime to their workers or to hire extra employees, even if they are less productive than the existing workforce. Another option made possible by higher price is to shift production from other products to rice. Lower prices are assumed to have the opposite effect. Hence the supply curve in Figure 3.4 slopes upwards.[3]

Now place the demand curve and supply curve together (Figure 3.5). Suppose price happened to be at P_1. At this price the amount supplied, OH, exceeds the amount demanded, OQ. Retailers will find inventories of the product rising. Producers will find orders slowing down and their own inventories will increase. Inevitably, someone will give the order to 'move' the product by reducing the price.

As price falls, two things happen. First, demand tends to rise: more rice is consumed because existing customers eat more and new customers appear on the scene. This effect is captured by the movement downwards along the demand curve from A to E. Second, supply tends to fall. The decline in the price spills back into lower profits. Some producers will go out of business; others will operate at a

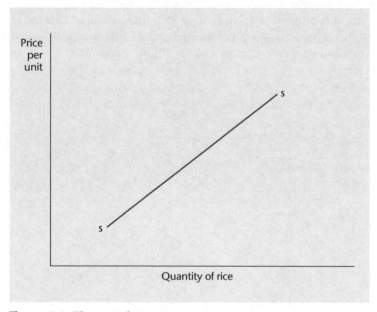

Figure 3.4 **The supply curve**

---

3 The sequence of events may not be that simple in practice. Thus, many firms find that more demand leads to a fall in unit costs which allows them to sell at a lower, not a higher, price. Their supply curves might be downward-sloping rather than upward-sloping. For a plant of given size, however, unit costs will rise after a certain point (machines will be operated too intensively, there will be administrative bottlenecks, etc.).

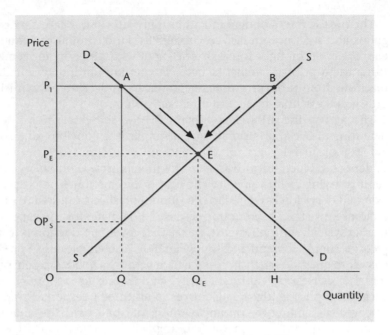

Figure 3.5 **Excess supply causes prices to fall**

reduced output level. This effect is captured by the movement downwards along the supply curve from B to E. Eventually, demand and supply are brought into equilibrium. *Market equilibrium* is reached at price OP_E and quantity of rice OQ_E. At this point, there is no tendency for price to either rise or fall. Provided the assumptions of the competitive market hold, there will be continuous pressure to move towards the equilibrium point.

The above analysis contains an implicit assumption about the adjustment process. We have assumed that if supply exceeds demand, price declines and, if demand exceeds supply, price increases. In other words, adjustment occurs via changes in price because of disparity between quantity supplied and quantity demanded at a particular price. An alternative adjustment process is via *changes in quantities*. We consider price disparities at a given output level instead of quantity disparities at a given price level. If, for any given quantity supplied, the supply price exceeds the price at which that quantity is demanded, then the quantity supplied will decrease. If the demand price exceeds the supply price, quantity supplied increases. For example, consider a given supply OQ in Figure 3.5. The price at which that quantity is demanded, OP_1, is higher than its supply price, OP_S. This means that quantity supplied will increase. Note that, as the curves are drawn, it makes no difference to the equilibrium outcome which of the two adjustment mechanisms is chosen.[4]

---

4 This is called the Marshallian adjustment process; that based on price movements is the Walrasian adjustment process. With differently shaped curves, specifically if the supply curve happens to be downward-sloping, it makes a difference which adjustment process is assumed from the point of view of the stability of equilibrium.

These basic forces of demand and supply affect all markets – not just consumer goods and services, but also raw materials, land, capital and labour. In all cases, equilibrium is brought into existence and is sustained by movements in price. In turn, these price movements help restore equilibrium by eliciting predictable reactions from profit-maximising producers and utility-maximising individuals. This is the essential feature of a market system.

The above discussion has explained how the price of a good or service is determined. The analysis may appear simple, even obvious, and so in a sense it is. Yet it took many years for the mechanism of price determination to be fully understood. Much effort was spent by the classical economists of the nineteenth century trying to link price to the cost of production. The cost of a product was assumed to be closely related to the amount of labour required to produce it. Hence, a moral as well as an economic case could be made for the superiority of the free market system. With hindsight, we see that cost of production is just one side of the picture. Simple demand and supply analysis also enables us to provide a definitive answer to questions such as: Is price high because a good is expensive to make? Or is it high because people prize it greatly? Or does one go to a lot of expense to make it because its price is high? The answer to all three questions is *yes*. In a celebrated passage, the eminent economist Alfred Marshall used the analogy of a pair of scissors to explain how demand and supply jointly determine price. Which blade of a scissors cuts the page? One cannot say: both blades together do the cutting.

While prices are determined by supply and demand, they also act as *incentives* and as *sources of information*. They play an active as well as a passive role in the market system. Changes in price *bring about* equilibrium between demand and supply. When a gap threatens to appear between demand and supply, prices act as a signalling mechanism to bring them closer together. These signalling and incentive functions of price play a vital role in making the market system work.

3.3 Movements in demand and supply

Demand and supply curves do not stay permanently in the one position. Over time, demand will shift because of changes in:

- the level of income available to consumers,
- the price of substitute or complementary goods,
- the distribution of income among different classes of consumers,
- the demographic structure and age-trends,
- tastes and fashion,
- seasonal factors.

Each demand curve is defined relative to its own price for given levels of these other variables. If they change, the demand curve will shift. The term an 'increase' or 'decrease' in demand, by conventional usage, is used to denote an outward or inward shift in the demand curve.

Suppose real income in a country rises by 10 per cent. Demand for rice will increase. In Figure 3.6 we depict this as a shift in the demand curve from DD to

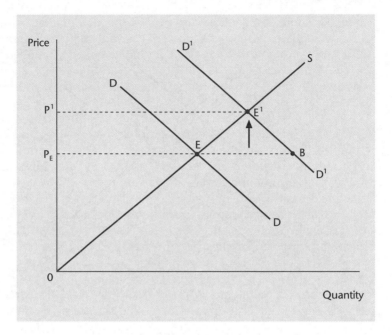

Figure 3.6 An outward shift in the demand curve

D^1D^1. At the initial equilibrium price OP_E, demand now exceeds supply by EB. This excess demand, $D > S$, will cause price to be bid up. It keeps rising until a new equilibrium E^1 is reached. This rise in price has caused a fall in demand, but only in the special sense that one moves upwards along D^1D^1 by the amount BE^1. At E^1, price is higher, having risen to OP^1. Output too is higher, having responded to the higher price by moving *along* the supply curve. The amount demanded has also risen, despite the higher price, reflecting the power of the income effect.[5]

Supply curves also shift position. Among the reasons for a shift in supply are:

- technological innovation,
- change in prices of labour, capital and material inputs,
- natural calamities and man-made disasters (war, weather, fire),
- strikes and government regulations,
- organisation and management restructuring.

Suppose scientists discover a cheaper way of producing a good. This means that, at each price level, more output can now be produced. We represent technological innovation of this type as an outward shift in the supply curve from SS to S^1S^1 (Figure 3.7). At the original equilibrium price OP_E, there is an excess supply of EB. Applying the adjustment-process rule ($S > D \Rightarrow$ price declines), price starts to fall. This stimulates demand which moves downwards *along* the (unchanged) curve DD to E^1. A new equilibrium is established at E^1. More is supplied (and demanded)

---

5 Studies of the demand for rice show that a 10 per cent increase in income can be expected to lead to a proportionally lower increase in the quantity of rice demanded.

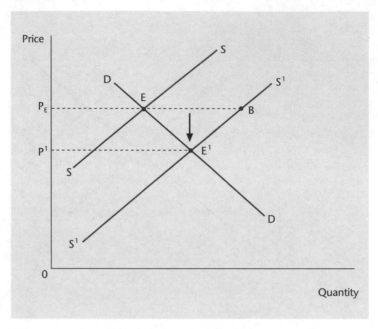

Figure 3.7 An outward shift in the supply curve

at a lower price as a result of the cost-reducing innovation, just as one would expect.

These examples illustrate the flexibility of the market system and its adaptability to change. Demand and supply curves can shift outwards and inwards. Provided prices are sufficiently flexible, markets will 'clear'. Everyone who wants the product, whether it be rice or wine or rented apartments, and is prepared to pay the prevailing price, will be able to buy it.

The practical significance of price flexibility within the market system needs to be emphasised.[6] For example, in former socialist countries, where the market system was absent, willingness to pay and the availability of goods in the shops were quite distinct concepts. One's pockets could be bulging with money, yet many products were unobtainable. Everything had to be booked well in advance; shop shelves were often bare; many products were unavailable because of

---

6 Commenting on the transition in Moscow to 'free-for-all capitalism', *The Financial Times* journalist Leyla Boulton listed among the advantages of the new lifestyle:

> the queues and the shortages at the local food shop have disappeared since the abolition of price controls in January 1992. Thanks to the liberalisation of imports decreed at the same time, Muscovites today are far better-dressed than in the Soviet Union and, despite (justified) grumbling at still very high prices, can find whatever they need in the shops and in the kiosks which have mushroomed in the capital. There is little that is not for sale in Moscow today. 'Afghan war veterans available for all manner of security services' says the advertisement on the trolley buses. ('Capitalism grew in my courtyard', *Financial Times*, Thursday, 25 August 1994)

As the author makes clear, there is also a negative side. Because of the weak institutional framework, identified later in this chapter as essential to the market system, Russia suffers many economic and social ills arising from an unbridled free market.

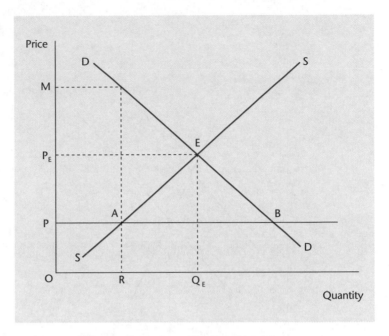

Figure 3.8 Effects of a price ceiling set at OP

administrative decisions. The system did not respond to market incentives but to bureaucratic dictates. The existence of excess demand was not easy to detect and was certainly not crucial to the supply decisions made by producers.

Attempts to replace the price system with administrative decisions, whereby suppliers were instructed how much to produce, led to major distortions and systematic inefficiency. Figure 3.8 illustrates what happens when there is interference with the price system. Thus, suppose a maximum price (or 'ceiling') of OP was set, administrators having (incorrectly) assumed that at price OP demand would have equalled supply at output OR. The mistake leads to excess demand AB. What happens? Utility-maximising individuals will rush to purchase more rice. Rice will be siphoned off the official market into the more profitable black market. The resultant price will rise towards OM, evidently offering ample scope for profitable dealing. The price cannot exceed OM, but it will lie well above the officially determined price OP. The authorities are likely to blame speculators for the resultant rise in price, but the blame is misdirected. Even in the absence of a black market, long queues and waiting lists for rice will occur. The problem is that the official price is not permitted to perform its coordinating function. By being artificially depressed, it is signalling a much greater abundance of the product than is in fact the case. With market liberalisation the equilibrium price would be OP_E with sales of OQ_E.

Suppose, to take another example, the authorities choose an administrative price with the intention of maintaining rice producers' income. They set a minimum price above OP_e and undertake to buy all the supply at that price. Now

57

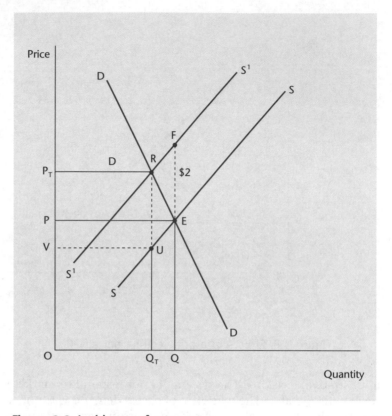

Figure 3.9 Incidence of a tax

excess supply appears. Stocks accumulate in shops (a familiar sight in countries with extensive price control; huge stocks of unwanted produce appear alongside lines of bare shelves). The surplus stocks will have to be: (1) sold off at lower prices, thus causing the administrative error to be explicitly exposed; (2) stored in warehouses in the hope of a shift in demand occurring at some future date; or (3) effectively destroyed in some manner (i.e. fish dumped in the ocean, fruit and vegetables fed to animals, wine converted into pure alcohol). These solutions are not theoretical curiosities. They have been resorted to on a regular basis in many countries. The EU's Common Agricultural Policy has led to an accumulation of surpluses, large unwanted stocks (butter mountains, wine lakes, etc.) and subsidised or 'dumped' exports, just as economic theory would lead us to expect.

Demand and supply curves can be useful in answering a question which business often has to address. Suppose a tax is imposed on an industry's output, who bears the burden? Is it the consumer, or the producer, or both? This is known as the problem of determining the *incidence of the tax*.

Suppose a sales tax of $2 per unit is applied to a product such as a bottle of wine (Figure 3.9). This can be depicted by a shift in the supply curve to the left. At the initial output OQ, the selling price rises to QF = (OP + $2), where FE represents the tax. At that higher price, supply exceeds demand and price falls. Eventually, equilibrium is restored at OP_T and OQ_T. From this it can be seen that: (1) quantity supplied and demand after the imposition of the tax falls to OQ_T; (2) government tax revenue is the area P_TRUV, i.e. tax of \$2 per unit (P_TV) multiplied by the amount sold ($OQ_T = UV$); (3) the price to the consumer has risen by PP_T, *not by the full amount of the tax*; and (4) the price has fallen by PV (to OV). Hence the burden, or the incidence, of the tax has been shared between the consumer and the producer.

The amount of tax raised depends on the slopes of the demand and supply curves. If the demand curve is steeply sloped, the government gets more tax and most of the incidence falls on the consumer. If, on the other hand, the demand curve is flat, the government gets less revenue and the incidence falls mostly on the producer. The slope of the demand curve depends on the availability of substitutes and/or of alternative sources of supply such as the shadow or black markets. Tax incidence problems loom large in industries such as alcohol, tobacco and petrol, and also in the labour market, where the incidence of income and social security taxes can have serious implications for labour costs and for demand for labour. In determining tax incidence effects, we need to know the precise shape of the relevant demand and supply curves.

A sales tax, or any other type of tax, affects not only the allocation of output but also income distribution. Economists take a close interest in the *incentive effect* of taxation. They spend a great deal of effort measuring the responsiveness of supply and demand to changes in price. Companies (and politicians) are, of course, interested in this aspect, but they will also be concerned with the *endowment* (or income distribution) *effect* of a tax. Thus, in Figure 3.9, the imposition of the tax leads to a decline in wine producers' revenue (net of the sales tax) from PEQO to VUQ_TO. This loss of revenue could have serious repercussions on the overall profitability of firms in the industry.

The above analysis of taxes can be extended to subsidies. Subsidies to certain types of goods and services are common: food, petrol, fertilisers, domestic heating. Often the intention is to reduce the price of goods that are important for the less well-off. Sometimes the objective is to reduce congestion and pollution (subsidies to urban transport). The incidence, incentive and endownment effects of a subsidy can be traced in exactly the same manner as taxes. Note that a subsidy involves an *outward* shift in the supply curve whereas a tax involves an *inward* shift.

Demand and supply conditions are in the process of constant change. Provided prices are flexible, the market system generates a new equilibrium price after the initial equilibrium has been disturbed. However, markets vary with regard to the timespan required for adjustment to take place. Financial markets, such as those in foreign exchange, adjust very rapidly – often within minutes. Others, such as the labour market, may take years to adjust. While the equilibrating characteristics are plausible and readily understood in the context of a single market, it is more difficult to show that the market *system* as a whole will possess these equilibrating characteristics. How can we be sure that markets for all goods and services together will succeed in generating a mutually consistent, unique and stable general equilibrium? To Adam Smith this was the work of the 'invisible hand', guiding market actors towards a socially efficient outcome. A formal proof of the stability of the market system was not worked out until the 1950s, but the assumptions required for this proof were highly restrictive. Experience shows, however, that the market system seems to react to changes in a broadly stable way and it has so far coped with disequilibrating shocks reasonably well. This gives grounds for confidence that our simple theoretical model captures important features of real world markets.

3.4   The role of traders and arbitrage

The analysis of demand and supply has so far assumed that producers deal directly with consumers. As we know, this is far from being the usual case. The ex-factory price often amounts to only a fraction of the final retail price paid by the consumer. The difference between price ex-factory and price over-the-counter to the consumer represents payments to the 'middleman': wholesalers, agents, accountants, transporters, retailers. Is this margin between the two prices a reflection of inefficiency, or exploitation, or does it simply represent a fair reward for the effort and risks of distributing goods?

Some people regard trading and arbitrage as somehow inferior to 'real' work, such as actually producing a good. The tendency to depreciate the role of the distributive sector has a long pedigree. The Physiocrats of the eighteenth century, for example, viewed agriculture as the only true source of a country's wealth, with distribution playing a derivative role. Adam Smith himself, normally a rock of common sense, made a distinction between productive and unproductive (i.e. services) labour which sounds very contrived to modern ears:

> The sovereign, for example, with all the officers both of justice and war who serve under him, the whole army and navy, are unproductive labourers. . . . In the same class must be ranked, some both of the gravest and most important, and some of the most frivolous professions; churchmen, lawyers, physicians, men of letters of all kind; players, buffoons, musicians, opera-singers, &c. . . . Like the declamation of the actor, the harangue of the orator, or the tune of the musician, the work of all of them perishes in the very instant of its production.[7]

He justified this view on the grounds that service workers did not produce a physical surplus which could be reinvested. Not only did service sector workers not add to the surplus, their wages were paid out of it, reducing the amount available for accumulation.

From a market perspective, classifying the service sector as unproductive or second class makes no sense. The reason was explained by Professor Alfred Marshall as follows:

> It is sometimes said that traders do not produce: that while the cabinet-maker produces furniture, the furniture-dealer merely sells what is already produced. But there is no scientific foundation for this distinction. They both produce utilities, and neither can do

---

7 Adam Smith, *Wealth of Nations* (1776), book 2, chapter 3, p. 352.

more: the furniture-dealer moves and rearranges matter so as to make it more serviceable than it was before, and the carpenter does nothing more.[8]

If the end of all economic activity is consumption, then the production of wholesale and retailing services is as 'useful' in economic terms as the production of goods.

The information industry is a case in point. It includes activities such as the compilation of massive financial databases, stockbrokers' information sheets for clients, reports on firms, industries and economic surveys. There are consumer guides of various types, ranging from the *Which?* magazine reports of the Consumers' Association to travel guides, designed to help the consumer make informed decisions. All this activity helps to make the market operate more efficiently. Advances in communications technology have played an important role in easing the problem of *asymmetric information.* This problem arises when one party to a transaction possesses more information of its true value than another.

Consider, for example, a small firm seeking a bank loan. The firm has intimate knowledge of its own financial state of affairs, but the bank knows much less. In an effort to correct this asymmetry, the bank must engage in protracted information-gathering on the past financial performance of its prospective borrowers. It will ask for audited accounts and a business plan before making a decision on the loan. These services inputs are a valuable and necessary element in an efficient market system, not a superfluous frill.

Popular opinion in some countries persists in viewing manufacturing as the key to prosperity, with other related activities regarded variously as derivative – or, worse, exploitative – and as such either irrelevant or harmful to growth. Former socialist countries went so far as to exclude services from GNP altogether, using the gross material product concept instead. The practical significance of this exclusion is far from trivial.

The proportion of the EU workforce employed in services exceeds 60 per cent, up from 53 per cent in 1980. In the US and the UK, over 70 per cent of the workforce is employed in the services sector. Furthermore, the percentage of employment in services is increasing rapidly (Table 3.2) and has risen by about 50 per cent since 1960. Many of those so employed are facilitators, intermediaries and arbitrageurs. It makes no sense to suggest that these people do not contribute to GNP. Such an attitude, if carried over into policy, can cause governments to underestimate the importance of an efficient and productive services sector in a modern economy. This neglect can have a detrimental impact on the competitiveness of the manufacturing sector. Some of the negative perspectives of services in the past may have arisen as a reaction to monopoly elements in that sector. Companies and professional groups in the services sector were often insulated from competition by protective legislation, and used their position to 'corner' the market and extract excessive prices from the consumer. The solution to this problem, however, is to expose their activities to competition, not to deny that the activities themselves enhance utility.

---

8 Alfred Marshall, *Principles of Economics* (London: Macmillan, 1920), p.53.

Table 3.2 Employment in services as a percentage of civilian employment

	1960	1980	1990	1998
US	56.2	65.9	70.9	73.8
Japan	41.3	54.2	58.7	60.6
Germany	39.1	51.0	56.8	62.1
France	39.9	55.4	64.0	70.7
UK	47.6	59.7	68.9	71.0
Italy	33.5	47.8	58.6	60.0
Canada	54.1	66.0	71.2	73.8
EU	39.1	52.7	61.1	63.6

Source: OECD, *National Statistics*; OECD, *Employment Outlook* (June 2000); and author's own estimates.

3.5 The efficiency of the market system

In Chapter 2 we defined the concepts of productive efficiency and allocative efficiency, and mentioned that, under certain conditions, the free market could be shown to bring the economy to an efficient point so defined. The analysis of the market system in this chapter enables us to provide an intuitive explanation of why this might be the case.

Consider, first, the demand curve. It shows how much people are willing to purchase at each price. The person who bought the OQth unit of the good in Figure 3.10 did so because the utility received from it made it just worth the price OP. The consumer tries to ensure that the extra utility obtained from an additional purchase is proportional to its price. This extra utility is termed *marginal utility*. When deciding how to allocate our income among competing desirable items, we implicitly compare marginal utility and price. If pears cost twice as much as oranges, we assume that, in a free market, utility-maximising consumers will arrange their purchases so that the marginal utility provided by the last kilogram of pears purchased is double the marginal utility of the last kilogram of oranges. Suppose this condition were breached and the utility of pears were four times the marginal utility of oranges. Then the consumer could add to utility, within a fixed budget, by buying more pears and fewer oranges. The utility-maximising assumption will dictate a continuance of this reallocation until the 2 : 1 ratio is reached. Free market prices reflect marginal utilities.

Next, consider the supply curve, SS. This represents the cost of producing the product. The extra cost of producing the OQth unit of output, otherwise known as its *marginal cost*, is QS. The supply curve slopes upwards because, in the short run, unit costs are assumed to rise as output increases. Hence, at a higher price it becomes profitable to produce more output and firms continue producing more until marginal cost equals that higher price. The connection between costs and price at firm level will be explained fully in Chapter 5. For the present, all we need is to understand that the supply curve indicates the marginal cost of producing any given level of output.

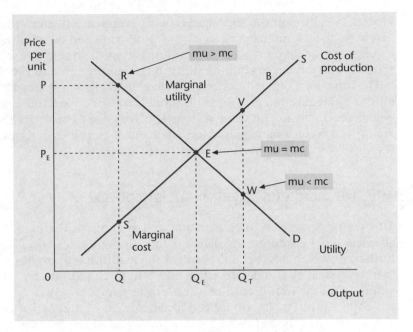

Figure 3.10 Price, marginal cost and marginal utility

Consumption at R (of output OQ at price OP) is not efficient. This is because the marginal utility derived from consuming the OQth unit exceeds the marginal cost of producing the OQth unit. Ideally, we would want to expand production until the point is reached where price and marginal cost are equal. That is, the marginal cost of producing the last unit of output is exactly proportional to the utility derived from it. In Figure 3.10, such a point is reached at E, where output is OQ_E and price is OP_E. That equilibrium is clearly superior to the OQ–OP combination, because for each unit between OQ and OQ_E, the marginal utility exceeded marginal cost. It would not be desirable to produce beyond OQ_E because then the marginal cost would exceed the marginal utility. At output OQ_T, for instance, marginal cost $Q_T V$ exceeds marginal utility $Q_T W$.

If points such as E are reached for every product, then we know that marginal utility (which is proportional to price) will also be proportional to marginal cost.

As we have seen, *the free market system with competition will provide precisely that outcome*. Market forces drive each market to equilibrium at points such as E. This is achieved not because market participants are consciously striving to achieve an efficient outcome in the economist's sense. Rather, they are being driven by the desire on the part of consumers to maximise utility and on the part of producers to maximise profits. We are back to Adam Smith's 'invisible hand', leading market agents to a socially beneficial outcome which was no part of their original intention. Competition leads profit-seeking producers to provide what consumers want to purchase at the lowest possible price. While free market competition tends to lead the economy towards *static* efficiency, it also has important *dynamic* efficiency effects. Over time, pressures of competition will ensure that costs are kept to a minimum. A free market with competition gives firms a powerful incentive to seek more effective ways of producing and distributing their output, through rationalisation and innovation. For most industries, we think of this process as involving continuing shifts of the supply curve to the right.

The case for competition and the free market as a generator of economic efficiency is subject to many qualifications. The 'invisible hand' is itself in need of guidance. Discussion on these matters is a live issue as many industrial countries attempt to become more market-oriented and as countries in transition decide on the type of market institutions most suited for their needs.

3.6 The free market system in social context

This chapter provides an explanation and analysis of the market system. Later chapters will expand on the demand and supply framework. Before proceeding further, however, it is useful to consider the institutional conditions needed if the market system is to operate efficiently. These conditions are easy to take for granted, but the transition from socialism to a market system in many countries has shown just how important the social context of the market can be.

First, the price system presupposes a *stable and reliable medium of exchange*. This implies the existence of a secure and widely acceptable currency. A monetary economy differs from a barter economy in that it allows exchange to occur even in the absence of a coincidence of wants between the buyer and the seller. For example, a car worker can sell labour to the employer in return for money, which can then be spent on goods and services at the individual's discretion. By contrast, exchange will take place in a barter economy only if someone is willing to take exactly what another has to offer – one needs what is called in the jargon a *double coincidence of wants*. Also, if the general money price level is rising rapidly and unpredictably, people get confused about the *real* price level and are unable to distinguish between an absolute rise and a relative rise in the price of a good they are interested in trading. Rapid price changes involve great uncertainty.[9] (We discuss inflation in Chapter 12.) Such confusion breaches the assumption of full information, the absence of which can be very damaging to effective economic performance.

Second, there must be active competition and full information. The market cannot work well if consumers are ignorant of the qualities of the good or service being purchased – lack of such knowledge explains why so much of the health service has been taken over by the state and why there is such intensive regulation of the banking and insurance industries. Also competition among firms is needed in order to ensure that they respond quickly and efficiently to price signals (see Chapters 6 and 7 for discussion of this point).

---

9 A business graduate from the National University of Cujo, Argentina, explained the frustrations of trading during the period of hyperinflation of 1989–90 as follows. To purchase an automobile tyre, one had to seek quotations from a number of suppliers. Wide price variations – of as much as a 3:1 ratio – were not uncommon, even within the same city. After spending considerable time obtaining the various quotations, one frequently found that the lowest price supplier had changed the price in the interim and the search had to be started all over again.

Box 3.2

A market economy

Is one where:

> Exchange is mediated through markets in which prices play a decisive role.

To work smoothly and effectively, a market needs:

- A medium of exchange – stable and reliable.

- Competition and full information – transparent prices, well-informed consumers, free entry and exit.

- Strong institutions – a body of law which protects property rights and ensures that contracts are enforceable.

- A supportive framework of social custom – markets will not function efficiently without standards of truth, trust, acceptance and obligation.

- Income redistribution – sufficient to create consensus and to confer legitimacy on social order without destroying incentives to perform.

Third, we need strong institutions, in particular the *institution of private property* and a *legal framework*. At one time, proponents of market socialism believed that market mechanisms could apply while retaining state ownership. But experience showed that this was not a practical proposition. Bureaucrats 'bargaining' with other people's goods and services will rarely act in the same manner as rational consumers and producers would in a free market. Individuals will save only if there is a real prospect of their being able to use their savings to acquire property. Entrepreneurs will invest only if the profits they earn can be spent as they wish, either to reinvest or to pass on to future generations – or even to 'waste' on luxuries. Private property is needed if the investment and saving decisions of the market system are to be efficient. In addition to private property, one needs a broad legal framework covering bankruptcy, competition law and contract enforcement. Limited liability, patents and the public company are examples of legal constructs which have exercised enormous influence on the process of industrial development. Without them, the market system as we know it today could not have developed.

Fourth, markets will not function properly without *certain minimum standards of truth, trust, acceptance and obligation*. Where these are missing, either transactions do not take place or else they take place at great cost in terms of legal, financial and security precautions. Such costs inhibit the ability of the price system to signal scarcities and surpluses. The growth of business ethics courses reflects an appreciation of the practical importance of ethical standards in the market system. Where such standards are high, customers trust a label, believe that freshly baked bread means just that, accept a buyer's word – without the necessity of personal verification. In a practical way, this saves resources and enhances efficiency.

Finally, one needs an equitable distribution of *wealth and income* to confer legitimacy on the social order. To some extent, this involves a curtailment of the right to private property. Private property can, and may even have to be, compulsorily acquired by the state in order to ensure social harmony. The extent of state involvement needed to achieve this objective is a matter of debate. What is clear is that governments can affect income distribution in a myriad of ways: by imposing progressive income taxes (rich people pay a higher proportion of tax on their income than poor people), by targeted spending on education, health and housing, and by the provision of social welfare income 'floors' and 'safety nets' for the poor. These measures are not always as effective as appears, and they can have unwanted and often unexpected side-effects such as the adverse effect of highly progressive taxation on entrepreneurial incentives. Some critics argue that the search for social justice is a mirage. An individual's income, they claim, is acquired by hard work, luck and inheritance; attempts to alter the balance between rich and poor will turn out to be counterproductive and ineffective in the long run.[10] Clearly, there is room for much disagreement on these issues.

3.7 Conclusions

One of the best-known passages in the *Wealth of Nations* (1776) describes how the pursuit of self-interest leads to social benefit:

> It is not from the benevolence of the butcher, the brewer or the baker that we expect our dinner, but from their regard to their own self-interest. We address ourselves, not to their humanity, but to their self-love (Adam Smith, *Wealth of Nations*, book 1, chapter II, p. 18)

In retrospect, we see that the imposition of centralised decision-making on an economy can achieve short-term successes. Among them might be included the transformation of the Soviet economy under Stalin and the restoration of full employment in Germany by Hitler. But history suggests that the successes of such centralisation are ephemeral. The postwar experience of Central Europe confirms this conclusion. Decades of socialism left this region weakened by an inefficient allocation of resources, by the erosion of innovation and by technological obsolescence.

One striking consequence of the neglect of the price system by the socialist countries was the dramatic contrast between energy consumption patterns in Eastern and Western Europe. Between 1965 and 1985, the energy intensity of GDP fell from 0.52 to 0.38 per cent in the West, while actually rising in the East over the same period from 0.73 to 0.78 per cent.[11] Because internal energy prices in the

---

10 F.A. von Hayek, *The Fatal Conceit: The errors of socialism* (London: Routledge, 1989).
11 B. Heitger, 'Comparative economic growth: East and West', in B. Heitger and L. Waverman, *German Unification and the International Economy* (London: Routledge, 1993).

Eastern economies were not set at the prevailing international levels, the increase in world energy prices in the early and late 1970s, 'signalling' the need for energy conservation, was not transmitted to their firms and consumers. As a result, industrial energy intensity in the 1990s was five times higher in Poland than in the US and, five times higher in Hungary than in Germany. The economies of the Czech and Slovak Republics are eight times more energy-intensive than Italy. Low energy prices are considered the principal reason for such high energy use.[12] The high level of energy intensity not only implied a waste of energy due to underpricing, but also encouraged the growth of heavy pollution industries and gave insufficient incentives to the development of less energy-intensive methods of production.

Writing of the contrast between East and West Germany, John Kay has remarked that:

> Whatever the superficial attractions of central direction and control, in practice it literally failed to deliver the goods. The immediate contrast between East and West Germany provided as close to a controlled experiment as social science is ever likely to see. The results of that experiment, and its dramatic end, imply that for the foreseeable future the private value-maximising corporation will be the principal engine of commercial activity in Europe.[13]

The 'private value-maximising corporation' is the same as the profit-maximising firm which determines supply. Given the increasing range and scope of the market system, it has become more than ever important to understand this system and the role of the firm in its working.

Where the institutional prerequisites are absent, however, market capitalism can get a bad name. Essentially, the point is that the free market will not perform efficiently without moral restraints. A legal system, for example, based on the principles of profit-maximisation, would deliver little justice. Judges would deliver judgments on the basis of the highest bribes. Paradoxically, the market system and the pursuit of self-interest will operate effectively only when a significant proportion of the workforce puts duty and propriety ahead of personal advancement and prosperity. It has often been remarked that the *definition of property rights based on the market system depends precisely on the lack of universality of private property and the motivations of the market system*. An efficient economy needs an incorruptible judiciary and civil service. An interesting question is whether the market itself tends to undermine some of the values of trust, incorruptibility and restraint which we have identified as essential to its proper functioning. Evidence from the history of economic development suggests that, while it may be relatively easy to pull down the monolith of central economic control and to reinstitute private property and free exchange, it takes longer to develop the cultural and social structures necessary to sustain a truly successful society.

---

12 F. Juhagz and R. Ragno, 'The environment in Eastern Europe: From Red to Green', *OECD Observer* (April/May 1993).
13 John Kay, *Foundations of Corporate Success: How business strategies add value* (Oxford: Oxford University Press, 1993), p. 321.

✔ Summary

1. The market system comprises three major markets – the product market, the labour market and the capital market; two primary sets of participants – firms and households; and two subsidiary participants – government and the foreign sector. The market system is characterised by a set of interconnecting relations. The interdependence of the market system is reflected in the circular flow of income between the different market participants and from one market to another. Households sell their labour to firms and use their earnings to purchase the output of these firms. Households save for the future and their savings are deployed by firms, thereby adding to society's capital stock. Failure of any one market to 'clear' affects the other markets.

2. Many useful economic activities are not included in the market economy, such as household duties or voluntary community work. Shadow, or 'black' economy activities, by contrast, can be included in the definition of the market economy, although they often fail to be recorded in official estimates. The shadow economy has been estimated to account for up to 30 per cent and more of officially recorded national production.

3. Price is determined by supply and demand. Provided prices are flexible, markets will 'clear' automatically, meaning that the amount supplied just equals amount demanded. The market system also ordains that price changes act as a signal or incentive. Thus, a rise in price calls forth additional supply and gives consumers an incentive to reduce consumption and to divert expenditure to substitute products. Shifts in the demand or supply curves cause a change in price. In the real world there is no single stable equilibrium price because demand and supply curves are in a constant state of flux.

4. Demand and supply curves can be used to analyse the effects of the imposition of a sales tax or subsidy, or to estimate the consequences of different scenarios of shifts in incomes, technology and similar factors.

5. Agents and middlemen make a positive and important contribution to the functioning of a market system. Generally, the provision of services is the largest sector by far in industrial countries, much of it consisting of facilitator-type activities. In the US and Britain, over 70 per cent of the total workforce is now employed in this sector. There has been sustained growth in service activities such as transportation, recreation and personal services – ranging from hairdressing, health and education to banking and insurance.

6. Competition and the market system leads profit-seeking entrepreneurs to produce what consumers want to consume and secures an economically efficient level and distribution of output. But to do so, there must be an appropriate institutional background and value system. Capitalism, although useful, is unlovely and badly needs the protective social framework it constantly tends to undermine.

? Questions for discussion

1. Discuss the preconditions necessary for the smooth functioning of the market system.

2. Does the existence of a shadow or 'black' economy imply that the price system is not working? Is its existence consistent with the laws of demand and supply?

3. Discuss what you would consider to be the main determinants of demand and supply of rented apartments. Suppose the government decides that rents are too high and sets a maximum rent. What would you expect the consequences of this action to be for (a) apartment owners, (b) existing renters, and (c) future renters?

4. The government gains revenue by imposing a sales tax. Who stands to lose the most, the consumer or the producer, or both?

5. Discuss the role of the 'middleman' in the distribution of goods and services.

6. It is often claimed that market forces, with their emphasis on selfish motivation and profit-maximisation, undermine ethics, yet arguably an ethical approach towards contracts and employees by business is essential for the market system to function. Is the first assertion simply wrong?

Exercises

1. At the beginning of January 1992, price controls were lifted in Russia. Within a day food prices had increased by 250 per cent, but the food queues vanished overnight. Using demand and supply curves, explain what happened. How would you expect the supply of food to have been affected – in the short term and in the long run? Which groups in society gained, and which lost, as a result of the abolition of food price controls?

2. We know that the number of personal computers being sold has increased, yet the price is falling. Use supply and demand curves to explain how this can happen.

3. Consider the supply curve of oil for central heating. In each of the cases below, indicate whether there is a movement along the supply curve (and in which direction) or a shift of the supply curve (and whether left or right): (a) new oil fields start up in production; (b) the demand for central heating rises; (c) the price of coal falls; (d) oil companies anticipate an upsurge in the demand for central heating oil; (e) the demand for petrol rises; (f) new technology decreases the costs of oil refining; (g) oil products become more expensive.

4. The following table contains data on price, quantity supplied and quantity demanded.

   (a) Draw a diagram showing the demand and supply curves.
   (b) With this diagram, estimate the new equilibrium price and quantity after the imposition of a tax of £2 per unit.

Price £	Quantity Supplied (units per week)	Quantity Demanded (units per week)
10	500	800
11	550	750
12	600	700
13	650	650
14	700	600
15	750	550
16	800	500

(c) Comment on the incidence of the tax.

(d) Show how producers' sales are affected and how much tax revenue accrues to government.

5. Suppose buyers' tastes change in favour of fresh vegetables and simultaneously there is an advance in vegetable-growing technology. Show how the supply and demand curves would be affected. What would be the effect on the equilibrium price and quantity? Do we know?

   Suppose instead of an improvement in technology, vegetable producers were hit by adverse weather. How would your diagram change? Would you be able to say whether the new equilibrium price would be higher or lower than the original equilibrium? What would be the effect on equilibrium quantity?

6. (a) Consider the economic consequences of a prohibition on the consumption of alcohol. What happens to the supply curve? What happens to the demand curve? How will the prohibition affect equilibrium consumption and price? What further indirect effects are likely to follow? (According to some writers, 'prohibition is likely to raise the level of violence by increasing the marginal benefits, and lowering the marginal costs, of breaking the law'.)

   (b) Suppose the head of an anti-drugs enforcement agency reports, as evidence of the agency's success in deterring drug users, that the street price of drugs has fallen. Is this evidence conclusive? What other factors might have caused the fall in price?

7. The minimum price set by the European Commission for many foodstuffs and dairy products is set above the market clearing equilibrium price. The objective of this price floor is to support farm incomes. Use a supply and demand diagram to illustrate the effects of setting the minimum price on (a) food prices; (b) farm incomes; (c) government spending.

Further reading

The European Commission's *Panorama of EU Industry* is a useful source of information on the output, employment and competitive structure of European industries. There is an extensive literature on what has been variously called the 'shadow', 'black' or 'hidden' economy. A useful, if rather inconclusive starting point is the special feature 'Controversy; On the hidden economy', *Economic Journal* (June 1999). Professor Friedrich Schneider is a leading authority on the subject (see Box 3.1 for references). Demand and supply curves and the determination of price are standard fare in introductory economic textbooks. D. Begg, R. Dornbusch and S. Fischer, *Economics*, and John Sloman, *Economics* (Harlow: Financial Times Prentice Hall, 4th edn, 1999), cover the topics in this chapter effectively. The relationship between economics and business morality is discussed in W. Baumol, 'Smith vs Marx on business morality and the social interest', in W. Baumol (ed.), *Microeconomic Theory: Applications and origins* (New York and London: Harvester Wheatsheaf, 1986).

Chapter 4

MARKET DEMAND AND THE PRICING DECISION

Introduction

The market demand curve is important for business in two practical ways. First, the decision to invest in expanded production capacity or in a marketing campaign requires a close analysis of the expected growth of demand over time. Second, the firm's pricing decision depends on the nature of the demand curve for the firm's products. The pricing decision, of course, is not determined solely by demand-side considerations – the company's cost function and profit objectives, and the reaction of competitors, have also to be taken into account – but demand analysis plays a crucial part in the decision.

This chapter provides an economic analysis of market demand. This is an important starting point, both for understanding the economy and for the study of marketing.

Chapter outline

1. Assumptions about the behaviour of 'rational' consumers.
2. How to construct a market demand curve from a set of individual demand curves.
3. The concept of elasticity of demand, price, income and cross price elasticity.
4. How demand curves are estimated in practice.
5. The relevance of market demand characteristics to the firm's pricing decision.

4.1 What is a 'rational' consumer?

The theory of demand explains how an individual responds to changes in key economic variables such as prices and income. Five major assumptions about consumer behaviour are made which elaborate on the hypothesis that consumers are utility-maximisers. These assumptions can be summarised under the headings of *comparability*, *non-satiation*, *consistency*, *convexity* and *independence*.

> *Comparability*: Consumers can, and do, compare and rank different combinations of goods and services in terms of utility. If offered two baskets, A and B, of goods, the individual is sufficiently well informed to be able to declare a preference for A over B or for B over A, or express indifference between the two.

Non-satiation: Consumers' wants are unlimited. More is always preferred to less. If basket A contains more of every good and service than basket B, then A must be preferred to B.

Consistency: Consumers are consistent. If A is preferred to B, and B is preferred to C (where C is a third basket of products), then A must be preferred to C.

Convexity: As an individual consumes more of a particular good relative to other goods, its utility falls relative to those products. This assumption is similar to the assumption of diminishing marginal utility, which states that the more one has of a commodity, the less utility or satisfaction one derives from an incremental unit of that commodity. Consider the example of a cyclist returning home after a long journey. The first glass of orange tastes wonderful; the second glass, great; the third glass, good. Note how the extra utility per glass progressively declines. By the tenth glass, it may be near zero or even negative! The convexity assumption is consistent with the highly diversified character of most people's consumption patterns. If the assumption were invalid, and marginal utility were increasing instead of decreasing, a utility-maximising individual would spend all income on a single product. Such behaviour is not generally observed. An exception may be addictive goods which have increasing marginal utility; spending tends to concentrate heavily on the object of addiction.

Independent utilities: Independence of individual utilities means that the utility a person derives from a good is independent of how much others may possess of the same good. In other words, the value attached to a good by a consumer is not affected either by its value to others or by the quantity consumed by others.

These assumptions are reasonable, but nobody would claim that they provide a completely realistic description of consumer behaviour. For example, when information is costly or difficult to acquire, we may not have sufficient knowledge to rank preferences in a comprehensive and consistent manner. When consulting professionals (for example, doctors and lawyers), we are often unable to assess the quality of the services they are offering. The cost of acquiring information may lead the consumer to use a rule of thumb, or to follow the crowd. In such instances, recourse may be had to a less ambitious definition of rationality, such as 'bounded' rationality, whereby the consumer is assumed to be able to rank *relevant*, *feasible* and *known* options rather than all possible options.

Another problem arises when the utility derivable from the consumption of a particular good or service is unknown or uncertain. Liberal and authoritarian ideologies clash as to whether people are the best judges of their own interests in such circumstances. For example, one reason often cited for supporting unpopular innovative cultural products is that they will generate better returns in the long run when people learn how to appreciate them. Such a 'failure' of appreciation on the part of the individual is ruled out by the assumption of comparability.[1] Of course, the current preferences of the arts lobby may not be necessarily more long-sighted

---

1 The debate about subsidies to the arts generates much controversy. See D. Sawers, *Should the Taxpayer Support the Arts?* (London: Institute of Economic Affairs, 1993). John O'Hagan *The State and the Arts: Key economic policy issues* (London: Edward Elgar, 1998) provides an authoritative overview of these issues.

than anybody else's. The point is that people do not always have a well-defined preference field. Tastes and preferences change over time and the consequences of many decisions in economic life cannot be predicted. We try to weigh uncertain future benefits against certain present benefits.

The assumption of independent utilities has also been challenged. The opposite proposition has been propounded: that much of the satisfaction we obtain from the consumption of a particular good or service derives precisely from the fact that others are unable to afford it. A large house in a good neighbourhood, or a Rolls-Royce, yields much less utility if everyone has one. Similarly, we give certain gifts because their cost is widely known and will be appreciated by the receiver rather than because of any intrinsic usefulness of the gift. This type of interdependence has important implications for pricing policy. 'Position', 'gift' or 'snob' goods may be positively, rather than negatively, related to price. Yet an upward-sloping demand curve is an exceptional case and valid only within fairly limited price ranges. At a price of £1 million each, even the demand for Rolls-Royces will start to decline!

Keeping in mind these qualifications, the type of behaviour implied by the above 'rationality' assumption is a reasonable approximation of reality. Consumers weigh up alternatives, seek out and choose larger and better 'baskets' whenever possible. More consumption is better than less consumption. There is sufficient independence of utilities to make economic growth and increased consumption a source of higher welfare. Formally, we can imagine each consumer as maximising utility, subject to a budget constraint (income). One interesting result of this exercise shows that this idealised consumer will maximise utility when the *ratio of marginal utility to price is the same for all products consumed*. This confirms the point outlined in Chapter 3 in our discussion of the efficiency of the free market.[2]

---

2 Suppose the consumer's utility function is $U = U(X, Y)$, where X and Y refer to volumes of each product. (We assume a two-product economy for simplicity.) The consumer is then assumed to maximise utility subject to the budget constraint, where M is the consumer's income and Px, Py is the price of X and Y, respectively:

$$PxX + PyY = M.$$

To maximise U subject to this constraint, we form the Langrangean function

$$L = U(X, Y) - \lambda(PxX + PyY - M)$$

where λ is the Langrangean multiplier. The first-order conditions for a maximum are

$$\frac{\partial L}{\partial X} = \frac{\partial U}{\partial X} - \lambda P_x = 0$$

$$\frac{\partial L}{\partial Y} = \frac{\partial U}{\partial Y} - \lambda P_y = 0$$

from which it follows that

$$\frac{\partial U}{\partial X} \div P_x = \frac{\partial U}{\partial Y} \div P_y$$

or

$$\frac{\text{marginal utility of } X}{P_x} = \frac{\text{marginal utility of } Y}{P_y}.$$

4.2 Deriving the market demand curve

The assumptions of economic rationality enable us to conclude that, if the price of a good falls, other things being equal, the consumer will respond by demanding more. At worst, the consumer will not respond by demanding less. Hence, the individual demand curve will be downward-sloping or vertical, as shown in Chapter 3.

The *market demand curve* is derived by the addition of individual demand curves in a process of *lateral summation*, described in Figure 4.1. Suppose there are two individual consumers in the market. We begin by taking a price (OP) and asking how much each individual will demand at that price. At a given price per unit (OP), individual J demands OJ of a given product and individual H demands OH. Market demand at price (P) is therefore equal to (OJ + OH) denoted by point R (see Figure 4.1). This gives a point K on the market demand curve. Other points can be generated by setting new prices and adding J and H's consumption at each price. Thus, if price rises to OP^1, market demand falls to OS (= OJ^1 + OH^1).

Given that individual demand curves have a negative slope, the market demand curve should also be downward-sloping. This property, however, could be jeopardised by a large shift in income distribution between individuals with different tastes and priorities. Suppose that a society was divided into two groups – book-lovers and food-lovers. Any redistribution of income from book-lovers to food-lovers will have an impact on demand. Hence the demand for books depends not just on price and total income, but on the distribution of income. This potential difficulty must be kept in mind when analysing market demand in the context of changing macroeconomic aggregates.

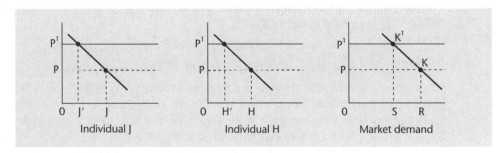

Figure 4.1 Derivation of the market demand curve

4.3 Elasticities of demand

Elasticity of demand is a shorthand way of characterising the sensitivity of demand to changes in its price, the level of income and other determining variables. Three types of elasticity are especially relevant to demand analysis: (1) price elasticity of demand, (2) income elasticity of demand, and (3) cross-price elasticity of demand. We shall discuss each type in turn.

Price elasticity of demand

A fall in price has two opposing consequences for sales revenue. First, sales revenue *increases* because more units are sold to existing customers, and new customers will be tempted to make purchases as a result of the lower price. Secondly, revenue *decreases* in that the price obtained on the original volume of sales has fallen. The balance between these two forces determines whether the reduction in price leads to an overall increase or decrease in total sales revenue. For example, suppose the figures are as follows:

Unit price	Quantity sold	Total revenue
$5	4	$20
$4	6	$24

The reduction in price from $5 to $4 involves an *increase* in revenue of $8 arising from the sale of 2 extra units at a price of $4 each, and a *loss* of $4 revenue because of the price decline of $1 on the original 4 units sold. The net revenue effect is ($4 × 2) − ($1 × 4) = $4.

In this example, the reduction in price yields a net revenue gain. In other circumstances, customers will not respond equally strongly to the fall in price and net sales revenue may fall. Depending on the degree of sensitivity of quantity demanded to price, we know that (1) cutting prices can sometimes be a mistake, (2) on occasion it may be possible to raise price and increase sales revenue at the same time, and (3) there may be a time-lag before the reduction in prices has its full effect on the quantity sold, because customers are slow to realise that price has fallen and to adjust their purchasing habits.

Price elasticity of demand measures the sensitivity of quantity demanded to changes in price and is defined as:

$$E(p) = \frac{\% \text{ change in quantity demanded}}{\% \text{ change in price}}$$

Since price and quantity changes are negatively related, $E(p)$ is negative. However, in discussing critical values of the formula, it is customary to use absolute values. Thus, we say that a good with a price elasticity of 5 has a higher elasticity than a good with elasticity of 2, notwithstanding that $-2 > -5$.

Reverting to the above arithmetical example, as price falls from $5 to $4 $E(p) = [(6 - 4)/4]/[(4 - 5)/5] = 0.5/-0.2 = -2.5$.

Elasticities are defined exactly only for small changes in price around the prevailing level, i.e. to changes *in the neighbourhood* of existing prices. The sensitivity of the elasticity estimate to the base can be illustrated by considering the effect of raising price from $4 to $5, instead of reducing it from $5 to $4, as in the above example. Elasticity then becomes:

$$E(p) = [(4 - 6)/6]/[(5 - 4)/4] = -0.33/0.25 = -1.32$$

Also, price elasticities can change as one moves up or down the demand schedule. In the case of the linear demand curve of Table 4.1 and Figure 4.2, the

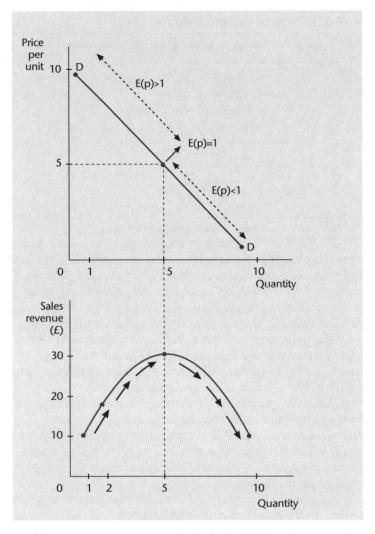

Figure 4.2 Price elasticity and total sales revenue

slope is constant. Every one unit rise in price leads to a loss of one unit of quantity sold. But a rise in price from 1 to 2 involves a decrease in volume sold of only 10% (from 10 units to 9 units), while a 1 unit rise in price, from 6 to 7, results in a 20% cutback in sales volume. Hence, as price increases, we see that the value of the price elasticity rises. Although it is common practice to list different products according to '*the*' value of their price elasticities (as if they were unique), this is a convenient approximation and caution should be exercised when using such elasticity estimates.[3]

---

3 By translating value into logs, demand curves of constant elasticity can be constructed. Elasticity estimates are often derived from such data transformations.

Table 4.1 Price elasticity and total revenue

Price	Quantity sold	Sales revenue	Marginal revenue	Price elasticity of demand*
10	1	10	10	
9	2	18	8	
8	3	24	6	> 1
7	4	28	4	
6	5	30	2	
5	6	30	0	=1
4	7	28	−2	
3	8	24	−4	< 1
2	9	18	−6	
1	10	10	−8	

*Elasticities are defined in absolute values; negative sign is ignored.

A crucial cut-off point in price elasticity analysis is a value of unity. If the value of the price elasticity of demand for a good exceeds unity (> 1) in absolute terms, the demand for that good is said to be price-elastic. That means that a given percentage decline in price will elicit a larger percentage increase in sales, and total sales revenue will increase. If the price elasticity is less than unity (< 1), a given percentage decline (rise) in price will stimulate a less than proportionate rise (decline) in quantity demanded, the demand for the good is said to be price-inelastic, and sales revenue will diminish (rise) as price declines (increases). If the absolute value of price elasticity is equal to unity (= 1), prices and quantities demanded move in inverse proportion; sales revenue for small changes around the prevailing price remains constant.

Price elasticity of demand can be further explained with a simple arithmetical example (Table 4.1). Suppose we take a range of prices from £10 per unit to £1 per unit and, at each price, estimate how many units would be demanded. *Total sales revenue* at each price is price times quantity. *Marginal revenue* is defined as the additional, or incremental, revenue obtained from the sale of the last unit. Referring to Table 4.1, we see that at price £10 only 1 unit is sold. Total sales revenue is £10. If price is reduced to £9, 2 units are sold. The marginal revenue obtained by reducing price from £10 to £9 is (£18 − £10), or £8. If we cut price to £8, 3 units are sold and sales revenue increases from £18 to £24. Marginal revenue from selling the third unit is (£24 − £18), or £6, and so on.

This information can be translated into price elasticities by noting that for prices above £6 per unit, the percentage change in quantity demanded exceeds the percentage in price. For example, a 10 per cent reduction in price, from £10 to £9, leads to a 100 per cent increase in quantity demanded (from 1 to 2 units). Marginal revenue is positive. The elasticity is 10. By contrast, at the bottom of the table, a 50 per cent fall in price from £2 to £1 results in only a 11 per cent increase in quantity demanded. Marginal revenue is negative and the elasticity is 0.2. Elasticity is equal to unity at a price of £5. At this price, quantity demanded is 6 units. The marginal revenue from the sale of the sixth unit is zero. Sales revenue is maximised at this price.

There are four main determinants of a product's price elasticity. First, the range of available substitutes for a good – the more close substitutes there are for the product, the greater is the price elasticity of demand. If the price of a product increases, buyers will switch to these substitutes. If its price decreases, buyers will switch to it from the substitutes. For example, if the price of a software program rises, buyers can easily turn to alternative software packages. At the other extreme, the demand for life-saving drugs such as insulin and Beta Interferon is likely to be highly price-inelastic, since there are few alternative treatments.

Second, the narrower the definition of the product, the higher the price elasticity. Thus, the demand for Irish whiskey is more price-elastic than the total market demand for whisky. In turn, the demand for whisky is more price-elastic than the demand for spirits as a whole.

Third, the share of spending on the good in the consumer's budget affects elasticity. The larger the share of one's budget spent on a good, the greater the elasticity of demand for it. A 10 per cent increase in the price of commodities such as pepper or salt will have little effect on consumers' behaviour, given the small fraction of income spent on these products. By contrast, a 10 per cent increase in the price of clothing or automobiles will impact more severely on the average consumer's budget. Consequently, demand for such products may be expected to be more price-elastic.

Fourth, elasticities are generally higher in the long run than in the short run. People need time to adjust to a new price, to find acceptable substitutes and to alter spending patterns.

Price elasticities have several important practical uses:

- *Governments* have a keen interest in price elasticities. They help to determine both the products on which to levy taxes and the rate of tax to impose. Clearly, products with low price elasticity of demand, such as tobacco, alcoholic drinks and energy, are the ones to tax. Imposition of a tax on such products has a small effect on quantity and hence proves a lucrative source of tax revenue. Luxury goods are attractive to tax authorities for the same reason. Knowledge of demand theory and empirical estimates of the shape of the demand curve also help to determine the rate of tax to levy. As prices rise as a result of indirect taxes, price elasticity tends to increase. After a point, a rise in tax could lead to a fall in total tax revenue. This is particularly likely where taxes can be evaded by smuggling.
- *Business organisations and industry associations* use elasticities to estimate the effects of changes in price and taxes on their members' sales revenues. Also, in advocating lower corporate tax rates, recourse might be had to estimates of the elasticity of investment in response to such tax changes.
- *Central banks* use elasticities to estimate the effects of changes in exchange rates on imports and exports, and more broadly in assessing the effects of movements in an economy's cost competitiveness on GDP and employment.
- *Energy pricing policy* would be difficult to formulate in a coherent way without good information on the relevant price elasticities of different products.
- *Trade economists* use elasticities to estimate the effect of trade liberalisation on imports, exports and domestic production. Price elasticities are also intensively used in evaluating agricultural policy options.

Thus, there is practical value in understanding the interactions between tax rates, the consumer price, the producer price, sales revenues, and profits. As we saw in Chapter 3, an indirect tax can be represented as an inward shift in the supply curve. The *incidence of the tax* is shared between producers and consumers, and depends on the slope and position of both the demand and the supply curve. In general, the more inelastic the demand for the product, the larger the proportion of the tax shifted forward to consumers, and the smaller the decline in equilibrium quantity. For those reasons, it pays industries affected by indirect taxes to keep close watch on such matters.

Income elasticity of demand

The income elasticity of demand is defined as:

$$E(y) = \frac{\% \text{ change in quantity demanded}}{\% \text{ change disposable income}}$$

This measure indicates the responsiveness of demand for a particular product to changes in income. Interpretation of the coefficient is straightforward: if $E(y) > 1$, the percentage demand for the product grows faster than the percentage change in disposable income and the product is defined as a *luxury good*. If $E(y)$ lies between 0 and 1, demand for the product grows, but at a less than proportionate rate than income. A product with such an income elasticity is called a *necessity*. Demand for some goods actually declines as income rises ($E(y) < 0$). These are called *inferior goods*. Examples include potatoes, dairy products, black and white television sets, table wine. Knowledge of how demand responds to changes in income is a vital ingredient in long-term planning. But, as in the case of price elasticity, the larger the company's share in the overall market, the more useful the information will be. If a company has only 1/1000th share of the total market for a particular product, it is likely to concentrate more on expanding its market share than in expanding the total market. Estimating the expansion or contraction in the total market response to price would be an academic exercise for such a firm. By contrast, a trade association, representing the entire industry, would be extremely interested in the overall income elasticity.[4]

Cross-price elasticity of demand

The cross-price elasticity of demand measures the relationship between the quantity of a product demanded and the price of related products. The related products can be *substitutes* or *complements*.

---

4 Sometimes income and price effects interact in a curious manner. A famous example is that of the Giffen good, where a fall in price could, in theory, lead to a decline in demand. If the product absorbed a large proportion of an individual's income, a major fall in price could have a significant impact on income. Now suppose that the good is 'inferior', so that the rise in income caused by the price decline would lead to a fall in demand. For sufficiently large income effects and price changes, it is conceivable that a fall in price could lead to a fall in quantity demanded. In other words, the demand curve could be upward-sloping. Although of great theoretical interest, the Giffen good case is virtually irrelevant from a practical point of view.

$$E(x, y) = \frac{\% \text{ change in quantity demanded of } x}{\% \text{ change in price of } y}$$

A good x is a substitute for y if an increase (decrease) in the price of y causes an increase (decrease) in the demand for x. A good x is a complement for y if an increase (decrease) in the price of y causes a decrease (increase) in the demand for x. The relationship should be reciprocal for the effects of changes in the price of x on the quantity demanded of y.

An example of substitutes is two competing personal computers such as Gateway and Dell. A rise in the price of one leads consumers to buy more of the other. An example of complements is printers and personal computers. A rise in the price of computers leads to a fall in demand for printers. Why? Because fewer computers are demanded and each PC user needs access to a printer. Cross-price elasticities of demand provide a useful point of departure for defining the market of a particular good and indicating which products should be included in a given market. This can be important in cases involving competition law, where a firm's share of 'the' market can be relevant evidence (see Box 4.1 for the famous cellophane case).

4.4 Estimating the demand function

A firm might want to quantify the relationship between sales volume, product price, price of substitutes and complements, national income, advertising expenditure, etc., for several reasons. For example:

- A tobacco company might want estimates of the effect of an increase in government taxes on sales.
- An electricity company may be planning to build a new power station and would like to know how demand for electricity is expected to develop over the next ten years.
- A brewery might want an estimate of the effect of income growth and a changing age-structure of the population on the demand for beer.
- A clothing manufacturer might want an estimate of the future increase in demand for imported textiles as restrictions on imports are relaxed.
- A computer firm might want to know the consequences of lower price and high national income growth on the demand for microcomputers.

To derive this information, it will be necessary to estimate a demand function for the product concerned.

How to estimate demand functions

There are six steps involved in estimating a demand function and using it for forecasting purposes (Box 4.2). First, the variables likely to influence demand for the product must be identified. Own price, income, price of substitutes are obvious candidates, but there may be other specific factors influencing demand. The next three steps are technical in nature. They concern the form of the demand function,

Box 4.1

The cellophane case

The use of cross-price elasticities of demand for the purpose of market delineation received the endorsement of the United States Supreme Court in a landmark judgment, *U.S.* v *E.I. Du Pont de Nemours and Company* (1956).

At that time, Du Pont produced 75 per cent of total sales of cellophane in the US and received royalties from the remaining 25 per cent, which were produced under licence. Prices of cellophane were between 2 and 7 times higher than those of substitute products. Du Pont was accused of using monopoly power to maintain this price differential. Du Pont defended itself against the anti-trust suit on the grounds that the market in which it was competing was not that for cellophane itself but for all feasible wrapping (e.g. aluminium foil, wax wrappings, and so on). In that broader market, Du Pont held only an 18 per cent market share. Clearly, whether Du Pont had monopoly power would depend on how the relevant market was defined.

Goods belonging to the same market have high substitutability. A key measure of the degree of substitutability is the cross-price elasticity of demand. In this case it was decided that the cross-elasticity between the price for cellophane and other wrappings was sufficiently high to justify the broader definition of the market, and this allowed Du Pont to win the case. The judgment proved to be controversial: there was reference to the 'Cellophane fallacy'. The decision as to when a particular cross-elasticity becomes 'large' must, of necessity, be arbitrary. The US Supreme Court has adopted a 'reasonable interchangeability' criterion for defining the extent of a market, measured by reference to cross-elasticities.

The issue of defining the relevant market is crucial to competition law, mergers control legislation and business strategy. It regularly features in competition cases. A recent example is the protracted legal dispute between the Anglo-Dutch conglomerate, Unilever, and the US private corporation, Mars. Legal proceedings began in 1990 and are still ongoing. Mars complained that Unilever had created barriers to entry to the impulse-purchase ice-cream market. The legal battles were fought in two jurisdictions of the European Union: Germany and Ireland. Unilever had a dominant share of the impulse-purchase ice-cream market in both these countries, which Mars was anxious to break into. In the Irish case, Unilever (through its subsidiary HB) pleaded that the relevant market was not the total sales of impulse ice-cream, but rather sales of all convenience products sold through small stores. This meant that soft drinks, candy and other confectionery belonged to the same market as ice-cream. Unilever's evidence was based on qualitative and opinion-based estimates. Mars argued that the narrower definition of the market was the correct one to use and adduced econometric estimates of cross-elasticities in support of its case. In this case, the trial judge took the view that, in contrast with the Du Pont case, the narrower definition should prevail: the relevant market was defined as the impulse sales of wrapped ice-cream products. It is not clear to what extent this decision was based on the economic evidence. According to McDowell, European case law has not been based to any significant extent on the evaluation of statistical and econometric estimates in defining the relevant market.

Source: William F. Shank and Noel Roy, 'Market direction in the analysis of United States groundfish demand', *The Antitrust Bulletin* (Spring 1991); Moore McDowell, 'An ice-cream war: bundling, tying and foreclosure', *European Journal of Law and Economics* (3, 1996)

Box 4.2

Estimating a demand function

Think of a demand function of general form:

$$Q_i = \alpha_0 + \alpha_1 Y - \alpha_2 P_i + \alpha_3 P_s - \alpha_4 P_c + \alpha_5 Z + e$$

where: Q_i = quantity demanded of good i
Y = real income
P_i = price of good i
P_s = price of substitute(s)
P_c = price of complement(s)
Z = other relevant determinants of demand
e = error term representing random factors
α_1, $\alpha_2 \ldots \alpha_5$ can be interpreted as elasticities (assuming logs instead of absolute values are used).

Then follow these steps:

1. Identify independent variables: income, own price, price of substitutes and complements, other influences.
2. Decide on form of function: linear, log linear, translog; lag structure; prior constraints.
3. Determine statistical estimation techniques: ordinary least squares is one of a large number of possible estimation techniques.
4. Derive parameters: often reported as short-term and long-term elasticities.
5. Evaluate results and cross-check with other procedures: surveys, marketing tests, managers' opinions.
6. Set up different scenarios of future Y, P and Z. Use simulations to derive forecasts for Q.

the statistical estimation techniques used (usually regression analysis of some type) and the derivation of statistically reliable estimates of the parameters. Thus, in the equation in Box 4.2, an actual number will be estimated for the value of α_1, α_2, etc. These parameters will enable quantitative statements to be made (within a defined range of possible error) about how demand for the product will be affected by changes in the independent variables. This information is often presented in the form of elasticity estimates. Step 5 involves careful evaluation of the results, including comparison between the consultant's estimates and those of other studies. If the objective of the study is to examine the sensitivity of demand to a particular variable(s), the exercise might end here. However, if the objective is to derive a demand forecast, the final step – step 6 – is to construct a range of scenarios involving prices, income and other (Z) variables such as advertising and demographic changes, and to estimate the level of demand corresponding to each scenario.

Clearly, liaison is required between management and the consultant in deciding what variables are relevant for the estimates of each good, how such variables should be measured, what statistics are relevant and for which period. Attention should be drawn to any unusual features of the data due to exceptional events such as strikes, adverse weather or changes in compilation methods. The statistical procedure will then generate estimates of the net effect of each variable on quantity demanded. In the case of elasticities, while their derivation is largely technical, evaluation will require dialogue and cross-checking with other procedures such as consumer surveys, marketing tests and the opinions of management. At all times it is important to bear in mind that econometric results are highly tentative and sensitive to the specification of the equation. Normally a range of estimates should be compiled on the basis of different assumptions about the future evolution of income and so on. If the company is the sole seller in the market, the market demand for the product will be the same as the company's demand curve. If, however, as is usually the case, the company is one of a small number of suppliers, additional analysis is required. The effects of a change in the company's price will be influenced not by the nature of the market demand curve alone, but also by the reaction of competing firms to any change in the firm's price.

Forecasting demand for a firm's product is a necessary exercise, but is fraught with uncertainty. The statistical analysis provided by economists helps to identify the structure and driving forces of market demand. Knowing these basic determinants of demand, the manager is in a better position to react to a changing future environment. But statistical analysis relies on historical market data. It should be supplemented by qualitative analysis based on customer interviews, market surveys, managers' views, regular monitoring of current sales volumes and trends, and price experiments. As an example of the last, Dolan and Simon (1996) cite the case of a German mobile phone manufacturer who kept price constant in one region but allowed it to vary up and downwards in other regions. By studying the regional response rates, this experiment enabled the firm to implement a successful nation-wide price strategy.[5]

Empirical findings

Empirical studies show that price and income elasticities tend to vary considerably between different goods and services. In general, price elasticities for food, fuel, health and housing services are found to be low (< 1); while price elasticities of demand for clothing, communications and purchased transport tend to be high (> 1). Even at this broad level of generality, there are sharp differences in elasticity values for the same products across countries. Elasticities are also sensitive to the precise specification of the product. The price elasticity of demand for haddock has been estimated at 2.2, much higher than the price elasticity of fish and even higher still than the elasticity of food (estimated at zero for the UK and 0.87 for the US).[6] Services have been found to have a low price

5 R.J. Dolan and H. Simon, *Power Pricing: How managing price transforms the bottom line* (New York: Free Press, 1996).

6 A. Deaton and J. Muelbauer, *Economics and Consumer Behaviour* (Cambridge: Cambridge University Press, 1980).

Table 4.2 Price and income elasticities for the service sector

	Price	Income
Services		
Housing	−0.73	1.186
Health	−0.82	1.582
Purchased transport	−1.11	0.955
Communications	−1.63	1.315
Recreation	−0.97	1.410
Education	−0.55	0.959
Government	−1.36	1.071
Total services	−0.32	0.979
Mixed (industry and services)		
Fuel and power	−0.86	0.967
Other household	−1.28	0.986
Transport	−1.24	1.418
Total Services and Mixed	**−0.28**	**1.013**

Source: R.E. Falvey and N. Gemmell, 'Are services income-elastic?: Some new evidence', *Review of Income and Wealth*, September 1996.

elasticity in general (0.32), but individual items have much higher elasticities, such as recreation (0.97). Within recreation, the price elasticity of demand for movies has been estimated at 3.7 (Table 4.2).[7]

Income elasticities tend to be higher than unity for books, health services, communications, consumer durables and recreation, while significantly below unity (but positive) for food (0.17 in the UK, 0.95 in the US). A selection of estimates for service industries is provided in Table 4.2.

A detailed study of the drinks industry provides further insight into the uses of elasticity estimates.[8] Table 4.3 shows estimates of own-price and income elasticities in Canada for beer, spirits and wine published in the early 1990s. The dependent variable is consumption of beer, spirits and wine per capita. Annual observations are taken for the period 1953–86. To explain movements in consumption, a number of determinants (independent variables) were tested:

■ own-price,
■ income per capita,
■ weather conditions (relevant to beer),
■ minimum legal drinking age.

The objective of the study was to establish if, and to what extent, changes in the minimum legal drinking age affected consumption.

Different forms of the estimated equation were examined. Indeed, four estimates of each parameter are shown in the original publication. The results

---

7 Edwin Mansfield, *Applied Microeconomics* (New York, London: W. Norton, 1994), p. 4.
8 J. Johnson *et al.*, 'Short-run and long-run elasticities for Canadian consumption of alcoholic beverages', *Review of Economics and Statistics* (February 1992).

Table 4.3 Consumption of alcoholic beverages: short-run and long-run elasticities for beer, spirits and wine in Canada

		Short run		Long run
Beer	Price	−0.27	Price	−0.28
	Income	0.48	Income	0.46
	Warm days	0.03	Warm days	0.10
Spirits	Price	−0.45	Price	0.84
	Income	0.85	Income	1.33
Wine	Price	−0.86	Price	−1.26
	Income	1.33	Income	2.59

Note: Based on average data for 1956–83.
Source: J. Johnson et al., 'Short-run and long-run elasticities for Canadian consumption of alcoholic beverages', Review of Economics and Statistics (February 1992).

show that price elasticities for alcoholic beverages tend to be low. In the short run, a 1 per cent increase in price is estimated to reduce per capita consumption of beer by about 0.3 per cent, and of spirits and wine by about 0.5–0.9 per cent, respectively. Income elasticities vary considerably between the three products. Wine emerges as a luxury good with an income elasticity of 1.33 in the short run and 2.59 in the long run. Beer's income elasticity is low ($E(y)$ is 0.48 in the short run and 0.46 in the long run), which is sufficiently low to justify its classification as a necessity (in economic terms at least). Income elasticity for spirits lies somewhere between the values for beer and wine. (Note the marked difference between short-run and long-run elasticities in this instance). Warm weather leads to more beer-drinking, but seems to have little effect on spirits or wine consumption. Using this information, the study concluded that an increase in the legal drinking age by the one year would lead to a short-run reduction in beer consumption of 2–3 per cent, with a slightly larger effect on wine. There is no evidence of a significant effect on spirits (which suggests that young people consume only small quantities of spirits). In this instance, the long-run effects were found to be even less important than the short-run effects.

These results are of obvious interest to companies in the drinks industry, as well as to the tax authorities and to the road safety organisations that were concerned with the high accident rates of young drivers. An unusual finding was that long-run price elasticity for spirits turned out to be positive. The study described this as a 'disappointing' and 'implausible' result (p. 72). Another counter-intuitive feature is that the long-run price elasticity for beer is lower than its short-run elasticity. Usually, the relationship is the other way round. We mention these aspects to underline that econometric estimation rarely 'lets the statistics speak for themselves'. Quirky and idiosyncratic results are not unusual and the researcher who is frank about them deserves credit rather than censure. There is a danger of trying too hard to find estimates which the researchers will consider 'plausible' and accord with 'intuition' based on economic theory.

Box 4.3

Which market, which elasticity?

When markets are segmentable, the definition of the market to which the elasticity applies becomes rather complicated. The relevant elasticity in the use of the football stadium is not tickets as such, but each particular *type* of ticket.

The complexity can be illustrated by an example, drawn from the hotel industry.

Most capital cities offer the traveller various types of accommodation. The traveller can either stay in a hostel or make use of the wide range of 1–5 star hotels.

The 4 and 5 star categories are typically represented by a small number of hotels all belonging to well-known domestic or international chains, usually situated in or near the city centre. The demand for accommodation in 4 and 5 star hotels comes from various types of buyers, from the 'classic' tourist who books a room directly at the hotel to the business executive whose secretary organises the trip and the wholesaler who asks for big discounts. The choice of each buyer for one particular hotel of this category is not only a question of personal preference, but also of the buyer's budget. Buyers will try to maximise their utility; and hoteliers their profits. The following table roughly outlines the main segments of the market for 4 and 5 star city hotels and their prices in London:

Segment	Average price of room per night
Individual tourist	£285
Corporate clients	£250
Packages	£210
Wholesaler/travel trade	£170
Government	£150
Airlines	£100

Although a hypothetical case, the range of price variation is similar to the range found in many capital cities.

To attract each market segment efficiently, the hotel must differentiate its rates according to the type of consumer. It is not unusual for a hotel to quote around 60 different prices for the same room, depending on the client, the number of room nights and the time of the year. The individual tourist, for example, may be willing to pay the highest rate for luxury accommodation, but the demand of this segment is not large enough to fill a hotel. Only about 5–8 per cent of the yearly occupation can be secured from this source. In contrast, an airline which contracts to purchase 15 room nights daily and stay with the chain on a worldwide or national basis throughout the year will demand, and obtain, a much lower price. This leads to differences in rates of up to 200 per cent for the same room. The most important customers for the 4 and 5 star hotels are corporate clients. They promise the largest volumes at a relatively high average rate. Companies sometimes book high-class hotels in order to give their employees an incentive and because of prestige reasons. Normally hotels offer one-year contracts with fixed rates to this segment, in order to bind the company to the hotel. The following market demand curve might characterise the market in simple terms:

▶

Box 4.3 continued

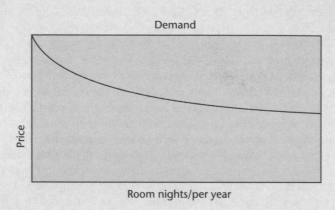

The demand curve is non-linear. Since only a few customers are willing to pay the highest rates, a rise in price results in a relatively small loss of room nights sold to this segment of the market. At the lowest end of the market, demand is more price-sensitive. Customers who normally stayed in 3 star hotels are more willing to switch hotel grade. As can be implied from the graph, the demand for rooms can be very price-elastic and differs from segment to segment.

The hotel has to consider how many rooms it will offer to each segment without losing customers and impairing its image as a first-class hotel. A business executive, for example, would be disturbed by a busload of tourists causing congestion at the reception desk. The individual tourist would be upset on discerning that most of the other guests are paying less. With low-budget tours organised by a tour operator, the hotel is fully booked, but other bookings are jeopardised. These situations can lead to long-term problems in the high-price segment of the market. The development of a strategic business mix requires knowledge of the market, experience, and risk awareness. Elasticities are only one of a number of ingredients which go into determining the price structure of the hotel. However, they are an important element in the equation. The point of the exercise is to increase margins (maximise profits) by selling as many bookings as possible to the high-price segments such as corporate clients and individual tourists. Bookings from airlines and the lower-price segments are taken only in order to maintain good business relationships or to promote one's 'image'.

Finally, some further warnings about the reliability of elasticities should be noted. Most elasticities are estimated on the basis of historical experience. They may prove to be unstable, since the past is not always the best guide to the future. Also, elasticities are defined in relation to a particular market but, as we have seen, the relevant market segment has to be found by careful analysis. The manager of a football stadium, for example, may find that different groups have quite different price elasticities, depending on how stadium seats are organised and segregated. Similarly, a theatre or a hotel will explore opportunities for segmenting the market (see Box 4.3). From a revenue-maximisation point of view, the more degrees of segregation the better. Another important point is that markets are dynamic entities. Demand for products can be cyclical, leading to systematic changes in elasticity values over time. Sometimes, though rarely, the advent of a new product can lead to an increase in demand for a product which is consumed jointly with it, such as happened to the cassette market following the success of the Sony Walkman. Elasticities change in value over time. Markets are evolutionary not static. Finally, businesses that are interested in elasticities of a much narrower segment of the market than is amenable to standard econometric analysis will have to resort to more informal estimation methods.

4.5   Price elasticities and the pricing decision

Elasticities are of most interest to larger firms and to trade and industry organisations which face a downward-sloping demand curve for their sales. Such firms are, by definition, important players in the market and their sales constitute a significant portion of total demand.

If the firm is one of many and each firm accounts for a minute part of the market, as postulated in the definition of the competitive market in Chapter 3, then each firm's demand curve will be very flat and its price elasticity of demand will be very high. In such circumstances, there is a 'going price' in the market. If a firm charges above this price, customers will vanish. If it reduces the price below the going rate, it is inundated with customers. Such a firm is unlikely to be interested in having its demand curve estimated. The product's income elasticity of demand is also of little concern to the firm since its share of the total market is so small. In such cases, only individual industry associations and business organisations will be concerned with elasticities and demand analysis.

Firms are always trying to escape the bind of perfect competition, to make their demand curves inelastic to some degree, to enhance their market range so that they can raise their prices above the going rate. This is what finding a *market niche* means. Once the niche has been found, price elasticities become highly relevant. Firms with well-established market niches must constantly review possibilities of market segmentation in order to exploit any opportunities for revenue increases. Although firms may not express it that way, they are, in effect, seeking to separate high and low price elasticity segments of the market. This is the basis of the distinction between business and economy-class air travel, between 'reserved stand' seats and terraces in a football match, between the dress circle and the stalls in theatres.

Take, for example, the case of the owner of a football stadium who is organising a special charity match. The objective is to maximise gate receipts for the good cause. The question is what price, or profile of prices, to charge in order to achieve this objective. The additional costs of opening the stadium and operating it for the match are small in relation to the expected revenue. For simplicity, let us assume that they are zero. The problem then becomes one of maximising sales revenue.

Suppose that the market demand curve is estimated as DD. What price will maximise revenue? To answer this question, we need to construct the *marginal revenue curve*. Marginal revenue is the net change in total sales revenue resulting from the sale of an extra unit of a good. It equals the price obtained from sale of the marginal unit *less* revenue lost as a result of having to reduce the price on existing sales. Hence the marginal revenue curve is below the demand curve in Figure 4.3; that is, the marginal revenue received by the producer for each extra ticket sold is less than the price charged for that ticket.

Sales revenue will be maximised when marginal revenue equals zero. In the case of a linear demand curve, such as Figure 4.3, this happens when OQ tickets are sold. At that point, marginal revenue has fallen to zero and elasticity of market demand is equal to unity.[9] If price were lowered any further, more tickets would indeed be sold, but total sales revenue would fall.

That might seem to be the end of the story. However, suppose the market could be segmented further. Instead of charging a uniform price, different prices could be charged to different groups of spectators. Essentially, we offer slightly superior seats in the stadium at a much higher price to one segment of the market which is less price-sensitive than the other segments. When the markets are segmented, the definition of the market to which the elasticity applies becomes rather complicated. The relevant elasticity in the case of the football stadium is not tickets as such, but rather each particular type of ticket. Segmentation is enforced easily by checking tickets against seats and ensuring that the lower-price ticket holders cannot occupy the high-price seating. The lower the price elasticity of demand of a group, the higher the price it will be profitable to charge. Hence the effort to segment the market, and to reinforce the loyalty of each segment by relatively inexpensive ploys, such as frequent-flyer miles allowance to business class airline travellers, greeting passengers by name, provision of free in-flight programmes and roomier seats.

In attempting to understand the effects of price changes on volume sold, however, customer reactions are not the only factor for a firm to consider. Competitor reactions also need to be taken into account. If competitors feel threatened as a result of the price cut, they may follow with cuts of their own. This could lead to a price war. Competitor reactions are also relevant in estimating the consequences to the firm of raising its price. If they keep their price constant, the firm may lose customers. If they do follow, the net effect on demand may be very

---

9 This can be explained also by simple calculus. Sales revenue (R) is, by definition, price (p) times quantity (q): $R = p.q$. To find the revenue-maximising price, differentiate with respect to p:

$$dR/dp = q + dq/dp.p = 0$$
$$1 + dq/dp.p/q = 0$$
$$dq/dp.p/q = -1$$
$$[dq/q]/[dp/p] = -1$$

But this last expression is the definition of the price elasticity. So the price which maximises revenue is reached when the price elasticity equals (minus) unity.

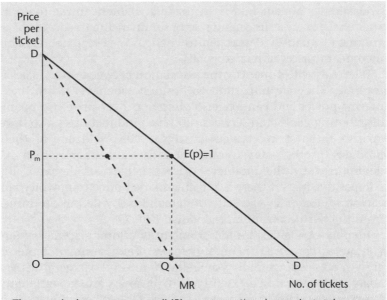

The marginal revenue curve (MR) measures the change in total revenue corresponding to a marginal change in quantity of sales. More quantity can be sold only by lowering price. To the right of Q, MR>O implies that such a strategy increases sales revenue. After sales volume, it leads to lower sales revenue.

Figure 4.3 Demand curve and the marginal revenue curve

small – at least in the short run. In the longer run, the price increase may stimulate new entrants.

These considerations underline the inevitable uncertainty surrounding the price–volume relationship at firm level. The demand curve facing the firm is unknown, apart from one point: the present sales volume and price. It is unlikely to have the nice smooth features of the textbook market demand curve. Also, it will be likely to change over time and to be sensitive to the stage of the business cycle. To add to the complexity, it can change over the course of the product cycle of the good itself.

4.6 Conclusions

Demand analysis can make an important contribution to a firm's understanding of its market. It helps to identify the key variables that can influence demand for a product and provides an empirical quantification of their influence. But it is only one of a number of techniques that managers use in formulating sales and pricing strategy. It needs to be combined with other methods of assessing the market. Statistical analysis is designed to complement, not act as a substitute for, liaison with those close to the market.

Elasticities of demand are an essential element in the tool-kit of an economic analyst. They are a shorthand way of summarising the degree of sensitivity of sales volume or quantity demanded to changes in designated variables such as price, income, or prices of related goods.

Price elasticities quantify the association between prices, sales volume and sales revenue. They are important to business whenever a firm has some degree of market power and can exercise discretion over price. Companies producing or distributing goods and services subject to indirect taxes also have good reason to take an interest in elasticity analysis. The incidence of the tax as between producer profits, sales volumes and the consumer is to a substantial extent determined by the product's price elasticity of demand. By contrast, in a competitive market there is a 'going' market price from which no single producer can stray. The price elasticity of demand is, by definition, infinite when viewed from the perspective of an individual firm.

Income elasticities are important in developing scenarios for growth of sales volume as consumer income increases. They summarise the effects of income growth on sales. Again, they are relevant mostly to larger firms or to industry-level analysis. They are used extensively by business and governments for forecasting. Cross-price elasticity of demand has been employed in anti-trust (fair competition) cases and in investigations of the sensitivity of the demand for one good to the price of others. The elasticity concept can be used to measure the effects of other variables on demand as well as price and income.

We have emphasised the need for caution in using elasticity estimates. Great care must be taken to define the market one wants to have investigated and to allow for changing market structures and elasticity values over time. Elasticity analysis is only a subset of a fully-fledged analysis of demand.

The economic analysis of demand is sometimes criticised for focusing too much on price and not enough on quality. It seems to suggest that price, and price only, keeps demand and supply in line with one another and that price competition between firms is the only kind of competition that matters. There is some validity in this criticism. In economies, 'price' is used for purposes of simplicity as a proxy for non-price variables as well as price. These non-price factors include product quality, after-sales service, prompt delivery and suchlike. In practice, we know that getting the quality decision right may be as important, and often is more important, for sales and profits as getting the pricing decision right.

A business student will also be struck by the way economic analysis of demand tends to take the demand curve as a given. By contrast, strategic management and marketing theory is all about finding out how to change the demand curve. The inventor of Coca-Cola, John Pemberton, confided to his nephew in 1887 that, if only he had the proper capital, he could make a fortune out of Coca-Cola: 'If I could get $25,000', he wrote, 'I would spend $24,000 on advertising and the remainder on making Coca-Cola'.[10] Advertising and sales promotion are powerful

---

10 Mark Prendergast, *For God, Country and Coca-Cola: The unauthorised history of the world's most popular soft drink* (London: Weidenfeld & Nicolson, 1993), p. 73. Coca-Cola has learnt the lesson. It spends hundreds of millions of dollars on advertising and public relations annually.

tools in influencing a firm's demand curve. Product innovation is also important. In such instances, a firm might have to forecast demand without having historical data to guide its pricing decision.[11] We discuss ways of promoting and protecting market power in a later chapter. But while advertising and sales promotion are powerful tools in influencing a firm's demand curve, price still matters and the market can be highly price-sensitive.

✔ ## Summary

1. Economics assumes that the typical consumer is 'rational'. That is, the consumer is capable of making comparisons between different groups of purchases, has consistent preferences and always prefers more to less, has a diversified pattern of spending, and derives utility from consumption independently of what others consume.

2. The market demand curve is conceptualised as the sum of individual demand curves for the good or service. It shows the relationship between changes in price and change in quantity demanded.

3. Price elasticities of demand are a shorthand method of describing the sensitivity of consumer demand to a change in price. Income elasticities of demand refer to the association between changes in income and quantity demanded. Cross-price elasticities of demand refer to the effect of a change in the price of one good on the amount purchased of another good. Each of these elasticities provides useful information to the firm.

4. Firms, industry associations and governments go to considerable trouble to estimate demand functions. The estimates so obtained yield insights into the market profile of the good which can be useful in production, marketing and pricing decisions. They are frequently used as a basis for forecasting exercises. Statistical estimation techniques have become immensely sophisticated, but unfortunately are highly prone to error. They need to be supplemented by on-the-ground information and managers' judgement.

5. Market segmentation is an important element of pricing and marketing strategy. If different groups of consumers have different price sensitivities, it pays to identify and separate them and to charge them different prices. Hotels, theatres, football stadiums and airlines utilise such policies in their pricing. For instance, it is not unusual for a hotel to quote as many as sixty different prices for the same room, depending on the type of client, the time of the year and the number of room nights.

---

11 One way of resolving this problem is to break down the new product or service into its component parts or *characteristics* (which pertain to currently produced goods and services) and to use these for historical analysis.

? Questions for discussion

1. Define the concepts: (a) price elasticity of demand; (b) cross-elasticity of demand; and (c) income elasticity of demand. How are these elasticities estimated? Explain why it might be important for a firm to know their values.

2. In what respects would you expect determinants of the demand for computers to differ from the determinants of the demand for milk?

3. A study of electricity consumption shows that the income elasticity of demand is 0.3 in the short run and 0.6 in the long run, and that the price elasticity is −0.1 in the short run and −0.3 in the long run. Why, in your view, are long-run elasticities usually higher than short-run elasticities?

4. Regarding the cellophane case outlined in Box 4.1, Du Pont claimed that cellophane had close substitutes such as aluminium foil, waxed paper and polyethylene, and cited in evidence the high cross-elasticity of demand for cellophane. Against Du Pont, it was argued that a high cross-price elasticity between Du Pont's cellophane and other products would be expected since Du Pont would have an incentive to keep increasing price until some good became a substitute. Which argument do you find more convincing?

    The Supreme Court found in favour of Du Pont.

5. In May 2000, a five-star London hotel quoted a mid-week nightly rate of £285. The same hotel was offering an Easter weekend rate of £165 per night. What does this tell you about the hotel's assessment of the price elasticity of demand of weekenders relative to mid-week occupants? (See Box 4.3.)

    Is there any rate (price per night) below which hotels would not be prepared to sell rooms?

☞ Exercises

1. Draw a graph showing the demand curve and the supply curve of personal computers. How would your graph be affected by:

    (a) a rise in the price of software,
    (b) a rise in the price of electric typewriters,
    (c) a fall in the price of desktop printers,
    (d) an expected increase in next year's PC prices,
    (e) a 10 per cent sales tax on computers,
    (f) a fall in income tax?

2. A retailer has purchased 500 software packages, which are non-returnable to the distributor. The retailer's supply curve of these products is therefore vertical. It finds that the equilibrium price is £150. Draw a supply and demand curve diagram showing this equilibrium.

    Suppose there was a fire at the store and 100 packages were destroyed. Show the new equilibrium position on the diagram. If you are told that the price elasticity of demand is 2, by how much will price rise as a result of this fall in supply?

3. Which of the following are likely to have a positive cross-price elasticity of demand?

    (a) fishing rods and fishing permits,
    (b) imported rice and domestically produced rice,
    (c) taxi and bus fares,
    (d) cars and tyres,
    (e) beer and wine,
    (f) cameras and films.

4. Suppose a government wanted to reduce petrol consumption by 10 per cent. You are told that the price elasticity is 0.3. You are asked to evaluate two possible ways of achieving the target:

    (a) by means of a tax on petrol, or
    (b) by rationing.

    Which policy would you recommend and why?

5. Suppose for health reasons a tax is placed on tobacco consumption, with the objective of reducing the demand for cigarettes. The cigarette industry objects to this tax and argues that, since the price elasticity of demand is very low, the only effect of the tax will be an increase in government revenue. Use diagrams to analyse this situation. What other measures could the government use to achieve its objectives?

6. Imagine that you are responsible for running a bus company and you have access to the following information about the elasticities of demand for bus travel:

    (a) income elasticity $= -0.4$,
    (b) own-price elasticity $= -1.2$,
    (c) cross-price elasticity with respect to rail fares $= +2.1$.

    How might this information be of use to you in circumstances when your company is running a service which is currently making a loss?

7. You have been hired as an economic consultant by OPEC and given the following statistics showing the world demand for oil:

Price (dollars per barrel)	Quantity demanded (millions of barrels per day)
10	60,000
20	50,000
30	40,000
40	30,000
50	20,000

Your advice is needed on the following questions:

(a) If the supply of oil is decreased so that the price rises from $20 to $30 a barrel, will the total revenue from oil sales increase or decrease?

(b) What will happen to total sales revenue if the supply of oil is decreased further and the price rises to $40 a barrel?

(c) What is the price that will achieve the highest total sales revenue?

(d) What quantity of oil will be sold at the price that answers (c) above?

(e) What are the values of the price elasticity of demand for price changes of $10 a barrel at average prices of $15, $25, $35 and $45 a barrel?

(f) What is the elasticity of demand at the price that maximises total sales revenue?

(g) Over what price range is the demand for oil inelastic?

📖 Further reading

The analysis of consumer behaviour can be extended in many directions, including indifference curve analysis, allocation of consumption over time, choice in the face of risk and uncertainty, and the effects of advertising. These issues are treated in D. Laidler, *Introduction to Macroeconomics* (London: Philip Allan, 1985), and H. Varian, *Microeconomic Analysis*, 3rd edn (London: W.W. Norton, 1992). The price–quantity relationship which economics focuses on is only one of many aspects of the firm's pricing decision. N. Hanna and H.R. Dodge, *Pricing, Policies and Producers* (London: Macmillan, 1995), offer a marketing specialist's review of these issues and place the price–volume relationship in a broader marketing perspective. R.J. Dolan and H. Simon, *Power Pricing: How Managing Price Transforms the Bottom Line* (New York: Free Press, 1996) provides a lively practitioners' perspective on this subject.

Chapter 5

THE FIRM IN A COMPETITIVE MARKET

Introduction

In Chapter 4 we examined the determinants of market demand. Now we ask what lies behind the market supply curve. This involves a study of the motivation of firms and their cost structure. We maintain the assumption of perfect competition, but this will be relaxed in later chapters.

It is easy to see why a demand curve is downward-sloping. The reasons for a supply curve being upward-sloping are less straightforward. In one scenario the upward slope can be explained easily. A rise in price will induce firms to supply more. A rise in price may even be a necessary condition of more output in the short run, since employees may have to be paid overtime and material inputs may have to be purchased on less favourable terms. As output increases, so too does unit cost, and hence the firm's supply curve slopes upwards. By adding together the supply curves of the individual firms we derive the market supply curve, and it too slopes upwards.

Complexities arise if increases in output lead to a fall in unit cost. This happens quite often because of *economies of scale*, and it is especially likely in the long run. As markets expand, the scope for exploiting economies of scale expands. To be able to exploit scale economies and to have vigorous competition at the same time requires even larger markets still. Scale economies have implications for the competitiveness of national industries and for the viability of national markets, as well as for the slope of the supply curve.

The textbook model of competition assumes that all firms are profit-maximisers, that they all produce the same product and that each firm accounts for a small fraction of the total market. Thus, the individual firm has no market power. This assumption is rather extreme, but approximates the position facing many firms which operate in highly open and competitive markets. Exposure to global competition means that they have to supply at world market price or else lose sales. By assuming zero market power initially, we are able to explore important features of the market system. One such feature, familiar to business strategists, is the tension between the individual firm's efforts to acquire market power (through product differentiation, takeovers and alliances) and the prevalence of market forces tending to undermine that power.

Chapter outline

1. Profit-maximisation as the objective of the firm.
2. The implications of profit maximisation for the behaviour of the firm.
3. The cost structure of the firm, economies of scale and scope.
4. The role of transactions cost in explaining firm size and organisational mode.
5. Empirical evidence on cost functions.
6. The derivation of the market supply curve from individual firm supply curves.

5.1 Profit maximisation

Firms seek to maximise profits. Like the assumption of utility maximisation, this assumption has to be interpreted as a general tendency, a reasonable hypothesis, rather than a statement that all firms are guided only by this consideration. In the short term, the acquisition or defence of market share may often necessitate taking price and quality decisions which conflict with profitability and may even involve short-term losses. Also, opportunistic behaviour is rarely the best foundation for long-term profits. The firm that avails itself of every opportunity to take maximum advantage of its customers, employees and suppliers will sooner or later ruin its reputation and lose business.

When originally conceived, the idea of profit maximisation applied to a world of owner-managers of small firms. Provided the owner-manager did not have too strong a preference for leisure and the good life, the assumption that he or she would try to maximise profits seemed reasonable. Difficulties arose with the growth of the public limited liability company and the replacement of owners by professional management. Owners (the shareholders) might still safely be presumed to want maximum profits. But managers might want to maximise something different – their salaries, for instance, or their executive power. Since, in a typical limited liability firm, ownership is often fragmented, shareholders are unable to monitor and judge performance as closely as the executives. With the possibility of conflicting objectives between owners and managers, the firm might not always behave in the way one would expect on the basis of the profit-maximisation assumption. In the words of Herbert Simon, a pioneer in the theory of organisational behaviour:

> Most producers are employees, not owners of firms. Viewed from the vantage point of classical [economic] theory, they have no reason to maximise the profits of the firms, except to the extent that they can be controlled by owners. (H. Simon, 'Organisations and markets', *Journal of Economic Perspectives*, Spring 1991)

The divorce in objectives between owners and managers gives rise to a *principal–agent problem* (see Box 5.1). A firm's profits are assumed to be related to managerial effort, but owners are unable to monitor and measure this effort. Hence they must think of ways of motivating executives to maximise profits rather than their own utility.

Box 5.1

The principal–agent problem

Principals:

- Shareholders

In order to control the actions of their agents:

- Board of Directors
- Senior Executives

Require instruments:

- Management incentives
  - pay related to profit
  - share options
  - fixed-term contracts

- Threat of takeover

One start to resolving this problem is to appoint a Board of Directors, elected by and answerable to the shareholders. But this redefines rather than resolves the principal–agent problem since non-executive directors, like any other agent, may have their own agenda (including the desire to 'keep in' with the management). They have limited time to devote to board business and their financial stake in the company may be relatively modest.

There are two further ways of tackling the problem. First, owners (the principal), through the Board of Directors, can devise 'price' incentives which will motivate executives (their agent) to pursue the principal's objectives of profit maximisation. Second, if they are unable to do this, owners can sell their shares to other owners who will find ways of utilising the firm's assets more profitably. The threat of a takeover, and the consequent prospect of a new management team, can be a powerful spur to performance by executives. We consider each of these possible solutions in turn.

Management incentives

Owners pay executives a base salary, but they also tie remuneration to profits by payment of various forms of profit-related incentives. Examples include profit bonuses, fixed-term contracts which are renewable if a profit target is reached, and share options. Share options are both a reward for past performance and an incentive to future effort, since a rising share price will increase the value of the options. Another possibility is for shareholders to apply the 'stick' of critical review of management performance at annual general meetings.

Profit-related incentives are only a partial answer to the problem of divergent objectives.[1] First, the link between executive pay and managerial effort is difficult to quantify. At the time of the takeover of Chrysler in 1998, Daimler executives were surprised to discover that the compensation package given to one senior Chrysler executive exceeded the collective remuneration of Daimler's entire executive Board ($13m). Did the Chrysler executives really work all that much harder as a result? They certainly worked less effectively, since Daimler was taking them over (*International Herald Tribune*, 14 August 1998).

Second, a more difficult problem is that the relationship between a firm's profitability and managerial effort can be erratic. Profits can rise or fall because of macroeconomic developments or because of a run of good or bad luck. The 1990s was a prosperous decade for business: recovery from recession, low inflation, and falling unemployment. Profits boomed as did corporate pay, but it would be hard to argue that the high remuneration caused the economic boom. Proof of the pudding in this instance may well be executives' reluctance to rely too much on profit or share-price-related remuneration. Remuneration committees dominated by company executives have been known to award hefty executive pay increases despite falling profits. Minimum service contracts and 'golden parachutes' (payments to the executives in the event of their being made redundant or dismissed) can further moderate the impact of profit-related incentives. Not surprisingly, empirical studies indicate that the correlation between executive pay and company performance is weak.[2]

Despite these qualifications, shareholders continue to pay high levels of remuneration to their executives. Compensation of the highest paid executives has escalated and the gap between executive and shopfloor pay has widened. In the 1970s, the typical chief executive of a large American company earned about 40 times more than the average factory worker. During the 1990s, the same executive earned over 400 times more. Executive pay was rarely out of the news in the UK, with attention focusing on the pay of senior executives of several privatised industries. Executive share option schemes have soared in the US over the past decade. In 1998 alone, 92 of America's 200 leading chief executives were given options with an average minimum value if exercised of $31m.[3] Of course, high executive remuneration may prove a good bargain for the owner-shareholders if they achieve even a mild motivation effect. Shareholders may also acquiesce in high pay for their executives because, being dispersed and

---

1 Kevin Murphy, 'Executive compensation', in O. Ashenfelter and D. Card (eds), *A Handbook of Labour Economics* (Amsterdam: North Holland, 1998).

2 A survey of 169 companies by the National Institute of Economic and Social Research (NIESR) in the UK concluded that the pay of top executives responded positively to growth in sales, but was only weakly correlated to returns for shareholders. Another finding was that executive directors' pay grew faster in firms which grew by acquisition rather than by organic growth, and in firms which funded their expansion by borrowing rather than by use of shareholder funds. Inclusion of the value of executive share options in the calculations would, by definition, have brought executive remuneration and company performance (defined often in terms of share value) less out of line. But the link between even total executive compensation and company performance remains extremely weak.

3 The figures in this paragraph are taken from 'Share options', *The Economist* (7 August 1999).

> ## Box 5.2
>
> ## Profit maximisation in action
>
> A history of the Coca-Cola Corporation reports that Roberto Goizueta, newly appointed CEO in 1981, was frustrated by Coke executives' varied reactions to competition in setting their goals: 'some going after increased sales, some market share, and *only a few concerned over return on capital*' (my emphasis). Goizueta believed something had to be done. At the heart of his new strategy lay the profit target: 'a rate substantially in excess of inflation, in order to give our shareholders an above average total return on their investment'. This emphasis on profitability was instrumental in raising earnings per share by 10 per cent per year. The price of Coca-Cola stock shot up from $35 in 1980 to $120 in 1986, an increase well above the stock market average for the period. The value of management share options followed suit, bringing significant benefits to the chief executive and to his team in the process. The moral of this story is that failure to maximise profits will eventually be detected and corrected by market forces.
>
> *Source*: Mark Prendergast, *For God, Country and Coca-Cola* (London: Weidenfeld & Nicolson, 1993), p. 374.

numerous, they have little economic incentive to monitor management directly. An individual shareholder will bear heavy costs for organising such monitoring, but the benefits will accrue to all other shareholders. Hence each individual shareholder has an incentive to sit tight and hope that another shareholder will take the initiative. This is an instance of a pervasive problem in economic life called *the free-rider problem*.

Institutional reform can also help to bind executive pay more closely to performance. The Cadbury Committee, for example, recommended that company remuneration committees should be composed primarily of non-executive directors who will not themselves benefit directly from awarding higher compensation to management.[4] The Greenbury Report (1995) on corporate governance made further recommendations, one being full disclosure of directors' remuneration as a way of enhancing accountability.

Threat of takeover

Even if all the above measures fail, the threat of takeover acts as one further discipline on management. If management persistently underutilises the company's resources, the threat of a takeover by another management team will be accentuated, with potentially adverse consequences for incumbent executives. While even the best-run companies can become a takeover target, the probability of this unpleasant outcome can be minimised by earning high profits. This raises the share price and makes the firm too expensive for predators.

---

4 Cadbury Committee Report, *The Financial Aspects of Corporate Governance* (London, 1992).

The takeover threat is particularly relevant to countries with a highly developed stock market culture, such as the US and the UK. Of course, management has devised many ingenious ways of reducing the potency of this threat. Among the more familiar schemes are *greenmail* (where incumbent management buys off the raider with company money), *white knights* (where the assistance of a friendly outsider is enlisted to ward off hostile bidders) and *poison pills*. Poison pills refer to provisions whereby, in the event of a merger/takeover, shareholders can acquire shares in the surviving firm at a substantial discount from market price. This acts as a disincentive to such takeovers by making them more expensive. Executives are aware that these measures offer no foolproof defence. Replying to a question about a possible takeover of the company, the chief executive of a major materials multinational, CRH (Cement Roadstone Holdings), commented:

> A company is always vulnerable if it performs badly. A good performance is the best protection against acquisition. It means that someone else has to prove to shareholders that they can run your business even better.[5]

Market forces, therefore, in the form of both the 'carrot' of incentives and the 'stick' of the takeover threat, impose a discipline on management and penalise the systematic neglect of profit maximisation. At the limit, there is the threat of bankruptcy, a real danger for an underperforming firm. Even in the public sector, state-owned commercial enterprises can be given an incentive to act like a profit-maximising firm through the imposition of 'hard budget constraints' linked to a targeted return on capital.

In recent years the rising power of institutional investors relative to individual investors has given greater weight to shareholder interests over those of corporate executives. Large investors are more able to wield power and are better organised than traditional small private shareholders. Because of their size, they are able to surmount both the transactions cost and the free-rider problems.[6] This accretion of shareholders' control has been driven by the pressure placed on investment managers themselves to perform well. Investment and pension fund trustees are more astute, are less inclined to entrust all their funds to one manager, are more likely to compare the performance of different fund managers and are more prepared to shift their funds from one manager to another than small private investors. Thus, while the volume of capital available to investment managers has reached unprecedented heights, so too has the competition for managing it. This makes fund managers more demanding in terms of shareholder returns.

Alternatives to the assumption of profit maximisation have been explored. For example, that executives try to maximise sales, subject only to a minimum level

---

5 Cited in J.A. Murray and A. O'Driscoll, *Managing Marketing* (Dublin: Gill & Macmillan, 1993), p. 378. Note, however, that good performance does not guarantee immunity from hostile bids. See T. Franks and B. Mayer, 'Hostile takeovers and the correction of managerial failure', *Journal of Financial Economics*, 40 (1996).

6 M. Useem, *Executive Defence: Shareholder power and corporate reorganisation* (Cambridge, MA: Harvard University Press, 1993), discusses this issue. It has been estimated that two-thirds of the equity market of the UK and one half of the US market are controlled by professionally managed institutional investors. Individual ownership of UK shares fell from 54 per cent in 1963 to 18 per cent in 1993.

of profit to keep shareholders happy. This assumption is plausible in certain circumstances, but as a generalisation it is hard to argue its superiority over profit maximisation. Unless long-run profits are maximised, the forces of competition threaten not only the jobs of management, but the survival of the firm.

Besides, profit maximisation does not necessarily conflict with the objective of keeping or expanding market share. The firm making the largest sustained profits will be best equipped to survive in the long term. Of course firms will continue to emphasise factors such as product quality but this preference for product quality might reflect a contrasting management style and time-horizon, rather than deviation from the long-run objective of profit maximisation. For instance, it is often said that Japanese firms take a longer-term view than their American counterparts, and wait until then to reap their profits. Japanese firms are certainly world leaders in one essential characteristic of a profit maximiser – the minimisation of costs per unit of output. The contemporary profit-maximising firm, in summary, may have a sophisticated agenda. A former chief executive of the Bank of Montreal objectives as follows:

> In rating my bank's performance, I assign only 40% weight to the bottom line. Customer satisfaction, employee competence and public image count for 60% for they are the indicators of future profit and future shareholder value.[7]

Anglo-American firms may discount the future more heavily than German and Japanese firms. But most remain profit maximisers. Some just place more weight on future profits than others.

5.2 Rules for maximising profit

The profit-maximisation assumption is important, because it has strong implications for how firms behave. These implications apply both to the pricing decision and to the output decision. Where competition is intense, the firm has little or no discretion over price. It takes price as given. The key decision becomes how much to produce. The company must also decide what techniques to use in its production: how much labour, how much machinery and buildings, how many raw materials. In making these decisions, a profit-maximising firm will be guided by certain rules.

The first rule is that the firm must produce up to the point where *marginal revenue (MR) equals marginal cost (MC)*. Recall from Chapter 4 that marginal revenue equals the increase in total revenue derived from the sale of one additional unit. Marginal cost is defined analogously as the increase in total cost incurred by the production of one additional unit. Suppose the marginal revenue from an additional unit of sales is £10 and marginal cost (the extra cost of producing that unit) is only £5. Clearly, it is profitable for the firm to produce that unit. Suppose that the next unit also earns a marginal revenue of £10 but that its marginal cost rises to £8. It is profitable to produce that unit also. The firm will

---

7 M. Barrett, 'Practical idealism in banking', *Irish Banking Review* (Autumn 1994), p. 77.

Box 5.3

Derivation of profit-maximisation rule

The profit-maximisation rule can be derived formally as follows:

By definition $\quad \pi = TR - TC$

where: π = profits
   TR = total revenue
   TC = total costs

The first-order condition for profit maximisation is:

$$\frac{\partial \pi}{\partial q} = \frac{\partial TR}{\partial q} - \frac{\partial TC}{\partial q} = 0, \text{ where } q = \text{ unit of output} \qquad (1)$$

i.e. $\qquad \dfrac{\partial TR}{\partial q} = \dfrac{\partial TC}{\partial q}$

$\qquad$ MR = MC

This is the rule that *marginal revenue must equal marginal cost.*
   The second-order condition for a maximum is:

$$\frac{\partial^2 \pi}{\partial q^2} < 0$$

i.e. $\qquad \dfrac{\partial MR}{\partial q} - \dfrac{\partial MC}{\partial q} < 0$

$$\frac{\partial MR}{\partial q} < \frac{\partial MC}{\partial q} \qquad (2)$$

This means that the MC curve must cut the MR curve from below. From a practical point of view, it is not so important. Businesses are highly unlikely to choose minimum profit points!

increase production up to the level where the marginal cost and the marginal revenue are equal. At any lower output, marginal revenue exceeds marginal cost and unexploited opportunities for profit would be ignored. At any higher output, marginal cost exceeds marginal revenue. The firm incurs losses at the margin, and that too is inconsistent with profit maximisation. This rule is derived formally in Box 5.3.

Second, the firm *minimises the cost of producing any given level of output.* It minimises costs by applying the rule: *purchase each input up to the point where the net value of the output produced by that input equals the cost to the firm of purchasing it.* The input might be the services of an employee, a new machine, additional quantities of raw materials or more warehousing space. The marginal cost of the

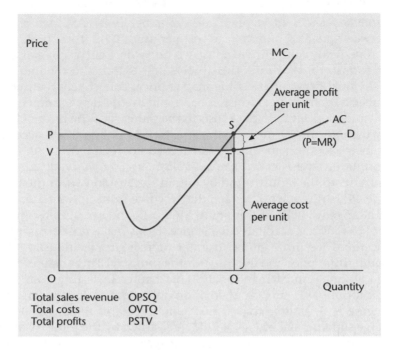

Figure 5.1 **Cost curves of the firm**

input to the firm is the price paid (assuming price is insensitive to the amount of the input demanded by the individual firm). The value of the extra output produced by each input to the firm equals the extra output multiplied by price (in technical jargon, the value of its marginal product).

Suppose this were not the case. Say the value of the marginal product of an employee is £100 per day (net of material costs), while the cost of hiring him or her is £60 per day. At the same time, the marginal product of the new machine is £60, but the cost of running it is £100 per day. Then, assuming no other costs, the firm is making £40 per day profit from the marginal employee and losing £40 per day from the marginal machine. The profit-maximising firm should hire more labour and fewer machines!

A third rule is that a *technically inefficient (in an engineering sense) production technique should not be used*. If 100 units of output could be produced by using (a) 80 units of labour and 100 units of capital, or (b) 60 units of labour and 90 units of capital, technique (b) will always be chosen by the profit maximiser.

The logic of the MR = MC rule is illustrated in Figure 5.1. An individual firm in a competitive market, by assumption, faces a given market price. Each additional unit it produces can be sold at a constant price OP. Hence the extra revenue earned by an additional unit of production (marginal revenue) equals price. The firm's demand curve can be depicted as a horizontal straight line. In this instance, the demand curve and the marginal revenue curve are the same. Profits are maximised when MC intersects the firm's MR line, PD, at S. At that point, OQ is produced and sold at price OP. Profit per unit is ST, which is the difference between price QS and average cost per unit (TQ).[8] Total profits are PSTV.

A perfectly competitive industry is one where entry and exit are free. If firms in an industry make profit, this attracts new entrants to the industry. Although no individual firm can affect the market price, collectively their entry does have an impact. Eventually, expansion of supply by the new entrants will cause price to fall and, possibly, also raise costs in the industry as the price of inputs is driven up by the industry's growth. In the long run, equilibrium will occur when profits are reduced to the bare minimum needed to retain firms in the industry. This minimum level is called *normal profits*. *Supernormal profits* are bid away by new entrants to the industry and by output expansion within the industry. The price line, PD, shifts downwards and the AC curve shifts upwards, until eventually AC is at a tangent to PD. At this point, MC = MR and average cost (including a normal rate of return on capital) equals price. Firms make no 'excess' profits. There is no incentive for firms either to enter or to exit the industry. We have reached equilibrium price and quantity for the industry. This analysis can be related back to the supply and demand analysis of Chapter 3. Starting from initial price/output equilibrium at E, suppose there is an outward shift in the demand curve to D^1D^1 (Figure 5.2). Assume that at first supply remains fixed at OQ. Price rises to OP. Large supernormal profits of PAEC are earned by the industry at that price, just as they are by our individual firm in Figure 5.1. These supernormal profits attract new entrants to the industry as well as encouraging existing firms to expand. Supply increases along the SS curve. As it does so, downward pressure is brought to bear on price. Eventually equilibrium is reached at E^1, where there are no longer supernormal profits.

Thus, in competition, the unrelenting search for profits leads to their eventual erosion. From the point of view of the firm, this outcome is both unintended and undesirable. From society's perspective, it is the great advantage of competitive markets.

The rules for profit-maximising behaviour are plausible, but they need to be interpreted with care. First, 'profits' in an economic sense are not the same as profits in a company's profit and loss statement (see Box 5.4). Second, empirical measurement of marginal costs and of the marginal product of an employee may be subject to a wide margin of error. Third, firms may have insufficient information on demand conditions to determine marginal revenue.[9] This last problem can be particularly acute in circumstances where the reaction of competitors has to be estimated as well as the reaction of customers. Intuition and guesswork then have to supplement more systematic information.

---

8 The relationship between average costs and marginal costs can be explained as follows. Average total costs include fixed costs plus the sum of marginal costs. If the marginal cost is above average cost, average cost must rise: if below, average cost must fall. This point can be illustrated by a simple example. Suppose a person of 7 feet is added to a class with an average height of 5 feet. The average height of the class is raised. Likewise, if a person 4 feet tall joins the class, the average class height falls. For the same reason, if marginal cost is lower than average cost, average cost is falling.

9 R.S. Kaplan and A.A. Atkinson, *Advanced Management Accounting* (Hemel Hempstead: Prentice Hall, 1989), p. 179.

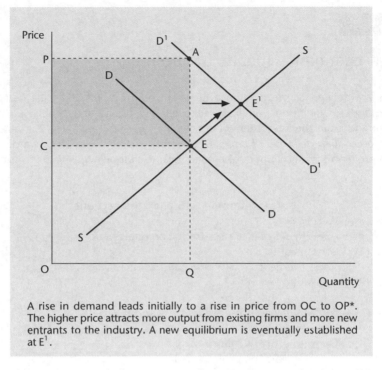

A rise in demand leads initially to a rise in price from OC to OP*. The higher price attracts more output from existing firms and more new entrants to the industry. A new equilibrium is eventually established at E^1.

Figure 5.2 How industry responds to an increase in market demand

Given these practical difficulties in making the MR = MC rule operational, it is not surprising that firms use rules of thumb to determine sales and pricing. *Mark-up pricing* or cost-plus pricing is one such commonly used alternative. However, the size of the mark-up varies considerably by product which indicates that, in deciding on the mark-up, managers may implicitly be using the marginal rules. Another pricing strategy, the Japanese practice of *target pricing*, consists of taking a competitive market price as given and working backwards to determine the target cost for the product. This proactive approach to costs is also compatible with adherence to the marginal rules for profit-maximising behaviour.[10] Finally, some forms of widely observed price behaviour such as *below-cost selling* superficially appear to contradict the profit-maximisation rule. But such is not necessarily the case. The practice of loss leading by large multiples can be shown to be perfectly compatible with profit-maximising behaviour.

---

10 T. Hiromoto, 'Another hidden edge: Japanese management accounting', *Harvard Business Review*, 66(2) (1988), pp. 22–6. Over the years, economists have contributed to the literature on business pricing decisions, beginning with a classic study by R.L. Hall and C.J. Hitch, *Price Theory and Business Behaviour* (Oxford: Oxford University Press, 1939).

Box 5.4

What economics means by profit

Profits are defined as the difference between total revenue and total costs. The key to understanding the distinction between economic profits and profits as defined by an accountant lies in the interpretation of costs.

The *accounting definition of profits* is, of course, far from straightforward. A simple pro-forma profit and loss account might look similar to that below, with six possible versions of profit.

Pro-forma Profit and Loss Account

	Turnover	1000
	less direct cost of sales (including depreciation)	900
(1)	**Gross profit**	**100**
	less overheads (distribution and administration)	60
(2)	**Operating profit**	**40**
	less exceptional items[1]	2
(3)	**Operating profit before interest and taxation**	**38**
	less interest	4
(4)	**Operating profit before tax**	**34**
	less corporation profits taxation	10
(5)	**Operating profit after tax**	**24**
	less (net) minority interests[2]	4
(6)	**Profits attributable to ordinary shareholders**	**20**
	less extraordinary charges[3]	3
(7)	**Profits for the financial year**	**17**
	Dividends	10
	Balance to reserves	7

Gross profits are defined as the difference between sales revenue and variable costs. *Operating profits* are obtained by deducting overheads (or fixed costs in our terminology).

The existence of operating profit does not *per se* indicate that other firms would be eager to enter the business. The reason is that capital has been invested in the firm, in respect of which investors expect a certain level of return. This expected or 'normal' rate of return would *at minimum* equal the yield on a fixed-interest government bond. Instead of investing in the company, investors could have obtained this (riskless) return by buying government bonds. Given that business is risky, some premium over the bond rate would be required to keep investors satisfied. This risk premium will differ from industry to industry. Compared with, say, a government bond yield of 8 per cent, return on capital of between 12 per cent and 20 per cent would be the expected norm in industries. Return on capital employed (ROCE) equals operating profits before interest and tax divided by the value of total assets.

From operating profit before tax, therefore, we should deduct an amount representing a 'normal' return on capital to shareholders before profit, in the economist's sense, is earned. It is the presence or absence of economic or supernormal profits which determines whether

Box 5.4 continued

firms will enter or exit the industry. *Supernormal profits*, not operating profits in the accounting sense, perform the signalling function of the market system.

The *economic definition of profits* incorporates the idea of *opportunity costs*. It takes into explicit account that capital employed in a firm has alternative uses. There is a cost to society of deploying it in the firm. That cost is determined by considering the 'best' alternative use – defined in terms of the best cash yield ratio – to which it could have been put.

Two aspects of economic profit merit comment. First, the standard economic analysis of the firm focuses exclusively on profits. *Cash-flow* does not appear in the calculations. Yet many firms argue that a cash-flow statement showing movements of cash within a company reveals more about the firm's viability than declared profits. In theory, a profitable firm ought to be able to raise cash, given a perfect capital market. In practice, this is not always the case, especially in instances where the firm is part of a group which is cash-negative or where there is a long gap between the timing of initial investment and inflow of cash return. Being wholly dependent on shareholders or financial institutions for cash is not a sustainable long-term position and may even be difficult in the short term. The importance of cash-flow tends to be neglected in the economic analysis of the firm.

Another qualification concerns the *role of taxation*. Economic profits are defined before deduction of tax. We assume that all firms face the same tax regime and that different initial positions regarding tax credits and write-offs can be ignored. We also assume that corporation profits tax does not affect the profit-maximising level of output. These initial assumptions can, however, be relaxed to take account of both regional tax incentive schemes – 'signals' devised by national or regional authorities to attract inward investment – and of the complex interplay between corporate profits tax, depreciation and inflation on the cost of capital to the firm.

To conclude, there is no single universally applicable measure of profits in either accountancy or economics. The substantive conceptual difference between the two disciplines' approach is the deduction in the economics definition of normal return to shareholders on operating profits. The resultant (positive or negative) 'supernormal' profits perform the signalling role for enterprises that prices perform for individuals.

Notes:
1. Defined as material items of a non-recurrent nature arising out of the ordinary activities of the business.
2. Profits arising from activities in which the firm has a minority shareholding.
3. Defined as highly abnormal, non-recurring items arising from transactions which fall *outside* the ordinary activities of the company.

5.3   Cost structure of the firm

A firm's costs are divided into *fixed costs* and *variable costs*. Fixed costs consist of pre-committed outgoings, which are payable regardless of the level of output. Variable costs represent outgoings, such as materials, energy and distribution costs, which rise and fall in accordance with the volume of output. Fixed costs can be subdivided into *sunk costs* and *other fixed costs*. Sunk costs refer to past expenditure on fixed assets which have no alternative use and the cost of which can be amortised or recouped only by trading. Examples of sunk costs include the costs of a nuclear power station, large steel plants or the Channel Tunnel. By contrast, the cost of the lease of an office building is a fixed cost, but is not a sunk cost, since the building could be sub-let to another firm. Sunk costs play an important role in determining the firm's output and price strategy. Over time, all costs except sunk costs become variable. In economics jargon, the long run is defined precisely as that period of time over which fixed costs can be converted into variable costs.

The cost structure of a firm is illustrated in Figure 5.3. Costs are measured on the vertical axis and level of the firm's output on the horizontal axis. Fixed costs have to be paid regardless of the level of sales and are depicted by a straight horizontal line. Total variable costs are shown as an upward-sloping line, reflecting the fact that variable costs are a positive function of output. Thus, a rise in output from 500 units to 600 units raises total costs from £10 million to £12 million. The variable costs incurred in adding 100 units of output amount to £2 million.

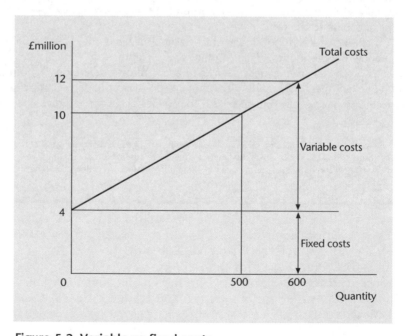

Figure 5.3 Variable vs fixed costs

The breakeven chart is a graphic representation of the relationships between costs, volume and price and shows the effects of short-run variations in output upon a firm's profitability. A typical breakeven chart might look as follows:

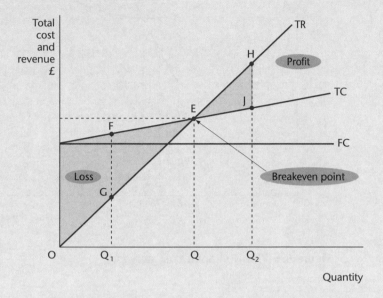

Total fixed costs (FC) are constant over a range of output, while total variable costs start at zero when output is zero and increase with output thereafter. Total costs (TC) are the sum of fixed and variable costs. Since selling price is constant, the total revenue (TR) line starts at zero and increases proportionately with output and sales volume.

The firm breaks even (makes neither a profit nor a loss) at output OQ. At output less than this, say OQ_1, total cost FQ_1 exceeds revenues GQ_1, resulting in a loss of FG. At outputs greater than the breakeven output, say OQ_2, total revenues HQ_2 exceed costs JQ_2, resulting in a profit of HJ. Profits or losses at other output levels can be similarly determined.

Figure 5.4 The basic breakeven chart

In calculating the contribution of a new product to profits, variable costs are sometimes assumed to be linearly related to output (i.e. they are assumed to rise by a constant amount per unit of output). The *breakeven chart*, for example, includes information on costs and revenues, and depicts a situation where a certain minimum level of sales is required for the firm to break even (Figure 5.4). After this point, the firm enters a profit zone, with profits being calculated as a constant contribution per unit. Breakeven charts are used to estimate the effects on profits of variations in sales volumes around the breakeven point.

Studies of cost structures, however, suggest a more complex picture than the linear relationship suggests. The key point is that variable costs per unit of

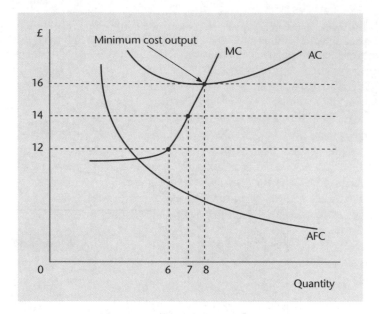

Figure 5.5 The U-shaped cost curves

output are not constant as output increases. In the short run, they tend to fall. Then, beyond a certain output level, they begin to rise. A simple starting point is to depict the relationship between unit costs and sales volumes by a U-shaped curve (Figure 5.5). The initial cost decline is attributed to *economies of scale*: the flattening, and eventual rise, of the unit cost curve is explained by the growing weight of *diseconomies of scale*. These concepts, which occupy a central role in our understanding of the size and cost structure of firms, now need to be explained.

Economies of scale and scope

First, there are *indivisibilities*. Indivisibilities are costs incurred in large non-incremental amounts, such as the cost of constructing a tunnel or a nuclear energy plant. A half-built tunnel is costly to make, but useless. A half-built nuclear reactor is likewise costly, but dangerous. Each project becomes useful when the entire project is completed. Completion may be a large-scale and expensive exercise. The Channel Tunnel between England and France cost more than £10 billion sterling to construct. These *sunk costs* had been incurred, and the accompanying debt remained to be serviced, without a single train or passenger having passed through. As the 'output' of the tunnel increases, the fixed costs are spread over a larger volume of traffic. Average fixed cost per unit of output (AFC) falls. Hence total cost per unit declines. The more passengers using the tunnel, the lower the cost per unit.

Indivisibilities are encountered in many areas of business. For example, the costs of R&D and product design have to be incurred long before production begins. As the product reaches the market and is sold, these initial fixed costs are spread over a larger volume of output. The cost of developing a new car and bringing it to the market can involve an outlay of more than $1 billion over a period of two or more years before a single car is sold.[11] The average pre-tax cost of developing a successful drug is $150m, which rises to $500m if costs of failures are included. As test procedures become more demanding and as science tackles more complex diseases, these indivisible costs are rising all the time. From the author's point of view, it costs the same to get one copy of a book ready for publication as 1000 copies. To get a new food product onto a UK supermarket shelf can cost as much as £3 million in marketing, advertising and promotion expenditure. The essential feature of these expenditures is their 'indivisibility'.

Another source of scale economy is *increased specialisation*. Adam Smith observed that, as a firm's output increased, its cost per unit declined because employees would become more dextrous and skilled and, by focusing intensively on a narrow range of activities, would be able to suggest improved ways of performing their work and even devise better machinery to assist them (see Box 5.5). Skinner's concept of a *focused factory* puts these ideas into modern garb:

> A factory that focuses on a narrow product mix for a particular market niche will outperform the conventional plant, which attempts a broader mission. Because its equipment, supporting systems and procedures can concentrate on a limited task for one set of customers, its cost and especially its overheads are likely to be lower than those of a conventional plant. But, more important, such a plant can become a competitive weapon because its entire apparatus is focused to accomplish the particular manufacturing task demanded by the company's overall strategy and marketing objective.[12]

Two modern versions of Smith's scale economies through specialisation focus on the development of *core competencies* and *learning-by-doing*. The core competencies version states that a firm must attain a certain minimum size in order to give employees scope to concentrate their efforts and to develop specialised skills. Learning-by-doing economies arise because of growth in the firm's *cumulative output*. The longer the firm remains in business, the more technical and marketing experience accumulates, which translates into lower unit costs. A 'learning' elasticity of 0.2 has been estimated for the aircraft production industry; production costs decrease by 2 per cent, with a 10 per cent rise in

---

11 K.B. Clark and T. Fujimoto, *Product Development Performance: Strategy organisation and management in the world auto industry* (New Haven, CT: Harvard Business School Press, 1991).

12 Wickham Skinner, 'The focused factory', *Harvard Business Review* (May–June 1974), p. 41. Skinner went on to observe that focused manufacturing plants are 'extremely rare' in the US. The conventional US plant, in his view, undertook a multiplicity of tasks motivated by the desire to achieve economies of scale and utilise its overheads to the maximum. Adding more products to the firm's product range yielded scale economies in one sense – more intensive use of capital equipment – but it undermined them in a more important sense by distracting human and organisational resources from the core task.

Box 5.5

Adam Smith's division of labour

Adam Smith's classic text, *An Inquiry into the Nature and Causes of the Wealth of Nations*, was published in 1776. A major theme of the book, sketched in the opening chapters, is that wealth consists of a nation's productive power, not its stock of gold. In Smith's view, the source of 'the greatest improvement in the productive powers of labour' is the *division of labour*. Nowadays, we use 'specialisation' and 'economies of scale' instead of 'division of labour'.

Smith identified three ways in which increased specialisation leads to higher productivity: first, it enhances the dexterity of the workforce; second, it saves time lost in passing from one type of work to another; and third, it leads to the invention of 'a great number of machines which facilitate and abridge labour and enable one man to do the work of many'. Interestingly, Smith believed that inventions were likely to be suggested by the workers 'who, being employed in some simple operation, naturally turn their thoughts towards finding out easier and speedier methods of performing it' (p. 13).

To illustrate the benefits of specialisation, Smith took the celebrated example of the pin factory. By specialising the tasks of each worker, the factory produces 4800 pins per worker per day, but if each worker tried to produce pins on an individual basis they could produce only a fraction of that amount. More than 200 years after the publication of *The Wealth of Nations*, the output of pins per worker in Britain had risen to 800,000 per day. This converts to an annualised average 2.6 per cent growth rate in labour productivity (close to the national average for all industries!).

Not all of this productivity growth can be ascribed to specialisation within the pin industry. For instance, employees are now better educated than in the past – though this superior education reflects specialisation in a separate sphere itself. Technical progress also derives from division of labour.

The figures illustrate the immense significance of an apparently modest productivity growth – if it is sustained over a sufficiently long span of time. The structure of the pin industry has also changed markedly since Smith's time. Whereas in 1776 there were 100 or more small firms in Britain producing pins, in 1976 all pins in the United Kingdom were produced by just two firms.

Source: C.F. Pratten, 'The manufacture of pins', *Journal of Economic Literature* (March 1980).

output. Know-how and technological expertise embodied in the workforce rise with the number of aircraft that have been produced.[13]

The statistical *law of large numbers* is another factor helping to reduce unit costs. The optimum level of inventories grows with the square root of sales (the stock inventory rule), not proportionally with sales. *Economies of increased dimension*, or *'engineering' rules*, also account for the reduction in unit costs with extra sales

---

13 G. Klepper, 'Entry into the market for large commercial aircraft', *European Economic Review*, 34(4) (1990), p. 777.

volume. This source of scale economies is important for storage and transport activities. Capacity increases with *volume*, while cost is more closely related to *area* – hence the economies of huge warehouses, supertankers, pipelines and beer-vats. Imagine a box $2 \times 2 \times 2$ with a volume of $8\,m^3$. The area of the box consists of six sides, each of which is $4\,m^2$. Total area = $24\,m^2$. Now consider the effects of doubling the dimensions of the box to $4 \times 4 \times 4$. Each side of the box now measures $16\,m^2$. Total area = $96\,m^2$, but cubic capacity increases to $64\,m^3$. Thus, while storage capacity increases eight-fold, costs (assumed to be related to area) increase only four-fold. Another example of this phenomenon is the tendency for the cost of operating a machine to vary by 0.6 times the capacity of the machine – the Haldi–Whitcomb '0.6 rule'.[14]

Finally, *economies of scope* arise when the cost of providing two or more distinct goods from the same firm is less than the cost of producing them separately. Economies of scope are common in distribution and retailing. In the case of photocopiers, for instance, it is more economical for one firm to supply toner and paper together rather than to have them supplied separately by different firms. Likewise, it is sometimes more cost-effective to distribute different but related products, say refrigerators and washing machines, together than to distribute each separately. Economies of scope are crucial to understanding the cost–benefit of developing global brands. Hamel and Prahalad explain by citing the example of Yamaha.

> Yamaha makes and markets a broad range of musical instruments under a single brand (including guitars, pianos, trumpets, organs and violas). It is inherently better positioned to build a significant market share than single instrument competitors ... which cannot amortise their brand investments across multiple product categories. (*Competing for the Future*, Boston Harvard Business School Press, 1994, p. 282).

Economies of scope are also common where networks exist. Information technology and telecommunications are outstanding examples of networks which allow the owner of the network to push down unit costs as more customers use the network's facilities. Joint distribution of bank and insurance services makes it possible to spread costs by using distribution networks more intensively. The removal of rules restricting the provision of these products led to the development of the bancassurance industry in Europe in the 1990s. Another example is the benefits to an airline of an extended flight network. Although some services may not be individually profitable, they may still add to overall company profits if customers using them are attracted thereby to profitable parts of the airline's network. Airlines often offer highly competitive fares for short-distance flights to hub airports in order to induce customers to avail themselves of the firm's more profitable long-haul flights.

---

14 The Haldi–Whitcomb study researched the cost structure of 687 plants. They found that 94 per cent had economies of scale. They estimated the equation $C = ax^b$, where C = cost of operations and $x =$ output capacity of plant. The coefficient of b was estimated at 0.6 – hence the 0.6 rule.

These varied sources of scale economies explain why average cost per unit of output can fall when total output rises.[15] After a certain level of output, however, the forces reducing costs cease to dominate. The average cost curve flattens out and then starts to slope upwards. In technical jargon, diseconomies of scale begin to outweigh economies of scale.

Diseconomies of scale

Unit costs tend to rise in the short run because, among other reasons, employees will have to be paid overtime. A point may even be reached where they start to get in each other's way. As output increases, there is a build-up of stress and friction on managers, machines and materials as they are pushed to the limit. Also, standard scale economies become less effective. Learning-by-doing in any particular activity occurs at a declining rate and eventually reaches zero. Employees too can become over-specialised, leading to loss of adaptability and initiative.

In the long run, these problems can be addressed by expanding the size of the plant, buying more machines and adding to staff. Management systems can be developed, and bottlenecks and constraints can be systematically addressed. The long-run overall average cost of the firm may continue to slope downwards for a considerable range of output. Successful firms tend to see a continuous downward trend in unit costs. Yet the constraints on minimum efficient size eventually become binding, at different scale-levels in different industries. (In other instances, unit costs continue to decline until a monopoly position is reached, at which juncture competition legislation rather than scale constrains the size of the firm.)

After a certain output level, diseconomies of scale swing into action. These involve *increases* in unit costs as output rises. *Diseconomies of scale* take a number of forms.

1. *Informational requirements* grow as the firm becomes larger. Instead of the informal communication system of a small firm, larger firms have to employ special systems to disseminate information.

2. *Management control* becomes more difficult as firms get bigger, leading to higher unit costs.

3. *Industrial relations problems* can become more acute, and disproportionate effort has to be devoted to motivating staff and cultivating corporate *esprit de corps*.

4. As firms become larger they suffer a *loss of flexibility*. Customised demand becomes harder to cater for.

5. *Transport costs set limits to size in some industries*. For this reason, corrugated cardboard manufacturing and construction materials, such as cement and

---

15 It is tempting to add the economies of bulk order purchasing as another source of scale economies. These are called pecuniary economies of scale. To be sure, bulk ordering provides the keenest input prices to the larger firms, and businesses identify this as a major advantage of larger size. But lower price through bulk orders reflects, rather than constitutes, an economy of scale. Alternatively, it could represent exploitation of market power (monopsony) which has nothing to do with scale economies, although both are cost-reducing for the firm.

gravel, usually have to be installed more closely to the consumer than many other industries. This sets a limit on plant size.

The scope for exploiting scale economies and for avoiding diseconomies of scale is in a constant state of flux. 'New wave' manufacturing strategies, variously labelled as world-class manufacturing, lean production, flexible specialisation, post-Fordism and Total Quality Management, can restore economies based on new forms of work organisation. To raise productivity, teams or groups can be formed around the production of common parts or the search for customers.[16] Lean production, for example, much used in Germany, Japan and the US, is based on teams of multi-skilled workers and flexible automated machines. It is 'lean' in that it uses fewer inventories, less space and more teamwork, with an objective of zero defects and minimum inventory. It strives to combine the advantages of mass production and craft production.

In some industries the optimum scale of operation (from a cost per unit perspective) is increasing, but in others the advent of new technology has given a renewed lease of life to smaller firms. Computerised reservation systems provide special advantages to larger airline carriers, but information technology has improved the ease and cost of access of smaller firms to data which previously only a large firm could have afforded to acquire. Major drug companies find that they can control the rising cost of innovation by contracting out research to smaller specialised medical research companies. Chiroscience and Celsis, two of Britain's most successful medical research companies in the 1990s, founded by biotechnology entrepreneur Chris Evans, were started in this way. Quality control, likewise, in the sense of quality assurance and strategic quality management, has become less expensive at smaller scale of output as a result of computer-aided design and the microcomputer. Flexible batch production has reduced the plant size at which the minimum cost point, or the minimum efficient scale of operations (MES), is attained. Changes in telecommunications technology, such as the development of mobile phones and satellite communications, have exposed many state-owned monopolies in Europe to competition from smaller competitors. The telecoms industry no longer requires enormous sunk costs in the form of cables linking every receiving household.

The shape of the cost curves – short run and long run

Thus, both managerial and technical factors explain why the average cost curve may, after a certain level of output, level, flatten out and then slope upwards. Firms, of course, try to circumvent these constraints. Much organisational innovation and experimentation, ranging from franchising to cooperatives and multidivisional planning, is targeted at overcoming potential diseconomies of scale. The net effect of these measures on the evolution of optimum firm size defies simple generalisation. As we shall see in a later chapter, there is no universal

---

16 J. Storey (ed.), *New Wave Manufacturing Strategies: Organisational and human resource management dimensions* (London: Paul Chapman, 1994).

trend towards larger firm size. There indeed seems to be a large range of output where the average cost curve is flat and the optimum firm size remains indeterminate. Many different sizes of firms can be equally efficient. This is consistent with the observation that both small and large firms are able to coexist profitably in many industries.

5.4 The transaction costs approach

A second implication is that the long-run average cost curve is likely to be much flatter than the short-run cost curve. In the long run, firms can adjust their plant size and try to deal with congestion problems. Hence the rise in costs will be less pronounced. Fewer costs will be fixed in the long run.

A curious feature of a market economy is that the price system is used to allocate resources everywhere – *except within the firm itself*. Within the firm, the allocation of resources, the assignment of functions and the distribution of rewards are determined by management. Professor Ronald Coase elaborated on this point in a well-known passage:

> Outside the firm, price movements direct production, which is co-ordinated through series of exchange transactions on the market. Within a firm, these transactions are eliminated and in place of the complicated market structure with exchange transactions is substituted the entrepreneur co-ordinator, who directs production. It is clear that these are alternative methods of co-ordinating production. ('The nature of the firm', *Economica*, November 1937)

Why is coordination the work of the price system in one case and of management in another? Coase's response was that firms exist because they economise on *transaction costs*. For example, an employee in a firm agrees to work for a certain remuneration and, in return, undertakes to carry out whatever reasonable tasks are assigned by management. This saves two types of cost, which would have been incurred had each of these tasks been negotiated through an item-by-item market contract: (a) special contracts do not have to be made with each factor with which labour works (owner of machinery, landowner, supplier of inputs); and (b) the cost of specifying future duties is avoided (the services to be provided by the employee are expressed in general terms). Thus, by hiring an employee on an annual or permanent basis, the firm economises on transaction costs.

Two types of transaction costs are of particular relevance to the firm:

1. *Motivation costs*, which arise because of asymmetric information. For example, by hiring on a long-term basis, with a promotional 'ladder', the employer hopes to give the employee a stake in the business which will cut down on monitoring costs and minimise costly arrangements for protecting the firm against *opportunistic* behaviour, or *shirking*, on the part of employees.

2. *Imperfect commitment*: two parties may wish to bind themselves to honour promises they would like to make but which, having made, they may later have an incentive to renounce (e.g. a housebuilder's guarantee). The market

system may not be able to provide them with such an arrangement. A firm can get around this difficulty, however, by building up a reputation for reliability through repeated execution of contracts and fair dealing with customers and staff.[17]

The diverse nature of transaction costs enables us to explain the reasons why firms exist, why the optimal size of the firm is bigger in some industries than in others, and why firms choose different modes of organisation. Certain types of activity will be conducive to the formation of cooperatives; others to cottage industry; some to public ownership; others to private ownership. The transactions approach can be used to explain why some people are hired on one-off contracts, while others are offered long-term contracts. Tasks can be subcontracted through the market system and agents motivated by *franchises* and *licences* rather than by outright hiring as employees. Another implication of the theory is that, as technology and markets change, the organisational mode can also be expected to change.

Transaction costs explain why different *size* of firms will be a feature of a market system, complementing the analysis of economies and diseconomies of scale. Consider, for example, the analysis of the takeover of a supplier's business in preference to procurement of these supplies through the market system. The advantages, from a transaction cost perspective, of such forms of vertical integration arise for three reasons:

- better coordination and better protection of specific investments can be achieved, especially where specialised know-how is involved.
- the supplier may not be able to assess the value of its market power and hence it can be taken over at a cost less than its value to the buyer.
- scale and transaction economies can be obtained. These will enable the firm to consolidate its market power. (This topic is treated in Chapter 7.)

After a certain stage, the larger firm begins to encounter diseconomies of size. Not just because of the type of managerial diseconomies described earlier in this chapter, but also because of problems such as the loss of the benefits of competition among suppliers, distraction from the 'core competencies' of the firm and the problem of 'double marginalisation' (Case Study 5.1).[18] All these, taken together with the growing demand for customised goods and services from a more affluent society, diminish the appeal of vertical integration and add to the attraction of contracting out. The *core competence* argument, useful as a source of scale economies up to a point, can be converted into an argument for downsizing after that point is passed. Many corporations in the late 1980s and early 1990s explained their reduction in scale on this basis.[19] Asea Brown Boveri's decision to

---

17 P. Milgrom and R. Roberts, *Economics, Organisation and Management* (Hemel Hempstead: Prentice Hall, 1992).

18 The double-marginalisation case is analysed in Case Study 5.1.

19 G. Hamel and C.K. Prahalad, 'Core competences of the corporation', *Harvard Business Review* (1990); and *Competing for the Future* (New Haven, CT: Harvard Business School Press, 1994).

subdivide into 1300 separate companies and 5000 autonomous profit centres can be seen as a way of addressing this problem.[20]

5.5 Empirical evidence on cost functions

Economies of scale are easier to describe than to measure. Estimates of scale economies tend to be imprecise and heavily qualified. Yet measurement is important if we want to find out more about trends in firm size, about the number of firms likely to survive in specific industries and about the economic benefits of a larger market.

Three main estimation techniques have been used. First, cost functions, using historical cost and output data, analogous to the demand functions described in Chapter 4, can be estimated by *econometric techniques*. Second, these results can be extended by means of *engineering estimates*, based on information obtained from managers, engineers, economists and accountants with experience of running or constructing plants of different size. Relationships between unit costs and various dimensions of scale can then be established. Third, industrial census data can be used to identify the type of enterprise that is gaining an increasing share of industrial output – the *survivor technique*. It tries to identify the most efficient size of firm *ex-post* on the grounds that the most efficient-sized firm will survive the longest. This method is constrained by the inadequacies of output volume data and by the difficulty of separating technological improvements from scale economies. However, it avoids the bias created by the tendency of engineering estimates to overlook the organisational costs of larger scale.

Empirical studies enable the researcher to determine (a) the minimum efficient scale (MES); and (b) the slope of the average cost curve at output levels below the MES. Thus, the minimum point of the average cost curve can be estimated as well as the additional unit costs incurred when operating at a given percentage above or below that point. Estimates of scale economies based on the engineering approach are presented in Table 5.1. Industries are ranked according to the degree they are affected by scale economies. The MES for each industry can be compared with the overall size of any particular market (e.g. the UK and the EU). Within industry groups, there are large variations in the incidence of economies of scale. For example, in the case of cars, the optimal scale is estimated as 2 million cars per year, while for tractors, the MES is attained at an output of only 90,000 tractors per year. Scale economies are particularly important for the petrochemicals aircraft, and synthetic rubber industries. Clothing, textiles, timber and wood do not feature in the table because scale economies are only weakly identified. Minimum unit cost in producing footwear is estimated to be reached at a production of only 4000 pairs a week. Spreading first-copy and set-up costs are very important in the book trade – at 50 per cent of MES, the unit cost of a hardback book rises 36 per cent and a paperback 20 per cent above the minimum unit cost.[21]

---

20 'Does size matter?', *The Economist* (11 June 1994).

21 These estimates are taken from C.F. Pratten, 'A survey of economies of scale', in *Research on the 'Cost of Non-Europe'*, Vol. 2, Studies on the Economics of Integration (Brussels: Commission of the European Communities, 1988).

Table 5.1 Unit cost increase at half the minimum efficient scale (MES) for selected products

Product	Unit Cost Increase at half MES	MES as a % of production UK	EU
Cars	6–9	200	20
Rolled aluminium	8	114	15
Trucks	7.5	104	21
Computers	5	>100	n.a.
Aircraft	20	>100	n.a.
Tractors	6	98	19
Refrigerators	4	85	11
Steel	6	72	10
Electric motors	15	60	6
Washing machines	4.5	57	10
Large turbine generators	5	50	10
TV sets	9	40	9
Synthetic rubber	15	24	3.5
Petrochemicals	12	23	3
Ball bearings	8–6	20	2

Source: 'The economies of 1992', European Economy (Brussels, March 1988). Based on C.F. Pratten's estimates.

The quantification of scale economies was an important element in the evaluation of the effects of the EU's single market programme which was formally completed in 1993. The removal of trade barriers increased the size of the market to which European firms had secure access. If they were able to sell more as a consequence of this better access, and if unexploited scale economies still remained, unit costs would decline and their competitiveness *vis-à-vis* third countries would increase. Clearly, a substantial increase in market size was involved. According to C.F. Pratten, cost reductions at firm level of 9 per cent on average were achievable by moving from one-half MES to the MES itself. He found that in most industries the European market could support 20 or more MES plants, whereas individual countries such as Germany, France and the UK could, on their own, support only four plants. This turned out to be a major constituent of the total estimated benefit of the programme (see Chapter 17). The figures indicated that the single market was likely to be a significant source of unit cost savings for computers, cars, turbo generators and videos (mainly because the MES is large in these industries relative to the overall size of the European market). By contrast, no advantage was predicted for industries such as bricks, crisps and footwear.

Economies of scale are important in most economic activities. According to OECD estimates, economies of scale are the primary factor affecting competitiveness in about 30 per cent of manufacturing output in the major industrial countries. Scale economies are also important in the services sector, particularly banking, insurance, telecoms and the media.[22] Where the MES is large relative to the national market, monopoly elements will enter the market and this makes the measurement and analysis of scale economies highly relevant to competition authorities. Analysis of scale economies can also act as a warning to business of the need for restructuring if the size of domestic firms is significantly smaller than the MES of the industry in competitor countries.

5.6 From cost structure to supply curve

Marginal cost and supply

Suppose one accepts the general proposition that costs per unit initially decline and after a certain point start to rise. Two implications follow. First, an optimal firm size becomes possible to determine analytically. It is located at the level of output where MC = MR and AC = price. Second, a link can be directly established between the firm's supply and the industry supply.

The link between the individual firm's supply curve and the industry supply curve can be illustrated by imagining the reaction of the firm to changes in price. Returning to Figure 5.5, at a price of £12, six units are produced. A higher price of £14 leads to seven units; at £16, eight units are produced, and so on. Thus, the MC curve can be interpreted as the supply curve of the firm.

To derive the market supply curve, the supply curves of the individual firms are laterally summated (see Figure 5.6). This is depicted in just the same way as individual demand curves were laterally summated in order to derive the market demand curve. The resultant upward-sloping market supply curve reflects two main influences. First, a rise in price elicits more supply from each firm in the industry in accordance with the profit-maximisation rule. Second, a rise in price,

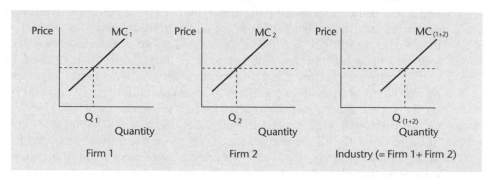

Figure 5.6 Deriving the market supply curve from individual firm supply curves

---

22 This assessment may be qualified somewhat by John Kay's observation: 'I have yet to encounter a firm or an industry where managers did not initially overestimate the importance of scale economies' (p. 172). One explanation for this may be that firms often find they are profitable when overtrading and incorrectly ascribe this to economies of scale. John A. Kay, *Foundations of Corporate Success: How business strategies add value* (London: Oxford University Press, 1993).

by raising the profitability of the industry, *attracts new entrants*. These two effects – more output from firms in the industry and still more from new entrants – are incorporated in the industry supply curve. They illustrate how a shift in market demand can, through the price mechanism, attract more supply from the industry.

As the industry gets larger, various influences begin to impinge on the firm's MC curve. First, the price of inputs into the industry might be bid up. If this happens, the supply curve will shift upwards. Second, scale economies will also have to be taken into account. They could involve downward shifts in the supply curve over time.

External economies of scale

As an industry grows, an additional class of scale economies often emerges, namely, *external economies and diseconomies of scale*. Although internal to the industry, they are external to the individual firm. External or *agglomeration economies* are relevant to understanding the pattern of location of industries, the tendency of some industries to form clusters, and the reinforcing of competitive advantage through clusters of activities related to a specific industry.

Expansion of a particular sector in a location means that skilled personnel are attracted to that location and a specialised R&D capacity may develop. Subcontractors find it worthwhile to locate nearby. The development of a centre of excellence reduces costs for all firms in the industry, but the cost reductions happen only because of the expansion of the industry as a whole in the region. Growth feeds on growth, in a virtuous circle of cumulative and circular causation. Instances of the practical significance of external economies of scale are easy to list:

- The cases of the flower industry in the Netherlands, ceramic tiles in Italy, the Swiss watch industry and the German printing press industry are much cited examples of industries that have drawn competitive strength from external scale economies. Their experience has been documented in Michael Porter's classic study, *The Competitive Advantage of Nations*.[23]
- The regions of north-central Italy (the Third Italy) are another much studied instance of external economies in action.[24] For example, the growth of the Emilia-Romagna region, based on small, heavily localised firms with a high proportion of owner-managers, owes much to regional support mechanisms which generate substantial external economies of scale. Trade associations provide marketing,

---

23 M. Porter, *The Competitive Advantage of Nations* (London: Macmillan, 1990).
24 M.H. Best, *The New Competition: Institutions of industrial restructuring* (Oxford: Polity Press, 1990). The benefits of extended market size can be illustrated also from the example of Koni, a major producer of shock absorbers. Koni can concentrate on R&D on shock absorbers today, better than Ford could in the early days of automobile production when the market was so small that Ford had to produce every component for itself (the engine, gearbox, steering wheel, shock absorbers and so on). Only with an increased size of market does it become profitable for a separate firm like Koni to specialise in shock absorbers, producing them more efficiently than Ford ever could – this advantage further enhanced by concentrating on R&D for this component alone. Division of labour at work once again! (I am indebted to Professor Jacob Kol of Eramus University for this example.)

technical information and training facilities. Financial cooperatives are a vehicle for guaranteeing loans to individual artisans. External economies of scale enable small firms to compete and to attain very high levels of productivity.

■ The concentrated location of the entertainment industry in Hollywood, high tech in Silicon Valley and international banking centres in London, Luxembourg and Dublin is heavily influenced by external economies of scale.

■ Similar effects have been observed in the Languedoc-Roussillon region of France and in the Jutland region of Denmark, where inter-firm cooperation has been found to play a vital role in overcoming the disadvantages of small firm size.

External scale economies can be incorporated into the supply curve by imagining outward shifts in the curve occurring as output expands. The key feature of external scale economies is that they impact favourably on *all* firms in the industry and, therefore, do no violence to the assumption of a competitive market. They can be treated more or less the same as technology improvements. Such improvements lead to a downward shift in the cost curves of all firms in the industry.

5.7   Conclusions

The chain of causation, from market demand to the supply decision of an individual firm, is simple in outline. But to establish the link, assumptions have to be made concerning the motivation of the firm as expressed by the actions of its executives, the nature of the firm's cost structure and the degree of market power. Each assumption is open to modification. Nevertheless, the actual behaviour of many firms in a modern economy conforms quite closely to the theoretical model outlined in this chapter. Shifts in demand elicit changes in supply more or less automatically, sooner or later, motivated primarily by the dictates of profit maximisation.

In a competitive market, management's objectives and the firm's cost structure determine the size of the firm. Economies and diseconomies of scale, both at firm level and at industry level, are key determinants of this cost structure. Indirectly, they help to explain why some industries are more concentrated (i.e. have fewer firms, accounting for a larger share of industry production) than others. But new ways of exploiting these economies, and of overcoming diseconomies, are constantly being discovered. Also, the scope for exploiting them differs markedly between industries, with aircraft production at one end of the spectrum and *haute couture* fashion clothing at the other. As the possibility of applying scale economies increases, even comparatively large countries, such as the UK or Germany, do not offer sufficient size to permit complete exploitation of scale for some industries. National markets are too small to support enough MES firms to ensure a healthy degree of competition. Hence the drive for the European single market. In order to help their domestic industries to achieve optimal scale and minimum costs, governments are being driven to negotiate better access to export markets. In return, they are obliged to reduce their own trade barriers against foreign goods and services. The pursuit of unit cost reductions through greater scale is a major explanatory factor underlying the growth of the multinational firm and the globalisation of business.

Yet the trend towards bigness is not uniform across countries. Technology and customised demand are moderating influences. They enable small firms to engage in activities where bigger is not better. Small and large firms can coexist within the same industry, each category operating profitably. External economies of scale can also help small firms to overcome the disadvantage of small size.

The cost structure of firms and industries, and consequently the shape of the industry supply curve, has a strong time dimension. Throughout this chapter, the distinction is repeatedly drawn between *short-run* and *long-run* cost profiles. The short run is characterised by the dominance of fixed costs. The firm's location, its plant and machinery, its managerial staff and structure are relatively fixed and cannot be altered in response to surges or restrictions in demand. In the short run, once capacity levels are reached, the supply curve is upward sloping, as more expensive labour time, less efficient workers and/or less efficient firms have to be brought in to increase output. Over time, however, a firm can exercise discretion over these fixed price costs. The plant can be closed and production transferred to another location. New machinery can be ordered to replace the old and the structure of the workforce can be altered. Formerly fixed costs can become variable. As we have seen, the long run is defined as a period when all costs, except 'sunk' costs, have become variable. The long-run cost function shows the minimum cost at each output level, when the desired plant size, technology and human resources structure can be freely chosen. Generally, this function will be flatter than the short-run cost function. It could even be downward sloping. Costs will rise less steeply as output increases beyond the minimum-cost point because, over time, it will be possible to build a larger plant and also external economies may develop, both of which will tend to reduce unit costs.

This chapter has focused on the competitive market model. Most managers, however, operate in markets in which they possess some degree of market power. Faced with aggressive competition, firms try to evade it by repositioning themselves in the market. The essence of this repositioning is a search for monopoly power. We shall discuss what happens in these less competitive markets in the next chapter.

✔ Summary

1. Just as consumers are assumed to maximise utility, so firms are assumed in economic analysis to maximise profits. The profit-maximisation assumption is justified on the basis that firms which neglect profitability either become vulnerable to takeover or run the danger of becoming bankrupt. Executives can be induced to maximise profits on behalf of owners by specially designed managerial incentive schemes. In this way, the principal–agent problem is largely circumvented.

2. If a firm is a profit maximiser, it must act according to certain key rules. First, it will sell output up to the point where the marginal revenue obtained on the last unit sold exactly equals the marginal cost of producing it. Second, the firm minimises the cost of producing any given level of output. It will combine intermediate and factor inputs in such a way that the extra profit brought into the firm by the last unit of each input equals its cost to the firm. Third, the firm must reject all technically inefficient production techniques.

3. A firm's cost structure is conventionally depicted as being U-shaped, or L-shaped, with declining unit costs being succeeded by a tendency for unit costs to rise or, at least, to flatten out. The main reasons for declining unit costs are economies of scale and scope. Standard economies of scale are those arising from indivisibilities, greater exploitation and cultivation of specialised skills, learning-by-doing and economics of increased dimension. Economies of scope apply to networks which allow different products to be supplied more cheaply through a common network than through a separate network for each service.

4. Diseconomies of scale set limits to the expansion of large firms. They are evident in the loss of operational flexibility and the mounting informational requirements as firms grow in size.

5. The long-run average cost curve is likely to be flatter than the short-run curve because, in the long run, non-sunk fixed costs can be transformed into variable costs. Fixed assets, plant and labour can be sold off and redeployed in line with a firm's changing needs.

6. The optimal size and organisation structure of the firm can be analysed by the transactions costs approach. This approach enables us to weigh up the merits of buying in a good from outside the firm versus making it itself, and proceeds to study the strength and weakness of different modes of organisation: long-term contracts, joint ventures and franchising, for example. This approach asserts that the firm is not merely a profit-maximising entity responding to a fixed set of opportunities and constraints. It is also a set of governance structures in which diverse motives operate. Transactions analysis complements the classical analysis in a significant way.

7. Scale and scope economies are an important feature of economic life, and they play a crucial part in determining industrial structure and the size distribution of firms in different economic sectors. Empirical measures of economies of scale have been used to estimate the effects of the opening of internal markets to competition such as the EU's single market programme.

8. External economies of scale can explain why small firms may coexist with, and even thrive against the competition of, very large firms. Examples include the Marche regions of northern Italy, Jutland in Denmark, Languedoc-Roussillon in France and Silicon Valley, California.

? Questions for discussion

1. Economics assumes that firms try to maximise profits. Review the arguments used to justify this assumption. Do you find them convincing?

2. It is often argued that the MR = MC rule is of no practical use because firms do not know the values of the marginal cost and marginal revenue of their output. Is this a criticism of the economic theory of the firm, or of the firm's accounting system?

3. In industries such as the automobile industry, economies of scale have increased enormously as a result of vertical integration and automation. New entry to the industry has virtually stopped. Yet Jaguar (which was taken over by Ford in 1989) announced a major investment programme in 1995 for two new luxury models with annual volume of a modest 70,000 cars per year. If a model can be viable with such a small production run, why do large firms dominate the market?

4. In banking and insurance, economies of scale, obtained by the takeover and control of distribution networks, deter new entrants. Banks and insurance companies have been amalgamated into giant bancassurance companies. What types of economies of scale are likely to be most relevant to this sector? What types of diseconomies of scale would you expect?

5. 'Rarely is a firm efficient because it is big. Rather, it becomes big because it is efficient.' Do you agree?

☞ Exercises

1. 'The mere threat of a takeover acts as a powerful force motivating top corporate managers to pursue value-maximising business strategies.' Explain why this should be so. What takeover defences can management devise to reduce the threat of takeover?

2. 'In the economists' perfectly competitive industry, jockeying for position is unbridled and entry to the industry very easy. But this kind of industry structure offers the worst prospect for long-run profitability' (Michael Porter). Identify some industries which are close to being perfectly competitive. Why do new firms enter them if the long-run profits outlook is so poor?

3. Show with the aid of diagrams how firms in a competitive industry will respond to a decrease in market demand.

4. Suppose that a firm, with a total cost structure as shown in the table below, can sell as much output as it wants at a price of £10.

   (a) Derive its MC curve.
   (b) At what level of output will the firm reach the point of maximum profits?
   (c) Compute the average costs per unit at each output level. Is the firm making a profit or a loss at the 'profit-maximising' level of output?

(d) Suppose price were to rise to £14, what difference would this make to output and profit?

Output	0	1	2	3	4	5	6	7	8	9	10
Total cost (£)	10	25	36	44	51	59	69	81	95	111	129

5. The table below shows a firm's total costs over a range of output and the price corresponding to each quantity sold. Find out its profit-maximising level of sales and the corresponding price. (Compute the firm's total revenue, marginal revenue and marginal cost schedules.)

(1) Output (goods produced per week)	(2) Total costs (£ per week)	(3) Price (received per unit)
0	10	–
1	25	21
2	36	20
3	44	19
4	51	18
5	59	17
6	69	16
7	81	15
8	95	14
9	111	13
10	129	12

6. (a) Calculate the marginal and average costs for each level of output from the following data.
    (b) Explain how marginal and average costs are related.
    (c) Costs of £12 are incurred in the initial position, even though no output is being produced. How can this be explained?

Output	0	1	2	3	4	5	6	7	8	9
Total cost (£)	12	40	53	64	73	83	93	104	120	145

7. Suppose a firm discovers that the marginal product of a unit of machinery is twice the marginal product of a unit of labour. You are told that the cost of labour is £6 per unit and the cost of machinery is £3 per unit. Is the firm minimising costs in accordance with the rules for profit maximisation? If not, how can it reduce them?

8. Suppose two firms produce the same product and have exactly the same marginal cost curve but their average fixed cost is different. Will they produce the same level of output?

9. Assume that a manufacturer of food-mixers has the following costs and price:

Food-mixer price	£70
Variable cost per unit	£40
Unit contribution	£30
Total fixed costs	£60,000

    Assuming both price and unit variable costs are constant, how many food-mixers would the manufacturer have to sell in order to break even? (See Figure 5.4.) Suppose it was judged impossible to attain a sufficient sales volume to break even, what should the firm do?

10. (a) Sketch the average fixed cost curve, the average total cost curve and the average variable cost associated with Figure 5.3.
    (b) Is this cost structure consistent with the widely observed association of higher profits with higher levels of economic activity?
    (c) What are the limitations of the breakeven chart approach in comparison with the U-shaped analysis?
    (d) Is the U-shaped analysis also consistent with the cyclical behaviour of company profits?

11. Examine Figure 5.1 carefully to show that maximising total profits is not the same as maximising average profit per unit. Explain why this is the case.

📖 Further reading

A good place to start is Adam Smith's *Wealth of Nations* (1776), notably the still interesting and percipient introductory chapters on the division of labour and the size of the market. Topics such as economies of scale and market power are addressed comprehensively in texts on the economies of industrial organisation. R. Clarke, *Industrial Organisation* (Oxford: Basil Blackwell, 1985), is a good general treatment. On transaction costs, a classical source is O.E. Williamson, *Markets and Hierarchies: Analysis and anti-trust implications* (New York: Free Press, 1975). For an up-to-date assessment, see the conflicting exchanges between S. Ghoshal, Peter Moran and Oliver Williamson in the *Academy of Management Review*, 21(1), 1996. An excellent review of business and organisation is provided in P. Milgrom and J. Roberts, *Economics, Organisation and Management* (Upper Saddle River: Prentice Hall International, 1992), especially chapter 16.

Case study 5.1

Applying the MR = MC rule within a vertically integrated firm

This case study illustrates the complexities behind the simple MR = MC rule in the context of a vertically integrated business. It is not an easy read, and provides food for thought rather than any single conclusion.

The MR = MC rule has been explained in the context of 'arm's length' market transactions between the firm and the customer. What happens, however, if the customer happens to be not a series of independent individuals outside the firm but an associated company? Such intra-firm transactions are a common feature of the market system. Many large firms are vertically integrated. When one firm in the group – say, the upstream division – supplies an input to another firm in the same group – the downstream division – what principles of pricing should apply? The short answer is that MR = MC remains the guiding principle. However, its application can involve some difficult calculations. We illustrate by reference to what is called the *double-marginalisation problem*.

We start with a vertically integrated firm. The upstream division states the price at which it will supply an input to the downstream division, and then the downstream division decides how much to buy. Suppose the downstream division markets the final product directly to the consumers outside the firm at a constant cost c per unit. It faces a demand curve that is downward-sloping. Production of a unit of a final product requires one unit of the intermediate good, which can be produced at a cost of d per unit. Thus, the total cost of the final good to the firm as a whole is $(c + d)$ and the firm would want the quantity sold of the final good, and thus the amount transferred of the intermediate good, to be determined by the condition that the marginal revenue on final sales be equal to $(c + d)$.

For example, if the final demand curve is given by the equation $P = 10 - Q/16$, where Q is the amount sold at the price P, then total revenue is $PQ = 10Q - Q^2/16$. Total revenue is maximised when MR = $10 - Q/8$. (This can be quickly obtained by differentiating the total revenue function.) If the value of c is 2 and that of d is 1, then the marginal cost to the firm as a whole is 3. Equating MR to marginal cost gives $10 - Q/8 = 3$, or $Q = 56$, which means the final price should be $P = 6.50$. These calculations are shown in the first column of the table below.

To achieve this in a divisionalised firm under the given procedure, the transfer price should be $T = 1$, or more generally, $T = d$. Facing this price, the manager of the downstream division will see a marginal cost to the division of $2 + T = 2 + 1 = 3$, the actual cost to the firm. The manager will then select $Q = 56$ (where MR = $2 + T$) and order this many units of the intermediate good from the upstream division. If any other value of T is selected, the downstream manager will buy and produce an amount that does not maximise corporate profits. If T is set at 4, for example, then the manager downstream will face a marginal cost of $2 + 4 = 6$ and will select $Q = 32$, where MR equals the marginal cost he or she faces. This would

Case study 5.1 continued

lead to less profit for the firm. Entering different values for T in the second column of the table gives the quantities that result.

An example of double marginalisation in transfer pricing:

	Integrated firm	Downstream Division	Upstream Division
Demand	$P = 10 - Q/16$	$P = 10 - Q/16$	$T = 8 - Q/8$
Total revenue	$10Q - Q^2/16$	$10Q - Q^2/16$	$8Q - Q^2/8$
Marginal revenue	$10 - Q/8$	$10 - Q/8$	$8 - Q/4$
Total variable costs	$3Q$	$(2 + T)Q$	Q
Marginal revenue	3	$2 + T$	1
Quantity	56	$8(8 - T)$	28
Price	6.50	8.25	$T = 4.50$

At a transfer price equal to its constant marginal cost, however, the revenues of the upstream division are just equal to its total variable costs. Its manager, being evaluated on the division's profit, would do better with a higher transfer price, even though this hurts corporate profitability. For example, if the transfer price is set at 4, the downstream division will demand 32 units and the upstream division will show a net profit of $(4 - 1).32 = 96$.

More generally, the relationship $MR = c + T$ defines how much the downstream manager will want to sell on the final market and thus how much the upstream manager can sell internally at any transfer price T. Equating the marginal cost of $c + T$ to the marginal revenue of $10 - Q/8$ leads to $Q - 8(8 - T)$. This formula indicates the amount the downstream division will want to sell as a function of the price charged for the input and thus the amount of input it will buy. This is effectively a demand curve for the upstream division and is entered accordingly in the first row of the third column. For the upstream division to maximise profits, its manager will equate the marginal revenue facing the upstream division to its marginal cost, c. The fact that the upstream division considers the marginal revenue of the firm as its (inverse) demand curve and looks to the curve that is marginal to it in computing the transfer price is the source for the term *double marginalisation*.

The inverse demand corresponding to a demand of $Q = 8(8 - T)$ is $T = 8 - Q/8$. This gives a marginal revenue of $8 - Q/4$. With a marginal cost of $c = 1$, this yields $Q = 28$, $T = 4.50$ as the optimal choice for the upstream division (see third column of the table). This gives the upstream division profits of $28(4.50 - 1) = 98$. With only 28 units rather than 56 being transferred, however, final goods output is half what it takes to maximise corporate profits. Corporate profits, which would have been $56(6.50 - 3) = 196$, are now only $28(8.25 - 3) = 147$, where 8.25 is the price the downstream division charges in the final market when it faces a transfer price of 4.50 and correspondingly chooses to sell 28 units.

▶

Case study 5.1 continued

There is no easy answer to this double-marginalisation problem. Clearly, the profit-maximising rule is still valid. But managerial incentives have to be carefully tailored. One cannot assume that instructing each divisional manager to maximise profits and to price intra-firm transactions accordingly will yield the best solution for the group as a whole. A set of incentives will have to be devised, based on cost minimisation. One possibility is to enlarge the number of upstream subsidiaries in the company and make them compete among each other for the downstream divisions' orders. The firm could also decide to purchase from outside suppliers and use their price as a benchmark for the upstream division. 'Competition by comparison' is used widely as a method of stimulating competitive behaviour.

Source: Paul Milgrom and John Roberts, *Economics, Organisation and Management* (Prentice Hall Inc, Upper Saddle River, NJ, 1992), pp. 550–1.

Chapter 6

THE ECONOMICS OF MARKET POWER

Introduction

Competition is an enduring and pervasive fact of business life. Although the intensity of competitive pressure varies according to type of industry and stage of the business cycle, most managers recognise a broad similarity between their own experience and many aspects of the competitive model of the previous chapter. High profits attract new entrants; losses lead to exits. Prices cannot be realistically altered without regard to the 'market' rate, and so on.

Yet one important aspect of business reality is *market power*. Up to now, we have assumed that firms have negligible market power. Each firm is so small in relation to the total size of the market that it takes the going market price as 'given' and can safely ignore other firms' reactions to its sales or price decisions. There are too many (uncoordinated) producers to make any such interdependence worthwhile considering. This assumption is now relaxed. Firms are allowed to have monopoly, or market, power.

The way firms use, and maintain, market power is the subject of this chapter.

Chapter outline

1. Evidence on the proportion of economic activity that can be classified as monopolistic.

2. How firms behave in situations where they possess market power, the case of a *single-firm monopoly*, the most extreme instance of market power, and comparison between this situation and the case of competition.

3. How monopoly profits act as a magnet to new entrants. In trying to gain a share of these profits, the new entrants tend to erode them. In a dynamic market system, monopolies are always under threat. How firms protect a monopoly position – or 'market niche'.

4. The analysis of *oligopoly* markets, where a few firms have a significant share of the market.

6.1 Firm size

The facts

'Corporate giantism' is a feature of many parts of the economy. In the car, aircraft and oil industries, large scale is the norm rather than the exception. Wal-Mart Stores employ over one million people – a workforce more than half the size of the total working population of a small country such as Ireland. Among Europe's major employers, Daimler, Siemens and Unilever have become household names (Tables 6.1 and 6.2), as have the state-owned communications and transport companies. Numbers employed in each of the national railway companies of the UK, Germany and France exceeded 200,000 prior to the privatisation programmes.

At the opposite end of the spectrum are the small and medium-sized enterprises (SMEs), defined as enterprises employing 500 persons or less. In 1993, there were 17 million such enterprises in the European Union (EU). Although only a fraction

Table 6.1 The world's 10 largest corporations

1999	Employees (000s)	Revenue $USbn
1 Sinopec	1,172	41.8
2 State Power	1,149	36.0
3 Wal-Mart Stores	1,140	116.8
4 US Postal Services	906	62.7
5 Industrial and Commercial Bank of China	549	20.1
6 China Telecommunications	529	18.5
7 Agricultural Bank of China	500	14.1
8 DaimlerChrysler	467	159.9
9 Siemens	443	75.3
10 Hitachi	398	71.8

Source: Global Fortune 500, *Fortune* (July 2000)

Table 6.2 Top industrial employers in Europe, 1998

	No. of employees
1 Siemens	382,000
2 Daimler-Benz	295,514
3 Unilever	287,000
4 Philips Electronic	268,431
5 Volkswagen	256,132
6 Fiat	242,748
7 Nestle	225,808
8 Deutsche Telekom	222,259
9 Asea Brown Boveri (ABB)	213,057
10 Vivendi	193,320

Source: Company web pages

Table 6.3 Number of enterprises and employment by sector of industry, EU-12, 1990

	Number of enterprises (000s)	Micro 0–9	Small 10–99 (% share)	Medium 100–499	LSEs ≥500	Total employment (million)	Dominance
Extraction	150	7	17	15	61	4.3	large
Manufacturing	1,750	15	28	21	37	27.4	large/SME
Construction	1,890	44	34	11	10	8.8	micro/small
Wholesale trade	1,510	34	35	22	9	7.6	micro/small
Retail distribution	3,530	58	20	9	14	12.1	micro
Transport/communication	910	19	16	9	56	7.1	large
Producer services	1,830	28	20	15	37	11.3	large/micro
Personal services	4,210	49	23	13	15	15.8	micro
Total	**15,780**	**32**	**25**	**15**	**28**	**94.6**	

Source: European Network for SME Research (FNSR), *The European Observatory for SMEs Annual Report* (Zoetermeer, The Netherlands)

of the total number of enterprises, the 12,000 large-scale enterprises (LSEs), defined as enterprises with more than 500 employees, accounted for 28 per cent of the EU's workforce in services and industry of 100 million.[1] Enterprises employing up to nine persons ('micro'-firms) employ 32 million or one-third of the total. Micro-firms are heavily represented in retail distribution, construction and personal services (Table 6.3).

Data in Table 6.4 show that the proportion of the workforce in large enterprises (500+ employees) tends to vary considerably across European states. In Germany, 43 per cent of employees are working in such enterprises, whereas in the Mediterranean countries, Greece, Portugal and Spain, the corresponding figure is only 21 per cent. Italy remains something of an exceptional case. Reflecting its reputation as a home for a vibrant and successful small enterprise sector, no fewer than 80 per cent of employees work in enterprises employing less than 500 people.

The majority of US firms are small. Firms with fewer than 500 workers account for 50 per cent of private sector employment. The vast majority of US firms had sales below $10 million per year.[2]

Firm size, concentration ratios and market power

Some rough indication of the proportionate strength of competitive forces in the economy can be gleaned from examining the proportion of small relative to large firms in an economy. Suppose one starts with the assumption that sectors with large numbers of small enterprises are more likely to have the characteristics of a competitive market than sectors dominated by the larger enterprises. On this

---

1 European Network for SME Research, *The European Observatory for SME Third Annual Report* (Brussels, 1995).

2 William Shepherd, *The Economics of Industrial Organisation* (Hemel Hempstead: Prentice Hall International, 1990), p. 128.

Table 6.4 Employment share of large enterprises

	Employment share of enterprises by number of employees (% share)	
	0–499	500+
Belgium	73	27
Denmark	70	30
France	66	34
Germany	57	43
Greece	79	21
Ireland	49	51
Italy	80	20
Luxembourg	71	29
The Netherlands	60	40
Portugal	79	21
Spain	79	21
UK	59	41
EU	66	34

Source: European Network for SME Research (FNSR) *The European Observatory for SMEs Fifth Annual Report* (Zoetermeer, The Netherlands, October 1997)

basis, since 72 per cent of the EU workforce is employed in SMEs, we could infer that 72 per cent of total marketed activity approximates the conditions of the competitive market and the remaining 28 per cent could be classified as monopolistic. This is a crude indicator, however, since, as we have seen, on the one hand large firms are not incompatible with competition and on the other the prevalence of small firms does not guarantee competition.

Another approach is to focus on *concentration ratios*. Concentration ratios are a commonly used measure of the degree of market power at industry level. These ratios measure the percentage share of industry sales, or employment, accounted for by the largest companies. A C4 of 70 per cent, for example, indicates that the largest four firms account for 70 per cent of industry sales. A C10 of 85 per cent indicates that the ten leading companies account for 85 per cent of industry output. The concentration ratio is a widely used measure of the degree of market (or monopoly) power in an industry.[3] Typical illustrations of information expressed in this way: six firms (including Polygram, Sony, EMI, Warner, BMG and RCA) accounted for 80 per cent of world-wide music sales in the mid-1990s, while one firm (Unilever) accounts for 40 per cent of the global tea distribution market.

Inferences based on concentration ratios are subject to many caveats. For one thing, they *overestimate* the degree of market power in so far as they ignore the exposure of even the largest enterprises, and the most concentrated sectors, to

---

3 Many other ways of doing this have been proposed. The Hirschman–Herfindahl index, for example, measures the degree of monopoly power as the sum of squared values of market share of all firms. Use has been made of other 'comprehensive' indices, but none has proved demonstrably superior to the standard concentration ratios. The HHI index tends to be used in the US, while the concentration ratio is more used in the EU.

foreign competition. In a world of free trade and mobile foreign investment, the strongest European enterprises can no longer treat their domestic market as safe. Domestic sales meet with stiff competition from Japan and the United States at one end of the market and the newly industrialising countries at the other. Global competition has also affected the giants of the American market such as General Motors, General Electric and IBM. A significant proportion of these firms' product range is sold in highly competitive markets. IBM's strong market power in mainframes, for example, does not extend to other products in its range such as PCs and software. For this reason, high domestic market shares may be a misleading indicator of market power. This caveat is particularly necessary in the case of small open economies. Their small size means that concentration ratios are likely to be high; their openness means that they are bound to be far more exposed to competition than the concentration ratios will suggest. Thus a high concentration ratio in a sector is a necessary, but not a sufficient, condition for monopoly power (Box 6.1).

Some degree of *underestimation* of market power arises to the extent that small enterprises are under the direct or indirect control of a larger company. An enterprise is defined as the smallest unit which has a separate legal entity. As we have already seen in the case of *Asea Brown Boveri*, parent companies often deliberately subdivide their operations into semi-autonomous enterprises as a means of avoiding organisational diseconomies of scale. The bargaining power of large companies can be underestimated by mistakenly regarding its small subsidiaries as fully autonomous entities. Concentration is always greater if calculated by reference to firm size rather than enterprise size. Account must also be taken of the many formal and informal links between major suppliers and retail outlets in some sectors, which may give a misleading impression of the degree of competition. McDonalds' franchisees, petrol stations and 'tied' UK pubs are subject to much less competition than might appear.

Assessing the 'amount' of competition in an economy, therefore, cannot be decided on the basis of a simple formula. A broad overview based on firm size analysis and concentration ratios suggests that as much as 75 per cent of the European and the US markets could qualify as 'effectively' competitive.

Table 6.5 Market structure in the US economy, 1939–80

Share of Each Category in National Income	1939	1958	1980
		(percentage shares)	
Pure monopoly[a]	6.2	3.1	2.5
Dominant firm[b]	5.0	5.0	2.8
Tight oligopoly[c]	36.4	35.6	18.0
Effectively competitive[d]	52.4	56.3	76.7

Notes: (a) Pure monopoly: One firm has 100 per cent of the market.
    (b) Dominant firm: One firm has 50 –100 per cent of the market and no close rival.
    (c) Tight oligopoly: The leading four firms combined have 60 –100 per cent of the market.
    (d) Effectively competitive: Many competitors, all with negligible market share.

Source: William Shepherd, *Economics of Industrial Organisation* (London: Prentice Hall International, 1990)

Box 6.1

US government v Microsoft – competition among the few?

Small numbers of firms in the industry is a necessary but not a sufficient condition for market power. And possession of market power is not the same thing as abuse of market power. Both these issues came to the forefront during the competition case, *US government v. Microsoft*, initiated in 1998 by the US government which sued Microsoft, the world's largest software company, on grounds of abusing its market power. The main focus of the case was on Microsoft's response to the emergence of Netscape's Navigator browser. In response to the threat, Microsoft developed its own browser (Internet Explorer) and gave it away for free. In addition, the US Justice Department argued that Microsoft had forced PC makers to install Internet Explorer as a condition for obtaining a Windows operating licence (i.e. a case of 'bundling' Internet Explorer and Windows).

Microsoft's Windows operating system dominates the personal computer (PC) market. It is installed on 8 out of 10 PCs in use. Apple's Mac OSX is also a competitor and Linux is a recent arrival on the scene. Rivalry exists between makers of PCs themselves as well as among software firms producing products such as spreadsheets and operatng systems.

The case revealed interesting evidence on the forces leading to large size in high-tech industries. Some years ago, Professor Brian Arthur of Stanford identified three in particular:

- *Up-front costs* – the first disk of Windows to be sold cost Microsoft $50m. The second and subsequent disks cost $3.
- *Network effects* – the more users, the more likely the language or a standard emerges as *the* standard. Hence the more people who use the standard the more useful it becomes. Consumers of a product gain from it being used by *other* consumers
- *Customer groove-in* – high-tech products are difficult to use. Training costs are high initially but thereafter only updating is needed (e.g. learning to use Word or teaching pilots to fly Airbus planes)

These scale economies act as a barrier to entry for any newcomer and explain why first movers in the sector are hard to displace.

The barrier to entry that was judged to favour Microsoft was termed the *applications barrier*. It arises because operating systems provide value to the consumer through running applications. Since the development of software in applications involves high sunk costs in preparation but low marginal costs in production and distribution, applications developers have a strong incentive to write for the operating system with the most users; that way, the fixed costs will be recoverable from a larger number of users. This network externality effect enhanced the power of the largest firm, Microsoft, and was bad news for producers of competing operating systems. US anti-trust officials argued that the integration of Microsoft's Internet browser with its operating system was stifling competition in Internet software. Thus monopoly power in one segment of the market (operating systems) could be used to expand dominance in other areas such as Internet software. In short, Microsoft was able to use network externalities and lock in to exert market dominance and exclude competitors.

Box 6.1 continued

The case poses a certain dilemma. On the one hand, market power can be abused to keep out competitors with predictable consequences for price and quality in the long run. On the other hand, as Microsoft CEO Bill Gates argued, government regulation could curb innovation. There are three main possible responses to these arguments: (a) do nothing, on the grounds that one operating system may be the most efficient outcome, (b) regulate Microsoft's prices and practices, as is done in the case of utilities, or (c) split Microsoft into two separate companies in order to create competition. Industry economists have different views on this, but the do-nothing option seems to have been ruled out and regulation has few advocates.

Sources: Brian Arthur, 'Increasing returns and the new world of business', *Harvard Business Review*, July–August 1996; Findings of fact (5/11/99) *USA v. Microsoft* (www.usdoj.gov); R. Schmalensee, Direct testimony in *USA v. Microsoft* (www.microsoft.com)

'Effectively competitive' means more than four competitors, all with small (<50 per cent) market share. On this definition, relatively high effective competition is found in the wholesale and retail trades, finance, insurance and real estate services. This leaves the remaining 25 per cent of market activities being transacted in monopoly or oligopoly market structures. 'Tight oligopoly' sectors, defined as those sectors in which the leading four firms have 60–100 per cent of the market and between which collusion is therefore 'relatively easy', accounted for 18 per cent of total market activity in 1980, compared with 36 per cent in 1958. Examples of tight oligopolies in the US economy include breakfast cereals, soft drinks, cigarettes, copper and soaps. The extractive industries emerge, surprisingly, as more market-competitive in the US than in Europe.

'One capitalist always kills many'

The share of big firms in economic activity appears to have been declining rather than increasing over time. Total employment in the 500 largest US companies fell from more than 14 million in 1984 to 12 million in 1994, during which time employment in business services doubled to over 6 million.[4] Figures for the UK reveal a similar picture. While between 1935 and the 1970s the share of the 100 largest UK firms in total manufacturing output rose from 24 to 41 per cent, the concentration ratio declined significantly in the 1980s, especially if allowance is made for the increased exposure of the UK market to foreign trade.[5] This is reflected in the increase in the proportion of UK manufacturing employees at work in plants with fewer than 200 employees from 27 per cent to 39 per cent between 1976 and 1987. US Bureau of the Census figures show that the share of

4 'Outsourced and out of luck', *Business Week* (17 July 1995).
5 Roger Clarke, 'Trends in concentration in UK manufacturing 1980–89', in M. Casson and J. Creedy (eds), *Industrial Concentration and Economic Inequality* (Aldershot: Edward Elgar, 1993). S.J. Prais, *The Evolution of the Giant Firm in Great Britain* (Cambridge: Cambridge University Press, 1976).

> ### Box 6.2
>
> ## Six factors tending to intensify competition
>
> 1. Technology factors favourable to small firms
> 2. More demand for customised goods
> 3. Anti-trust actions and merger restrictions
> 4. Deregulation
> 5. Globalisation of trade and foreign investment
> 6. Shift to service industries

small firms (<500 workforce) in total manufacturing employment rose from 24 per cent in 1972 to 38 per cent in 1991.[6]

That concentration ratios, measured in terms of numbers employed, sales or capital assets, appear to be on a downward trend is an important finding. It contradicts the Marxian prediction that big business, driven by the interaction of economies of scale and the single-minded pursuit of profit, would eventually dominate the industrial economies. In this view, larger firms, with low unit costs, would have been expected to put smaller firms out of business. 'One capitalist always kills many' (Karl Marx, *Capital*, vol. 1, p. 36) – the prediction being that economic power would become steadily more concentrated. This has not happened, notwithstanding popular concern about the sheer size and power of the new global corporations.

Monopoly power and the relative growth of big business has been restrained by six factors (see Box 6.2). *First*, in the previous chapter we referred to the role of technology in facilitating small businesses. *Second*, this effect is strengthened by the growing demand for customised goods. *Third*, anti-trust and merger legislation has made monopoly power more difficult and costly to maintain (see Chapter 7). *Fourth*, deregulation has exposed many formerly closed sectors to competition. *Fifth*, the globalisation of trade and investment has impacted very strongly on the market power of domestic firms. *Sixth*, and finally, the shift in demand in industrial countries towards services may also be a significant factor. Concentration is considerably lower in services than in manufacturing. For instance, establishments with <100 employees account for 64 per cent of non-manufacturing employment, but only 28 per cent of manufacturing employment.

These trends are consistent with the empirical finding that bigger size does not always imply better profitability. The performance of industrial conglomerates in profit terms has been very mixed. Mergers have had modest long-run effects, suggesting that efficiency gains from mergers are small. Periods of merger frenzy tend to be succeeded by downsizing and a reversion to smaller scale and more

---

6 William J. Dennis Jr, Bruce D. Phillips and Edward Starr, 'Small business job creation: The findings and their critics', *Business Economics* (July 1994), p. 25.

Table 6.6 Growth of employment, output and productivity
in EU enterprises 1988–98

	% growth p.a.	
	SMEs	LSEs
Employment	−0.1	−0.3
Real turnover	2.1	2.4
Labour productivity	2.1	2.8

Source: *The European Observatory for SMEs, Sixth Annual Report* (Zoetermeer, The
Netherlands, July 2000)

focused activity. Successful conglomerates do exist (for example, in the media and
entertainment sector), but they are the exception rather than the rule. Perhaps
the only consistent beneficiary of all the takeover activity has been the deal-
maker. Size alone, even within a single industry, is neither a necessary nor a
sufficient condition for sustained competitive advantage.

Contrasting with the performance of large firms, SMEs have been a major
source of job creation and entrepreneurial innovation. The Birch Report found
that two-thirds of the increase in US employment between 1969 and 1976 was in
enterprises with less than 20 workers.[7] This finding has attracted intense scrutiny.
The US Small Business Administration, on the basis of more extensive data
covering the period 1976–88, concluded that small enterprises employing fewer
than 20 workers provided 37 per cent of new jobs over this period, while
accounting for just under 20 per cent of total US employment. These statistics are
less startling than Birch's, but confirm the important role played by small
business in new job generation. There is continuing controversy about the correct
measurement of the small business contribution.[8]

The European Observatory for SME Research reached similar conclusions to the
Birch Report. In the EU, micro and small enterprises have generally proved more
dynamic in creating job opportunities than larger firms. The superior
performance of SMEs has been attributed to active labour market measures and
tax concessions, in addition to the long-term forces referred to above.[9] Growth
rates of employment and output for SMEs exceeded those of larger firms through
the period 1988 to 1998 (Table 6.6).

The potential contribution of SMEs to easing the EU's unemployment problem
has been stressed throughout the past decade. SMEs are especially significant in
qualitative terms because they provide many young people with their first job.
The European Commission White Paper *Growth, Competitiveness Employment*
(1993) called for policies 'to underpin the dynamism of SMEs' (p. 64). This

---

7 D.L. Birch, *The Job Generation Process* (Cambridge, MA: MIT Program on Neighborhood and Regional
Change, 1979). See also D. Storey, *Understanding the Small Business Sector* (London: Routledge, 1994).

8 For a critical view of Birch's and subsequent authors' estimates, see Steven J. Davis, John
Haltiwanger and Scott Schuh, 'Small business and job creation: Dissecting the myth and reassessing
the facts', *Business Economics* (July 1994).

9 European Network for SME Research, *The European Observatory for SME Second Annual Report* (Brussels,
1994), p. 13.

dynamism derives from the flexibility of production methods and labour deployment in these enterprises. To assist their continued growth, the White Paper recommended: (1) support for cooperation between firms, (2) introduction of new financial facilities for SMEs, and (3) support for improvement in management quality.

This positive assessment of the dynamism of small business is subject to one major qualification: small firms generate new jobs at a faster rate than big firms, *but they also have a high mortality rate*. A detailed study of small firms in the German economy, for example, shows that only about 40 per cent of establishments in each cohort are still operating eight or nine years after start-up.[10] Again, this conclusion is quite general: there is an exceptional amount of 'churning' in the employment record of small firms.

The era of the mega-plant employing thousands of workers seems to have ended some time in the 1970s for many industries and countries. The typical large firm is no longer associated with giant manufacturing plants, but rather with a multitude of decentralised, moderate-sized and specialised plants managed from a small and equally specialised head office. And side-by-side with that large firm, a surprisingly large number of independent small firms compete and coexist.

6.2 The economics of market power

The theory of monopoly

All firms seek to obtain, consolidate and expand market power. Many firms have some degree of market power but, in the majority of cases, not sufficient to cause significant deviations from a competitive market outcome. A minority of firms occupy strong monopoly positions. Firms in this category account for a significant, if not strictly determinable, proportion of total marketed activity. To understand the market system in its entirety, therefore, we need to know how the system functions when individual firms possess significant market power. Specifically, we need to know (1) the consequences of this power for the firm's price and output decisions, (2) how market power is attained and sustained, (3) the systemic implications of market power, and (4) how policy-makers should respond to it. We discuss the first two issues in this chapter and the others in Chapter 7.

The consequences of market power can be explained with the analysis of the firm described in Chapter 5. For simplicity, we take the extreme case of a single-firm monopoly. We assume its costs are U-shaped (Figure 6.1). Demand conditions are represented by the demand curve DD, from which the marginal revenue curve MR can be derived. Applying the profit-maximisation rule MR = MC gives the equilibrium output of OQ_m. The market-clearing price for that output is OP_m. The average cost at that output level is SQ_m. Monopoly profits are then the average profit margin RS multiplied by output OQ_m. They are represented by the area of the rectangle P_mRSF.

10 T. Boeri and U. Cramer, 'Employment growth, incumbents and entrants', *International Journal of Industrial Organisation*, 10 (1992), pp. 545–65.

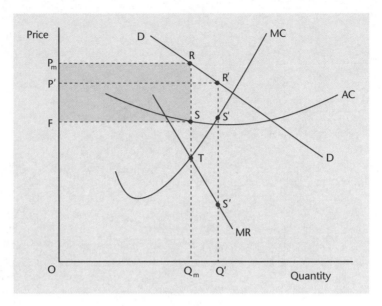

Figure 6.1 The single monopolist

Market power means that an individual firm's output affects price. Thus, suppose production were raised above OQ_m to OQ'. Price would have to fall to OP'. Corresponding to that price and output, we have $MC = Q'S'$ and $MR = Q'T'$. Note that $MR < MC$. This implies that the net increase in revenue obtained by raising output by Q_mQ' is less than the cost of producing that extra output. Hence total profits must be lower at output OQ' than at OQ_m. The profit-maximising monopolist, therefore, will cut back sales to OQ_m. The profit-maximising rule prevents the firm from selling either more or less than OQ_m. This is why Q_m and P_m are monopoly equilibrium price and quantity.

The economic consequences of the monopoly are estimated by reference to the benchmark case of competition (Figure 6.2). We start off from the monopoly equilibrium. Only this time, for convenience of exposition, constant costs over the relevant output span are assumed (i.e. $AC = MC$). (We can imagine the monopolist as a multi-plant firm, able to increase output by adding to the number of plants without affecting unit costs.) The monopoly sells OQ_m at price OP_m. Now assume that competition is introduced into the industry. Each plant is taken over by an independent owner. The plants are numerous, so each single owner can have no influence on price. Hence, $MR = P$ for each individual firm. The profit-maximising rule leads each firm to produce up to the point where $P = MR = MC$. In Figure 6.2, this corresponds to point S, with output OQ_c (higher than monopoly output) and price OP_c (lower than monopoly price). The welfare loss of monopoly is the triangular area RTS. Intuitively, this represents the total utility derived from the addition of Q_mQ_c to extra output, measured by Q_mRSQ_c *less* the actual resource cost of producing it represented by the area under the MC curve, Q_mTSQ_c. *The creation of this so-*

143

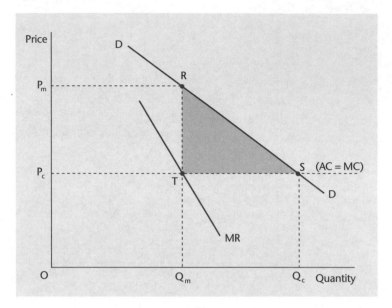

Figure 6.2 Monopoly v. competition – same costs

called 'dead-weight' loss of monopoly (the triangle RST) constitutes the standard 'static' argument against monopoly. It captures what most people believe is wrong about monopoly: price is higher and output lower than would be the case if competition were introduced.

One core issue has been left offstage. That centres on the *cost* position in the two situations: monopoly and competition. Figure 6.2 assumes that costs are the same under both market structures. But if, as seems likely, cost levels differ between the two situations, the net welfare effects will have to be revised accordingly. Suppose, for example, that monopoly leads to 'managerial slack', defined as a lackadaisical attitude to costs and innovation. The cost curve in conditions of monopoly would then lie *above* the cost function for competition (Figure 6.3). The change from monopoly to competition would in these circumstances not only yield the welfare triangle RTS, but also a significant cost-saving *rectangle*, ASVB, plus an extra small triangle SVZ. These combined elements can amount to a significant efficiency gain. Competition among firms is one of the most powerful forces stimulating innovation and investment in technology in modern industries.[11]

The economic losses of monopoly have to be analysed on an empirical case-by-case basis, as is done every day by law courts and by competition authorities. The weight of evidence is that monopoly frequently involves *higher* costs than the

---

11 Michael Porter, *The Competitive Advantage of Nations* (London: Macmillan, 1990), p. 636. If, however, scope for exploiting economies of scale and innovation capacity is greater under monopoly than under competition, these dynamic gains would also have to be included in the cost–benefit analysis of monopoly. We shall discuss these further in Chapter 7.

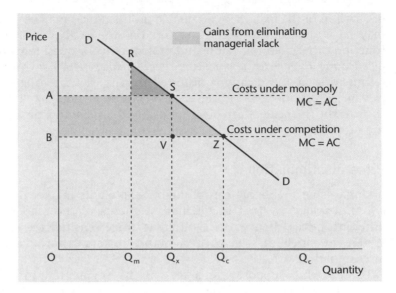

Figure 6.3 Monopoly v. competition – different costs

welfare triangle because costs under monopoly are higher than under competition. This is particularly likely in state-owned monopolies or in companies that are insulated from the threat of takeover, since elsewhere the desire to avoid attracting predators will force the monopolist to be as cost-efficient and profitable as possible.[12]

So far, the economics of monopoly has been analysed in terms of its *efficiency* effects. The effects on *income distribution* must also be taken into account. Clearly, the *owners* of the firm benefit; indeed, the analysis of Figure 6.2 suggests that they obtain all of the monopoly's profits. In reality, monopoly profits, or 'rents', tend to be distributed more widely than that. For example, *employees* gain a share of the benefits in the form of better working conditions and above-average remuneration.[13] Managers and staff, being under less pressure to perform and to keep up with best practice, can enjoy a utility-generating, easy-going lifestyle. The 'managerial slack' or 'X-inefficiency' thereby created absorbs considerable amounts of monopoly rents. Sometimes monopoly profits may not be that high because of wasteful use of raw materials and poor maintenance of machinery. A portion of the excess profits might also go to ensuring that the monopoly position of the firm is sustained. Strategic entry deterrence techniques involve some

---

12 A potential disciplining mechanism on a monopoly firm in the private sector is the fear of takeover. Any sign of management taking life too easy will attract the corporate raider. A monopolist does not always enjoy a quiet life.

13 This does not imply that competitive firms must necessarily be worse employers than monopoly firms. There are sound microeconomic efficiency arguments for being a 'good' employer. Competition gives firms an incentive to think more carefully about the optimum remuneration pattern for employees.

dissipation of the maximum attainable profits. Prices may be cut. Lobbying costs may be undertaken to keep regulators on side. Activities that serve no social function other than to acquire and protect rents or quasi-rents have been called *rent-seeking or directly unproductive profit-seeking (DUP) activities.* The costs of resources used and decisions distorted in this way are called *influence costs.* A private sector monopoly, however, must ensure an adequate return on influence costs. If the financial return does not justify the spending, profits will decline and the monopoly again leaves itself vulnerable to takeover.

Price discrimination

A single-seller monopoly can profitably exploit its market power by practising *price discrimination.* That is, different segments of the market can be charged different prices; hence their different price-sensitivities can be exploited. Wherever price elasticity of demand differs, there is scope for price discrimination.

To see why, suppose a market can be segmented into two parts: one representing high-elasticity customers and the other consisting of customers with a low-price elasticity of demand. The respective demand curves are D_1 and D_2 (Figure 6.4), with the corresponding marginal revenue (MR) curves MR_1 and MR_2. We assume, for simplicity, that the monopolist's MC curve is constant and the same for each market.

In order to maximise profits, the monopolist must set price such that its MR in each market equals its constant MC. The exercise will involve computing the MR curve corresponding to the demand curve in each market. A combined MR curve can be derived as a lateral summation of the MR curve in each market. The combined marginal revenue curve, CMR in panel (c) of Figure 6.4, is derived in this way. When CMR cuts MC, the firm's maximum profit point is attained.

In Figure 6.4 (panel (c)), the MC and the CMR curve intersect at E. Profits are maximised when marginal revenue equals OC. In market 2, we see from panel (b) that the level of output/sales corresponding to $MR_2 = OC$ is OQ_2. At that sales level, a price of OP_2 can be charged. In market 1, marginal revenue of OC is earned

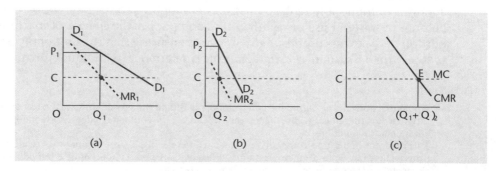

Figure 6.4 Monopoly price discrimination

on the OQ_1th unit of sales. The price obtainable in this price-sensitive market is only OP_1. The firm's profits are therefore maximised by selling:

OQ_1 at price OP_1 in market 1,
OQ_2 at price OP_2 in market 2.

Price discrimination is common practice wherever monopoly power exists. In Chapter 4 we introduced the theory of market segmentation and the pricing decision in the case of hotel rooms, football stadiums, theatres and suchlike. Utility companies, such as gas, electricity and telecoms, also resort to elaborate forms of price discrimination, and successful exporters are regularly accused of 'dumping' – i.e. selling cheaper in the (price-elastic) world market than in their (price-inelastic and protected) domestic market. But a price-discriminating firm must be careful that the markets are truly segmented, i.e. it must not be possible to arbitrage between them. Otherwise, an intermediary could make money by buying the good in market 1 at OP_1 and selling it into market 2 at OP_2. Assuming zero impediments between markets, this arbitrage would continue until the prices in each market were equalised. The presence of impediments, or transaction costs, gives scope for divergence in price between one market and another. A firm obviously has an incentive to spend resources on *creating* market segmentation, through advertising campaigns and improved quality. Cosmetic changes to the product may be made in order to avert accusations of exploitation or unfairness. This would mean that the MC differs in each market and allowance would have to be made for this in deciding the optimal sales level in each market. But the principles guiding the decision would remain unchanged – it boils down to ascertaining the level of MR through careful demand analysis, supplementing it with reliable cost information and applying the appropriately adjusted marginal cost – marginal revenue rules.

Price discrimination can also be incorporated into a monopolist's pricing strategy through charging two-part tariffs. Typical examples include telecom charges involving a fixed rental per quarter plus a price per call; or of professional associations which charge a membership fee allied to a concessionary members' fee for conferences, journal issues and other services. The net effect is that different users are charged different amounts for the same service. The practices of 'bundling' or 'full-line forcing', whereby a firm requires the customer to stock a range of its products or refuses to sell on a single item basis, are other forms of price discrimination. These practices all presuppose the presence of some monopoly power.

Price discrimination is widely practised. This is because it can be important for the bottom line. Dolan and Simon observe that, for given costs structures, a 1 per cent boost in average price yields a net profit increase of 12 per cent to the average US corporation (*op. cit.*, p. 4). Readers can check this by taking 1 per cent of net sales of any company and adding it to net profit. At the same time, price discrimination can be hard to document. Fear of adverse consumer reaction and of attracting the attention of the competition authorities makes firms cautious about publishing details. They are more likely to try to explain price discrimination by claiming that the dearer product is of superior quality or that the costs of supply and distribution vary between markets. Of course, if the products are not identical, prices could diverge without this constituting price discrimination in the economist's sense.

Multi-product and multi-plant monopolists

Occasionally, some parts of a monopolist's product range are sold under highly competitive conditions, while other items are sold under monopoly conditions. In that event, the MR = MC rule continues to apply, with allowance being made for the different demand conditions in each market.

Take, for example, the pricing policy of a large supermarket. Part of its sales consist of products, the price of which is well known, such as milk, bread, hamburgers. These are called known-value items (KVIs). Also on the supermarket's shelves are many goods whose price is not familiar to the average customer (non-KVIs). Once inside the store, the customer is likely to purchase both types of good. In a one-stop shop, KVIs and non-KVIs are complements. The supermarket can be viewed as being able to exercise a certain degree of monopoly power (spatial monopoly) over its customers, *once they are inside the store*. In such circumstances, it can be shown that the supermarket's profit-maximising strategy might lead it to charge below-cost prices for the KVIs in order to attract customers and recoup these losses through sales of non-KVIs at monopoly prices (see Box 6.2).

A loss-leader price strategy can, therefore, be compatible with profit maximisation. In this instance, the important point is to ensure that the MR of KVIs is properly defined so as to include the revenue obtained from additional sales of non-KVIs to customers attracted to the supermarket as a result of the loss leaders.

A multi-plant monopolist, by contrast, faces a single MR, but a different MC schedule in each plant. The profit-maximising rule ordains that the cost of producing the last unit in each plant should be the same for all plants and equal to the common MR:

$$MR = MC_1 = MC_2 = MC_3 = \ldots = MC_n$$

where n is the number of plants. Suppose this rule were breached. MR was £10; MC_1 was £8 and MC_2 was £12 in plants 1 and 2. By transferring production from plant 2 to plant 1, profits could be increased. Such allocation will continue until the MCs are equalised. This rule can have important practical application when allocating quotas between different participants in a cartel (see Case Study 6.1).

Box 6.3

When competition induces pricing below cost

Loss-leading is a pricing strategy which is widely used in multi-product retailing. It involves the sale of a subset of 'traffic building' items at below-cost prices. This appears to contradict the rule of profit maximisation. Another interpretation is that it is an outcome of anti-competitive behaviour, i.e. large firms price below cost in order to drive the weak out of business. However, closer analysis shows that it is perfectly consistent both with profit maximisation and with competition in the market. The critical issue in selecting the optimal price of a retail product is the correct definition of marginal revenue. In multi-product retailing the marginal revenue of any one product must incorporate the spillover effects arising from the pricing of other products in the store. These effects include the mark-up earned on goods purchased by customers attracted to the store by loss leaders.

Loss-leading is an inherent feature of grocery retailing. The distinguishing feature of the retail grocery market is the vast range of product categories and different brands offered to the consumer. The average American supermarket of 40,000 square feet typically carries between 20,000 and 30,000 different products ('Survey of retailing', *The Economist*, 4 March 1995). Consumers will only have prior knowledge of prices in a subset of known-value-items (KVIs) that are characterised by frequently-purchased standardised staple products such as bread and milk. The prices of all other products, non-KVIs, will be unknown to the customer prior to entering the store.

Consumers are rational and enter stores that are deemed to offer lower retail prices. Given the costs and disutility associated with acquiring price information, customers' entry decision will be based upon their *perceived* value for money from shopping in a particular store, as indicated by KVI prices. Retailers will therefore compete for market share on the basis of KVI prices. The information costs that are associated with finding out the relative price of non-KVIs in different stores generate switching costs for consumers. Once consumers have entered the store, therefore, switching costs result in spatial market power that allows the retailer to extract price-cost mark-ups on non-KVIs.

These features of imperfect information allow retailers to sell certain 'traffic building' items below-cost in an endeavour to attract consumers into the store, and to charge higher prices on other goods.

Product margins are not completely independent of one another. The concept of one-stop shopping results in a positive link between the demand for KVIs and non-KVIs in the sense that lower prices on the former will enhance customer entry and hence sales of non-KVIs. To this extent, they may be considered complements and optimal margins must incorporate this product demand dependency.

The optimal KVI pricing strategy for the multi-product retailer under conditions of imperfect information is illustrated in the figure below.

In the absence of interdependent demands, aggressive price competition between stores for market share results in continual price undercutting on KVIs that ensures pricing at marginal cost and zero economic profit at q_0. However, optimal pricing of KVIs must take into account the demand interdependency between KVIs and non-KVIs. For complementary products this has a positive impact on revenue. The greater the market share attracted by

Box 6.3 continued

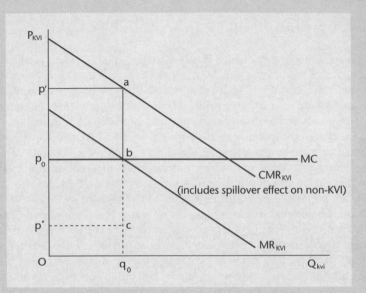

KVI pricing, the greater the sales of non-KVIs with high price–cost mark-ups due to retailer market power once the customer has entered the store.

The marginal revenue curve must be amended to incorporate this additional net revenue impact from non-KVI products, and hence the corrected marginal revenue curve CMR will lie above the original MR. The effective marginal revenue resulting from selling q_0 KVIs thus exceeds marginal cost by (p^1-p_0), and the retailers earns profits $(p^1 abp_0)$. Given these profits, the retailer has an incentive to price undercut its rivals by reducing the price of KVIs slightly below p_0 in an endeavour to increase market share. All retailers face the same incentive. Once again intensive price competition between stores for market share results in continual price undercutting on KVIs by all retailers until it is no longer profitable to do so. The additional profits generated by the complementary sale of non-KVIs are fully dissipated by price cuts on KVIs. These are priced below cost (p^* is below MC) to protect market share. In equilibrium, the resultant loss on KVIs ($p_0 bcp^*$) will just equal the profit ($p'abp_0$) earned on non-KVIs. Competition over the consumer base ensures that overall profits remain at zero and output at q_0. We make the realistic assumption in other words that the market price elasticity of demand for KVIs such as butter, margarine, basic vegetables is close to zero, while being very high for any individual retailer.

The extent of below-cost selling depends upon the spillover effect that the pricing of KVIs has on non-KVI products. This will be contingent upon the cross-price elasticity of demand and share of expenditure on non-KVIs relative to KVIs. Higher cross-price elasticity values will result in a greater impact on sales volume for non-KVI complements and hence on effective incoming revenue. This positive effect is enhanced for high prices of non-KVIs, where a larger unit increase in revenue is obtained for a given rise in sales volume. The scope for below-cost selling in the grocery market is therefore apparent. The benefits of one-stop shopping and the costs associated with shopping around result in a high cross-price

Box 6.3 continued

elasticity between KVIs and non-KVIs. In addition the extensive range of products carried by retailers and the limited capacity of consumers to remember all of these prices imply that the proportion of non-KVIs to KVIs is large, while the ability of retailers to exercise some degree of market power over non-KVIs once customers have entered suggests that the mark-up on non-KVIs is larger compared with KVIs. Relative expenditure on non-KVIs is therefore large.

Overall, competition for consumers will reduce margins on KVIs to the lowest possible value so that the sum of margins over all products will just cover costs and retailer profits will be zero. Below-cost selling on certain known-value-items is an outcome of competition under conditions of imperfect consumer information, interdependent demands, and intensive price competition over the consumer base.

Source: Ciara Whelan, Trinity College Dublin; P.P. Walsh and C. Whelan, 'Loss-leading and price intervention: welfare outcomes in a second best world', *The International Review of Law and Economics*, 19 (3), 1999.

6.3 How to sustain monopoly power

Monopoly profits act as a beacon to potential entrants to the industry. If they succeed in gaining entry to the industry, monopoly profits will be competed away. Strategic management textbooks advise firms on how to protect and insulate themselves from potential entrants. Economic analysis has the opposite concern. It focuses on the need to keep open the possibility of entry, to maintain contestable markets, so that firms will operate efficiently.

Another term for market power is *competitive advantage*. Competitive advantage, in turn, is related to: (1) the threat of substitute products not being imminent, (2) a low degree of rivalry for market share among existing producers, and (3) the threat of new entrants. It can be achieved in a number of ways:

- *Economies of scale*, if sustained over a sufficiently large range of output, give big firms a cost advantage over smaller competitors. Eventually, this could result in just one firm serving the market (single-firm monopoly). More usual is the situation where a few firms dominate the industry.
- *Government policies* such as provision of a patent, nationalisation, or regulation, create monopoly situations. For example, until recent times, private buses were prevented from competing with the state-owned bus monopoly in many European cities.
- *Ownership of know-how* can confer market power even in the absence of specific legislation and economies of scale. This know-how could embody organisational, marketing or financial procedures, as well as technological leadership.
- *Ownership of natural resources* – such as oil, diamonds, uranium, etc., where the number of producers is limited by physical constraints.

The way in which market power can be *sustained*, once it has been acquired, needs careful attention. Many firms fail to sustain market power. In Britain, GKN,

Courtaulds and British Leyland (and its predecessors), and in Germany, AEG and Mannesman, are examples of once great companies which survive in much diminished shape or have fallen by the wayside. Sustaining market power involves three primary elements:

1. *Architecture*: The network of relational contracts written by or around the firm. Companies such as IBM and Marks and Spencer exemplify strong architecture in that they have established *a structure, a style, a set of routines*, which motivate employees and suppliers. These routines resulted in exceptional corporate results over many years and through many changes in the economic environment. (Although, as IBM's difficulties in 1994 and Marks and Spencer's in 1999 demonstrated all too well, no position is permanent.)

2. *Reputation*: Relevant in markets where quality is important, but is verifiable only through long-term experience. Examples include car hire, accountancy services and international hotel chains. In these markets, reputations are costly and difficult to create but, once established, can generate substantial market power. Reputation is bolstered by advertising and development of brand names.

3. *Innovation*: Development of product differentiation and patents, as already noted, are a source of market power, but many types of innovation are not protected by patent. The key issue is how to protect a specific innovation in a world where innovations – from software to personal stereos to cream liqueurs – are difficult and expensive to protect through legal measures. The most powerful means of protection usually is to combine innovation with architecture and reputation, much as, say, Coca-Cola combines its patent with its sedulously created marketing and distribution.

Architecture, reputation and innovation together give a firm what Professor John Kay has termed *distinctive capability*, which in the long term sustains its monopoly power.

Market power can also be preserved by *strategic entry-deterrent measures* such as (1) setting price deliberately below the profit-maximising level in order to reduce the attractiveness of the industry to outsiders (limit-pricing), (2) concealing profit figures for monopolised parts of its business – a common practice in the case of subsidiary operations of large companies, (3) below-cost selling, predatory pricing and dumping, and (4) deliberate over-investment in capacity and extension of product range.

To sum up, what matters in terms of exercising market power is the firm's ability to earn above-average profits without attracting new entrants into the industry. If entry is not too costly and cannot be deterred, even a 100 per cent market share may leave the incumbent firm with little market power. A high firm concentration ratio will signal market power only if it is accompanied by a low degree of *contestability*.

6.4 Market power with few firms – the case of oligopoly

The case of monopoly, in which just one seller dominates the entire market, is useful for illustrative purposes. However, in reality single-seller monopolies are the exception. More common is the case of markets dominated by a few large firms. Economists call this oligopoly. Oligopoly and monopoly are close cousins from an economic viewpoint. For example, a firm needs to supply only one quarter of the total market in order to be characterised by the UK's Office of Fair Trading as possessing a 'monopoly position'.

Oligopolies come in many guises. There are different ways in which market power can be exercised when interdependence between the small number of firms prevails in the market. Firms might try to form a *cartel*, whereby price, market share and investment decisions are made collectively, with the objective of maximising profits. At the international level, the best-known cartels include OPEC (once a dominant force in the oil industry, but now greatly weakened) and the De Beers diamond 'monopoly'. Within the EU, cartels have been found in a diverse range of industries: cases involving dyestuffs, quinine, low-density polyethylene and cement have come to attention in recent years.

Suppose there are two producers, firm 1 and firm 2. They form a cartel in order to avoid competing away their profits. Total profits are maximised when MR = MC for the industry as a whole. This is the level of profits the profit-maximising cartel will seek to earn. To determine the marginal cost curve for the industry, each firm's MC curve is laterally summated by finding out how much output can be produced in each firm at each MC level. The MR curve is derived from the industry demand curve, estimated by the techniques described in Chapter 4. The profit-maximising output for the two-firm cartel in Figure 6.5 is OQ and price OP. Total industry profits are represented by the area PRSF.

The cartel then has the task of determining production quotas for each firm (market-sharing). This is not an easy task. One possibility would be to order each firm to sell at OP and to allocate a quota of OQ_1 to firm 1 and OQ_2 to firm 2. Because of firm 1's lower cost structure, however, it earns more profits than firm 2. Some haggling might take place as to the share-out. Each participant has

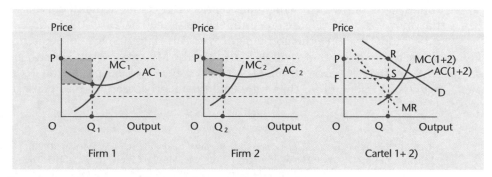

Figure 6.5 How a cartel determines profit-maximising output

a selfish interest in the other participant being reasonably satisfied with the outcome, but the unbalanced nature of the distribution in Figure 6.5 may lead to tension. If this imbalance is not corrected, firm 2 will be tempted to 'cheat', i.e. to sell a few extra units at OP, in order to obtain a larger share of the cartel's profits. This will be a profitable exercise for firm 2 if undetected, since MC is well below OP at its assigned production level OQ_2. Of course, if everyone cheats, the cartel's effectiveness diminishes and may even disappear entirely. Hence a mechanism for detecting and limiting cheating is an essential requirement for a cartel. Many cartels have self-destructed because of their inability to implement such a mechanism. (We explain in Case Study 6.1 how the troubled but still surviving De Beers diamond cartel has coped with this problem.)

In some instances, rather than form a cartel, oligopolists may decide to allow a dominant firm to assume a leadership role. If the leader raises price, the others follow, and vice versa in the event of a fall in price. The *price leader* then decides on the price that maximises its profits, on the assumption that all other producers will sell as much as they find profitable at the price chosen by the leader. The net result is a higher price and more profits for all in the industry. It is not as advantageous for the producers as a cartel, but it is less transparent and, therefore, less likely to encounter legal problems. Too blatant price leadership behaviour can, of course, attract attention. In the US, the Department of Justice has taken exception to 'conscious parallelism' of price decisions, even in the absence of overt collusion – and hence can object to the leader advertising price changes.[14] A well-publicised example of price leadership is the case of ICI and British Salt. The two firms accounted for a 45 per cent and 50 per cent share, respectively, of the UK market. In its 1986 *Report on the UK Salt Market*, the Monopolies and Mergers Commission criticised British Salt for having chosen to 'follow' the price increase of ICI. The Commission recommended that the price of salt should be controlled through the use of an index, based on the costs of the more efficient producer, British Salt.[15]

A variant of the price leadership model is the kinked oligopoly model. According to this model, if, at a given ruling price OP, an oligopolist reduces price, the fall in the price will be followed by its competitors, but if it increases price, competitors will not follow. They will prefer to see their market share increase at the expense of the firm which raised price. Hence the demand curve is relatively flat above price OP (Figure 6.6) and relatively steep below OP. The *kinked oligopoly curve* model explores the consequences of this rigidity. One consequence is that, at the ruling price, there will be a break in the MR curve. At this point, an upward shift in the MC curve from MC_1 to MC_2 may not be passed on to price. An aggressive trade union, therefore, could demand a rise in remuneration without

---

14 H. Michael Hayes *et al. Business marketing: A global perspective* (Chicago: Irwin, 1997), p. 297.

15 J. Sutton, *Sunk Costs and Market Structure* (Cambridge, MA: MIT Press, 1991), p. 195. The salt market is dominated by two firms in the UK (a *duopoly* case) and, in the US, the four-firm concentration ratio approximates 100 per cent.

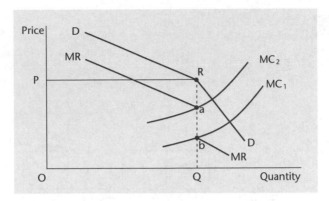

Figure 6.6 **Kinked oligopoly curve.**

any repercussions on output or price. The theory tells us nothing about how the going price itself is determined, only that once set it will tend to be stable. Firms in the industry will be slow to pass on increases in costs of production to the consumer. Price changes in such circumstances are likely to occur in discrete jumps and to be accompanied by uncertainty and even 'price wars' before a new 'going' price becomes accepted.

Price competition is often shunned by oligopolists. Because of a fear of the unpredictable consequences of price changes and the danger of sparking off a series of disequilibrating 'follower' price-cuts, the ambitious firm may prefer to engage in less quantifiable, less transparent and consequently less easily followed forms of *non-price competition*: advertising, provision of better quality service and marketing strategies designed to create customer loyalty and tie in more customers.

The analysis of interdependence can be extended well beyond the standard cases of cartel, price leadership and kinked oligopoly demand curves. The implications of strategic interdependence in markets with few producers have been extensively explored in game theory. Game theory analysis develops the idea that, if interdependence exists, firms' decisions on production and pricing will be affected by what they believe their competitors will do in response.

A standard example starts with a two-firm industry. Each firm can choose a 'high' or a 'low' price (Box 6.4). If they both choose high prices, they make profits of $3 million each. With low prices, they make only $2 million each. But if one sets a high price and the other a low one, the low-price firm makes $4 million while the high-price firm gets only $1 million. Although the firms would do best if they both set high prices, they will not do so. If firm A sets a high price, firm B's best strategy is to undercut it. Firm B will then make $4 million, rather than $3 million. If firm A sets a low price, firm B's optimal strategy is to do the same. It will earn $2 million instead of $1 million. Thus, each firm will be driven to opt for a low price regardless of what the other firm chooses. They each choose the low price and make only $2 million each. This is called a *Nash equilibrium*. No

Box 6.4

Price strategies and profits

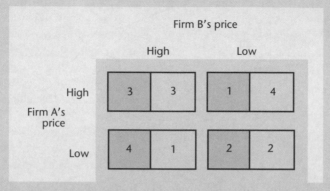

In each box, firm A's profit is on the left and firm B's profit is on the right. Firm A's dominant strategy is low price and high output. (This is better for A whether B's price is high or low.) Likewise, firm B's dominant strategy is low price. Hence, low–low is Nash equilibrium. It is the strategy which is best for each firm when the other firm's strategy is taken as given. We assume a non-cooperative game. If the two firms cooperated, they could reach (3,3), a superior outcome.

A cooperative solution is possible provided there is :

1. pre-commitment, i.e. an agreement is made;
2. credible threat, i.e. the commitment will be *binding* and enforceable.

firm wants to change strategy, given full knowledge of the other firm's strategies.[16]

A key aspect of this situation is that firms cannot make *binding commitments* to collude. Even if they did make a commitment to charge the higher price, they would each have an incentive to cheat. And the commitment, since it involves collusion, could not be enforced in the courts. (On the contrary, if discovered, the parties to the agreement could end up in trouble since any such agreement might be deemed illegal.) Game theory has gone on to explore ways in which a more

---

16 This case is otherwise known as the prisoners' dilemma. Two prisoners having committed a crime are kept in separate cells. If they both keep silent, they will be acquitted – hence the importance of keeping them apart and ensuring that there is no collusion. If one confesses and the other keeps silent, all the blame falls on the latter, who gets a heavy sentence, while the prisoner who confesses receives a light sentence. Each prisoner is likely to conclude that to confess is the optimal strategy. This is the Nash equilibrium. Thus they both confess, they incriminate each other and get a moderate sentence each. The optimal position from their joint perspective is not chosen – much to the relief of the honest citizen, one may add! The more prisoners involved in the crime, the more likely they are to confess. From society's perspective, large numbers make for a superior outcome, though each prisoner acts solely out of self-interest. This echoes Adam Smith's analysis of the market system.

advantageous outcome from the firms' point of view could be achieved. If the game is repeated often, as happens usually in real life, each firm can find ways of testing each other's good faith. Firms might be able to keep profits up by setting high prices and building up a reputation for keeping them there, regardless of how other firms react (the price leadership model). Game theory has also been applied to monopoly theory to explain how the monopolist is likely to respond to new entrants and how it might plan to neutralise rivals. Although game theory addresses problems with which business can readily identify, it has been less successful at giving governments and firms practical advice. Game theory was given a signal boost by the award of a Nobel prize in 1995 to the three economists most closely associated with its development over the past 50 years: two Americans, John Nash and John Harsanyi, and a German, Reinhard Selten. Business too has become more aware of the usefulness of a game-theoretic approach in deciding whether to enter a market, or how to defend a market position. Game theory can also be useful in devising bid systems. The design of the multi-billion auctions of radio spectrum for mobile phones in the UK in 2000 and in the US in 1994–95 was influenced by game theory, as was the mobile phone companies' participation in the auction. The application of auction theory to such practical transactions continues to the present day.

6.5 Conclusions

Market structures vary a great deal. They range from perfect competition at one extreme to a single-firm monopoly at the other. In between there is a continuum. At one end of the range there is monopolistic competition, where there are many firms, each with some small degree of product differentiation but with little ability to fix price, and relatively easy entry and exit. Small retail businesses, restaurants and small clothing firms have these characteristics, and are included in the 'effectively competitive' sectors. At the other end of the spectrum are cases of oligopoly, where a few firms exercise a dominant position in an industry and where the actions of each individual firm have a perceptible impact on market price.

It is easy to describe a market morphology in general terms. More problematic is the task of identifying the extent of market power exercised by individual firms in specific industries. We conclude that large sections of modern industrial economies can be described as 'effectively competitive' in the sense of being highly exposed to competitive pressure and with individual firms having limited market power. Moreover, the proportion of the economy falling into the effectively competitive category seems to be increasing. With increased prosperity there is a shift to the services sector, where the optimum scale is smaller than in industry. Technology also seems to be helping the survival and growth of many small firms. Also, as the world economy becomes more open, more firms are exposed to competition. For example, in the late 1950s the automobile industry counted four or five major world players. Today, about twenty automobile firms are capable of competing on a global scale, although at a national level, there is continuing rationalisation of the industry. In the European market, the removal of trade barriers following the 1992 programme has led to a significant erosion of individual companies' market power. Another factor contributing to a higher incidence of competition is the break-up of large, state-owned companies as part of many countries' privatisation programmes and the rapidly proceeding deregulation of the telecoms, post, energy and transport industries. The growing sophistication of the market also opens opportunities for an increased number of market participants. The top selling auto model in the US market in the 1990s sold 400,000 units, compared with 1.5 million units in the late 1950s. All major automobile manufacturers produce a higher number of models than previously and a smaller volume of sales of each model.[17]

Yet monopoly influence and market power are important realities in the business world. The flourishing amount of anti-trust and competition law cases testifies to that fact. Analysis of monopoly theory shows why there is a general presumption that monopoly will be inefficient relative to competition. Reference was made to both the static inefficiency losses and to the potentially more important, but difficult to measure, dynamic efficiency losses. Objections to monopoly are also frequently made on equity grounds. Establishing a sense of 'fairness' is essential to the proper operation of the market system. Consequently, the general presumption is that monopoly has detrimental effects on economic performance. But each case has to be judged on its merits. In some circumstances, scale economies and an innovation programme can best be developed within a monopoly market structure. In such cases, without monopoly there may be no market and hence it makes good economic sense to treat the monopoly as the lesser of two evils.

Summary

1. Monopoly in various forms is a common feature of a modern economy. At least a quarter of economic activity in the EU and US is transacted in what can be described as predominantly non-competitive markets. The proportion of manufacturing that can be characterised in this way is higher than the economy average. However, in an economy, there is a continuum between perfect competition and the single monopolist at opposite ends of the spectrum. Neither model is completely 'realistic'. Which activities are grouped at each end of the spectrum has to be decided case by case.

2. Forces of competition have been kept strong by advances in technology and the growth of the services sector, which have been conducive to the development of small independent firms. Other factors underlying this trend are trade liberalisation, the deregulation and privatisation of the former state-

---

17 This does not *necessarily* prove that the market has become more competitive, since brand proliferation could reflect an entry-deterrent strategy on a non-competitive market. The above data are taken from Kim B. Clark and Takahiro Fujimoto, *Product Development Performance: Strategy, organisation and management in the world auto industry* (Boston: Harvard Business School Press, 1991).

owned monopolies and the demand for customised products. Competition policy has played a role (to be further discussed in Chapter 7).

3. The motivation of monopoly is to earn superior profits to that obtainable under perfect competition. Economic analysis shows that monopoly involves more than the mere redistribution of income from the consumer to the monopolist. It can also lead to static and dynamic efficiency losses for the economy. It is a *negative-sum game*; the monopolist's gain is less than the economic losses of the rest of society.

4. Monopoly profits attract would-be entrants. In order to survive, the monopolist must continually upgrade and maintain technological leadership. It must build up and sustain its competitive architecture.

5. Oligopoly exists where an industry is dominated by a few firms which have to take account of interdependence between their decisions. Industrial organisation theorists have outlined many possible modes of strategic behaviour and interaction. There is no unique generalisable model of behaviour, analogous to perfect competition or the monopoly model. The measurement of market power in such cases can be difficult and instances of the abuse of such power hard to detect. Each case must be examined on its own merits.

6. Economic analysis helps us to understand how monopolists and oligopolists will behave under different market conditions. Non-competitive behaviour is generally expected to lead to an inferior outcome relative to competition, although there are some exceptions, notably when economies of scale require very large size relative to the extent of the market.

Questions for discussion

1. Suppose a firm acquires a monopoly position in an industry by buying out all previous suppliers in the market.

   (a) Give three reasons why a Competition Authority might object.
   (b) What arguments may the firm use to justify the takeover?

2. 'The key to growth – even survival – is to stake out a market position that is less vulnerable to attack from opponents, whether established or new, and less vulnerable to erosion from substitutes and other competitors.' What methods can a firm use to establish such a position?

3. 'Collusion is difficult to achieve and even more difficult to maintain.' Explain these difficulties.

4. Large firms usually account for a much greater share of a country's exports than of its domestic market. Can you suggest reasons why this should be so?

5. (a) A monopolist sets a lower price in one market than another for the same good. Is this consistent with profit-maximisation?

(b) You are now told that the lower price has been set below both average and marginal costs and that the firm is engaged in *predatory pricing*. Should the firm be prohibited from setting price this way? Could this price behaviour be consistent with profit-maximisation?

6.   Discuss the main factors tending to intensify competition in the global economy. Are there any countervailing forces tending to undermine competition?

☞ Exercises

1.   Consider an industry with which you are familiar. How would you assess the degree of competition in that market? Is the market becoming more or less open to competition? What are the consequences of this for economic efficiency?

2.   The table below shows a demand curve facing a monopolist who produces at a constant marginal cost of £5.

Price (£)	9	8	7	6	5	4	3	2	1	0
Quantity	0	1	2	3	4	5	6	7	8	9

Calculate the monopolist's marginal revenue curve and its profit-maximising price and output. What would be the equilibrium output and price for a competitive industry with an identical cost structure (MC = £5 at all levels of output)? Explain why a monopolist produces a lower output and charges a higher price.

    Suppose that, in addition to the constant marginal cost of £5, the monopolist has a fixed cost of £20. What difference would this make to the monopolist's output, price and profits?

3.   Suppose there are ten identical producers of spring water. The constant marginal cost of extraction of the water is £1 per litre. The maximum extraction rate for each firm is 10 litres per day. Suppose the market demand curve for this water is as follows:

Price (£ per litre)	Litres demanded per day	Price (£ per litre)	Litres per day demanded
11	0	5	6
10	1	4	7
9	2	3	8
8	3	2	9
7	4	1	10
6	5		

(a) If the firms form a cartel, what will be the profit-maximising price and output for the industry, and for each firm?

(b) Suppose that one of the firms secretly breaks the rules of the cartel and reduces its price. What effect will this have on its profits?

(c) How might the remaining nine producers respond?

(d) If the cartel broke up and firms competed against each other independently, what will be the equilibrium amount of water supplied and demanded, and what will be the price? How much will each firm produce?

4. An author receives a royalty equal to 10 per cent of the revenue obtained by the publisher from sales of a book. Use a straight line demand curve to illustrate the point at which the author's royalties will be maximised. Show that the author's preferred price will always be lower than the price level which maximises the publisher's profits.

5. An industry has a demand curve as follows:

Price (£)	10	9	8	7	6	5	4	3
Quantity	1	2	3	4	5	6	7	8

(a) Suppose the industry is composed of a monopolist with a constant MC equal to £3. What price and output are chosen?
(b) Now suppose there are two firms, each with MC = AC = £3. What price and output will maximise profits if they collude?
(c) Why do the two firms have to agree on the output each will produce?
(d) Suppose a third firm entered the industry who could supply the industry at a constant MC of £4. How would that affect the monopolist/cartel's calculations?

📖 Further reading

There are numerous texts on the economics of industrial organisation. An overview of the basic models of monopoly and oligopoly, and the pricing behaviour of firms in different market structures, is provided in William Shepherd, *The Economics of Industrial Organisation* (Hemel Hempstead: Prentice Hall International, 1996); and D. Hay and D. Morris, *Economics of Industrial Organisation* (London: Oxford University Press, 1993). An excellent discussion of how firms can best sustain their monopoly power is John Kay's *The Foundation of Corporate Success* (Oxford: Oxford University Press, 1995). For a detailed discussion of the role of small firms, see contributions to the July 1994 issue of *Business Economics*. John Vickers provides a summary of advances in oligopoly and competition theory in 'Strategic competition among the few – Some recent developments in the economics of industry', *Oxford Review of Economic Policy* (1985), reprinted in S. Estrin and A. Marin, *Essential Readings in Economics* (London: Macmillan, 1995).

Case study 6.1

The diamond cartel

'A diamond is forever' boasts the glamorous advertisement of De Beers. But diamonds are valued mainly because they are considered a sound investment, relatively immune from the vagaries of economic ups and downs. Diamonds are cheap to produce and would be lower in price but for the global cartel operated by De Beers. The cartel has protected its market monopoly by flattening out short-term fluctuations in supply, and to some extent demand, with the aid of a huge buffer-stock.

The diamond cartel was set up by Sir Ernest Oppenheimer, a South African mining magnate, in 1934. The cartel is the vehicle through which over 80 per cent of world rough sales are marketed and administered.

Unlike other commodity cartels, the diamond cartel both controls supply and influences demand, combining the roles of major distributor, marketing agency and buffer-stock manager. It has developed an expertise in matching supply to demand and the financial strength to hold diamonds temporarily off the market.

Structure of the diamond market

Diamond mines are relatively few in number, are easily identified and cannot be increased at will. The major producers are South Africa, Botswana, Namibia, the former Soviet Union and Australia. Owing to the wide variation in diamond quality, a country's volume of output is not an accurate indicator of the value of its production. For example, Australia is the world's largest producer of diamonds in volume terms but, because of the low average price of its output, it ranks much lower in terms of value.

Major diamond producers ranked by volume and value

	% share of world production (Vol)	Volume		Value	
		mn carats	1997	US$	1997
Australia	34.7	40	1	322	6
Congo	19.1	22	2	897	4
Botswana	17.3	20	3	1650	1
Russia	12.5	14	4	1305	2
South Africa	8.6	10	5	983	3
Angola	4.6	5	6	410	5

Source: Various, as indicated at end of text.

The industry's major producer is the De Beers corporation, which has direct and indirect interests in mines throughout the world, as well as in South Africa.

Case study 6.1 continued

The structure of supply is quite complex. Each diamond has to be classified and valued individually, and different diamonds of the same price are not necessarily tradeable substitutes. At the micro-level, the diamond market is not a single market, but embraces many sub-markets, with different prices, and distinctive supply and demand characteristics. Price differentials exist for different product grades in most commodity markets. The lack of homogeneity in diamonds is such that there is no single price which acts as a reliable benchmark for the market as a whole. The market is highly segmented and prices range from $1 to tens of thousands of dollars. This has important implications for their marketing by the cartel.

Good stones are relatively scarce – around 10 per cent of the market by volume accounts for 50 per cent of the market by value.

Industrial diamonds refer to stones that are too small or flawed and too opaque and imperfect to be saleable as polished stones. Historically, industrial diamonds have formed about 80 per cent in volume and 20 per cent by value of all diamonds found. This segment of the market is also served by synthetic diamonds. Natural industrial diamonds nowadays probably account for less than half of all diamonds sold by volume and for less than 5 per cent by value. De Beers and General Electric dominate the world market for industrial diamonds.

De Beers sorts diamonds into boxes and sells them to sightholders who represent the main cutters. These cutters and polishers of diamonds are spread around three main centres: Antwerp, Tel Aviv and Bombay. They sell the polished stones to polished diamond buyers who in turn supply the retail trade.

Structure of the diamond market

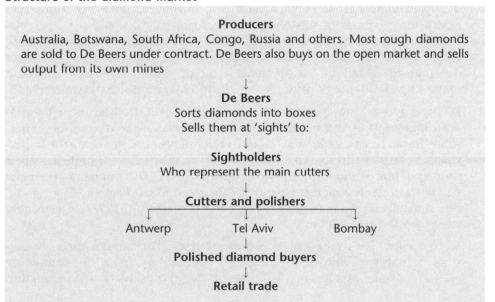

Producers
Australia, Botswana, South Africa, Congo, Russia and others. Most rough diamonds are sold to De Beers under contract. De Beers also buys on the open market and sells output from its own mines
↓
De Beers
Sorts diamonds into boxes
Sells them at 'sights' to:
↓
Sightholders
Who represent the main cutters
↓
Cutters and polishers
Antwerp   Tel Aviv   Bombay
↓
Polished diamond buyers
↓
Retail trade

Case study 6.1 continued

Certain key characteristics of the market make it susceptible to cartelisation. First, there are a small number of significant suppliers and rigorous physical barriers to entry. Second, the product is durable, has a high value to volume ratio and is easy to store. Third, the demand for jewellery quality gems, which make up 90 per cent of the $5 billion rough diamond market, is relatively price-inelastic. The rewards to a cartel from controlling supply are therefore likely to be considerable.

How the system operates – control production, dominate the trade, influence demand

The Central Selling Organisation (CSO), based in Switzerland and London, is the collective name of companies controlled by De Beers and its associates. It buys rough diamonds from the mines, valuing them and selling them to sightholders. CSO sales peaked at $6.7 billion in 1997. By keeping rough prices at the highest sustainable level, the cartel aims to achieve long-run profit-maximisation over the demand cycle rather than short-run market clearing at spot prices. The key characteristics of the cartel are:

1. The system of *producer quotas*. Most significant producers have a long-term and exclusive contract to supply a certain proportion of De Beers' annual diamond sales.

2. The cartel has created a strong antidote to any individual producer's *incentive to cheat*. De Beers backs up the carrot of higher prices with a powerful stick – its ability to release from its stocks a supply of any type of diamond. Every diamond mine has its own characteristic output. If De Beers chooses to release more stones of this characteristic from its stockpile, the stockpile-supported price can drop dramatically. Success in regulating and controlling supply has come about primarily as a result of the cartel's strong grip over distribution, aided by its financial strength, administrative skills and marketing experience of diamonds with particular or unusual characteristics.

3. De Beers acts as a *swing producer*. In a buoyant market, De Beers benefits from both higher prices and stock appreciation as goods are sold from the buffer-stock. But in a depressed market, it bears the full brunt of financing the buffer-stock. It can play this role credibly since its own mines are one of the cheapest sources of fine diamonds in the world and because of the company's financial strength. When the market is weak it can afford to cut back production and this cutback makes a material difference to the market. In 1997, De Beers held stocks worth US$4 billion.

4. *Market control* is exercised at the wholesale level. The cartel's role as buffer-stock manager is reinforced through its external buying offices, competing with independent traders for diamonds produced outside its own production

Case study 6.1 continued

network. When markets are weak it absorbs excess supply. Conversely, when markets are strong, it stays out of the market.

5. The system is also designed to *encourage participation by the wholesalers*. The stones are sold by De Beers at 'sights', where trade buyers are offered boxes which more or less fit their requirements. A box must be accepted or rejected in full. Price haggling is not permitted. This unusual method of supplying the wholesale market is integral to balancing the preferred mix of diamond at retail level. During the 1980s slump, the supply of big diamonds was curtailed. By limiting their supply, the cartel kept up their retail price, at the expense of allowing its own stockpile to grow. Price paid to the mines was maintained despite the adverse market circumstances. This type of action builds up reputation, and encourages loyalty on the part of cartel members.

6. The cartel pays careful attention to *demand management*. It spends over $150 million a year on advertising. This focuses consumer attention on the stones which De Beers needs to sell. This could turn out to be a two-edged sword since strong demand would also benefit any prospective defector from the cartel. Hence the importance of the cartel's ability to control cheating.

Threats to the system

Any interference with the market system runs the danger of encouraging unintended countervailing and competing reactions. An official price ceiling gives an incentive to sell diamonds outside the system (to 'cheat'); while minimum prices encourage over-supply. The diamond cartel is not exempt from these tendencies and its operations are under periodic threat.

1. Advertising can influence demand, but its effects can easily be overwhelmed by business cycles and by the ebb and flow of fashion. If De Beers expects a glut of a certain type of diamond, it will stop putting it in boxes, but months can pass before the effect of the move is felt in the market for polished stones.

2. De Beers' sway over customers for rough diamonds is not matched by its influence on customers for polished diamonds – jewellers and their suppliers. This makes it difficult for De Beers to control prices to the end-buyer.

3. New entrants add uncertainty to the diamond market. A new diamond mine in Canada will account for six per cent of world supply. Political instability in Africa and in Russia can also create problems by magnifying the incentive to cheat and favouring short-term over long-term perspectives of national interest. This explains why De Beers has embarked on a marketing campaign to create a De Beers brand rather than to promote diamonds in general.

4. De Beers' main concern is the confidence of its members. If they sense that the cartel lacks the strength needed to fulfil its role as swing producer, cartel

▶

Case study 6.1 continued

members will be tempted to sell their diamonds before others do the same. The main cement to this cartel, as to others, is the conviction that centralised selling and buffer-stock management are in its collective interest.

Sources: 'The cartel lives to face another threat', © *The Economist* (London 10 January 1987); 'The diamond business: glass with attitude', © *The Economist* (London 20 December 1997). I am grateful to MIB participant Roderigo Carillo de Albornoz for assistance with this box.

Questions for discussion

1. Suppose you were asked to estimate a demand curve for diamonds, what variables would you include? In what respects would you expect the demand for a long-lasting good such as diamonds to be different from the demand for nondurables such as wine and food?

2. How would you draw up a supply curve for the diamond industry? What relevance would such information have for the cartel?

3. How might the cartel determine the profit-maximising price?

4. Who gains and who loses from the cartel? Is there an economic case for trying to break it up? If yes, is there any way of doing it?

Chapter 7

COMPETITION POLICY, PRIVATISATION AND REGULATION

Introduction

When competition prevails, firms have limited discretion over price. Profit maximisation leads them to equate marginal cost to marginal revenue and, because price is more or less 'given' in a competitive market, price equals marginal revenue. Also, competition forces firms to minimise costs and to search relentlessly for new and better ways of doing things. Competition encourages innovation. For these reasons, maintaining a market structure that is open to competition is of the utmost importance to an efficient economy.

Our *first* task in this chapter is to define the characteristics of a market that encourges competition.

Our *second* task is to discuss competition policy. Competition policy refers to the rules governing the conduct of firms in a market. Without well-developed and effective competition rules, the market system will not function properly. Yet a competition regime has to balance the need for active competition on the domestic market with the equally pressing need to allow firms to attain a minimum efficient scale and be able to match international competition. On occasion, it may make sense to tolerate, even encourage, high concentration ratios in the domestic market. The extension of competition policy to deal with state aids to industry, and particularly support for state-owned enterprises, is also examined. We illustrate these issues with examples from the competition policy of the EU.

Third, the move to privatisation is analysed. Starting in the 1980s in the UK and New Zealand, privatisation programmes have been implemented throughout the world economy. 'New consensus' thinking goes far to explaining the rapid spread of these privatisation programmes, in particular the desire to introduce competition where it was absent as well as assisting governments to improve their financial situation.

The degree of popular enthusiasm for competition has waxed and waned. Proponents of competitive market structures are now in the ascendant. In order to understand why, we must understand the origin of this pro-competitive viewpoint. It is not necessarily pro-business, though it has coincided with a strongly pro-business trend in other areas of economic policy. Most businesses feel under threat from competition. They are more likely to believe that their problems derive from excess competition rather than an insufficiency of competition. They argue for space and time to adjust to the pace of technological advance and to build up competitive advantage. Getting the balance right between sectoral strength and optimal competitive pressure is vitally important for economic performance.

Chapter outline

1. Market structure and competition.
2. The main features on competition policy.
3. Privatisation programmes, their rationale and effectiveness.
4. Regulation.
5. Conclusions.

7.1 Market structure and competition

Market structure is defined in terms of a set of market attributes:

- numbers and size-distribution of sellers and buyers,
- characteristics of the product and degree of market segmentation,
- barriers to entry into the industry,
- barriers to exit from the industry.

The textbook definition of a competitive market is one where there are large numbers of firms selling a homogenous output in an industry with no entry or exit barriers. At the other end of the spectrum is monopoly. In between, there is a large array of complex market structures. These are defined by reference to the industry's concentration ratios and the characteristics of the product, the latter being measured in terms of degree of differentiation, price elasticity of demand, and sensitivity to business cycles. Account must also be taken of the degree of vertical and horizontal integration within the industry (i.e. the extent to which firms own or control 'downstream' intermediate goods industries or related, horizontal products and services), and ease and expense of entry and exit.

Corporate strategy theory provides an important critique of the market structure approach by stressing that management should not take market structure as 'given', as part of an unchangeable 'external' environment. Corporate strategy analyses how corporate conduct can be framed so as to bring about *changes* in that environment. It shows how management can restructure the market in a partisan fashion. There is clearly a two-way process at work. More generally, business decisions about pricing and other matters are often determined less by the present market structure than by the structure the firm is seeking to establish in the future.

There are further limitations to any approach that seeks to link market structure with a firm's conduct and performance. *First*, firms may be few in number and yet competition and rivalry can be intense. As we have seen (Box 6.1), the software market is dominated by Microsoft, but small firms continue to chip away at the leader's sales. This rivalry could be all that is required for efficieny. Hence, Schumpeter's famous assertion that the 'the textbook case of perfect competition has no title to be set up as the ideal model of efficiency' (1942, p. 106).

Second, whereas the standard approach emphasises the efficient allocation of a *given* set of resources, Schumpeter stressed the importance of innovation as a vital generator of the *growth* of resources. Successful firms are typically characterised by a capacity to engage in research, to innovate, to hire entrepreneurial managers and to enjoy sufficient profit margins to finance such overheads. These firms are often large corporations enjoying significant market power. Unlike the stereotypical monopoly, however, this market power does not necessarily insulate them from competition. Pressure on the Schumpeterian firm comes from:

> competition from the new commodity, the new technology, the new source of supply, the new type of organisation ... competition which strikes not at the margin of the profits and output of existing firms but at their foundations and very lives.[1]

Third, innovation, technological diffusion among firms and the evolutionary development of industry also have a bearing on market structure. The free enterprise system is one of a continuously uncertain and shifting equilibrium:

> The essential point to grasp is that in dealing with capitalism we are dealing with an evolutionary process. ... Capitalism never can be stationary. ... The fundamental impulse that sets and keeps the capitalist engine in motion comes from the new consumers' goods, the new methods of production or transportation, the new markets, the new forms of industrial organisation that capitalist enterprises create (Schumpeter, 1942, p. 85)

Any weakening in the firm's impulse to innovate will lead to its displacement by new, aggressive competitors, searching for enhanced market share. Leadership and dominant market position do not necessarily provide a safe refuge from competition in a capitalist system – unless state regulation protects existing firms by creating artificial barriers to entry.

Thus one needs to use a broad perspective in assessing market structure and its consequences for efficiency. What matters is that the threat of competition and new entrants is kept alive, while existing firms are not denied the means of defending themselves against the threat. Regulation should not be based solely on rules about numbers of competitors and concentration ratios but should take account of the overall degree of contestability from domestic and international competitors.[2] There is continuing debate, however, over the type of market structure most conductive to *innovation*.

---

1 J. Schumpeter, *Capitalism, Socialism and Democracy* (London: Allen and Unwin, 1942), p. 84.

2 The notion of hyper-competitive rivalries has Schumpeterian overtones. D'Aveni describes the process in these terms in his much acclaimed book: 'As long as one wild-card player may try to enter the market, the market is contestable; so it is no longer a safe haven. Thus, even where we observe that entrants have not attacked yet, we can't be sure that they won't enter in the future. The mere threat of their entry is enough to force firms to act like they have entered.' Richard D'Aveni, *Hyper-competitive Rivalries: Competing in highly dynamic environments* (New York: The Free Press, 1995), p. 96.

Some argue that more competition produces greater incentives to innovate, some that monopoly power is a necessary condition for innovativeness and some that the truth is in the middle. Important assumptions explaining the differences in results pertain to the likelihood of technology spill-over and to capital availability. Empirical evidence on the issue is conflicting.[3]

The reason for this conflicting evidence may be simply that some industries use high profitability to finance innovation, while others deploy their profits largely to the protection of their monopoly. In the pharmaceutical industry, for example, some persistently profitable firms with high market shares derive their profits from the discovery of new drugs. Most patent applications emanate from large firms. Companies with more than 1000 employees account for two-thirds of Europe's new patents. But against this, a large number of market leaders in the consumer goods area do not conform to the image of a Schumpeterian innovator but behave like the textbook monopolist – building their market position on advertising, brand loyalty and distribution chains, and generating very few social benefits in the process. Clearly the ideal market structure will vary from industry to industry. The key requirements are that the markets should be *contestable* – new entrants should not be excluded by monopoly pricing or other strategies – and that they should *encourage innovation*. These guiding principles are worth keeping in mind when evaluating competition policy and when devising a privatisation programme.

7.2 Competition policy

General principles

Competition law is one of the most important points of interaction between business, law and economics. Firms need to understand the rationale and practice of competition legislation and rules. Competition law is also important because it impinges so closely on the welfare of the consumer and the dynamism of the business sector. Badly framed competition policy will bring relatively few benefits to the consumer at a high cost to business. These costs include not only the costs of taking or defending a competition case, but the costs arising when a firm is uncertain about the applicability of the law to its behaviour.

Competition policy draws sustenance from economic theory of the firm. The analysis of the costs of monopoly has been influential in persuading the US authorities of the merits of a compulsory break-up of large monopolies such as Standard Oil and AT&T into smaller independent units. Exception clauses to the general ban on monopolies owe something to the Austrian model, which tends to the view that the free market will police itself. EU competition law allows for exemptions where it is judged that a forced break-up of a monopoly or prohibition of a cooperative practice could adversely affect efficiency.

---

3 P. Stoneman and P. Diederen, 'Technology diffusion and public policy', *Economic Journal* (July 1994), p. 923.

Competition policy is based on a belief in the *economic* benefits of competition. The starting assumption is that market forces are the most effective means of ensuring efficiency in the allocation of resources, of adapting to change and, ultimately, of maximising consumer welfare. A much quoted passage from the European Commission's first report on competition policy (1972) reflects this basic philosophy:

> Competition is the best stimulant of economic activity since it guarantees the widest possible freedom of action to all. An active competition policy pursued in accordance with the provisions of the Treaties establishing the Communities makes it easier for the demand and supply structures continually to adjust to technological development. Through the interplay of decentralised decision-making machinery, competition enables enterprises continually to improve their efficiency, which is the *sine qua non* for a steady improvement in living standards and employment prospects within the countries of the Community. From this point of view, competition policy is an essential means for satisfying to a great extent the individual and collective needs of our society.[4]

Thus, competition has three major advantages over monopoly:

- it makes organisations internally more efficient by sharpening incentives to avoid slackness;
- it allows the more efficient organisations to prosper at the expense of the inefficient (the selection process); and
- it improves dynamic efficiency by stimulating innovation.

The above arguments emphasise *efficiency*. *Equity* is another important consideration in competition policy. Governments enforce competition policy in order to protect weaker companies against the abuse by monopolies of their dominant market position. Support for the free market presupposes 'fair' trading rules and a level playing field. Defining 'fairness' is not, of course, always easy. Moreover, the dictates of fairness, efficiency and competition sometimes pull in different directions. Efficiency may require a more concentrated industrial structure than a government concerned with equity might want to tolerate. Somehow, consistent rules must be formulated which encourage competition, allow business a reasonable degree of certainty, but which have enough flexibility to deal with cases where market power may be necessary on technical grounds.

Competition policy has been afforded priority in the EU. New competition regimes are being introduced in Eastern Europe and in many developing countries where the framework for competition is being created from scratch. The EU has been influential in their introduction, linking them to free trade accords. While individual countries have their own distinctive competition regimes, four general principles underlie competition policy:

1. Highly concentrated market structures are more likely to be monopolistic than less concentrated structures. Competition policy tends to focus on the former.

---

4 European Commission First Report on Competition Policy (1972).

Box 7.1

EU competition law – Articles 81 and 82

Article 81 (formerly Article 85 of the Treaty of Rome)

1. The following shall be prohibited as incompatible with the common market: all agreements between undertakings, decisions by associations of undertakings, and concerted practices which may affect trade between Member States and which have as their object or effect the prevention, restriction or distortion of competition within the common market, and in particular those which:

   (a) directly or indirectly fix purchase or selling prices or any other trading conditions;
   (b) limit or control production, markets, technical development or investment;
   (c) share markets or sources of supply;
   (d) apply dissimilar conditions to equivalent transactions with other trading parties, thereby placing them at a competitive disadvantage;
   (e) make the conclusion of contracts subject to the acceptance of other parties of supplementary obligations which, by their nature or according to commercial usage, have no connection with the subject of such contract.

2. Any agreements or decisions prohibited pursuant to this article shall be automatically void.

3. The provision of paragraph 1 may, however, be 'declared inapplicable' in the case of any agreement, decision or concerted practice which contributed to improving the production or distribution of goods, or to promoting technical or economic progress, while allowing consumers a fair share of the resulting benefits, and which does not:

   (a) impose on the undertakings concerned restrictions which are not indispensable to the attainment of these objectives;
   (b) afford such undertakings the possibility of eliminating competition in respect of a substantial part of the products in question.

Article 82 (formerly Article 86 of the Treaty of Rome)

Any abuse by one or more undertakings of a dominant position within the common market or in a substantial part of it shall be prohibited as incompatible with the common market in so far as it may affect trade between Member States.

Such abuse may, in particular, consist in:

(a) directly or indirectly imposing unfair purchase or selling prices, or other unfair trading conditions;
(b) limiting production, markets or technical developments to the prejudice of consumers;
(c) making the conclusion of contracts subject to the acceptance of supplementary obligations which, by their nature or commercial usage, have no connection with the subject of such contracts.

2. Competition law is applied to a wide range of markets, i.e. to public sector commercial services and non-profit organisations, as well as to the private sector.

3. The benefits of competition include direct benefits to the consumer. But its indirect effects on upstream and downstream markets have also to be taken into account. An inefficient telecoms industry, for example, affects both the individual telephone user and also the pattern of comparative advantage, through raising communication costs.

4. Case-by-case studies are necessary to quantify the net economic benefits and costs of a monopoly.

Competition policy – the example of the European Union

The EU's competition regime provides a practical illustration of the general principles of competition policy.[5] Competition policy is a complicated subject requiring a knowledge of law, accounting and economics. Conflicting interpretations can arise relating to the definition of a monopoly and what constitutes proof of abuse of monopoly power and collusion. As economies become more exposed to foreign competition, the definition of the relevant market widens; and it may be appropriate to take a more tolerant view of 'cooperation' among domestic firms. The economic effects of monopoly can also be the subject of dispute.

The principles of the EU's competition policy are contained in articles 85 to 94 of the Treaty of Rome. Since the Treaty of Amsterdam came into effect in 1999, these have been renumbered articles 81 to 90. To avoid confusion, we use the post-1999 numbering in this chapter. These articles cover both uncompetitive behaviour between firms and state aids that affect trade between member states. The objective of keeping the EU market open and free from distortion is addressed by two key articles, articles 81 and 82 (Box 7.1).

Article 81 prohibits *restrictive agreements* relating to price, market shares or production controls, *unless specifically exempted or licensed*. Exemptions can be given by the Commission if the restrictive agreements can be shown to (a) improve efficiency, (b) allow consumers a 'fair' share of the resulting benefits, and (c) do not eliminate competition entirely. The exemption clause has been frequently and successfully invoked.[6] For example, selective and exclusive dealerships for new car sales are permitted by virtue of this clause (Box 7.2).

---

5 Within the EU, national competition rules coexist with the common EU regime but, in the event of conflict between them, EU law takes precedence. For a good summary, see W. Santer, 'Competition policy' in A. El Agraa (ed.), *The European Union: Economics and Policies* (Financial Times Prentice Hall, 6th edn, 2001).

6 Case of *Vacuum Interrupters* [(0) 1977 L48/32]. The Commission declared the joint venture a restrictive agreement, but granted an exemption on the grounds that technological and economical progress would be enhanced by the joint venture.

Box 7.2

Exclusive dealing in the European motor trade

EU law bans any agreement between firms intended to prevent or distort competition. But 'selective and exclusive dealerships' (SEDs), the arrangements which govern all new car sales, are exempt under what is known as Rule 123/85. A typical European new car dealer offers models of only one, or a few select, makes. The customer cannot cross the street and buy the same car more cheaply because, by agreement, the next dealer will probably be located several miles away. The rule also applies to spare parts. Manufacturers can refuse to sell to wholesalers or can 'advise' their equipment producers against reaching agreements with them unless certain terms are agreed.

SEDs are examples of what economists call *vertical restraints*. Vertical restraints involve agreements between producers of complementary goods. They are distinguished from *horizontal restraints* which relate to agreements between producers of the same good or close substitutes. Thus if a car manufacturer places a limit on what retailers sell and how they sell the product, that is a vertical restraint. Agreements between car manufacturers themselves as regards price or market share is a horizontal restraint. Generally, vertical restraints are considered innocuous for competition (but see below for qualification). By contrast, there is a presumption that horizontal restraints are harmful to competition.

An SED typically specifies what retailers sell and how they sell it. Under 'selective dealership', a producer uses only those retailers who agree to support its brand in specified ways – perhaps by giving information to potential customers or providing after-sales service to those who buy. 'Exclusive dealerships', as the name suggests, commit retailers to selling one brand. They often go hand-in-hand with 'full-line forcing', under which retailers stock a manufacturer's whole range, not just one or two products.

Other vertical restraints include 'exclusive territories', which limit a retailer's sales to a particular area (hotel firms or fast-food chains rarely put two outlets in the same part of town) and 'franchise fees', which are sometimes paid to manufacturers for the right to sell their wares or to put their logos above the shop door (some high street shops are run this way). Producers may also try to fix retail prices, either by controlling discounts or by demanding that retailers sell minimum quantities of their products.

At first sight, these devices look like a conspiracy against consumers. Consumers can indeed be disadvantaged by vertical restraints. Yet sometimes they can also end up better-off, because contracts with vertical restraints are often the most efficient way for producers to get their products to the customer. In other words, anti-competitive practices can sometimes yield large efficiency gains.

A manufacturing firm can sell through an independent retailer or by setting up its own retail network. At one end, independent retailers may have stronger incentives than employees to maximise retail profits and they may know more about local markets. Retailers may like this arrangement too, because they keep some strategic leeway. Yet, it is often inefficient to sell to entirely independent retailers.

The reason for this inefficiency is that retailers, left to themselves, may set prices higher than producers (and consumers) would like. Suppose producers sold their goods to retailers at a uniform wholesale price. If retailers have some monopoly power in their local markets, they can set retail prices above wholesale prices (plus retail costs). But manufacturers would

Box 7.2 continued

like prices to be lower: that would expand retail sales, reduce unit costs, and boost the manufacturer's sales and profits. One of several ways around this is to demand that retailers pay a franchise fee for the right to sell the product and, in return, to cut wholesale prices. Payment of a franchise fee does not affect the dealer's profit-maximising level of sales. But a lower wholesale price does, and gives an incentive to the dealer to cut the retail price and raise sales volume.

Independent retailers may also give customers less information on the brand or spend less on after-sales service than the manufacturer would wish. They may be unduly influenced by competition from other franchisees selling the same brand. To circumvent this problem, manufacturers can impose quality standards. Also, by granting each dealer an exclusive territory, they ensure that the dealer has an incentive to build up a reputation for quality. This is the justification for selective dealership in the case of the automobile trade.

Complaints against vertical restraints might still be valid in that consumers' range of choice is being restricted. However, if there are many competing producers, retailers, even with exclusive territories, do not have much market power. True, they face no competition from others selling the same brand. But other local retailers are selling competing brands, curbing their ability (and that of producers) to exploit consumers.

If there are few brands – or if brands are not close substitutes – vertical restraints can keep competition out and prices up. Retailers with exclusive dealerships and territories do not have to compete. Without these arrangements, they would have to fight for custom.

Exclusive dealerships commit retailers to selling one product range. They often go hand-in-hand with 'full-line forcing' and 'exclusive territories'. These vertical restraints appear contrary to the public interest, but they are often a means of ensuring good after-sales service and lower price. Hence the rationale for exempting them under the competition regime. This exemption was extended for a further ten years in 1994. Current economic thinking stresses the importance of market structure. The more competition between brands, the more likely that pro-competitive and efficiency effects of vertical restraints will outweigh any anti-competitive effects.

Sources: 'Restraints of trade?', © *The Economist*, London 24 September 1994; D. Salvadori, 'The automobile industry', in D. Mayes, *The European Challenge: Industry's response to the 1992 programme* (Hemel Hempstead: Harvester Wheatsheaf, 1991). For an updated account, see L. Peeperhorn, 'The economics of vertical restraints', *Competition Policy Newsletter* (Brussels: European Community, June 1998).

Article 82 addresses the problem of *abuse of dominant position*. It outlaws unfair trading practices, unjustified tie-in clauses and similar arrangements. Concepts such as 'dominant position' and 'market abuse' have been subjected to different interpretations. Some indication of the complexity of the issues is given in the summary of the judgment in the *Woodpulp* case (Box 7.3).

These articles apply in principle to vertical as well as horizontal agreements between firms. *Vertical restraints* (VRs) are contracts between firms at different stages of the production chain that specify more detailed commitments on the parties than simply to exchange a given quantity of goods or services at a given price per unit. Examples include selective and exclusive dealerships (SEDs)

Box 7.3

EU competition law – the *Woodpulp* case

According to the Commission, whenever a producer has charged the same price as another producer for a given product in a given region and during a given quarter, it must, in principle, be regarded as having 'concerted' i.e. colluded with the other producer. But parallel conduct cannot be regarded as furnishing proof of collusion unless collusion constitutes the only plausible explanation for such conduct. Also, although Article 85 of the Treaty prohibits any form of collusion which distorts competition, it does not deprive economic operators of the right to adapt themselves intelligently to the existing and anticipated conduct of their competitors. (European Court of Justice ruling on *Woodpulp*, 1993)

This case gives the flavour of the problems that can arise in trying to resolve difficult economic issues in a legal framework. In March 1993, the European Court of Justice finally closed one of the longest running cases in competition law, the *Woodpulp* case, nine years after the original decision by the Commission! This was a case where the Commission had found that a group of Scandinavian, Canadian and US woodpulp producers had operated a price cartel over a sustained period. The parties challenged the Commission decision.

First, they challenged it on grounds of jurisdiction. However, because the arrangements challenged in the decision had *effects* within the Community, the Court found that the Commission had been perfectly entitled to make a ruling on it, regardless of the place of origin of the parties or of where the agreements were actually drawn up and signed.

Second, the parties claimed that 'parallel price behaviour' did not amount to collusion. They claimed that it could be explained by the operation of legitimate market behaviour. This turned into the key issue.

Eventually, the Court commissioned two reports by economic consultants to help them come to a ruling on the case. The first report dealt with parallelism of prices and, in particular, whether the evidence justified the findings of parallelism of announced prices and transactions prices. The second report analysed the woodpulp market during the period in question.

According to these reports, the system of price announcements agreed between the parties to the arrangement was introduced in response to the producers' customers. The quarterly cycle was the result of a compromise between the consumer's desire for a degree of predictability as regards the price of pulp and the producer's desire not to miss any opportunities to make a profit in the event of a strengthening of the market. The simultaneity or near-simultaneity of the price announcements could be explained as reflecting a high degree of market transparency.

On the parallelism of announced prices, the experts concluded that this could be plausibly explained by market conditions rather than collusion. The market in question was oligopolistic on the producers' side and also on the customers' side. This led to a situation where prices were slow to react in the short term.

On the basis of the expert reports, the Court upheld the appeal by the companies and quashed the fines imposed by the Commission.

Box 7.3 continued

This case illustrates the complexity of competition cases. The judicial process on competition cases can be protracted and uncertain. Note also that the remit of the economic consultants advising the Court was to discover whether a restrictive arrangement existed. Had they been asked to quantify the effects of such a possible arrangement, the exercise would have been even more prolonged than it was.

discussed in Box 7.2, retail price maintenance, service requirements e.g. undertakings to spend on advertising and after-sales service, and two part (non-linear) pricing involving a fixed charge and a fixed price per unit. VRs essentially involve agreements between producers of complementary goods. They are distinguished from *horizontal restraints* (HRs). HRs relate to agreements between producers at the same stage of the production chain.

Competition law tends to take a permissive view of VRs. The reason for this is that abuse of market power by one producer (say the car manufacturer) damages the producer of the complement (the dealer). Thus any limit to sales by the manufacturer to exploit monopoly power reduces sales and profits of the dealer. And vice versa in case of use of monopoly power by the dealers. Hence both parties are driven by self-interest to an efficient outcome, very much in the spirit of Adam Smith, and no intervention by the Competition Authority is needed. In judging VRs, the EU takes a permissive view provided efficiency is in fact achieved. Also it adds two other criteria: (a) equity – protection of small enterprises, and (b) promotion of market integration – hence any measure preventing 'parallel' imports (imports of the same product from different national markets) is unfavourably regarded. The more inter-brand competition in the market, the less the danger of a VR being in breach of competition law.

Another instrument for maintaining competition is *control of mergers* regulation. A merger comes within the scope of this regulation if it exceeds a certain size – the aggregate world turnover of the merged units must exceed ECU 5000 million and the Community-wide turnover of at least two of the undertakings must exceed ECU 250 million. Proposed mergers have to be notified to the Commission. Sometimes they are rejected, sometimes approved, and on other occasions approved with qualifications (Box 7.4). Merger policy in the EU, as in many other countries, is predicated on the assumption that, provided no significant increase in market power ensues, mergers are efficiency-enhancing. Entrepreneurs are considered better equipped to judge the future economies to be gained from a merger than outsiders – though they are far from being infallible in this regard, as we have seen. (According to one authority, the 'only effect' of many mergers is 'to increase company size and to produce economic inefficiency'![7])

7 D.C. Mueller, 'Mergers', in *The New Palgrave Dictionary of Money and Finance* (London: Macmillan, 1992), p. 705.

Box 7.4

Mergers with conditions

In January 1996, after five months' investigation, the Commission approved the proposed merger between Kimberly-Clark Corporation (USA) and the Scott Paper Company (USA). These firms are major tissue paper and related product manufacturers. Together they will become the No. 1 tissue paper producer at both the world and the European levels.

However, this approval was granted only after the parties agreed to make substantial modifications of the merger in the United Kingdom and Ireland. The modifications were required because the two firms had control of two leading brands of consumer tissue products (Kleenex and Andrex), as well as a large share of private-label products (i.e. sold under the retailer's name). The original proposal would have led to the creation of a dominant position and a sharp diminution of inter-brand competition.

The conditions for approval of the merger were that the parties had to agree:

(a) to divest all of Kimberly-Clark's branded consumer toilet tissue business sold under the Kleenex brands in the UK and Irish markets. The new purchaser would be allowed to use these brand names for a maximum 10-year period.
(b) Scott's brands for facials and hankies also to be sold and the Andrex trademark for consumer facials and hankies not to be used for an indefinite duration.
(c) Kimberly-Clark's 80,000-ton tissue facility at Prudhoe (England) to be divested. This will reduce the firm's share of tissue paper production capacity to 40 per cent.

According to the Commission, had action to force divestment not been taken, 'consumers would have had to pay too high prices for basic tissue paper products and the benefits to consumers of further innovation and product quality improvement would have been lost'.

Source: Competition Policy Newsletter (Spring 1996), p. 27.

State aids appear prominently in the industrial and regional policies of many member states. Government aid which distorts competition and which affects cross-border trade is regarded as incompatible with the common market. The main thrust of policy has been to ensure that state aids are transparent, monitored and subjected to upper limits. Any new state aids likely to affect trade between member states have to be notified and approved by the Commission. The Commission has tried to curtail the amount of subsidies and other indirect supports provided by member states. Of course, political and economic considerations can conflict on these issues, and the Commission has been criticised for being overly influenced by political pressures, particularly where powerful state companies are involved (such as the state airlines).

The European Commission sometimes acts on its own initiative and at other times responds to complaints from the public or competitors concerning the abuse of monopoly power. Sometimes action is triggered by tip-offs from insiders.

Its investigative powers are considerable. These include 'dawn' raids whereby its officials arrive without prior notice at the premises of companies in order to search for evidence. Executives can have their offices searched, an alarming experience, and can be subjected to oral questioning even before any charges are brought against the company. Telephone print-outs, possession of competitors' business cards and even invitations to business lunches can be used as indirect evidence of 'concertation'. The scale of the dawn raids can be considerable. A dawn raid was carried out in April 1995 on the offices of forty newsprint producers in seven European countries suspected of price collusion. After all this, the Commission can order firms to refrain from certain practices which it deems anti-competitive. It can also impose fines of up to 10 per cent of a company's world-wide turnover, as some major EU firms have discovered to their cost. Fines of ECU 248 million (equivalent to about 6 per cent of turnover), for example, were imposed on thirty-three European cement producers in November 1994, on the grounds that they used secret agreements to reduce price differences between them in order to protect their national markets. Prestigious companies such as Blue Circle (UK), Italcementi (Italy) and Lafarge (France) were among the accused.[8] (Box 7.5).

The European Commission has tackled the monopoly power of many public utilities by application of competition law combined with specific legislation. The Rail Directive of December 1991 is one of many examples of action to enhance competition in Europe's state-owned infrastructure companies. The Directive sought to introduce greater financial discipline and more operational competition within member states and across borders. National railways were pressed to separate track infrastructure from train operations and to produce transparent accounts revealing the respective costs and revenues attributable to *infrastructure* and to *services*. This approach was based on the belief that the provision of rail *services* on that infrastructure, for freight and passengers, can, and should, be opened to competitive tender. Germany's Deutsche Bahn has been split into three businesses: one for rail track, one for passengers and one for freight. The former British Rail was also split into a separate track-owning company, Railtrack, together with three rolling stock leasing companies and a plethora of franchise holders operating services alongside rival independent operators.[9] Similar initiatives were taken in the case of energy, telecoms and postal services.

In addition to the 1992 programme, the EU is committed to further trade liberalisation following the Uruguay Round (see Chapter 17). The expectation is that exposure to global competition – increasing the degree of contestability of the European market – will make European industry more efficient. More concentration and rationalisation at a domestic level may be a fall-out of this policy and need not necessarily be a cause of concern. A more open market is, by

---

8 This case has been appealed by the producers.
9 Some separation of track and service operations has been implemented in Scandinavia and New Zealand, among others. France is opposed on the grounds that separation involves loss of economies of vertical integration.

Box 7.5

The case of the cement industry

Competition is the underlying principle behind the single market and is paramount to building an integrated market between the European economies. The European Commission has the task of safeguarding the competitive climate. On occasion, it has taken a tough stance with firms or undertakings which it believes have violated EU competition law. Large penalties have been imposed on firms which breach these rules. At the same time, competition policy is heavily politicised, much more so in the EU than in the US.

The authorities usually learn of violations of competition law through voluntary notification or through complaints from aggrieved third parties.

Following extensive investigation, penalties were imposed on a cement producers' association, called CEMBUREAU, during 1994. It was ordered to pay a fine amounting to ECU 248 million, equivalent to 6 per cent of its members' turnover.

CEMBUREAU is the European Cement Association. Its members included eight national cement associations and 33 European cement producers, among them prestigious companies such as Blue Circle (UK), Italcementi (Italy) and Lafarge (France). The firms accounted for almost half of the Community supply. Supply in the cement industry is particularly concentrated at a national level, with only one producer in operation in some countries. Economies of scale and high entry/exit costs make the industry prone to high levels of concentration. This might explain why the alleged collusion can occur, despite comparatively high (33) numbers of firms. Usually, a cement works is located close to its raw materials, due to the heavy transport costs. However, investigation showed that varying cost structures in different firms made exports profitable for some firms. Hence there was an incentive to arrange market-sharing deals and take joint action to prevent 'disruption' of the market. In the case of CEMBUREAU, the Commission alleged that the members of the cartel had agreed to confine sales within their own national borders, allowing each producer to maintain their dominant position in their national market. The nature of the alleged infringements originated from market-sharing agreements, transnational restrictive practices and restrictive practices relating to exports. EU law forbids any agreement or collaboration between businesses or individuals which could affect the trade between member states.

The investigation took five years to complete, which shows how difficult it can be to gather evidence of anti-competitive practices. The case is being appealed in the European Court.

Source: 'Press releases issued on the most important developments', *EC Competition Policy Newsletter*, Vol. 1, No. 3 (Autumn/Winter 1994).

definition, a more competitive market and the competition authorities' job is done for them by the market. This saves on the high compliance costs attached to enforcement of competition by legal means. However, as the global reach of firms in many industries increases, the need for a supranational competition authority will become more acute.

Although this section deals only with EU practice, competition law is applied with increasing rigour across a growing number of countries. The 1998 Competition Act, regarded as the biggest shake-up in British competition law in twenty-five years, brought UK competition law into line with that of the European Union for the first time. It gave sweeping new powers of investigation to the Office of Fair Trading (OFT) and opened the way for massive fines if companies break the rules. Directors and employees can be sent to prison for obstructing investigations. The OFT has been given powers to demand information and carry out dawn raids if it suspects anti-competitive behaviour. Interestingly, earlier that year the loss to the UK economy from monopolistic behaviour was estimated at 1 per cent of GDP or about £7.6 billion in 1996 prices (*Journal of Industrial Economics*). In 1999, two of the top European companies, Roche of Switzerland and BASF of Germany, were fined a record $725 billion by the US authorities for their part in a nine-year world-wide arrangement to control the market in vitamins. A former executive was sentenced to jail for four months and fined $100,000 for his part in the cartel. 1999 was also the year that the mighty Microsoft ran foul of the US anti-trust authorities. Judge Thomas Jackson began his 207-page ruling with a four-word sentence 'Microsoft enjoys monopoly power' (its Windows operating system runs on eight out of ten personal computers). He went on to rule that the company used his power to eliminate competition from a range of rivals across the industry, particularly from Netscape. Needless to say, Microsoft has challenged this finding. Whatever the outcome, these cases demonstrate how essential it is for executives to be aware of the rules of competition in their own country and in foreign countries they do business with.

Competition and globalisation

The increasing openess of national markets is having the effect of imposing competition. This increased globalisation of national economies is having several different effects. First, high concentration and rationalisation at a domestic level need not necessarily be a cause of concern. A more open market is by definition a more competitive market. Openness may encourage such concentration but the openness itself is doing the competition authorities' job for them automatically. Second, national industries are becoming more sensitive of the need for a 'level playing field'. If country A has strict competition rules and country B has lax rules, this could mean that B's producers are able to set up arrangements to reserve B's markets for themselves, while enjoying free access to A's market. This will not seem fair to A's producers. For this reason pressure is growing for similar competition rules to be introduced in countries participating in world trade. Third, as the global reach of firms in many industries extends, what can be done to prevent abuse of monopoly power by giant multinationals? Mega mergers between companies in different parts of the world create corporations of global dimensions. Even when not having an actual production presence in countries, firms can form strategic alliances that enable them to penetrate foreign markets with international partners. This is particularly true of information technology, entertainment, air transport and pharmaceutical industries, but high levels of global concentration are also found in less glamorous products such as tea and bananas. In these circumstances, coordinated action by competition authorities on an international scale is necessary if the enhanced opportunities which free trade provides are not to be undermined. The formulation of global competition laws is high on the agenda for many countries, including those of the EU.

7.3 Privatisation

Privatisation has become an integral part of most countries' pro-competition programme and has now become a familiar feature of new consensus economic policy. It is defined as the transfer of state owned assets to private control. This can be achieved through direct sale of the assets to the private sector. Another possibility is to transfer the administration of these assets to the private sector (by competitive tender for example) but for the state to retain ownership. This section focuses on privatisation in the former sense.

The move to privatisation began in the UK and New Zealand in the 1980s; it spread to continental Europe in the 1990s and is now taking a front seat in a large number of developing countries ranging from India to Morocco. The US was a significant absentee from this trend, largely because it had so few nationalised industries to privatise. World-wide revenues from privatisation amounted to $600 billion between 1990 and 1999, two-thirds originating in industrial countries.

Reasons for privatising

The motivations for privatisation have been diverse. Underlying most of them has been a certain disillusion with the capacity of nationalised industries to deliver efficient services to the public and to achieve the social goals they were set up to attain. For state companies the principal agent problem discussed in Chapter 5 was particularly acute. The objectives of the politicians who owned the companies were often conflicting and volatile, the government department in charge of the company added another layer of complexity, with the result that management had no clear objectives and no sustained incentive to perform. One major objective of privatisation therefore was to make the company more efficient and to change its ethos.

Second, closely related to the above, governments wished to introduce competition into sectors hitherto dominated by state utilities. If this was done while the companies remained in state ownership, their chances of succesfully coping with competition would be increased by being run by the private sector rather than the public sector.

Third, many nationalised industries were notorious losers of money. The liberalisation of trade threatened even further losses. Selling them was seen as a way of stopping the haemorrhage from the current state budget. Fiscal benefits could also accrue on the state's capital account from the sale of the assets. Obviously the proceeds from sale of profitable state companies or from those with potential to earn more under private sector management such as telecoms and energy utilities promised to be especially large. The proceeds from privatisation yielded £65 billion to the UK exchequer up to 1997. During the five years, 1995–99, Italy's privatisation proceeds came to $80 billion. According to OECD estimates, revenues from privatisation during the period 1990–98 amounted to 24 per cent of Hungary's 1998 GDP, 20 per cent of Portugal's and 15 per cent of New Zealand's. Many developing countries saw privatisation as a golden one-off opportunity to reduce public sector debt and to set in motion a lower tax environment without damaging increases in budget deficits.

Fourth, politicians, supported by public opinion, became converted to the view that the balance of the mixed economy had shifted excessively towards the public sector. This belief was fortified by the abuse of power by many public sector trade unions with frequent use of the strike weapon and outmoded attachment to demarcation and other restrictive practices in the workplace.

Former communist countries have been profoundly affected by the privatisation of their economies. However, the origin of their privatisation programmes and the context in which these are being implemented are obviously very different to those in the West. For one thing, these countries were being transformed from a situation in which virtually the entire economy was state-owned. For example, by 1995, Treuhandanstalt, the agency in charge of privatisation in Eastern Germany, had privatised some 12,000 firms, about 85 per cent of all firms in the previous regime operating under state ownership. In many of these countries, governments had large budget deficits and a limited capacity to raise revenues through higher taxes. Privatisation, to them, was seen as a way of disposing of loss-making entities and providing desperately needed revenues to the state.

There is something paradoxical about privatisation of state-owned companies in Western countries. After all, these companies were originally set up to resolve an economic problem not to cause one! Many were established in response to situations of private monopolies or of 'excessive' competition among private firms. Nationalisation was designed to encourage exploitation of scale economies and to ensure that monopoly profits, to the extent that they existed, would accrue to the state, which would distribute them in a socially optimal way. In retrospect these expected advantages failed to materialise. Too often nationalised firms abused their monopoly power. They gave bad service at high prices. They suffered extensive X-inefficiencies. Although they tended to 'featherbed' their employees, they were prone to surprisingly bad industrial relations. Against this background it is easy to believe a European Commission estimate that complete liberalisation of the European airline industry would bring about a 10 per cent decline in costs and prices, implying benefits of some $1 billion per year, obtained through lower pay costs, more efficient deployment of the workforce and lower overheads.[10]

---

10 F. McGowan and P. Seabright, 'Deregulating European airlines', *Economic Policy* (October 1989).

Effects of privatisation

Privatisation programmes come in diverse forms and many are of too recent vintage to determine their success or failure. Studies of the UK experience suggest a mixed bag of results. Some privatised companies have achieved a highly successful turnaround, notably British Telecom and British Airways, but the verdict on the privatisation of British Rail and the water industry is far less flattering. *The Economist* described the privatisation of the former as a disaster! Experience also differs between countries. In a highly generalised way, one might say that privatisation has been succsessful in the UK while unsuccessful in Russia.

The effects of privatisation can be evaluated under several headings: effects on *efficiency*, effects on *government revenue* and effects on *income distribution*.

A key consideration is the effect of privatisation on efficiency, i.e. on measured labour productivity or better still total factor productivity. The resultant fall in unit costs can be passed on to the consumer in terms of lower prices and better quality. In the UK, it was estimated that telephone charges fell by 35 per cent in real terms between 1984 and 1994. According to the US Department of Justice Antitrust Division Annual Report 1994, increased competition in the US telecoms industry hastened the introduction of fibre optic technology and spurred an increase in technological innovation. Electricity charges also declined in real terms. As a general rule, experience shows that the more competition in the privatised companies the greater the likelihood of a positive outcome. This is just as economic theory would predict. A policy environment that encourages long-run investment in the privatised companies is also important.

The effect of government revenue is more complex than might appear. In the case of an outright sale, the gain to the state cannot be equated with the sale price. The state has just replaced one asset (the state company) with another (cash). To calculate the net financial gain to the state, we must compare the present value of the stream of net revenue expected from the firm had it remained in state ownership with the proceeds from the sale. (The concept of present discounted value is explained in Chapter 10.) The price paid for the company is thus a crucial variable. If under-priced, the privatisation programme could end up worsening instead of improving government finances in the long term. Also there must be some assessment of how this extra cash accruing to the goverment is being used. It is being spent on building up military power or on consumer handouts or on long-term investments for the future?

Last, one must consider the income distribution effects. There are at least four parties to consider: the state, employees of the privatised firms, the consumer, and the new owners. The mode of privatisation has an important bearing on the outcome. Share flotation is one mode, often associated with a certain predetermined allocation to existing employees (British Telecom 1984, British Gas 1986). Direct sale to private sector business has also been used (National Coal Board 1994, Rover cars to British Aerospace). Management buy-outs are another possibility (National Freight Corporation 1982 and several bus companies). In each case, careful analysis is needed in order to assess the resultant income distribution effect. It is obviously easy for the state that is strapped for cash to be induced into selling too cheap (as happened in Russia and in many fomer Communist countries). Also shares can be sold too cheaply to the public in order to curry popular favour or to ensure that the flotation will be a 'success', as happened in several Western European countries.

There is little doubt that in most instances privatisation has brought benefits to the consumer, not just in terms of lower price but also in terms of improved quality of service and efficiency. There are many areas of the economy to which the ethos of a state company is particularly unsuited and where privatisation has yielded unambiguous benefits. State-owned hotels and restaurants, for example, or manufacturing industries, where quickness of response and an entrepreneurial approach is especially important. State farms, created on the grounds of economies of scale, have never become successful enterprises. To some extent, governments have voted with their feet. The number and scope of privatisation programmes around the world shows that finance ministries are convinced that the potential benefits exceed any potential losses. Experience to date would support this verdict. But it will take time before the dynamic efficiency effects of privatisation can be fully evaluated.

7.4 Regulation

Regulatory reform and natural monopolies

Regulatory reform is designed to promote competition, regardless of whether the industry is in state or private ownership. In principle it is a separate issue from privatisation. Yet, in practice, reform of government regulation of industries, particularly state-owned utilities such as elasticity, gas and telecoms, has been associated with the issue of privatisation. For that reason we introduce the subject at this stage of the discussion.

Suppose a state-owned company exists in a context where competition is not apparently possible. Economies of scale are so preponderant that it is not profitable for more than one firm to operate in the industry. This is the case of a *natural monopoly*. The state may still wish to privatise in the hope of securing a change in the 'managerial culture' of the organisation, or to add to government revenues, even though the privatised firm will continue to retain monopoly power. How do costs and benefits stack up in this instance? Clearly there are benefits from privatisation, but these will be achieved only if there is also some state regulation of the privatised entity. How should the privatised monopoly be regulated? The economics of regulation now enters the picture.

Natural monopolies were until recently regarded as dominant in the energy, transport and telecom industries. In addition, private sector competitors were often excluded by law from trying to compete with the state monopoly in these sectors. But banning competitors would be redundant if economies of scale were really that powerful, so the existence of legal restrictions suggests that the monopoly was not so 'natural' after all. When such is the case, one solution is to remove the restrictions on entry, subject to the new entrants satisfying some basic minimum operating criteria such as prudential reserve ratios, safety provisions, and so on. Privatisation can then proceed, though whether *deregulation* comes before or succeeds privatisation can have an important bearing on how much revenue is obtained from the sale.

Deregulation has been applied to many industries in addition to those controlled by state monopolies. Major changes have been made in the rules governing banks, stock broking, insurance, and radio and television boadcasting. These initiatives were inspired by belief in the merits of the free market. No less important was technological change. In some industries, it has made restrictions on new entrants unenforceable; in other it has made small production units more efficient. For example, technical advance has now made even very small electricity generating plants more efficient than previously. The combined effects of deregulation and technology have opened up many hitherto restricted markets. The resultant increase in contestability has brought about huge improvements in efficiency.

However, there remain some important sectors where the monopoly proves to be genuinely 'natural' and where consequently the degree of competition is limited. There are two major steps in dealing with the situation. The first step is to break down or to 'unbundle' the services provided by the monopoly into component parts so as to isolate the core natural monopoly element in the industry. In electricity, for example, the real monopoly element is not power generation or power distribution but the transport of electricity through a network. By unbundling the industry into its different potentially competitive and natural monopoly components, efficiencies can be secured through the market system. The potentially competitive parts can be sold to the private sector, or put into competitive play by out-contracting or competitive tendering.

The second step is how to deal with the natural monopoly element. This involves three interrelated strands: pricing, access and quality of service. We briefly review each off these, recognising that the relevance of each aspect will differ according to sector and the period of time since the liberalisation process was begun.

Pricing

Incentive regulation refers to the design of incentives to ensure that producers keep prices and costs as low as possible. The underlying assumption is that costs are not given but are influenced by the incentives set by the regulatory authorities. If there was no regulation the privatised monopoly might well slip into the same bad habits as the state company it replaced. Whether the new regulation achieves a superior outcome to direct provision of the good or service by the state company depends on the effectiveness of the regulatory system.

In the UK, following the privatisation of telecoms, gas, water, electricity and railways, regulatory bodies were set up for each industry (with acronyms such as

Ofgen, Ofgas, Ofwat and so on). Their task was to prevent the abuse of monopoly power and to find ways of promoting competition. This sounds easy, but regulators frequently get into hot water in trying to achieve this objective.

There are several ways of regulating a privatised industry with strong monopoly elements.

(a) Price = Marginal cost

One simple way would be to oblige the monopoly firm to charge a price equal to marginal cost, and provide a subsidy for any ensuing loss. The drawback is the cost of the subsidy and the difficulty of determining marginal cost.

(b) Break-even or average return on capital

Alternatively the regulator could insist on a price that allows the firm to just break even. This eliminates 'monopoly' profits but leaves wide open the opportunity to reap the rewards of monopoly in other guises (such as the quiet life and X-inefficiency). Some regulators use a formula related to *rate of return on capital* which the monopoly would not be permitted to exceed. This avoids the problem of direct price control, but has the disadvantage of reducing the incentive to firms to minimise costs, once the permitted profit rate has been attained. Rate of return controls have been applied extensively in the US. Not surprisingly there have been frequent disputes over the definition and measurement of rates of return in these cases.

(c) RPI minus X

Another possibility is to set maximum prices. The UK authorities have taken this approach. Various types of price-capping formulas have been used, known as '*RPI minus X*', wherby the regulator permits the firm's price to rise by no more than x percentage points below the retail (consumer) price index (RPI). In a multi-product monopoly, such as telecoms, the regulator may opt for a tariff-basket method, whereby the authorities decide which products are placed in the basket and how the various prices are to be weighted. This usually means permitting lower prices for price-elastic services (say international phone calls by business customers) and relatively higher prices on the price-inelastic part of their active (say domestic customers). While providing flexibility, regulation can be highly controversial. The public will often perceive such pricing structures as unfair, even if based on sound economic principles. Where the output is more homogeneous, such as gas and electricity, the regulator may use an average revenue target, whereby the predicted rise in average revenue in the firm is not permitted to exceed RPI minus X.

A key problem of incentive regulation is to determine the efficiency factor x. If x is set too low, the firm will make excessively large profits ('rents') and the regulator will lose face. If it is set too high, the firm will become unviable. In deciding on the right value of x, the regulator may have to be guided by the expert, but hardly disinterested, knowledge of the regulated firm. Relations between the regulated and the regulator may become too close and cordial (this phenomenon is called *regulatory capture*). Another problem is that the formula could act as a disincentive to efficiency if more efficient performance were to lead to subsequent upward revision of *x*. In practice, rate of return considerations are implicit in setting *x*. Even the most expert and experienced regulator can make mistakes. The UK electricity regulator, for example, had to undertake a full-scale review less than a year after establishing new price-caps because the regulated firms' financial performance was much better than estimated. Opportunistic behaviour by the regulator can be highly destabilising.

Access and quality of service

Each of the above techniques refers to ways by which the regulator can prevent abuse of monopoly power in the form of excessive charges to the consumer and excessive profits. But monopoly power can also be curbed by determining the conditions of access to the service or sector. For example, in the case of network operators in electricity, gas, telecoms or air transport, the monopolist has an obvious incentive to provide access to its network on unfavourable terms. To counteract this, the regulator must devise and open a fair and transparent licensing scheme for new entrants. Considerable research has gone into establishing how *access charges* for connection to networks should be determined. The *efficient component pricing rule* (ECPR) has been developed to deal with such situations. It provides that new entrants must pay an amount to cover the marginal cost of access to the network plus some contribution towards fixed costs of setting it up which were borne by the original state firm. This rule has many flaws, and there is no simple rule of thumb for determining the relevant fixed and marginal costs. Another factor here is that some providers may have universal service obligations, i.e. an obligation to provide a minimum set of services of specified quality to all users at an affordable price. The regulator must also have regard to the quality of service offered by existing and new operators to the consumer and by the network owner to competing operators. The existing operator must not be allowed to favour its own downstream (retail) arm over competitors. Finally, there is usually provision for complaints procedures and for the development of customer charters.

The above considerations demonstrate that regulation may be necessary, and better than no regulation, but it is by no means costless. Regulators do not come cheaply. They need large staffs of economists and lawyers. Regulators can be of variable quality and regulatory capture is an ever-present danger. Their decisions can always be subject to long and expensive appeal, just as in the case of competition law.[11] Regulation cannot be considered a satisfactory substitute for

---

11 Inevitably, decisions on how to deal with monopolies have an arbitrary element. In the UK, these decisions can be appealed if the regulated firm considers them unduly harsh. 'Taming monopolies', *The Economist* (13 August 1994); M. Beesley (ed.), *Regulating Utilities: The way forward* (Institute of Economic Affairs, August 1994).

competition. The high cost of imposing regulation underlines the importance of competition as an alternative, more efficient, policing device for curbing excessive profits. In short, the best regulator will often be one that succeeds in making itself redundant. Over time, emphasis must be placed on deregulation and exposure to international competition as the most efficient way forward.

7.5 Conclusions

When thinking of competition most businesses see their problem as one of excess competition, not a lack of it. This is understandable from the perspective of an individual firm already established in an industry. Competitive pressure has increased in most industrial societies. But the notion of competition being 'excessive' sits uneasily with much economic thinking on the role of free markets. Competition affords opportunities for new firms to enter the industry. From these firms' perspective, the problem may appear one of too little, not too much competition. Competitive pressure gives firms an incentive to search more vigorously for ways of protecting their domestic market, by developing market niches and, if necessary, by circumventing competition legislation. As a result, new entrants to an industry can be deterred by unfair trade practices, and financially weaker (often small) firms can be discriminated against in the process, unless protected by law. The consumer, too, can suffer discrimination as larger firms build up their war chests and tighten their hold on their market share. In short, despite the increased openness of industrial economies, competition policy is still needed.

The new competition requires competition policy that ideally should be transparent, easy to implement and predictable. The need for case-by-case assessment, taking account of each market's special features, can result in complex legal cases and much uncertainty. Competition policy is not a flawless set of precepts which can impose competition in a costless way. It can be expensive and inefficient to enforce and can be subverted and distorted. Yet, for all that, the secretary general of Unice, the federation of European industry, reflected the weight of business opinion in his assertion that *the essential corollary of competitiveness [is] strong competition policy.*[12]

State-owned enterprises in formerly non-traded sectors of the economy – telecoms, transport, energy and public utilities – have become a focus for competition policy in recent years. These enterprises were once regarded as 'natural' monopolies, but thinking has changed. Governments have become convinced of the efficiency gains that can be obtained through a more market-oriented framework. The European Commission has been particularly active in promoting competition in these sectors through the use of competition law.

Competition policy has been further bolstered by setting limits on the amount of state aid provided by member states to various industrial and regional initiatives. This type of action is welcomed by the weaker member states because

---

12 Reported in *The Financial Times* (5 December 1994).

they are unable to afford the cost of matching the subsidies offered by richer member states. The EU's strategic policy to favour competition is also evident in its support for SMEs.

A degree of tension between competition and industrial policy is to be expected. Prior to the Second World War, cartelisation was seen as a way of building up more efficient and technically progressive industries in Germany and Switzerland. Japan also had a tradition of looking with suspicion on 'excessive' competition because of its possible detrimental effects on an industry's capacity to exploit fully the economies of scale. According to one authority, the Japanese authorities feared 'excessive' competition as much as monopoly as a potential source of inefficiency.[13] Their predilection for limiting competition and encouraging mergers, vertical and horizontal firm groupings, and inter-firm operating agreements, has been fundamentally at odds with anti-trust policy. In the case of the automobile industry, for example, the Ministry for International Trade and Industry (MITI) sought to limit production to one firm and, failing that, a target of 'at most' three firms was set. It proved impossible to restrict competition in this way, however. The vigorous competition between domestic firms that prevailed in postwar Japan proved to be an important source of vitality for the Japanese economy. Yet, to this day, some countries maintain a more tolerant approach to cartels than would be countenanced by most European countries. Keeping the domestic market contestable often entails an element of compromise between the objective of avoiding market dominance and allowing a technically efficient size of firm.

The suggestion has been made that internal competition rules should be extended to incorporate an international body of rules on competition law, under the framework of the World Trade Organisation (see Chapter 17). In a globalising economy, stronger enforcement against the abuse of monopoly power by powerful multinationals will need to be established.

Competition policy, by correcting market distortions, is designed to maintain the efficiency of the market system. Firms need to be careful that they do not infringe competition law. Economics and law interact very closely in relation to market power, and managerial decisions on restructuring, mergers and acquisitions should take this into account.

---

13 R. Komiya, *The Japanese Economy: Trade, industry and government*, University of Tokyo Press, 1990), p. 297. For an early treatment of 'excessive' competition, see also K. Rothschild, 'The waste of competition', in E.H. Chamberlin (ed.), *Monopoly and Competition and their Regulation* (London: Macmillan; New York: St Martin's Press, 1954).

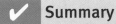

Summary

1. Competition law derives motivation and sustenance from economic principles. But putting these principles into a legally coherent framework is not easy. Application of competition law can be complicated, uncertain and highly expensive.

2. EU competition law applies to restrictive agreements, abuse of dominant position, control of mergers and state aids. The European Commission sometimes acts on its own initiative and at other times acts in response to complaints. It has played a very proactive role in introducing competition into Europe's state-owned service industry monopolies such as telecoms, post, air and rail transport, and energy.

3. There are several motives for privatisation, only one of which is the promotion of competition. Fiscal and political considerations also figure largely in the cost–benefit calculations. Privatisation programmes, like competition policy, are being introduced in conjunction with new consensus policies. On balance, they are seen as a way of improving the structure of the economy. Evidence to date suggests that they have, on the whole, proved successful in raising efficiency. But the privatisation experience has not been universally beneficial.

4. Regulatory reform is another key element in a pro-competition policy. The regulator has the task of setting objectives and targets for profits and prices. There is no easy formula to guide action in this area and the performance of the regulator has proven a contentious issue. In Britain, there has been sustained criticism of the regulators for allowing privatised firms to earn too much profit, pay over-generous executive salaries and provide poor quality service. This has stimulated interest in finding ways of replacing regulation by market forces – by de-bundling the services of such natural monopolies and exposing them to competition.

Questions for discussion

1. Suppose a group of firms organises a market-sharing agreement. They arrange not to compete with each other on their local markets. What would be the effect of such an agreement on the industry's profits? Why should a competition authority object? What arguments might the chief executive of the new group use to defend the agreement?

2. Why is it necessary to have competition legislation? What would prevent market forces from eroding the market power of a monopoly or oligopoly?

3. Innovation is a core ingredient of faster economic growth. What contribution can competition policy make to encouraging innovation?

4. Comment on the motivations for privatisation in your country and compare them with those outlined in this chapter.

5. What gains can be expected from a policy of privatisation? Which, if any, of these gains arise because of the transfer from public ownership to private ownership? Do you agree with the argument that what really matters is that competition is introduced or extended as a result of the privatisation?

6. Suppose a state-owned monopoly has been privatised. After privatisation, the problem of regulating the now private sector monopoly rests with a regulator appointed by the government. What guiding rules would you suggest for the regulator? Should the objective of the regulator be to call the shots in pricing or to try to introduce competition into the industry? Would the latter policy have the same effect in the long term as price controls would have in the short run?

7. According to the British Nobel prize-winner, Sir John Hicks, 'the best of all monopoly profits is a quiet life'. Compare this view with Schumpeter's hypothesis that firms with monopoly power were the driving force in innovation.

Exercises

1. Write a memo to a newcomer on a competition authority explaining why and under what circumstances monopoly is inferior, from an economic point of view, to competition. In your memo, comment on the EU Competition Commissioner's assertion that 'competition policy plays a key role in creating an environment that is favourable to business, this being crucial to lasting growth and job creation' (*XXVth Report on Competition Policy*, Brussels, 1995).

2. In the light of the following summary, comment on the motivation and effectiveness of the East German privatisation programme.

   In 1990 the Treuhandanstalt was the world's biggest holding company, with 12,370 businesses from coalpits to a Berlin horse-track. By the end of 1994, all but 100 had been sold or liquidated. The larger companies were sold mainly to West German or other European investors which were in the same industry. The smaller ones were bought by their managers.

   Initially, the Treuhandanstalt expected to raise DM 600 billion, but instead it raised only one tenth of that amount and left the state with a debt of DM 270 billion. It tried to pass on the businesses as a going concern. In many cases it had to pay investors – by assuming the company's debts or environmental liabilities – to take the companies off its hands. It was a buyer of management, technology and marketing skills for its companies rather than a seller of assets. It helped to subsidise investments in shipyards at a rate of DM 800,000 per job.

   Yet, even with this selective subsidisation, more than 60 per cent of the four million people Treuhandanstalt firms once employed have been made redundant. This loss is blamed on the overvalued currency and high labour costs (relative to East German productivity).

   A remarkable feature of Treuhandanstalt is the speed at which it worked and its short lifespan. It closed its doors in December 1994.

3. In March 1996, two Swiss giants of the drugs industry, Ciba and Sandoz, announced a merger. This was a merger of record size, the combined market values of the two companies being $64 billion (£42 billion). By contrast, the value of Glaxo's bid for Wellcome in 1995 amounted to only £9 billion.

    After the merger, the new company, Novartis, would rank as the world's second largest drug company, next to Merck and ahead of Roche and Johnson & Johnson, with a 4.4 per cent share of the prescription drugs industry.

    The case for the merger was that (a) synergies created by merging with another Swiss company would be greater than with an American, British or German giant, (b) the merger would create a single company with vast financial resources, (c) cost savings worth an estimated £1 billion could be made – mainly through shedding 10,000 jobs worldwide, (d) pressures on healthcare costs have brought profit margins under pressure and have forced drug companies to seek savings through consolidation, and (e) the rising cost and complexity of medical science means that huge sums (amounting to £1 billion per year in the case of Novartis) have to be spent on R&D.

    After the announcement of the merger, the stock of Ciba and Sandoz rose by 28 per cent and 20 per cent respectively.

    The deal had a wide-reaching impact on other firms in the industry. Shares in Zeneca and Warner Lambert rose because of their prospect of becoming takeover targets. Shares in companies such as Glaxo fell because the market suspected it might make a bid for other firms in response to the Swiss merger.

    The chief executive of Zeneca, a firm with a market value of some £30 billion and 1.4 per cent of the prescription drugs market, commented that large size is irrelevant because success in this industry depends on scientific innovation and there is no evidence that R&D productivity increases with size. Small companies such as Astra of Sweden and Amgen of America had grown rapidly in the decade to 1996. But other industry experts argue that only giant firms will be able to survive in such a fast-changing, R&D intensive industry.

    (*Source*: *The Sunday Times*, 10 March 1996)

    (a) Comment on the possible benefits of the merger.
    (b) Evaluate the possible downsides of the merger.
    (c) Was the rise in the share prices of Ciba and Sandoz linked to the announced downsizing of the workforce? If so, could this be viewed as evidence of conflict of interest between capital and labour?
    (d) How do you explain the initial rise in Zeneca's share price?
    (e) What light does this example throw on the existence of economies and diseconomies of scale?

4. In Box 7.2, the statement is made that 'payment of a franchise fee [i.e. a fixed amount of money regardless how much of the product is sold] does not affect the dealer's profit-maximising level of sales. But a lower wholesale price does'. Explain this assertion with the aid of a diagram, using U-shaped cost curves.

5. Early in 2000, Brazil's Economic Defence Council, the anti-trust agency, was asked to approve a merger between Brazils' two top brewers to form a powerful new company AmBev (*Business Week*, 27 March 2000). The new company would have a 70 per cent share of the Brazilian beer market. The argument in favour of the merger was that scale

economies would enable AmBev to become sufficiently strong to withstand competition on the home market from imported beers and to prevent them being taken over separately by foreign multinationals. AmBev would also have the financial power to invest abroad and achieve multinational status itself. Brazil's number 3 brewer, Cervejarias Kaiser, objected that the merger would reduce competition and raise prices. The issue was a sensitive one, since an upsurge in foreign investment inflows had resulted in a sell off of large numbers of Brazilian-owned companies. Mergers were proposed in airlines and steel for reasons similar to those prompting the formation of AmBev. The Council approved the merger in March 2000. From an economic point of view, did it do the right thing?

Further reading

J.S. Bain's *Barriers to New Competition* (Cambridge, MA: Harvard University Press, 1956) is a classic, and still highly readable, source on this subject. For a good contemporary review, see D. Jacobson and B. Andréosso-Callaghan, *Industrial Economics and Organisation: A European perspective* (Maidenhead: McGraw-Hill, 1996). The reports of national competition authorities such as, in Britain, the Monopolies and Mergers Commission, are the best source of information on recent cases and will illustrate how cases are adjudicated on in practice. *Competition Policy Newsletter*, published by the European Competition Policy Directorate, contains summaries of recent competition cases and also special articles on EU competition policy. For analysis of vertical restraints, see EU Commission *Green Paper on Vertical Restraints in EC Competition Policy* (Brussels: EU Commission, 1997). Important advances have been made in public policy towards firms with market power, in particular regulatory theory. These aspects are presented in a non-technical manner in F.M. Scherer and David Ross, *Industrial Market Structure and Economic Performance* (Boston: Houghton Mifflin, 3rd edn, 1990). For an *ex-post* review of the experience of privatisation, see David Parker (ed.), *Privatisation in the European Union: Theory and policy perspectives* (London: Routledge, 1998). A readable and insightful account of the application of new thinking on competition policy and regulatory reform to transition economies is provided in J. Fingleton *et al.*, *Competition Policy and the Transformation of Central Europe* (London: Centre for Economic Policy Research, 1996).

Chapter 8

GOVERNMENT INTERVENTION AND THE MARKET SYSTEM

Introduction

Government plays a major role in the economy. The share of government spending in GDP ranged from 30 per cent in the US to just under 55 per cent in Sweden in the late 1990s.[1] In addition to this, the authorities affect the business environment through a myriad of taxes, rules and regulations. The purpose of this chapter is to analyse the contribution of government to economic welfare and the business environment.

The objectives of government and business are to some extent in opposition. The social objectives of government policy can impose restraints on a firm's behaviour in relation to employees and investment. Competition policy limits the scope of business to acquire and exploit monopoly power, environmental legislation can impose heavy financial burdens on industry, and progressive income taxes impact severely on executive salaries. However, governments and business also share much common ground. Both have an interest in fostering growth, securing high levels of employment and promoting social harmony. Hence, business should not allow itself to be cast in the role of opposing all public intervention. Much of this intervention is desirable, necessary and directly beneficial to business. This much has always been recognised in economics. Adam Smith himself devoted a long chapter to discussing the various functions of government. In addition to the provision of defence and justice, he asserted that 'the sovereign or commonwealth' had a duty to erect and maintain

> those public institutions and those public works which, though they may be in the highest degree advantageous to a great society, are however of such a nature that the profit could never repay the expense to any individual or small number of individuals. (Adam Smith, *Wealth of Nations*, 1776, Vol. 2, p. 244)

The debate has come a long way since then, as we shall see.

For four decades after the Second World War, the influence of government in the economy grew at an unprecedented rate. Some of this growth was fuelled by Keynesian ideas of macroeconomic management. We defer discussion of this aspect of government intervention until Part II. This chapter focuses on the microeconomic considerations that prompted governments to play a more active role in the economy.

---

1 *OECD Economic Outlook* (December 2000).

The economics of government intervention has undergone extensive review in recent decades and the tide of government expansion has turned. Whereas fifty years ago governments regarded nationalisation as a solution to market imperfections, nowadays the debate is about privatisation. Many no longer see the welfare state as the solution to the problem of poverty, but rather as a possible source of its exacerbation. Instead of providing people with pensions, governments are encouraging people to make provision for the future for themselves. Changing ideas have spilled over into changing budgets. Government spending as a percentage of GDP has stopped increasing and in some countries has declined (see Chapter 15).

Chapter outline

1. The case for *income redistribution*. A large proportion of public spending is motivated by the desire to help the poor. This is because the free market system may result in considerable income inequalities. Intervention then may be desirable as a means of securing social solidarity, and thereby helping to secure faster and more sustainable growth.

2. The problem of *market failure*. Four types of 'failure' are discussed: (a) monopoly power, (b) externalities, (c) public goods and (d) lack of information. Business will certainly be familiar with these reasons for government intervention. The case of monopoly, discussed in Chapters 6 and 7, touches many firms directly or indirectly. Also, business benefits from government subsidies – this subvention being justified by the externalities argument or by the desire to redistribute jobs and incomes to poor regions. Correction of market failure for reasons of public good and information may have less agreeable consequences for business. Thus, firms may find themselves subject to regulations and controls regarding pollution, consumer protection, fire and health provision. A manager needs to understand the economic causes and consequences of the market failure that gives rise to such intervention.

3. The instruments of *government intervention*. Should intervention take the form of tax and subsidy incentives, regulation, or direct state provision?

4. The problem of government *failure*. Although a case for intervention may exist on first principles, in practice government intervention may create its own equally damaging set of distortions. This possibility could arise if, say, income taxes had to be raised in order to provide industrial or regional assistance. The gains to the economy through provision of this assistance could be offset by the disincentive effects and compliance cost of the higher taxes. The cure might end up being worse than the disease.

8.1   Income distribution and the equity–efficiency trade-off

Economics seeks to improve society's material welfare. This seems a reasonable definition of the aim of economic activity, although at various times in the past other objectives have taken precedence. To some, economic activity was useful primarily as a means of securing and maintaining political power. Colbert, the influential finance minister of Louis XIV, saw as the main purpose of his subjects' labour not the increase in their own happiness, but the enhancement of the glory and power of their sovereign, who personified the Nation. Despots, through the centuries, have viewed economic activity primarily as a means of securing and extending their power rather than of improving the welfare of the masses. Even those who agree with the objective of maximising individual utilities may disagree over the interpretation of what truly gives utility to us as human beings and who is best equipped to judge.

The value judgements underlying modern economics are derived from a philosophy of individualism and liberalism. *Individualism* means that what ultimately counts is the utility every individual attains and that the utility of each individual should be given an equal weight. *Liberalism* signifies that individuals should be free to decide what provides the greatest utility. Individual preferences are taken as a given. The task of the economist, in this view, is to advocate structures which ensure that they are satisfied to the maximum extent, not to pass judgement on them.

It is important to distinguish between utility and income. The standard assumption underlying economic reasoning is that the marginal utility of income is positive, but decreases as income rises.[2] 'Economic man' always prefers a higher income to a lower one, but the intensity of this preference diminishes as income rises. Ascetics, who are happiest with a minimal income, and Scrooges, for whom income becomes more important the more they have of it, are both excluded by this definition. A systematic relationship thus links utility to income. On the face of it, the individualist principle of treating the utility of every person equally, coupled with the assumption of declining marginal utility for all individuals, would imply that the total utility in society is maximised when income is distributed perfectly evenly. Nevertheless, even while accepting these two behavioural assumptions, utilitarians generally do not advocate total income equalisation.

There are two reasons for this. *First*, different people derive different amounts of satisfaction from the same income levels. Material wealth does not matter equally to all. However, since utility cannot be objectively measured and compared among individuals, there is no way of finding out who derives how much utility from various levels of income. *Second*, policies to achieve greater equality have an adverse effect on incentives to work and enterprise and may, after a point, lead to a fall in total income. The size of the cake to be distributed may be affected by how the cake is sliced. In this metaphor, the slicing pattern represents the egalitarian or equity factor and the size of the cake stands for the second major

---

2 This is the axiom of dominance, as described in Chapter 3.

criterion of economic judgement: efficiency.[3] If the unweighted utility sum in a society can only be maximised by allowing a degree of inequality, then the inequality outcome might be preferred to perfect income equalisation.

There are, none the less, strong egalitarian tendencies in popular debate on economic issues, dating back to the eighteenth-century English philosopher Jeremy Bentham, the founder of utilitarianism. The assumption of decreasing marginal utility implies that when we take an equal amount from the rich to give to the poor, the rich will have suffered less of a utility loss than the utility gain enjoyed by the poor. A utilitarian asked to choose between a perfectly equal distribution of income, and an unequal distribution *of exactly the same total income*, would favour the equal distribution. Egalitarian predispositions also emerge from other philosophies and schools of thought. Some argue that society should give the utility of the poor greater weight than the utility of the rich on grounds of need, regardless of fine points about diminishing utility.[4] Others, such as the philosopher John Rawls, have pushed this line of judgement to the extreme, arguing that any economic change which increases inequality would be acceptable only if it serves to make the poorest better off also.[5] This implies that the utility of the worst-off individual takes precedence over all others. In opposition to the egalitarian presumption, Robert Nozick and others argue that what matters is not how much utility individuals currently attain, but how they have got to this point. If the individual's income has been obtained legally, no one is entitled to deprive him or her of any of it, hence *ex-post* redistribution of income is unjustified.[6] Note that these are all individualistic philosophies. None of them, however, has rivalled the impact on economic thinking exerted by utilitarianism.

The equity–efficiency trade-off remains a controversial topic. There are undoubtedly situations where the criteria of equity and efficiency conflict. Too much equality reduces the incentives to work and can thus lead to inefficient outcomes. Yet too much inequality can lead to a waste of human resources and lack of productive investment. The even spread of the fruits of growth has been identified by the World Bank as a factor favouring rapid development (see Chapter 2). There is increasing concern about the growth in inequality in countries such as the US, the UK and New Zealand, which have been at the forefront of free market policies. As Box 8.1 shows, two of the most unequal societies in terms of income distribution are the US and Switzerland. In Switzerland's case, the inequality can mainly be attributed to the presence of a small number of extremely wealthy people, against a background of a very broad well-off middle class and little absolute poverty. In the US, the high inequality

---

3 Utilitarian political philosophy considers a third major criterion for judging economic systems: individual liberty. We assume in this chapter that governments are democratically elected and civil rights are respected. Hence, the 'state vs market' distinction does not mark a choice between an authoritarian and a liberal system.

4 Abram Bergson, 'A reformulation of certain aspects of welfare economics', *Quarterly Journal of Economics*, 53 (1938).

5 John Rawls, *A Theory of Justice* (Oxford: Oxford University Press, 1971).

6 Robert Nozick, *Anarchy, State and Utopia* (Oxford: Basil Blackwell, 1974).

The equity–efficiency trade-off

Economics is the study of trade-offs between different uses of scarce resources. Firms continuously trade off current benefits from the distribution of dividends against future benefits from retaining these profits and reinvesting them in the business. Managers and workers trade off the career fruits of long and hard working hours against the joys of leisure time. Consumers trade off the utility that could have been attained by buying good X or Y for the utility derived from purchasing good Z instead.

Arguably, the most important, and certainly the most hotly debated, economic trade-off is the political choice between equity and efficiency. Conventional wisdom suggests that more equity leads to less efficiency, because equalisation of income and wealth among individuals can reduce work incentives, as well as the aggregate level of savings and investment (since rich people tend to save more). Conversely, unrestrained market forces result in inequitable outcomes or, in the famous words of Arthur Okun, 'dollars transgress on rights'.[1]

Economists have attempted to check the link between equity and efficiency empirically. This entails finding satisfactory measures of the two concepts. Efficiency is usually measured by reference to average GNP per capita.

Measuring equity is trickier. Economists associate equity with an even distribution of income and wealth among individuals. The main measure of income distribution is derived from the Lorenz curve, presented in Diagram 1.

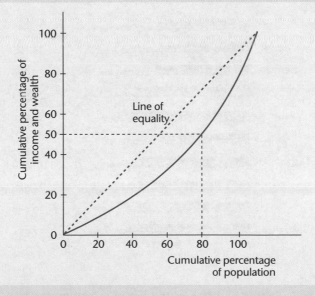

Diagram 1 **The Lorenz curve**

Box 8.1 continued

The Lorenz curve plots the cumulative share of income and wealth in ascending order against the cumulative percentage of population. In the above diagram, for instance, 80 per cent of the population receives only 50 per cent of the total income, while the richest 20 per cent enjoy the remaining 50 per cent of the pie. The poorest fifth of the population receives a mere 3 per cent of national income and wealth. This Lorenz curve thus depicts a society with considerable inequality. A country with perfect equality of income and wealth, where each individual controls the same amount of material goods, exhibits a straight Lorenz curve, called the 'line of equality'.

The more strongly the Lorenz curve diverges from the line of equality, the greater the degree of inequality. This can be captured by a simple measure. The Gini coefficient is the proportion of the area delimited by the line of equality and the Lorenz curve, relative to the total area between the line of equality and the horizontal axis. The index can take values between 0 and 1, where 0 means perfect equality and 1 represents complete inequality (one individual gets the whole pie).

Diagram 2 shows Gini indices for a selection of high-income countries. The black bars represent the distribution of disposable income among individuals. The blue bars show what level of income inequality would have prevailed in the absence of government redistribution through progressive taxes and welfare benefits.

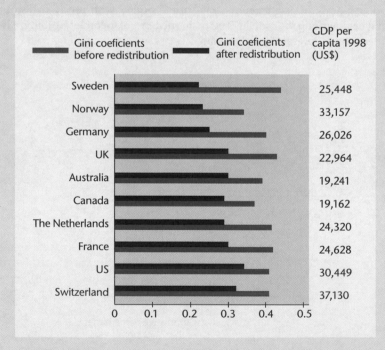

Diagram 2 **Slicing and size of the pie in ten countries**

Sources: A Atkinson, *Income Inequality in OECD Countries: Evidence from CIS data* (Paris: OECD, 1995).

Box 8.1 continued

Three important conclusions can be drawn from Diagram 2.

1. Market forces alone produce highly unequal income distributions. The 'before redistribution' Gini indices for the ten sample countries are contained in the range 0.33–0.44.
2. Post-tax distributions are much less unequal than pre-tax distributions. The 'after redistribution' coefficients lie in the range 0.20–0.34. Tax and welfare payments reduce inequality to a significant extent.
3. Countries that espoused 'new consensus' policies with most enthusiasm (US, UK, New Zealand) have more unequal distributions than other countries.

Yet, equity and efficiency do not necessarily conflict. The ten countries in Diagram 2 are all among the world's very richest. An extended study of 56 countries found that income inequality is bad for economic growth.[2] The study provides comprehensive statistical evidence that countries with more evenly spread income tend to grow faster than countries with a large gap between the incomes of the poor and of the rich. It is argued that big income differentials reflect underinvestment in education and divert government efforts from investment and growth-promotion towards the abatement of social conflict.

The relationship between equity and efficiency ultimately depends on individual attitudes and culture. In some societies, income inequalities are condemned less, and financial work incentives valued more, than in others. A political philosopher stated that 'the combinations of equity and, say, economic growth attainable in a competitive market economy full of individualistic materialists might be rather different from those attainable in a co-operative economy run by and for ascetic altruists'.[3] A poll conducted in 1990 showed that only 29 per cent of Americans thought it was the government's job to reduce income differentials, while 60–70 per cent of Germans and Britons, and over 80 per cent of Italians and Austrians, were of that opinion.[4] The debate will go on.

Notes:
1. Arthur M. Okun, *Equality and Efficiency: The big trade-off* (Washington, DC: The Brookings Institution, 1975).
2. Torsten Persson and Guido Tabellini, 'Is inequality harmful for growth?', *The American Economic Review*, 84, 1994.
3. Julian Le Grand, 'Equity versus efficiency: The elusive trade-off', *Ethics* (1990).
4. Reported in *The Economist*, 5 November 1994.

index arises because of major population groups at both extremes of the income spectrum. There is a sizeable group of very rich and an even more numerous cohort of very poor people. This shows some of the ambiguity in conventional measures of income distribution and indicates how difficult it is to reach definitive judgements about the optimum degree of inequality. Perhaps the more fruitful line of enquiry is to examine how assistance might be most efficiently channelled to those most in need, rather than what abstract degree of inequality society should be prepared to tolerate.

Such reasoning has motivated policy-makers to focus on the efficiency criterion. Efficiency is less ambiguous an objective than equity. Any improvement in efficiency produces a net increase in income and, hence, it is in principle possible by income distribution to make all people in the community better off – or at least to ensure that nobody is made worse off. An outcome is defined as efficient when it is impossible to make one person better off without making at least one other individual less well off. Devised by the nineteenth-century Italian economist Vilfredo Pareto, any outcome which passes this efficiency test is said to satisfy the *Pareto* criterion. A corollary to the Pareto criterion is the *compensation principle*, which says that if an outcome is more efficient, it should be feasible for the gainers to compensate the losers. The implicit assumption is that compensation can be, and is, arranged for the losers from economic change. The arranger in this instance is the government. In that case, if the entire cake grows bigger, everybody's slice will also grow.

The above approach focuses on the degree of equality of *outcomes* of the market process. But the *process* may be fair, even if it generates unequal outcomes. Much modern debate focuses on this – i.e. inequality may be less objectionable if the process is fair (equality of opportunity, level playing field) than if it is unfair. For example, people with different levels of stamina, ambition, attitudes and willingness to work engage in market activities. Provided there is equality of opportunity, a meritocratic approach would not object to inequality of outcome in such circumstances.

8.2 Market failures

Economic theory has shown that a perfectly competitive economy, guided by Adam Smith's 'invisible hand', attains a Pareto-efficient allocation of resources. But most real-world markets violate at least some of the assumptions which underlie the economists' idealised free market model. Such deviations of real markets from the efficient model economy are called 'market failures'. Market failure can arise for four main reasons: (1) monopoly power, (2) externalities, (3) public goods, and (4) information asymmetries.

Monopoly power

The distortionary effects of monopoly have already been analysed (Chapter 6). Monopoly involves a breach of the rule, marginal cost = price, by introducing a wedge between marginal cost of production of a good and the utility it provides the marginal consumer as measured by prices. Monopoly pricing also creates an income distribution effect. Monopoly profits are earned at the expense of the consumers, who pay a higher price relative to what they would pay in a competitive market. This is the reason why consumer organisations oppose monopolies and cartels, and lobby their governments for stricter competition legislation.[7]

---

7 Another redistributive effect of monopoly power is that rival firms might be pushed out of a market by a more powerful competitor, not because of the latter's superior product, but because of the monopolist's ability to enhance a dominant position even further, be it through advertising, below-cost pricing or government lobbying.

However, the gain of firms at the expense of consumers is not what lies at the heart of the economic case against uncompetitive behaviour. The distribution of gains between firms and consumers can only be judged on equity grounds, and is thus entirely subjective. The real problem is that economic efficiency is reduced when firms attain monopoly power. As we move from a competitive situation, with a large quantity supplied at a low price, to a monopoly, where a smaller quantity is supplied at a higher price, what occurs is not a zero-sum redistribution of income from consumers to producers, but a net loss of utility to society at large. This has been described as the 'dead-weight loss' of monopoly.

The dead-weight loss, as described above, is a static phenomenon relating to the market situation at one point in time. Empirical estimates of the dead-weight losses caused by existing monopolies or oligopolies typically amount to only a few percentage points of the values of total sales in the particular industry. A forerunner in trying to measure the dead-weight loss, Arnold Harberger was surprised to find that such welfare losses amounted to a mere 0.1 per cent of US national income in the 1920s.[8] A later, more detailed study, however, estimated the dead-weight loss arising from uncompetitive behaviour in the UK to have ranged between 0.2 and 7.2 per cent of private sector output.[9] The size of this estimation interval indicates the difficulties of estimating welfare effects empirically.

As readers will recall from Chapter 7, the chief efficiency losses from monopoly occur over time. Monopolists or oligopolists have less of an incentive than competitive firms to maintain efficiency, to innovate and to improve their services. Indeed, as Hicks once noted in a famous dictum, 'the greatest of monopoly profits is a quiet life'.[10] This is a central theme of the Austrian School. The pressure of competition forces firms to aim at lowering their (marginal) costs continuously, while sheltered firms do not have to be so concerned about their costs and the improvement of output quality. The losses due to such so-called X-inefficiencies are even more difficult to estimate empirically than dead-weight losses. Nevertheless, in many circumstances they outweigh the dead-weight losses stressed by economic theory. The Cecchini Report, for example, estimated that the X-efficiency losses of non-tariff barriers on intra-European trade amounted to 2 per cent of GNP in the late 1980s.

Externalities

A second important source of market failure are *externalities* or 'spillover effects'. These arise when an economic activity affects a third party who had no say in the effect-creating action. The perfect competition model assumes that no such external effects exist. Both producers and consumers bear the entire cost and enjoy the entire benefit created by their economic actions. This assumption is frequently breached in practice. The resulting spillover effects reflect an inefficiency of the free market system.

8 Arnold Harberger, 'Monopoly and resource allocation', *American Economic Review*, 44 (1954).
9 K. Cowling and D. Mueller, 'The social costs of monopoly power', *Economic Journal*, 88 (1978).
10 J.R. Hicks, 'Annual survey of economic theory: The theory of monopoly', *Econometrica* (1935).

	Origin	
	Production	*Consumption*
Positive	Training employees in general skills	Vaccine against contagious disease
	Aesthetic company headquarters building	Neighbour's well-kept garden
Negative	Air water and noise pollution	Congestion
	Ugly factory buildings	Radio noise

Figure 8.1 The four categories of external effects

Externalities can be either positive or negative. Positive externalities, also called external benefits, bestow a benefit on a third party (e.g. a firm trains an employee in computing technology, which skill can then be passed on at zero cost to another firm if the employee changes job). Correspondingly, a negative externality, also referred to as an external cost, imposes a cost on a third party, involving a loss of utility (a classical example being the chemical plant which causes water pollution – see below).[11] A further distinction can be made between producers and consumers. Externalities can result either from the consumption activities of some individuals or from the production process of firms.

The different types of externalities are summarised in Figure 8.1. Examples are given for each of the four categories. All four types of externalities lead to inefficiencies when the market system is left to operate freely. The free market provides too little of the activities providing positive externalities and too much of those with negative externalities. In that sense, 'positive' externalities are just as 'inefficient' as 'negative' externalities.

To illustrate the efficiency loss from spillover effects, we begin with the classical example of a *negative production externality*. Imagine a chemical plant which channels its polluted effluents into the nearest river. Imagine also that, downstream, there is a factory which needs clean water, and, therefore, must incur costs in cleaning the water. Finally, assume that the resulting loss in profits for the downstream factory can be measured in money terms and is a constant fraction of the factory's output. This situation is represented in Figure 8.2.

The chemical factory, operating in a perfectly competitive market, faces a horizontal demand curve and thus a given price, OP, for its output (in this case, therefore, price = marginal revenue). Its marginal costs increase with output. The

11 The use of this example, of course, does not imply that all chemical plants are polluters.

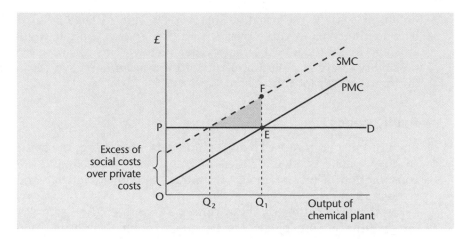

Figure 8.2 A negative production externality: chemical plant polluting river

production costs borne by the firm are denoted PMC, which stands for private marginal costs. Profit maximisation drives the firm to produce up to OP = PMC, hence the amount OQ_1 of chemicals is produced. However, the factory's operating costs do not encompass the totality of costs created by the manufacture of its output. External costs borne by the downstream factory (incurred in cleaning the water) arise in addition to the firm's outlays. The money value of the profit loss per unit of chemical output suffered by the downstream factory is represented by the vertical distance EF in the diagram. In order to represent total production costs per unit, we add EF to PMC to obtain SMC, the social marginal cost. In the case of a negative production externality, the social cost is greater than the private cost of production. From society's point of view, the costs to the downstream factory should be added to the outlays of the chemical company. Hence, the optimality condition is that OP = SMC. It would thus be socially optimal to produce OQ_2 rather than OQ_1.[12]

This example shows that, in the presence of negative externalities, the free market leads to an over-provision of the goods concerned. In the opposite scenario – where the production or consumption of a certain good creates external benefits – a free market results in too low a level of production or consumption.

Note that economics tends to resist any absolutist approach to the pollution problem. The existence of external costs such as pollution does not generally provide an economic justification for the total suppression of the underlying activity. In our example, the closure of the chemicals plant is not required for efficiency, merely a reduction in output (and hence in pollution) to the level OQ_2. There is a trade-off between the utility lost by the sufferers of pollution and the utility gained by the producers and consumers of the good whose production gave rise to the externality. Some pollution is, for this reason, usually better than no

---

12 The net welfare gained by a move from OQ_1 to OQ_2 is equal to the shaded triangle, which represents the dead-weight loss caused by the existence of the external effect.

pollution. Only if the negative spillover EF were so large as to push up SMC beyond the demand curve over the whole range of output would it be most efficient to shut down the factory completely. This is not just a theoretical possibility – several polluting plants of Central Europe have been closed down during the 1990s for this reason.

Public goods

The third main category of market failure arises because of the existence of *public goods*. A public good is defined as being *non-excludable* and *non-rivalrous* in consumption. A private good, by contrast, is both excludable and rivalrous in consumption.

For the explanation of these concepts, consider the example of an army, representing a pure public good, and an apple, a private good. A good is excludable if individuals can be prevented from enjoying its benefits. It is easy to withhold an apple from someone, hence it is excludable. However, if an army successfully defends a country against an invading force, then all inhabitants of the protected country necessarily benefit (assuming none of them sympathises with the invader) and no one can be excluded. National defence is thus non-excludable.

Non-rivalry means that the consumption of a good by an additional person does not preclude someone else also consuming it. Put more technically, a non-rivalrous good is subject to a zero marginal cost of consumption. If one individual eats the apple, this precludes anyone else eating it. Apples are thus rivalrous goods. If the army protects the nation, however, all citizens are free to enjoy the feeling of security that protection engenders. The fact that I feel secure does not in any way preclude your feeling secure, nor does it add to the security bill. Consequently, national defence is also a non-rivalrous good.

Public and private goods do not constitute sharply-delineated categories. There is a continuous range of products between the two opposite poles, pure public goods and pure private goods. Figure 8.3 tentatively places some examples of different goods within this continuous range, differentiating between the intensity of rivalry and the degree of excludability of these goods. The fact that most goods are roughly situated around the diagonal starting at the origin illustrates that there is a strong link between (non-)rivalry and (non-)excludability.

In the bottom left corner of the diagram are listed some pure public goods. If a country's air is clean, if its territory is safe from foreign armies and if its currency is stable, then the benefits of these achievements can be withheld from no citizen of this country, nor does it cost more to provide them if the resident population grows. They are, therefore, unambiguously non-excludable and non-rivalrous. At the other extreme are pure private goods, situated in the top right corner of Figure 8.3. Apples, cars and books are clearly excludable and rivalrous. The most interesting cases, however, are located between these two poles. Museums and art galleries are to some extent non-rivalrous. My enjoyment from viewing a Caravaggio today in no sense diminishes the possibility of your enjoying it tomorrow – hence it is non-rivalrous. But if everybody crowds into the gallery at

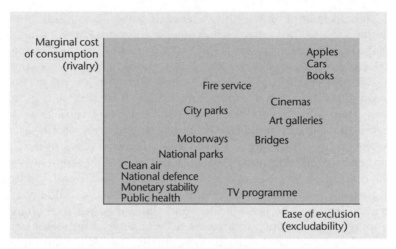

Figure 8.3 Private goods and public goods

the same time, each person's enjoyment will diminish and, in that sense, the art gallery becomes a rivalrous good. It is also excludable – one can change the admission fee to the gallery.

Another example of a good which is only partly 'public' by nature is a motorway. Again, up to a certain point of congestion, additional users cause only minor, if any, diminution of existing users' utility. It is also possible to exclude certain drivers from the use of these roads by setting up checkpoints or toll booths. Obviously, it is more costly to control the access to a motorway than to monitor the entrance of a museum or art gallery. A motorway is thus less 'excludable' than a museum. This is important, because very few things are technically non-excludable. As technology changes, some things become less excludable (e.g. defence) and some more excludable (e.g. urban roads, pay TV). The real issue is the *cost* of exclusion, which is an example of *transaction costs*. Also, improved technology and income growth have made some hitherto non-rivalrous goods become rivalrous (e.g. air space for planes, ocean fishing).

Markets fail in the presence of pure public goods because of the so-called 'free-rider' problem. It may be very costly to provide a public good (think of an army!), but everyone can benefit from it no matter whether he or she has contributed to its financing. Self-interested individuals have an incentive to avoid paying for the good in the hope that others will provide it. In other words, utility-maximising individuals try to free-ride on the others. If all individuals reason in that fashion, none of the public good is produced, even if the aggregate cost of providing the good is much lower than the sum of potential utility gains. The market, a system based on non-cooperative interaction of selfish individuals, leads to zero provision of pure public goods. If the aggregate benefit potentially derived from the public good exceeds its total cost of provision, this could be a very inefficient outcome. The non-rivalrous character of a public good means that the market should produce more than it does, while its non-excludable character means that the market will never have the incentive to do so.

Markets fail not only in the presence of pure public goods, but whenever a good shares some of the characteristics of a public good. For example, suppose a good is excludable but non-rivalrous (MC = 0). Provision by the free market at a positive price is non-optimal. Since MC = 0, P should also = 0, i.e. the good should be provided free of charge. Market provision implies prices above the socially optimal level. Take the example of a bridge. If the bridge is provided by a private firm, then a fee has to be charged to the crossing vehicles so that the firm can cover the costs of building the bridge and earn a profit. As we have shown, however, once the bridge has been built, the most efficient outcome occurs at the point where the social marginal cost and marginal benefit curves intersect. Since the marginal cost curve of a bridge is virtually zero for all additional crossings up to the point of traffic congestion, the price charged should be zero. Obviously, no private firm will be prepared to build the bridge without charging a toll for all crossings. The levy of a toll has two effects. First, it implies a transfer of resources from the users of the bridge to the supplying firm (a redistributive effect). Second, charging a fee also implies a dead-weight loss of efficiency, conceptually similar to the dead-weight loss arising from monopoly. Therefore, compared to the potential optimum, provision of such a public good through the market system leads to a net loss of economic efficiency.[13]

Public goods are not the same as publicly provided goods. Even though public goods are usually provided by the government, many goods and services currently provided by the state do not conform to the economic definition of a pure public good. Services such as health, education, housing, all come under the heading of *merit goods*. Merit goods are goods that society wishes everyone to consume, regardless of what an individual's preferences for that particular good are. For instance, most countries have a law which dictates that children must attend school until they reach a certain age; this is society's way of ensuring that everyone consumes a certain amount of education, because it is seen as good. There also exist *merit 'bads'* (e.g. heroin) which society believes that each individual should not consume (because they are bad), regardless of the individual's preferences. With merit goods, society can have a different view of the consumption of these goods than the individual. The case for merit goods implies some qualification of the basic assumption that social welfare is an aggregate of individual welfare and that the individual is the best judge of the latter.

Information failures

The fourth type of market failure arises because real-world consumers and producers are not perfectly informed about all goods and prices. Where lack of such knowledge is significant, *information failure* leads to an inefficient outcome in a market system. A good example is the health effect of tobacco consumption. In a free market, no firm has an incentive to circulate information about the

---

13 This is a frequently used example, but it is tricky because the concept of MC is ambiguous when the unit of production is different from the unit of consumption. The same applies to seats on a train.

hazards of smoking. It is obvious that tobacco companies will abstain from such activity. The reason why no other firm will undertake an advertising campaign is that knowledge about the effects of smoking is a public good – hence no selfish individual will be prepared to pay the private firm for the enlightenment it offers. Information failures also provide a rationale for public sector involvement in activities as diverse as drugs testing, health inspection of restaurants, banking regulation and the provision of job search centres for the unemployed.

These four sources of market failure point to the need for government intervention. The form of such intervention is the subject of the next section.

8.3 Government intervention

The public sector constitutes the major alternative to free private markets. Hence, a call for government intervention is generally regarded as the logical consequence of the diagnosed market failures. As we have seen, public sector activity accounts for sizeable proportions of all real-world economies. Even in a country as market-oriented as the US, government expenditure accounts for a third of GDP.

Governments can influence economic activity in three major ways: *taxation and subsidisation*, *regulation* and *public provision*. Together, they constitute the main elements in the government's microeconomic policy.

In evaluating the different modes of intervention, attention is focused on their efficiency effects rather than the income distribution effects. Of course, in many instances the modality of intervention may be determined by equity or, indeed, purely political considerations. For example, it may be 'easier' in political terms to boost farm incomes by raising food prices than by providing highly transparent subsidies of an equivalent amount. For that reason, arguments about the inefficiency of one mode of transfer over another may often fall on deaf ears. Yet research on more effective ways of intervening, and on the costs and benefits of different forms of intervention, clearly helps rational decision making.

Taxes and subsidies

Taxes and subsidies are used extensively to distribute income (food subsidies, education grants to the lower income groups, progressive income taxes, etc.). Subsidies require taxes to finance them, and this raises questions concerning the optimal structure of taxes. We have already referred to the rules which should govern indirect taxes: impose high tax rates on activities with low price elasticity of demand and low broadly-based rates on all other activities (Chapter 3), assuming that the motivation for imposing taxes is simply to obtain revenue for the government.

While most taxes are imposed for this reason, there is another motivation which merits discussion. Taxes can sometimes be imposed not primarily in order to collect revenue, but to direct resources in a particular direction – e.g. a pollution tax. In other instances, the two motives overlap (a tax on tobacco yields large revenue and also discourages consumption of cigarettes).[14] By the same token, while the bulk of subsidies are transfer payments to lower income groups, many are provided in order to encourage particular activities and regions (industrial grants and regional assistance).

Returning to the example of the polluting chemicals factory, it is easily shown that, if the government taxes the plant by the amount EF for every unit produced, the firm's private marginal cost is increased and equals the social marginal cost, leading the firm to produce the socially optimum output level of OQ_2. By taxing the polluter by exactly the value of the damage caused, the government is said to have 'internalised' the externality. In general, an optimal government policy taxes firms or individuals for the value of the external cost they cause and subsidises them to the value of the external benefit they create. This is the rationale underlying, for instance, taxes on fuel, and subsidies for education and industrial training.

The desirability of government intervention in the presence of externalities has been questioned by Ronald Coase and his successors. His work in this field, resulting in the formulation of the 'Coase Theorem', earned him a Nobel prize in 1991. Coase's theorem states that the market system can be efficient even in the presence of spillover effects, provided that property rights on these effects are clearly defined and that negotiation between the concerned parties is costless. Returning to the example of the polluting factory, the Coase Theorem states that the optimum output level OQ_2 of Figure 8.2 would be achieved if the property rights for the clean river were assigned either to the chemical plant or to the downstream firms (and any other parties affected), and if negotiation among them was costless. If the plant is given the right to pollute the river, the downstream users can get together and 'bribe' the firm to reduce its output and the ensuing water pollution. Starting at output level OQ_1, the downstream users' gain in utility from reduced effluents (EF per unit of output) exceeds the firm's forgone profit from reduced output up to the point OQ_2. At production levels below OQ_2, the firm's forgone profits through further output reductions (OP − PMC) are greater than the downstream additional utility gains (EF). Hence the plant will be 'bribed' to limit its output to point OQ_2. If the property rights for the river are allocated not to the firm but to the downstream users, then the starting point is at zero output, because the latter's preferred situation is one of no pollution. However, up to point OQ_2 the chemical plant gains more in profits by increasing its production than the others lose in utility. Hence, the firm will find it profitable to 'bribe' the downstream users to allow output up to a level OQ_2. In consequence, the efficient output level OQ_2 will be attained independently of who owns the rights over the river.

The Coase Theorem provides a fascinating insight into the complexity and ingenuity of the market mechanism. But it is subject to two major qualifications. First, while for Coase's model the distribution of property rights does not affect efficiency, it certainly does matter in terms of equity. There is a distributional difference between the scenario where the downstream users have to compensate

---

14 Note that these objectives conflict.

the firm for reducing pollution, and the situation where the firm is forced to compensate the downstream users for directing its effluents into the river. Society at large might have a preference in this respect, and thus expect the government to intervene. An example of such a state-imposed allocation of property rights is the 'polluter pays' principle enshrined in article 130r of the Maastricht Treaty:

> Community policy on the environment shall aim at a high level of protection taking into account the diversity of situations in the various regions of the Community. It shall be based on the precautionary principle and on the principle that preventive action should be taken, *that environmental damage should be rectified at source and that the polluter should pay.* (emphasis added)

Society at large is implicitly given the property rights for clean air and water, and it is up to the polluter to pay compensation rather than society having to 'bribe' the polluters to reduce emissions.

Second, Coase's result hinges on the assumption of zero costs of negotiation. Such transaction costs, however, are a considerable obstacle to many negotiated settlements in the real world. It might be a costly and time-consuming endeavour for the downstream factory, anglers and others to organise themselves and to negotiate with the firm. If we think of external costs such as air pollution, it is obvious that to organise all consumers of air is a sheer impossibility. Furthermore, anybody trying to coordinate the public interest would have to confront the free-rider problem, since reduced air pollution is non-excludable.

This leads to the conclusion that government intervention is still needed to deal with externalities, particularly where these spillovers affect large numbers of otherwise unrelated individuals. Coase's Theorem is instructive, however, in suggesting ways in which this problem might be approached and alerts us to the importance of securing maximum involvement of the affected parties.

Regulation

Regulation involves, first, direct control or prohibition of certain actions; and second, the creation of incentive programmes using taxes, subsidies and other measures in order to guide behaviour to socially superior outcomes. Competition policy is a form of regulation, and we have already seen in Chapter 7 how it can be applied to moderate uncompetitive behaviour of private firms. Environmental and planning legislation is an everyday feature of life for a modern business (to be discussed in the following chapter). Regulation of natural monopolies and the supervision of the bank and insurance industries are familiar examples of government interference in the market system. Even though regulation involves an infringement on the workings of the market system, it may be justified on efficiency grounds.

Regulation is never costless and frequently involves a perpetual game of leapfrogging between the regulator and the regulated. The former sets down rules of behaviour which the dictates of profit maximisation often lead the regulated to circumvent. For this reason, the belief is gaining ground that 'command-and-control' regulation should be replaced as much as possible by regulation based on taxes/subsidies and other incentives. This amounts to harnessing the coordinating powers of the price mechanism on the government's behalf. A charge could be levied, for instance, on output equivalent to the amount of pollution in excess of certain agreed norms, as outlined in the analysis of the chemical plant. Of course, taxes will often not be a feasible option for practical and administrative reasons. Pollution, then, has to be held in check by regulation; for example, by the imposition of emission standards or by issuing tradeable emission permits further discussed in Chapter 9.

State provision

The main policy instrument to achieve an efficient procurement of pure public goods is *state provision*. We have shown above that the free-rider problem inhibits private markets from providing pure public goods, even where these are clearly in demand. For this reason, for instance, national security is never left to private provision. Much government spending on justice, defence or fundamental research could be attributed to public goods. Next to social welfare, these tend to absorb a high share of government spending in most industrial countries.

Many goods fall into the intermediate class between the purely public and the purely private in nature (see Figure 8.3). For these, various forms of public and private provision can be appropriate, depending on the extent and nature of the good's 'publicness'. Thus, there are strong efficiency grounds for assigning responsibility to the public sector for keeping our cities clean – but does this mean that all street cleaning and rubbish collection must be undertaken directly by the public sector? For a long time the answer was thought to be yes. It is now realised that many of these activities can be contracted out to the private sector, with major savings in cost without losses in service quality.

How government intervention can help a country to get on board the knowledge economy is another important topic. One way is for the state to provide more education, especially at second and third level. Another possibility is to establish research institutes that would be required to liaise with industry as, for example, agricultural research institutes with the food industry. An alternative to direct provision of new tech activities is to provide tax incentives to 'new economy' activities in the hope of obtaining knowledge spillovers from domestic and foreign-owned 'new economy' businesses.

There is room for debate about the desirable levels and types of government intervention in these different situations. In most cases, the probability of the government's achieving an efficient and equitable outcome must be balanced against the efficiency of private markets in terms of cost minimisation and speed of innovation. The latter aspect indicates that government intervention, like the market system, is susceptible to various failures.

8.4 Government failure

So far we have implicitly assumed that governments are omniscient, altruistic bodies striving to lead the economy to equitable and efficient outcomes where private markets fail to do so. This is obviously an unrealistic assumption. Led by William Niskanen at the University of California in the 1970s, economists began to scrutinise the behaviour of public sector employees more closely. Rather than assume bureaucrats know everything and aim only at the social good, recent studies have applied the same behaviour assumptions to public sector workers as to those in the private sector. Public servants – like private sector workers – are assumed to look for high pay, high job security and good promotion opportunities. Once this is done, one finds that, unlike in a competitive market, there is no 'invisible hand' in a bureaucracy to lead self-interested individuals towards an efficient output mix. In the private sector, managerial advancement is correlated with the profitability of the employing firm, albeit somewhat imperfectly, through the takeover threat and profit-related performance incentives. In the public sector, however, no such constraints apply. The main source of advancement lies in the growth of the agency or the commercial state company in which the individuals are employed. Self-interested public sector employees thus strive towards the expansion of their department or company. Niskanen has formalised a 'Parkinson's Law' of ever-increasing numbers of government officials into a theory of public sector which has an insatiable tendency to grow, and hence to interfere with the economy beyond the point of optimal intervention.

Niskanen's model captures an important part of the truth, but hardly the whole truth. Many politicians and civil servants act impartially and unselfishly. Yet, even if bureaucrats were altruistic, government failure might occur. The problem lies in the absence of full information being available to the authorities to enable intervention to be imposed at just the right level. How, for instance, can a government find out the value of the external cost caused by the chemicals factory discussed above? Even a perfectly well-intentioned government, aiming to levy a unit output tax corresponding to the distance EF in Figure 8.2, will find it difficult to estimate EF in practice. If the officials ask the downstream firms for their valuation of the river pollution, they are likely to obtain an exaggerated estimate. These firms have an incentive to overstate their utility losses in the hope of greater compensation or greater output reduction. The chemicals firm, on the other hand, will do its best to understate the value of the external costs it causes in order to minimise the tax it will be charged. Imperfect information in the real economy prevents governments from intervening in an optimal fashion.

Government failure can also arise because of lack of correspondence between politicians' objectives and those of the electorate. The *theory of public choice* explores the implications of the idea that politicians, like voters, are rational utility-maximising individuals. Political representatives, however, are motivated by the desire to be re-elected into office. They maximise utility by maximising votes, and this may lead to different actions and different outcomes than those required by the long-run interests of society. The fundamental hypothesis has

Box 8.2

Industrial subsidies in the European Union

The European Commission produces periodic estimates of the value of subsidies to industry. These estimates include not only the grants paid, but also implicit subsidies in the form of soft loans – which are very important, in France and Denmark – and tax concessions, which are used relatively more by Germany and Ireland. According to this comprehensive definition, the average rate of industrial subsidy in the EU amounted to 3.7 per cent of value added in the early 1990s.

State aid to manufacturing in the European Union (*yearly averages* 1996–98)

	Million euro	Value added (%)	euro per person employed
Belgium	732	1.9	1,093
Denmark	712	2.9	1,433
Germany	11,463	2.6	1,434
Greece	616	4.9	997
Spain	1,800	2.1	691
France	4,481	2.0	1,131
Ireland	416	1.9	1,458
Italy	8,864	4.4	1,955
Luxembourg	48	2.3	1,476
Netherlands	629	1.1	735
Portugal	195	1.0	188
UK	1,454	0.7	334
EU (15)	32,639	2.3	1,113

Source: *Eighth Survey on State Aid in the European Union* (Brussels: European Commission, April 2000).

There are wide variations in subsidy rates (see table) among EU countries, but state aids for selected businesses are a favourite dish on the microeconomic policy menu of most European governments. Why do they subsidise industry to this extent?

The major justification is provided by the externalities argument. For example, R&D brings benefits which the firm undertaking it cannot fully appropriate, hence the subsidisation of 'techno-parks'.

A special case of externality is employment creation in depressed areas. In Europe, the biggest subsidies have been flowing to declining industries such as coal, steel or shipbuilding, which often happen to be located in economically disadvantaged areas. While unbridled market forces would have driven many firms in these industries out of business long ago, governments have supported them in order to slow down the process of job shedding and to provide time for alternative employment sources to replace the declining industries. The externalities corrected by the support of declining industries in depressed areas relate to (a) excess of private over social cost of labour if the alternative to a job in supported industries is unemployment, and (b) congestion costs avoided in the

Box 8.2 continued

centre by keeping employees at work on the periphery. There may also be non-economic considerations such as social harmony and regional balance in the country. *Efficiency* arguments can be complemented by a case on *equity* grounds, particularly if employees in declining industries possess skills which are specific to their jobs and cannot be transferred to alternative employment.

Another reason invoked to justify industrial subsidies is asymmetric information. Take, for example, the case of SMEs seeking investment finance. It is often asserted that SMEs have to pay too high a rate of interest because lenders have a less clear appreciation of the riskiness of their projects than borrowers. As the firm grows, and establishes a track record and *reputation*, the problem eases considerably. But in the early stages some intervention may be warranted, such as the provision of interest relief on loans to SMEs. The action can be rationalised as a response (a) the information problem – the government might have a better idea of private and public returns on SME investment than private lenders – and (b) to externalities – small firms, if they manage to survive and grow, may confer social as well as private benefits because of their flexibility and regional dispersion.

Many other arguments, some quite ingenious, have been invented to justify state subsidisation. Yet often subsidies are disbursed not for rational and high-minded reasons but because of politically motivated alliances between politicians and the lobbying firms. The European Commission is trying to make subsidies more transparent, so as to bring them within the ambit of public debate, and to limit their amount, in order to minimise their distortionary effects on the private sector and to prevent the spectacle of rich regions outbidding poorer regions for much-needed investment projects. The Commission has achieved some success in this endeavour. Subsidies, as a percentage of value added, have fallen from 3.7 per cent in the early 1990s to 2.3 per cent at the end of the decade.

been described by one of the early writers on this topic, Professor Anthony Downs, as being that *political parties formulate policies in order to win elections, rather than win elections in order to formulate policies.*[15] Politicians may wish to be elected so as to benefit from the power, prestige and perks associated with a particular political office. Political parties may be inclined to put policies in place which will enhance the party's popularity and win votes for the next election, rather than those based on macroeconomic prudence.

To complicate the analysis even further, government intervention may not only be incapable of relieving market failures, it might even give rise to new ones. The classic example is taxation. Subsidies, losses by state enterprises and the costs of public sector employees in regulatory activity have all to be financed sooner or later by taxes. Taxation of income, however, creates obvious distortions. It encourages leisure relative to work, the black economy instead of the official economy and tax avoidance rather than productive market-driven activity. Indirect taxation can also, after a certain point, lead to high compliance costs,

---

15 A. Downs, *An Economic Theory of Democracy* (New York: Harper, 1957), p. 57.

avoidance and evasion. Another problem with both taxation and regulation is to enforce and oversee compliance by all firms. Large corporations frequently complain that smaller firms find it easier to avoid certain taxes, safety standards or social regulations.

Because government intervention is subject to inefficiencies, there are situations where the cost of attempting to 'correct' the free market distortion is greater than the cost of the original distortion itself. There was indeed a widespread belief that the European economies in particular had become overtaxed in the 1980s for these reasons. In developing countries, the problem of government failure cane be particularly acute. Higher taxes all too often lead to tax evasion, corruption and maladministration. Hence the general movement towards lower tax rates, accompanied by much stronger control of government spending.

Subsidies also lead to problems by cultivating a dependence mentality in their recipients. Subsidised intervention designed to correct a particular externality can take on a life of its own and continue in existence, even if the original cause of the externality has ceased to exist. Rather than adapting to change, firms and individuals may find it easier and more lucrative to devote their efforts to obtaining special government concessions. Such behaviour of 'grantepreneurs' is yet another instance of 'rent-seeking' and can be extremely inefficient. It can also lead to bribery and corruption, and thereby undermine the quality of governance. This has proven a major problem in many transitional and developing economies.

8.5 Conclusions

Asked how big government should be, a British politician, Enoch Powell, once answered:

> This is one of those questions which have the appearance of being capable of an experimental or objective answer, but which, on examination, refer us back to matters of opinion and intent. It is a proposition in a debate which mankind will never conclude and in which the tides and currents will continue to flow back and forth.[16]

This chapter has shown that there are good reasons for not expecting easy answers to such general questions. Government intervention exists in all countries and successful countries tend to have widely divergent degrees of intervention. The optimal degree of intervention varies among countries and within countries over time. There is some evidence based on World Bank studies, referred to in Chapter 2, that lower government: GDP ratios are associated with higher growth. There is also evidence that, while the huge postwar growth in the public sector in Western Europe was at first highly successful in stimulating economic growth, by the 1980s it had started to produce diminishing and even negative returns. Public sector trade unions became more powerful, bad industrial relations and inefficient practices became institutionalised, and tax burdens became too heavy.

---

16 P.H. Douglas and J.E. Powell (eds), *How Big Should Government Be?* (Washington, DC: American Enterprise Institute, 1968), p. 41.

There is nothing in economic theory to support the view that business should be 'opposed' to government or relentlessly hostile to its expansion. The case for some government intervention in the economy is strong. Provision of education and physical infrastructure are obvious examples, no less than public support for R&D. The achievement of regional balance in an economy and the minimising of congestion are important objectives which government alone can address. Governments have a role to play in creating national priorities. Michael Porter instances the campaign by the Japanese government to elevate national attention to quality and overcome the stigma of 'cheap' Japanese goods. The Deming Prize was identified as 'one of the most visible elements of the programme'. This prize 'carries enormous prestige' and 'sends a strong signal to all Japanese firms about the requirements of competitive success'.[17]

Business can play an important role in stimulating and leading debate on how government could be made more efficient and how intervention can be effected with least cost.

Even though it acknowledges a role for state intervention, economics probably disposes to a more favourable view of the potential of competitive markets than of public sector involvement. This predisposition lay at the heart of the general policy shift towards stronger emphasis on market forces. Its most prominent advocates in the 1980s were Ronald Reagan and Margaret Thatcher, but the pro-market consensus has by now spread to all continents. Wherever feasible, state-provided services are being privatised and competitive elements are being introduced into the most unlikely quarters, even into the workings of the civil service itself.

Efficiency is only one of the two criteria framing economic judgement. Equity considerations often favour more rather than less state intervention. Real-world free markets generally may maximise the size of the economic cake, but they also tend to produce some very small slices. The decision on what level of equity to aspire to cannot be made by either the economist or business, but must be decided by the electorate.

✔ Summary

1. The free market system may bring about considerable income inequalities which, if widely perceived as 'unfair' outcomes, may require intervention to correct. Government intervention to protect the poor through disaster relief and basic anti-poverty programmes is quite consistent with 'new consensus' policies. In redistributing income, however, account must be taken of adverse effects on incentives and efficiency. Also, there is much ambiguity associated with conventional measures of income distribution. Inequality may be less objectionable, for instance, if the *process* is fair, even if it generates unequal outcomes. There may be a trade-off between equality of opportunity and equality of outcomes.

---

17 Michael Porter, *The Competitive Advantage of Nations* (London: Macmillan, 1990), p. 681.

2. A Pareto-efficient outcome is defined as one such that nobody can be made better off without making at least one other individual less well off. Free markets can fail to deliver efficient outcomes for four main reasons. First, when firms attain monopoly power, economic efficiency is reduced as monopolies tend to produce lower quantity at a higher cost than a competitive situation. Second, positive or negative externalities can be an important source of market failure if the market system is left to operate freely. A third source of market failure arises because of the existence of public goods and the associated free-rider problem. Fourth, information asymmetries lead to market failure when consumers and producers are not perfectly informed about all goods and prices. These sources of market failure point to the need for government intervention to bring about equality between social costs and social benefits.

3. Governments can influence economic activity in three major ways: (a) taxes and subsidies, (b) regulation, and (c) public provision. Taxes and subsidies are used extensively to distribute income. Both can also be used in order to direct resources in a particular direction or activity. Regulation involves direct control or prohibition of certain actions. Even though regulation involves an infringement on the workings of the market system, it is justifiable in certain circumstances. Public provision is the main policy instrument to achieve efficient procurement of pure public goods. However, the provision of many goods which fall between purely public and purely private goods can be contracted out to the private sector, with major savings in cost and without losses in service quality. In any particular instance, the precise form of intervention may be determined by equity or political considerations, as well as by the efficiency effects.

4. The public sector is prone to 'government failures' just as the incentives driving the private sector can lead to market failures. Government failure can arise because of the absence of full information by the authorities on the 'right' level of intervention or lack of correspondence between politicians' objectives and those of the electorate. Government intervention may not only be incapable of relieving market failures, but might give rise to new ones. The cost of attempting to 'correct' free market distortions can be greater than the cost of the original distortion itself. Even though economics acknowledges a role for state intervention, it probably disposes to a more favourable view of the potential of competitive markets than of public sector involvement.

❓ Questions for discussion

1. What is the economic case for government intervention in a market economy?

2. What is meant by government 'failure'? Why does such failure happen?

3. The Delors White Paper (1993) identified as one of the 'fundamental imbalances' in the EU economy the fact that

current levels of public expenditure, particularly in the social field, have become unsustainable and have used up resources which could have been channelled into productive investment. They have pushed up the taxation of labour and increased the cost of money.... As a result, the level of long-term investment has fallen and the lack of confidence among those involved in the economic process has caused demand to contract. (p. 40)

Comment on this assessment.

4.   Give reasons in support of the view of EU business organisations, such as UNICE, that government spending's share of GDP in Europe should be reduced to the United States' level in order to speed up EU growth. Do you agree with this view?

5.   Using the arguments for state intervention outlined in this chapter, make a case for government support for:

(a) small and medium-sized enterprises (SMEs),
(b) urban transport,
(c) railways,
(c) education.

6.   Sometimes government intervention to correct an externality (say, a subsidy to tertiary education) has an adverse impact on its income-distribution objective (children of the better-off have a disproportionate probability of entering universities). What combination of measures might a government use to deal with this problem?

Exercises

1.   Give examples of government interventions in your business which have been (a) helpful, and (b) unhelpful to the firm. Justify or criticise this intervention by reference to the analytical framework of this chapter.

2.   Compare cleaning an office building with improving the air quality of a major city. Which is a public good and which a private good? Why?

3.   The Commission for Social Justice Report, November 1994 (London: HMSO), drew attention to the following:

(a) The richest 20 per cent of the UK population had 7 times the post-tax income of the poorest 20 per cent in 1991, compared with a multiple of 4 in 1977.
(b) The 1991 multiple of the richest 20 per cent over the poorest 20 per cent was 25 in terms of pre-tax income.
(c) Between 1973 and 1991, the income of the bottom 10 per cent of Britain's population rose by 10 per cent; the income of those in the top 10 per cent of the income distribution rose by 55 per cent.
(d) The most pronounced increase in income inequality was observed in the UK, New Zealand and the US.

Comment on the implications of each of these findings. How would you respond to the criticism that further tax reductions will increase inequality and social divisiveness instead of promoting enterprise?

4. According to the Delors White Paper (1993), low-cost efficient infrastructure is essential to promote competitiveness. With this in mind, it proposed a trans-European transport and communications network (TENS). List some of the reasons why government support is considered necessary for this type of investment. What types of infrastructure can be supplied by private enterprise?

Further reading

There are many good texts on the economics of government. C.V. Brown and P.M. Jackson, *Public Sector Economics*, 4th edn (Oxford: Basil Blackwell, 1990), provides a comprehensive analysis and list of references. The first systematic attempt to apply economic theory to bureaucratic organisation was W. Niskanen's *Bureaucracy and Representative Government* (Chicago: Aldine Press, 1971), which has been reprinted and updated in W. Niskanen, *Bureaucracy and Public Economics* (Aldershot: Edward Elgar, 1994). A witty and forceful statement of the need for state intervention and of the consequences of its absence ('private affluence, public squalor') is provided by J.K. Galbraith, *The Affluent Society* (Harmondsworth: Penguin Books, 1950). For a withering attack on the abuses to which state intervention can lead, see Deepak Lal, *Against Dirigisme* (San Francisco: ICS Press, 1994) and *The Depressed Economy* (Aldershot: Edward Elgar, 1993). The World Bank view is presented lucidly in *World Development Report 1997*, 'The state in a changing world' (Washington DC; 1997).

Chapter 9

BUSINESS AND THE ENVIRONMENT

Introduction

As industrial output and world population continue to grow, people are becoming more conscious of the strains being placed on the environment. Business too is affected by these concerns. Environmental laws and policies have been adopted in virtually all industrial countries and they impinge profoundly on many sectors of industry. Spending by industry on pollution control has averaged 3 per cent of total sales revenues, and this figure has risen to 20 per cent or more for some of the more polluting industries such as chemicals, paper and mining.[1] But while some firms have seen their costs escalate as a consequence of having to conform with more rigorous environment regulations, other firms have been favourably affected. Suppliers of pollution abatement equipment and pollution monitoring systems have found themselves in a rapidly growing market. Many companies have discovered that going 'green' can be a profitable way of doing business.[2]

Environment problems relate primarily to issues such as water reserves and water quality, air quality, soil contamination, disposal of waste and depletion of natural resources. At one time, depletion of non-renewable resources, in particular fossil fuels, was regarded as the major physical constraint on economic growth. Today, the focus of concern has shifted towards the deterioration in air and water quality, the disposal of waste and the protection of natural areas.

The environment has a strong economic, as well as scientific, dimension. From an economics perspective, the problem is that ownership of fresh air and good water supplies is not clearly vested. Access to ocean fisheries and large tracts of natural rain forest is unrestricted because there is no clear owner of these resources. Environmental goods and services are not supplied in the shops like apples or computers. Consumers might care desperately about the quality of the environment, but there is no market through which they can express their preferences. Environmental quality confronts us with extreme examples of public goods, externalities and market failure as outlined in Chapter 8. Because there is

---

1 Jean-Claude Paye, 'Investing in a clean environment', *The OECD Observer* (February/March 1996), p. 4.
2 There is strong competition among large, consumer-oriented firms for leadership on environmental issues. What began for many firms as a government-regulated burden has become a way of reducing waste, conserving resources, improving public image and making profits.

no well-defined market for environmental goods, nobody has an incentive to ensure that these resources are carefully husbanded. *The absence of a market price means that the scarcity value of these resources is not signalled to the consumer. This means that they will tend to be abused and overexploited.*

Because the optimal allocation of vital natural resources cannot be assured by the free market, government intervention is necessary. But for government intervention to be effective and efficient, ways have to be found of inferring the value consumers place on non-market goods, and then of imposing the requisite taxes and subsidies to correct these externalities, where feasible, and using direct regulation where it is not. Finding the optimum mix of these measures is important for economic efficiency.

There is a global, as well as a national, dimension to the environmental problem. Traditionally, economists took an unending supply of clean water and air for granted. These were labelled 'free' goods, to which no price was applied because there was no scarcity. This was an acceptable assumption when world population was little more than a billion and when industrialisation and energy consumption were a fraction of their level today. We know now that these resources are not infinite. The water table in many parts of India and China has fallen steeply in the past two decades, as it has in southern Spain, the Aral Sea and in parts of the US. Under the North China plain, including Beijing and Tienjin, the water table is disappearing by 1–2 metres per year. The area covered by the Aral Sea dwindled by 40 per cent between 1960 and the late 1980s, mainly because of the draw-down of irrigation waters from the rivers flowing into the sea. As world population continues to grow – it has now reached six billion people and is predicted to reach ten billion by 2050 – the air quality in the world's mega-cities and the quality of water supply have become major issues. Acid rain, global warming, through the release of greenhouse gases, and the depletion of the ozone layer are also entering the debate. These problems have a predominantly international dimension and need to be tackled on a multilateral basis. They also raise deeper issues concerning the extent to which the global ecosystem, which has finite absorptive and accommodating capacities, will impose an ultimate limit to economic growth.

Chapter outline

1. The relationship between economic growth and the environment.

2. Setting and attaining environmental objectives.

3. Instruments of environmental policy, distinguishing between market incentives and the traditional regulatory approach of setting quantity-based pollution emission standards.

4. Implications for business.

9.1 Economic growth and the environment

It is sometimes argued that economic growth and improved environmental quality are irreconcilable objectives; that economic growth must inevitably lead to further environmental degradation. However, this view takes account of only one of the links between the environment and economic growth. In reality, the environmental impact of economic growth is more complex than this.

1. Economic growth entails increased pressures on the environment if there are no changes in the way the economy operates. Hence it leads to a decline in environmental quality via a *scale effect*.

2. The *composition* of economic activity changes with the various stages of economic development. When economic growth takes off, economies move out of agriculture and into manufacturing, thereby increasing the resource and pollution intensity per unit of production. As income levels grow even higher, service activities increase their share in the economy. Because services are generally characterised by low pollution levels per unit of production, this slows down pollution.

3. As economies expand, *technology* reduces pollution per unit of product. In market economies, the drive to minimise production costs gives an incentive to energy efficiency and reduced material intensity.

4. *Environment policy* comes into play. The willingness to pay for environmental quality grows with income. Environmental policies affect behaviour. They favour clean activities and penalise pollution-intensive activities (by mandating abatement efforts which raise the cost of production). Technology and innovation are stimulated in a certain direction by the resulting change in explicit and implicit price structures. Higher energy prices, for example, stimulate research into more fuel-efficient cars and machinery. Consumers may also directly affect this trend by increasing their demand for environmentally friendly products.

Empirical data show a complex set of correlations between economic growth and different types of environmental pollution. Air and water quality indicators reveal considerable diversity in effluent patterns as countries become richer. In Figure 9.1, the quantity of effluents is graphed on the vertical axis and GNP on the horizontal axis. In the early stage of development, the strain on the environment grows rapidly. Industrialisation initially inflicts severe damage on air quality and the physical urban environment. Yet the graph indicates that, while some aspects of the living environment change for the worse, some basic indicators of local pollution (such as access to safe drinking water) improve at a very early stage in the growth process.

Once a certain income level is reached, growth not only tends to raise citizens' preferences for a clean environment, but also provides the financial resources for taking effective policy action. The output of certain effluents has an inverted U-shaped pattern over time. Pollution levels rise, stabilise and then decline. The turning point for the majority of pollutants occurs at an income per capita level of

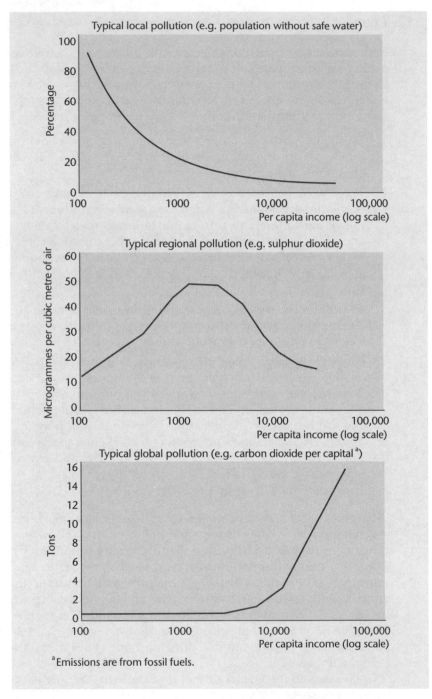

Figure 9.1 A stylised view of the relations between economic growth and the environment

Source: Based on World Bank, *World Development Report* (1992).

around $10,000. Suspended particle matters, sulphur dioxide, airborne lead, carbon monoxide, nitrogen dioxide, faecal coliform and oxygen-depleting substances in rivers follow such an inverted U-shape. Smoke and lead emissions emanating from some of Europe's main cities (London, for example) are about half what they were 25 years ago, and the quality of European rivers and lakes has also improved in certain respects during this period. The layout of housing estates and urban landscapes has improved as a result of tighter and more enlightened planning requirements. The concentration reversal shown by the inverted U is due, in order of importance, to: (a) the compositional effect, i.e. the shift from manufacturing to services, (b) tighter regulations, and (c) new technologies. In industrial countries, the inverted U-shape has largely hinged on the changing composition of aggregate production.[3]

In contrast with this reassuring picture, some types of effluent concentrations increase monotonically with development: e.g. greenhouse gases (carbon and nitrous oxides) and municipal wastes. Problems of diminished biodiversity, depletion of the ozone layer, acid rain and, in certain areas, a falling water table also continue to worsen. Transport pollution, in general, has proven resistant to control. Road-vehicle traffic continues to grow and the energy intensity of transport has not improved.

Industrial countries typically spend around 1.5–2.0 per cent of their national income on pollution abatement.[4] Provided pollution abatement policies are based on proper cost–benefit analysis, however, the benefits from improved environmental quality should outweigh the costs and there should be a net welfare gain. Contrary to common belief, environmental protection is not job-destroying. If account is taken of new jobs generated by the environment protection industry itself, environmental policies have had, overall, *a beneficial (although small) impact on employment.*[5]

As countries become richer, they first clean up the most pressing environmental problems that pose direct health hazards and fall exclusively within the national domain. At a later stage they turn to the more complex threats to the regional and global environment. Economic growth assists this process by generating the means to finance pollution abatement and to consider environment-improving strategies.

It is clear from the above that environment is not just a matter of concern for developed economies. It also affects developing countries. Developed countries are responsible for more than two-thirds of greenhouse emissions at present; but developing countries are growing fast and are consuming more energy. By 2025, today's *developing countries will account for two-thirds of global greenhouse emissions.* This will have major implications for their own citizens as well as for the global ecosystem (*The Economist*, 11 October 1997).

---

3 G. Grossman and A. Krueger, 'Economic growth and environmental quality', *Quarterly Journal of Economics* (110, 1995).

4 R. Turner, D. Pearce and I. Bateman, *Environmental Economics: An elementary introduction* (Hemel Hempstead: Harvester Wheatsheaf, 1994), p. 240.

5 Jean-Claude Paye, 'Investing in a clean environment', *The OECD Observer* (February/March 1996), p. 5.

9.2 Environmental policies

Setting objectives

It is not easy to set quantifiable objectives for environment policy. *First*, scientists disagree about the extent and consequences of environmental degradation. Anyone attending a public hearing on the environmental impact of a motorway, a chemical plant or a new mine will be struck by the contradictory evaluations of the different parties' environmental impact statements. *Second*, the impact on the *global* environment is even more complex to evaluate than the *national* or the *local* impact. *Third*, it can be difficult to disentangle disagreements about the consequences of pollution from objections to the income distribution effects of measures to deal with them.

To illustrate the problem, consider the topical issue of how to deal with greenhouse gases. The *greenhouse effect* refers to the concentration of greenhouse gases (such as carbon dioxide, nitrous oxide, chlorofluorocarbons (CFCs)) in the atmosphere leading to global warming. Fossil fuel industries and agriculture are the two industries most likely to generate such emissions. According to some mainstream scientists the greenhouse effect is already having a visible impact on the economy through flooding and extreme weather conditions across Europe and elsewhere. Initially, global warming may have a favourable impact on parts of the world (higher agricultural output, less need for energy) but, as temperatures increase, the costs will become apparent as populations in low-lying areas are displaced and drought begins to affect many regions. There are likely to be serious income distribution effects. Low-lying Bangladesh, Egypt and the Netherlands will be adversely affected, while higher-lying areas in cold climates will benefit. Other countries may experience extremes of heat and cold, with unpredictable consequences.

In such circumstances, the objective of policy is determined by weighing the benefits to society of reducing greenhouse emissions against the cost of controlling them. In order to do this, first we need to estimate the benefits to be obtained from reducing/avoiding damage due to greenhouse gases; and, second, estimates must be made of the cost of controlling these emissions.

The benefits to society of control of greenhouse gases are represented by BB in Figure 9.2. BB is downward-sloping because, once emissions have been reduced beyond a certain level, the marginal benefits of further reductions in greenhouse gases decline. The marginal social cost of reducing emissions is drawn as the upward-sloping curve CC, reflecting the hypothesis that increasing amounts of economic activity have to be curtailed in order to squeeze out the last vestiges of greenhouse gases. The two curves intersect at E*, indicating an optimal level of reduction in pollution of OQ. To insist on a higher rate of reduction would involve greater marginal costs than benefits. To choose a lower rate than OQ would mean allowing more pollution than is socially desirable.

By this reckoning, OQ is the objective, the optimal level of greenhouse gas emissions. By conceptualising the problem in this way, we find, repeating the lesson of Chapter 8, that a complete ban on emissions would be sub-optimal. The optimal level of emission is not zero.

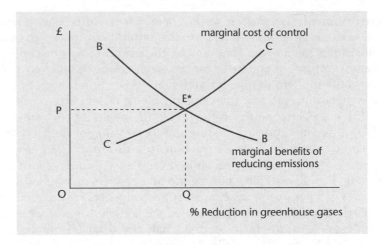

Figure 9.2 **Costs and benefits of reducing greenhouse gases**

But how do we assign actual numbers to costs and benefits? Often, we do not have sufficient empirical information to identify the exact location of point E. In the greenhouse gases case, there have been many estimates of the CC curve. Most economic studies of global warming have focused on ways of minimising the cost of achieving a given reduction in greenhouse gas emissions, through a combination of fiscal and regulatory instruments. But estimating BB has proven difficult.

One way forward is to adopt a '*no regret*', *or precautionary, principle*. Thus, even a very low risk of catastrophic damage should induce society to take countervailing action. In the case of greenhouse gases, the Kyoto conference (December 1997) committed most industrial countries and some transition economies to limit greenhouse gas emissions to 5 per cent below the 1990 level by the year 2010, while the Montreal Protocol (1987) and its successive amendments envisaged the complete phasing out of CFC emissions. Progress could also be made by governments correcting local externalities which have an incidental effect of reducing emissions. That way, even if concern about greenhouse gases were to turn out to be mistaken, minimal economic loss would be incurred because the measures taken would be justifiable in their own right. For example, the removal of subsidies to coal could be justified on the grounds that coal-burning causes local air pollution.

Various methods have been proposed to measure the benefits of an environmental resource. Take, for example, the recreational use of a lake created by a dam. One way of finding out its value to the public would be to ask individuals, by means of a questionnaire, how much they would be prepared to pay for such use. This is the *contingency valuation method*. Another method of inferring values is by *hedonic pricing techniques*, used to estimate the disutility of airport noise, bad air quality in cities or the value of a woodland amenity. Here we compare house prices near airports (say) with those, equal in other respects, in a quiet area. The difference can be indicative of the capitalised value of a quieter

227

environment. A *production function approach* can also be used whereby we assign a value to the environment equal to the amount consumers pay in order to produce substitutes themselves. For example, the amount spent by consumers on domestic water purification apparatus for tap water could be taken as a rough indicator of the value to them of higher water quality. The amount spent on noise insulation may be an indicator of the value people in cities place on being insulated from traffic noise. Depending on the problem, one might use one or a combination of these three methods of assessing the social value of the environment.

The depth and extent of reaction to a diminution in environmental quality *from those who are themselves unlikely to be directly affected by it* can be surprisingly strong. People who have never gone on a safari worry about wildlife, and stay-at-homes can get just as upset as seasoned travellers by the erosion of the Nepalese valleys. The resultant value is called *the non-use value of a resource*. The utility of non-users accounts for more than half the total economic value of wilderness areas and better water quality in lakes and rivers.

Setting measurable environmental objectives places a heavy demand on statistics. The development of environmental indicators, satellite accounts to existing national accounts and, in the long run, integrated economic/environmental national accounts are essential to this exercise and are being developed. Environment impact studies are now compulsory for state-aided projects in the EU and will help to provide a statistical foundation for a national accounting exercise. From a business perspective, it is important to ensure that there is a strong economic input in specifying the optimal level of pollution and quantifying the economic costs of attaining environmental objectives.

9.3 Policy instruments: design and effect

Government environmental policy has been described as *an effort to put a green thumb on Adam Smith's 'invisible hand'*. In the past, the emphasis was on regulation rather than prevention and on administrative controls in preference to market-based incentives. Over time, these regulations have become increasingly onerous because of:

- high administrative costs,
- insufficient flexibility in implementation,
- stultifying effects on industrial innovation.

The economic reasons for preferring market incentives to regulation can be illustrated with a simple example (Figure 9.3). Imagine a paper mill, the output of which is linearly correlated with the amount of pollution. On the horizontal axis we measure quantity of the firm's output, for which there is a corresponding amount of pollution generated. Draw the marginal profit curve of the firm, MP. It is downward-sloping because, as output increases, profits per unit are assumed to fall. The firm continues production up to output OQ. At that point, any further increase in sales will yield negative profits (loss). In terms of Chapter 5, it represents the point where private MC = MR.

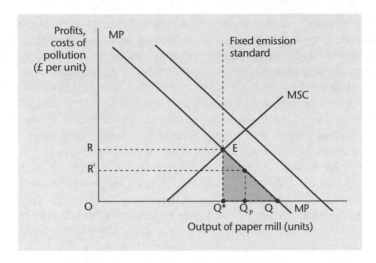

Figure 9.3 Regulation v tax to reduce pollution

Source: Adapted from R. Turner, D. Pearce and I. Bateman, *Environmental Economics: An elementary introduction* (Hemel Hempstead: Harvester Wheatsheaf, 1994)

Next, the marginal social cost of the pollution created by the factory is represented by the upward-sloping curve MSC. These social costs are external to the firm – private costs are already taken account of in the firm's profit-maximising calculus.

The socially optimal equilibrium point is reached at output OQ*. However, the private profit-maximising firm will want to produce at OQ. To reduce the firm's output, the government could use regulation or market incentives.

The government could tackle this problem by setting a fixed emission standard for each firm in the industry. Assume it had perfect information and chose the right level OQ*. Each firm is instructed not to produce more than OQ*. What is wrong with this solution? First, the firm has an incentive to evade the regulation. Profit maximisation requires output OQ, not OQ*. Profits forgone as a result of this restriction amount to the area QEQ*. Second, as a consequence of this incentive structure, firms will have to be monitored. Forms will have to be filled in, factory visits made, etc. This will involve compliance costs for the firm and administrative costs for the authorities. Third, penalties will have to be introduced in order to ensure compliance. If the financial cost per unit of these penalties to the firm is less than OR per unit, it will pay the firm to produce more than OQ*. At penalty level OR' per unit, it would be profitable for the firm to produce OQ$_p$, thus breaching the optimal level.

Suppose that a tax OR were imposed instead of the 'command and control' fixed emission standard. The firm would respond to the tax by cutting back output to OQ*, the optimal output level. One advantage of the tax is that the firm will be *motivated* to reduce output by the dictates of profit maximisation. At output OQ*, marginal profits are zero; hence the introduction of tax of OR makes production beyond OQ* uneconomic. The same applies to all output in the range

Q*Q. Second, because of this, close monitoring of each firm's output will not be necessary. Government can focus on the problem of getting the overall tax and pollution level right and let individual firms produce as they like. Third, compliance and administrative costs will be minimised.

A disadvantage of a tax relative to command and control regulation is that it may give the authorities insufficient control over the *absolute* level of pollution. Suppose, for example, the MP curve shifted outwards because of an increase in demand or a reduction in input costs for paper. For a given tax level, the firm's output will increase and also the level of pollution. In cases where it is important that absolute levels are not breached, say for reasons of community health, this would be a consideration in favour of regulation (see below).

Over and above these theoretical issues, the rising cost of environmental regulation has forced governments to reconsider the merits of market incentives. Market-based instruments refer to price incentives such as pollution taxes, subsidies, deposit-refund systems and tradeable permits. (*Tradeable permits* consist of permits for a specified level of pollution, allowing firms to trade the permits to the highest bidder.) The US, Canada and the Scandinavian countries have been to the fore in employing these measures and their use is being extended to developing countries, including Chile and Mexico. The European Commission has also proposed to use tradeable permits with the aim of helping to cut emissions of greenhouse gases by 8 per cent between 1990 and 2012. The incidence of such measures has grown in recent years. The most pronounced increase was in energy taxes aimed at reducing carbon emissions in the Scandinavian countries and the Netherlands. *Deposit-refund systems* in packaging have also become more common. They are designed to encourage people to return empty bottles and cans. Some countries offer subsidies on trade-ins of old cars in order to prevent owners dumping them in the countryside.[6]

Market-based incentives have many advantages over the 'command-and-control' approach of direct regulation. Use of the price mechanism enables costs and benefits to be weighed by each individual firm and consumer, thereby increasing the probability of achieving a given pollution abatement at least cost. Environmental measures which use the price mechanism have the added advantage of integrating environmental concerns into the design of products and into process innovation (see Box 9.1). As a European Commission report expresses it:

> By ensuring that prices reflect underlying scarcities, governments can give consumers, as well as industries, incentives to limit the environmental consequences of their behaviour. The principal advantage of this approach is that the right signals are given to decision-takers. Instead of mandating specific technologies, this policy integrates the environment into everyday decision-making and leaves it to individual agents to find the most promising solutions to environmental problems without compromising their international competitiveness. By drawing upon the full knowledge base of society rather than upon the technical know-how of a limited number of regulators, such a strategy is often likely to generate least cost solutions. Furthermore, as environmental

---

6 OECD, *Managing the Environment: The role of economic instruments* (Paris: OECD, 1994).

Box 9.1

Taxing unleaded petrol

Pollution arising from exhaust emissions is one of several examples of externalities associated with motoring. Motorists take no account of the effect on society of this pollution unless they are charged for it. One way of charging them is to tax petrol. Furthermore, if the emissions from leaded petrol are more dangerous than emissions from unleaded petrol, leaded petrol should be taxed more heavily than unleaded petrol. The rationale behind this action was that lead pollution had adverse effects and, in particular, that it might inhibit children's intellectual development.

Applying the precautionary principle and the polluter pays principle, governments tried to persuade people to buy less leaded petrol. This was done through a combination of tax and subsidy incentives, and also by regulation.

In the UK there is a tax differential in favour of unleaded petrol. Germany also has a tax differential and, in addition, provides a subsidy to catalytic converters. (Once fitted with a catalytic converter, a car has to use unleaded petrol as lead poisons the catalyst.) An EC directive ruled that, from 1990 onwards, all new cars sold in the EC have to be able to run on unleaded petrol. By 1996, 16 OECD countries had introduced a tax differential between leaded and unleaded petrol.

These measures resulted in a rise in the share of unleaded petrol in total petrol sales between 1990 and 1998 from 34 per cent to 78 per cent in the UK and from 68 per cent to 100 per cent in Germany. When goods are close substitutes, as are leaded and unleaded petrol, market incentives can be very effective. Differentiation of fuel taxes enabled most EU countries to phase out completely the use of leaded petrol by 1999. Developing countries are introducing similar measures. By 2005, India plans to have completely phased out the use of leaded petrol.

Source: Laura Blow, 'Fuel for thought', *Economic Review* (September 1995); Jean-Philippe Barde and Jeffrey Owens, 'The evolution of eco-taxes', *The OECD Observer* (February/March 1996).

improvements are rewarded, a powerful incentive is given to develop clean technologies and production processes. This, in turn, might trigger further improvements in technology via a trickle-down effect and bolster the position on international markets.[7]

The European Commission has introduced a macroeconomic rationale for more intensive use of green tax/subsidy measures by pointing out that they could have the added advantage of alleviating unemployment, if revenue from eco-taxes could be applied towards reducing taxes on labour. In its 1993 White Paper, *Economic Growth, Competition and Employment*, the Commission referred to the 'under-use' of labour combined with 'over-use' of environmental resources. Yet taxes on labour, a factor we want business to hire in greater numbers, yield ten

---

7 European Commission, 'Economic growth and the environment: Some implications for economic policy-making' (Brussels: 1994, COM 94/465), p. 10.

Table 9.1 Tax structure in the European Community, 1992

	Total revenues (%)	GDP (%)
Taxes on consumption	26.3	10.9
Taxes on labour	56.7	23.4
Taxes on capital	17.0	7.0
Total	**100.0**	**41.3**
Of which:		
Revenues from taxes linked to environmental problems	6.33	2.66
– Transport (vehicle ownership and purchase, vehicle fuels)		2.37
– Energy		0.21
– Pollution and others (e.g. soil, air, water, noise)		0.07

Source: European Commission, Economic Growth and the Environment: Some implications for economic policy-making (1994).

times more tax revenue than taxes on the environment, which we want business to utilise less intensively (Table 9.1).

In a speech on 2 August 1995, the British Chancellor, commenting on his new landfill tax proposal, said that by raising revenue from waste disposal, Britain would be able to make further cuts in employers' insurance contributions and so create more jobs: 'We will tax waste more and jobs less.' The benefits from such re-orientation of policy could be significant. By relieving the unemployment problem, economic growth in Europe could be increased at the same time as improving the environment. Furthermore, the quality of economic growth could be enhanced and the connection between growth and human welfare brought closer together.

By far the most widely discussed economic instrument for the environment in Europe has been a carbon tax. The tax is to be levied on the carbon content of fuels in order to cut back the amount of carbon dioxide released into the atmosphere. This proposal has been criticised on several grounds. First, inadequate 'ring-fencing' – critics argue that additional revenues from carbon taxes would be used to bolster government spending instead of reducing labour taxes. Second, if Europe introduced stiff carbon taxes without parallel action in competitor countries, energy-intensive sectors could suffer competitive losses, with potentially damaging consequences to jobs. Third, to achieve carbon reduction targets, high tax rates would have to be imposed. According to one estimate, an increase in oil prices of 128 per cent in real terms would be required in order to bring about a 20 per cent reduction in the carbon content of fossil fuels in the UK.[8] Although the Scandinavian countries have introduced a form of carbon tax, agreement on the desirability, not to mention the level and application, of such a tax has still to be achieved at EU level.

---

8 A. Ingham and A. Ulph, 'Carbon taxes and the UK manufacturing sector', in F. Dietz, F. van der Ploeg and J. Van der Straaten (eds), Environmental Policy and the Economy (Amsterdam: Elsevier, 1991).

Effects of intervention

Despite the many advantages of market-based measures, regulatory intervention, enforced by penalties, is necessary in some cases. Regulation may be superior where:

- major health risks are involved (e.g. toxic waste),
- risks of catastrophic failure are present, such as nuclear power plants,
- the amount of pollution generated by the polluter (i.e. at the level of an individual plant) cannot be measured precisely.

However, government intervention, whether market-based or regulatory, can 'fail'. Lack of information, the danger of regulatory capture, intrusiveness of bureaucracy and rent-seeking by lobby groups all serve to diminish the effectiveness of such intervention. 'Failure' can apply both in the process of specifying the target levels of pollution (which may be set too high in response to green lobbies or too low in response to industry lobbies) and in deciding the level of incentives or penalties needed to attain these targets. Often, intervention in one sector of the economy frustrates the effectiveness of environmental efforts in another. Agricultural supports led to over-use of chemicals, over-grazing and water pollution. Subsidies to irrigation have accentuated the problems of salination and water shortage in many developing countries. Energy subsidies have led to over-use of fossil fuels, thus exacerbating the pollution problem.

But, for all the qualifications, intervention has been superior to inaction. One of the success stories is the reduction in lead and smoke emissions in urban areas in many industrial countries. Also, because European post-tax energy prices have been 25 to 50 per cent higher than the US, the EU can produce a unit of GNP with less than 60 per cent of the energy it requires in the US.

9.4   Impact on business

The new approach to environmental issues has had a profound impact on business. Although originally the concerns of environmentalists and industrialists were regarded as antithetical, attitudes have changed considerably. Many firms now pride themselves on their green image. Business organisations have pledged their support for environmental improvement. Groups such as the Business Council for Sustainable Development (BCSD) and the 'Responsible Care' programme set up by US chemical manufacturers have compiled 'good practice' guidelines for environmentally friendly behaviour by companies. Some involve firms committing themselves to tracking the environmental impact of their products right through their lifecycle, from manufacture to final disposal.

Frances Cairncross has identified five positive motivations for this about-turn in business attitudes:[9]

---

9 Frances Cairncross, *Green Inc.: A guide to business and the environment* (London: Earthscan, 1995), p. 64.

1. *Employee morale*: employees want their firm to have an environmental record of which they can be proud. They dislike being associated with a 'dirty' industry.

2. *Consumer tastes*: shoppers are more interested in 'green' products (though often, surprisingly, unwilling to pay for their green preferences) and respond positively to favourable publicity.

3. *Good publicity* strengthens the corporate image. It can be important for multinationals selling directly to the consumer (such as McDonalds), to companies subject to government taxes and hence vulnerable to political pressure (petrol companies, brewing), and to firms in the mining, oil and chemical business, which frequently interact with planning authorities where their 'reputation' may be an important aspect of the final decision. The fear of bad publicity, even if undeserved, led Shell to abandon its plans to sink the Brent Spar oil rig at sea in 1995.

4. *Cost savings*: companies have found that reducing waste and conserving energy and raw materials can be profitable, especially in view of the rising costs of waste disposal. 3M's 'Pollution Prevention Pays' scheme claims to have saved some $500 million since 1975. Tough environmental policies can save firms money.

5. *Market niche*: a 'green' image can be important for sales of food and disposable products, and can be an effective way of establishing a strong market niche.

These positive factors are important for firms which are subject to public scrutiny and where information on their 'greenness' can be compiled. But, given the unwillingness of many customers to pay a large premium for green products, the movement would have been much slower and less decisive in direction had it not been buttressed by government legislation and enforcement. In this regard, the *threat of litigation* has added a powerful incentive to firms to conform to environmental regulations. Litigation has become a major worry for firms, and for their insurers, because it can be immensely costly as well as generating negative publicity (regardless almost of the verdict). It also creates uncertainty; firms can be liable for damages and clean-up costs of not only present but also past pollution, for which the current management of the firm may have had no responsibility. Litigation can be initiated by environmental authorities and even by individuals who take action against the authorities for not enforcing their rules with sufficient zeal.

Environmental policy affects business in many different ways. *First*, it reduces costs for some business inputs. A fishing hotel on a lake will benefit from tighter rules on sewerage disposal in nearby towns. German paper companies have benefited from the recycling laws which have increased the supply of cheap recycled pulp. A country's food and drinks industry may gain from the improvement of a country's green image.

Second, environment consciousness may encourage innovation, with the possibility of discovering new and more efficient processes and products, and/ or creating new markets for a company's products. Johnson Matthey benefited

Box 9.2

Green as a selling point

During the 1980s, detergent manufacturers began to find ways to use the environmental properties of their products as selling points. One was Procter & Gamble (P&G). In the early 1980s, a technician at its French division came up with the idea of the flexible plastic 'dosing' ball. It had two advantages: it stopped powdered detergent from blocking the dispenser and it allowed a highly concentrated washing solution to engulf the clothes for the first 10 minutes of a wash. The ball stimulated P&G to develop concentrated liquid detergent that could be sold in a recyclable plastic container. Also, the firm developed a refill carton, thereby reducing household packaging waste. As a result, liquid detergents increased their market share. Refill cartons proved popular with environmentalists and also with the supermarkets, partly because they take up much less shelf space per wash than concentrated powders.

Source: Frances Cairncross, *Green Inc.: A guide to business and the environment* (London: Earthscan, 1995).

from the growth of catalytic converters since it mines platinum and palladium, key ingredients in a catalyst. By adjusting its product design, Procter & Gamble benefited from the shift in preferences to greener products (Box 9.2). Professor Michael Porter, a strong advocate of the benefits of environmental regulation for industry, cites other cases of what he calls *innovation offsets*:

> Process changes to reduce emissions frequently result in increases in product yields. At Ciba-Geigy's dyestuff plant in New Jersey, the need to meet new environmental standards caused the firm to re-examine its waste water streams. Two changes in its production process – replacing iron with a different chemical conversion agent and process changes that eliminated the release of toxic products into the waste water stream – not only boosted yield by 40 per cent but also eliminated wastes, resulting in annual cost savings of nearly $1 million.[10]

Generally, firms involved in innovative techniques for waste disposal, energy efficiency improvements, leisure industries with minimal adverse environmental effects, firms specialising in environmental audits, environmental impact studies, eco-labelling and suchlike can be expected to have improved opportunities. Automobile firms which are successful in developing environmentally friendly cars can anticipate substantial returns. Case studies confirm that it is possible that innovation offsets, even under a strict regulatory regime not intended to encourage innovation, can provide benefits in excess of compliance costs to the affected firms. Early development of new products with attractive environmental features can give companies an 'early mover' advantage, such as that enjoyed by Scandinavian pulp and paper manufacturers, and by some German firms in

10 Michael E. Porter and Claas van der Linde, 'Towards a new conception of the environment–competitiveness relationship', *Journal of Economic Perspectives* (Fall 1995), p. 102.

package-intensive products. A key requirement for this to happen is that national environmental standards should anticipate international trends in environmental protection.

Third, tighter environmental regulation can in some circumstances give one company or industry a lead over its rivals. Thus, the major chlorofluorocarbon (CFC) producers, such as DuPont and ICI, were influential in backing the Montreal Protocol, the treaty to reduce the use of CFCs through aerosol propellants, refrigerants and solvents. As well as producing CFCs, these firms also happened to be the main producers of the nearest chemical substitute to CFCs. But since the substitute was also more expensive than the CFCs, they had an obvious interest in securing a properly enforced global agreement on CFCs. A national ban by one government alone would have exposed domestic producers of the expensive substitute to unfair competition from CFCs made in other countries. Hence a company that has developed substitutes will do well from tighter regulations or changes in tastes, provided the regulations or taxes are universally applied and consistently enforced. Environmentally clean firms may also benefit by attracting ethical mutual funds. This could be advantageous to these firms' reputation, albeit not necessarily providing them with cheap capital. Ethical funds to date have not earned notably lower rates of return than other funds.

Since the establishment of the Toxic Release Inventory in 1986, more than 20,000 American manufacturing plants have a legal obligation to publish details of their releases of some 320 hazardous chemicals. In the belief that attack is the best method of defence, a growing number of American companies have responded by including an environmental audit in their financial statements. In Europe, this practice has gained some adherents. Norsk Hydro, for example, a chemical and fertiliser manufacturer, publishes reports with detailed figures on emissions and discharges, measured against authorised limits. British Gas publishes an environmental review of its approach to subjects such as contaminated land and energy efficiency, and the Chartered Association of Certified Accountants holds an annual competition for the best environmental reports.

Fourth, environment policy can have an important impact on a firm's international competitiveness. High product standards can sometimes restrain foreign competition. For example, the European Commission's ban on the use of certain growth hormones prevents US hormone-treated meat from competing with EU producers. In other circumstances, rules relating to production processes and methods applied in the home country can give a competitive advantage to firms producing in countries with less stringent standards. As noted above, environment policy has strong sectoral effects. Firms in polluting industries find their cost structure has risen. The consequences can be seen in the opposition to the proposed carbon tax in Europe from energy-intensive building materials and transport industries which perceive (rightly) that the measure will lead to higher energy costs, and hence to higher prices and diminished demand for their products. The nuclear industry, on the other hand, is supportive of the proposal since it sees the carbon tax as promoting its cost advantage relative to power generators using coal or oil. These sectoral conflicts are an inevitable consequence of any economic change.

Environment policy has implications for income distribution within countries. A tax on energy may make sense in environmental terms, but it will be unpopular with those directly affected. Unfortunately, many eco-taxes hurt the poor proportionately more severely than the better-off. They are examples of *regressive* taxes.[11] The attempt by the UK government to raise value added tax on energy consumption in the mid-1990s generated such an electoral backlash that the proposal had to be effectively abandoned. Attempts to compensate the losers proved ineffective, and the gainers – the environmental lobby – failed to support the measure.

9.5 Conclusions

The concept of an environmentally sustainable growth rate has captured the attention of economic policy-makers. The Earth Summit at Rio de Janeiro in 1992 exposed an entire generation of politicians and citizens to environmental ideas. However, the relationship between economic growth, the environment and human welfare is more complex than headlines or political slogans suggest. Higher GNP and a better environment can in many respects be complementary objectives. Prosperity allows people the luxury of becoming more environmentally conscious and makes them better able to afford higher environmental standards. It is extreme poverty (i.e. the lack of GNP) that creates the mind-set of short time-horizons and a lower propensity to plan far into the future.

Improving environmental performance is not inconsistent with a firm maintaining competitive advantage. At the extreme, environmental catastrophes such as at Bhopal (1984), the *Exxon Valdez* (1989) and *Diamond Grace* (1997) can have dramatically adverse effects on a firm's financial viability, and environmental strategies are needed to find cost-efficient ways of minimising these risks. Moreover, environmental regulation often encourages firms to use their resources more efficiently. Many forms of environmental pollution by firms, whether in the form of discharges, toxic materials or discarded packaging, are simply waste in a different guise. Opportunities exist to eliminate such waste through redesigning products and processes, and through innovative ways of reorganising operations. Through innovation, some environmental problems at least can be reduced or eliminated without incurring substantial costs. There are instances where a reduction in environmental pollution has even reduced business costs and improved product quality.

Throughout Part I of the book we have emphasised the role of the market and the importance of competition in an efficient economic system. Environmental

---

11 In calculating these income distribution effects, one has to have regard of the ultimate incidence of the tax. As we saw in Chapter 3, just because a tax happens to be levied on the supplier (say, an electricity generating station), that does not mean that the supplier suffers the whole incidence of the tax. The incidence will depend on the price elasticities of demand and supply.

economics addresses the problems that arise when the market 'fails' – either because property rights are not defined, as in the ocean fisheries, or because of the intrinsic nature of environmental goods. Government intervention becomes essential to an optimal outcome. But government intervention does not mean ignoring altogether the market mechanism. Good environment policy consists in setting objectives and using market mechanisms to achieve them. This is easier said than done. A strong state sector does not guarantee a good environment, as the degradation of the environment in many countries testifies.

✔ Summary

1. The integration of environmental and economic policies is important for achieving sustainable growth. Measures in place are already having a major impact on business. Business cannot afford to neglect environmental concerns.

2. The relationship between quality of the environment and economic growth is complex. After a certain level of prosperity has been reached, some forms of pollution seem to abate. This happens partly because of shifts in the composition of demand away from manufacturing towards less polluting services and partly because richer countries are able to afford to give higher priority to pollution control. In many respects – water quality and clean air in urban areas, for instance – the quality of the environment in the advanced industrial countries is better than it was at the start of this century. In developing countries, by contrast, the early stages of industrialisation and the development of agriculture have been associated with environmental degradation. One billion people still lack adequate supplies of drinking water.

3. The relationship between economic growth and problems such as global warming is still not known with precision. Yet there is support for countervailing action on the basis of the precautionary principle.

4. Environmental priorities should be set so as to equate the cost of cleaning up, or preventing, an additional unit of pollution with the benefit of higher output to society. Various techniques for measuring these benefits and costs have been developed. There is a need for an extensive statistical base on environmental quality to make environmental impact assessments more accurate and useful.

5. The instruments of environmental policy include market incentives and regulation. Both have a role to play in achieving policy objectives. Regulation has been costly to implement, and there has been a swing towards market-based incentives through policies of the 'polluter pays' type.

6. The impact of environmental policy on business is a thorny question. Some argue that environment policy can be a spur to innovation and can force industries into efficiency. Others worry about the costs and the delays caused by this policy. All agree that there are strong sectoral effects and, as with economic policies generally, well-defined losers as well as gainers. Firms with

a positive approach to environmental issues can benefit through improvements in reputation, in employee morale and in product quality.

? Questions for discussion

1. The costs of environmental protection are perceived as being too burdensome for many businesses confronting international competition in an increasingly open economy. It has also been argued that many governments struggling with large budget deficits cannot afford high environmental standards. Yet there is a bedrock of public support for environmental goals. Discuss the economic costs and the benefits of environmental improvement from:

   (a) a business perspective,
   (b) an overall economy perspective.

2. Give examples of ways in which environmental protection can be profitable for business. Under what circumstances can environment policy damage business?

3. Outline the main advantages and limitations of the 'polluter pays' principle.

4. Discuss possible sources of 'government failure' in the application and administration of environmental policy.

5. 'Market prices should as far as possible be made to reflect the external costs to society of economic activity.' What methods can governments use to 'internalise' the social costs of environmental damage?

6. Many studies have shown that the application of nitrogen fertilisers to agricultural land causes pollution. What measures could be taken to reduce this pollution?

7. If people travel on a bus that causes pollution, should government try to reduce the emission from the bus by taxing the transport company or the bus passengers?

☞ Exercises

1. Many corporations, especially those in environmentally sensitive industries, allocate a section of their Annual Report to explaining their environmental policy. Describe and evaluate such a policy statement in a firm of your choice.

2. According to some estimates, a $200 carbon tax would cut carbon dioxide emissions by four to five times as much as an equivalent $200 devoted to subsidising energy conservation. Why might this be so?

3. The Swedish sulphur tax is estimated to have triggered a 40 per cent decline in the sulphur content of fuel oil between 1990 and 1992. The tax accomplished its environmental objectives, but yielded less revenue than the Treasury expected. Why might the Treasury have preferred a lower rate of tax than the Environment Department?

4. Consider a tax on petrol, imposed because of concern about air quality. The objective of the tax is to reduce vehicle emissions. Given that the price elasticity of demand for petrol is well below unity, examine the effects of the tax under each of the following headings.

   (a) Does it discourage an activity that causes environmental harm?
   (b) Does it place a burden on those responsible for the environmental problem?
   (c) Does it minimise administrative costs to government and to payers of the tax relative to the benefits expected?
   (d) Does it provide a dynamic incentive for petrol refineries and car manufacturers to innovate and upgrade product quality?

5. It is often claimed that multinational subsidiaries apply higher environmental standards in the host country than domestically owned competitors. Give reasons why this might be the case. Would you expect multinationals to apply different standards in plants in the host country to those in the home country?

6. Explain why the ocean fisheries are more likely to be over-fished than a privately-owned lake.

📖 Further reading

A readable introduction to environmental economics is provided in R. Kerry Turner, David Pearce and Ian Bateman, *Environmental Economics: An elementary introduction* (Hemel Hempstead: Harvester Wheatsheaf, 1994). For an overview of the issues from a business perspective, an excellent source is Frances Cairncross, *Green Inc.: A guide to business and the environment* (London: Earthscan, 1995). The OECD has an ongoing stream of publications on this topic, as does the European Commission. See, for example, 'Economic growth and environmental sustainability – a European perspective', *European Economy*, Brussels, 71/2000. Those interested in environment project appraisal should consult *The Economic Appraisal of Environmental Projects and Policies: A practical guide* (Paris: OECD, 1995); also, Nick Hanley and C.L. Spash, *Cost–Benefit Analysis and the Environment* (Aldershot: Edward Elgar, 1993).

Chapter 10

HIRING LABOUR AND THE INVESTMENT DECISION

Introduction

Previous chapters have been concerned with how much output a firm produces, what price it charges and, when discretion over price is lacking, what other measures can be used to boost profits. This chapter considers how the firm should determine the amount of inputs to purchase. By this we mean the number and quality of employees, the amount of plant and machinery, the quantity of energy and commodity and intermediate materials, and so on. Since the same basic principles apply to all inputs, we confine discussion to the economics of hiring labour and the investment decision. Both these subjects are treated in depth in human relations, industrial organisation and corporate finance courses, and no claim is made in this chapter to provide a comprehensive analysis. Yet much light can be thrown on these subjects by the application of the simple economic principles developed in the previous chapters.

Chapter outline

1. The hiring decision.
2. The firm's investment decision.

10.1 The hiring decision

The classical theory

It follows from the principle of profit maximisation that the firm's demand curve for labour is driven by the rule: hire employees up to the point where

total remuneration costs = the marginal revenue product of labour.

That is, the firm should, first, compute all the costs of hiring an extra unit of labour; second, calculate the net value to the firm of that unit of labour's output; and third, continue hiring up to the point where costs and benefits are equal. If the cost of hiring an extra employee is £1000 per month and the output of that employee contributes £1500 to profits, the firm should add to its staff. If the marginal revenue product is only £500, the firm should reduce its staff. Equilibrium is reached at the point where costs equal extra revenue.

The marginal revenue product (MRP) depends on several variables. First, it depends on the degree of competition in the product market. If the firm operates in a perfectly competitive market, all its output can be sold at the going market price, and hence the value of the marginal employee is found by multiplying the employee's marginal product by the market price, i.e. $MRP = MP \times P$. If the marginal employee produces 10 units of output at a price of £150, its marginal revenue product is equal to the value of its marginal product, i.e. $10 \times £150 = £1500$. (For simplicity, we assume zero materials cost.)

If, on the other hand, the price were to fall as a result of the extra 10 units being offered on the market, the loss in revenue on existing sales would have to be incorporated in the calculations, by computing marginal revenue (as discussed in Chapter 4). The marginal revenue product from these 10 units is then:

$$MRP = MP \times MR.$$

Second, account must be taken of the decline in marginal productivity as more units of labour are applied. If the law of diminishing marginal productivity applies, after a certain point successive increments of labour yield a diminishing return, assuming all other factors such as size of plant, number of machines, etc., remain unchanged. Hence the marginal product curve is assumed to slope downwards. Since the firm's demand curve for labour (DD) depends on the marginal product of labour, it too is downward-sloping (Figure 10.1).

Third, the supply of labour to the firm must be considered. If the firm is a small player in the market, it takes the going 'rate for the job' as given. It can obtain all the employees it wants at that rate, and so will not offer more. Were it to offer less than the going rate, nobody would be willing to work for it. In such circumstances, the supply curve of labour to the firm is a horizontal line (W_1 W_1 in Figure 10.1). Equilibrium occurs when the firm's supply and demand curves for labour intersect, at point E_1.

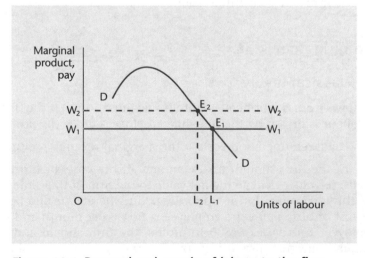

Figure 10.1 Demand and supply of labour to the firm

This simple analysis yields important but familiar conclusions about the relationship between pay and numbers employed by the firm:

1.   A rise in pay leads to a fall in the demand for labour. If the ruling pay level were to be OW_2 instead of OW_1, the equilibrium would change to E_2, with OL_2 instead of OL_1 units of labour demanded.

2.   A fall in pay, for the same reasons, leads to a rise in the amount of labour demanded.

From firm to industry

It is possible to progress from the individual firm's demand and supply of labour to an industry supply and demand curve. The industry demand curve is obtained by the lateral summation of individual firm demand curves. The procedure is the same as that used in deriving market demand curves. The aggregation exercise, however, relies on several strict assumptions about the independence of a firm's demand from the overall level of demand for labour. The industry demand curve, like the individual firm's, is downward-sloping.

The industry supply curve is different from the firm's supply curve. It is no longer horizontal because, while labour might be available to an individual firm at the going rate, the going rate itself is determined by supply and demand at the industry level. Instead, it slopes upwards, reflecting the assumption that higher pay will attract more labour supply. As pay levels increase, more people are attracted to the industry, existing employees are more reluctant to leave the industry and also some may work longer hours. All this is consistent with our model of the rational individual, maximising utility in the workplace.

In this way, we obtain the industry's supply and demand curve. Equilibrium pay is OW, and OL units of labour are demanded and supplied at that pay level (Figure 10.2).

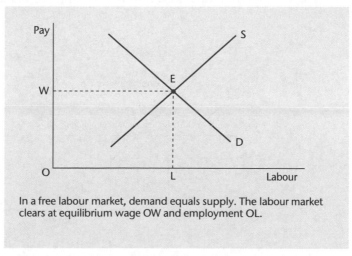

In a free labour market, demand equals supply. The labour market clears at equilibrium wage OW and employment OL.

Figure 10.2 Industry demand and supply curves for labour

Disequilibrium in the labour market

The above analysis depicts a market-clearing situation. Pay flexibility ensures that everyone who wants work can find it, provided they are prepared to accept an appropriate level of pay. In practice, there are many impediments to adjustment.

Labour markets, for example, can be affected by *trade unions* which exert monopoly power in order to raise pay levels. The labour supply curve then no longer reflects the sum of independent individual utility-maximising decisions, but rather the collective preferences of unions. It becomes a pay-setting schedule, determined by union–management bargaining strategies.

Labour supply can also be distorted by *minimum wages*, by the *tax system* and by other *cost-increasing rigidities*. These prevent, or slow down, the process of adjustment between labour demand and labour supply, and can exacerbate the unemployment problem (we discuss this further in Chapter 14).

Suppose, for example, the labour market was in equilibrium at point E_1 where the pay level is OW_1, and OL_1 are employed (Figure 10.3). The government now decides that this is the minimum pay which employees should ever be asked to accept and enacts legislation accordingly. Pay OW_1 becomes the minimum rate.

Now assume that the demand for labour curve shifts downwards from D_1D_1 to D_2D_2. This could happen because of the announcement of slower growth, which leads to pessimistic expectation for future sales. With a free market, the fall in demand leads to:

- a new equilibrium at E_2,
- a fall in pay to OW_2,
- a fall in employment to OL_2,
- a decline in labour supply of L_1L_2 in response to lower pay level.

As a result of the minimum wage legislation, however, the new equilibrium is at E^* instead of E_2. Pay does not fall (which is good news for the 'insiders', OL^*, who are fortunate to hold on to their jobs). Numbers employed fall to OL^*. The burden

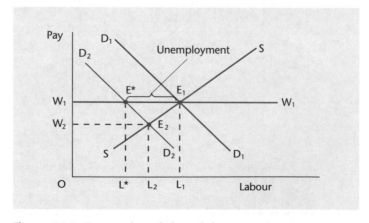

Figure 10.3 **Economics of the minimum wage**

of adjustment to the decline in demand, in other words, falls entirely on the numbers employed rather than on pay.

In discussion of this type, the term *pay rigidity* is used as an umbrella term to denote all conventions, institutions and legal measures which set an externally imposed 'floor' to pay levels. Some European governments are concerned that the EU's Social Charter, by imposing minimum standards for working and living conditions (hours worked, treatment of part-time workers, provision of benefits), will tend to aggravate the unemployment problem. Considerations such as this prompted the British government to insist on an 'opt-out' clause enabling it to reject initiatives based on the Charter. However, these fears may prove unfounded. European governments are conscious of the need to reduce the indirect costs of hiring labour. France and Germany have both made efforts to roll back some of the more significant cost-increasing features of their social welfare systems.

Extending the model

The textbook model is a useful starting point, but it needs extensive modification before becoming a useful guide to the operation of the real-world labour markets.

One obvious objection is that labour should not be treated as analogous to a commodity. Employees depend on pay for their livelihood and on their jobs for a feeling of well-being and inclusion. There is a social as well as an economic dimension to the labour market.

Even more serious is the objection that the classical model conceptualises labour as something that can be bought and traded at will, more or less as farm workers once were at hiring fairs or dock labourers at the turn of the century. Hiring a new staff member in today's world is a different matter.

- *First*, the firm is purchasing a stream of labour services over time, often over many years. It has to assess the pattern of productivity during this period. The productivity pattern can itself be affected by the type of pay structure the firm offers. If a firm does not want to hire an employee, it can call on the services of a consultant or it can decide to contract out. This gives it the flexibility envisaged in the model.
- *Second*, the productivity of the employee cannot be known with certainty in advance of actually being at work in the firm and, even after that, productivity is difficult and expensive to monitor. An employee is not a machine which performs according to instructions. A firm has to consider how to motivate its staff. Compensation schemes have to be devised which will encourage maximum participation by the employees and transform them from 'compelled performers' to 'willing contributors'.
- *Third*, employees, like machines, have to be upgraded (trained) but, unlike machines, they can choose to leave their employer after the upgrading.

The standard analysis of the labour market treats marginal productivity of labour as given, once the amount of capital, land and training made available to an employee is given. Business, by contrast, sees marginal product as something that is the manager's job to raise. The level of remuneration is seen as a crucial instrument for raising productivity. Also, it is clear that the whole remuneration 'package' has an important bearing on employee morale and motivation. An attractive pay structure, defined in terms of its progression over time, pension rights, procedures for promotion and separation, etc., can help a firm to attract and retain the right people in the business. These considerations are especially important when work itself requires intellectual effort and commitment, which cannot be accurately measured and is more difficult to monitor. This is the typical case in high-tech industries. For them, human relations (devising ways of motivating highly skilled and mobile staff) is as much a part of the firm's technology as its patents and machinery.

In deciding how many people to employ, the firm must consider more than the current pay. It needs to calculate the stream of net revenues likely to be generated by the employee over time. From this it must deduct the stream of costs associated with that employee (pay, employer social security, social provision such as holidays, maternity leave). Further deductions must be made in respect of up-front outlay for searching, screening and interviewing. All the above must be discounted at an appropriate rate (see below), and then the impact on profits after tax must be assessed.

From the employee's perspective, accepting a position with a firm also involves long-term consequences which an investment approach is best suited to analyse. Hence a recent graduate may be happy to accept a job in a well-known accounting or law firm for lower pay than in a less prestigious firm, because higher future earnings are expected to result from the prestige of having passed the former's stricter screening process. Also, skilled employees, on leaving their jobs, do not necessarily take the first alternative offered. To take a job which fails to utilise their skills could lead to an erosion of these skills, and also to a loss of status and reputation. Instead, they search around until a better option is found, balancing the lost revenue from being unemployed (net of any unemployment benefits) against the prospect of a better job and a superior flow of future earnings. This leads to the phenomenon known as *search unemployment*, a voluntary withdrawal from the workforce which is entirely consistent with utility-maximising principles.

10.2 The investment decision

Rental cost of capital

Investment consists of an addition to capital stock. Net investment refers to the accretion of capital in a firm, after deducting depreciation. We have seen that, in the case of labour, a profit-maximising firm will apply the rule: wage = marginal revenue product, subject to the various qualifications just outlined. The same rule applies to its purchase of raw materials or intermediate materials. In any well-run company, details of marginal revenue product and marginal cost will be properly recorded.

An investment decision by the firm involves the purchase of a machine or a new plant (*physical* investment), or allocating funds to training and upskilling the workforce (*human* investment). In principle, the familiar profit-maximising rule applies. We work out the marginal revenue product of the capital used for the investment and compare it with the cost of capital. Because investment involves a long time-dimension, future returns are hard to define and to measure. Marginal revenue product refers to the stream of net earnings generated by the project over its lifetime. We must find a way of expressing this profile as a single average annual return.

In addition, we must find a formula for deriving the cost of capital. In simple terms, what is called *the rental cost of capital* is determined by three main factors. First, the rate of interest. Suppose the investment cost the firm £C. Had the firm invested the cash in bonds (or given it to shareholders to invest as they wished), this capital would have earned i.£C annually. If the investment fails to earn more than this, management should not proceed with it. Second, account must be taken of the depreciation of the asset, which we might compute as an annual charge of δ.£C. Third, an adjustment might have to be made for inflation, π. Assuming the price of the asset rises in line with the general price level, this will result in an annual rise in the nominal value of the asset of π.£C. Fourth, allowance will also have to be made for taxes on profits of the project, less any capital grants. This can be done by either deducting from the MRP or adding to the estimate of the rental cost of capital. Amalgamating the first three factors gives us an equation for the rental cost of capital, R, as follows:

$$R = (i.£C + \delta.£C - \pi.£C) = £C(i + \delta - \pi)$$

The profit rule states that the firm should continue investing up to the point where this R equals MRP.

To summarise, an investment decision involves the acquisition of an asset which will provide a flow of future benefits, which has to be weighted against an up-front capital outlay and future annual costs. *A key variable in determining the rental cost of capital, and hence the profitability of investment and the demand for investment capital, is the rate of interest.* This negative relationship is the analogue of the relationship between the wage rate and the demand for labour.

The rental cost of capital approach is an intuitively reasonable, but unfamiliar, way of assessing investment. We now proceed to other ways of calculating returns on investment which draw on the same basic framework but which are more widely used in business.

Techniques for investment appraisal

Any firm has a large number of projects in which it might invest. Each of these projects is an option available to the firm. Some of these options are profitable and some are not. Economic principles offer guidance as to which ought to be chosen. In this context, three main techniques are used for measuring the return on investment:

- net present value,
- internal rate of return,
- pay-back.

One of the most important techniques for the evaluation of investment projects is that of *net present value (NPV)*. This approach can be defined as follows:

$$\text{NPV} = x_0 + \frac{x_1}{(1+r)} + \frac{x_2}{(1+r)^2} + \ldots + \frac{x_n}{(1+r)^n} + \frac{J}{(1+r)^n}$$

where NPV = net present value, x is the net cash flow from the project in year i (i.e. after correcting for inflation), r is the interest or discount rate, n years is the life-span of the project and J represents the scrap value of the investment at the end of the investment period. This technique involves prediction of the annual net cash flows of the project over its lifetime. These cash flows are exclusive of interest payments. The corporation is assumed to supply all investment funds from debt and equity sources. They are then discounted back to the present in order to give the present value of the investment. In NPV calculations, the interest or discount rate to be used for the test is selected in advance. Management decides the appropriate discount rate. It is the minimum rate of return on capital employed which the firm is prepared to accept. As such it includes the cost of capital and also a risk premium. (For some projects, e.g. oil in politically unstable parts of the world, the risk premium could be a multiple of the firm's cost of capital.) Projects may receive the green light if the NPV discounted at this rate is positive. If there are more such projects than the firm is able to finance, it will most likely choose those projects which have the highest return. The NPV technique, in summary, by translating future net cash flows of an investment into current value, represents the capitalised values of this stream of cash. In financial appraisals of investments, this technique is usually referred to as *discounted cash flow (DCF)* analysis.

Another indicator of the return on a project is the *internal rate of return (IRR)*. This is closely related to the NPV technique and is defined as the discount rate (r^*) that reduces the net present value of a project to zero:

$$\text{NPV} = 0 = x_0 + \frac{x_1}{(1+r^*)} + \frac{x_2}{(1+r^*)^2} + \ldots + \frac{x_n}{(1+r^*)^n} + \frac{J}{(1+r^*)^n}$$

where x is the net cash flows after subtracting input costs, and $r^* = $ IRR. This is similar to the formula used for NPV calculations, except that the discount rate r^* is computed so as to equate NPV to zero. A decision rule might be to approve the project provided the IRR is equal to or greater than an agreed discount or interest rate.

The internal rate of return seems to be a convenient way of summarising the returns of a project, and in practice it sometimes makes no difference whether one uses IRR or NPV to rank projects. However, in the cases where it does make a difference, notably when there are negative cash flows later in the project's life (e.g. strip mining and oil industry projects), the IRR can give the wrong ranking. Also, some projects may have more than one IRR, so it is not clear which specific one to choose. Problems with IRR can arise where a project receives positive cash flows in some years, followed by negative cash flows. All in all, NPV is the more reliable indicator (Box 10.1).

In a large company with many investment opportunities, there are two stages in the process of investment appraisal: first, screening and second, ranking. Oil companies, for example, usually set a high IRR threshold (screening) and then use NPV and some form of Profitability Index (such as NPV/Capital Expenditure or NPV/Maximum Exposure) to rank projects and decide which to accept (ranking). With high inflation it is important to distinguish between MoD (Money of the Day) and RT (Real Terms or constant purchasing power) cash flows. Pay-back is sometimes included in the screening process and projects are rejected if pay-back is greater than two years, say, for a small project, longer for a really major, strategic project.

IRR is widely used, but it should not be relied on as the sole decision criterion for investment projects.

The *pay-back period* is another common guide for investment appraisal. The pay-back technique simply considers the number of years that must elapse before the net income from the investment pays back the initial outlay – in other words, the number of years before the cost of the investment is recovered. An investment goes ahead if the pay-back is less than some pre-specified number of years. Because of the increasing uncertainty of future revenue estimates beyond a certain period, this technique is often regarded as a valid way of appraising investments. The advantages of the technique relate to its simplicity and its use in highlighting the risks in a project.

Box 10.1

Weakness of pay-back and IRR techniques

The annual flow of revenue for three projects is shown below. Each project involves an initial outlay of £1 million. Project A pays back quickly (four-year pay-back period if undiscounted, five years if discounted at 5 per cent) but has a short lifetime. Project B pays back more slowly (five-year pay-back period undiscounted) but continues to provide net revenue for many years. Clearly, it would be a mistake to select project A over project B because of its shorter pay-back period.

Project C illustrates some of the pitfalls that may be encountered by the user of IRR. This project is the same as project B except that there is a large negative flow in the last period, reflecting, say, environmental clean-up obligations. In fact, project C has two IRRs, at 9.68 and 12.75 per cent. If the discount rate were 5 per cent, the analyst might be inclined to recommend proceeding with project C. But this would be a serious mistake. Because of the last period's negative flow, the NPV of project C is negative for any discount rate below 9.68 per cent. A lower discount rate implies that relatively greater attention must be paid to distant events, such as the clean-up cost. Depositing the funds at 5 per cent will be a better strategy than investing in project C, given the clean-up costs that would be faced in 20 years. The IRR of such a project shows the rate at which the project will break even; it fails to reveal that, at a lower discount rate, the project may be unprofitable.

Box 10.1 continued

Annual cash flows for three projects

Year	A	B	C
0	−1.00	−1.00	−1.00
1	0.25	0.20	0.20
2	0.25	0.20	0.20
3	0.25	0.20	0.20
4	0.25	0.20	0.20
5	0.25	0.20	0.20
6		0.20	0.20
7		0.20	0.20
8		0.20	0.20
9		0.20	0.20
10		0.20	0.20
11		0.20	0.20
12		0.20	0.20
13		0.20	0.20
14		0.20	0.20
15		0.20	0.20
16		0.20	0.20
17		0.20	0.20
18		0.20	0.20
19		0.20	0.20
20			−4.50
Pay-back (years)	4	5	5
Pay-back (discounted)	5	6	6
NPV at 5 per cent	0.08	1.42	−0.28
IRR (%)	8.0	19.3	12.8; 9.7

Source: Alan W. Gray, *EU Structural Funds and Other Public Investments: A guide to evaluation methods* (Dublin: Gill & Macmillan, 1995), pp. 28–31.

Pay-back rules have, however, several limitations. One is their short-termist bias. By ignoring cash flows beyond the specified cut-off date, the pay-back technique biases investment decisions against projects with long-term benefits. Thus, take two projects with different estimated lifetime scales. The pay-back technique automatically tends to support the project with the shorter pay-back period. If the first project was at the end of its life after five years, while the second project provided annual benefits for another 15 years, the mistake of ignoring benefits after the pay-back period is clear. For this reason, use of the pay-back period criteria is not to be recommended. Yet it remains widely used in the UK and the US.

Both the NPV and the IRR method indicate that the relationship between the interest rate and the demand for investment funds is negative. Consider two

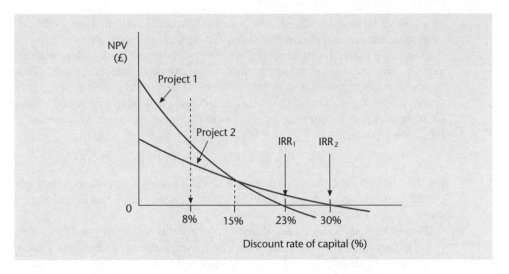

Figure 10.4 Net present value (NPV) and internal rate of return (IRR) on two projects

projects, 1 and 2, with NPV and IRR as in Figure 10.4. Project 1 has an IRR of 23 per cent, Project 2 of 30 per cent. At low rates of interest, however, NPV is superior on Project 1, while at rates above 15 per cent, the NPV of Project 2 is above that of Project 1. Which project do we choose? At any discount rate below 15 per cent – say 8 per cent – it may be better business to choose Project 1, even though its IRR is lower than Project 2. If, however, Project 1 had more time-dependent risk (e.g. a change in government or in legislation were in the offing), some further risk analysis would be required before making a final decision. Project 2 has the advantage of earning its revenue earlier than Project 1.

Extensions

The investment decision involves a great deal of uncertainty. Future net flows are subject to wide margins of error. Among the sources of uncertainty are:

- price trends/exchange rates,
- changes in tax rates,
- cost trends,
- depreciation,
- scrap value of the investment,
- interest rates,
- catastrophic loss due to accidents/acts of God,
- risks of nationalisation.

This endemic uncertainty, combined with the greater openness of capital markets, has made business conscious of the need to earn a healthy return on capital employed. Some firms expect new investment to earn as much as 20 per cent on shareholder capital. The profitability of the project can be critically influenced by the interest rate on borrowed funds. For example, the present value of £100 in 10 years is £56 at a 6 per cent discount rate, but only £39 at a 10 per cent discount rate and £16 if discounted at a 20 per cent rate.

Firms use many techniques for dealing with uncertainty. One possibility is to take a range of likely outcomes and assign probabilities to each. For example, suppose you judged that a project, at best, might yield an NPV of £20,000 and, at worst, a loss of £4000 and that you considered each outcome equally likely. Then, by weighting each outcome by its probability of realisation, an *expected return* can be computed as:

$$E(R) = 0.5(£20,000) + 0.5(-£4000) = £8000$$

Further refinement may be necessary to take account of risk aversion on the part of the firm, i.e. it may want to weigh losses more heavily than gains of the same size.

The expected return can then be compared with the riskless return on a government bond. If the return on the investment project is less than the bond rate, the firm should give the money back to its shareholders rather than invest it itself. In practice, executives are extremely reluctant to do this. They would regard it as a serious reflection on their own entrepreneurial acumen.

Another way of dealing with risk is by investing abroad in different markets with non-synchronised cycles. Then, when one market is experiencing a slump and is causing the firm to lose money, there is a good chance that the other market is performing well and adding to profits. Firms also reduce risk by investing in different products, although as we have seen in Chapter 6, conglomerate investments have tended to yield disappointing returns – risk reduction is bought at a heavy price in average returns. Risk can be diluted by joint ventures or by pooling. Dozens of banks, for example, shared the risk of the Channel Tunnel.

Equilibrium

So far we have addressed the determinants of demand for investment funds. Given a world of full information and certainty, one could laterally summate all individual firms' demand functions to derive an industry or economy demand for capital as a function of the rate of interest.

The classical model also postulates a link between the supply of capital and the rate of interest (allowing for risk). It is generally assumed that the two are positively associated, but the relationship is not well defined. Level of income is clearly another important determinant of the supply of capital, as are expectations regarding inflation and tax.

Putting demand and supply factors together, we can sketch out a theory of the rate of interest analogous to the theory of pay determination. The equilibrium interest rate is one which brings the supply of investment capital into balance with the demand for investment capital. The interest rate, like the level of pay, plays an important role in determining the structure of an economy and is highly pertinent to the conduct of monetary policy. We shall return to this aspect in Part II of the book.

10.3 Conclusions

This chapter has shown that, under certain assumptions, the profit-maximising firm will pay factors of production the value of their marginal product. It is a short step from this to asserting that, under a free market system, labour and machines and other inputs are paid what they are worth to society. The marginal productivity theory invites normative inferences. Some nineteenth-century economists concluded from it that workers who formed trade unions were in effect trying to extract a reward for their labour in excess of their 'true' contribution to society, as determined by the invisible hand. Left to itself, the market determines each person's salary. Everyone gets paid what they are 'worth' – as decided by the market. If anyone believes they are being paid too little, the theory suggests an immediate remedy: move to another job where their output would be more highly valued. If no such job can be found, the market is conveying a clear message: you are not being underpaid.

As we have seen, the marginal productivity theory is an incomplete theory of how factors are rewarded. Unlike machines, people need to be motivated and the structure of their pay packet over time plays an important role in this. Marginal productivity is not determined by technical factors only, but also by a firm's total remuneration package. Also, free competition does not prevail in labour markets. To understand how pay is determined in any real situation, careful attention must be devoted to analysing market structures. Nevertheless, the fundamental principle that, *ceteris paribus*, pay levels and the demand for labour are negatively correlated is a good starting point for discussions of employment and unemployment policy. It has practical, far-reaching implications.

Likewise, the negative association between interest rate and investment emerges from the marginal productivity theory of capital. Different types of problem arise in applying this rule to the real world. Account must be taken of the extreme uncertainty of marginal productivity estimates in the context of long-run projects. Nowhere is this uncertainty more evident than in the valuation of 'new economy' firms. Prior to its going public, accountants valued Netscape at $112 million. A few months later, following, following its IPO, the market valued it at $2.1 billion. Such astonishing lack of concordance between accounting and market valuations are commonplace in the knowledge economy. Uncertainty about projected future earnings is only part of the problem. Evaluating the human capital assets of a firm also presents novel, and as yet unresolved, problems of valuation.

✔ Summary

1. Profit maximisation and competition lead the firm to hire labour up to the point where the cost of hiring equals the marginal revenue product to the firm. The cost of hiring includes all direct and indirect costs associated with an additional member of staff. Marginal revenue product equals the extra output produced by the marginal employee multiplied by the net marginal revenue derived from it.

2. This analysis carries the important inference that pay and numbers employed are negatively correlated. A rise in pay, other things being equal, leads to a fall in employment. By allowing pay to fall, employees can price themselves into a job. The labour market model has been influential in persuading some governments to view with suspicion 'social' initiatives which could threaten jobs.

3. Labour market analysis has to take into account the increasing similarities between hiring labour and the investment decision. A firm's decision to employ a person involves a commitment over time, involving costs and benefits to the firm. These need to be properly calibrated and discounted.

4. Economics takes marginal product of labour as exogenously determined by technology and by the amount of cooperant factors at its disposal. In fact, labour productivity is often highly endogenous. Management's task is to convert 'compelled performers' into 'willing contributors'. Pay levels and pay structures can contribute to this transformation.

5. The investment decision is driven by the need to equate return on capital with the cost of capital. The cost of capital can be defined as the rate of return expected by shareholders and the return on capital can be interpreted as return on shareholder capital. Firms ration investment funds by insisting on a minimum rate of return on capital employed (ROCE).

6. Three widely used techniques for investment appraisal are: net present value, internal rate of return and pay-back period. Of these, the net present value – or discounted cash-flow method – is superior on analytical grounds.

7. No appraisal method can conceal that investment involves heavy risk. There are ways of coping with risk, but not of eliminating it. The riskiness of investment explains why investment spending fluctuates so markedly relative to other types of spending.

❓ Questions for discussion

1. Why does marginal revenue product decline as the quantity of labour employed by the firm increases? How do you reconcile this with the observed increase in the productivity of labour over time? How useful is the 'pay = marginal revenue product' rule as a guide to business?

2. Does the practice of paying an employee increments for each year of service conflict with the profit-maximising rule: wage = marginal revenue product?

3. How, in your view, would a monopoly trade union determine its objectives in pay negotiations? Would it aim to maximise pay per person employed or the number of persons employed, or something in between? How would the answer affect the level of pay demanded by the trade union for its members?

4. The Cambridge economist Alfred Marshall wrote that 'highly paid labour is generally efficient and therefore is not dear labour'. Do you agree?

5. The principal–agent problem was discussed in Chapter 4. The way of resolving it is to draw up contracts which will protect the principal from the opportunism of the agent through (a) provision of incentives to the agent, (b) monitoring of the agent's performance, and (c) penalising the agent if there is non-performance. Compare and contrast the agency theory approach with the standard demand and supply model of the labour market in this chapter.

6. Is the economist's approach to the investment decision consistent with the analysis of a corporate finance or management accounting specialist?

 ## Exercises

1. Suppose a firm's output–labour input relationship was as follows:

Number of employees	Total output produced
1	20
2	50
3	90
4	120
5	145
6	165
7	180
8	190
9	195

(a) Calculate the marginal product of labour at each employment level.
(b) If price per unit was £1000 and the pay level was £20,000 per year, how many employees would the firm hire?
(c) If pay levels increase to £31,000 per year, what would be the impact on employment?

2. Suppose the price of a computer is £10,000. Its effective life is two years. Its marginal revenue product to the firm is £5000 for each year and its scrap value at the end of the period is £2000. The interest rate is 6 per cent per year. Calculate (a) the present value of the flow of marginal revenue product, and (b) the net present value of the investment.

3. Suppose you are asked to decide whether a new machine should be purchased. Projected net returns (sales less costs) over the four-year life of the machine are: year 1, £2000; year 2, £4000; year 3, £4000; year 4, £6000. The machine costs £10,000. The firm uses a 10 per cent discount rate. Should it proceed with this project? Assess by reference to (a) NPV, (b) IRR, and (c) a two-year pay-back period.

4. An investment project yields a revenue stream of £100 per year for 10 years. The cost of the project is £500. Suppose the pay-back period rule is four years, would you accept this project? What is NPV if the discount rate is 10 per cent? What is the IRR?

📖 Further reading

A good textbook on labour economics is D. Sapsford and Z. Tzamatos, *Labour Economics* (Basingstoke: Macmillan, 1993). P. Milgrom and D. Roberts, *Economics, Organisation and Management* (Hemel Hempstead: Prentice Hall, 1992), begins where the standard analysis ends and shows how useful economic concepts can be in explaining pay structures. This new approach to explaining pay, hiring and pensions policy is developed in E.P. Lazear, *Personnel Economics for Managers* (New York: John Wiley, 1998). Useful sources on investment appraisal include S.A. Ross, R. Westerfield and B. Jordan, *Fundamentals of Corporate Finance*, 2nd edn (Boston: Richard D. Irwin, 1992), and Richard Pike and Bill Neale, *Corporate Finance and Investment: Decisions and strategies* (Harlow: Prentice Hall, 1999).

Part II

THE MACROECONOMIC FRAMEWORK

Introduction to Part II

The overriding task of macroeconomic management is to provide a stable economic framework. This means low inflation, fiscal responsibility and steady economic growth. Low inflation is needed so that the price system can carry out its functions efficiently. Fiscal responsibility is necessary to ensure that a sustainable tax and government spending regime is in place that will encourage enterprise and innovation. Fiscal balance is also required in order to maintain price stability. Steady economic growth is desired in order to avoid the misery of another Great Depression similar to that of the late 1920s and early 1930s, and to escape from the cycle of boom and bust. Business fluctuations are a reality, but we need to minimise their amplitude and encourage business investors to take a long-term perspective. The implicit assumption of macro-economics is that steady growth will mean a higher long-run trend growth.

This is a perspective which modern business would strongly endorse. Most firms have to cope with enough uncertainty at market level, without the addition of gratuitous uncertainties arising from government mismanagement of the macroeconomy. In preparing their sales and profit forecasts, however, firms cannot simply assume that the macro-environment will remain stable. They must contribute to making such stability happen by influencing economic policy. To do this effectively requires an understanding of how the macro-economy operates, and of the dogmas and assumptions which influence the policy choices of economists.

Our starting point (Chapter 11) is a discussion of how output is determined in the short run. We study the determinants of aggregate supply and aggregate demand, and consider the relationships between the real part of the economy and monetary variables. The contribution of Keynesian analysis of demand to our understanding of the economy is explained.

With this analytical foundation, we proceed to analyse two key macroeconomic problems: inflation (Chapter 12) and unemployment (Chapter 14). The former problem, a central preoccupation of modern macroeconomics, appears to have eased considerably, even to the point where the question 'Is inflation dead?' has been seriously raised. Unemployment, however, remains high in many countries. The danger to economic and social stability from a persistently high level of long-term unemployment has obvious implications for business.

The nature and effectiveness of fiscal and monetary policies is the subject of Chapters 13 and 15. We argue that the primary focus of monetary and interest rate policies should be on maintaining price stability. This places the duties of central banks, as the relevant authority, in a higher profile than before. Fiscal policy, traditionally considered as a solution to the problem of unemployment, is now seen as having contributed to the problem. The reduced effectiveness of fiscal measures can be traced to the growth of public debt, itself the consequence of excessive budget deficits incurred over many years (Chapter 15).

This leads to an analysis of business fluctuations and economic forecasting (Chapter 16). Initially, we assume that government intervention is completely absent. Is the system very unstable in such circumstances? Or are there strong self-adjusting mechanisms at work? Then intervention by the authorities is allowed for. We conclude that some degree of intervention is desirable in cases of extreme shocks to demand or supply (such as, for example, the collapse in the stock exchange on 'Black Monday', 19 October 1987, the currency crisis of the 1990s and Japan's collapsing aggregate demand since 1991)), but that the scope for counter-cyclical action is much less than it used to be.

Business forecasting is then discussed. Managers need to understand how forecasts are formulated and to develop some 'feel' for the important qualifications attached to them. The task of converting macroeconomic forecasts to company forecasts involves analysis not only of overall GNP growth, inflation and interest rates, but also of overall market developments, evolution of the company's market share and specific marketing or product quality initiatives

The objective of this section is to provide the reader with an understanding of:

- Key economic concepts: GNP, GDP, purchasing power parity, aggregate supply and demand.
- Recent economic thinking on the role of central banks and governments in dealing with inflation, unemployment and other macroeconomic problems.
- A knowledge of how monetary policy is formulated, and its implications for interest rates.
- The extent and causes of unemployment and possible solutions.
- The strengths and limitations of monetary and fiscal policies, and how they impact on the economic environment.
- The reasons for business cycles, the scope for reducing their amplitude, the nature of economic forecasting and how to translate macroeconomic forecasts into meaningful information for the company.

Chapter 11

AGGREGATE SUPPLY, AGGREGATE DEMAND AND THE PRICE LEVEL

Introduction

Macroeconomics differs from microeconomics in a number of respects. First, macroeconomics is concerned with the functioning of the economy *overall*. Instead of examining how an individual market works it studies how markets interact. It focuses on aggregate variables such as national output, employment and the general price level.

Second, government and public institutions occupy a more central place in macroeconomics than in microeconomics. The high profile of government in macroeconomics stems in large part from the intellectual origins of the subject. Macroeconomics developed from the writings of the British economist John Maynard Keynes on the Great Depression of the 1920s and 1930s. Keynesians argued that state intervention on a macro-scale was necessary if capitalism was to be saved from self-destruction. They showed how the amplitude of business fluctuations could be reduced by macroeconomic policy and that higher long-term growth could be achieved as a result.

Third, macroeconomics is a more controversial subject than microeconomics. There are disagreements about the role of monetary variables, the causes and cures of unemployment, and the effectiveness of fiscal policy. The reader must not expect to find a single 'right' answer to current macroeconomic problems. There are numerous schools of macroeconomic thought.[1] Because macro-economics is closely involved with government policy, political, social and economic objectives intermingle and can sometimes conflict. Controversy also arises because of the intrinsic complexity of the subject. There is no single 'true' model of the economy.

Readers often complain that, in macroeconomics, 'everything seems to depend on everything else'. The complex chain of interdependence between macro-variables explains why macroeconomics is so difficult and, at times, frustrating. Yet macroeconomics, at its best, can provide solutions to practical problems. These solutions have had a tremendously positive impact on living standards during the past five decades.

---

1 No fewer than seven (respectable) schools of macroeconomic thought have been identified: Keynesian, traditional monetarist, new classical, new Keynesian, supply-side, neo-classical and structuralist. See Edmund S. Phelps, *Seven Schools of Macroeconomic Thought* (Oxford: Clarendon Press, 1990).

Chapter outline

1. Description of gross domestic product (GDP), gross national product (GNP) and how they are estimated

2. Analysis of the concepts of *potential* GDP and *GDP at purchasing power parity*.

3. Outline of a simple (classical) economic framework, beginning with the aggregate supply (AS) curve. The shape of this curve has a direct bearing on the effectiveness of standard macroeconomic policies.

4. Derivation of the aggregate demand (AD) curve. The role of monetary variables enters the analysis at this stage.

5. How the equilibrium level of output and the equilibrium price level are determined. Equilibrium occurs at the point where the AS and AD curves intersect.

11.1 How is gross domestic product (GDP) calculated?

Gross domestic product (GDP), as we saw in Chapter 2, refers to the output of goods and services produced in an economy during a specific period of time.[2] GDP estimates are published on an annual, and sometimes a quarterly, basis. GDP *less* depreciation is *net national product*. The latter is equivalent to *national income*, which in turn is defined as the total of all payments for productive services accruing to the residents of a country.

GDP statistics matter to business for at least four reasons. First, forecasts of future aggregate demand are usually expressed in terms of projected growth in GDP. These forecasts are relevant to the firm's forecast of its own future sales. Second, assessments of the current state of the economy are based on the current and recent past level of GDP. The financial markets scrutinise GDP growth trends with particular care. An acceleration in growth, for instance, could signal an increase in inflation and, in due course, a tightening of monetary policy and higher interest rates. Likewise, slower growth could mark the beginning of a recession. (A recession is technically defined as a fall in GDP in two successive quarters.) Third, movements in GDP can have political implications. Fast growth is perceived as an electoral plus; weak growth an electoral minus. Fourth, international comparisons of aggregate market size are based on GDP data.

---

2 It can be defined formally as:

$$p^1x^1 + p^2x^2 + \ldots + p^nx^n$$

where x^i = quantity of the ith good or service produced
  p^i = the price of the ith good or service
  n = the number of goods produced
  i = 1, 2, ..., n

Real and nominal GDP

Nominal GDP is the current value of goods and services produced in an economy. It is the product of two variables: price and quantity. If we are analysing the change in nominal GDP between one year and another, we need to separate the effect of price changes from volume of output variations. The concept of *real* GDP is designed to provide this information. Change in real GDP is computed by valuing the quantities of goods and services produced in the two periods with the same set of prices. It acts as an indicator of changes in volume of output.

Suppose two goods, x and y, are produced. In year 1, GDP comprises 10 units of x and 12 units of y, at prices £5 and £8 per unit respectively. GDP equals:

$$5x_1 + 8y_1 = 5.(10) + 8.(12) = 50 + 96 = £146$$

In period 2, quantities produced of x and y increase to 11 and 14 units. At the same time, the price of good x rises to £6 and good y to £9. Nominal GDP rises to:

$$6x_2 + 9y_2 = 6.(11) + 9.(14) = 66 + 126 = £192$$

Nominal GDP has increased by $(192 - 146)/146$ or 31.5 per cent. This increase reflects the combined effects of a rise in the average price level and a rise in volume of output. To calculate real GDP in period 2, we compute the value of period 2 quantities at period 1 prices, i.e.:

$$p_1x_2 + p_1y_2 = 5.(11) + 8.(14) = 55 + 112 = £167$$

The increase in real GDP is given by $(167 - 146)/146$, or 14.4 per cent.

Dividing nominal GDP by real GDP yields a figure known as *the implicit GDP deflator*. This indicates by how much the *average* level of prices of goods and services included in GNP has risen since the base year. The implicit deflator closely resembles the more familiar consumer price index which will be discussed in the next chapter.

GDP price deflator = (Nominal GDP ÷ Real GDP) × 100

	Nominal GDP (1)	Real GDP (at p_1) (2)	Implicit GDP Deflator (1) (1)/(2) × 100
Year 1	£146	£146	100
Year 2	£192	£167	115
% increase:	31.5%	14.4%	15%

Since there are different ways of measuring the increase in an economy's price level, care must be taken in choosing the index itself and the base period from which the calculations are made.

GDP and GNP

Gross national product (GNP) refers to output produced by productive factors *owned by permanent residents of a country*. Gross domestic product (GDP) is output produced by productive factors *located in the country*, regardless of their owners' nationality. The need for this distinction arises when domestically owned productive factors generate income for domestic residents from economic activity carried out abroad. For example, the repatriated profits of a Japanese automobile subsidiary located in the UK are included in Japan's GNP, but excluded from its GDP. In the UK's accounts, they are included in GDP, but excluded from GNP. For most countries, the gap between GDP and GNP is very small (for instance, it is only 0.3 per cent of GDP in the US). But for countries with large net income from migrants (Mexico), or with an extensive presence of multinationals (Singapore, Ireland) or with high dividend income from capital held abroad (Kuwait), the gap can be as high as 10 per cent of GNP. Both measures are useful in their own way. GDP is a better measure of the amount of productive activity in a country; GNP is a superior measure of a country's standard of living. Summing over all countries, global GNP is in principle exactly equal to global GDP.

How to compute GDP

Statisticians compile GDP statistics using three separate data sources: (1) output, (2) income and (3) expenditure. In principle, all three sources should yield the same answer, since they measure the same thing, but because of statistical discrepancies this rarely happens in practice. The details of each method of compilation need not concern us, but the methodology throws light on the different components of these important national account aggregates.

The *output method* calculates the value of the output of goods and services produced in the economy over a specified period of time. Given that many firms' output is another firm's input, to avoid double-counting, only the value added at each stage of the production process is counted. *Value added* is defined as gross sales minus cost of raw materials and intermediate inputs. For an individual firm, value added, computed as: gross sales minus cost of intermediate inputs and raw materials equals, by definition, wages and salaries plus rent plus interest payments plus profits.

Since value added comprises wages, salaries and profits, GDP estimated by the output method should give exactly the same figure as the sum of wages and salaries, rents and corporate profits. The *income method* of computing GDP focuses on this latter aspect. In turn, since income is earned as a result of someone else spending, the addition of all sources of national spending should in theory provide the same GDP estimate as the previous two. (The pro forma statement of the national accounts using the income approach is presented in Box 11.1 for illustrative purposes.) The *expenditure method* adds up all spending on final goods and services, i.e. on investment goods, on consumer products, and on government-supplied goods and services. These three approaches underline the essential circularity in the flow of income and output through an economy. Firms generate value added, the

Box 11.1

National income, gross national product (GNP) and gross domestic product (GDP)

There are three key elements in the national account totals: national income, gross national product (GNP) and gross domestic product (GDP). This table shows how they are derived, using the *income* approach.

1. **Employees' compensation**
2. **Income of self-employed**
3. **Corporate profits**
4. **Rents and interest**
National Income
5. **Indirect taxes (+) less subsidies (−)**
Net National Product at Market Prices
6. **Capital depreciation**
Gross National Product (GNP)
7. **Net payments (+)/Receipts (−) of income from abroad**
Gross Domestic Product (GDP)

The main components of the accounts are:

1. *Employees' compensation* includes pay (before income tax) and employees' social tax contributions. In industrial countries, this amounts to over 60 per cent of national income.
2. *Income of self-employed* refers to income of farmers, retailers, professionals (lawyers, doctors etc.) and partnerships.
3. *Corporate profits* are profits before tax as defined by the tax authorities.
4. *Rents and interests* represent the returns to land and capital, respectively.

   National income, the sum of the above items, is defined as income earned by residents from current production of goods and services in the economy. National income is significantly lower than GNP at market prices. To derive GNP, two further items must be added: net indirect tax revenues and capital depreciation.
5. *Indirect taxes less subsidies*. Output valued at current market prices includes indirect taxes and excludes subsidies. Indirect tax represents a transfer to government which is collected by business on behalf of the state. It is not part of business income nor is it a receipt in respect of a service rendered. Hence, to reconcile national income and national production data, an adjustment must be made for these indirect taxes and subsidies.

> **Box 11.1 continued**
>
> Adding indirect taxes to national income yields an estimate of *net national product (NNP)*. To derive GNP, one further adjustment is required.
>
> 6. *Depreciation* is defined as the amount set aside for the maintenance of capital stock. It is computed as the amount of depreciation allowed for tax purposes in the case of business firms. In the case of government-owned assets, depreciation has to be estimated.
>
> Net national product plus depreciation equals *gross national product.*
>
> Finally, *gross domestic product* is obtained by adding to GNP income earned by non-residents in the national territory, such as repatriated profits of foreign subsidiaries, and subtracting income earned by nationals abroad. GDP can be higher or lower than GNP.

counterpart of value added is wages and profits, and wages and profits, in turn, are the mirror image of national consumption and investment. These interlinkages are an important feature of an industrial economy.

Composition of GDP

There are five components of national expenditure:

1. Consumption $= C$
2. Investment $= I$
3. Government purchases $= G$
4. Exports $= X$
5. *Less* Imports $= M$

$$GDP = C + I + G + X - M$$

Note that exports are entered with a positive sign and imports with a negative sign. GDP does not measure total spending *by* domestic residents, but total expenditure on *goods and services produced by domestic residents.*

Consumption consists of purchases of non-durable goods, such as food and fuel; consumer durable goods, such as washing machines and cars; and services, such as holiday spending, insurance and travel. The main determinant of consumption expenditure is the level of national income.

Investment consists of additions to capital stock or, in economics jargon, increases in *real* capital formation. (This is not to be confused with financial investment, which consists of the transfer of existing assets from one person or institution to another.) Investment is divided into three categories: (a) plant and machinery investment, (b) residential and office investment, and (c) additions to inventories. Government spending on infrastructure, such as roads, railways and ports, is also included. Forecasters watch investment in inventories carefully – an unplanned build-up of inventories is a classic signal of a weakening in demand.

Government spending consists of current spending on goods and services, such as health, justice, security and education. Only spending which involves a direct purchase of goods and services is included in the GDP figure. Social welfare payments, industrial subsidies and interest payments on the national debt are omitted. Such transactions are called *transfer payments*, i.e. they involve the transfer of purchasing power over existing resources, from one household to another, rather than spending on additional production. Rather misleadingly, education is treated as current spending although arguably, being investment in human capital, it should be included as part of national investment.

Exports refer to spending by foreigners on domestically produced goods and therefore must be included in GDP, whereas for the same reason *imports* are excluded.

In summary, GDP represents total spending on domestically produced goods and services by both residents and foreigners:

$$GDP = [C + I + G - M] + X$$

$$\downarrow \qquad\qquad \downarrow$$

| Spending by residents on home-produced goods and services | Spending by foreigners on home-produced goods and services |

These statistical conventions for measuring GDP have many conceptual and practical limitations. The major conceptual issues have already been discussed in Chapters 2 and 3. Measurement difficulties include: (1) the omission of unpaid household and other voluntary work; (2) the incomplete coverage of underground economy activities; (3) the classification as outputs of what arguably are inputs, such as expenses on crime prevention and depletion of the environment; and (4) the absence of specific provisions for the run-down of non-renewable resources. These qualifications are not trivial. The value of unpaid (non-market) housework in the major industrial countries has been estimated to be worth more than one fifth of GDP.[3]

11.2 Potential GDP, actual GDP and GDP at purchasing power parity (PPP)

Potential and actual GDP

Potential GDP is a concept of crucial significance in macroeconomics. It is defined as:

> the maximum output that an economy can produce if capital, labour and other factors of production are fully utilised, consistent over the medium term with low inflation.

---

3 See A. Chadeau, 'What is households' non-market production worth?', *OECD Economic Studies* (Spring 1992). As the percentage of women entering the workforce increases, this source of bias will diminish.

Potential GDP is not the same as the maximum attainable level of output in an engineering sense. The qualifying clause 'consistent with low inflation' suggests that potential GDP will be lower than the engineering maximum. As the physical maximum is approached, productive factors become more scarce, prices are bid up and an inflationary cycle could be set in motion. Deviations from potential GDP in either direction can cause problems.

> If actual exceeds potential GDP, price stability is placed in jeopardy; if it is less than potential GDP, there is unemployment and resources are being wasted. Macroeconomics studies ways in which divergences of both types can be minimised.

There are two main ways of estimating potential GDP. One is to estimate a trend growth rate from past data. This method can be sensitive to choice of base year and takes no account of new resources. Another method is the 'production function' approach, which relates potential output directly to changes in available factor resources and their utilisation rate. To estimate potential GDP by this method, output is divided into a business sector and a government component.[4] Given the difficulty of measuring government output, actual output in this sector is usually assumed to be equal to its potential. Attention then focuses on ways of measuring the business sector's potential output. This exercise involves four steps: (1) the growth of productive inputs, such as labour, capital and energy, is estimated; (2) an estimate is made of the utilisation levels of these inputs consistent with low inflation; (3) the productivity of these factor inputs is assessed, i.e. an estimate of total factor productivity growth is derived; (4) these three steps are combined to obtain an estimate of the potential growth of business sector output. The process is illustrated in Figure 11.1.

Estimates of potential output based on the production function approach are regularly published and are used as a guide to macroeconomic policy. Attention is paid to the sign and size of the *output gap*, defined as the difference between actual and potential GDP. OECD estimates for the year 2000, show that Japan was operating at 3.4 per cent short of its potential, Italy 2.6 per cent and Belgium 0.7 per cent (Table 11.1). In other cases, notably in the US, actual economic growth exceeded total potential growth. But no one knows for sure what the potential growth rate in an economy is. Estimates for the US economy used to cluster in the range 2–3 per cent, but increases in productivity fed by technology advances have spawned a series of 'new economy' estimates of 3–4 per cent. Final judgement on the level of potential GDP has to depend on judgement as well as on technical analysis.

Macroeconomic policy focuses on the relationship between actual and potential GDP. By maintaining a stable economic framework, governments hope to achieve close concordance between the two series, thereby also ensuring that the trend growth rate will reach its optimum level.

---

4 R. Torres and J.P. Martin, 'Measuring potential output in the seven major OECD countries', *OECD Economic Studies* (Spring 1990). Potential output has also been defined as: the level of output which the economy could produce if capital and labour were fully utilised, with a margin of slack to accommodate short-term increases in demand.

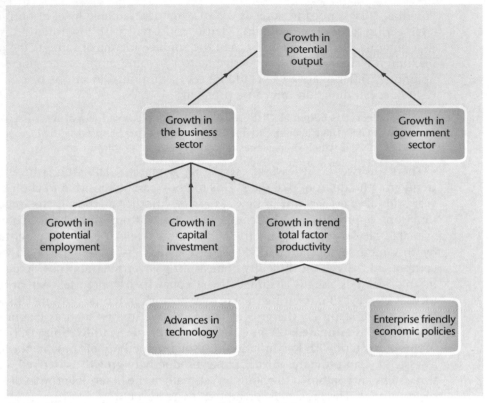

Figure 11.1 Decomposition of growth in potential output

Table 11.1 Output gaps for the year 2000

US	2.2
Japan	−3.4
Germany	−2.3
France	−0.6
Italy	−2.6
UK	1.1
Canada	0.2
Austria	0.8
Belgium	−0.7
Denmark	−0.6
Finland	0.8
Ireland	5.5
Netherlands	1.2
Norway	−0.7
Spain	0.7
Sweden	0.7

Notes: Output gap = deviations of actual GDP from potential GDP as a percentage of potential GDP.

Source: OECD, *Economic Outlook*, December 1999. Author's estimates.

GNP at purchasing power parity (PPP)

In making international comparisons it is necessary to convert all nominal GNPs into a common currency. More often than not, the common currency will be the US dollar. In this context, it is common to distinguish between *GNP at current exchange rates* and *GNP at purchasing power parity* (PPP). The two GNPs often diverge quite markedly. For instance, India's GNP per head in 1998 was US$440 at nominal exchange rates but $US2060 at PPP (World Bank *World Development Indicators*, 2000). Which statistic is 'right', and why do they differ?

- To understand the difference, imagine this simple four-step experiment. Begin by compiling a *representative basket* of goods and services. A representative basket might, for example, contain:

> 2 kilos of rice
> 1 kilo beef
> 5 inner city bus rides
> one month's rent of a two-bed apartment
> 1 personal computer
> 2 visits to doctor
> etc.
> (the list could run into hundreds of items)

- Ask an individual to purchase this basket in Washington DC. Assume that the cost happens to amount to the convenient figure of US$1000.

- Find out the cost of buying *exactly the same basket* in India. Suppose it turned out to be 8540 rupees. Then we say that the *Purchasing Power Parity (PPP)* rate of exchange is 8540 rupees divided by $1000 i.e.

PPP 8.54 rupees = $1

- India's national accounts show that GNP per head in 1998 was 17,600 rupees. Divide by 8.54 to derive GNP per head in US dollars at PPP as *$2060*. This is the World Bank figure. To derive GNP per head in US dollars, divide 17,600 by 40 (the current exchange rate per dollar) to get *$440*.

The main reason for the difference is that current rates are determined by trade in goods and by mobile capital flows. Services (cost of drivers, barbers, helpers, etc.) that cannot be traded do not enter the picture. But they are invariably much cheaper in developing countries than in better-off countries. Poor countries are still poor, but much less so than comparison on the basis of current exchange rates would appear to suggest. World Bank PPP estimates indicate that countries such as China and India are three to four times better off than would appear on the basis of GDP at nominal exchange rates (see Table 11.2).

To compare living standards in different countries, purchasing power parity is the more accurate indicator. Thus, executives or diplomats from a relatively poor country posted to a relatively rich country have a strong interest in consulting the

Table 11.2 Comparison between GNP per capita at current exchange rates and at PPP

Country	GNP per capita (current prices and exchange rates)	GNP per capita (PPP)
India	440	2060
Morocco	1240	3188
Argentina	8030	11728
Mexico	3840	7450
China	750	3051
UK	21410	20314
France	24210	21214
Canada	19170	22814
US	29240	29240

Source: World Bank, *World Development Indicators* (Washington DC, 2000)

type of dedicated purchasing power parity indexes that are available from consultants since they will require an upward adjustment in their salaries if they are to provide equivalent living standards to those available at home. For foreign investors interested in repatriating profits from a developing country, nominal exchange rates are what matter, not PPP. We discuss purchasing power parity again in Chapter 21.

11.3 The aggregate supply (AS) curve

Our next step is to construct a model showing the determinants of aggregate supply and demand. Aggregate supply (AS) can be regarded as a rough proxy of potential GNP.

The aggregate supply (AS) curve shows combinations of real output (y) and the price level (p) which are consistent with equilibrium in the economy. A vertical AS curve shows that a given level of real output, y_0, is consistent with many possible price levels (Figure 11.2(b)). A positively-sloped AS curve shows that a rise in the price level from, say, p_0 to p_1 is consistent with a rise in output from y_0 to y_1 (Figure 11.2(a)).

The price on the vertical axis of the AS curve is the *general price level*. This contrasts with the industry supply curves in Chapter 3, where price of the industry's output is on the vertical axis. The industry supply effect arises because the price of the industry's output is defined relative to prices in other sectors. All other prices are assumed to remain constant. In the case of the AS curve, the general price level is defined relative to prices of productive factors such as labour. A rise in the general price level relative to nominal wages would, on this reasoning, have a positive effect on aggregate supply. The AS curve will be positively-sloping. If, on the other hand, one believes that the price of labour (and other productive factors) is linked to the general price level – because, say, employees demand higher pay to compensate for inflation – it will be impossible to have any relative price effect and the AS curve will tend to be vertical. This line of reasoning, as we shall see, has important implications for macroeconomic policy.

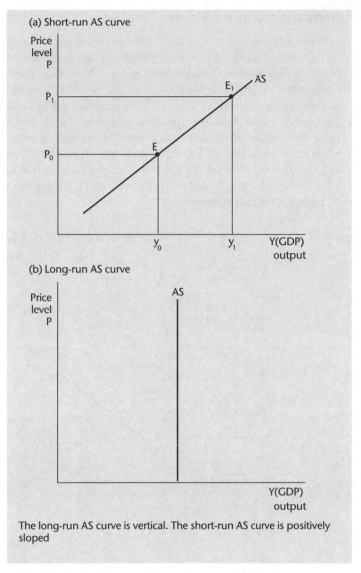

(a) Short-run AS curve

(b) Long-run AS curve

The long-run AS curve is vertical. The short-run AS curve is positively sloped

Figure 11.2 Aggregate supply curves

The AS curve provides a conceptual framework within which the viewpoints of the various schools of macroeconomic thought can be analysed. The shape of the curve is a controversial subject. The new consensus view depicts it as being near-vertical. Keynesian economists, by contrast, believe that the AS curve is near-horizontal up to the point of full capacity output. The debate hinges critically on one's view about the response of employees to changes in the cost of living and of firms to changes in costs.

Derivation of the AS curve

To derive the classical AS curve, we start with the assumption that individuals are utility-maximising, firms are profit-maximising and that they operate in a competitive market. Markets for factors of production are also assumed to be competitive. Hence each productive factor will, in equilibrium, be paid the value of its marginal product. Figure 11.3 illustrates the case with respect to labour. Supply of labour depends upon the real wage (w/p). As we saw in the last chapter, the curve slopes upwards because employees supply more hours of work if the real wage rises. Demand for labour is determined by the value of its marginal product. We recall the rule that a profit-maximising firm hires labour up to the point at which the value of the output produced by the marginal employee equals the cost of hiring that employee:

wage = marginal product of labour × price of output

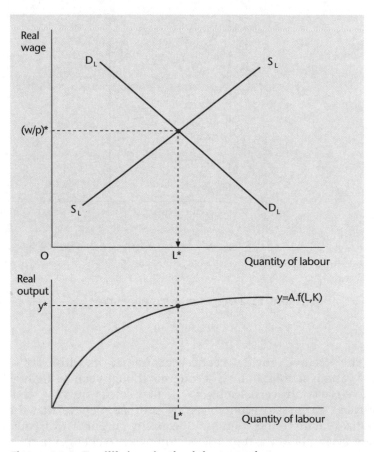

Figure 11.3 Equilibrium in the labour market

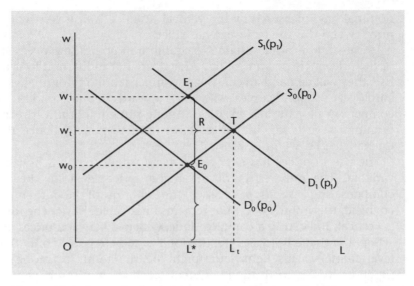

Figure 11.4 A nominal price increase – effect on the labour market

Assuming that all markets clear smoothly, equilibrium in the labour market occurs where the demand and supply curves for labour intersect. In Figure 11.3, this occurs at a real wage $(w/p)^*$, and with OL* units of labour employed.

Having determined equilibrium real wage, the level of output can be read off from the production function. The production function indicates the level of output that can be produced by each level of labour input, assuming it is combined with a fixed capital stock (K), technology and other factors (A). Thus, it shows that an output of y^* can be produced by the input of labour, L^*.

The next question is to determine how equilibrium output, y^*, changes in response to changes in the price level. A fundamental implication of the classical model is that *in the long run, equilibrium output (y^*) is invariant with respect to the general price level p^**. This conclusion draws heavily on the assumption that individuals and firms behave *rationally*. They calculate, bargain and decide if and how much to work, on the basis of the real wage (w/p), not the nominal money wage (w). In technical jargon, all market participants are assumed to be free from *money illusion*.

The role of the money illusion can be clarified by drawing nominal wage, instead of real wage, on the vertical axis (Figure 11.4). Then, *for any given price level, p_0*, we can draw a demand and supply curve for labour as before. Consider now the effect of an increase in the price level from p_0 to p_1.

Initially, the rise in the price level shifts the demand curve for labour outwards to $D_1 (p_1)$. This happens because firms will observe that price of output has increased relative to nominal pay. Profits will increase and firms will want to hire more labour. If workers were ignorant or unconcerned about the fact that prices had gone up, a new equilibrium could happen at point T. At T, more labour would be employed (OL_t) and the nominal wage would rise to w_t. Since the rise in nominal pay (measured by the vertical distance E_0R) is less than the rise in the price level, E_0E_1, the real wage has fallen.

However, w_t is not a sustainable equilibrium point. Employees are not ignorant of the price increase and, being rational, are not indifferent to it either. As prices rise, they will demand an equivalent compensation in nominal wages. Over time, employees' supply curves will shift upwards by an amount which exactly compensates for the rise in prices. A long-run equilibrium is reached at E_1. The nominal wage is w_1, but prices have risen to p_1 and hence the real wage is unchanged: i.e. $w_1/p_1 = w_0/p_0$.

The rise in prices has changed *nominal* values, but has not affected any *real* variable. The only effect of the higher price level has been to prompt a compensating rise in pay. Since the amount of labour employed has not changed, the volume of output remains unaffected. Hence the long-run AS curve is vertical, indicating a complete independence between prices and real output.

Suppose that employees are 'irrational' and behave as if only the *nominal* wage level matters. This behaviour might be the result of money illusion or of rigidities in the institutional system (such as minimum pay) which prevent

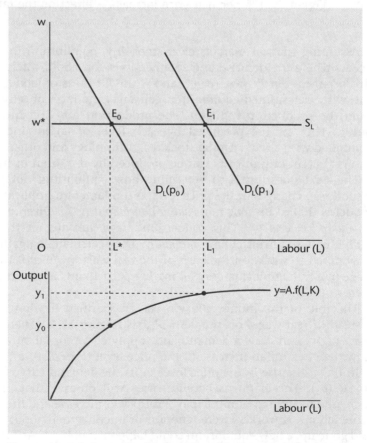

Figure 11.5 Labour demand and nominal money wages

employees from accepting or being offered a wage below w^*. This situation is illustrated in Figure 11.5, where the *nominal* wage is measured on the vertical axis and the supply of labour is assumed to be perfectly elastic at the going money wage, w^*. In this situation, an increase in the price level from p_0 to p_1 shifts the demand curve for labour outwards. Employers respond positively to the fall in the real wage. But employees do *not* respond to the fall in their real wage. A new equilibrium occurs at E_1. The amount of labour employed increases to L_1. There is a corresponding increase in output. Using the production function, the consequent increase in output can be estimated. The new equilibrium point is reached at output y_1 and price p_1. The price level is higher and so is output. The rise in the price level has a significant *real* effect in that the quantity of real output produced has increased. By tracking the effects of different price levels and joining the points together, the short-run AS curve can be derived. It is positive-sloping and becomes steeper as full employment is approached.

While the labour supply curve is assumed to be horizontal with respect to the nominal wage initially, this assumption becomes more and more untenable as the economy approaches full employment. Labour's supply reactions then become increasingly like the classical model. Once full employment is attained, the AS curve becomes vertical, even in the short run.

Short-run v long-run AS curve

The distinction is often drawn between the long-run AS curve, which is vertical, and the short-run AS curve, which is upward-sloping, as in Figure 11.6. A rise in prices could lead to higher output if wages were 'sticky' in nominal terms in the

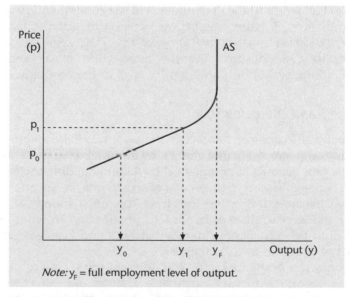

Note: y_F = full employment level of output.

Figure 11.6 Short-run aggregate supply curve

short run. This 'stickiness' might be present because the rise in price was unanticipated, or because of fixed-term pay deals. Employees might require time to absorb the implications of the rise in price and may react more slowly than firms to the new price level. For these reasons, price changes can have 'real' effects on output and employment in the short term.

The existence of rigidities and short-term 'wage stickiness' may be intuitively acceptable as a working assumption of how the labour market operates in the short run. But such irrational behaviour cannot be indefinitely sustained. Eventually, employees will respond in the 'classical' manner. That still leaves open the question of how long it will take them to respond. The length of the short run is not generally agreed; it is likely to vary from country to country, and even from region to region. Empirical evidence suggests that a period of 1–2 years is a reasonable definition, although some economists of the 'new classical' school argue that it is much shorter than that. They believe that economic agents react so quickly that the short-term concept has no practical relevance to economic policy.

11.4 Aggregate demand (AD) and money

We now turn to the demand side of the economy. As we have seen, aggregate demand comprises consumption, investment, government spending and net exports (exports *less* imports). To keep matters simple, assume a *closed* economy, i.e. one which conducts no foreign trade. Since the larger the economic entity, the lower the trade:GNP ratio, the closed economy assumption approximates the position of the larger industrial countries or blocs, such as Japan, the US and the EU.

We shall return to the determinants of the components of aggregate demand in later chapters. For the present, we focus on identifying *the relationship between aggregate demand, money and the price level*. The aggregate demand (AD) curve traces this relationship. And the intersection of AS and AD indicates the equilibrium level of output and price level in the economy.

Money and the price level

Virtually all economic transactions in an industrial economy involve the use of money. Suppose we define money as the stock of notes and coins held by the public plus deposits in commercial banks and building societies. If people do not have 'enough' money, they cut back spending in an attempt to add to their money balances. If they feel they have 'too much' money, they go out and spend it on goods, or equities or bonds, etc., in an effort to reduce their money stock. This link between desired money balances and aggregate spending is a major focus of attention in this analysis.

Money can be defined in several different ways. One commonly used measure (known as M0) defines it as including (a) notes and coins held by the public, and (b) commercial bank balances with the central bank. The definition can be broadened to include a greater range of financial assets. For example:

M1 = currency held by public plus current accounts held by deposit-taking institutions;

M2 = M1 + deposit accounts;

M3 = M2 + deposits with a wider range of financial institutions and a broader definition of deposits;

M4 = M3 + deposits of building societies.

Definitions differ between countries, but it is unnecessary for the reader to grapple with these fine distinctions. Suffice it to say that the boundary line between money and non-money assets is arbitrary.

The demand for money

Consider now what determines the amount of money people want to hold. This is not just an academic question. In the UK, the amount of money (M3) amounts to £826 billion compared with a GDP of £924 billion. If, tomorrow, people were for some reason to feel that they had 'too much' money and decided to spend half of their money stock on goods or equities instead, this would have a dramatic impact on the level of aggregate demand.

Individuals hold a certain amount of cash on hand and a balance on deposit in the bank. The decision to hold this amount has been influenced by two main variables:

(1) *The level of income.* The richer you are, the more money you are likely to hold in absolute terms (though the proportion of your total assets held as money may fall). Individuals hold currency to finance daily transactions. They use bank accounts to cover items such as monthly credit card charges, telephone and other bills which fall due for payment on a regular basis. Companies require money for much the same reasons. We call this the *transactions* motive for holding money.

(2) *The price level.* If, tomorrow, all prices were to double, you would feel that you did not have 'enough' money, and to get more you would cut down on spending. If, tomorrow, all prices fell by 50 per cent, people would have a surfeit of money and would most likely embark on a shopping spree. Hence the close link between the price level and aggregate demand.

> For a given money stock (or money supply), the higher the price level, the lower the volume of spending and the lower the level of aggregate demand. And the lower the price level, the higher the volume of spending and the higher the level of aggregate demand. The AD curve is downward-sloping.

(3) *The interest rate.* No interest is on paid on currency, and demand deposits often receive only a token rate of return. Higher interest rates, therefore, increase the opportunity cost of holding money and reduce the demand for it.

Other variables, such as inflationary expectations and credit card technology, also affect the demand for money but we will ignore them for now in order to avoid unnecessary complications

The supply of money

The supply of money is assumed to be determined 'exogenously'. By this we mean that the central bank can decide how much to provide. If it thinks there is too much money in the system, it can reduce the stock. It can add to the stock if it thinks there is not enough money in the system.

The central bank controls the supply of notes and coins. By law, it is the body with authority to issue them. But currency today accounts for only a small fraction of total money supply (well under 5 per cent in most countries). Hence, the really important question is how deposits in commercial banks are controlled.

Assume an economy with a central bank and one commercial bank, the latter to be taken as representative of the whole commercial banking system. *Deposit-creation* refers to the process whereby the commercial banking system is able to create new deposits and hence increase the money supply. The methods by which money is created can be described as follows.

Suppose an individual places £300 cash in a current account in the commercial bank. This deposit creates an asset and a liability for the bank. The deposit is a liability in that the amount is owed to the depositor, who can demand repayment at any time. The deposit is also an asset of the bank in that it has more currency in its vaults. So far, this transaction is not profitable for the bank. It has to bear the cost of managing the customer's account, while it earns nothing on the currency deposited. Hence it has an obvious incentive to use the asset. One profitable way is to give a loan to another customer.

By lending to customers, the bank creates a further asset and a liability. The asset is the customer's obligation to repay the loan to the bank at some date in the future. The corresponding liability is the credit balance placed on the customer's account with the bank. This is a profitable transaction from the bank's point of view, since it charges interest on the loan. Clearly, the bank will want to make as many loans as it prudently can. Its ability to make loans in practice will be constrained by one key obligation: the bank has to stand ready to convert deposits into cash at the request of the customer, more or less on demand. While the bank knows that only a fraction of loans will translate into a demand for cash at any one moment in time, it has to be able to satisfy that demand as required. To be safe, it must maintain a certain *reserve ratio*, i.e. ratio of reserves to deposits. The reserves in question are cash in vaults and balances with the central bank. If a bank has excess reserves, it is able to create money by making loans. If it is short of reserves, it must cut back on loans. Since the counterpart of loans is a deposit, changes in loans directly affect the money supply. The amount of new deposits the banking system as a whole can create depends on the size of its reserves and its required reserve-asset ratio.

Suppose that on average a 10 per cent reserve ratio is sufficient to meet all normal demands for cash. That means that the bank will have to keep 10 per cent of its deposits in cash on hand or as deposits with the central bank. The balance sheet of the commercial bank might then be as below:

Commercial Bank Balance Sheet			
Assets	£	*Liabilities*	£
Cash (notes and coin in vaults		Deposits	3000
and balances with central bank)	300	Capital employed	500
Advances	3000		
Fixed assets	200		
	3500		3500

Suppose now that reserves were increased from £300 to £400. Assuming the reserve ratio remained constant, the bank would have an incentive to lend more to its customers since interest on loans exceeds the return on reserves. With reserves of £400, deposits could increase to £4000 without breaching the reserve requirement. These additional deposits could be created by the extension of new credit to customers. We could expect the new balance sheet to look like the following:

Commercial Bank Balance Sheet			
Assets	£	*Liabilities*	£
Cash (notes and coin in vaults		Deposits	4000
and balances with central bank)	400	Capital employed	500
Advances	3900		
Fixed assets	200		
	4500		4500

Deposits have increased by £1000, advances by £900 and reserves by £100. Supply of money has increased and the bank has created money by making loans. Clearly, therefore, the amount of reserves or the *monetary base* has a pivotal role in determining money supply.

The monetary base and the central bank

Let us now assume that the central bank can control the monetary base. This is not wholly true, but it is close to the truth.[5] The monetary authorities can affect

---

5 An insider view of the operational difficulties in controlling the money supply in the case of the Bank of England is provided in J. Dow and I. Saville, *A Critique of Monetary Policy and British Experience* (Oxford: Clarendon Press, 1990).

Box 11.2

Open market operations

Suppose the central bank purchased bonds worth £105 million from the public and paid for this purchase in newly issued notes. This might lead to the following sequence of effects:

1. The public decides to hold an extra £5 million in cash and to deposit the remaining £100 million with the commercial banks.
2. The commercial banks' balance sheet initially rises by £100 million.

Assets		Liabilities	
Notes on hand	(+) 100	Deposits	(+) 100

3. The commercial banks now have excess reserves.
4. They will seek to expand credit by advertising the availability of loans, by reducing lending rates.
5. An equilibrium will be reached when the correct reserve ratio of, say, 10 per cent is restored. Loans of £900 million will have been generated by the initial injection of £105 million.

Assets		Liabilities	
Notes on hand	+100	Deposits	1000
Loans	+900		
	1000		1000

---

the monetary base in several ways. We outline the main ones briefly here, leaving further discussion until Chapter 13 on monetary policy.

First, the central bank could require the commercial bank to hold a certain minimum ratio of reserves to deposits. By raising the *reserve requirements*, say from 10 per cent to 15 per cent in our example, the amount of deposits which can be sustained by a given monetary base will decline and money supply will fall. (In practice, reserve ratios are much lower than this.) If the required reserve ratio is lowered, the commercial bank will be able to lend more and money supply will rise.

Second, the central bank may resort to *open market operations*. Open market operations involve the sale or purchase of government bonds, which alters the amount of cash held by the commercial banks and thus their ability to create credit (Box 11.2). The central bank could, for instance, purchase a government bond from an individual and pay for it in currency notes. The seller of the bond will deposit the notes in the commercial bank, and the process of lending and deposit expansion, as described in the numerical example above, gets into motion. If the central bank wishes to expand the money supply, it will *purchase* bonds, so increasing the reserves available to the banking system. If its intention is to reduce the money supply, it will *sell* bonds, so reducing the liquidity base of the banks. In each case, there is a pronounced multiplier effect. Money supply expands or contracts by a multiple of the original injection, the precise amount depending on the reserve ratio.

Third, the central bank could change the *interest rate* attached to the commercial bank's balances with it. Commercial banks cannot always judge their required reserves with perfect accuracy and, when they run short, they have to borrow from the central bank. The interest rate the commercial banks pay when borrowing from the central bank is called the *discount rate* or *marginal lending facility*. By raising the discount rate, the central bank is making such emergency loans more expensive. This induces the commercial banks to hold more of their assets in liquid form, i.e. as reserves, and hence to restrict the expansion of their non-liquid assets, such as loans to customers. In that way, the supply of credit is restricted. In addition, banks will try to pass on the extra interest cost to the customer by charging higher interest on loans. This will make borrowing less attractive to businesses and households. A similar sequence of events follows, *mutatis mutandis*, in the case of lowering the discount rate.

The above analysis of money supply consists of a simple sketch of what is in fact a complex process. The multiplier approach can be extended to take account of both the bank's reserve ratio and the public's propensity to hold cash relative to deposits (Appendix 11.1), and more complicated multipliers can easily be imagined. A key issue for monetary policy is to find out how stable these multipliers are. Another complication flows from the various degrees of 'moneyness' of different financial assets. So far, we have distinguished between the monetary base and the larger monetary aggregate represented by deposits in commercial banks. There are, however, many intermediate types of deposits and correspondingly diverse definitions of money supply. Many types of money are aggregated in the broad money supply and, for this reason, this statistic must be interpreted with care. Sometimes shifts between different components of 'the' money supply can be as significant as shifts in the aggregate figure itself. The dividing line between financial assets which fall within the definition of money and those which fall without is quite blurred. The essential point is the importance of the monetary base. If we assume that this variable can be controlled by the monetary authorities and that the behavioural and money reserve ratios used in the money multiplier do not change too unpredictably, the authorities will be able to control the broader money supply. The significance of this power will be explained later.[6]

Money supply, money demand and the interest rate

Interest rates come in different forms – short run, long run, nominal and real – but we assume for simplicity that there is only one (see Chapter 13 for more). The equilibrium interest rate is the rate of interest that equates the supply of money and the demand for money.

The relevant supply and demand curves are drawn in Figure 11.7, with stock of money (S) on the horizontal axis and the interest rate (R) on the vertical axis. We

---

6 Different monetary variables are used as indicators or objectives by central banks. The ECB uses M3; the UK, M0 and M4; the US, M2, M3 and TNDS (total domestic credit); Japan, M2 plus CDS.

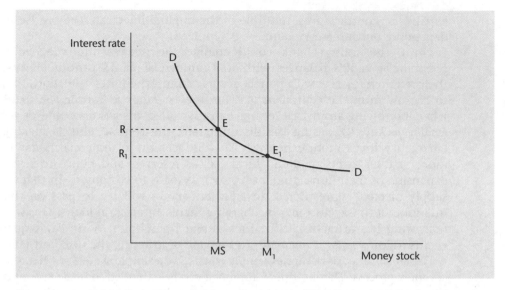

Figure 11.7 Money supply and demand: a stock (liquidity preference) approach

assume that prices are constant and that the supply of money is determined by the central bank. Money supply can thus be depicted by the vertical curve in Figure 11.7.

The demand curve for money is determined by the interest rate and other factors such as income, technology and so on. Assuming these other factors are constant, and focusing just on the interest rate relationship, the demand curve for money (DD) will be downward sloping for reasons already discussed. Hence equilibrium will be at E, with interest rate R.

Suppose the central bank wanted to reduce the interest rate. It could use open market operations to expand the money supply, shifting it from OM to OM_1. The economy is now far more liquid than before, people have an incentive to put their excess cash balances into more remunerative outlets such as government bonds. Money starts flowing into the bond market, bond prices rise and the interest rate falls to R_1. The fall in interest rate in turn will have a positive impact on aggregate demand. The transmission mechanism running from money supply to interest rate to aggregate demand is in practice very complex; it occupies a central role in studies of monetary policy.

Two further observations are necessary at this stage. *First*, the analysis, although simplified, illustrates the basic thinking behind central bank policy. By increasing money supply, the bank reduces interest rates and stimulates demand. By curbing money supply, it raises interest rates and reduces demand. Central banks seeking 'soft landings' for an overheated economy, where actual GDP exceeds its potential level, must try to work out how much of an interest rate hike is needed to achieve balance between the two. This requires in depth knowledge of money demand curves and, further down the line, detailed understanding of the interaction between interest rates and the different components of aggregate demand. No wonder central banks have large research departments.

Second, in Figure 11.7 we use what is known as the liquidity preference framework to explain interest rates. This is a stock approach. Another approach is the loanable funds or credit flows analysis used in Chapter 13. There we focus on supply and demand for credit and the role of the interest rate in bringing them into equilibrium. This is a flow approach. To achieve equilibrium, both markets must be in balance. Hence the two approaches are complementary.[7]

The aggregate demand (AD) curve

The aggregate demand (AD) curve shows the relationship between real expenditure, or output (Y), and the price level (P) consistent with equilibrium in the money market. That is, at each point on the AD curve, money demand equals money supply. The curve is based on the assumptions that (1) the level of money supply (Ms) is determined by the monetary authorities, and (2) that money demand depends on the level of output and the price level. The AD curve is downward-sloping (Figure 11.8).

Suppose that the initial equilibrium at (Y_0, P_0) is disturbed by a fall in the price level to P_1. This brings the economy to point A in Figure 11.8. Point A, however, is

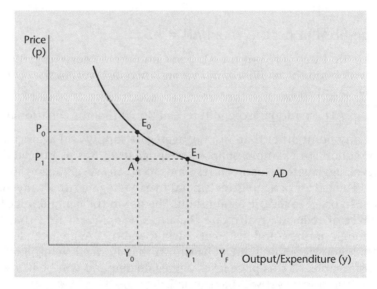

Figure 11.8 Aggregate demand curve

---

7. To see this, think of something closer to individual experience than monetary economics, house prices, for example. The equilibrium house price does two things: (a) it keeps demand for the housing stock equal to the demand for it and (b) it ensures equality between supply of new houses (housing completions) and demand for new houses. Equilibrium in market segment (b) is not sustainable without equilibrium in (a).

not an equilibrium point. The fall in the price level has reduced the transactions demand for money. Given that money *supply* remains unchanged, the fall in money demand implies that money supply is greater than money demand. There are excess money balances in the economy which individuals will want to convert into goods or other assets. Assuming the price level stays at P_1, the excess demand can only be eliminated if real spending increases from Y_0 to Y_1. At this higher level, people will want more cash to finance their transactions. The increase in real expenditure, by increasing the demand for money, yields a new equilibrium point E_1. By joining all such points together, we derive the AD curve.

The negative relationship between changes in price and change in aggregate demand can also be explained by the *real balance effect*. This effect can take two forms:

1. A fall in the price level means an increase in the purchasing power of financial assets. As the price level declines, the 'real' value of these assets, including the money stock, increases, people feel better off and want to spend more. Hence a fall in prices will be associated with a rise in real expenditure.

2. A rise in real money balances resulting from a fall in the price level causes an outward shift in the money supply. This leads to a fall in the interest rate. Investment and consumer spending will be stimulated. Again, the fall in price will be associated with a rise in aggregate demand..

Equilibrium occurs when AD = AS

The final step is to put the AD curve and the AS curve together (Figure 11.9). We then obtain the equilibrium price and income levels in the economy at (p_0, y_0). At that point (E_0),

AD = national expenditure = national income = national output = AS

At any point other than (p_0, y_0), aggregate supply and aggregate demand will not be equal. For example, suppose the price level was p_1 instead of p_0. At that price level, aggregate demand corresponds to y_1. However, aggregate supply remains at y_0. The excess of aggregate demand over aggregate supply means that prices must rise in order to restore equilibrium. The rise in the general price level will have the effect of reducing real money balances. People will find that they do not have enough money and will cut back spending. Aggregate demand will fall. By analogous reasoning, it can be shown that a price level p_2, greater than p_0, is not sustainable. At this price level, aggregate demand will be below aggregate supply and the price level will have to fall.

The AD curve could shift outwards or inwards as conditions change. For example, an outward shift could be caused by any of the following:

- an upsurge in business expectations leads to higher investment,
- consumers decide to increase their spending,
- people's preferences for holding money change,
- the monetary authorities increase the supply of money.

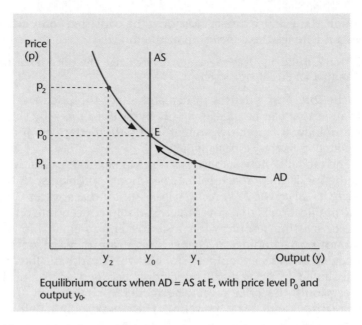

Equilibrium occurs when AD = AS at E, with price level P_0 and output y_0.

Figure 11.9 **Aggregate demand and aggregate supply**

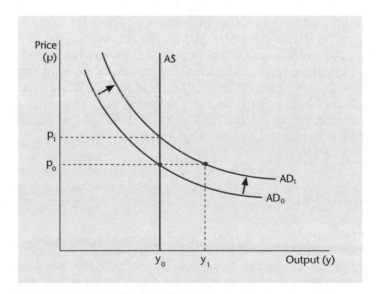

Figure 11.10 **Shift in aggregate demand**

Referring to Figure 11.10, an outward shift of AD means that, at the original price level p_0, demand will increase from y_0 to y_1. However, at this level of demand, aggregate supply is only y_0. Hence the price level must rise. Sustainable equilibrium is not reached until prices reach p_1. A shift in the demand curve to the left of AD_0 will, by similar reasoning, be consistent only with a lower price level than p_0. Hence the conclusion of the model:

> shifts in the aggregate demand curve change the price level, they do not affect real output and real living standards.

In the long run, changes in demand affect the price level, not 'real' variables. 'Real' output can be increased only by 'real' factors – by shifts in the production technology, by more investment, or by the better operation of the markets for productive factors, especially labour.

The model sketched above is a *classical model*. It captures the essential features of the modern approach to macroeconomic problems. *Its central message is that aggregate supply can be increased only by shifting the aggregate supply curve to the right.* The implication is that governments should concentrate on encouraging efficient use of existing resources, on fostering entrepreneurship and investment, and promoting technological change. Aggregate demand does not feature in this model as an independent force for growth. Because the long-run aggregate supply is assumed to be vertical, interaction between aggregate demand and supply affects only the price level. The model is simple, but the policy conclusions emanating from it are powerful. They have dominated the economic policy debate since the 1980s.

To dismiss aggregate demand as a factor relevant to the objective of securing higher output may well be to push the argument too far. Shifts in demand can, and do, affect output in the short run. The assumption of independence between real and monetary variables rests on the assumption that AS is vertical. If the AS were positively sloped, shifts in AD would affect the price level and *there would also be effects on real output.* Even if these effects are transitory, they could have a significant influence on an economy's trajectory. Much current macroeconomic controversy concerns arguments about the shape of the AS curve, the demarcation between the short run and the long run, and the interconnections between short-run and long-run economic growth.

11.5 Conclusions

> The ideas of economists and political philosophers, both when they are right and when they are wrong, are more powerful than is commonly understood. Indeed, the world is ruled by little else. Practical men, who believe themselves to be quite exempt from any intellectual influences, are usually the slaves of some defunct economist. I am sure that the power of vested interests is vastly exaggerated compared with the gradual encroachment of ideas. (J.M. Keynes, *The General Theory*, p. 383)

The above passage from the *General Theory* is by now so celebrated as to have become almost a cliché. Yet it contains an enduring truth: ideas about how an economy works matter. The study of macroeconomics provides an opportunity of engaging in dialogue with those who determine economic policy. This chapter sets the scene for later discussion by outlining the main features of the classical macroeconomic model which dominates today's economic thinking.

Macroeconomics grew out of two 'priors': (1) that deviations between actual and potential GNP occur and can persist, and (2) that something can be done to bring them closer together. That 'something', according to the Keynesian school, was management of aggregate demand. In recent times, the consensus has shifted to the view that attempts to manage aggregate demand can easily be counterproductive. Furthermore, attempts to manage it distract attention from aggregate supply, which *is* susceptible to policy initiatives. An extreme view is that aggregate demand hardly matters at all. Knowledge of the classical model enables us to understand why. If we do not agree, there are useful analytical tools with which to criticise the model and to explore alternatives.

The nub of the classical position is that the AS curve is vertical in the long run. If this is true, shifts in aggregate demand affect prices, not quantities. They affect not real output and employment, but inflation. Anyone who studies the speeches and statements of central bankers will detect a familiar echo at this juncture. An expansion of the money supply or a fall in interest rates, they say, will do nothing for long-term unemployment, or for economic growth, if it endangers price stability.

In the next chapter we study the topic of inflation. Inflation threatens when the economy 'overheats' and when growth temporarily exceeds its long-run potential. But, in certain circumstances, inflation can occur even if the economy is operating below capacity. Supply-side shocks can generate pass-through effects and, in economies with rigid structures, these shocks can generate an inflationary spiral. 'Stagflation' is how this conjunction of stagnant economic conditions and inflation has been described. A central platform of the current orthodoxy is that inflation, whatever its origin, is a 'bad thing', to be resisted if necessary at some short-term cost. Another is that, regardless of how inflation is initiated, whether by a demand shock or a supply shock, inflation can be sustained only if monetary policy and the monetary authorities allow it to continue. These propositions will be investigated next

✔ Summary

1. GDP refers to the output of goods and services produced by permanent residents of a country. Nominal GDP is the current value of these goods and services produced. Real GDP measures volume of output and is computed by valuing the quantities of goods and services produced in two periods with the same set of prices, thereby neutralising the influence of changing prices. There are three methods of measuring GDP: (1) the income, (2) the output, and (3) the expenditure methods, each of which should in principle yield the same figure.

2. Potential GDP is defined as the maximum output that an economy can produce when factors of production are fully utilised while maintaining low inflation. This will be less than the maximum attainable level of output. It can

be estimated by extrapolating growth from past trends or, alternatively, by a production function method. Macroeconomic policy focuses on minimising the gap between actual and potential GDP. Estimating potential GDP is a critically important exercise for economic authorities and central banks.

3. The distinction is made between GDP at nominal exchange rates and GDP at purchasing power parity (PPP). For less well-off countries, the difference can be appreciable. GDP per person at PPP is the better measure of real living standards across countries

4. The aggregate supply (AS) curve can be regarded as a rough proxy of potential GDP. It shows the combinations of real output and the price level which are consistent with equilibrium in the economy. A near-vertical AS curve is based on a classical model of long-run equilibrium. Because all market participants are assumed to be free from money illusion, the classical model concludes that equilibrium output is invariant with respect to the general price level. A distinction is drawn between the long-run AS curve, which is vertical, and the short-run AS curve, which could be upward-sloping. Keynesian economists concentrate on the short-run AS curve, which they believe is relatively flat up to the point of full employment. Nowadays, many economists argue that the AS curve is near-vertical, even in the short run. Important practical policy conclusions flow from different views on this question.

5. Aggregate demand (AD) comprises consumption, investment, government spending and net exports. The AD curve is downward-sloping and shows the relationship between real income and the price level consistent with equilibrium in the money market. Thus, at each point along the AD curve, money demand equals money supply. The assumptions underlying the AD curve are that (1) the level of money supply is determined by the monetary authorities, and (2) that money demand depends primarily on output, the price level and the interest rate.

6. Money supply can be regulated through a number of mechanisms: reserve requirements, open market operations and the interest rate, all of which affect the monetary base.

7. Equilibrium levels of price and income are determined by the intersection of the AD and AS curves. The AD curve can move outwards or inwards as economic conditions change. If the AS curve is vertical, shifts in the AD curve change the price level but not 'real' variables. Output can only be increased in a sustainable way through outward shifts in the AS curve. Aggregate supply in the economy can be increased when technology improves, more capital becomes available, labour supply increases or when the labour market becomes more flexible. In the short run, shifts in the AD curve can affect output. There are disaggreements about how great that effect can be. The new consensus urges extreme circumspection in deploying aggregate demand management.

? Questions for discussion

1. Considerable resources are spent by the statistical authorities in deriving estimates of GDP. From a business perspective, would you say that this exercise is a worthwhile and valuable one?

2. What is the difference between *actual* GDP and *potential* GDP? How is potential GDP calculated? Of what practical use are potential GDP estimates?

3. Discuss reasons why the aggregate supply curve might be vertical. Do you find them convincing?

4. What is the aggregate demand (AD) curve? Why does it slope downwards? What might cause it to shift outwards?

5. What is money supply? How might it be controlled by the authorities? What forces in the economy tend to bring money supply and money demand into equilibrium?

6. In the short run, the AS curve is often drawn as upward-sloping. What is the reason for this? What is the economic significance of this?

☞ Exercises

1. Which of the following transactions should be included as part of GDP?

   (a) A consumer pays £10 for a meal at a restaurant.
   (b) A company buys a plant from another firm for £1 million.
   (c) A supplier sells computer chips to a firm that makes personal computers.
   (d) A person buys a second-hand car from a dealer for £5000.
   (e) A person buys a new car for £15,000.
   (f) A factory, which produced £2 million worth of PCs each year, closes down.

2. A person saves £10,000 of this year's income and spends it on new machinery. Explain how this would be recorded in the national accounts. Another person takes £10,000 from under the mattress and buys shares on the stock market. Would this be recorded in GDP?

3. Consider an economy with only three goods. Their market prices are $P_1 = 5$, $P_2 = 10$ and $P_3 = 15$. The production (and consumption) of each good during 1995 was $Q_1 = 20$, $Q_2 = 25$ and $Q_3 = 10$.

   (a) What is the value of nominal GDP?
   (b) Assume that in 1996 prices rise to $P_1 = 6$, $P_2 = 12$ and $P_3 = 17$, and quantities produced (and consumed) go to $Q_1 = 21$, $Q_2 = 27$ and $Q_3 = 11$. Calculate the value of nominal GDP. Compute real GDP, using 1995 prices as the base year. What is the rate of inflation? What is the real rate of growth of the economy?
   (c) Calculate the change in real GDP using 1996 prices as the base year. Explain why your answer is different to that in (b).

4. Take any country listed in Table 11.2. Explain the difference between its GDP per head at purchasing power parity and at nominal exchange rates rates. Using data on the actual 1998 nominal exchange rates, compute the implicit PPP exchange rate for any three countries. Comment on the results.

5. Use diagrams to explain the following statement:

   Outward shifts in the aggregate demand curve affect output only temporarily, whereas outward shifts in the aggregate supply curve affect output permanently. And, whereas a positive demand shock raises prices, a positive supply shock reduces them.

6. Suppose the national accounts for a country showed the following figures:

wages and salaries	£400
investment	£200
money supply	£450
corporate profits	£100
rents and interest	£150
depreciation	£50
indirect taxes less subsidies	£70
dividends sent abroad	£50
income from agriculture	£70

   Compute the value of GNP and GDP.

7. Explain how you would expect a stock market boom to affect (a) aggregate supply and (b) aggregate demand. Is a stock market boom 'good' for an economy? How would a fall in the stock market affect the macro economy?

📖 Further reading

There is no shortage of macro textbooks, but it is difficult to find one that combines comprehensiveness with accessibility for a business-oriented reader. Perhaps this is because the subject-matter of macroeconomics is so difficult. M. Burda and C. Wyplosz, *Macroeconomics: A European text* (Oxford: Oxford University Press, 1997), has a welcome emphasis on the open economy, with useful case studies of European economic problems. C. Pass, B. Lowes and A. Robinson, *Business and Macroeconomics* (London and New York: Routledge, 1995), covers some of the same ground as Parts II and III of this book. A concise, historically minded account of the development of macroeconomics is provided by J.A. Sawyer, *Macroeconomic Theory: Keynesian and neo-Walrasian Model* (Hemel Hempstead: Harvester Wheatsheaf, 1989).

Appendix 11.1: The money supply process

A simplified model of the money supply process can be formalised as follows:

1. $M = Cp + D$
   where: M = money supply
   Cp = currency held by the non-bank public, and
   D = deposits of the commercial banking system.

2. $C = Cp + C_b$
   where: C_b = currency held in bank vaults.

Next we assume that:

3. $Cp = cD$ and $C_b = bD$
   where c is the fraction of its deposits the public holds in cash and b is the fraction of deposits the commercial banks hold in cash.

Substituting 3 into 1 and 2 gives:

4. M = $cD + D = D (c+1)$
5. C = $Cp + C_b = cD + bD = (c + b)D$
   M/C = $(c + 1)/(c + b)$
   M = $C[(c + 1)/(c + b)]$

This is the formula for the *money multiplier process*.

For $c = 0.05$ and $b = 0.1$, it tells us that an increase in *high-powered money* (C) will increase the money supply by a multiple of that initial increase, i.e. by a factor of 7, using the formula:

$$M/C = (0.05 + 1)/(0.05 + 0.1) = 1.05/0.15 = 7.$$

This multiplier formula is a useful teaching device. However, in practice the ratios can prove highly unstable, thereby making the size of the multiplier difficult to predict.

Chapter 12

PRICE STABILITY, INFLATION AND CENTRAL BANKS

Introduction

Inflation is a global phenomenon. However, the severity of inflation differs from country to country. Extremely high rates of inflation have prevailed in parts of Latin America and in the emerging market economies of the former Soviet bloc. Among the industrial economies, Japan and Germany have consistently managed to keep inflation low. While some European countries, such as Greece and Italy, had high inflation in the past, they had attained price stability by the end of the 1990s. Indeed price stability rather than inflation is now becoming the norm world-wide (Table 12.1).

Industrial countries experienced low inflation in the 1960s, high inflation in the 1970s (sparked off by the oil price rises of 1973–4), lower inflation in the 1980s and relative price stability in the 1990s. A banner headline in the mid-1990s proclaimed Britain's success in controlling inflation, with the celebratory statement 'INFLATION HITS 27-YEAR LOW'. Similar headlines greeted inflation

Table 12.1 Inflation rates in major industrial countries

	1961–70	1971–80	1981–90	1991–2000	Peak rate since 1970
Germany	2.8	5.2	2.6	2.3	8.8 (1974)
UK	3.9	13.3	6.1	3.2	23.5 (1974)
France	4.3	10.0	6.3	1.7	14.8 (1974)
US	2.7	7.1	4.7	2.7	10.7 (1980)
Japan	5.6	8.7	2.1	0.9	21.0 (1974)

Source: World Economic Outlook, IMF, October 1999.

Table 12.2 Latin American inflation

	1980–85	1986–90	1991–96	2000	Peak rate since 1970
Chile	21.3	19.3	13.2	5.0	505 (1974)
Bolivia	611.0	46.5	20.7	3.1	11,705 (1985)
Mexico	60.8	69.6	14.9	9.1	132 (1987)
Argentina	322.5	584.0	15.1	−0.5	4,924 (1989)
Brazil	149.0	657.5	720.0	5.5	2,407 (1994)

Source: 64th Annual Report, BIS; author's estimates for year 2000.

Table 12.3 Inflation in Central and Eastern Europe

	1991–95	1996–99	1999	Peak since 1989
Albania	75.4	16.9	2.0	226.0 (1992)
Czech Republic	21.5	7.6	2.5	56.7 (1991)
Estonia	290.7	11.4	3.3	1,076.0 (1992)
Hungary	104.9	16.3	9.0	35.0 (1991)
Latvia	258.4	8.2	2.2	951.0 (1992)
Lithuania	353.5	10.0	1.6	1,021.0 (1992)
Poland	41.7	13.4	7.0	586.0 (1990)
Slovak Republic	23.6	7.3	10.6	61.2 (1991)
Slovenia	78.5	11.8	7.5	1,306.0 (1989)

Source: European Bank for Reconstruction and Development, Transition Report 1999.

figures in many other industrialised countries. For them, the challenge has become that of maintaining price stability and ensuring that there is no return to the inflation rates of the past.

Other countries have had a less happy experience. As Table 12.2 shows, Brazil struggled with an annual inflation rate exceeding 2400 per cent as recently as 1994. Happily, it has since subsided to single-digit figures. At the end of the 1980s, at least four countries were experiencing runaway inflation in excess of 1000 per cent per annum (Argentina, Nicaragua, Peru and Yugoslavia). Among the former socialist countries, Georgia, Russia and the Ukraine have suffered serious depredations on the value of their currency (Table 12.3). Prices continue to rise at around 80 per cent per annum in Turkey. High inflation has damaged these economies and has distorted the business environment.

Many economies have introduced successful counter-inflationary programmes during the past decade. Argentina's inflation reached nearly 5000 per cent in 1989 but, following its stabilisation programme, it fell to 3 per cent. Bolivia, Chile and Israel are other examples of successful stabilisation. However, experience warns against complacency. Inflation can be easily ignited. Japan's inflation averaged under 2 per cent in the 1990s, but had been as high as 21 per cent in 1974. UK inflation reached 24 per cent in 1975 and registered double-digit figures again in the late 1980s. The US's peak inflation rate was 11 per cent as recently as 1980.

Inflation is difficult and costly to subdue. It feeds on itself – the so-called *inflationary spiral*. Higher prices lead to higher pay; higher pay raises costs of production leading to further price rises; these price rises fuel further claims by employees for compensation, and so the spiral continues. Once caught in a spiral, it is hard to escape. Deflation too can be a major problem as Japan's experience in the past decade demonstrates.

Price stability has become a major policy objective of government. The monetary authorities in the euro area, New Zealand, Canada and the UK are formally committed to maintaining stable prices. Most other countries have a strong public commitment to keeping inflation low, although less formal targets are set. Price stability being a public good, the public authorities are necessarily involved in its supply.[1] Keeping the price level stable is a major task for government. It is an essential element in a healthy business environment.

Chapter outline

This chapter proceeds as follows.

1. Price stability and inflation: definition and measurement.

2. The determinants of inflation, distinguishing between the proximate causes (excessive increase in money supply or a slack exchange rate regime) and the ultimate causes (what makes governments acquiesce in a particular monetary or exchange rate policy).

3. The benefits of price stability, and the adverse economic effects of inflation and deflation.

4. Policies for achieving sustainable price stability.

5. Price stability and exchange rate 'anchors'.

12.1 What is price stability?

Price stability is defined as the sustained absence of both inflation (prices rising too fast) and deflation (falling prices). Since inflation is more common than deflation, and since some degree of price increase may be consistent with price stability, we focus on the issue of inflation. Inflation is a *persistent* rise in the *general* level of *money* prices. Consumer price inflation is defined by reference to the total money cost of a *basket* of consumer goods and services. The components of the basket and the weights attached to them are designed to reflect the type of goods and services consumed by a typical individual or household. In 1914, the UK retail price index contained 80 items, most of them food products, but also including necessities such as candles, starch and washing soda. Nowadays, the index contains around 600 items. Many new products have been added such as video recorders, CD players, microwave ovens and mobile phones. In all, some 150,000 price quotations are obtained each month from various types of sales outlets in different regions of the country. The US consumer price index (CPI) is derived from price quotations on 71,000 goods and services collected at about 22,000 retail outlets.

The number of goods and services in the sample basket is necessarily an incomplete inventory of output in the economy. Opinions differ as to what should be included in the price index. For example, the UK is one of the few countries to include mortgage interest payments in its index. The method of introducing new goods is also problematic, though much of the improvement of living standards in modern economies derives from new products. Another issue is the weighting to be attached to the various items in the basket. As the standard

---

1 For a definition of this term, see Chapter 8. Price stability is non-rivalrous (one person's enjoyment of its benefits does not limit any other person's) and non-excludable (people cannot be prevented from enjoying the benefits of price stability, regardless of whether or not they have contributed to its provision). Hence, a market system will not on its own produce an optimal supply of this good.

of living rises, basic necessities – such as food and fuel – become proportionately less important in household consumption. Although the composition of the household 'basket' is revised periodically in order to reflect the changing pattern of household spending, the timing and extent of such revision can create biases in the resultant price index.

Inflation statistics are affected by three main sources of bias:

1. *Composition bias* arises because of the delay in incorporating new goods into the consumer basket. They tend to be included in the CPI only after some years have elapsed. Typically, their price will have fallen during this period, sometimes by 80 per cent or more. (Mobile phones were not included until 1998, thus the index missed the substantial price reductions of this product during the previous decade.) The delay in including new products in the CPI basket leads to a systematic overestimation of true inflation.

2. *Quality bias* occurs because there is insufficient adjustment of price increases for improvements in quality. Thus, a new car model might be more expensive than the old model, but if the rise in price is due to higher quality living standards the CPI should register no change. The statistical authorities try to adjust for quality improvement, but generally the adjustment has been found to be insufficient, particularly in the case of personal computers, household appliances and medical care – where quality improvement is occurring at a very rapid rate.

3. *Substitution bias*: As prices increase, people shift spending from goods which have become relatively dear towards cheaper goods and services, and from more expensive to less expensive retail outlets (this is called *outlet bias*). The share of spending on individual components of the consumer basket changes in response to changes in relative prices. Since spending tends to shift from goods with the most rapid price increase towards goods with the lower price increase, failure to take account of this will result in an upward bias in the inflation index.

The precise empirical importance of these various sources of measurement bias is not known. Studies of the consumer price index suggest a total upward bias of around one percentage point each year. Although this bias may seem small, if inflation is running in low digits the bias may amount to a large fraction of actual inflation. A study of the British retail price index concluded that substitution bias was not a substantial source of error, but that composition and quality biases could lead to a 'significant', but at present unquantifiable, overstatement of the true price increase. In the US, the Advisory Commission to Study the Consumer Price Index (CPI) concluded that the CPI overstated the change in the cost of living by about 1.1 percentage points per year: 0.5 percentage points due to substitution bias and the remainder due to quality and composition bias.[2]

---

2 M. J. Boskin *et al.*, 'Consumer prices, the Consumer Price Index and the cost of living', *Journal of Economic Perspectives* (Winter 1998); N. Oulton, 'Do UK price indexes overstate inflation?', *National Institute Economic Review* (May 1995).

Because of these biases, price stability is defined as an inflation rate in the range 0 to 2 per cent.

The consumer price index can be a politically sensitive statistic.[3] It has a direct bearing on the living standards of the majority of households and employees. Pay, pensions and social welfare increases are often directly tied to this index, with significant consequences for public finances. Two issues arise because of this. *First*, should there be a different 'representative basket' to reflect the spending pattern of different segments in society? A senior executive has a different consumption pattern from that of a young trainee. A poor person's consumption basket will be more affected by price changes of basic necessities than the representative household. However, because, in the long run, most prices rise more or less proportionately, the biases arising from these different consumption patterns will usually be small.

A *second* issue is whether *asset prices* such as house and share prices should be included in the index. Many people might feel that changes in house prices, for instance, would impact significantly on living standards, yet they are excluded from the consumer price index. The statisticians would reply that what matters for living standards is the cost of *housing services*; i.e. rents on rented accommodation, the cost of housing repairs and in some countries (the UK, for instance) mortgage payments, rather than the price of a house *per se*. Likewise a stock market boom means that buying shares is more expensive, but share prices are not included in the consumer price index. Were they to be included a problem would arise in so far as a rise in share prices, unlike a rise in food prices, may not be a 'bad' thing for the consumer. Changes in asset prices are by no means irrelevant to inflation. They can impact in an important way on pay costs and total spending. But their impact is measured indirectly rather than directly in the consumer price index.

12.2 What causes inflation?

To control inflation, we must understand its causes. The *monetarist* view of inflation, encapsulated in Milton Friedman's dictum, *inflation is always and everywhere a monetary phenomenon*, has been enormously influential. Inflation occurs when the growth of the money supply persistently exceeds the growth of real output. Theories of inflation focus on (a) how 'shocks' on the demand-side (a rise in confidence) or the supply-side (a commodity-price boom) can impart an upward twist to the general price level; and (b) how that initial price level rise can generate an inflationary spiral through accommodating monetary supply increases.

---

3 So much so as to cause the resignation of Brazil's finance minister in September 1994. In a private conversation mistakenly broadcast by satellite television to a bemused audience throughout Latin America, he remarked that when it comes to inflation indices: 'I don't have any scruples. What is good, we use – what is bad, we hide' (*Financial Times*, 5 September 1994).

Money supply and inflation

If each of us woke today with twice as much money as yesterday, two things could happen: (1) we could spend some of the extra money on goods and services to celebrate our good fortune; or (2) we might invest part of the money in government bonds or similar financial assets. In the latter case, the resultant upsurge in asset prices would boost demand for goods and services. Hence prices would be 'driven' up – assuming a fixed aggregate supply.

This higher level of spending does not reduce the *total* holding of money, but merely transfers money from one person to another at a more rapid rate than before. Nominal money stock remains at twice its original level. As prices rise, however, a given amount of money will buy fewer goods and services. The real purchasing power of money declines. The initial equilibrium is restored when prices and income in money terms are about twice as high as they were originally. Only then will people be willing to hold the higher supply of money. This explains why inflation cannot continue without a sustained increase in the money stock and why continued excessive increases in the money stock are invariably followed by inflation.

The chain of causation may be sketched using the AS/AD framework of Chapter 11. A rise in money supply from M_0 to M_1 shifts the AD curve outwards from $AD(M_0)$ to $AD(M_1)$. The eventual equilibrium will move from E_0 to E_1 and prices will rise from P_0 to P_1 (Figure 12.1). Further increases in money supply will lead to corresponding price increases, and so on.

In the short run, as we have seen, the AS curve may be positively sloped rather than completely vertical. In that event, a rise in the money stock will cause higher prices, but it will also lead to more output. The output effect occurs because of

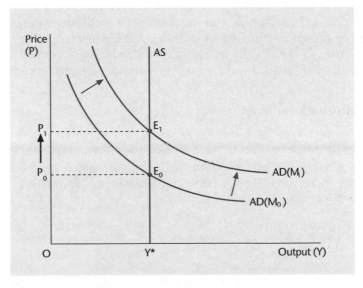

Figure 12.1 A rise in money supply causes a rise in prices

short-term rigidities, reflecting employees' inability to respond instantaneously to the decrease in the real wage caused by the increase in the price level. In the longer term, pay levels will 'catch up' on inflation and, over time, they will respond more quickly to it. The economy then approximates more and more closely to the vertical AS.

This approach is consistent with the *quantity theory of money*. This theory is constructed on the basis of the highly simplified equation:

$$MV = PT$$

where M = the money supply; V = the velocity of circulation of money; T = the amount of transactions; and P = the price level. The amount of transactions can be approximated by the volume of real output (Y).

Suppose that the money stock (M) in an economy is £1000 and the velocity of circulation (V) is 2, the Quantity Theory tells us that, in equilibrium, the annual value of GNP (i.e. PY) must equal £2000. This is consistent with any number of combinations of price and quantities. If the price (P) is £4 per unit, then Y must be 500 units. If price falls to £2 per unit, volume of output can rise to 1000 units, and so on.[4] Clearly, a great deal of theorising is going on behind the equation, but for the present we simply accept it at face value.

If the further assumption is made that Y and V are given, a direct link is established between changes in M and changes in P. This can also be expressed in percentage terms. Other things being equal (notably, the velocity of circulation and trend growth in income), the higher the growth of money supply, the higher the rate of inflation. Hence the popular description of inflation as 'too much money chasing too few goods'.[5]

The Quantity Theory is a useful start to a theory of inflation, but it leaves many questions unanswered. It oversimplifies the causal interactions between money supply and real output. It places all the emphasis on money supply without explaining the economic and social factors which determine how and why money supply should be allowed to increase. A fully fledged theory of inflation would also have to explain the determinants of velocity of circulation and probe more carefully the justification for assuming that it remains 'constant'.

Inflationary 'shocks'

A common type of inflationary shock is a surge in demand caused by over-optimistic expectations in the private sector. British inflation in the late 1980s, for example, was fuelled by a housing boom, stimulated by tax-cuts and a feel good factor, and financed by excessive credit expansion. Deregulation had loosened the

---

4 The Quantity Theory can be converted into rates of change of the variables as follows:

$$m = p + y - v$$

where lower case letters refer to rate of change over time.

5 To keep matters simple, we have assumed that the coefficients of p and y are unity. This assumption can be changed without affecting the conclusion.

Bank of England's control over lending by financial institutions. It took time before the monetary authorities were able to rein in the money supply.

Demand pull inflation can also be sparked off by excessive *government budget deficits*. For example, the government might try to stimulate demand in order to achieve a reduction in unemployment. As demand expands, labour and commodity markets tighten, and prices could be driven up. Also the deficit could affect the liquidity base of the economy, in effect increasing the money supply, lowering interest rates and giving an additional boost to the economy. In transition economies, the sudden liberalisation of the economy was associated with a huge increase in the deficits of state firms and corresponding build-up of overdrafts in the banking system. Governments were unable to stem these deficits (the soft budget constraint). Being underpinned by state guarantees, these overdrafts were in effect 'monetised'. The resultant expansion of credit constituted a significant demand shock to the economy and directly contributed to inflation.

Another source of shocks is supply-side disruption. *Energy-price shocks*, *sudden shortages of key materials* and *trade unions* can 'cause' inflation by persistently raising costs ahead of the level of productivity. Traditionally, this was termed *cost-push inflation*. But the verb 'cause' has in each case to be carefully qualified.

From an inflation perspective, the key point to remember is that, in each case, inflation will be sustained only if the rise in spending is accompanied by an increase in the money supply.

The inflationary process

In order to translate a one-off general price increase into sustained inflation, the Quantity Theory tells us that something else must happen: money supply also has to rise on a sustained basis. The monetary authorities have to acquiesce in a continuously rising money supply. A political decision might be taken that the short-run costs, in terms of civil strife, unemployment and disruption, of refusing to validate the inflation are greater than the economic costs of inflation (about which more later).[6] Nothing better illustrates this point than the contrast between the reaction of Britain and Germany to the oil crisis of the 1970s. Up to 1973, the UK inflation rate had only been marginally higher than Germany's. After 1973, Britain's inflation rose to more than double Germany's. The British authorities decided to validate the inflation, whereas in Germany the authorities made clear their intention not to validate it, and German employers and trade unions responded by keeping tight curbs on prices and nominal incomes. In Germany, determination not to increase the money supply dampened inflationary expectations and moderated pay claims. This made it easier to curb inflation. In Britain, responses to the initial price rise appeared to weaken the

---

6 Exchange rates have to be introduced in order to explain inflation in open economies. These economies are exposed as much to external as well as to internal inflationary pressures. The extent to which inflation is imported from the rest of the world, then, hinges crucially on the exchange rate regime adopted by the small country. We defer consideration of this issue until later.

authorities' will to control the money supply, which made control of inflation harder, and inflation escalated.

An anti-inflation strategy should be based on a proper understanding of the economic costs of inflation. This will help to provide the authorities with a democratic consensus needed to take the sometimes unpleasant actions required in order to make the strategy work. Germany's successful postwar inflation record, for example, owes as much to the public's aversion to inflation as to the skill of its monetary authorities in regulating the money supply. But institutions also play a vital role. Monetary institutions and fiscal policies must both be geared to give a high priority to price stability. Monetary institutions derive their status, power and priorities from government, and are heavily influenced by societal values.

A key element, therefore, in understanding inflation is to understand why a price shock in one country translates into an inflationary spiral, whereas in another it leads to a one-off rise followed by a return to price stability. The answer seems to be that the capacity of a country to resist inflation depends on its institutions, and on their credibility and reputation in restraining inflationary impulses. These institutions include, of course, the monetary authorities, but trade unions and government also form a vital part of the relevant institutional infrastructure.

The proximate economic causes of inflation are comparatively easy to analyse in the context of a Quantity Theory approach. Its ultimate causes are more complex. Nobody believes any more that inflation is exclusively associated with excess aggregate demand – the prevalence of *stagflation*, i.e. recession combined with inflation, has seen to that. Nor is it inevitable that a supply-side shock will generate an inflationary spiral. Excessive money creation does not take place in a vacuum. Inflation is caused by the interaction between monetary policy, institutions and political calculation.

12.3 Benefits of price stability and costs of inflation

Price stability means avoiding the costs of inflation. On a broader canvas, it is the essential backdrop for many of the benefits of the market system and competition outlined in Part I. As mentioned in Chapter 3, without a secure medium of exchange, prices cannot perform the signalling function that is key to the efficiency gains of a market system, and hence the market cannot deliver on its potential. Exactly the same argument applies in the case of the gains from trade. A stable domestic price system helps to ensure that international exchange is conducted on the basis of a correct knowledge of prices and alternatives.

Why is inflation considered harmful? Why is its control treated as a priority? Why do the monetary authorities take the risk of reducing short-term growth in order to prevent inflation? Inflation has implications for efficiency, income distribution and growth. Articulating and quantifying these implications, however, can be difficult. It has been said with some justice that *most people think that inflation is a bad thing for very bad reasons*. Yet there are good reasons for believing inflation is a bad thing. Its economic costs can be assessed under five main headings.

(1) *Rapid changes in the general price level obstruct the efficient working of the market system.*
Relative price changes and shifts in the composition of demand can be obscured by inflation. Consumers and producers will, as a result, suffer some degree of 'money illusion'. They confuse general price level changes with relative price movements. This leads to a blurring of the signals and a distortion of the incentives on which the market economy depends. A World Bank report commented that:

> Rapid and accelerating inflation undermines allocative efficiency because it increases uncertainty and induces savers to invest in unproductive 'inflation hedges' such as real estate, consumer durables, gems and foreign currency deposits. Some countries have developed complex systems for indexing wages and prices to compensate for inflation, though this is administratively costly and tends to penalise those (mostly poor) people outside the indexation system. Where indexation does not exist, the 'inflation tax' contributes to a growing sense of social and economic injustice.[7]

In addition to making the price system function less efficiently, inflation imposes an administrative cost. The *menu cost* of inflation refers to the time and bother of having to change prices frequently in markets where price, in the normal course of events, is kept unchanged for some time. Examples of such 'customer' markets include labour markets, retail and wholesale trade, pay telephones and parking meters. Obviously, these menu costs are greater the higher the rate of inflation. Another type of efficiency loss consists of what are known as 'shoe-leather costs' of inflation. These arise because of the complexity and inconvenience of transacting business when inflation is rampant.

(2) *Inflation impacts on the distribution of wealth.*
Unless loans are perfectly indexed, inflation will redistribute resources from lenders to borrowers by reducing the real value (in terms of goods and services) of debt which is denominated in money terms. It will also tend to redistribute income from those whose incomes are fixed in nominal money terms, or which lag behind inflation, to those whose incomes are indexed to inflation. The elderly (who have accumulated assets) may also lose from inflation to the young (who are, in general, net debtors). Most of these redistributions reflect either an inability to adjust to a higher rate of inflation or, more likely, a lag in adjustment. Inflation-indexation schemes are not only administratively costly, but are also likely to be applied only to a proportion of the workforce, more often than not those in secure sectors of the economy with strong trade unions. The income-distributive effects of inflation are not just a simple question of reallocating income from poor to rich, elderly to the young, government to private sector.

---

7 World Bank, *World Development Report* (Washington, DC, 1983), p. 59.

What is really damaging is the haphazard and uneven incidence of this redistribution within and between different classes. The eminent Hungarian economist, Janos Kornai, describes inflation as a disaster which *descends mercilessly on the population, leading to perpetual unrest as people see the savings they have scraped together melt away in their hands.*[8]

(3) *Inflation hinders economic growth.*
The causal link between inflation and growth is easier to establish in theory than to identify empirically. Economic growth is determined by a multitude of factors, including a country's initial income and its economic policies. It is revealing that Japan and Germany, countries with a strong commitment to low inflation, have fared better in the growth league than the higher inflation UK and US through most of the postwar period. However, this type of evidence remains plausible rather than compelling.

Multi-country studies of inflation and growth suggest two main conclusions: (a) low inflation is associated everywhere with strong growth performance; and (b) hyperinflation is associated with economic decline.[9] For countries in between, with moderate rates of inflation, statistical analysis is less conclusive. The high-growth East Asian countries fit into this category, with inflation of 6–10 per cent p.a. since the 1970s (Table 12.4). Harder evidence has emerged from recent studies which report reductions in productivity growth in the range 0.05–0.10 per cent for each additional percentage point of inflation.[10] These results imply significant losses from inflation in the long run. In developing countries, inflation deters foreign investors and gives domestic investors an incentive to accumulate their wealth in the form of unproductive 'inflation hedges' such as real estate, precious

Table 12.4 Inflation in selected Asian economies

	1971–80	1981–90	1991–95	1996–2000
China	2.8	6.0	11.7	2.1
Hong Kong	9.4	6.7	8.1	2.5
India	4.8	7.9	9.7	6.7
Indonesia	8.0	5.5	8.5	20.2
Malaysia	8.0	6.0	4.4	4.0
Taiwan	9.7	8.0	3.7	4.1

Source: World Development Report, *The Economist*; IMF; www.ado.org.

---

8 Janos Kornai, *The Road to a Free Economy* (London: Norton, 1990), p. 108.
9 International Monetary Fund, *World Economic Outlook* (Washington, DC, May 1990).
10 T. Gylfason, *Principles of Economic Growth* (Oxford: Oxford University Press, 1999) outlines recent literature on this topic. He concludes: 'Experience thus seems to indicate that high inflation hurts growth, but where the threshold between high and low inflation lies in this context – at 40 per cent per year? 20 per cent? 10 per cent? – is not yet known' (p. 93). This degree of agnosticism might appear somewhat alarming to devotees of a price stability target of 0–2 per cent! However, few economists would argue that inflation is good for growth, even if evidence that mild inflation is bad for growth is hard to establish.

metals, consumer durables and foreign currency, rather than in more socially productive assets. The unstable environment produced by rapidly rising prices also leads to the shortening of the time-horizons within the community. Rather than focusing on opportunities with a medium-term or long-term payback, attention and effort is switched to short-term, speculative 'deals'. Thus, inflation impacts negatively on the capacity of society to generate wealth, by causing the misuse of capital and by distorting the behaviour of entrepreneurs.

(4) *The redistribution of wealth and the economic turmoil associated with inflation can cause major social tensions and threaten democratic institutions.*
Resentment among the losers and uncertainty among other members of the population can enhance the appeal of populist and totalitarian parties which provide simplistic answers to economic problems. There are many examples in history of democratic regimes which collapsed in the aftermath of inflation. Italy during the 1920s when Mussolini took control, and Germany in 1933 when Hitler gained power, are instances of this. Some Latin American countries have experienced similar crises. Inflationary spirals, where prices, salaries and wages chase each other upwards in a mutually self-reinforcing circle, have had dire social and economic consequences. The disastrous consequences have been summed up in a famous quote from Keynes (himself drawing on Lenin):

> There is no subtler, no surer means of overturning the existing basis of society than to debauch the currency.[11]

(5) *Inflation once started is costly to reduce.*
Experience shows the painful withdrawal symptoms which accompany the breaking of the inflation habit. These occur because of slow adjustment in labour and goods markets to the lower rate of inflation and to continuing uncertainty about whether this lower rate will be maintained. Once it gets out of control, the policies required to check inflation can be very costly. They involve strict fiscal policies and a tight monetary regime, and – regrettably often – a reduction in economic activity in the short run. For example, the restrictive policies in the UK during the period 1989–93, which were introduced in order to reduce inflation, led to an increase in the unemployment rate from 7 per cent to 12 per cent from 1990 to 1993, and to real short-term interest rates exceeding 9 per cent in 1990.[12] If the monetary authorities proceed too rapidly in trying to cut the inflation rate, without the necessary complementary policies being in place and public opinion being properly primed, lower inflation will be secured at the cost of unemployment in the short run.[13]

---

11 J.M. Keynes, 'The social consequences of changes in the value of money', in *Collected Economic Writings*, Vol. IX (London: Macmillan, 1971), p. 60.
12 *European Economy*, 'Annual economic report for 1993'. Of course, this does not necessarily have to be the case. See Box 12.4 on Argentina later in this chapter.
13 The process of reducing inflation is called *disinflation*, and the relationship between inflation and unemployment is measured by the *Phillips curve*.

Box 12.1

The costs of deflation

Deflation, defined as a persistent decline in the general price level, is a rare phenomenon. Since 1950, prices have risen almost continuously in industrial countries, apart from a brief interlude in Japan and Germany in 1986–87. The prolonged and widespread price decline that occurred in Japan in the 1990s was a novel experience for a modern industrial country. The experience throws light on the difficulties created for business by falling prices.

Between 1990 and 1995, Japanese commercial property prices tumbled more than 50 per cent, while by August 1995 the Tokyo stock market had fallen 54 per cent below its recorded high in 1990. Land prices more than halved in value. The collapse of asset prices, reinforced by the rising value of the yen, exerted a strong downward pressure on the general price level. Wholesale prices fell for four consecutive years, and consumer prices started to slide in 1994, affecting a diverse range of products: food, drink, clothing, machine tools and computers. The consumer price index showed inflation in the range 0–1 per cent. However, the Japanese consumer price index tends to overstate inflation for two reasons. First, like all such indices, it fails to take full account of quality improvements and substitution possibilities. Second, the upward bias in inflation statistics is thought to be bigger in Japan than elsewhere because of the shift in spending from traditional retailers to cheaper discount stores. Some estimates suggest that average consumer prices, when measured correctly, may have fallen by as much as 5 per cent in 1995.

The case for price stability is usually made by reference to the economic costs of inflation. But the case could equally be made by reference to the cost of deflation. Some of these costs are evident in Japan. Among the problems attached to a falling price level are:

1. Declining prices lead to major, haphazard changes in the distribution of wealth. Borrowers find that the real burden of debt has escalated beyond their expectations. High debt : income ratios, combined with falling asset prices, lead to a 'debt trap', whereby servicing debt becomes increasingly difficult. Problems of negative equity for households can have disastrous consequences for consumer confidence and business expectations.
2. The counterpart of borrowers' real loss is lenders' gain. But lenders benefit only if the borrowers are able to pay. Japanese banks have suffered huge write-offs from non-performing loans.
3. Profits have been squeezed between price declines and wage and other costs, which are relatively inflexible. Industry is experiencing a 'Darwinian shake-out'. Market shares are under threat.
4. Nominal interest rates cannot be negative. If prices fall, real interest rates become higher than appears. Real long-term interest rates in Japan reached as high as 5 per cent. This has an adverse impact on investment.
5. Investment is further discouraged by the collapse in profits. Even if wages were flexible, one could still have problems. Money illusion might lead wage earners to feel worse off. This could generate a deflationary spiral and serious output loss.

Box 12.1 continued

6. Consumers find it difficult to estimate relative price changes against a backdrop of rapid overall price declines.

Even at the end of the 1990s, it was still unclear whether Japan had pulled out of its deflationary slump. GDP declined in 1993 and remained relatively stagnant thereafter. Fears were expressed that a sustained fall in prices could initiate a vicious circle of lower domestic consumer spending and even greater pressure on prices, profits and the battered financial system. At one juncture, the Bank of Japan was urged to initiate a small inflation – a rather uncongenial policy prescription for such an eminent institution!

While deflation has been unusual, *disinflation* – defined as reducing a high rate of inflation to an acceptable 2 per cent level – has been a common experience in recent decades for both developed and developing countries. It involves a milder version of the problem of deflation. Adherence to a price stability objective seems to be the best recipe for avoiding the twin problems of inflation and deflation, and for deriving maximum benefit from 'new consensus' economic policies.

Source: IMF, *World Economic Outlook* for statistics.

Writing sixty years ago, Keynes observed that:

> each process, inflation and deflation alike, has inflicted great injuries. Each has an effect in altering the distribution of wealth between different classes. Each has an effect in over-stimulating or retarding the production of wealth. *Both evils are to be shunned.*[14]

Inflation creates problems. For similar and symmetrical reasons, so does deflation, defined as a persistent fall in prices (Box 12.1). The solution is for governments to ensure that price stability, once restored, is thereafter maintained.

Some qualifications to the case against inflation can be made without detriment to the general thrust of the argument. The harmful effects of inflation will be reduced to the extent that inflation is correctly anticipated, and contracts and loans are properly indexed. But this is not easy to do. Inflation is mostly unpredictable and uncertain. Another extenuating argument is that inflation might help business by lowering the real value of debt and that large nominal rises in company profits resulting from inflation may flatter managers and keep shareholders happy. Similarly, it may be easier to save jobs in weak firms by freezing nominal wages in conditions of rising prices than by reducing real wages by the same amount through nominal pay reductions in conditions of price stability. Employees resist nominal wage cuts, for understandable reasons. For governments, tax bands are often not indexed and so, if inflation occurs, extra revenue may be generated without the political cost attached to raising tax rates.

---

14 J.M. Keynes, 'Economic consequences of the peace', in *Collected Economic Writings*, Vol. II (London: Macmillan, 1971), p. 149.

Mortgage holders on fixed-interest and inflation-indexed salaries will not be unhappy at the prospect of higher inflation. However, all these are short-run arguments. It is questionable if 'money illusion' can persist for long among consumers, producers and voters in the face of a persistently rising level.

12.4 Central banks, institutional reform and the control of inflation

The control of inflation involves a broad spectrum of economic policies.

(1) There must be *political commitment* to low inflation. This has to be made manifest in strict control of public finances, since excessive government deficits almost inevitably result in excessive monetary expansion. An informed public opinion is also important. Popular aversion to inflation, fed by the memories of the disastrous hyperinflation in the inter-war period, has been a hallmark of Germany's successful anti-inflation strategy. Widespread understanding of the costs of inflation is necessary in order to ensure sufficient public support for the sometimes unpalatable measures needed to keep inflation low.

(2) There must be an *appropriate institutional framework* to buttress this political commitment and to give it credibility. The elements of such an institutional framework have been the subject of much debate in recent years. The proposed new institutions of the EU provide an interesting case study in this matter. In seeking to establish a single currency, the requirement that such a currency would be stable was deemed of paramount importance. The Maastricht Treaty (1993) specified procedures for restraining government borrowing and for ensuring that the European Central Bank (ECB) should be independent of governments, with price stability as its primary objective (Box 12.2).

(3) *Central banks should be largely independent of political control.* The level of central bank independence varies widely. In some instances, the central bank plays a clearly subordinate role, as for example in the relation of the Bank of England to the Chancellor of the Exchequer up to the early 1990s. In other instances, for example in the case of Germany, the monetary authorities have enjoyed considerable autonomy.

The evidence indicates that independence rather than management by politicians is the optimal strategy for low inflation (Figure 12.2). Political control may lead to policies such as a pre-election cut in interest rates (to help the electoral prospects of the incumbent party), which results in higher inflation at a later stage. Many countries have acknowledged this danger and are responding by measures to increase the autonomy of the monetary authorities. The French government, for example, greatly extended the independence of the Banque de France in 1994. New Zealand has been to the fore in delegating responsibility for maintaining stable prices to its central bank.

(4) *Central banks need a clear statement of their policy objective.* Ideally, this objective should be to maintain price stability. Central banks, as the guardians of monetary policy, may be asked to carry out unpopular tasks. For instance, the objective of

Box 12.2

The European Central Bank

A landmark event in Europe's monetary history was the establishment of the European Central Bank (ECB) on 1 January 1999. The ECB, with its unqualified objective of price stability and elaborate guarantee of independence, incorporated new thinking on monetary economics as well as the old-fashioned commitment to sound finance of the Bundesbank.

The primary objective of the ECB is to 'maintain price stability' (art. 105). It must also 'support the general economic policies of the Community', but this is to be done 'without prejudice to the objective of price stability'. The ECB is independent from political control. Community institutions and the governments of the member states undertake 'not to seek to influence the members of the decision-making bodies of the ECB in the performance of their tasks' (art. 107). Reflecting the strong liberal market principles of the Community's founders, Europe's new monetary authorities are enjoined to act 'in accordance with the principle of free competition, favouring an efficient allocation of resources' (art. 105).

The Governing Council of the bank consists of:

(a) an executive board, appointed by common accord of the member states, for an eight-year non-renewable term, consisting of a president, a vice-president and four other members;

(b) governors of the national central banks.

The ECB is required to submit an annual report to the Council and to present it to the European Parliament. Members of the executive board may be asked to appear before the European Parliament.

Given the numerical weight of the national governors in the decision-making process, it is necessary that their independence of national governments must be clearly established. Hence the Commission's concern to ensure that national central banks are independent.

The ECB's tasks are:

- to define and implement the monetary policy of the Union,
- to hold and manage the official foreign reserves of the member states,
- to promote the smooth operation of the payment systems,
- to conduct foreign exchange operations in a manner consistent with 'the general orientations for exchange rate policy' as laid down by the Council (i.e. the finance ministers of the member states).

The tasks of the ECB are similar to those of national central banks. Note that the European Council retains control of exchange rate policy, though it is specifically stated that the Council shall do so without prejudice to the primary objective of maintaining price stability (art. 109). This is a sensitive issue and the relationship between the Council and the ECB is not one which can be defined precisely in formal treaty language. Only by practical experience will the balance of responsibilities be determined.

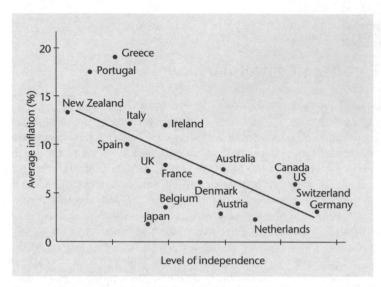

Figure 12.2 Central bank independence and inflation, 1950–90

Source: Robert J. Barro and Vittorio Grilli, *European Macroeconomics*, London: Macmillan, 1994, p. 444

maintaining low inflation may require higher interest rates at a time when the government's desire for faster short-term growth might dictate keeping interest rates low. In such a case, there is a danger that neither objective will be satisfactorily achieved. Long-term interest rates will fall only if markets are assured that the monetary authorities are determined to keep inflation low. New Zealand gave a strong signal to its central bank of the goal which it was expected to follow by linking the pay and job security of the governor and staff inversely to the rate of inflation.

(5) *Governments must not finance their budget deficits by borrowing from the central bank.* Borrowing from the central bank is, as we have seen, equivalent to printing money. It directly increases the money supply and is highly inflationary. If excessive money creation is the cause of inflation, a primary requirement for controlling inflation is control of the money supply.

These general principles are useful guides for an anti-inflation strategy. However, they must be bolstered by an institutional environment conducive to price stability, and its relevant requirements will vary from country to country. (See Box 12.4 for a discussion of the Argentinian experience.) Procedures for pay negotiations or *incomes policy*, agreed between the state and the private sector, may be important in some countries as a direct means of curbing an inflationary wage–price spiral and of defusing inflationary expectations.[15] Maintaining a

---

15 Incomes policy can be particularly useful in countries with strong and highly organised labour unions. If a large section of the workforce pre-commits to a low level of pay increase, that ensures a broad level of support for anti-inflation policies. Austria has used a form of national pay agreements as part of its successful price stabilisation strategy. Incomes policy can also be used as a way of minimising the costs of disinflation.

strong competition policy can also be a way of restraining inflation. For example, the British economy was able to grow faster in the 1990s without igniting pay inflation because labour markets have become less influenced by trade union monopolies, and more flexible in relation to types of work and hours worked. Improved efficiency at the micro level and breaking up monopolies make it hard to pass on price increases to the consumer.

Equally important is the need for capable policy-making *within* central banks. Central banks must know *when* to intervene and *how* to intervene. Although central bankers like to affect an aura of omniscience, the decision of when to 'put on the brakes' or to relax monetary policy is a matter of judgement as well as science.[16] A prime requirement for a central bank, therefore, is to develop an early warning system of impending inflation. Macroeconomic forecasting models and *lead indicators* of inflation are used for this purpose (Box 12.3). Experience in the late 1980s also showed the importance of asset prices as a source of inflation, in particular stock price indices and house prices. We need better understanding of the processes by which these prices feed into an inflationary psychology. It is also important to have reliable information on *actual* and *potential* GDP.

The next task is to decide on the policy instruments to use in controlling the money supply – interest rates, open-market operations, reserve requirements – and to understand their likely effects on the economy. These are discussed in the next chapter. As we shall see, controlling the money supply has been made difficult by deregulation and global capital mobility, further compounded by technical advances. For example, automatic teller machines (ATMs) enable a fixed supply of cash to be used more efficiently. Other innovations, such as smart cards and credit cards, substitute for cash. The ratio of cash to consumption spending in Europe fell between 1970 and 1990 from 13 per cent to under 8 per cent. The possibility of a cashless society has become closer as technology advances.[17] The evolution of mutual funds has also impaired the capacity of central bankers to control money supply. In terms of the Quantity Theory of Money equation, all these changes in the financial system have led to a higher and less predictable velocity of circulation (V), and hence have weakened the relationship between money supply (M) and the price level (P).

Central banks are beginning to adopt a more pragmatic approach to controlling money supply than in the past. Nowadays, many central banks use inflation-targeting rather than control of the money supply as the primary instrument for maintaining price stability.

---

16 A Swiss authority on monetary economics, Professor Jürg Niehans, expressed the view that 'economists should be under no illusion that central banking will ever become a science. ... However far monetary theory may progress, central banking is likely to remain an art': J. Niehans, *The Theory of Money* (Baltimore, MD: Johns Hopkins University Press, 1978), p. 294.
17 Committee of Governors, 'Payment systems in EC member states' (September 1992).

Box 12.3

Forecasting inflation by lead indicators

The main objective of monetary policy is the control of inflation. This is the core responsibility of a central bank. However, there is a significant time-lag between the implementation of a monetary policy change (say, a rise in the interest rate) and the subsequent effect that change has on the rate of inflation. For this reason, it is vital that central banks have early advance warning of inflation so that countervailing action can be taken in good time. To this end, monetary authorities monitor a wide range of indicators of future inflation. These are called *lead indicators*. Movements in these indicators tend to precede movement in the inflation rate. Sometimes a composite leading indicator is derived which combines individual indicators into a single index.

The most widely used lead indicators of inflation are:

- overtime payments,
- order books,
- capacity utilisation (usually available for manufacturing only),
- growth of aggregate money supply and private sector credit,
- commodity prices (oil and non-oil),
- stock market indices,
- labour earnings in service industries,
- house prices (new and second-hand),
- long-term bond yields (nominal),
- exchange rates.

Statistical techniques are used to estimate the power of these possible indicator variables in predicting future changes in inflation. The calculations will associate each indicator with a certain 'lead' value. Thus, new house prices '*with a lead of two years*' may be chosen. This tells us that house price changes this year correlate closely with changes in the consumer price index in two years' time. Sometimes it is possible to go further and estimate by how much and over what precise time-period the consumer price index will be affected by a change in a lead indicator, e.g. 'a 5 per cent devaluation in the exchange rate will lead to a 2 per cent increase in inflation within eighteen months'.

In particular, it is important to identify lead indicators which will be effective in picking up *turning points*, i.e. points when a recession is turning into a boom; or a boom turning downwards. Straightforward extrapolation techniques will give satisfactory estimates of what prices would be, given a combination of past trends. The major contribution of lead indicators is their ability to signal changes from past trends or turning points. Needless to say, no indicator is perfect, and the length of the 'lead' time and the significance of variables will change as the economy changes. For example, the increasing flexibility of labour markets (and high unemployment) in the UK and other Western European countries has weakened the hitherto very close relation between movements in the exchange rate and subsequent inflation. In former days, employees might have received full and automatic compensation for any rise in these prices following devaluation. The rise was then 'passed on' to other domestic prices, promptly and entirely. By the mid-1990s, the pass-through mechanism was operating much more weakly.

12.5 Inflation and exchange rate anchors

Monetary policy as described above is relevant mostly to large countries with autonomous monetary policies. The euro area, Japan and the US obviously fall into this category. For smaller countries, however, a different approach may be necessary. One major difference is the importance to them of exchange rate policy as a means of attaining price stability. By attaching its currency to an anchor currency, that is, by tying its currency to a stronger and low-inflation currency, a small country can 'lock' its inflation rate into a lower level. Provided the anchor currency's monetary authorities are firmly committed to low inflation, the smaller country attached to it will do likewise.

To explain inflation in small open economies (SOEs), we begin by noting that these economies, being heavily dependent on trade, are highly vulnerable to external inflationary pressures. The extent to which inflation is 'imported' from the rest of the world then hinges crucially on the exchange-rate regime adopted by the small country. If the exchange rate is *fixed* relative to a weighted average of its trading partners, domestic inflation is largely determined by inflation in these countries. If they have high inflation, it will be transmitted to the small country; if they have low inflation, the small country will have low inflation. (The theory behind this will be explained in Part III.)

Why choose another currency as an anchor? One reason is that anchoring the value of your currency in terms of a major international reserve currency gives an anti-inflation policy a great degree of credibility. It is an easily understood signal to impress the public and trade unions. It provides a clear message to the market that the state is serious about stabilising prices. If successful, product and factor prices will adjust quickly to the lower inflation regime and expectations will be moderated accordingly. Using a single-currency anchor is, for this reason, superior to using a trade-weighted multi-currency anchor. The single-currency anchor gives a much clearer signal of a government's anti-inflationary intentions and thus garners credibility in the capital and labour markets.

There are many examples of countries using exchange rate anchors to combat inflation. In the past, Austria, the Netherlands and Belgium have all used a Deutschmark link to achieve consolidated low inflation rates. In West Africa, the former French colonies were linked with the French franc through the CFA

Box 12.4

How to stop hyperinflation: the example of Argentina

There is wide agreement on the stabilisation package which nations suffering from hyperinflation ought to adopt. This package should consist of four main elements:

1. the use of a nominal exchange rate anchor to break inflationary expectations;
2. the use of restrictive fiscal policies;
3. the adoption of tight monetary policies by independent monetary institutions;
4. the introduction of microeconomic structural reforms. These include competition, trade liberalisation, deregulation of labour markets, and the liberalisation of capital and foreign exchange controls.

Some countries have dealt successfully with hyperinflation using this approach: Argentina, Chile and Israel, among others. The Argentine experience is an example of an ambitious and radical stabilisation programme which has dealt successfully with the problem of hyperinflation.

Argentina's economic progress from 1988 to 1994 is recorded in Table 12.5. The jump in prices in 1989 was a 'classical' manifestation of inflation caused by excessive money supply, as the government financed its yawning budget deficit by printing money. The costs of hyperinflation are illustrated by the contraction of national income in 1989 by 6.2 per cent alongside an inflation rate of 3079 per cent. (Some estimate that it reached as high as 5000 per cent that year.)

In late 1990 and early 1991, serious attempts to counteract this massive inflation began. The new government, led by Carlos Menem, tackled the problem with a policy package made up of a mixture of fiscal and monetary measures. This involved a major ideological U-turn for the Peronist Party which had, up until then, displayed a hostility towards free market ideas.

Menem's principal innovation in monetary policy was the introduction of a law in April 1991 which introduced a new currency unit, the peso, and fixed it at a one-to-one exchange rate with the US dollar. The law obliged the central bank to sell or exchange its reserves at the ratio of 10,000 Australs (1 peso) per US dollar. Hence, monetary expansion could no longer be used as a 'soft option' for financing government expenditure without incurring debt (denominated in a hard currency) or raising taxes.

The new regime also took strong measures to deal with the underlying fiscal problem. On the revenue side, there was, in general, no rise in the rate of taxation, but a concerted effort was made to ensure greater tax compliance. On the expenditure side, there were cuts in spending in several areas. Public capital expenditure was severely reduced. Loss-making semi-state bodies were restructured and either wholly or partly privatised. Powerful interest groups, such as the defence forces, also suffered cutbacks. Military expenditure, as a percentage of GDP, fell by a third (from 3 per cent to 2 per cent) over the period 1990–92.

The net impact of these measures was such that, by end-1993, Argentina was running a fiscal surplus in a relatively low inflation environment.

In one sense, the effect of these contractionary fiscal and monetary measures on output was contrary to intuition. In a Keynesian framework, one would expect that, as government

Box 12.4 continued

spending fell, taxes increased and money supply curtailed, the economy would suffer a recession. Instead, quite the contrary happened. The economy stopped shrinking and began to grow. One possible explanation for this is that the creation of a stable macroeconomic environment led to an increase in investor and business confidence which, in turn, stimulated private sector investment and growth. Also, the restructuring and privatisation of large sectors of the economy under state control may have led to large efficiency gains in the use of these productive assets. Greater labour market flexibility helped to minimise the negative impact on employment of the cutback in government spending.

The political support of the ordinary citizenry and business community (as reported in opinion polls) gave the government vital encouragement. This strong consensus enabled it to override the opposition of politically entrenched interest groups. The reward for bringing inflation under control was significant, as is suggested by the 4.6 per cent per capita real growth in Argentina's national income up to 1998. However, inevitably, there were also costs, especially in terms of higher unemployment and slow export growth, as the strong dollar up-valued the peso to an unwarranted extent. Fears of de-linking led to a rise in domestic interest rates and further damage to the economy. To obviate interest rate problems, in 1999 the government floated the idea of replacing the peso with the US dollar as Argentina's official currency. Since Argentina's GDP amounts to 3 per cent of US GDP, the dollarisation proposal would have far-reaching implications, one being whether the US would agree to share the ensuing seigniorage gains on a currency base of $16 billion. Ecuador proceeded to full dollarisation of its currency at about this time.

Table 12.5 **Argentina, 1988–94**

	Fiscal balance as % of GDP*	Annual % rate of inflation	Annual % change in GDP
1988	−5.6	343	−1.9
1989	−0.6	3079	−6.2
1990	+1.4	2314	+0.1
1991	+1.7	171	+8.0
1992	+2.2	24	+8.7
1993	+2.2	10	+6.0
1994	+1.1	3	+4.5

* Including privatisations.

Source: *World Bank Development Report* (Washington, DC, 1995); 'A Survey of Argentina', *The Economist* (26 March 1994); S. Hawke. 'Dollarisation for Argentina', The Cato Institute (Washington, DC, 1999)

currency zone and since 1999 with the euro. The US dollar has been widely used as an anchor to achieve stabilisation. Argentina's one-to-one link between the peso and the dollar is a recent, and so far strikingly successful, example of a dollar-linked anchor (see Box 12.4). Mexico and Brazil have used it to stabilise inflationary expectations. For a period, the Canadian dollar was tied to the US dollar. From 1922 to 1979, the Irish pound was maintained at parity with the pound sterling.

Not all anchor regimes work out well. Adoption of a fixed exchange rate anchor without a complementary fiscal, monetary and microeconomic reform package can lead to major problems. One danger is loss of cost competitiveness. Suppose employees in the domestic economy demand salaries over and above productivity gains – this could lead to domestic costs getting out of line with the anchor currency. If domestic inflation exceeds that of the anchor economy, cost competitiveness of domestic producers will be eroded. Another difficulty arises if the anchor currency revalues and this erodes cost competitiveness of the domestic economy relative to its third country competitors. Thus, a strong dollar pulls up the Argentine peso and creates problems for Argentine firms competing against Brazilian firms. The French franc zone in West Africa delivered low inflation, but may have damaged these countries' long-term competitiveness. A second consideration follows from this. It is important that the link with the anchor currency is credible. Credibility in this context requires that the exchange rate is in line with the government's capacity and political determination to deliver complementary anti-inflation domestic policies. We shall return to this topic in the discussion of exchange rate systems and regimes.

12.6 Is inflation dead?

Following many years of struggle, by the mid-1990s inflation at last appeared to be under control in most industrial countries. So great has been the success in achieving price stability, in both developed and developing countries, that some have concluded that inflation is 'dead'. By this they mean that structural and institutional changes in the global economy have made a resurgence of inflation so unlikely that inflation can effectively be written off as a problem solved. There are several powerful factors behind this line of reasoning.

First, there is *strong public support* for price stability. In part this is explained by unhappy memories of past inflation and its association with low growth and high unemployment. Even more important, in developed countries, is the ageing of the population. The proportion of people relying on pensions that are not inflation-indexed and who have a strong interest in price stability has increased dramatically. Older people also tend to be lenders rather than borrowers, and – as we saw earlier – lenders are hurt by inflation.

Second, changes in the financial system have been conducive to price stability. Capital markets, not monetary authorities, excercise the dominant influence on long-term interest rates. The international market in bonds is highly inflation-averse. Policies that endanger long-term price stability in the pursuit of short-term economic goals will be swiftly 'punished' in the market through falling bond prices and higher interest rates. This will not be popular with domestic voters. Finance ministers have consequently become as fearful of market perceptions as of the censure of their own monetary authorities. The more open and competitive financial environment, in both national and international markets, has encouraged monetary authorities to take pre-emptive action against incipient inflation sooner than they might if they had full control over the domestic market.

Third, liberalisation of markets has led to *greater competition*. The power of special groups to pass on cost increases to the customer has diminished. Resistance to price hikes, whether by trade unions or oligopolies, has stiffened considerably in recent years.

Fourth, the major economies are now *less vulnerable to commodity price shocks* than they were in the 1970s and 1980s. In part this is because of the growth of the services sector, in part because advances in technology have reduced independence on material inputs. GDP becomes lighter as countries become richer.

Fifth, the potentially harmful effects of inflation on their nascent democracies have motivated many developing and transition economies to adopt price stability as a major objective.

At a theoretical level, we have seen that economists have become increasingly convinced that inflation must be confronted rather than accommodated. Politicians, motivated by practical considerations, have reached exactly the same conclusion, and price stability has now become a political priority:

> There is now more conviction among politicians of the electoral advantages of running an economy in a way that keeps inflation under wraps, with ageing populations in many countries providing a growing constituency in favour of low and stable inflation. Politicians seem increasingly more content to leave monetary policy to independent central banks. This favourable political background is enabling central banks to engage in pre-emptive strikes against inflation – a strategy that is, in the long run, likely to be much less painful than allowing inflation to emerge (possibly into double figures), then stamping hard on the brakes and bringing the economy crashing to a sudden halt. This new approach can only be good for inflation and, since low inflation and high output growth go together in the medium to long run, good for the overall economy.[18]

Although this may appear a reassuring conclusion, experience warns against complacency. The spectacular decline in the UK inflation rate from around 16 per cent in 1980 to under 4 per cent in 1986 was succeeded by a return to double-digit inflation 5 years later, a relapse for which macroeconomic policy had a large share of responsibility. Perhaps it is better to say that inflation is dormant, rather than dead. It is always only too ready to oblige with an encore.

12.7 Conclusions

The experience of the 1970s and 1980s has enhanced the status of price stability as a policy objective. It has also strengthened our understanding of the link between money and inflation.

Weak monetary authorities have exacerbated inflation by:

- misjudging the timing of monetary policy – being too lax when the economy is booming and too restrictive when the economy operates under-capacity,

---

18 F. Browne and J. Fell, 'Inflation – dormant, dying or dead?', Technical Paper, Central Bank of Ireland (October 1994).

- pushing too hard on the brakes once inflation has emerged, thereby raising the costs of disinflation.

Feeble governments have also caused inflation by:

- accommodating excessive pay demands and price increases,
- failing to control public spending,
- financing deficits by monetary means.

The world economy is now seeing a focused and determined effort on the part of the authorities to provide price stability – more so than ever before. One would hope that the decline in inflation has been associated with a demonstrable improvement in economic efficiency and social stability. Many experts believe that it has, and for good reason. However, causality is never simple in economics. Low inflation does not guarantee good economic performance, nor does every high inflation country grow slowly. However, in the latter instance growth occurs despite inflation, not because of it. Price stability certainly assists economic growth, while departures from price stability never actively help to improve economic performance.

 ## Summary

1. Inflation is a persistent rise in the general level of money prices. Consumer price inflation is defined by reference to the total money costs of a basket of goods and services consumed by the average individual or household. The composition of this basket is revised periodically in order to reflect the changing patterns of household spending. Because inflation statistics are affected by composition, quality and substitution biases, price stability is defined as an inflation rate in the range 0–2 per cent.

2. *Proximate* causes of inflation include the monetary view of inflation, associated with Milton Friedman, which asserts that inflation occurs when the growth of the money supply persistently exceeds the growth of real output. This approach is consistent with the Quantity Theory of Money: the higher the growth of money supply, the higher the rate of inflation, other things being equal. However, the Quantity Theory leaves many questions unanswered, such as explaining the economic and social factors which determine how and why money supply should be allowed to increase.

3. A sound strategy for price stability must be based on a proper understanding of the economic costs of deviating from stability. The costs of inflation can be classified under five main headings. Rapid changes in the general price level obstruct the efficient working of the market system. Inflation also impacts adversely on the distribution of wealth, as well as hindering economic growth. The redistribution of wealth and the economic turmoil which accompany inflation can cause major social tensions which threaten democratic institutions. Finally, once started, inflation is costly to reduce. The solution is for governments to ensure that price stability, once restored, is thereafter maintained.

4. Price stability involves a broad spectrum of economic policies. There must be political commitment to low inflation and, to buttress this political commitment and give it credibility, there must also be an appropriate institutional framework. Given that the evidence indicates that independence rather than management by politicians is the optimal strategy for low inflation, central banks should be largely independent of political control. Central banks as the guardians of monetary policy require a clear statement of their policy objective, which ideally should be to maintain price stability. Equally important is the need for capable policy-making within central banks regarding when and how to intervene. An anti-inflation strategy would also require that governments must not finance their budget deficits by borrowing from the central bank as this is equivalent to printing money.

5. Exchange rate policy is an important means of controlling inflation in small economies. Some countries have attached their currency to a stronger, low inflation currency in the hope of locking their inflation rate into a lower level. The advantage of such anchoring is that it can give an anti-inflation policy a degree of credibility. However, adoption of a fixed exchange rate anchor without the adoption of a complementary monetary, fiscal and microeconomic reform package can lead to major problems.

6. There are many factors explaining the priority being given to price stability: changes in public support, openness of financial system, more intensive competition, less vulnerability to 'shocks'. But inflation is not yet 'dead'.

❓ Questions for discussion

1. What is price stability? How is the inflation rate calculated? Why might standard measures of inflation overestimate the 'true' rate of price increase?

2. Discuss the reasons why one might expect, over the long run, countries with lower inflation to enjoy faster growth than those with higher inflation.

3. It is sometimes said that business tends to be soft on inflation because firms prefer an environment of rising prices to one of static or declining prices. Do you agree?

4. Why do monetarists believe that sustained inflation is impossible without the explicit or implicit acquiescence of the monetary authorities?

5. Inflation targeting by the monetary authorities involves three steps:

   (a) deciding on a target inflation rate,
   (b) forecasting inflation, and
   (c) formulating and implementing a policy response should the forecast inflation rate deviate from its target level.

   Comment on each of these steps.
   (*Note*: Further details relevant to part (c) of this question are provided in Chapter 13.)

6. Is inflation 'dead'? Evaluate the arguments in section 6 of this chapter.

Exercises

1. What has been the inflation rate in your country in the past decade? What have been the determinants of this inflation?

2. A central bank announces that inflation is 'public enemy number 1' and engages in restrictive monetary policy to reduce it from 6 per cent to 3 per cent.
    What would be the likely effects, if any, on output and unemployment? Would your answer be different in the long run and the short run? Can disinflation be costless?

3. Suppose the UK inflation rate were to rise from 2 per cent to 10 per cent. Indicate three sections of the community that would lose and three that would gain from this. List three reasons why a resurgence of inflation might be bad for the British economy.

4. Identify any developing country that has experienced high inflation and has implemented a successful stabilisation programme. Evaluate that experience in the light of the arguments of this chapter in favour of price stability.

Further reading

Central bank reports are the best source of up-to-date statistics and analysis of inflation. The *Bank of England Quarterly Bulletin* presents excellent statistical information and special articles. Roger Bootle's *The Death of Inflation* (London: Nicholson Brealey, 1996) explores the causes of inflation. J. Kornai's *The Road to a Free Economy* (London: Norton, 1990) looks at inflation from the perspective of the transition economies, while A. Blinder, who (like the author of this book) spent several years on a central bank's board, gives an intriguing account of life in the Fed in *Central Banking in Theory and Practice* (Cambridge, MA: MIT Press, 1998).

Chapter 13

UNDERSTANDING INTEREST RATES AND MONETARY POLICY

Introduction

Interest rates are important to business. Although interest payments constitute a small proportion of most firms' total costs, they are often highly significant in relation to profit. Because the corporate sector tends on average to be a net borrower, a rise in interest rates involves a direct deduction from profits. For a highly geared firm with a heavy debt, a rise in interest can lead to bankruptcy. Even a financially strong firm can find its bottom line severely dented by a change in lending rates.

Changes in the interest rate also impact on business indirectly. If a rise in interest rates causes an economic slowdown, the demand for products which are interest rate-sensitive (new houses, for example) will fall and firms supplying these products will suffer, even if they were net lenders. Some firms are vulnerable to this type of interest rate exposure; for them, the interest rate (and, by extension, monetary policy) must be factored into their value at risk. The large and growing volume of trade in interest rate futures is testimony to the importance business attaches to interest rate fluctuations.

Business and central banks frequently clash over the conduct of monetary policy. They have radically different perspectives on interest rates. Central banks are likely to regard fluctuations in economic activity with far greater detachment than the business sector. A central bank might even regard a slowdown in economic growth as a necessary, if regrettable, cost of maintaining price stability. A company put out of business by a recession is unlikely to take such a philosophical view of the matter.

This chapter explores the complex and circumscribed relationship between monetary policy, interest rates and economic activity. Although monetary policy has already been discussed in the context of inflation, the details of such policy and its relation with interest rates have yet to be fully examined. Our starting point is the Quantity Theory of Money from which are derived propositions about both the long-run 'neutrality' of money and the monetarist dictum that *inflation is always and everywhere a monetary phenomenon*.

Public opinion easily overestimates the power of the monetary authorities in relation to interest rates. They *influence*, rather than determine, the level of interest. Their power has been particularly circumscribed in the long end of the market, by mobile capital and financial technology. Inflationary expectations are crucial in explaining nominal interest rates, while at the same time nominal rates and monetary policy can play a key role in forming these expectations. Higher interest rates might be caused by fears of future inflation, but they could also be the consequence of a tight monetary stance designed to prevent such inflationary expectations taking root. On occasion, the authorities have engineered a rise in interest rates only to find that the market drives them higher still, fuelled by a fear that the initial rise was not enough!

Monetary policy and interest rates are analysed in this chapter in the context of a closed economy. The analysis is primarily applicable to policy in the US, Japan and the euro area. In such circumstances, foreign considerations exert only a subsidiary influence in determining domestic policy. By contrast, in smaller countries, the relationship between domestic interest rates and the exchange rate is far closer and would have to be viewed in the context of global capital markets. The analysis is extended to the open economy in Part III.

Chapter outline

1. Definition of different types of interest rate: nominal v real, short-term v long-term, and the meaning and significance of the term structure of interest rates.

2. The determinants of interest rates.

3. The effect of changes in interest rates – the chief weapon in the central bank's armoury – on levels of consumer spending and investment activity.

4. The framework of monetary policy in terms of the instruments at the central bank's disposal, and the use of intermediate targets and instruments.

5. The design of monetary policy, paying particular attention to the need to achieve balance between the long-term objective of price stability and short-run discretionary action.

13.1 Which interest rate?

Interest is payment for the use of funds over a period of time. The interest rate is defined as *the amount of interest paid per unit of time as a fraction of the balance outstanding*. Although, for convenience, we refer to 'the' rate of interest, in practice there are many different rates of interest, according to their maturity, marketability and risk of the financial instrument. 'The' interest rate is in fact a continuum of interest rates, extending from the short to the long run across a wide spectrum of degrees of riskiness.

Nominal v real interest rates

Suppose interest on a £1000 government bond is 10 per cent per year. An investor in this bond will receive £1100 at the end of the year. The *nominal* return is £100 and the nominal interest rate is 10 per cent. Assume inflation is 4 per cent p.a. and is expected to stay at that rate. This means that, at year-end, £1040 will be needed in order to maintain the real purchasing power of the £1000 principal. In other words, £40 of the £100 nominal return represents compensation for rising prices. To derive the *real* return, this £40 must be subtracted from the total nominal return. The real return is defined, according to the *Fisher relation*, as $£\left(\frac{100-40}{100}\right) \times 100 = £60$, or 6 per cent per year.[1]

real interest rate (r) = nominal interest rate (i) *minus* inflation rate (π)

Now suppose people expect that inflation will rise from 4 per cent to 8 per cent per year. A 10 per cent bond will still yield a nominal return of £100. However, the expected 8 per cent inflation rate implies that to buy the equivalent of £1000 worth of purchases this year will cost £1080 next year. In such circumstances, the real return will fall to (£100 − £80) = £20 per year. The real interest rate becomes (10% − 8%) = 2 per cent.

The fall in the prospective real interest rate will not go unnoticed. Financial markets are paid to be aware of such developments. As inflation expectations are adjusted upwards, they will be less willing to lend at 10 per cent since the expected real return has fallen. The fall in demand for government bonds will drive down the price and cause nominal yields to rise. Assuming that market participants do not suffer money illusion, bond prices will continue to fall until the nominal yield (or nominal interest rate) increases to 14 per cent. At that rate, the real interest rate has returned to its initial (equilibrium) level.

The real rate of interest is not directly observable. It is defined by reference to an *expected* inflation rate. However, one can infer its value by subtracting *current inflation* (or inflation one year later) from nominal interest rates. Defined this way, real interest rates can be negative. Real interest rates fell to −4 per cent in 1973, but rose to a level of 4–6 per cent in the 1980s. Since then, there have been signs of a slight moderation in interest levels. The range of variation across countries is quite marked. By the early 2000s, real long-term interest rates were as low as 2 per cent in Japan compared to 4 per cent in the US and France.

The negative real interest rate of the 1970s poses some intriguing questions. Why would anyone lend money at a negative real rate of interest? The most likely answer is that the lenders did not intentionally do so, but simply made a mistake in their inflation forecasts. The steep rise in inflation may have taken them by surprise; and, as the value of their fixed nominal interest bonds fell in real terms, they lost money. This loss in real earnings had an important implication for future behaviour. The next time inflation threatened, lenders were determined not to be caught again. Real long-term interest rates in the UK (5.6 per cent) and Italy (5.2 per cent) rose steeply during the period 1980–92, compared with countries with a low inflation record, such as Germany and Japan (4.2 per cent and 4.8 per cent

---

1 The relationship is named after Irving Fisher who was the first to provide a systematic analysis of the issue in 1896. This relationship holds exactly in theory. In practice, when tested against past experience, we find that, over long periods, changes in inflation have a less than point-for-point effect on nominal interest rates.

respectively).[2] Financial markets continued to have an aversion to even the mildest threat of inflation. Any suspicion that the authorities are taking a permissive approach to inflation immediately pushes up the nominal rates.

The Fisher equation implies that a 10 per cent interest with 4 per cent inflation is equivalent to 14 per cent interest and 8 per cent inflation. Since the real rate of interest is the same in both situations, borrowers might be thought to be indifferent between them. In practice, this is unlikely to be so. Cash flow is heavily influenced by the absolute level of the nominal rate. The higher the nominal rate, the greater the outflow (proportionately) in the early years of a loan. Many businesses, especially small firms, and mortgage holders are constrained by nominal limits on credit. Bankers respond to the cash-flow profile of a loan as well as to the long-run real rate of interest. The rise in the upfront burden of a rise in nominal rates, therefore, can affect business in ways which are ignored in the Fisher relation.

The term structure of interest rates and the yield curve

Interest rates differ according to the maturity of the loan. Bonds with a maturity of less than 1 year are considered short term; those with a maturity of 1–3 years, medium term; and those over 3 years, long term. The *short-term* rate is usually defined by reference to the yield on a 3-month interbank deposit or treasury bill; the *long-term* rate by reference to a 10-year government bond. Statistics for these rates in 2000 show that nominal long-term interest rates in the industrial countries exceeded short-term interest rates in most countries (Table 13.1). Real yields are also higher in the long run. Interest rates differ markedly between countries, but more so in the case of nominal rates than long-run real rates.[3]

Table 13.1 Interest rates and inflation in industrial countries, 2000

	Nominal interest rate			Real interest rate	
	Short term (1)	Long term (2)	Inflation (3)	Short term (1)–(3)	Long term (2)–(3)
US	6.31	6.37	2.4	3.91	3.97
Japan	0.12	1.70	−0.3	0.42	2.0
Germany	4.3	5.23	1.5	2.80	3.73
France	4.30	5.42	1.3	3.00	4.12
Italy	4.30	5.58	2.6	2.70	2.98
UK	6.30	5.24	2.5	3.70	2.74
Spain	4.30	5.53	2.8	1.60	2.73

Notes: Short term = 3-month interbank or certificates of deposit. Long term = 10-year government bonds.

Source: OECD, author's own estimates.

---

2 Figures taken from 'Are real interest rates high?', *OECD Economic Outlook* (June 1993).

3 Given high capital mobility, this is what one would expect. Theoretically, if inflation expectations were correctly measured and national governments were all equally creditworthy, market forces would tend to force real interest rates in different countries to converge.

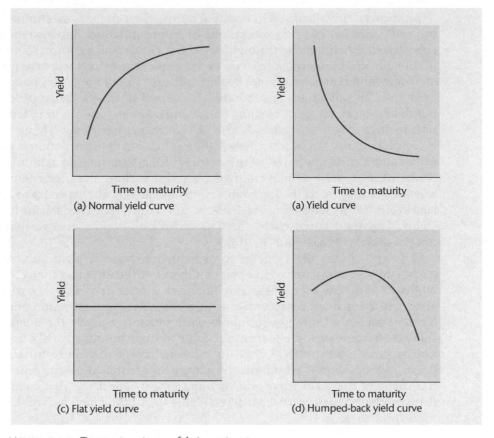

Figure 13.1 Term structure of interest rates

Three-month and 10-year yields are just two observations on a whole spectrum of maturities. One could add 6-month, 2-year and 5-year rates, and so on. The *term structure*, or time-profile, of interest rates is defined as the relationship on a specific date between interest rates for bonds with different terms to maturity that have similar risk. The curve connecting these interest rates, or yields, is called the *yield curve*.

The 'normal' shape of the yield curve is upward-sloping. The underlying theory is that people have a positive time preference. Consumption this year is better than the promise of the same consumption next year. A promise to pay next year is considered more valuable than a promise to pay in 10 years' time, even if the same guarantee is attached to each promise. Things can go wrong in the future; people discount accordingly, and require compensation for the longer 'wait' and the accompanying uncertainty. Because short-term bonds are more liquid than long-term bonds, investors buy them even though they yield a lower return. Hence, the normal expectation is that long-term interest rates will be higher than short-term rates. But this does not mean that yield curves in reality are always positive-sloping. They can have a diversity of slopes: downward-sloping, flat and, occasionally, hump-backed (Figure 13.1).

Yield curves are calculated in nominal terms. Their shape is determined jointly by 'real' variables and by expectations of future inflation. Suppose inflation is expected to rise. Following the logic of the Fisher relation, a corresponding rise in nominal interest rates will also be expected. Hence the market will *expect* the price of longer-term bonds to decline. Dealers will rush to sell long-term bonds and to hold cash, or buy short-term bonds. This drives down the price of long-term bonds and raises the price of short-term bonds. As the yield on long-term bonds rises relative to short-term bonds, the *yield curve becomes steeper* (Figure 13.1(a)).

Now take a situation when inflationary pressure has eased; inflation is predicted to fall and a consequent fall in the nominal long-term interest rate is expected. New investors want to move out of cash and to buy more long-term bonds, thereby 'locking in' to the high rate now available but not expected to last. This leads to a rise in long-term bond prices and a corresponding fall in long-term yields. The yield curve could then be downward-sloping and we obtain the 'reverse-yield' curve (Figure 13.1(b)).

The expectations theory helps to explain the shape of yield curves. But its explanatory power is limited in so far as it ignores the distinctive characteristics of bonds of different maturities. The financial market is highly *segmented*. Life assurance companies, for example, with predictable nominal future obligations, have a preference for long-term bonds with which to balance these liabilities. If these are in short supply, a succession of shorter-term bonds will make do, but will not be perfect substitutes. Other institutions have a preference for short-term bonds. Because bonds with different maturities are traded in different markets, the shape of the yield curve will to some extent reflect the particular supply–demand characteristics in each market. (Some might even have a shape like Figure 13.1(d).)

The shape of the yield curve is a matter of crucial significance for bond traders, corporate treasurers, investment banks and fund managers. Considerable resources are expended on predicting its shape. Good predictions can prove hugely profitable. If a bank believes that a positively-sloped yield curve is about to flatten, it will buy long-term bonds in the expectation that long-term interest rates will fall (and the capital value of the bonds will rise), and sell short-term bonds in the expectation that short-term interest rates will rise (so avoiding the prospect of capital loss).[4]

Central banks also keep watch on the term structure. The yield curve can serve as a lead indicator of inflation, or of inflationary expectations in the market. It can also provide useful information to a central bank on market perceptions of its policy. Suppose the bank raises short-term interest rates. If the market is reassured by this signal of the central bank's determination to keep inflation low, long-term interest rates will not increase proportionally, and may even fall. In that case, a negatively-sloped yield curve would reflect market confidence in the bank's anti-

---

4 This is not to suggest that the mix of short-term and long-term bonds will be dictated solely by the profit-maximisation principle. Portfolio investors must maintain liquidity and security as well as earn profits. Debt held in short-term instruments may be cheaper than longer-term debt, but it can expose a firm to considerable interest rate risk as it falls due and has to be rolled over.

inflation strategy. Economic forecasters also study the yield curve for indications of the markets' perception of inflation and growth prospects.

So much for the *slope* of the yield curve. We still have to analyse what determines its *position*, i.e. what makes 'interest rates' rise or fall. To study this issue, we return to the assumption of there being a single interest rate. Like any other price, this interest rate will be determined by the forces of demand and supply.

13.2 What determines interest rates?

The interest rate can be regarded as the 'price' that brings demand for credit into equilibrium with supply of credit. As interest falls, investment projects become profitable, housing becomes less costly to finance and people want to borrow more. Hence the demand curve for credit is downward-sloping with respect to the interest rate. The supply of loanable funds is assumed to respond positively to the interest rate. A higher interest rate means a better return on saving. People spend less now in the expectation of earning higher interest and being able to spend more in the future.

This theory, called the 'loanable funds' theory, is illustrated in Figure 13.2. DD represents the demand for credit and SS the supply of credit. Equilibrium occurs where supply equals demand, at point E*. Suppose interest strayed from equilibrium and went to r_2 instead of r*. At that higher interest rate, supply of funds would increase from r*E* to r_2v_2; while demand would fall from r*E* to r_2u_2. At this interest rate, supply of credit would exceed demand. To induce people to borrow more, interest will have to fall. As it falls, supply of credit will also decline,

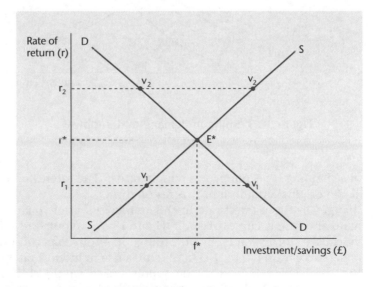

Figure 13.2 **Loanable funds theory of interest**

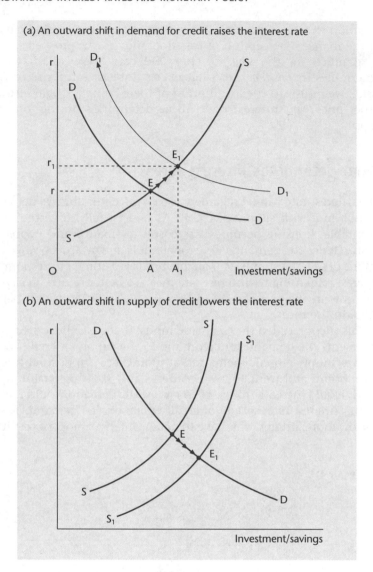

(a) An outward shift in demand for credit raises the interest rate

(b) An outward shift in supply of credit lowers the interest rate

Figure 13.3 **Shifts in demand and supply**

because lending is becoming less remunerative. The interest rate continues falling until the original equilibrium r* is restored.

Changes in the interest rate in this framework are explained by shifts in the demand and supply curves of credit (Figure 13.3). An outward shift in the demand curve caused, for example, by an upsurge in profit expectations, will move the demand curve from DD to D_1D_1 and cause a rise in interest rates from r to r_1. If the savings propensity increased, the supply curve would shift to the right and interest rates would fall. If the government budget deficit was increased, interest

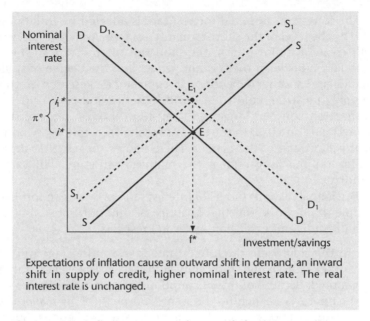

Expectations of inflation cause an outward shift in demand, an inward shift in supply of credit, higher nominal interest rate. The real interest rate is unchanged.

Figure 13.4 Inflation expectations and the interest rate

rates would also increase, given that a budget deficit is effectively a form of national dissaving, which shifts the supply curve to the left.[5]

Since saving and borrowing decisions are forward-looking, the nominal interest rate ought, in principle, to be adjusted for expected inflation. Inflation expectations will affect both the demand and the supply of credit.

Suppose we start in Figure 13.4 from an initial equilibrium at $E(i^*, f^*)$. Assume that, at this point, inflation is zero. Hence the real interest rate is the same as the nominal interest rate. Now suppose that, following a supply-side shock or excessive money growth, people expect an upsurge of inflation. This shifts the demand for credit curve outwards to D_1D_1, as borrowers will be prepared to pay more for credit in anticipation of higher sales revenues. But simultaneously the supply of credit curve will shift inwards to S_1S_1, as lenders will demand higher interest to compensate for the expected rise in prices. The new equilibrium will be realised at $E_1(i_1^*f^*)$. At this point, the *nominal interest rate has risen proportionally to the expected rise in prices, π^e. The real interest rate is unchanged.*

---

5 The relationship between budget deficits and the interest rate is complicated by the possibility that these deficits can affect the supply of credit, as well as the demand for credit. A European Commission study, based on data of the major industrial countries since 1980, finds that every 1 percentage point increase in the budget deficit/GDP ratio over a 1-year period raises long-term interest rates by 17 to 72 basis points. The overall impact depends on the level of the deficit/GDP ratio, as well as changes in this ratio: J. Nunes-Correia and L. Stemitsiotis, 'Budget deficit and interest rates: Is there a link?', *Economic Papers*, no. 105, Commission of the European Communities, November 1993. See also W. Tease *et al.*, 'Real interest rate trends: The influence of saving, investment and other factors', *OECD Economic Studies*, no. 17 (1991).

The long-term nominal interest rate is affected by inflation expectations, and also by the level of the short-term interest rate. Arbitrage between the two markets will create a spillover from the short-run interest rate to the long-run rate. The correlation between them is not perfect and the degree of spillover between one market and another depends on circumstances. Research on the experience of ten major industrial countries during the period 1970–90 showed a positive correlation between long- and short-term interest rates of 0.96 in the US, 0.51 in Germany and 0.30 in the UK.[6] As we shall see, monetary policy operates mostly at the short end of the market. These figures suggest that the effect of monetary policy on the long end of the maturity structure will vary from country to country.

The loanable funds model of interest rates provides an intuitively appealing and simple framework for the analysis of interest rates. But the theory needs qualification and extension in several respects.

(1) In this approach, the interest rate takes centre-stage in bringing savings and investment into equilibrium only because a *given* level of real output and income is assumed. Because of this assumption, an outward shift in savings leads to a fall in the interest rate. Behind the scenes, output is being *reallocated* from production of consumer goods to production of investment goods. Suppose, however, we remove the assumption of fixed output and that a rise in the propensity to save, represented by an outward shift from SS to S_1S_1, leads to a lowering of profit expectations – as in real life it easily could (Figure 13.5). The demand for loanable funds would then shift inwards from DD to D_1D_1. A new equilibrium occurs at E_1 at a lower level of investment and aggregate demand. There is a subsequent fall in real output and national income. Since savings are a function of income as well as interest rate, the fall in income leads to an inward shift in the savings function from S_1S_1 to S_2S_2. Eventually, a new equilibrium is attained at E_2. The interest rate may or may not fall, depending on the precise extent of the movements in the curves. The important point is that equilibrium has been brought about by two equilibrating factors rather than one: *changes in the interest rate and changes in income*. In the short run, changes in income would in fact bear the brunt of adjustment.

(2) The loanable funds theory concentrates on the mechanisms by which the interest rate brings *flows* of saving and investment into equilibrium. But the interest rate also performs an important function in relation to *stocks* of financial assets. At any one time, the term structure of interest rates determines the disposition of these stocks as between money at one end of the spectrum and long-term bonds at the other. Shifts in preferences between financial and real assets or between different types of financial assets could impact on the level of the interest rate, and a comprehensive theory would have to take this into account.

(3) The loanable funds theory ignores the long-run *dynamic* relationship between interest, investment and savings.

---

6 IMF, *World Economic Outlook* (May 1994).

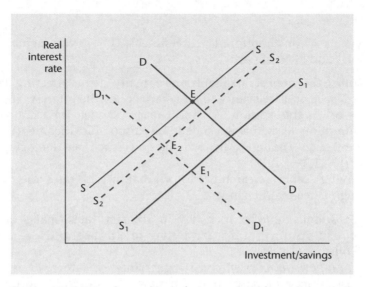

Figure 13.5 **Interdependence between supply and demand**

From a log-run point of view, savings are an essential prerequisite of investment. Investment generates economic growth, which will raise incomes and out of which will come future savings. This approach emphasises the importance of ensuring that savings are adequately and securely rewarded, and perceives no necessary contradiction in the long run between high real interest rates and high levels of growth and investment. Negative real interest rates may give a short-run stimulus to investment but, by undermining savings, may damage growth in the long run. A contrary view is that the propensity to invest, not the propensity to save, is in most urgent need of being protected; which implies that priority should be given to keeping long-run interest rates as low as possible. At this stage, it is unnecessary to do more than flag the issue and to note that interest rate policy has long-run as well as short-run implications for the economy.[7]

13.3 Interest rates and economic activity

To understand the channels through which interest rates affect economic activity, we focus on the direct links between interest rates and aggregate demand. There are also important indirect effects, via, for instance, changes in exchange rates, discussion of which is deferred to Part III.

Interest rates affect each of the components of aggregate demand in different ways. Recall that aggregate demand (GDP) can be broken down as:

---

7 The complexity of these relations is evident in the difficulties researchers experience in identifying any statistically robust relationship between long-run economic growth and the real long-run interest rate.

$$GDP = C + I + G + X - M$$

where: C = consumption, I = investment, G = government consumption, X = exports and M = imports.

Of course the interest rate is only one of many factors affecting these components, but because of its relevance to monetary policy the interest rate effect is what we focus on in this section. A typical macro model, for example, would specify consumption as being dependent on disposable income (Y–T), wealth (W), interest rates (i) and other variables (Z) such as demographic change, i.e. $C = f(Y - T, W, i, Z)$.

Delving deeper, research has shown that interest rates affect *consumer spending* through three main channels:

1. *Substitution effects*: increases in interest rates make saving (i.e. future consumption) more attractive for households relative to current consumption.
2. *Cash-flow (income) effects*: a higher interest rate reduces the cash flow of borrowers and raises the cash flow of lenders. If borrowers and lenders responded to changes in cash flow in the same manner, these effects would be symmetrical and offsetting. In practice, borrowers and lenders tend to have different spending propensities, and hence the redistribution of income following a rise in interest rates can, and does, impact on aggregate consumer spending. The magnitude of the net effect depends on household and business sector balance sheets, on the prevalence of fixed interest rate contracts and on propensities to spend (Box 13.1).
3. *Wealth effects*: a rise in interest rates lowers the value of housing, equities and bonds. A fall in asset values relative to borrowing can have a dramatic effect on consumer spending. In the mid-1990s, British consumers were still feeling the after-shock of the collapse in house prices five years earlier (Box 13.2). The Federal Reserve Bank estimates that the boom in asset values has added 1 percentage point to US aggregate demand each year during the late 1990s.

Investors tend to be far more sensitive to interest rate change than consumers. That explains why business has such a strong demand for interest rate forecasts. Again however, we note that interest rate is by no means the only variable to impact on the investment decision. A typical investment function would include a range of variables:

$$I = f(MPK, C)$$

where MPK = marginal product of capital,
C = cost of capital

Each of these variables has to be defined over a future time period and hence both marginal productivity of capital and cost of capital will be strongly affected by business 'sentiment' or expectations. In this respect, expected productivity (and hence profitability) of investment will be much influenced by prevailing ideas about the growth of the economy, so income variables also enter the picture

Interest rates and cash-flow effects

The cash-flow effects of higher interest rates depend on the net indebtedness of households and firms, and on the proportion of assets and liabilities which are interest-rate adjustable. This proportion varies sharply between countries. For example, two-thirds of lending to the private sector in the US is in the form of 'predominantly fixed interest', as compared with less than one-third in the UK, Australia and Italy. The higher the share of variable interest loans, the greater the extent to which borrowers will be affected by a change in interest rates. The potential importance of this cash-flow effect has been significantly magnified by the rise in the debt/income ratios of households in many countries during the past decade.

The impact of a change in interest rates has been found to be quite asymmetrical between borrowers and lenders. Not surprisingly, borrowers with a high debt/equity exposure cut back spending far more severely in response to a rise in the interest rate than lenders with substantial net wealth increase theirs. The age profile of borrowers and savers also has a bearing on the source of this asymmetry. Older people have a lower propensity to spend than younger people. They also have higher net savings. For example, almost 60 per cent of funds invested in British building societies are owned by investors over 55 years of age, but these account for only 15 per cent of borrowing. This may be a reason why an increase in deposit rates may have a different effect to an increase in lending rates of the same value.

The cash-flow effects of an interest rate change are more important in practice than the traditionally emphasised substitution effects. Cash-flow effects are especially important for business because firms in the non-financial sector are large net borrowers, while households are net lenders in aggregate.

either implicitly or explicitly. The interest rate is embedded in the cost of capital variable, along with depreciation, expected price changes in capital goods, and corporate taxes and investment subsidies (see Chapter 10).

Different types of investment have different interest rate sensitivities. Thus residential investment is very interest-sensitive because of the long lifespan of housing and the large initial outlay relative to income involved in a house purchase, whereas the link between interest rates and *business fixed investment* has proved surprisingly hard to quantify.

Two approaches have been used to study total business investment: the *neo-classical* model and *Tobin's q-theory*. The neo-classical model draws on the marginal productivity theory outlined in Chapter 10. The firm chooses a minimum cost combination of inputs to produce a given output. The desired level of the capital stock depends on the level of output and the cost of capital, where the cost of capital depends on the nominal interest rate, the price of capital goods, expected inflation, and tax rates and allowances. A negative relationship between interest rate and investment is predicted by this model. Tobin's *q*-theory of investment

Box 13.2

Effects of interest rate changes on consumer wealth

Interest rate changes affect investment levels. They also impact on consumer spending through net wealth effects. The latter are measured by changing asset prices. Asset prices in turn change because the discounted present value of future income pertaining to that asset has changed.

Take, for example, the bond market. Because of the fixed coupon rate on bonds, bond prices and the rate of interest are inversely related. Consider a 1-year bond, sold for £1000 and on which the borrower/issuer offers an 8 per cent return. After one year, the bond yields £80 to the lender, as well as the redemption of the original £1000.

The price of the bond equals the present discounted value of the bond. The present value is what would be paid today for the promise of money in one year's time and it is discounted because the value today is less than the promised payment in a year's time. Denoting the 1-year interest rate by i, the actual yield payment by U and the redemption value of the bond by B, we can write the present discounted value of the bond as:

$$PDV = \frac{U + B}{1 + i} = \frac{80 + 1000}{1.08} = £1000$$

Now, suppose that the interest rate on 1-year bonds increases, how much would anyone be willing to pay for the promise of receiving £1080 in one year's time? Because this promise will be discounted at the now higher rate of, say, 10 per cent, this must mean that the present discounted value, and hence the price of the bond, will fall:

$$PDV = \frac{U + B}{1 + i} = \frac{80 + 1000}{1.10} = £981$$

Because the market yield rate has increased from 8 to 10 per cent, the value of this bond must fall until the yield rates are equalised. *An increase in interest rates will therefore lead to a fall in bond prices, and vice versa.* A fall in bond values will lead to a fall in consumer wealth. Given that wealth is an important determinant of consumer spending, a fall in consumer wealth will be followed by a decline in consumption expenditure.

Similar effects of interest rate changes are evident in the equities market. A rise in the interest rate on financial assets leads to a rise in the returns investors require from equities. If the interest rate on bonds rises, equity holders will move their wealth out of equities. By selling their equity shareholdings they depress equity prices. Share prices will fall until equity returns are brought into equilibrium with bond returns. Conversely, a fall in interest rates will lead to a corresponding switch towards equities and a rise in share prices. According to the direction of the interest rate change, asset holders are likely to feel either wealthier or poorer and, in consequence, either expand or reduce their spending.

Further effects will also be evident in the housing market. One of the most important determinants of housing demand is the real interest rate. Most prospective homeowners require mortgages to buy their homes and the interest rate is the cost of these loans. Hence, an increase in the interest rate will lead to a corresponding fall in housing demand. This will be felt in the new housing sector, but it will also lead to a fall-off in the number of people willing to 'trade up' to larger houses. Even homeowners with no mortgages will respond to

comes to the same conclusion by a rather different route. It hypothesises that new investment depends on the gap between the market value of industry's capital assets and the replacement cost – the quotient of these two values is the *q* ratio. If the market value exceeds the replacement cost, profitable opportunities exist for new investment to exploit this gap. A rise in the interest rate, by lowering the market value of capital, therefore weakens the incentive to invest. A fall in the interest rate, by raising the market value of capital, stimulates investment. Although intuitively appealing, neither of these theories has stood up well to empirical testing. Even the association between interest rates and *inventory investment*, which one would have expected to be very strong, has proved hard to pin down.[8]

The impact of interest rates on *government spending* is a comparatively neglected topic, but for heavily-indebted governments, a potentially important element in the overall picture. The direct impact of an interest rate change falls on debt-servicing costs. A rise in these costs tends to have a negative impact on public sector spending as well as on general market sentiment. Relations between central banks and governments can become quite tense when the latter is heavily indebted. A decision to change interest rates can have a major impact on budget arithmetic in such countries. Interest payments on debt still account for over 20 per cent of government revenue in countries as diverse as Egypt, Morocco, Guatemala, India and Pakistan. In developed countries too, from Canada to Italy and the US, the ratio exceeds 15 per cent.

The modest effects revealed by econometric investigations into the effect of interest rate changes contrast with the weight attached to interest rate changes by the media, business organisations and politicians. Taken at face value, they suggest that we might agonise too much about the interest rate. The occasional much publicised disagreements about interest rate policy are usually about proposed adjustments in the interest rate of less than 1 percentage point. Why so much fuss if the impact on total spending is not appreciable?

There are several ways of answering this question. *First*, the cumulative effect of an interest rate change on aggregate demand may be greater than the sum of the effect of each component of demand. The British Treasury's model, for instance, suggests that a 2 percentage point rise in the interest rate causes consumption to be $1\frac{3}{4}$ per cent lower after two years than it would otherwise be. Add in the hard-

---

8 See A. Blinder and L. Maccini, 'Taking stock: A critical assessment of recent research in inventories', *Journal of Economic Perspectives* (Winter 1991).

to-quantify investment effects and one is talking about a significant effect on aggregate demand. *Second*, movements in interest rates have a strong effect on expectations. The interest rate acts as a signal. An interest rate increase comes with an implicit warning that, if the economy does not slow down, further action will be taken by the authorities. Likewise, a lowering of interest rates by the monetary authorities can be interpreted as a signal of easier money and more aggressive stimulation of aggregate demand.

13.4 Monetary policy and interest rates

Interest rates are an important tool in a monetary authority's armoury. Sometimes the central bank may directly change the short-term rate; at other times its actions will have an indirect effect on the interest rate structure. In assessing and guiding monetary conditions, the bank has regard not just to the level of interest, but also to money supply, lead inflation indicators and the exchange rate. To implement their policies and alter monetary conditions, monetary authorities have a variety of instruments at their disposal, direct controls and 'market-based' instruments.

Price stability – the ultimate objective

The ultimate objective of monetary policy is price stability.[9] Most central banks publish explicit inflation targets; virtually all regard control of inflation as a high priority (Box 13.3). This objective is based on the conviction that high inflation at best contributes nothing positive to, and will likely impede, economic growth and full employment. An explicit low inflation objective for monetary policy minimises uncertainty.

Monetary policy operates with a delayed reaction of 1–2 years. If inflationary pressures are building up, central banks need to take countervailing action before these pressures are translated into actual inflation. Prevention is better than cure. From a central bank's view, early response to a build-up of inflation signals a determination to maintain its *credibility*. If the proposed measures are seen as effective, the bank's credibility is strengthened. As a result, the bank's advice and opinions will carry greater weight with business, employees and government. By accurate diagnoses of what needs to be done, and implementation of the necessary measures, a central bank over time builds up *reputation*. This further strengthens its influence.

Experience shows that bad monetary policy can cause inflation. The chain of causation is outlined in Box 13.4. Suppose a central bank misreads the indicators

---

9 The Federal Reserve's objective is specified differently as that of ensuring full employment, rapid growth and price stability. Of course, US central bankers assert that price stability is the best way of achieving full employment and that there is consequently no conflict between these objectives. From time to time there have been proposals to redefine the objectives of the Fed in order to give price stability specific priority.

Box 13.3

How central banks define their objectives

Euro area

Price stability is the primary objective of the European Central Bank. The Bank has defined price stability as

> *a year on year increase in the harmonised index of consumer prices for the euro area of below 2 per cent.*

According to President of the ECB, Willem Duisenberg, this definition mirrors the Bank's aversion to both inflation and deflation. Neither price increases persistently above 2 per cent, nor price declines, could be deemed consistent with price stability.

UK

The Bank of England Act 1998 also defines the objectives of the Bank as being to maintain price stability. But the Chancellor of the Exchequer, not the Governor, determines the operational expression of the price stability target. Since June 1997, this has been a symmetric target of a 2½ per cent annual increase in the retail price index minus mortgage interest payments (RPIX).

US

The mandate of the Federal Reserve System was most recently defined in the *Humphrey-Hawkins Act*, passed by Congress in 1978. The Act requires the Fed to

> *maintain long-run growth of the monetary and credit aggregates commensurate with the economy's long-run production potential so as to promote effectively the goals of maximum employment, stable prices and moderate long-term interest rates.*

Japan

The new Bank of Japan Law was passed by the Diet in June 1997. The objective of monetary policy under the new law is

> *to contribute to the sound development of the national economy through the pursuit of price stability.*

As remarked by Yasuo Matsushita, Governor of the Bank of Japan

> *The sound development of the national economy is a common objective of all economic policies. As the objective of monetary policy is to contribute to the achievement of this ultimate objective through price stability, its direct objective will be to ensure price stability.*

Source: 'A New Framework of Monetary Policy under the New Bank of Japan Law', speech by the Governor of the Bank of Japan to the Yomiuri International Economic Society in Tokyo, 27 June 1997; Willem F. Duisenberg, 'The euro: The new european currency', speech at the Council of Foreign Relations in Chicago, 1 February 1999.

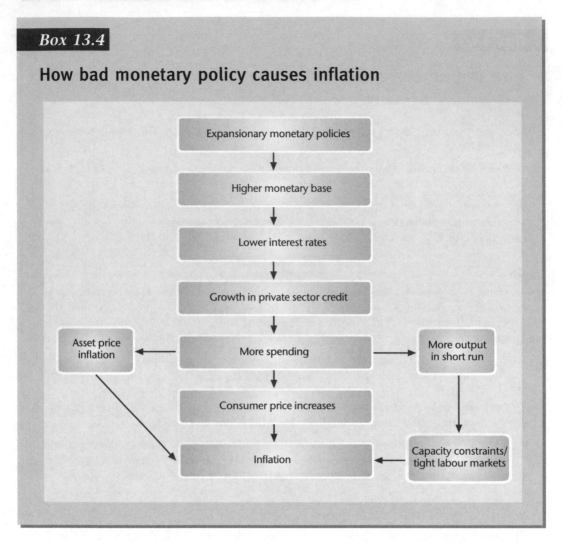

Box 13.4

How bad monetary policy causes inflation

and adopts an expansionary monetary policy while the economy is operating at potential. The monetary base increases and interest rates fall. This leads to growth in private sector credit, a rise in asset prices and an upsurge in spending. In the short run, it may be possible to achieve more output by running the economy at over-capacity. The one certain outcome of this process is a rise in the price level; and the probable beginning of an inflationary spiral.

Intermediate targets

Intermediate targets are variables that the central bank seeks to control in order to achieve its inflation objective (Box 13.5). The Bank of England, for example, has identified low long-run inflation as its ultimate objective. Its main focus, however, is not *current* inflation, which is a given and which it is powerless to

Box 13.5

The basics of monetary policy

Objective	$\longrightarrow$	Price stability	
Intermediate targets	$\longrightarrow$	■ Money supply targeting ■ Inflation targeting	
Policy instruments	$\longrightarrow$	■ Direct	Credit guidelines/ quotas Interest regulations Selective credit controls
		■ Market-based	Open-market operations Discount rate/short-term credit facilities to banks Reserve requirements

do anything about, but *future* inflation, 1–2 years ahead, which can be changed by today's policy actions. Money stock and credit aggregates are used as intermediate targets. Published monetary objectives include a wide diversity of measures. In using money supply as an intermediate target, the central bank derives an estimate of money demand (consistent with its inflation target) and then announces a target money supply to match it. A typical demand for money function will take the form:

$$\log m = a + b \log y + c \log p - d \log i$$

where m = nominal money supply, i = nominal interest rate, y = real income and $\log p$ = per cent annual increase in p, the price level.

The monetary authorities proceed by (i) estimating the parameters of the demand for money function (a, b, c, d), (ii) inserting values for potential economic growth (y) for the coming year, and (iii) specifying its target (or maximum) level of inflation. The rate of interest is a policy instrument, which can be taken as given for the initial calculations. From this exercise will emerge the level of money demand in the economy, and hence the required money supply increase to match this demand, i.e. resulting in the published money supply target.

Money supply targeting was the central tool of counter-inflationary policy during the 1970s and 1980s. To be applied successfully, two conditions are necessary. First, the money demand function has to be stable and predictable.

That is, the parameters of the money demand equation must be constant. If they changed in an unpredictable way from year to year, a rate of money supply growth which was just correct in one year might be quite inflationary in another year. The central bank would be unable to predict the 'right' rate of expansion of money supply. Second, money supply obviously has to be controllable by the authorities. They must be able to achieve the announced target.

The relationship between money supply and the national income has become less predictable than it once was. In the course of a review of UK monetary policy, Professor Mervyn King of the Bank of England concluded flatly that: *there is no longer any time-invariant mechanical link between the change in a given monetary aggregate and the subsequent out-turn for inflation.*[10] The speed at which money circulates (the *velocity of circulation*) has changed markedly. This means that the amount of economic activity which a given money supply can sustain has become highly variable. To complicate matters further, the velocity of circulation appears to have changed in different directions for different parts of the UK money supply. The velocity of circulation of the narrow money supply (M0) curve has *risen*, as new ways are discovered of economising on money balances (which attract zero, or minimal, interest), while the velocity of wider money supply (M4) has *declined*, as interest rates on bank deposits are forced upwards by competition with other financial institutions.

One reason for the weakening association between money supply and inflation is the deregulation of the financial sector. Financial innovation has also contributed. Increased competition has led to new ways of obtaining credit, and innovations have enabled a given supply of currency to finance a larger amount of transactions. The globalisation of capital markets has further weakened the hold of central banks on domestic money supply. Given these difficulties, the usefulness of money supply as an intermediate target has been questioned in the well-developed economies, and also in countries in transition where institutional change has been rapid. Also, the private sector often deliberately takes action to circumvent the monetary restrictions set by the authorities. As Goodhart's Law warns: *any monetary variable which the authorities seek to control instantly becomes meaningless.* Yet some central banks, including the ECB, continue to take a positive view of the merit of a money supply target.

Inflation targeting is widely used either as an alternative to money supply targeting, or to complement it.[11] This approach focuses on identifying lead indicators of inflation that will help to alert the authorities when inflationary or deflationary pressures are building up. These can then act as signals for pre-

---

10 M. King, 'Monetary policy in the UK', *Fiscal Affairs* (August 1994). Work continues unabated on estimating demand functions for money. Some are able to find stable values of the parameters, but only with the help of considerable ingenuity in constructing special variables to capture innovation, deregulation and tax effects: R. Thomas, 'Understanding broad money', *Bank of England Quarterly Bulletin*, 36(2) (May 1996).

11 See M. Artis, P. Mizon and Z. Kontolemis, 'Inflation targeting: What can the ECB learn from the recent experience of the Bank of England?', *Economic Journal* (November 1998); L. Svensson, 'Inflation-forecast targeting: Implementing and monitoring inflation targets', *European Economic Review*, 41 (1997).

emptive action on monetary policy. Inflation targeting requires good inflation forecasts. Hence, care must be taken to establish the variables that impact on future prices and the time lags between change in the target and change in the price level. For small countries such as New Zealand with floating exchange rates, the exchange rate will be a leading indicator; commodity prices such as oil are another; and capacity utilisation, unemployment, yield curves, earnings increases are others that can be useful. To work well, inflation targeting requires an independent central bank that has discretionary power to take unpopular action (and raising interest rates almost never pleases the public or the markets) when it believes action is necessary. Also there must be consistency among policy objectives. A government might want to have both price stability and a fixed exchange rate *vis-à-vis* its trade partners. But if the trade partners have high inflation, these two objectives are mutually inconsistent. The European Central Bank has adopted both money supply and inflation forecasts in setting its monetary policy. The two pillars of its strategy for price stability are (a) a 'reference value' for growth of money supply and (b) an assessment of the outlook for future price developments.

Policy instruments

The monetary policy instruments at the disposal of the central bank can be classified into two broad categories: *direct controls* and *market-based controls* (see Box 13.4).

Direct controls were once used very widely but, since the 1970s, they have become increasingly unfashionable and ineffective. They include measures such as:

- overall credit ceilings or guidelines, sometimes imposed on a bank-by-bank or sectoral basis,
- administrative controls on the level of interest rates and the spread between retail and wholesale rates,
- bank-by-bank rediscount quotas,
- moral suasion (sometimes called 'window guidance').

Direct controls seek to bypass the market mechanism. As such, they suffer from the predictable problems of all quantitative controls. They tend to be inefficient and their effectiveness tends to erode over time. This is because of the problem of *disintermediation*. The term *disintermediation* originates from the definition of the function of the banks, which is to intermediate between savers and lenders. Regulation gives lenders and borrowers an incentive to bypass the banks and get together directly through other means. Hence they are engaged in *dis*intermediation. If domestic banks' lending is restricted by central bank guidelines, borrowers will seek funds directly from the public or from banks overseas, or from financial institutions not covered by a central bank's regulations. While direct controls are still used in developing and transition economies, greater reliance on market-based controls has become a universal trend.

339

Market-based controls consist of open-market operations, the discount rate and reserve requirements. In industrial countries, *open-market operations* are used extensively. They are the most effective means of supplementing or withdrawing liquidity from the system. The most common method of effecting open-market operations is through repurchase agreements (repos). Repos involve the purchase of assets by the central bank under a contract providing for their resale at a specified price or on a given future date. Reverse repos involve the sale of assets by the central bank.

Liquidity can also be controlled by altering the terms on which the central bank offers credit to commercial banks. The *discount rate* is the rate at which the central bank provides reserves for the commercial banks. An increase in the discount rate, in addition to raising the cost of credit to banks, has an 'announcement' effect. It alerts the market to the central bank's view of the liquidity situation. Combined with open-market operations, an increase in the discount rate will be transmitted to other parts of the system. Thus, a tightening of liquidity through open-market operations can oblige banks to borrow from the central bank at the high interest rate. The banks will then pass on the interest rate rise to their customers.

Third, the central bank may affect liquidity directly by imposing *minimum reserve requirements* on the commercial banks. Reserve requirements have become less used in recent years. The UK has dispensed with them entirely for monetary control purposes. Changes in these requirements can be costly and disruptive to banks and, like direct controls, they encourage disintermediation.

13.5 The design of monetary policy

Monetary policy grows out of history and institutions as much as out of rulebooks. There is no universal blueprint for an optimal monetary policy. The search for better ways of managing monetary affairs, of course, continues. It has centred on four key issues: active v passive policy; rules v discretion; the supervisory role of the central banks; and the optimal balance between secrecy and transparency in central bank operations. We shall briefly discuss each of these in turn.

Active v passive

An *active* monetary policy is one which adopts a strong counter-cyclical role. It seeks to adjust monetary policy in accordance with short-term variations in economic circumstances. If the economy appears to be heading for a recession, an active monetary policy would loosen conditions; and, if the economy was heading for a boom, it would tighten monetary conditions. By contrast, a *passive* monetary policy focuses on the medium to long term and disclaims any responsibility for correcting short-term cyclical downturns.

The justification for a passive policy is not that cyclical downturns are a matter of no concern, but rather that monetary policy will prove to be ineffective in offsetting them. This pessimistic assessment of the role of short-term monetary policy is based on four considerations:

1. *Monetary policy operates with long and variable lags.* Monetarists argue that, because of these lags, stabilisation policy will be ineffective at best, damaging at worst. Because of the inability to predict precisely the time-profile of its effects, an activist policy could be destabilising.

2. *Information on the present state of the economy and on future trends is insufficiently precise*, given our current understanding of the economy, *to guide counter-cyclical monetary policy*, even if problem (1) did not exist.

3. There is a danger that *repeated and unsuccessful efforts at short-term stabilisation will cause monetary policy to lose touch with its primary objective of low inflation.* The economy might then end up with a double negative: no price stability and no stability in output.

4. *Inflation itself is one of the prime causes of cyclical fluctuations.* Surges of inflation cause booms, and disinflation causes recessions. If inflation is controlled, the need for counter-cyclical policy will diminish.

Despite the weight of these arguments, complete passivity in the face of short-run shocks is not always the right policy. At a time of crisis, activism is obviously justifiable and may be essential. One such episode was the reaction of the Federal Reserve Bank to the Wall Street crash of October 1987. On 'Black Monday', 19 October, the Dow Jones fell by 23 per cent – the largest one-day decline in stock market prices of the twentieth century. However, the real crisis came after that Monday. In order to keep the stock market functioning, brokers needed to extend massive amounts of credit on behalf of their customers for their margin calls. But banks were understandably reluctant to lend to the securities industry. To avert a threatened liquidity crisis, the Federal Reserve announced its readiness to serve as a source of liquidity to support the economic and financial system. This deliberate loosening of the money supply was paralleled in other countries. A major crisis of confidence, and a potentially damaging recession, was averted. Here was a case of successful monetary activism. Again, following the currency crises of the 1990s, monetary policy was used aggressively in the US and elsewhere in order to stave off contagion effects.

By contrast, calls for activism during Europe's currency crisis of 1992–93 were resisted by the German central bank. In the second half of 1992, monetary growth in excess of the target range, accompanied by price and wage pressures and high rates of domestic bank lending, were a concern to the German authorities. Yet Germany was being urged by some member states to cut interest rates in order to boost trade and ease their unemployment problem. The Bundesbank took the view that German money supply was still growing rapidly despite the economic slowdown, and that to reduce interest rates in such circumstances would endanger its credibility. A telling point is that, if the financial markets interpreted the easing of monetary policy as a sign that the authorities were 'going soft' on inflation, *intervention by the Bundesbank in the short end of the market would have had no impact on long-term rates. Since business investment is linked in Germany to long-term rates, economic recovery would have been delayed, instead of accelerated, as a result of the precipitate monetary easing.* In the

341

Bundesbank's view, these considerations justified rejecting calls for steep interest rate cuts. Instead, a series of small interest rate reductions were gradually implemented during 1993 and the first half of 1994. This strategy was vindicated in the subsequent slowdown in monetary growth and in the favourable evolution of wage and price inflation thereafter.[12]

The 'right' amount of activism in any particular situation is a matter for judgement. Generally, one can say that central banks have become more sceptical about the scope for successful short-term intervention. Forcing interest rates down too quickly can feed fears of inflation, raise long-term interest rates and deliver precisely the opposite of the intended effect. Raising them too abruptly can bring a boom to a premature end and cause a recession. There is a strong case for monetary policy being focused primarily on medium-term targets, subject to short-term adjustments in case of extreme necessity.

Rules v discretion

The dichotomy 'rules v discretion' is somewhat artificial, although it raises interesting issues from a policy view. One rule advocated by monetarists in the 1960s is that money supply should be increased by the same fixed percentage amount each year, determined by reference to the expected long-run growth potential of the economy. It was assumed that potential growth changed only gradually and that the demand curve for money was stable. Given these assumptions, the monetarist rule would ensure low inflation in the long run. Another example of a monetary rule is that domestic currency must be fully backed by foreign currency. It is comparable to exchange rate 'rules' such as those whereby one currency is pegged at a fixed rate to another.

Pre-commitment to policy rules, 'tying one's hands', has the advantage of discouraging speculation. If adhered to rigidly, a rule 'never pay blackmail to a kidnapper' will deter kidnapping much more effectively than a policy of treating each case individually on its merits. Similarly, a rule that monetary policy will *never* accommodate inflation means that economic agents know where they stand. Public commitment to rules also guards against what is known as *the time-inconsistency problem* in economic policy. This problem arises because, having promised to achieve something ('inflation will never be allowed to exceed 2 per cent') and having convinced everyone to believe in it, the authorities have an incentive to renege on this promise. They can use discretion to push up inflation and thereby gain a transient increase in output (and, in the process, perhaps win an election or secure their position for another term). Time-inconsistency tells us that this use of discretion, by catching people unawares, may well result in a one-off advantage. But, understanding that policy-makers may be inconsistent over time, private decision-makers are led to distrust policy announcements. Next time, the authorities will not be believed. People will see that the government has an incentive to use discretion. Those who lost out from their misplaced trust will

---

12 R. Corker *et al.*, 'United Germany, the first five years: Performance and policy issues', *IMF Occasional Paper*, no. 125 (Washington, DC, May 1995).

come to regard the authorities' discretionary power as a threat, not an advantage. To be effective, monetary policy would have to become increasingly unpredictable, making it harder for the private sector to make informed decisions. *Such discretionary policy choices will be inefficient.* They will tend to generate higher average rates of inflation, with no compensating increase in output.[13] Only by adherence to a fixed rule, publicly committed to and from which it can only deviate with the greatest difficulty, will the policy become fully credible.

The time-inconsistency literature draws attention to the adverse long-term consequence of apparently successful short-term policy expedients. Reference has been made already to the high real interest rates of the 1980s and the 1990s which have penalised governments for the high inflation and the negative real interest rates suffered by holders of fixed interest bonds during the 1970s. Countries with an historical record of broken promises may obtain a larger payback from fixed and binding rules than more stable countries. The latter may conclude that, used prudently, discretion is preferable to fixity, given the many uncertainties involved in interpreting monetary conditions. Recognition of these uncertainties has prompted central banks to adopt a more 'eclectic' approach to monetary policy, drawing on a number of indicators besides money supply, and to use 'evolutionary' money supply targets which take account of changes in velocity of circulation.

Central bank as supervisor of credit institutions

The central bank is concerned with the stability and efficiency of the financial sector. This is the context in which monetary policy functions and the structure of financial markets affect the way in which central bank policies operate. The supervision of the financial markets is entrusted to a central bank in some countries, to the ministry of finance or a separate institution in others. The liberalisation of international markets and the demise of unspoken rules of good behaviour have made the supervision of credit institutions an exacting responsibility. Such supervision includes the design and implementation of regulations covering bank operations, limits on competition perceived as dangerous to the stability of banks, rules on what banks can own, who can own them, and even the type of business they can engage in. The collapse in 1995 of Barings Bank, one of the City of London's most prestigious and respected merchant banks, and of the no less prestigious US hedge fund Long Term Capital Management (with an economics Nobel prize winner on its board), demonstrated the potential vulnerability of financial institutions to speculative ventures. Central banks are drawn into the resultant crises and have to be prepared to deal with them. The supervisory duties of a central bank are absorbing increasing amounts of time and attention.

---

13 The 'time-inconsistent problem' was first analysed in F. Kydland and E. Prescott, 'Rules rather than discretion: The inconsistency of optimal plans', *Journal of Political Economy* (June 1977).

Transparency v secrecy

Central banks are often very secretive. Critics accuse them of using secrecy to conceal a lack of clarity in their objectives and as a means of absolving themselves from the necessity of having to explain, and justify, their policy stance. Secrecy can be a means of concealing mistakes. An argument in favour of explicit policy objectives is that they neutralise these problems. Thus, money supply targets, or a transparent obligation to give priority to price stability, are examples of measures to tie the hands of the monetary authorities, to discourage them from over-ambitious targets, and force them to take unpopular action when necessary. Most important of all, published inflation or money growth targets are a way of exposing the authorities to monitoring and criticism.

Central banks have become conscious of the need for transparency and accountability in communicating their policy stance to the public. An instance of this is the publication of the minutes of the monthly meetings between the Governor of the Bank of England and the Chancellor of the Exchequer. The chairman of the Federal Reserve is frequently called to address Congress. In the course of 1999, the Bank of Japan Governor went to the Diet no less than 115 times to explain his bank's policies. Central bank governors regularly appear before parliamentary committees. Central bank reports are widely circulated and are often informative on the bank's views of the economy and on the direction of policy. The advantage of such transparency has to be weighed against the downside, from the central bank's view, of occasionally getting egg on its face because of poor forecasting – or tendering what, in hindsight, turns out to be bad advice.

Secrecy and reticence are still required, however, in some areas. First, the precise timing of its market-sensitive actions must be kept confidential. Any information leakages on such matters could call into question the bank's standing and weaken its reputation. Second, policy stances should not be made so transparent and specific as to give markets an incentive to test them and enjoy the luxury of a one-way bet. There is sometimes a need for a calculated degree of vagueness, especially in relation to exchange rate targets. Uncertainty about where exactly the central bank's break-points lie can help it to manage the market more effectively. Third, the central bank, as the government's banker, must afford government the same confidentiality as to any other customer, and many communications have to be kept secret for this reason.

13.6 Conclusions

Monetary policy is in practice conducted by using a mix of formal models, rules of thumb and market intuition. Monetary policy interacts with business in many different ways, most visibly through its effect on interest rates, and ultimately through its effect on inflation. Business needs to understand the factors determining interest rates in order to understand the monetary policy debate. While monetary policy is only one of many determinants of interest rates, it is crucially important in the short end of the market and can also exert a perceptible impact on the long end.

Interest rates affect the cost of working capital and the viability of long-term investment projects. They affect mergers and acquisitions activity, and can have an important bearing on stock market trends. Interest rates have a critical influence on the fortunes of bond traders, managers of hedge funds, mutual funds and other financial companies. The growing share of leveraged funds in the bond market makes that market highly vulnerable to unexpected changes in both the level and spread of interest rates. For instance, in 1994 the rise in 30-year US Treasury rates from 6.2 per cent at the start of 1994 to 7.75 per cent in mid-September 1994 was estimated to have reduced the value of bond holdings by as much as $600 billion. This massive loss was headlined by *Fortune* as 'The Great Bond Market Massacre'.[14] The initial hike in interest rates was prompted by the Federal Reserve's tightening in the short end of the market to head off incipient inflation.

While there is agreement that monetary policy operates through interest rates, there is continuing controversy about the channels through which interest rates affect household and business spending, the speed at which monetary policy affects real variables, the appropriate instruments and targets of monetary policy, and the optimal form of monetary policy. Notwithstanding these controversies, however, there is broad agreement on the analytical framework for analysing these issues.

In response to the question, 'How much do we really know about monetary policy?', Professor David Laidler replied: 'Enough to prevent it doing harm, but not enough to use it to do good.'[15] There is a valid political demand for short-run stabilisation policy, he argued, but this demand should not be met by monetary means. Adherence to this self-denying ordinance would prevent monetary policy from 'doing harm'. Not only that, but, by forging clear anti-inflation credentials, the central bank can 'do good' and provide a stable framework for growth.

Macro-stability is a necessary, but not a sufficient, condition for prosperity. A central bank's actions are based on a repugnance towards inflation which, in many real-life situations, may seem to take insufficient account of the cost of unemployment. Its actions are based on economic reasoning, accompanied by assumptions about the future. The penalty for mistaken judgements can be heavy. Together with the movement towards more independence for central banks, we can expect to see greater efforts to ensure accountability, and public explanations of the theory underlying central bank actions and of the methodology of its forecasts. Business has a part to play in this ongoing debate. If monetary policy objectives seem to require a tightening of monetary conditions, business must understand the motivation, and the instrumentalities, of monetary policy in order to offer a reasoned critique or to propose alternative strategies.

Given the limitations of monetary policy on the one hand, and the political demand for counter-cyclical actions on the other, we must consider what other

---

14 *Fortune* (17 October 1994).
15 David Laidler, *Taking Money Seriously* (New York and London: Philip Allen, 1990), p. 129.

policies might be used to stabilise the economy. The obvious candidate, and the subject of a later chapter, is fiscal policy.

 Summary

1. The interest rate is defined as the amount of interest paid per unit of time as a percentage of the balance outstanding. The real rate of interest is the nominal rate of interest minus the inflation rate. Although the real rate of interest is not directly observable, its value can be inferred by subtracting the current or forecast inflation rate from the nominal interest rates. Interest rates vary according to the maturity of the loan and its degree of riskiness. The term structure of interest rates is defined as the relationship on a specific date between interest rates for bonds with different terms to maturity that have similar risk. The curve connecting these interest rates is called the yield curve. Yield curves are calculated in nominal terms and are normally upward-sloping.

2. The loanable funds theory postulates that interest rates are determined by supply and demand of credit in an economy. Changes in the interest rate in this framework are explained by shifts in the demand and supply curve of credit. However, the theory ignores the long-run dynamic relationship between interest, investment and savings. Furthermore, the effects of changes in income and the influence of interest rates in relation to stocks of financial assets must also be considered.

3. A major tool of monetary control in industrial countries is the interest rate. Interest rates affect aggregate demand through three channels: substitution effects, where increases in interest rates make saving more attractive for households relative to consumption; cash-flow effects, where higher interest rates reduce the income of borrowers and increase the income of lenders; and wealth effects, where changes in interest rates affect the value of housing, equities and bonds.

4. The ultimate objective of monetary policy is price stability. Its intermediate targets are primarily money supply, interest rates and exchange rate levels. The monetary policy instruments at the disposal of the central bank can be classified as either direct or market-based controls. Direct controls seek to bypass the market mechanism, and include measures such as overall credit ceilings and administrative controls on the level of interest rates. Market-based measures act primarily through their effect on the interest rate. These include open-market operations, altering the discount rate and minimum reserve requirements.

5. There is no universal blueprint for an optimal monetary policy. The search for better ways of managing monetary policy continues. This has centred on issues concerning active v passive policy, rules v discretion, the supervisory role of the central banks, and the optimal balance between secrecy and transparency in central bank operations.

? Questions for discussion

1. In the present macroeconomic situation, the requirements of non-inflationary growth point to the importance of monetary policy in moderating demand where margins of spare capacity have virtually disappeared. ... It [monetary policy] should support a recovery of activity only where such margins remain large and there is little risk of inflation. (*OECD Observer*, August–September 1995, p. 48)

   Is it possible, or advisable, to attempt such fine-tuning for monetary policy? If the answer were yes, what monetary measures could be used to implement such a policy?

2. An investment report opened its 'investment outlook' section with the comment:

   We expect the global economic environment to be characterised by moderate economic growth and relatively low inflation, a combination which should lead to relatively low interest rates also.

   Is this statement referring to (a) the real interest rate, (b) the nominal interest rate, or (c) to both? Explain.

3. An investment report written in 1996 warned that:

   There is a fear that, for political reasons, the UK government will *'go for growth'* over the life of this Parliament by increasing spending and cutting taxes while being more lax about interest rates, thus fuelling inflation. That said, the feeling that interest rates have been raised at an earlier stage than in previous recoveries improves the likelihood that inflation will be kept under control.

   (a) Discuss the effects of higher expected inflation on bond markets.
   (b) Explain what the authorities might hope to achieve by raising interest rates at an early stage of the upward cycle.

4. Addressing a symposium in 1994, D.T. Brash, Governor of the Central Bank of New Zealand, remarked that 'the best contribution monetary policy can make to growth and employment is to maintain stability in the general level of prices' (Address to the Federal Reserve Bank of Kansas symposium, *Reducing Unemployment: Current issues and policy options*, Wyoming, 1994).
   Does attaining price stability implicitly mean that interest rates must be variable?

5. When the fiscal implications of German unification in 1990 became apparent, the yield curve steepened. Explain why this should have happened.

6. Suppose monetary policy 'eases'. How will the slope of the yield curve be affected? Explain how your answer might be influenced if the easing of credit led to a rise in expected inflation.

☞ Exercises

1. On 7 November 1991, the financial press reported:

   (a) The Federal Reserve sought to revive the US economic recovery by cutting the discount rate by 0.5 percentage points to 4.5 per cent, the lowest level in 18 years.

   (b) The Fed explained that the discount rate was cut against a background of 'sluggish' expansion of the monetary and credit aggregates, and 'abating inflationary pressures'.

   (c) The Fed's action was preceded by statistics indicating poor employment growth and faltering economic activity.

   (d) Mr Michael Boskin, the chief White House economist, said lower interest rates would help the economy, but warned that there might be a lag of one or two quarters.

   (e) *The Financial Times* reported that the Fed's action 'reflected growing evidence that the economic recovery has stalled' and 'followed heavy pressure from the White House which was "rattled" by polls indicating disapproval of President George Bush's handling of the economy'.

   Comment on (i) the reasons advanced for the Fed's cut in the discount rate, (ii) the likely effects of this action, and (iii) the sectors likely to be most affected by it.

2. 'The bond market lost its momentum as higher than expected inflation lowered expectations of another German rate cut.' Interest rate analysis stresses the role of market expectations. Explain the logical sequence behind this statement.

3. 'Monetary policy must be defined in terms of its final goal. For us, this final goal is, without any shadow of doubt, price stability' (Dr H. Tietmeyer, President of the Bundesbank, address to the Zurich Economic Society, November 1993).

   (a) What does price stability mean?

   (b) Comment on the usefulness of money supply targets as a guide for monetary policy.

   (c) In the speech from which the above quotation is taken, Dr Tietmeyer noted that 'the German money demand function has turned out to be stable'. Explain the significance of this remark.

   (d) Suppose money supply exceeds its target in a particular period. What action could or should a central bank take in response?

4. Write an assessment of the successes, failures and challenges of the European Central Bank since it began operations in 1999.

📖 Further reading

The big story in the late 1990s was the setting up of the ECB. See European Central Bank, *Monthly Bulletin* (January 1999), 'The stability-oriented monetary policy strategy of the Eurosystem', for a concise outline of ECB policy. The July 2000 Bulletin contains a disarmingly frank appraisal of current knowledge of the monetary transmission process. A. Chrystal and S. Price, *Controversies in Macroeconomics* (Hemel Hempstead: Harvester Wheatsheaf, 1994), offers a blend of theory and applied economics in the UK context. M. King, 'Monetary policy in the UK', *Fiscal Affairs* (August 1994), outlines Bank of England thinking on monetary policy objectives and instruments. Meanwhile, the main players in the world's monetary policy continue to be the heads of the three most powerful central banks: US, Japan and the ECB. Although carefully sanitised, readers might derive insights into the practicalities of monetary policy from the minutes of meetings between the Governor of the Bank of England and the Chancellor of the Exchequer (www.hm.treasury.gov.uk).

Chapter 14

UNEMPLOYMENT AND THE LABOUR MARKET

Introduction

High and prolonged unemployment is a sign of a malfunctioning economy. Being unemployed is, for most people, a highly distressing experience, and fear of becoming unemployed is a potent source of unhappiness and disutility. Moreover, unemployment causes damage in ways that cannot be measured by sheer numbers. Yet despite economic growth and rising per capita incomes, it is a more acute problem now than it was thirty years ago. The number of unemployed people in the OECD countries peaked at 38 million in 1994, up from just over 10 million in 1973. Although the OECD total had declined to 32 million in 2000, unemployment remains a particularly acute problem in Europe. France has seen the numbers unemployed increase from 530,000 in 1970 to over 3 million. Germany also has suffered a dramatic increase, from its level of below 2 per cent in the 1960s to 9 per cent in the 1990s. Meanwhile, unemployment has risen at a disturbing pace in the countries of Central Europe. This is a humbling reversal of fortune for Europeans who, for several decades after the Second World War, prided themselves on their low rates of unemployment.

An OECD study, published in 1994, described unemployment as the most widely feared phenomenon of the time:

> High unemployment creates insecurity and resistance to organisational and technical change. Long-term unemployment lowers self-esteem, is demotivating and self-reinforcing, and is associated with health problems. The rise in youth unemployment means that many young people are losing skills and employability. Groups in society that have never before faced a high risk of unemployment, such as white-collar workers, are losing jobs, with all the personal and societal costs that implies in terms of lost potential and lost investment.[1]

The incidence of unemployment has moderated somewhat in recent years, but its ill-effects continue to pose serious problems and represent a challenge to economic policy.

The adverse consequences of unemployment impact on business in several ways. They affect attitudes in the workplace, by making people less inclined to take their jobs for granted, but any advantage to business accruing on this score must be balanced by three offsetting factors. First, unemployment imposes heavy

---

1 *The OECD Jobs Study: Facts, analysis, strategies* (Paris, 1994), p. 41.

social welfare costs which have to be met by taxation; second, it places a great strain on government's economic policy; and third, it can be a cause of social and political instability.

Unemployment is a special problem of the industrialised countries because the unemployed in such countries are provided with an income by the state (unemployment benefit), but not a job. In order to qualify for unemployment benefit, the recipient must not be in paid employment. Sometimes the state benefit can amount to a significant proportion of the going pay rate, especially that available to an unskilled and poorly motivated worker.

In poorer countries, by contrast, unemployment benefit is either not provided or else provided at a very low level. As a result, most people are forced to find work. They are employed, but often at very low productivity levels. They may encounter extreme difficulty in finding a suitable job. Some experience long periods of involuntary inactivity (hawkers, casual labourers), but are not recorded as unemployed.

Socialist systems tended to be free of unemployment. People without work were assigned to state organisations. The state provided them with a job, regardless of whether there was any useful work for them to do. (In many cases there was not, as subsequent privatisation of socialist enterprises has revealed.) The unemployment problem, therefore, must be analysed in the context of specific institutions and societal values.

The problem of unemployment can be tackled in several ways. Much depends on the characteristics of the economy and its labour and product markets. This chapter provides the analytical framework needed to understand both the problem of unemployment itself and the rationale behind suggested ways of resolving it.

Chapter outline

1. The nature and extent of the unemployment problem.
2. The market approach to unemployment, drawing on the supply and demand analysis outlined in Chapter 10.
3. Short-run versus long-run perspectives on the unemployment problem.
4. The Keynesian contribution to solving the unemployment problem.
5. The relationship between technological change and unemployment.
6. Policies to alleviate unemployment. Falling unemployment rates in the late 1990s and the sustained full employment in some countries indicate that unemployment is neither inevitable nor ineradicable.

14.1 Facts about unemployment

Definition

The standard international definition, developed by the International Labour Organisation, identifies the unemployed as *those of working age who, in a specified period, are without work and are both available for, and have taken specific steps to find, work.* This sounds relatively straightforward, but numerous small differences of interpretation, compilation and data sources mean that national estimates often differ from international estimates. Even at the national level, estimates of unemployment differ, depending on whether one measures it according to the 'standardised' definition above or according to the number actually collecting unemployment benefit.

Standardised rates of unemployment in the OECD countries over the period since the 1960s are provided in Table 14.1.

The standardised definition of unemployment is not a comprehensive measure. For example, it does not include the following groups:

Table 14.1 Unemployment rates in OECD countries, 1960–2000

	1960s	1970s	1980s	1990	1994	2000
North America						
Canada	4.7	6.6	9.3	8.1	10.4	6.8
United States	4.7	6.1	7.2	5.4	6.1	4.0
Japan	1.3	1.7	2.5	2.1	2.9	4.8
Europe						
France	1.7	3.8	9.0	8.9	12.3	9.8
Germany	0.6	1.9	5.7	4.9	8.4	8.5
Italy	3.8	4.7	7.5	8.2	11.2	11.0
Netherlands	0.9	4.0	9.6	7.5	7.1	2.5
Spain	2.3	4.2	17.5	15.9	24.1	14.1
United Kingdom	2.0	4.4	10.1	6.9	9.6	5.7
Austria	2.1	1.6	3.3	3.2	3.8	4.2
Finland	2.1	3.7	4.9	3.4	16.7	9.2
Norway	1.7	1.6	2.8	5.2	5.5	3.5
Sweden	1.5	1.8	2.2	1.7	9.4	6.3
Switzerland	0.1	1.2	1.5	1.1	3.8	3.8
Australia	2.0	3.9	7.5	7.0	9.7	6.7
New Zealand	0.9	1.5	4.1	7.7	8.2	6.1
OECD	**2.8**	**4.3**	**7.0**	**6.0**	**8.1**	**6.5**

Source: OECD, *Implementing the Strategy* (Paris, 1995); OECD, *Economic Outlook* (various issues).

- Many part-time workers who would prefer to work full-time but are unable to find opportunities. Yet these 'involuntary part-time workers' are counted as fully employed.
- So-called 'discouraged workers'. These are people who report in the labour force surveys that they would like a job but are not currently searching for work, as they believe no suitable job is available.
- The standardised figures include people as unemployed who are in fact working full-time or part-time in the 'shadow' economy.

The net impact of these conflicting influences on the recorded unemployment rate is not known for certain. In the early 1990s, there were reckoned to be about 4 million discouraged workers and 9 million involuntary part-timers in the OECD, a significant number relative to official unemployment.[2] According to one study, discouraged workers and involuntary part-timers would have added 3 percentage points to the unemployment rate. But numbers unemployed are overestimated by virtue of the inclusion of people as unemployed who are in fact actively engaged in the underground economy.

Geographical distribution

Unemployment is a much more acute problem in Europe (10 per cent) than in the US (4 per cent) or Japan (5 per cent). In Japan, up to the mid-1990s, unemployment (at less than 3 per cent) could hardly be described as a major problem at all, but since then the situation has worsened. Although it is not without unemployed people, the US economy is in a state of virtually full employment. Within Europe there are wide variations in unemployment rates between Spain, Finland and France at one extreme, and Austria, The Netherlands, Norway and Switzerland at the other. There are also wide regional variations within countries. In the US, California has half the unemployment rate of Mississippi. In Britain, unemployment tends to be much higher in the north than in the south. Germany also has major regional disparities not only between east and west (17 per cent versus 8 per cent in 2000), but also within western Germany, where unemployment rates in northern regions like Bremen were up to three times higher than those found in the booming areas of the south such as Bavaria.

Transition countries suffered high unemployment during the 1990s. Starting from negligible or zero unemployment during the socialist regime, Albania, Latvia Romania and Russia had unemployment rates of 10–17 per cent by the end of the 1990s. For transition countries, the problem of unemployment is closely linked to structural change. Following the change in regime, whole sectors of industry proved to be unproductive and incapable of withstanding exposure to outside competition. As a result, in some transition countries people lost their jobs and became unemployed. In countries such as the Ukraine and Russia, there was less

---

2 John P. Martin. 'The extent of high unemployment in OECD countries', Federal Reserve of Kansas Symposium on 'Reducing unemployment: Current issues and policy options', Jackson Hall, Wyoming, 25–27 August 1994 (p. 11).

Table 14.2 Unemployment rates in transition economies

	1998
Estonia	9.6
Latvia	13.8
Lithuania	6.4
Albania	17.7
Czech Republic*	7.5
Hungary	9.1
Slovak Republic	11.9
Slovenia	7.9
Poland*	10.4
Russia	12.4
Ukraine	3.7
Bulgaria	12.2
Romania	10.3

* Figures relate to 1999 (OECD)

Source: European Bank for Reconstruction and Development (EBRD), Transition Report 1999, London 1999.

explicit unemployment. Workers continued in their jobs but were not paid or were forced to take administrative unpaid leave or decreased work hours. In the latter case, wages took the hit and the unemployment rate as such rose less than might be expected. There were many underemployed or unregistered workers. However accounted for in the statistics, much hardship and disillusion was caused. Transition from 'old' to 'new' competitive sectors continues to prove difficult. As Table 14.2 shows, high unemployment is endemic in these countries and, were it not for widespread labour hoarding, and non-payment of wages, the position would be much worse still. Unemployment may have different origins in these countries than in the West, but it is not the less painful for that.

Time dimension

Unemployment in industrialised countries was extremely low in the postwar period until the first oil price shock in the early 1970s. Since then, it has risen in three 'waves', corresponding to the two oil price supply 'shocks' of 1972–73 and 1979–80, and the demand 'shock' of 1990–92 (Figure 14.1). In many European countries, a strong ratchet effect was evident: unemployment rose after each shock, but did not revert to its original level once the shock had been reversed. The difficulty of a quick reversal is illustrated by the case of Finland. Following the break-up of the Soviet Union, Finland's unemployment rate rocketed from 3 per cent in 1990 to 17 per cent in 1994. It has taken 6 years to reduce it to its year 2000 level of 9 per cent. The last years of the 1990s, as Figure 14.1 makes clear, were associated with a general reduction in numbers unemployed, due in part to the implementation of better labour market and macroeconomic policies.

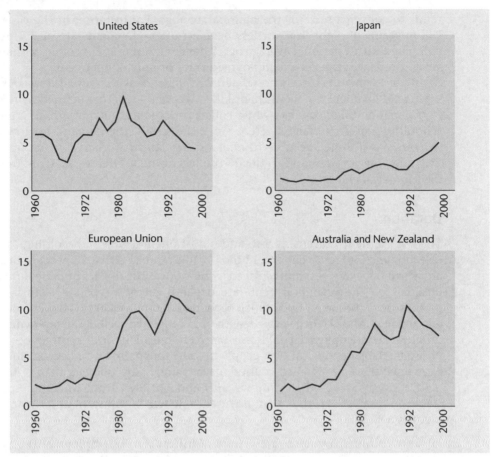

Figure 14.1 Unemployment rates in OECD regions, 1960–2000 (% of labour force)

Source: OECD CD-Rom

Composition

Young people, defined as those in the 15–25 age group, typically experience higher unemployment rates than other age groups, reflecting difficulties in the transition from school to first work experience. *Older workers* also experience an above-average incidence of unemployment, partly because they have to bear the brunt of job loss as industries are restructured. However, this does not always convert fully into the official unemployment figures because of early retirement schemes. *Females* experience higher unemployment than males in some European countries, but lower in many others, such as the UK, Japan and North America. *Lone parents* appear to be particularly vulnerable to unemployment. It also appears that *immigrants* experience more unemployment than nationals, a fact ascribed to their concentration in sectors which are cyclically sensitive and undergoing structural change. The figures also show that, with the passage of time, immigrants integrate more easily into the national workforce and their unemployment rate

355

tends to converge towards the national average. For instance, in the case of the US, migrants of eight years or less have an unemployment rate of 7.8 per cent compared with a national average of 5.7 per cent. But migrants of more than eight years' residence have an unemployment rate of only 4.9 per cent.

Unemployment is closely correlated with level of skills. *Unskilled workers* face a higher risk of unemployment than skilled workers – whether defined by reference to occupation (blue-collar vs white-collar) or to educational attainment (years of schooling, university degree, etc.). Since the 1980s, the demand for low-skilled workers has declined relative to demand for skilled workers and professionals. This decline in demand reflects the combined effects of structural and technological changes.

Duration

There is constant movement into and out of unemployment, according as people lose jobs and find replacements. In the US, it is estimated that 15 per cent of all jobs are wiped out every year and replaced by new ones. The impact of these inflows and outflows on the unemployment rate depends on two separate factors: (1) the proportion of the labour force which becomes unemployed between one time-period and the next, and (2) the average length of a completed spell of unemployment. The number of unemployed could rise between one date and another because an unusually large number of new people become unemployed, or because those who were unemployed at the first count remained unemployed longer than normally.

In a steady state, where inflows into and outflows from unemployment are stable and cancel out, the unemployment rate will be constant and the following identity will hold:

$$\text{Unemployment rate} = (\text{rate of inflow into unemployment})$$
$$\times (\text{average completed duration of period unemployed})$$

Thus, a given unemployment rate could be consistent with a high inflow rate and relatively short duration, or a low inflow rate and relatively long duration. This distinction can be important when analysing the causes of a change in the unemployment rate.

Long-term unemployed are defined as *those who have been unemployed continuously for one year or more*. The long-term unemployed typically suffer greater economic and personal costs than the short-term unemployed, e.g. through deterioration of their skills and loss of work motivation (loss of 'human' capital). Also, employers tend to use the duration of an unemployment spell as a screening device in their hiring decisions. As a result of these two factors, the long-term unemployed become 'outsiders' in the labour market, have little or no influence on wage determination and find it progressively harder to re-enter the workforce.

The incidence of long-term unemployment is particularly high in Europe (50 per cent of the unemployed in the EU are long-term, compared with only 12 per cent in Canada and 9 per cent in the US). Once unemployed, a worker in the EU has a relatively small probability of finding another job quickly. However, the comparatively low inflow rate into unemployment in Europe implies that the probability of *becoming* unemployed is lower for the European worker than in other industrial countries. Those with jobs – the 'insiders' – enjoy reasonable job security, while prospects for the long-term unemployed – the 'outsiders' – getting a job remain comparatively bleak. The US labour market has quite different characteristics. There, employees experience a more fluid, less secure situation where people lose jobs and find them more rapidly. It is hardly a coincidence that unemployment in the US is less than half the EU level. A European-style system of legal and collectively bargained restraints on hiring and firing, high levels of income support and high cost of employing labour has many attractions. But the cost can often be higher unemployment.

The measurement and interpretation of unemployment is a complex exercise. If the concern is with income distribution, social exclusion and discontent, or under-use of human potential, the standardised measure should ideally be supplemented by the inclusion of discouraged workers and involuntary part-timers. If one is concerned with explaining why the excess labour supply reflected in the unemployment statistics does not price its way back into jobs by lower pay, the standardised unemployment rate should be adjusted to take account of the proportion of long-term unemployed. The uncertainty surrounding the correct definition is not really surprising.

14.2 Supply-side approach and the market mechanism

The market mechanism

Unemployment can be analysed first in a demand–supply framework. The economy's demand for labour is derived from information on the production function, the stock of factors of production, and the level of output prices and wages. The demand curve for labour is assumed to be downward-sloping because of diminishing marginal productivity of labour. It shifts position in response to medium-term changes in technology, and in the quantities of capital stock and other factors of production. The supply curve is drawn with an upward slope, reflecting the assumption that labour supply responds positively to increases in real pay.[3] Employees in this model are assumed to be 'rational' – if prices rise by 10 per cent, they realise that their nominal pay will have to rise by 10 per cent in order to maintain their living standards. Agents bargain over real pay. They are free from 'money illusion'.

For a given demand curve DD, and supply curve SS, equilibrium pay is OW and, at that pay level, OL workers are employed (Figure 14.2). Supply equals demand and there is no unemployment. Shifts in demand and supply naturally occur over time. Supply can increase because of population growth, increased labour force participation, immigration and similar factors. Demand for labour could shift

---

3 Alternatively, it could be rationalised as a wage-setting schedule, showing how a higher level of employment causes pressure for higher real pay. But this would be in a union-bargaining model and/or an imperfect competition framework, not one in which the labour market clears in a classical sense.

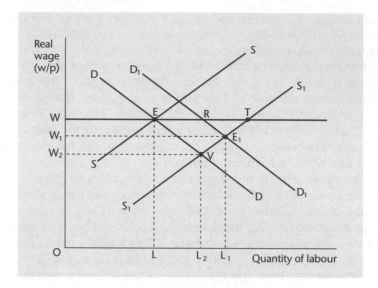

Figure 14.2 The labour market always 'clears' – in theory!

outwards as a result of increases in the capital stock, improvements in resource use or advances in capital-saving technology. The demand curve could also shift inwards because of a collapse in business confidence or the introduction of a new labour-saving technology. All these changes may have important implications for the level of pay. However, a central tenet of the market approach is that there is no *a priori* reason for believing that *any of these events should cause either labour 'shortages' or labour 'surpluses' (unemployment)*. Excess supply of labour can always be remedied by a fall in real pay; excess demand by a rise in real pay.

Thus, suppose there is an outward shift in supply from SS to S_1S_1. At the original equilibrium wage OW, labour supply now exceeds demand for labour by ET. If the market mechanism is allowed to do its work, this excess supply will drive down the real wage rate. A new equilibrium will be established at V. More workers will be employed at the new lower equilibrium wage OW_2. Thus, the increase in supply has been accommodated.

Suppose there is subsequently a shift in the demand for labour outwards to D_1D_1. Equilibrium will occur at the new pay level OW_1. More people will be employed at that pay level. Again, there is no unemployment.[4]

This way of analysing the market effectively treats employees in the same way as any other product or service. Price adjustments bring demand and supply into equilibrium. If the market for labour behaved like the market for goods, *unemployment would not be a problem*. This theory, of course, does not preclude the possibility that downward movements in pay might create

---

4 This point is overstated deliberately. The classical story does not imply that there would be *no* unemployment. Once allowance is made for turnover in a dynamic economy, and the fact that a *search* by both workers and firms takes time, there will be some equilibrium (sometimes called 'frictional') unemployment.

another set of problems, notably that of poverty, dead-end and low-productivity jobs. Market-minded economists, however, are disposed to regard such problems as less insidious than unemployment. Producing something, even at low productivity, is better, in this view, than being unemployed and producing nothing.

Labour market rigidities

If unemployment occurs, the classical model pinpoints the culprit as pay rigidities and, more generally, lack of labour market flexibility. Labour market flexibility is a term which can take many meanings (see Box 14.1). For convenience, we focus on the pay element. The flexibility problem then boils down to rigidity in real pay.

The 'real wage' or the real rate of pay (defined as the nominal cost of hiring labour deflated by the price of output) is the price which signals labour shortages or surpluses to the market. If the real wage is not flexible, the market cannot perform its function, and labour surpluses and shortages will persist. This process is illustrated in Figure 14.3.

Suppose labour demand shifts inwards because of a recession. The initial effect is to create a fall in the number of job vacancies at the going real wage. Given a constant flow of applicants, this excess supply leads to downward pressure on pay levels. As pay falls, the quantity of labour demanded increases along the lower

---

Box 14.1

Labour market flexibility

Labour market flexibility is a catch-all term (*un mot-valise*) which incorporates many different meanings. It could refer to one or all of:

1. pay flexibility of a firm's employees,
2. ease and cost of hiring and firing employees (quantity flexibility),
3. flexibility of hours worked,
4. ability to contract out services formerly provided in-house,
5. functional flexibility – ability of the firm to redeploy labour within the firm between different tasks and different locations.

Complete flexibility in relative and aggregate real wage averts the danger of unemployment resulting from excessive real pay per employee. But the economy is still vulnerable to the danger of unemployment (caused by an insufficiency of demand) and also to the problems of low-pay jobs and bad working conditions.

Sources: Denis Clerc, *Dechiffrer l'Economie* (Paris: Syros, 1994); B. Brunhes, *La Flexibilité de la Main-d'Oeuvre dans les Entreprises: Etude comparé des quatre pays européens* (Paris: OECD, 1989).

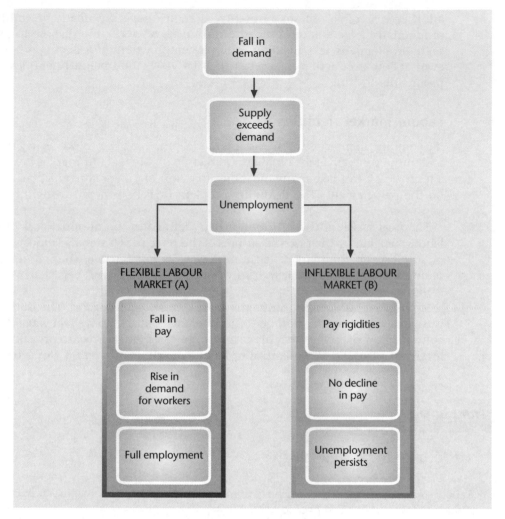

Figure 14.3 Adjustment to a fall in the demand for labour

demand curve. The process continues until eventually equilibrium is restored at a lower pay level. At that wage, everyone who wants a job will find one.

If pay does not fall, unemployment persists. A market perspective focuses on the reasons for these real pay rigidities and on methods of removing them. Among the more important rigidities analysed in Chapter 10 are:

Trade union power: Trade unions can force real wage rates above the point where supply equals demand. This pleases trade union members who retain their jobs, but limits the demand for labour and can result in lay-offs. A strong, centralised trade union movement might be able to anticipate this difficulty and pitch its demands at a level consistent with full employment. Austria is an example of a country with powerful trade unions and a highly centralised wage-bargaining system which has enjoyed near-full employment for many decades. But sometimes the preference of trade unions for higher pay, or simple miscalculation of the trade-off between pay and unemployment, leads them to insist on a higher level of remuneration than is consistent with full employment.

Minimum wages: If the minimum wage is set too low, it becomes redundant – the market-clearing real wage will be above the minimum. Set too high, however, a minimum wage can cause unemployment (or underground economy activity). Minimum wage legislation typically applies to only a small fraction of total employment, mostly in the lower skill and young categories. Sometimes it has unintended effects, benefiting middle-class teenagers who get casual work at the minimum rate, while excluding the really poor whom it was intended to help.

Replacement ratios: Replacement ratios are defined as unemployment benefit entitlements as a percentage of average earnings after tax. They set a floor below which the real wage rate cannot fall. Thus, suppose trade unions succeed in enforcing a pay claim above the market-clearing level. This leads to lay-offs. Laid-off workers then move into the non-unionised sectors. Pay levels in these sectors are driven down. Eventually, they reach the replacement level 'floor' where a person is as well-off unemployed as working. At this point, additions to the supply of labour into the non-union sectors cause unemployment. Replacement ratios also affect the time spent looking for an alternative job. They put upward pressures on real wages by reducing the economic cost of being laid off.

Replacement ratios (before tax) are higher in Europe than in North America (Table 14.3). They vary considerably according to family circumstances, being higher for people with large families and the unskilled. Economic theory demonstrates the potential conflict between providing a decent safety net to a person made redundant, and providing incentives to seek work and accept a job when it is offered.

Occupational and geographical immobility: The total labour market is highly segmented by both occupation and region. One can have excess demand for labour (shortages) in one part of the country and excess supply (unemployment) in other parts. It may take a considerable time before labour moves from areas where it is over-abundant to areas where it is scarce. Labour market flexibility within the different areas may not be sufficient to enable the imbalance to be overcome by regional variations in pay. For example, if pay is negotiated through a centralised negotiating system, and if welfare benefits and employment regulations are the same through all regions of a country, labour costs will also by definition be equalised at a regional level.

Employment protection legislation: Employment protection legislation is another source of labour market rigidity. In theory, its effect on unemployment is ambiguous, because it delays lay-offs (good) as well as discouraging recruitment (bad). Yet it is often cited in studies as a cause of unemployment.

Tax wedges: Income taxes and payroll taxes drive a 'wedge' between the cost of labour to an employer and the net after-tax income of the employee. When taxes

Table 14.3 Unemployment benefit replacement rates 1997

	Single	Married		Single	Married
Australia	37	73	Italy	28	54
Austria	54	70	Japan	32	65
Belgium	46	60	Netherlands	60	78
Canada	25	59	Norway	36	53
Denmark	48	96	Portugal	42	61
Finland	58	97	Spain	39	67
France	38	74	Sweden	58	84
Germany	57	68	Switzerland	61	91
Greece	8	11	UK	50	64
Ireland	33	62	US	7	48

Note: married = unemployed with 2 children.

Source: OECD web page (Social Policy: Benefit and work incentives in OECD countries).

increase, it often happens that businesses complain about the rising cost of labour, while *simultaneously* employees are aggrieved at their falling after-tax income. These two opposing perceptions are consistent. The effects of the higher tax are to (a) raise the cost of labour relative to other factors of production and relative to product prices, and (b) lower real after-tax pay (thus raising the replacement ratio). Higher labour costs to the employer dampen the demand for labour. Again, as before, inflexibilities in the labour market may prevent nominal wages falling sufficiently to compensate for the higher hiring cost. In these circumstances, a higher tax wedge will lead to unemployment. Higher taxes are likely to aggravate the situation further by weakening entrepreneurial incentives and stimulating the underground economy.

Rigidities in the product market: Product market rigidities exacerbate labour market rigidities. Monopoly rents extracted in final product or services markets can be shared with employees, leading to higher pay norms in these industries. This can have knock-on effects on unemployment in the same way that pay-hikes in a sector dominated by trade unions can cause unemployment. Monopolies in intermediate services industries (telecoms, electricity, transport), and regulated charging scales and minimum rates in professional services (legal and accountancy profession, medicine and veterinary services) raise the cost structure of an economy, thereby reducing the competitiveness of the traded sectors. Rigidities in the distribution sector – such as limits on opening hours – can also lead to the suppression of part-time jobs which cannot be replaced in other sectors of the economy. Finally, *'menu costs'* can be another source of rigidity. Changing prices can be expensive and, as a result, prices can be 'sticky'. Firms may prefer to keep prices fixed, forgo sales and cause higher unemployment, rather than incur the costs of varying prices frequently in line with fluctuations in demand. (Appendix 14.1 gives a practical example of a typical central bank's analysis of these rigidities and the resultant policy implications.)

14.3 Short-run versus long-run perspectives

Labour markets are more flexible in the long run than in the short term. Thus, suppose inflation rises unexpectedly from 4 per cent to 15 per cent. In a perfectly rational and rapidly adjusting system, employees would immediately raise their pay demands pro rata. In the real world, however, the pace of adjustment will be much slower. *In the short run*, employees will be tied into pay agreements; they and their employers will wait and see if the price increase is a flash in the pan or a long-run trend. Meanwhile, the sluggish response causes profits to rise, output and employment to increase, and unemployment to fall. *In the long run*, the story is different. Employees will insist on pay increases to compensate for the price rise. If full compensation is exacted, then real pay, and the level of employment and unemployment, will revert to their original level. A similar line of reasoning would apply in the case of an unexpected fall in inflation from 15 to 4 per cent, except that now employment will rise. This is one of the reasons why disinflation can be so costly in economic terms.

The idea of the existence of a trade-off between inflation and unemployment derived from a paper written by a New Zealand economist, Bill Phillips, in 1958 (see Appendix 14.2 on the Phillips curve). Originally it was thought that there might be a long-run trade-off between inflation and unemployment. The implication was that by being a little less fussy about inflation a country could achieve a long-run lower unemployment rate. Experience showed that this belief was seriously mistaken. The trade-off, such as it is, exists only in the short run and there is considerable scepticism about how significant even those short-run gains can be.

The idea can be related to our earlier discussion of the Aggregate Supply (AS) curve (Chapter 11). As long as there are nominal pay and price rigidities, the Phillips argument asserts that the AS curve will be positively sloped. What Phillips failed to take account of is that, in the long run, these nominal rigidities will be washed out of the system as economic actors' pay demands catch up with price developments. 'Rationality' will prevail, and the AS curve will revert to being vertical.

Consideration of short-run versus long-run perspectives leads to several implications. The *first* concerns the role of aggregate demand (AD). When the AS curve is vertical, as it is in the long run, changes in AD have no impact on output or employment, only on the price level. In Figure 14.4, the shift in AD to AD^1 leaves output (Y) unchanged. Once we allow for a positively sloped AS curve, however, the same shift in the AD curve increases real output from Y to Y^1, and in the process will reduce unemployment. AD thus becomes important in its own right as a factor in determining unemployment (a point discussed further in the next section).

A *second* issue concerns the location of the point at which the long-run AS curve intersects the horizontal axis, i.e. the long-run equilibrium level of output and the associated level of employment and unemployment. Nothing so far suggests that this point (Y in Figure 14.4) need coincide with full employment. The actual level will depend on the amount of distortions in the labour market such as those

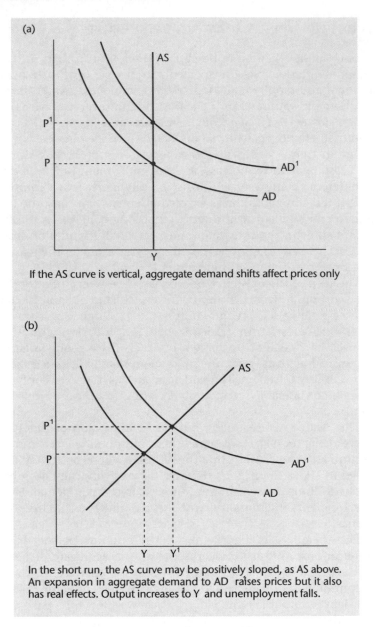

(a)

If the AS curve is vertical, aggregate demand shifts affect prices only

(b)

In the short run, the AS curve may be positively sloped, as AS above. An expansion in aggregate demand to AD raises prices but it also has real effects. Output increases to Y and unemployment falls.

Figure 14.4 Short-run versus long-run AS

mentioned earlier (trade union power, minimum real wages, replacement ratios, etc.) that do not have their origins not in short-term money illusion but are embedded in institutions and value systems. In the jargon of economics, this long-run unemployment is called the *natural rate of unemployment*, or the non-accelerating inflation rate of unemployment (NAIRU). The natural rate may be long run, but it is not time-invariant. It is amenable to policy action. Steps taken to reduce real rigidities in the labour market have had a significant downward impact on NAIRU in the UK, The Netherlands, Ireland and Denmark in recent years.

Third, a relatively recent discovery is that short-run unemployment can affect the long-run natural rate. The short run and the long run are not independant. Uncmployment, once created, might develop its own independent dynamic. *Higher unemployment may initially be caused by short-run factors, but prolonged periods of unemployment make it progressively more difficult for the unemployed to get back into the labour market.* Here short-run and long-run considerations tend to shade into one another

Hysteresis theory explains the dynamics of the natural rate in several ways. First, it refers to the fact that unemployment can be self-perpetuating both for the individual concerned (because of loss of skills and motivation) and for the economy in aggregate. The rise in the natural rate is ascribed to the erosion of human capital and the loss of the motivation of the unemployed, particularly of the long-term unemployed; the development of an under-class and a culture of dependency; increased power of insiders (those with jobs) relative to outsiders (the unemployed). Second, physical capital too becomes run down. Once a factory closes, it is difficult to reopen. Third, as time passes, insiders are able to strengthen their position *vis-à-vis* outsiders. These explanations of hysteresis focus on social dynamics and informational deficiencies that cannot be captured in the simple analytics of demand and supply.

While the Phillips curve addresses the problem of short-term rigidities, many rigidities have their origins in long-term, enduring distortions in the labour market. Some are the result of market failure. The *market for lemons* case draws attention to a source of dysfunction of the market arising from asymmetrical knowledge. Suppose a person becomes unemployed, walks into another firm, enquires about the going rate of pay and offers to work for, say, 30 per cent less than this. If the market system runs smoothly, this should lead to the offer of the job. However, the market may not run smoothly. The offer to accept lower pay may arouse the suspicion of the employer. Does it signal a deficiency in the applicant's qualifications or character? The more 'flexible' the applicant, the more these suspicions may seem to be confirmed. The basic problem arises because of *asymmetric information* between the applicant's self-knowledge and the employer's perceptions of the applicant. The employer knows very little about your capabilities and reliability – only a fraction of what you know yourself – and is likely as a result to clutch at straws. Willingness to work for less than the going wage rate in this instance may signal not so much cheapness as desperation and some hidden flaw. (Hence the term market for 'lemons', lemons being an American slang word for bad quality.[5])

---

5 The concept originated with G. Akerlof, 'The market for lemons: Quality, uncertainty and the market mechanism', *Quarterly Journal of Economics* (1970).

The *efficiency-wage theory* points to another type of rigidity deeply embedded in the market system. The theory states that employers often prefer to pay above the 'going' rate because, in so doing:[6]

■ they have a better chance of attracting and retaining better-quality employees;
■ they placate trade unions – or remove the incentive for employees to join trade unions;
■ they stimulate employees to work productively, with less need for monitoring (this is a variant of Henry Ford's 'economy of high wages' – Ford believed that paying higher wages gave his staff an incentive to work harder and more productively).

If one firm pays over the odds, there is no problem. But if all firms try to pay over the odds, the average level of pay rises. Eventually, equilibrium is reached at a higher-than-market-clearing wage, with residual unemployment. Efficiency-wage theory also offers an explanation of why pay levels may be rigid in the face of shifts in the demand curve – employers will be loath to be the first to cut pay.

The list of mechanisms interfering with the adjustment process of the market model can be extended, but the gist of the argument should now be clear. The different types of rigidities have different labels attached to them. Those emphasising the importance of state interference or monopoly power tend to be labelled 'classical'. Those emphasising not outside interference, but the rigidities arising from inherent failings in the market system itself (such as market for lemons, efficiency wages and menu costs) tend to be labelled (New) Keynesian. Each type of rigidity causes serious problems and is costly in a long-run dynamical sense, as well as in terms of short-run static efficiency.

New Keynesian rigidities are particularly difficult to deal with since they are less amenable to government action. They are more helpful in illustrating the complexity of the unemployment problem than in prescribing solutions for it. The policy implications of the demand and supply analysis, however, follow in a straightforward way from the diagnosis. Measures should be taken to reduce or eliminate labour market rigidities by:

■ promoting awareness in trade unions of the link between pay demands and unemployment, and restraining abuses of their power,
■ dispensing with statutory minimum wage legislation,
■ lowering replacement ratios (by reducing income and payroll taxes, targeting social welfare to those who need it most and making unemployment assistance less open-ended),
■ enhancing labour mobility through education, retraining and information,
■ making product and service markets more competitive.

---

6 J. Konings and P. Walsh identify the key feature of this model as the dual function of the wage from the employer's perspective: one function is to enable firms to attract the right type of labour, and the other is to create incentives for employees to work effectively, i.e. reduce efficiency costs: 'Evidence of efficiency wage payments in UK firm level plant data', *Economic Journal* (May 1994), p. 542.

This list of measures resembles the standard 'supply-side' economics programme adopted since the 1980s by the UK, the US, New Zealand and Australia whose example has won a world-wide following. A case could also be made for introducing special measures to deal with the hysteresis problem, e.g. by programmes targeted at the long-term unemployed (community employment schemes, workfare, special training and employment subsidies).

14.4 The importance of demand

John Maynard Keynes (1883–1946) was the most influential economist of the last century. Because of him, macroeconomics came into existence as an independent component of economics. His masterpiece, *The General Theory of Employment, Interest and Money*, published in 1936, took five years to write. With remarkable self-confidence, he confided in a letter to George Bernard Shaw:

> I believe myself to be writing a book on Economic Theory which will largely revolutionise – not I suppose at once but in the next ten years – the way the world thinks about our problems.

The classical approach, then as now, identified the key reason for unemployment as being that real wages were too high or that 'workers were pricing themselves out of jobs'. Yet in time of recession, the main problem, from a firm's perspective, is not so much that labour is expensive, but that there is insufficient demand for the firm's output. Focusing on the demand-side of the labour market, Keynes argued that the relationship between real wages and the aggregate demand for labour was more uncertain and unstable than the market model suggested.

His basic argument can be summarised as follows. Suppose that all employees agreed to a large cut in nominal wages, with the objective of reducing unemployment. The positive effect of this action would be that, at given product prices, the real wage is lowered and demand for labour increases. Employers move downwards along the demand curve. Unfortunately, there is also a negative side. As real pay declines across the economy, workers and their families have less money to spend. Aggregate demand for goods and services in the economy also declines. Retailers, finding that sales are sluggish, cut back orders. Manufacturers have, as a result, less demand for their output and begin to cut product prices. The burden of servicing corporate debt increases and future returns on investment are discounted more heavily. Expectations about the future become depressed and business investment declines. The indirect negative effect of these factors on the demand for labour could easily offset the positive effects of lower pay. Thus Keynes' 'fundamental' objection to the classical model: there are, he stated, *no grounds for the belief that a flexible wage policy is capable of maintaining a state of full employment* (p. 267).[7]

---

7 Indeed, if prices fall by more than the initial nominal pay cut, real wages may end up increasing instead of falling. This is what Keynes meant by the assertion that 'there may be no method by which workers can reduce real pay through nominal wage bargains'.

In an economy where the workings of the price mechanism were slow and uncertain, the fundamental reason for unemployment in Keynes' view was a lack of effective demand. The *General Theory* laid the foundations for a revolution in thinking and for the evolution of the Keynesian paradigm. Key features of this new paradigm can be summarised under four headings:

1. *Investment demand tends to be highly unstable.* Investors base their decisions on expectations for the future. These expectations are volatile and are heavily influenced by what is happening now. Falling demand leads to pessimistic expectations of future demand. Pessimistic expectations tend to be self-fulfilling. What Keynes termed *'the unstable character of business expectations and investment'* lies at the root of the unemployment problem in a market economy (*General Theory*, p. 279).

2. *Investment fluctuations have repercussions well in excess of the initial change in spending because of the multiplier effect.* Investment generates income for those engaged in construction, road-building, etc. This income is spent on consumption, which in turn creates income for someone further down the line, and so on (the 'multiplier effect').

3. *Self-adjusting forces in the economy are weak and slow-moving especially in the short run.* Keynes challenged not so much the logical coherence of the market approach as its practical relevance. Thus, he agreed that, as prices decline in a depression, the real value of money balances and government bonds increases and that, as a result, people will eventually spend more. Eventually, essential capital goods will also need to be replaced – such replacement can be postponed only so long. Eventually, too, business expectations will improve as sentiment that 'the worst is over' takes hold. But the fact that these equilibrating mechanisms operate in the long run may be small consolation to people now unemployed. *In the long run we are all dead* is a favourite quotation of the Keynesian School.

4. *State intervention may be needed to speed up the adjustment process.* It could achieve this by ensuring consistency between the propensity of investors to invest and the propensity of consumers to save. Over time, Keynes argued, 'comprehensive socialisation of investment may prove the only means of securing an approximation to full employment'.

Keynes made a significant and lasting addition to our understanding of the unemployment problem. His work sparked off a new research programme involving intense study of the components of total demand, the interactions between them, and the linkages between aggregate demand and the monetary sector of the economy. Keynes accepted that pay rigidities could cause unemployment and that a decrease in unemployment would most likely require a fall in real pay and a high level of business confidence. He stressed the importance of maintaining a stable aggregate demand as the key to low unemployment, and he envisaged an active role for government in moderating fluctuations in demand via fiscal and monetary policies.

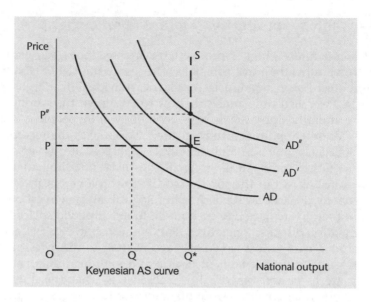

Figure 14.5 Aggregate demand and Keynesian aggregate supply curve

The Keynesian policy prescription can be illustrated by means of aggregate demand and supply analysis. Suppose the Keynesian aggregate supply curve (PES) is shaped like an inverted L, as in Figure 14.5. (This is, in effect, an extreme version of the positively shaped short run AS of Figure 14.4.) Up to the point of full employment output Q*, output can increase without initiating any increase in the price level. After Q*, any effort to stimulate demand will lead only to higher prices. Suppose the economy were at a point like Q, with unemployed resources. This would be the appropriate time for a fiscal stimulus. If it succeeds in its aim, aggregate demand will shift outwards (from AD to AD') and this will bring national output from OQ to OQ*, the full employment level. Thus, stimulation has been a highly effective instrument in this case. After Q* is reached, however, any further demand stimulus to AD", say, will be inflationary.

Keynesian economics has stimulated research on the full employment level of output, on the causes of wage and price rigidities, on the determinants of investment and on the different instruments which can be used to stimulate or contract the AD curve (tax reductions, direct spending by government, interest rate reductions). It provides important insights into the unemployment problem, not just in terms of short-term rigidities but also into the problem of extended demand stagnation such as that experienced in Japan during the past decade.

369

14.5 Technology, productivity and unemployment

At a micro-level, higher productivity and technological change often tend to destroy, rather than to create, jobs. The search for higher labour productivity and better technology, an imperative for the individual firm, leads managers to spend at least as much time analysing how to cut down the workforce as to add to it. More often than not, the decision to employ more people is taken as a last resort, after all other options have been tried. This makes the recommendations of the European Commission and the OECD urging greater investment in technology sound rather paradoxical.[8] It is all the more puzzling since these policies are advocated as part of the solution to the unemployment problem.

Nobody denies that modern technological advance is labour-displacing in the sense that PCs replace typists; household machinery displaces domestic servants; automation displaces operatives. This is the visible direct effect of improvements in productivity.[9] Most would also accept that, to the extent that these processes represent the replacement of boring and onerous human work by machinery, they are to be welcomed – in a sense, it is what the quest for higher living standards is all about. It would be perverse to prefer a situation in which more people were needed to complete a given task to one where fewer people were needed.

Yet technical progress can create serious distributional problems. If it proceeds too fast, those losing jobs may not be able to find alternative outlets in other industries. The problem can then be categorised as similar to that of skill or geographical mismatch and analysed in terms of the market model already described – an important transitional problem requiring flexible labour markets to resolve. Concern about the employment implications of technological advance is not something new to this generation; there have been many instances in history of opposition to new machinery on such grounds (see Box 14.2).

There is no compelling evidence to support the proposition that technical progress poses a long-term, systemic threat to the capacity of a modern economy to attain full employment. In the early 1800s, about 80 per cent of the UK working population was engaged in agriculture. The figure has now fallen to below 2 per cent. Rapid technical progress has made this massive shift possible. Fewer people are now engaged in producing food, and more are available for supplying other goods and services, such as comfortable housing and entertainment. Likewise, only 3 per cent of the US workforce is now required to supply most of America's food, while at the same time, millions of acres of arable land are deliberately kept out of production by set-aside programmes. Given sufficient time, major adjustment can take place without necessitating huge increases in unemployment. Such adjustment is not impoverishing: on the contrary, it is a necessary condition for attaining a higher living standard.

---

8 *OECD Jobs Study*: Delors White Paper: *UNICE Competitiveness Study*.

9 Although not as fast as one would think: 'we see computers everywhere but in the productivity statistics'. This statement by Robert Solow has become known as the 'Solow paradox'. Labour productivity growth fell rather than increased, despite the spread of computerisation. Only in the late 1990s did the long-awaited upsurge in productivity materialise.

Box 14.2

Technological change and employment: the lessons of history

Forecasts that the next wave of technological change will cause high unemployment have frequently been made in the past. Today, these fears take a variety of forms: beliefs that computers and robots will soon take the place of unskilled labour, or that the rate of structural change in the economy is too high and will lead to overwhelming dislocations through technological unemployment. Historically, such gloomy predictions have been wrong. Increased productivity has been accompanied by rising demand for labour and rising real wages.

In the 1820s, the 'Ricardian Socialists' argued that increased productivity from the introduction of machinery would reduce employment and put downward pressure on wages and on living standards. They were relying on an extended numerical example from chapter 30 of David Ricardo's revised *Principles of Political Economy*, after which Ricardo concludes: 'the opinion entertained by the labouring class, that the employment of machinery is frequently detrimental to their interests, is not founded on prejudice and error, but is conformable to the correct principles of political economy'.

Over the following half-century, capital accumulation and technical change caused average wages in the UK to more than double, while unemployment showed no appreciable rise.

In the 1860s, Karl Marx wrote in *Capital* that 'the greater the social wealth, the functioning capital ... the productivity of labour ... the greater the industrial reserve army [of the unemployed] ... the more extensive [are] the pauperised sections of the working class'.

As capital intensity and labour productivity continued to increase, average wages in the UK once again roughly doubled, and unemployment did not appreciably rise.

In the 1940s, after the Second World War, cyberneticist Norbert Weiner was forecasting that the invention of the computer would create massive technological unemployment. Over the following 40 years, average hourly wages in the US more than doubled, while unemployment increased by an average of 1 to 2 percentage points.

Source: *The OECD Jobs Study* (1994).

The main employment-creating aspects of advances in technology are indirect, and hence they are often overlooked:

(1) As productivity increases, employees earn higher salaries. This leads to what are called the *income-generating effects* of higher productivity. Higher purchasing power feeds into demand for goods and services (cars, videos, education, health). In this way, employment opportunities are created in a range of different industries. Historically, these income-generating effects on the demand for labour have tended to outweigh the direct labour displacement effects of new technologies.

(2) Advances in technology are usually associated with specific machines and production processes. Demand for the products embodying the technology grows rapidly. Semiconductors, scientific instruments, aerospace and computers are the fastest growing industries in the OECD in terms of employment. Thus, technology advance, growth in labour productivity and employment growth often go together. Employment in high-tech, high-productivity industries has risen from 15 per cent of the total manufacturing workforce in 1970 to over 20 per cent at present, whereas employment in the low-tech industries has fallen from 58 per cent to 50 per cent in the industrial countries.

Higher labour productivity can be stimulated not only by technology, but also by threat of competition from cheaper imports. The liberalisation of imports into industrial countries has no doubt had such an effect, but researchers differ on the weight to be attached to each factor. What is certain is that import penetration of low-cost countries in the industrial countries' markets for labour-intensive goods is increasing. This is forcing firms to rationalise and to raise productivity. Workers, especially those with a few or outdated skills, are put under enormous pressure in these industries. The transitional effects are evident in lower wages for the unskilled, especially in the flexible labour countries like the US, and by higher unemployment in Europe. The different behaviour of real wages of low-paid workers in the US and Europe during the 1980s offers revealing evidence of the effects of different degrees of labour market flexibility on the level of pay. In the US, real wages fell by over 1 per cent p.a., while in Germany they increased by nearly 3 per cent p.a. To anyone trained in supply/demand analysis, it comes as no surprise to find that private sector employment grew ten times faster in the US than in Europe between 1974 and 1992 (OECD, *Employment Outlook*, 1996).

The benefits of technological progress can be enjoyed in a number of different ways. For example, society could (a) produce the *same* output for *less* work, or (b) produce *even more* output for the *same* work, or (c) choose any number of intermediate output/work combinations. The third option seems to be the closest approximation of what has happened in most countries. Hours worked per person per year have fallen steeply, yet output per person has soared.[10]

The trend decline in hours worked has been seized upon to argue for job-sharing (moves to a 30 or 35-hour week, 4-day work weeks, week-on/week-off, etc.). But trade unions are less keen on accepting the cut in the real pay necessary to make such arrangements effective. In any event, the trend decline in hours worked has flattened in recent years. Also, a large number of part-time workers appear to want to work longer hours. Only a modest easing of the unemployment problem, therefore, can be expected from an increased recourse to leisure. In the meantime, it makes good economic sense to ensure that labour markets are kept

---

10 Between 1938 and 1987, annual total hours worked per person fell from 2316 to 1620 in Germany, 2267 to 1557 in the UK and from 2062 to 1608 in the US (A. Maddison, *Dynamic Forces in Capital Development*, Oxford: Oxford University Press, 1991).

Box 14.3

OECD jobs policy

The *OECD Jobs Study* stresses that solving unemployment requires a *set* of policies rather than one single policy. These policies can be summarised as:

1. Macro-stability – price stability and balanced budgets in the medium term.
2. Enhance the creation and diffusion of technological know-how.
3. Nurture an entrepreneurial climate.
4. Increase labour-cost flexibility.
5. Increase working-time flexibility.
6. Reform security of employment provisions (loosen mandatory restrictions on hiring and dismissals).
7. Reduce replacement ratios and other work disincentives.
8. Expand and enhance active labour policies (move from passive income support to 'active' measures such as job-creation programmes for the long-term unemployed, back-to-work plans and reorientation interviews).

The first three measures could be described as output-enhancing measures. The labour market flexibility measures could be classified as labour market policies. Demand management policy gets a brief and cautious acknowledgement under the first heading, but there is a strong emphasis on the need for inflation control.

Macroeconomic policy should focus on assisting recovery through faster non-inflationary growth of domestic demand when there is still substantial economic slack, while policies should be adjusted promptly to avoid a rekindling of inflation when recovery is well under way. (p. 44)

Source: The OECD Jobs Study: Facts, analysis, strategies (Paris, 1994).

flexible so that workers are free to express their preferences (through flexible hours, contracting out and work-sharing), and also to ensure that the adjustment costs arising from increased labour productivity are kept to a minimum.

This analysis suggests that the best response to advances in technology and productivity change is, first, to embrace such change by *getting the right framework for the 'new economy' industries to emerge*, and second, *to shift the focus of labour market policies* away from 'passive' income support to 'active' policies (improving skills, employment subsidies and special employment schemes).

14.6 Labour market policies

While details of policies differ among countries, there is nonetheless a striking consensus about the broad framework of an effective strategy against unemployment. This consensus focuses on three themes:

- the importance of macroeconomic stability,
- the belief that jobs for the unemployed must be found primarily through faster growth in the private sector,
- remove disincentives to work and to hire employees arising from the tax and social welfare system.

Each of these themes can be found in the conclusions of most policy-oriented studies of unemployment (see Box 14.3 and Appendix 14.1).

Macroeconomic policies

For a long time, roughly from the end of the Second World War to the oil crises in the early 1970s, Keynesian economics was seen as offering an effective and growth-promoting solution to the problem of unemployment. Whether it did so, in fact, is a matter of controversy. Indubitably, the heyday of Keynesianism coincided with record low unemployment. Equally, it would be hard to contest that Keynesian policies – and the widespread belief in the efficacy of these policies – kept business expectations high, helped investment and stimulated growth. Never before had the Western economies known such prolonged prosperity as that from the late 1940s to the early 1970s. Unfortunately, Keynesian economics lost its magic touch during the 1970s. We discuss why in the next chapter. Emphasis has now shifted to maintaining price stability so that both sides of the labour market can bargain over real prices and the forces of competition can be deployed to maximum effect. Government financial balance assists in keeping taxes on labour low.

Supply-side measures and private sector growth

Output growth, higher demand for labour and lower unemployment are obviously interlinked. The present tendency is to emphasise 'supply-side' policies. This includes not only encouragement of private sector growth by lower taxes, but also the elimination of rigidities in product markets such as monopoly in the services sector, or restrictive trading rules, which suppress job-creating opportunities. For example, state utility monopolies have tended to stifle the development of new private industries, and their employees, sheltered from competition, have been able to set pay trends which were inappropriate for the more exposed private sector. The ultimate losers from this process were the unemployed.

Reducing disincentives to work

This means ensuring a gap between after-tax pay and social security payments, avoidance of unemployment and poverty traps, curbing indirect costs of employing people (payroll tax, paperwork, social legislation), lowering standard income tax rates, reducing the power of trade unions and removing biases against labour in the industrial incentive structure. There must be incentives for employees to accept jobs at competitive wages and incentives for employers to take account of the interests of the unemployed (particularly in the public sector).[11]

Wage formation process

Small countries have found that collective agreements can internalise labour market pressures, thus increasing the sensitivity of real wages to 'shocks'. There is ongoing debate, however, about the relevance of such agreements to larger countries. The UK and the US would be resolutely opposed to them, while Germany, France and those espousing the European model are more favourably disposed.

Active labour market policies and the long-term unemployed

Flexible markets generate jobs, but slowly. For this reason, much experimentation has been made with 'active' labour market policies, which are often designed to address the problems of the long-term unemployed by direct intervention. Active policies can be categorised into three types: (1) *job broking* – measures to improve the flow of information about vacancies such as provision of job centres; (2) *training and education* – provision of special courses designed to upgrade the motivation and skills of the unemployed especially young 'drop-outs'; and (3) *direct job provision* through 'workfare' or public works programmes, often organised at community level, and special labour subsidies to the private sector attached to hiring long-term unemployed.[12]

The purpose of these policies is to reduce directly the number of unemployed people. One study showed that an increase in participation in active labour market programmes of 1 percentage point of the labour force reduces the unemployment rate by 1.5 percentage points.[13] But other studies show less positive results, perhaps because these programmes can have adverse as well as positive indirect effects on employment. The heavy costs to the government of

---

11 These issues have been exhaustively surveyed in R. Layard, S. Nickell and R. Jackman, *Unemployment* (Oxford: Oxford University Press, 1991). Dedicated to 'the millions who suffer through want of work' and citing some 500 references, the book wends its way through 580 pages of sophisticated economics to reach two broad conclusions about how to reduce unemployment. First, *reform the pay-bargaining system* in such a way as to secure lower pre-tax pay norms and achieve greater pay flexibility in response to adverse supply or demand shocks. Second, *revise the unemployment benefits scheme* by curbing open-ended duration of benefits: 'unconditional payment of benefits for an indefinite period is clearly a major cause of European unemployment' (p. 62). In place of open-ended benefit schemes, active labour market projects are recommended – the public sector should, if necessary, be prepared to act as employer of last resort.

12 L. Calmfors, 'Active labour market policy and unemployment – A framework for the analysis of crucial design features', *OECD Economic Studies*, no. 22 (Spring 1994).

13 This elasticity is taken from Calmfors (1994, p. 27). See also Layard *et al.* (1991).

implementing them (on average, active policies cost 1 per cent of GDP in developed countries) can *undermine employment elsewhere in the economy*. Also, too much emphasis on these schemes can lead to the neglect of the longer-term fundamental need to improve incentives and tackle rigidities.

14.7 Conclusions

A simple market approach argues that the key to reducing unemployment is (1) to enhance incentives for employers to expand their business, and (2) to achieve a reduction in the cost of hiring labour so that this extra business can be translated into more jobs. Policies are needed to address each of these requirements. In technical jargon, employers are discouraged by *product market rigidities* from expanding their business; and their extra business is not translated into enough expansion of employment because of *labour market rigidities*.

Labour market flexibility can be effective in generating jobs. However, higher paid and longer-lasting jobs require something more. Output-enhancing measures based on development of an entrepreneurial culture, adjustment to technological change and other 'supply-side' factors play an important role, as do effective education and training policies to upgrade skills. Incomes policy may also in certain circumstances be helpful. But if these measures are to succeed, pay bargaining must be attuned to the economy's needs. Collective pay deals can be useful in a crisis situation where one-off reforms in the labour market arrangements are being planned. They also are effective where trade unions and social partners are well informed, give genuine priority to unemployment and are able to deliver.

Market-based approaches do not imply that there is no role for government but, rather, that governments must act in concert *with* rather than *against* the market. Keynesian demand stimulation can work in certain situations. It is not coincidental that the Japanese government, the only government of a major OECD country to attempt to maintain high employment by fiscal expansion in the 1990s, started the decade with a debt : GDP ratio of only 20 per cent.

Labour market policies are not a panacea. One problem is that they tend to work slowly. Another difficulty is the limited effectiveness of labour market incentives when taken in isolation.[14] Studies of the effects of changes in payroll taxes, labour and social legislation, wage costs, income tax, employment subsidies, job training schemes and high replacement ratios often conclude that most firms are unaffected by the relevant measures, and that the number of jobs created by changes in the variable under study would be small.

It is important not to be discouraged by such findings. Even if the effects of any individual measure were negligible, the cumulative effect of a series of such

---

14 For example, Calmfors concludes: 'What contribution can active labour market policy make to fighting unemployment? On the basis of this exposition, my judgement would be that most countries in Western Europe could do better with more active programmes – if carefully designed – but not a lot better' (p. 38).

measures could be extremely significant. Thus, Elmeskov, Martin and Scarpetta (1998) in a review of the lessons of labour market reforms emphasise 'comprehensiveness', the need for 'a balanced mix of policies', which mutually reinforce innovative and adaptive capacity.[15] Active labour market policies – measures initiated in order to improve the functioning of the labour market – are an important element in such a strategy.[16] A comprehensive, sustained approach is necessary.

Some countries put more emphasis on maintaining a reasonable standard of living for the unemployed than others. But how is a 'reasonable' level to be defined and for how long should that level be maintained? The higher the level of social welfare and the more open-ended its duration, the higher the 'floor' on the wage level, since few will agree to work for less. Besides, given the high proportion of unskilled people among the unemployed, realistic alternative jobs will tend, at least initially, to be in the low-paid categories. Herein lies a serious dilemma for politicians. Another problem is that a policy of seeking to cut unemployment via labour market flexibility can often lead to an increase in job insecurity. This is not inevitable since, as we have seen, flexibility can come in many shapes besides labour turnover. Yet to many it is a worrying and unpopular outcome of the market approach. An article in *Time Magazine* refers to the 'temping' of America – the increasing proportion of the workforce engaged in insecure and impermanent jobs, with little or no *esprit de corps* and diminished job satisfaction. US Secretary of Labor, Robert Reich, has referred to the 'anxious class' of American workers. There is some evidence to support such a view. Part-time employment has accounted for a rising share of total employment, and the share of temporary work in total employment increased quite sharply in some countries such as France and Spain, where legislation regulating employment contracts was relaxed. As often in economics, one cannot give absolute priority to any one problem. Some compromise must be found between the brave new world of labour market flexibility, and society's need for commitment and cooperation.

---

15 J. Elmeskov, J.P. Martin and S. Scarpetta, 'Key lessons for labour market reforms: evidence from OECD countries' experiences', *Swedish Economic Policy Review* (Autumn 1998).

16 Unfortunately, the effectiveness of the different elements of an active labour market policy is difficult to estimate reliably. How can resources best be allocated between the various types of programmes discussed here? To go through existing micro-studies or surveys of such micro-studies only is, in Calmfors' words, 'a very distressing experience', because of the difficulties of generalisations (1994, p. 32). Differences in results within programme categories seem to be as large as differences between them. It is often not possible to explain variations in results by the differences in programme design. It also frequently happens that evaluations of the same programme, based on different methods, time-periods and country, can give conflicting results. But more evaluations are being done and we are slowly developing some guidelines on 'best practice' policies.

✔ Summary

1. The standard international definition of unemployment identifies the unemployed as those of working age who, in a specified period, are without work and are both available for, and have taken specific steps to find, work. There are wide variations in unemployment both between countries and within countries. Some sectors of the population, such as young people, migrants and lone parents, experience higher unemployment rates than others. Unemployment is also closely correlated with skill levels, with unskilled workers facing a higher risk of unemployment than skilled workers.

2. The market model analyses unemployment in a demand–supply framework. In this model, the labour demand curve is assumed to be downward-sloping and the labour supply curve upward-sloping. Provided prices are flexible, supply equals demand and there is no unemployment. Shifts in demand and supply, of course, occur over time, but there is no *a priori* reason for believing that any of these events should cause either labour shortages or labour surpluses (unemployment). If unemployment does occur, the model pinpoints the culprit as pay rigidities and, more generally, lack of labour market flexibility, usually referring to the problem of rigidity in real pay and conditions of work. Discussion of the problem of unemployment from this perspective focuses on the causes of these real pay rigidities and on methods of removing them. Sources of such rigidities include trade union power, minimum wages and tax wedges.

3. Labour market rigidities tend to be more severe in the short run than in the long run. In the short run, periods of inflation or disinflation can impact on real output and unemployment. In the long run there is no trade-off. Sometimes, however, short-run unemployment can spill over into long-run consequences, the *hysteresis* effect.

4. Focusing on the demand side of the labour market, Keynes argued that the relationship between real wages and the aggregate demand for labour was highly uncertain and unstable. In an economy where the workings of the price mechanism were too slow to ensure full employment, the fundamental reason for unemployment in Keynes' view was a lack of effective demand. While he accepted that pay rigidities could cause unemployment and that a decrease in unemployment would most likely require a fall in real pay, he stressed the importance of maintaining a high level of business confidence and aggregate demand as the key to low unemployment, and he envisaged an active role for government in moderating fluctuations in demand via fiscal and monetary policies.

5. Technological advance can be labour-displacing and concern about its employment implications is not something new to this generation. However, there is no compelling evidence to support the proposition that technical progress poses a long-term systemic threat to the capacity of a modern economy to attain full employment. 'New economy' activities create more jobs than they destroy.

6. Details of policies differ among countries, yet there is a striking consensus about the broad framework of an effective strategy against unemployment. This consensus focuses on the importance of macroeconomic stability, the belief that jobs for the unemployed must be found primarily through faster growth in the private sector, and the search for ways of minimising disincentives to work and to hire labour.

? Questions for discussion

1. Why should high unemployment be a matter of concern for business?

2. (a) Explain how the supply and demand curves of labour are derived in the standard model. Comment on the realism of the model's assumptions relating to the labour market.
   (b) Show how technological progress might affect the labour market in this model.

3. 'Unemployment is high because wages are too high and employees are pricing themselves out of a job' (business economist).
   'Reducing pay and employing people in low-wage jobs will depress national spending and make unemployment even worse' (trade union official).
   Evaluate these two opposing views of the unemployment problem.

4. A national minimum wage has been introduced by many countries as a solution to the problem of 'underpaid' workers. How would you expect such a measure to affect the level of unemployment?

5. What is meant by hysteresis in the context of unemployment? Discuss the importance of this concept in assessing the economic costs of unemployment.

6. Who are the 'insiders' in the labour market and who are the 'outsiders'? Discuss the relevance of this distinction to current unemployment in Europe.

7. Is faster economic growth the answer to Europe's unemployment problem?

☞ Exercises

1. Provide statistics on unemployment trends in a country of your choice. What policies are currently being applied for reducing unemployment? What other policies would you recommend? (A useful source is the OECD's annual publication, *Employment Outlook*.)

2. Explain how business decisions might be affected by a country's unemployment rate. If you were investing in a region or a country, would you be attracted or deterred by the existence of high unemployment?

3. Suppose there was a sudden and unexpected increase in wage settlements in the economy. What policies would you propose to deal with the threatened rise in unemployment and inflation?

4. Explain why the rate of unemployment is higher for unskilled workers than for the highly skilled. List some of the implications of this different incidence for policy.

5. How would you expect the following developments to impact on the NAIRU?

    (a) Greater anxiety on the workers' part about job security
    (b) A decline in the number of young entrants to the labour market
    (c) The growing importance of Internet job listings.

Further reading

A readable treatment of the theory of unemployment with a commendable historical perspective is J. Trevithick's *Involuntary Unemployment: Macroeconomics from a Keynesian perspective* (Hemel Hempstead: Harvester Wheatsheaf, 1992). A. Lindbeck and D. Snower have developed and popularised the insider–outsider model in *The Insider–Outsider Theory of Employment and Unemployment* (Cambridge, MA: MIT Press, 1989). A. Layard, S. Nickell and J. Jackson, *Unemployment: Macroeconomic performance and the labour market* (Oxford: Oxford University Press, 1991), has now become a classic text, with over 500 references and a masterly review of the literature, even if it proposes less than startling policy conclusions at the end of this enterprise. Readers should also dip into J.M. Keynes' *General Theory* to savour for themselves the flavour of this masterpiece. A good if slightly dated source for analysis and staistical overview is OECD, *The OECD Jobs Study: Facts, analysis, strategies* (Paris: OECD, 1994); also 'The challenge facing high and persistent unemployment', *European Economy*, 69, 1999. An update of the OECD study is provided in OECD, *Implementing the Job Strategy – Assessing performance and policy* (Paris: 1999).

Appendix 14.1: 'Dignity without responsibility'? A central bank view of the causes of unemployment

Central banks were widely criticised in the early 1990s for their slowness in reducing interest rates. Their dilatoriness, the critics argued, delayed the recovery of the world economy and prolonged unnecessarily the period of unemployment suffered by many millions in Europe. Nobel prize-winner Robert Solow accused the central bankers of enjoying 'dignity without responsibility'. His criticism drew a revealing reply from Dr Hans Tietmeyer, President of the German Central Bank, the Bundesbank.

The core of Dr Tietmeyer's defence was contained in his assertion that: 'monetary policy cannot be expected to make an active and direct contribution to a (lasting) reduction in unemployment'. This assertion would find much support among central bankers to this day, including the European Central Bank. The ECB's January 1999 monthly bulletin made the ringing assertion that 'the current high level of unemployment in the euro area is overwhelmingly structural in its origin. It is caused mainly by the inflexibility of euro area labour and goods markets. ... Attempting to reduce unemployment by an inflationary monetary policy would ultimately be self-defeating' (pp. 41–2).

Dr Tietmeyer expanded on his point by drawing attention to the comparatively minor influence exerted by the Bundesbank over the *long-term* interest rate which, in his view, is the crucial rate in determining business investment decisions. Even if the bank thought that this rate was too high, it did not follow that it had the power to reduce it. Its margin for manoeuvre was limited, since longer rates are dominated by expectations of inflation. The best contribution that a central bank could make, he argued, was to offer constant reassurance to the market about the commitment to low inflation. Once the credibility of the commitment to a low-inflation objective is achieved, lower expectations of inflation would then feed in to lower long-run interest rates. These rates were crucial to business investment decisions.

He also expressed the view that, in light of the budget deficits pertaining in 1994, no scope for expansionary fiscal policy existed. Again this view is re-echoed repeatedly in current ECB publications. Fiscal policy becomes less effective if the financial position of the government is perceived to be weak. The effectiveness of fiscal policy as a stabilisation tool is inversely related to the size of the national debt and the structural deficit.

Not satisfied with rebutting Solow's criticism that the Bundesbank was not 'doing enough', Dr Tietmeyer went on to outline his own views of the causes of Germany's unemployment. The direction of his recommendations can be guessed from his assertion that 'most [German] unemployment is structural, not cyclical'. The following specific measures were proposed, all easily recognisable as emanating from the labour market approach outlined in this chapter:

1. *Mismatch between demand and supply* of different skills: Demand for unskilled labour has weakened yet supply continues to increase. After a prolonged spell of unemployment, hysteresis effects make that unskilled labour hard to re-integrate.

2. *Poverty and unemployment traps*: 'Lessen the incentive to work, particularly among the lower income groups'.

3. *Labour legislation*: Employee protection in Germany 'seems to be so far-reaching in its social motivation' that it involves the 'unsocial outcome' of hampering employment.

4. *Cost of labour in Germany too high*: Hourly labour costs are among the highest in Europe and now too high in light of the need to absorb increased supply from eastern Germany.

Belief in the neutrality of money and the structural nature of the unemployment problem are hallmarks of the approach to unemployment now dominant in Europe. The implication is that solutions to unemployment must be sought in:

- moderate wage settlements,
- stronger work incentives,
- flexible pay arrangements for full-time and part-time employees,
- training and other 'active' labour market policies.

Sources: 'Dr Tietmeyer presents a German view of unemployment', *Bank for International Settlements Review* (12 September 1994). 'The stability-oriented monetary policy strategy of the Eurosystem', European Central Bank *Monthly Bulletin* (January 1999).

Appendix 14.2: Unemployment and inflation – the Phillips curve

Origins

The Phillips curve originated in a paper published in 1958 by Professor A. W. Phillips. The paper showed the existence of a strong negative relationship between inflation and unemployment in the UK for the period 1861–1957. Similar correlations were subsequently found to hold in other countries. Soon it was being suggested that governments could choose between different combinations of unemployment and inflation. Inflation-averse countries could opt for a point such as B with inflation of OP_b and unemployment of OU_b. Unemployment-averse countries might prefer a point like A, with unemployment of OU_a and inflation of OP_a. For some years, macroeconomic discussion focused on how to chose the most suitable point on the downward-sloping Phillips curve.

Two objections

From the late 1960s on, the Phillips curve came under fire on two counts. First, there were theoretical objections. In 1968, in separate articles, Edmund Phelps and Milton Friedman argued that there might be a short-run trade-off between unemployment and inflation but there was none in the long run.

Suppose the economy starts off at point A with an unemployment rate of 8 per cent and inflation of 2 per cent. The government wants to reduce unemployment form 8 per cent to 4 per cent. The Phillips curve shows that this can be achieved by allowing inflation to rise from 2 per cent to 5 per cent. In the short run the economy moves from point A to point B. At B we assume there is more inflation

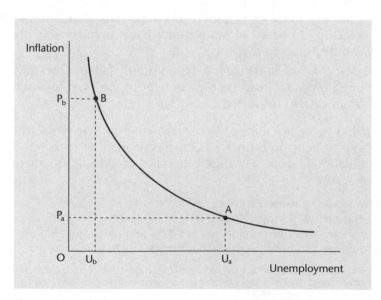

Figure A1 Phillips curve

but wages catch up slowly and real wages fall – this is what generates the fall in unemployment. There is a 4 per cent reduction in unemployment and inflation rises by 3 per cent.

However, *this position is not sustainable*. The Phillips curve analysis refers to the short run only. Sooner or later employees will demand compensation. They will realise that their purchasing power has been eroded as a direct result of the increase in inflation. Once compensation is acheived, real pay levels return to their original level and unemployment likewise. That is, the economy will move back to C, identical to A, only now, employees' expectations of inflation have increased to 5 per cent and the short-run Phillips curve (SRPC) is shifted outward and to the right. Unemployment returns to its original level of 8 per cent and inflation is at 5 per cent. Thus in the long run there is no trade-off between inflation and unemployment. Expansionary policies that aim to reduce unemployment by increasing inflation will be successful only in the short run.

The Friedman–Phelps critique states that individuals learn from past experience ('mistakes'). They do not suffer from *money illusion* in the long run. It is not *nominal wages* but *real wages* (nominal wages adjusted for inflation) that matter. By incorporating price expectations into the Phillips curve, the alleged trade-off between inflation and unemployment disappears: *the long-run Phillips curve is vertical*.

The second objection was that inflation could be caused by factors other than a lowering of the unemployment rate. Thus, a rise in oil prices causes an upward ratchet effect on consumer prices, which can easily feed into a wage spiral.

In formal terms the *expectations augmented Phillips curve* emerges as follows.

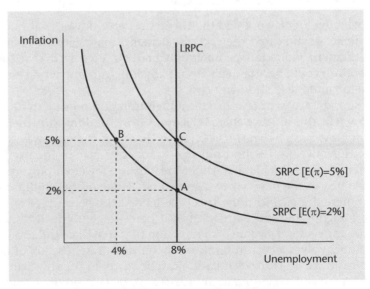

Figure A2 Short and long-run Phillips curves

Assume expected inflation for this year is the same as last year's

$$\pi_t^e = \pi_{t-1}$$

where π = price inflation and superscript 'e' = expected

The Phillips curve equation then becomes:

$$\pi_t = \pi_{t-1} - \beta(\mu_t - \mu_n) + v_t$$

Where μ_n = natural rate of unemployment
   v_t = supply side shocks
   μ_t = actual unemployment rate

Expected inflation can differ from actual inflation for two main reasons: aggregate supply side shocks (v) or aggregate demand shocks, which cause μ_t to exceed μ_n, the effect being determined by parameter β. Adaptive expectations implies that inflation next year will equal inflation this year provided $\mu = \mu_n$ and $v = 0$.

Structural unemployment and the natural rate

The long-run Phillips curve will be vertical at a point that is called the *natural rate of unemployment*. Regardless of the inflation rate, in the long-run the economy will return to its underlying *natural rate of unemployment* or *non-accelerating-inflation rate of unemployment (NAIRU)*. The actual unemployment level at that point is determined by the structural factors mentioned in the text such as replacement ratios, trade union influences, minimum pay levels and so on. Thus structural unemployment and NAIRU are closely related.

New consensus and the LRPC

The above framework laid the theoretical groundwork for new consensus macro policies. It indicated that activist demand management could not achieve any permanent reduction in unemployment. It suggested that low inflation (price stability) could be attained without any long-run impact on employment, though there would be a short-run cost.

Suppose we wish to move from high inflation point F to low inflation point G, how will this affect welfare? (Figure A3) In the long run there appears to be no costs; we move down the LRPC to G. However, the only way to get to G might be via H. Hence, in the short run significant costs may be incurred in terms of higher unemployment. This cost will be greater the slower employers and employees are to adjust to the new policy regime. Knowledge of the Phillips curve enables us to estimate the *sacrifice ratio*. This is defined as the percentage of real GDP that must be foregone to reduce inflation by 1 percentage point. Estimates of the sacrifice ratio range up to a value of 5, implying that to reduce inflation by one percentage point involves a cost in terms of discounted present value of about 5 percentage points of GDP. Thus, disinflation can be costly in the short run, as the experience of France and Argentina in the 1990s and the UK and the US in the 1980s testifies.

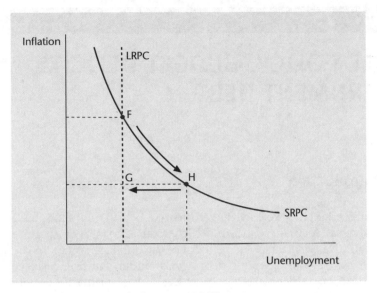

Figure A3 Long- and short-run Phillips curves

Phillips curve and the new economy

The Phillips curve remains an important concept. Generally, as labour markets tighten, earnings also rise and, for given productivity, this feeds into prices. During the 1990s, however, something strange happened in several western economies (UK and US in particular). Labour markets tightened, wages increased and unemployment fell, but *without the inflation that would have accompanied such an outcome in the past.* How to explain? One candidate is that new consensus policies (labour market flexibility, credibility of anti-inflation commitment, and the process of globalisation) have caused a steep decline in the NAIRU. A second factor might be the rise in productivity associated with the new economy (computerisation and the Internet). This has reduced unit costs, and hence held down price inflation, even though wages are rising rapidly. A third factor derives from the hysteresis argument. The boom of the 1990s led to a fall in short-term unemployment that in due course by changing attitudes and morale of the affected workers is translating into long-run improvements in the labour market. One small indicator of this is the finding that the 2.6 percentage point fall in the US unemployment rate between 1992 and 1997 accounted for a 3.0 per cent decrease in youth crime rate.

Sources: A. W. Phillips, 'The relation between unemployment and the rate of change in money wage rates in the United Kingdom 1861–1957', *Economica* 25 (November 1958); C. D. Romer and D. Romer (eds), *Reducing Inflation: Motivation and Strategy* (Chicago: Chicago University Press 1997); statistic in final sentence refers to paper by Richard B. Freeman and W. M. Rodgers quoted in *Business Week* August 21–28, 2000.

Chapter 15

FISCAL POLICY, BUDGET DEFICITS AND GOVERNMENT DEBT

Introduction

Budget deficits, excessive government debt and high taxes have become an almost universal focus of concern. Thirty years ago, governments worried much less about these matters. Management of the public finances, in the sense of balancing the books and keeping debt levels under control, was considered a rather pedestrian exercise. Fiscal policy was judged primarily in terms of its success in dampening economic fluctuations and maintaining full employment. In recent times, this counter-cyclical function of public finances has been downplayed. Keynesian economics, from which the era of fiscal activism drew its intellectual sustenance, has declined in prestige. Fiscal *balance* and fiscal *consolidation* have replaced fiscal *activism* as the conventional target of fiscal policy.

Why has *fiscal balance* become a policy priority in so many countries? It reflects a profound change in thinking about the role of fiscal policy in a modern economy. This change in perspective has had an important impact on the business environment, as is evident in the calls for smaller and more efficient government, lower taxes and more priority for the private sector.

Chapter outline

This chapter describes and explains the origins of this new fiscal policy environment.

1. The essential features of counter-cyclical fiscal policy.
2. The limits of fiscal activism, drawing on the concept of 'crowding-out'.
3. The burgeoning size of public sector debt and the constraints this imposes on fiscal policy.
4. New perspectives on fiscal policy: case study of the European Union.

15.1 Counter-cyclical fiscal policy

Counter-cyclical, or Keynesian, fiscal policy ruled supreme throughout most of Western Europe, and in many other countries, from the early 1950s to the mid-1970s. This period was a 'golden age' of full employment and rapid growth, and activist fiscal policy was given much of the credit for this success. The vocabulary and mode of thinking of Keynesian economics still remains influential, although much less so than in the past.

The basic message of counter-cyclical policy is that governments should run budget deficits in times of recession, and reduce them in times of economic boom. Counter-cyclical fiscal policy proved very attractive. It proposed an antidote to business fluctuations which both had a theoretical foundation and yet which, unusually for economics, was comparatively painless to administer. It suggested that government could spend more without the private sector having to spend less. Even more radically, it raised the possibility that, *because* the public sector increased its spending, the private sector would be able to spend more also. This happy message contrasted with the image of economics as the 'dismal' science, or the science of scarcity!

The problem addressed by Keynesian theory can be illustrated with an AS/AD diagram (Figure 15.1). The Keynesian AS curve is drawn with an inverted L-shape, flat up to the point of full-employment output, then vertical once this point is reached at y^*. Once full employment is reached, any further increases in aggregate demand, such as that from AD to AD', will result in higher prices. Real output cannot be increased beyond the full employment level. Hence, once the output gap has been reduced to zero (i.e. actual = potential GDP), expansion of demand through budget deficits will be inflationary.

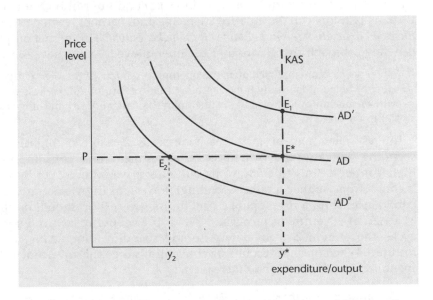

Figure 15.1 The Keynesian aggregate supply curve and fiscal policy

Now consider points to the left of full employment output. Keynes argued that an economy could become stuck at a point below full employment (such as y_2) for considerable periods of time. At this point, output is well below its 'potential' level (recall Chapter 11 on potential GDP). The problem at y_2 is one of insufficient *demand*, not insufficient *supply*.

The prescription for this situation is to increase the level of aggregate demand, i.e. to shift the AD curve outwards. This could be done by raising public sector expenditure or by reducing taxation. Fiscal expansion would stimulate, through a multiplier effect, consumer and investment spending. Such action would short-cut the need to wait for the longer term adjustment mechanisms of falling prices and wages to come into operation.

The fiscal rule suggested by this approach was *fiscal expansion* when the economy is operating below the full employment level, and *fiscal contraction* when the economy is at full employment.

One initial, and still heard, criticism of fiscal expansion is that the state could not 'afford' to raise spending. During a recession, tax revenues are low because of falling incomes and profits, while public spending is inflated because of higher unemployment payments. Expanding the deficit appears to be a recipe for making an already bad budgetary situation even worse. Also government borrowing to finance the higher deficit might pre-empt private savings, thereby leaving less funds available for private investors. Interest rates would be driven up and the private sector would be 'crowded out'. One way or another, an increase in public spending would have to be financed by a decrease in private spending. The *net* impact of a fiscal expansion, according to this view, would be to increase the size of the public sector, not the level of total output or aggregate demand.

Advocates of counter-cyclical policy argued that the 'affordability' of the fiscal expansion was the wrong issue to address. In conditions of high unemployment, fiscal expansion can be financed largely, and perhaps even entirely, *through increases in taxation revenue obtained from higher output*. This higher output could be generated through mobilisation of the unemployed. As Keynes pointed out:

> When we have unemployed men and unemployed plant, and more savings than we are using at home, it is utterly imbecile to say that we cannot afford these things. For it is with the unemployed men and the unemployed plant, and with nothing else, that these things are done.[1]

Interest rates may or may not increase as a result of higher government spending, but any adverse effects on investment and consumption through higher interest rates (the 'crowding-out' effect) would be offset by the boost to income from higher public spending, lower taxation and greater business confidence. Thus, a rise in public debt during a recession should not be regarded as a sign of government profligacy. When the economy is at the bottom of the cycle, the economy needs enterprise and spending, not saving, to restore its fortunes. When normal accounting conventions urge the government to cut back spending, that is the time to increase it.

---

1 J.M. Keynes, article in the *Evening Standard* in 1928. Quoted in R. Skidelsky, *John Maynard Keynes: The economist as saviour 1920–1937* (London: Macmillan, 1992).

The counter-cyclical fiscal model became an integral part of economics courses after the war. Keynesian fiscal theory transformed not only the way economists thought about fiscal policy, but also the way fiscal policy was conducted in industrial countries. Governments committed themselves to full employment and economists claimed to have the necessary technical tools to guide them to this objective, through active and vigorous use of fiscal policy.

Research on the application of fiscal policy during this period concentrated on three main issues: (1) the distinctive roles of fiscal and monetary policy had to be clarified; (2) some way had to be found of identifying accurately the shortfall, or excess, in aggregate demand that an economy was experiencing at any one time; and (3) the size of the fiscal 'injection', the net change in public spending needed to shift aggregate demand to the required degree, had to be determined.[2]

The policy mix

Fiscal policy was generally regarded as a more effective counter-cyclical tool than monetary policy. Recall the 'long and variable lags' in the operation of monetary policy which made it unsuitable for fine-tuning. Also, monetary policy is permissive only – an economy can be flooded with liquidity, interest rates may fall, but investors cannot be forced to invest. Nor, if the economy is booming and business expectations are buoyant, will interest rates be able, on their own, to halt an excessive increase in aggregate demand. Fiscal policy, by contrast, has a direct impact on demand. The government can build a road or an airport or new schools. Equally, it can directly switch off spending. Hence, it was argued that the proper policy mix is to combine an *active* fiscal policy with an *accommodating* (i.e. supporting) monetary policy.

How much extra aggregate demand is needed?

To be effective, counter-cyclical fiscal policy requires accurate information on the current level of GDP and on the gap between it and potential GDP. Identifying the size of the gap between potential and actual output, as we saw earlier, involves painstaking research and good judgement, and even then can be a hazardous exercise. Keynesian economics gave a tremendous boost to the development of applied macroeconomic research and national income accounting. Large econometric models of the economy were formulated, comprising hundreds of equations, and new ways of estimating their parameters were devised. The behaviour of the separate components of aggregate demand has also been extensively researched. Our knowledge of how the economy operates has been enormously enriched as a result. But, as the economy becomes more complex, the values of these parameters change in important but unpredictable ways. Hence

---

2 In terms of Figure 15.1, assuming that policy-makers knew that present output was y_2 and full employment (potential) output was y^*, how much injection of extra demand would be needed from government to ensure that the economy reached y^*? Recall that government intervention was needed since, by definition, the economy was locked into y_2 equilibrium by market forces. This was the 'under-employment equilibrium'.

the need for judgement. The problem for fiscal policy is that, unless the size of the required increment (or decrement) in aggregate demand can be accurately determined, active fiscal policy cannot be successfully applied.

How much fiscal impulse?

This is another thorny issue. Suppose actual GDP was £100 billion and potential GDP was £120 billion. At first sight, it might appear that a £20 billion injection of government spending would close the gap. But this is incorrect. According to the *theory of the multiplier*, aggregate demand would increase by a multiple of the initial injection. To see this, suppose the government were to spend an extra £20 billion on roads and imagine the following sequence of events.

- The initial injection of £20 billion accrues to employees and suppliers of materials. Suppose they spend £16 billion and save £4 billion. The amount saved 'leaks out' of the economy, but the £16 billion stays active and now constitutes income for other sectors of the economy.
- Employees on the road project may spend their additional income on automobiles or new houses. This gives a boost to the car industry and the construction industry, and to their employees and shareholders.
- Assume that the recipients of the £16 billion of extra income decide to spend £13 billion and save £3 billion. This £13 billion now constitutes income for somebody else.
- Suppose they in turn spend £10 billion and save £3 billion, and so on.

We see that the initial spending impulse of £20 billion has generated further spending of £23 billion (£13 billion + £10 billion), as well as £10 billion saving (£4 billion + £3 billion + £3 billion), and the process has by no means ended. Notice also that the additional savings will be available to buy the bonds issued by the government to finance the original £20 billion spending on the road project.

This description of the multiplier presents an intuitive and much simplified version of what in reality is a complex process. For one thing, account should be taken of 'leakages' from income into taxes and imports as well as savings. Also, different types of spending or tax concessions have different multipliers, since the propensity to consume differs among sectors of the economy and different income groups. Moreover, the linkage between the real and financial sectors has to be incorporated in the multiplier formula.

Before deciding on the amount of fiscal stimulus to provide, information is also needed on the present fiscal stance of the government, taking account of the economy's cyclical position. As the economy fluctuates, both government spending and taxation revenues behave in a way which tends to dampen these fluctuations. Thus, at given tax rates, tax revenues automatically get larger as the economy recovers, and fall as it declines. Government spending, on the other hand, tends to fall during an upturn and rise during a recession. The budget deficit, therefore, acts as an *automatic stabiliser*, contracting when the economy is expanding, and expanding when the economy contracts. Just because a government runs a deficit does not mean that it is pursuing an active counter-

Table 15.1 Industrial countries: budget balances (% GDP)

	1990	1993	1996	2000
European Union	−3.6	−6.5	−4.5	−0.6
Japan	+2.9	−1.4	−3.9	−8.4
US	−2.5	−3.4	−1.3	+1.0
Germany	−3.3*	−3.3	−4.0	−0.7
France	−1.6	−6.1	−4.0	−1.5
Italy	−10.9	−9.6	−6.7	−1.5
UK	−1.2	−7.8	−4.4	+0.2
Canada	−4.1	−7.3	−2.4	+2.3
Spain	−3.9	−7.5	−4.7	−0.8
Netherlands	−5.1	−3.3	−3.1	+0.8
Belgium	−5.4	−6.6	−3.2	−0.5
Sweden	+4.2	−13.4	−5.0	+2.0
Austria	−2.2	4.1	−4.5	−1.7
Denmark	−1.5	−4.5	−1.3	+2.0
Finland	+5.3	−8.0	−2.9	+4.6
Greece	−14.0	−12.1	−7.6	−1.5
Portugal	−5.4	−7.0	−4.0	−1.8
Ireland	−2.5	−2.7	−2.4	+3.2
Switzerland	−2.1*	−4.3	−2.7	−1.2
Norway	+4.2	−1.4	+3.8	+7.3
Iceland	−3.3	−4.5	−2.4	+0.8
Australia	+0.4	−3.9	−0.1	+0.3
New Zealand	−2.3	−0.7	+3.6	+0.3

Notes: * 1991 figure.

Negative sign equals a budget deficit; plus sign a budget surplus.

Source: IMF, *World Economic Outlook* (May 1996 and May 2000)

cyclical policy. It may simply be passively permitting the automatic stabilisers to do their work. Active policy is reflected in changes in *non-automatic* budget balances. This can be estimated by subtracting the automatic element from the deficit. The resultant estimate is called the *structural* deficit or surplus. It indicates the extent to which government is using discretion to moderate the impact of its net spending on the economy.

Examining the pattern of deficits and surpluses during the past decade, we see a marked shift towards fiscal conservatism (Tables 15.1 and 15.2). During the 1990s budget deficits were generally more pervasive than budget surpluses but towards the end of the decade the behaviour of the industrial countries had changed. *Thus in 1990 only five, and in 1993 only three, out of 23 industrial countries had budget surpluses. By the year 2000, the number of surplus countries had risen to 14.* Moreover, those countries with deficits at the start of the decade tended to reduce them over time. While buoyant economic conditions contributed to this turnaround, the adoption of new consensus policies with emphasis on macro stability played a more crucial role. In the EU in particular, the Maastricht criteria set strict limits on

Table 15.2 Fiscal policy stance, 1990 and 2000 (% of GDP)

	1990	2000	Change
Japan			
Total *of which*:	2.9	−8.4	−11.3
Cyclical	1.2	−1.8	−3.0
Structural	1.7	−6.6	−8.3
European Union			
Total *of which*:	−3.6	−0.6	+3.0
Cyclical	1.6	−0.4	−2.0
Structural	−5.2	−0.2	+5.0
United States			
Total *of which*:	−2.7	−1.0	+3.7
Cyclical	1.1	+0.5	−0.6
Structural	−3.8	+0.5	+4.3

Source: IMF, *World Economic Outlook* (May 1996, May 2000).

the size of budget deficits and member states were urged to achieve fiscal balance over the medium term.

One must be careful about reading off a country's fiscal stance from simple examination of its fiscal balance. A budget deficit is not conclusive evidence of an expansionary budget. For example, if the economy is in recession, a budget deficit will tend to happen because of the operation of automatic stabilisers. To discover the fiscal stance, we need to delve deeper and find out what, if any, extra measures the authorities have taken in response to the situation. To do this, the budget balance is decomposed into a *cyclical* component and a *structural* component. Suppose, for example, the overall budget deficit was £1000 million and the economy was in a recession. Now replace actual GDP with potential GDP, and estimate the level of public spending, tax revenues and budget deficit corresponding to that (higher) level of output. We assume unchanged tax rates and a given set of spending rules. The deficit so estimated is termed the structural deficit. Assume it amounted to £250 million. The cyclical deficit is defined as the difference between the actual deficit (£1000 million) and the structural deficit (£250 million), i.e. £750 million.

A country's structural budget balance shows the extent to which discretionary fiscal measures are being applied. The conservative trend in the EU and the US is evidenced in the reduced size of their structural deficits between 1990 and 2000. Japan is, of course, a dramatic outlier. Its fiscal situation changed from a surplus of 2.9 per cent of GDP in 1990 to a deficit of 8.4 per cent in 2000 (Table 15.2). This involved an extraordinary injection of spending into the economy, equivalent to 11.3 percentage points of GDP. Cyclical factors explain part of this movement from surplus to deficit. Because of the recession, automatic stabilisers injected extra demand equivalent to three percentage points of GDP. The real story, however, concerns the *structural* deficit, which moved from a surplus of 1.7 per cent in 1990 to deficit of 6.6 per cent in 2000, a cumulative shift of 8.3 percentage points. Japan's commitment to fiscal activism must count as by far the most striking example of counter-cyclical policy in recent times. The use of discretionary action has not solved Japan's economic problems, nor has it restored growth, but it averted what might otherwise have been a catastrophic slump with global repercussions.

The aggressive deployment of fiscal policy in Japan contrasts with its more cautious use elsewhere in the world. Our next task is to consider why governments have generally become more conscious of the serious limitations of fiscal activism and their reluctance to resort to it except in extreme circumstances.

15.2 The limits of fiscal activism

> The scope for using fiscal policy to stimulate economic activity in the short term, in the traditional sense of taking action that would widen budget deficits, appears to be very circumscribed at present. (OECD, *Economic Outlook*, July 1993)

Report after report on fiscal policy in the 1990s referred to the lack of *room for manoeuvre* in budgetary policy and to the likelihood that further deterioration in budget deficits *would depress overall demand through its negative effect on confidence rather than support it.*[3] The 'unsound financial position' of many industrial countries has led to a conservative approach to fiscal policy. The Delors White Paper on competitiveness, for instance, concluded that, over the long term, member states' *budgetary policy will have to contribute to increased national savings, implying budget deficits of 0–1 per cent of GDP.* Achieving this range obliged most European governments to put any proposal for counter-cyclical deficits on the back-burner for a considerable time.

The change in perspective on fiscal activism can be explained under five main headings: knowledge gaps and time-lags; political intervention; inefficiencies of a growing public sector; private sector reactions (the Lucas critique); and historical evidence. In the next section, we address a further limitation: the deterrent effects of the public debt overhang (see Box 15.1).

Knowledge gaps and time-lags

Fiscal activism, like any other type of policy intervention, works effectively only if the authorities have adequate information on the problem they are supposed to be addressing. In addition to accurate information on the current level of aggregate demand and reliable forecasts of aggregate demand, one also needs estimates of what are called *policy lags*. Policy lags refer to the lapse of time between recognition of the need for counter-cyclical action, actual implementation of the required measures, and the impact of these measures on the economy.

---

3 These were the actual phrases used in Commission of the European Communities, *Growth, Competitiveness, Employment* (Brussels, 1993) (Delors Report), pp. 52–3. Similar views were expressed in UNICE, *Making Europe More Competitive: Towards world class performance* (the UNICE Competitiveness Report) (Brussels, June 1994).

Box 15.1

The limits of fiscal activism

Knowledge gaps and time-lags

- What is potential GDP?
- Poor forecasting record.
- Recognition, decision and implementation lags.

Political intervention

- Deficits politically more attractive than surpluses.
- Political (electoral) cycles – spending decisions influenced by timing of elections rather than stage of the business cycle.

Inefficiencies of the public sector

- Growth in public spending leads to a heavy tax burden which penalises entrepreneurship and wealth creation.
- High labour costs.

Private sector response

- Lucas critique – zero trade-off between inflation and unemployment unless inflation is a one-off 'surprise'.
- Ricardian equivalence considerations.

Empirical experience

- Deficits do not cure unemployment.

Deterrent effects of public debt overhang

- Sustainable public debt.
- Generational accounting.

The amount of information available to the authorities often falls far short of these requirements. Fiscal policy, like monetary policy, operates with *long and variable lags*, and these lags hinder and can frustrate its effective deployment. The information problem is a valid qualification on the use of fiscal activism and is widely recognised as such. However, *on its own*, it does not amount to a compelling case against counter-cyclical policy. A dedicated Keynesian might infer that it simply signals the need to improve the quality and timeliness of the information. Also, informational deficiencies have beset the application of fiscal policy since its beginning. They have scarcely become worse over time and do not explain why counter-cyclical policies seem to have become less effective over time.

Political interference

In theory, it should be possible to manage fiscal policy in such a way that budget deficits in recession are followed by budget surpluses in boom, with a consequent rise and fall in public debt accordingly. Yet in practice, public debt tended to rise over time as a proportion of GDP in countries that pursued active counter-cyclical policies. There has been a systematic bias towards deficits in the operation of fiscal policy. One reason for this is that deficits are more popular politically than surpluses. A government which tries to retrench during a boom will appear 'mean' and doctrinaire. By contrast, an expansionary budget will nearly always be popular.[4] Spending projects initiated during the recession tend to take on a life of their own. They become difficult to switch on and off according to the vicissitudes of the economy, as the textbooks ordain they should do.

Another limitation on fiscal activism is the intrusion of explicitly political considerations in the *timing* of fiscal action. The popularity of expansionary policies tempts governments to apply them in the run-up to election, regardless of economic circumstances. These 'political cycles' create, rather than suppress, economic instability. Also, political considerations lead to some budget measures (particularly the unpopular ones) being taken immediately *after* an election in certain circumstances. For example, a newly elected government might wish to administer unpleasant budgetary medicine as soon as possible after an election in the hope that the public's recollection of its actions might have receded by the time of the next election. Economic and political motivations become interwoven. It is not surprising, therefore, that fiscal policy has often been found to operate in a pro-cyclical, rather than a counter-cyclical, manner.[5] When the government sector is small, this is not too serious a problem. When public spending reaches over 40 per cent of GNP, politically motivated fiscal action can have serious consequences for the economy. Fiscal activism, which originated as a solution to the problem of economic stability, itself becomes the problem.

Inefficiencies of the public sector

In Europe, government spending relative to GDP rose from 32 per cent in 1960 to under 45 per cent in 2000 (Table 15.3). In the early 1990s, the ratio in Sweden (67 per cent), Denmark (59 per cent) and Norway (58 per cent) was higher still. Most of the increase occurred during the 1970s and early 1980s. Since then, the upward trend has been halted, though the early 1990s saw a renewed surge in spending. A similar pattern of behaviour is observable in the US, though current spending is still much higher than its 1937 level of only 8.6 per cent of GDP.

High government spending relative to GDP became a source of concern for a number of reasons. First, it was associated with excessively high taxation, which

---

4 Arguably, the only time a contractionary budget becomes even mildly acceptable electorally is during a recession, when it is inappropriate from an economic viewpoint.
5 For example, a group of Scandinavian economists have blamed expansionary budgetary policy for 'overheating' the Swedish economy during the emergence of each crisis up to the 1980s: A. Lindbeck *et al.*, *Turning Sweden Around* (Cambridge, MA: MIT Press, 1994), p. 48.

Table 15.3 Government spending (% GDP)

	Pre-Second World War (about 1937)	1960	1970	1984	1990	2000
EUR	29.0	32.2	37.4	50.0	48.1	44.0
Japan	25.4	17.1	19.4	32.9	32.3	31.8
US	8.6	27.0	31.6	35.6	36.8	33.4
France	29.0	34.6	38.9	52.5	50.6	47.7
Germany	42.4	32.5	38.5	47.6	45.3	44.0
Netherlands	19.0	33.7	42.4	59.6	55.0	42.1
Ireland	...	28.0	39.6	51.3	40.0	29.5
Italy	24.5	30.1	34.2	49.4	53.2	44.2
UK	30.0	32.2	37.3	45.3	40.3	36.8

Note: EUR figures refer to average of twelve member states except for 1960, 1970 which include only nine member states, and 1937 refers to five states (France, Germany, Italy, UK, Netherlands). Any resultant distortions are very small. The 1995 figure for Germany includes the former East Germany and is not strictly comparable with figures for earlier years.

Source: *European Economy*, Annual Report No. 59, 1995; *European Economy*, Special Supplement, Spring 1995; OECD; pre-Second World War figures taken from Vito Tanzi and Ludger Schuknecht, 'The Growth of Government and the Reform of the State in Industrial Countries', IMF Working Paper, December 1995; *European Economy* no. 68 (1999).

undermined incentives to hire labour and to invest. Small businesses were particularly affected, since they lacked the capacity of large multinationals to avoid taxes through 'spreading' revenues and costs in different tax jurisdictions. Second, high spending on transfer payments created problems. Excessively generous 'safety nets' for less fortunate citizens eroded incentives to work. Third, the conviction took root that government was in some vague sense 'too big' and that substantial efficiency gains could be obtained by devolving some public sector activities to the free market. Australia, New Zealand and the UK took the lead in the 1980s in rethinking and redesigning the role of the state so as to prepare their economies for the greater competition of an open trade environment. Their example was rapidly followed. Even the Scandinavian countries, long regarded as the epitome of successful market socialism, began to reshape their economies in a more market-oriented way. They are still in the process of downsizing their public sectors. The UNICE Competitiveness Report (1994) expressed a business view of the effects of public sector intervention in the European economy in the following terms:

> [Growth in public spending] has resulted in a heavy tax burden which penalises entrepreneurship and wealth creation, makes labour costs too high via taxes on production, [and] is also a factor in reducing the attraction of Europe as a location for investment. (*Making Europe More Competitive: Towards world class performance*, UNICE Competitiveness Report, Brussels, June 1994, p. 51)

The report urged governments *to set a target reduction for the share of public expenditure in GDP by the end of the century*. Similar sentiments were articulated in the proposals of the Republican Party's 'Contract with America' in the US in the mid-1990s. These initiatives created a climate of public opinion that cleared the way for radical fiscal reforms.

The private sector response

A fundamental premise of counter-cyclical fiscal policy is that unemployed resources can be mobilised by expanding aggregate demand, without causing inflation. Nobel prize-winner Robert Lucas challenged this theory on the grounds that an expansionary policy would cause inflation (because the aggregate supply curve was vertical). Lucas developed the *theory of rational expectations* which pointed out that rational agents' expectations of inflation are not based exclusively on past behaviour, as had been previously assumed, but take account of the future impact of present policy changes. Any attempt to use output-stimulating policy today at the cost of higher inflation tomorrow would be instantaneously recognised by alert, 'rational' agents. Their expectation of inflation would at once increase. Nominal interest rates would rise and investment would be discouraged. The hoped-for demand stimulus would be pre-empted.[6] Consequently, past behaviour is a poor guide for future policy decisions because policy decisions – and prospective changes in policy stances – affect the parameters of private sector decisions. The structure of the model is not policy-invariant. An implication is that policy simulations based on models of past behaviour are, in Lucas' own word, 'worthless'. This is the so-called *Lucas critique*.

The historical evidence

One powerful critique of fiscal activism is that it no longer seems to work. During the 1960s and early 1970s, counter-cyclical policies basked in the glow of full employment and rapid growth. After 1973, which in retrospect appears as a watershed in the debate, we saw the emergence of the decidedly un-Keynesian phenomenon of unemployment combined with inflation (*stagflation*). Evidence indicated that expansionary fiscal policy did little to raise the real level of output in the medium term, but instead stoked up inflationary pressures. These perceived failures of Keynesian remedies gave birth to a whole new set of theories which questioned, weakened and, for some, fatally undermined the theoretical case for activist fiscal policies.

Much cold water has, therefore, been thrown on earlier optimism concerning the power of counter-cyclical policies to solve macroeconomic problems. This caution has been reinforced by consideration of the long-run consequences of budget deficits – specifically the problem of escalating public debt.

---

6 The Lucas critique originated in a paper by R.E. Lucas, 'Expectations and the neutrality of money', *Journal of Economic Theory* (April 1972).

15.3 Public debt and 'crowding out'

Public debt in the industrial countries reached a peak of 71 per cent of GDP in 1995, double the 1974 ratio. The escalation in the debt: GDP ratio began in the 1970s. Prior to that, the debt ratio had been relatively stable and, in some countries, had fallen significantly from the postwar peaks. Debt problems did not feature much in economic debate.

Opinions began to change as the 1970s progressed. Economic growth rates fell, growth in government spending continued unabated and taxation also increased, sufficiently fast to cause serious distortions in incentives, but not fast enough to keep up with spending. Finally, the debt problem hit the headlines. The cases of Mexico and Poland in the early 1980s sent shock waves through the world's financial system. Soon afterwards, a long list of developing countries had to arrange what was euphemistically called a 'rescheduling' of their debts. Lenders began to focus with greater intensity on the *sustainability* of debt. The need to reduce debt to sustainable levels 'crowded out' analyses of counter-cyclical fiscal policies. The debt crises prompted heavily indebted countries everywhere to assess their vulnerability to the market, and to review their fiscal procedures and policies. In addition to this, with the reduction and removal of international capital controls, countries have been forced to pay much greater attention to what world financial markets think of their macroeconomic policies. The ageing of the population in the developed world added a further layer of concern about the sustainability of the debt. Thus, since the mid-1990s there has been an improvement in the debt positions of most industrial countries. For example, US debt decreased from 75 per cent of GDP in 1995 to 60 per cent in 2000 and the EU average from 75 per cent to 69 per cent (Table 15.4). There have been some spectacular cases. Ireland, the Netherlands and Denmark have all experienced reductions of above 20 percentage points over a short time frame. Nevertheless, the problem of debt overhang remains acute for several EU countries, notably Belgium, Italy and Greece, all of which have debt: GDP ratios exceeding 100 per cent. Also, Japan's debt has moved in a contrarian way, rising from 76 per cent to 113 per cent during the past five years, reflecting slow growth and vigorous expansionary fiscal policy.[7]

'Crowding-out' problems

The scale of the debt build-up led to a radical review by economists of the theoretical interactions between debt, deficits and private sector spending. One important result of this rethink was the development of the concept of *Ricardian*

---

7 Japan's debt position is complex. Its debt: GDP ratio is extremely high, well in excess of 100 per cent, but its net debt excluding social security assets is comparatively modest – it is the only major industrial country where social security assets are so sizeable. Its net debt excluding these assets was 79 per cent in 1998 (comparable figures are for the US, 56 per cent; the UK, 42 per cent; Germany, 52 per cent; and Canada, 62 per cent). All indicators show Japan's debt is growing at an unsustainable rate.

Table 15.4 General Government Net Debt (% GDP)

	1978	1990	1995	2000
EUR (15)	23.9	40.8	75.2	68.5
Japan	11.3	9.5	76.2	112.8
US	21.3	31.5	74.5	60.2
Belgium	57.2	124.9	129.8	109.8
Italy	62.4	103.7	123.1	112.9
Greece	29.4	89.0	108.7	103.8
Netherlands	40.2	75.6	75.5	56.5
Denmark	21.9	65.8	73.9	50.8
Portugal	37.6	65.3	65.9	58.8
Germany	30.1	42.0	59.1	63.5
France	31.0	39.5	59.3	63.9
Spain	14.4	48.5	68.4	65.7
UK	58.6	39.1	58.9	49.7
Ireland	65.7	92.6	80.8	42.9

Note: The gap between gross and net debt is extremely wide in the case of Japan; its net debt deducts social security assets from gross debt.

Source: European Monetary Institute, First Annual Report, April 1995. OECD Economic Outlook, various issues.

equivalence. The idea behind Ricardian equivalence is that, as public debt is incurred, people realise that taxes will sooner or later have to be raised to service it. Hence, it is a matter of indifference whether the deficit is financed by taxes today or by borrowing (taxes tomorrow). In order to provide for these higher future taxes, 'rational' households will raise their savings ratio (Box 15.2). By contrast, Keynesian theory assumed that, if a tax cut was financed by bonds, these bonds would be considered by economic agents as an addition to private sector wealth. Consumption was supposed to depend on current disposable income, not on the stream of lifetime post-tax earnings which a rational utility-maximising individual would consider the appropriate yardstick.[8] If Ricardian equivalence is right, the stimulus to aggregate demand by *government dissaving* (i.e. by a budget deficit) will be offset by a rise in *private sector saving*.

The 'crowding out' argument, like Ricardian equivalence, explores the rivalrous nature of the relation between public and private sector spending. *Crowding out* refers to the various ways by which changes in public spending impact negatively on private sector spending. A certain degree of 'crowding out' has always been recognised as a side-effect of expansionary policy. For example, a higher budget deficit might easily lead to a rise in interest rates. However, it was believed that interest rate increases could be limited by an accommodating monetary policy. The 'crowding out' problem was regarded as a qualification, rather than a fundamental criticism, of fiscal policy analysis. But Ricardian

---

8 Robert Barro, 'Are government bonds net wealth?', *Journal of Political Economy* (November 1974), was the first to draw attention to this issue in modern times. But it was David Ricardo, a leading nineteenth-century economist, who first raised the conundrum in 1821 as a theoretical possibility. He concluded, unlike Barro, that it was of no practical importance.

Box 15.2

Ricardian equivalence

Current budget deficits increase future tax liabilities. If taxpayers make full provision for them now, there is no difference between a government financing its expenditure by taxation and by borrowing. The economic impact of each option is equivalent. This insight owes its name to the nineteenth-century economist David Ricardo, but it was Robert Barro who reintroduced the idea in 1974 and explained its implications for household and business behaviour, fiscal policy and the analysis of public debt.

To see how the mechanism operates, suppose the government lowers taxes by £100 million, financed by an increase in borrowing, keeping government spending constant. Assume that the borrowing is financed by issuing a bond with a 10 per cent yield (equal to the rate of interest). Assume, further, that the government will raise taxes to pay the interest on these bonds and that repayment of the principal is indefinitely postponed. In each future year, taxes rise by 10 per cent of £100 million, or £10 million. Rational taxpayers will appreciate this and will adjust their lifetime spending plans to take account of the higher tax burden. If they could, they would like to set aside a lump sum to cover the present value of this future burden. What is this sum?

By the standard rule, the present value of the future increase in the tax burden (PV) in millions is given by:

$$PV = £10m/(1 + r) + £10m/(1 + r)^2 + £10m/(1 + r)^3 + £10m/(1 + r)^4 + \ldots + £10m/(1 + r)^n$$

$$\Rightarrow PV = £10m/r = £100m$$

In other words, the present value of the future tax burden exactly offsets the tax giveaway in the current year. Taxpayers are neither better- nor worse-off. The remarkable conclusion is that: *whether the government chooses to finance a given level of spending by taxation or by borrowing, the effect is the same.* Hence the name for this effect: *Ricardian equivalence.*

Ricardian equivalence theory has been criticised on three main grounds. First, if public debt can be perpetually rolled over, the burden of debt servicing can be passed to future generations and will not affect this generation's spending. Second, if capital markets are imperfect, and households and firms are subject to credit limitations, they may be prevented from behaving 'rationally', even if they wished to do so. Suppose the government ran a budget surplus in order to repay public debt. Ricardian equivalence states that households, buoyed up by the anticipated decline in future taxation, will respond by spending more now. But credit controls may prevent them from borrowing enough to do so. Third, reactions to debt appear to be sensitive to its size. When the debt ratio is low, people do not worry much about it. Ricardian equivalence may apply only after debt has breached a certain threshold.

There is some limited empirical evidence in favour of Ricardian equivalence. Tests have examined the relationship between private savings and budget deficits (if Ricardian equivalence prevails, one would expect higher deficits to lead to higher savings). An indirect test of Ricardian equivalence is to check for a zero association between higher budget deficits and higher interest rates.

> *Box 15.2 continued*
>
> There is evidence of strong *threshold effects*. Only when public debt is perceived as high and threatening may budget deficits spark off a Ricardian reaction. Fear of political instability will weaken business confidence, drive up interest rates and make consumers cautious. In such circumstances, a fiscal stimulus will be ineffective and possibly even counter-productive. By the same reasoning, *a determined attack on a budget deficit – what appears as fiscal contraction – can, in these circumstances, be expansionary.*
>
> Overall, the econometric evidence appears to rule out *complete* Ricardian equivalence. Tax cuts are not entirely translated into extra savings. Budget deficits do have real effects. Hence, the real world may be one of Ricardian near equivalence rather than literal equivalence. This still makes Ricardian equivalence an important concept for fiscal policy.
>
> *Source*: A. Chrystal and S. Price, *Controversies in Macroeconomics* (Hemel Hempstead: Harvester Wheatsheaf, 3rd edn, 1994); G. Nicoletti, 'A cross-country analysis of private consumption, inflation and the debt neutrality hypothesis', *OECD Economic Studies*, no. 11 (Paris: OECD, 1988).

equivalence, taken literally, opened the door to a *policy-ineffectiveness* hypothesis, whereby a rise in the budget deficit could be wholly offset by contractionary private reactions which governments are powerless to counter. Thus, in a world where people take a long-run view of future liabilities, neither subtractions nor additions to public sector debt, caused by budget surpluses or deficits, will affect aggregate demand.

Sustainable and unsustainable debt

Public debt is *sustainable* when it stops rising as a proportion of GDP. If debt is growing at a non-sustainable rate, the financial markets are likely to become alarmed. First, they fear that debtor governments will be tempted to reduce the real value of fixed-interest debt by inflation. Second, they fear the possibility of debt default, rescheduling of debt or imposition of a moratorium on interest payments.

Some heavily indebted countries have begun to use the attainment of a sustainable debt ratio as a target for fiscal policy. A formula for determining the stability condition is outlined in Appendix 15.1. The rule for stabilising debt is that:

$$b = (i - g)k$$

where b is the *primary balance* : GDP ratio (the primary budget balance is defined as the budget surplus (+) or deficit (−) less interest payments), i is the nominal rate of interest on the debt, g is the nominal growth rate of the economy, and k is the initial size of the debt : GDP ratio. The interest rate variable (i) determines how fast debt is growing. Clearly, it helps to stabilise the ratio if the interest rate is close to, or less than, growth in nominal GDP. If the nominal interest yield on government bonds (i) exceeds the nominal growth rate (g), the debt will tend to

Table 15.5 Share of over-65s in the population (%)

	1960	2000	2050
US	9.2	12.4	21.2
Japan	6.1	16.5	30.4
EC15	10.6	16.1	27.6

Note: The elderly dependency ratio is the population aged 65 and over expressed as a percentage of total population.

Source: Eurostat.

grow faster than GDP and the debt ratio will increase over time, unless there is a primary *surplus* in the budget (i.e. the value of *b* must be positive). The bigger the initial debt ratio (*k*), the greater the required primary surplus. The advantage of the debt formula is that it helps us to identify the specific debt ratio or budget balance to target in order to achieve stability of the debt ratio.

Another issue is the *appropriate definition of a country's indebtedness*. One important item excluded from formal calculations of public debt is unfunded state pension liabilities. For many developed countries, these liabilities represent a large outstanding claim on future resources given the projected rises in the number of elderly people over coming decades. In the US, for instance, the share of persons aged over 65 years is expected to rise from 12 per cent in 2000 to 21 per cent in 2050; in Japan, from 17 per cent to 30 per cent (Table 15.5). In the EU, the proportion of elderly persons aged over 65 will also increase. Relative to the 'active' age group (15–64) the elderly population will more than double between now and 2040. In Germany the ratio will be 48 per cent; in Italy 55 per cent; and in Spain, 49 per cent. If account is taken of the trend towards longer periods of education and earlier retirement, the dependency ratio could rise even faster. For example, the average life expectancy of a person aged 65 in America has risen from 73 years in 1940 to 84 years in 2000. Today, there are almost five working Americans for every retired person. By 2030, there will be fewer than three. This is a worrying increase in the dependency ratio, even if less pronounced than in Europe and Japan.

Several estimates have been made of the 'true' debt of the public sector, by computing the present discounted value of future pension liabilities. Unfunded pension liabilities range from less than 50 per cent of 1990 GDP for the US, to around 200 per cent of 1990 GDP in Japan, France and Italy (Table 15.6).[9] Clearly the link between ageing population and fiscal balance is most acute in those countries where pensions provision is primarily provided by the state on a pay-as-you-go basis.

Such calculations of the 'true' level of public debt could be criticised for featuring just one of many unfunded liabilities of the state. Unfunded health

---

9 P. Van den Noord and R. Herd, 'Estimating pensions liabilities: A methodological framework', *OECD Economic Studies* (Winter 1994). CS First Boston, *The Reworking of Europe – Employment and Hidden Debt* (London, 1993).

Table 15.6 Public sector debt and net public pensions liabilities, 1990 (% GDP)

	Public debt	Net pensions liabilities	Extended public debt
US	56	43	99
Japan	70	200	270
Germany	44	160	204
France	47	216	263
Italy	101	233	334
UK	35	100	135

Note: Estimated on the basis of earnings-related benefits indexed on prices after retirement and a discount rate in the range 3–4 per cent.

Source: Van Noord and Herd (1994).

entitlements, for example, are another source of concern because of the escalating cost of medical care.

Research on *generational accounting* attempts to broaden the coverage of calculation to include all taxes and transfers, not just pension liabilities (although they omit consideration of the value of government's real investments to future generations). These accounts indicate:

- the present value of *taxes* that each generation or age cohort (say, all 30-year-olds today) will pay on average over their remaining life;
- the present value of the *transfers* each generation will receive from public sector sources, such as social security, disability, health benefits, etc.

On the basis of such calculations, it is possible to compute the net balance for each generation. These more comprehensive estimates confirm the existence of a significant intergenerational imbalance. Future generations in the US, for example, may have to pay considerably more in the form of higher taxes (111 per cent more according to one estimate) than current newborns in order to finance the same level of government benefits per person as are currently provided. Generational accounting is now routinely used by the US and it is also being developed by the EU, Japan and Norway.[10]

On balance, the scale of unfunded liabilities and entitlements constitutes another powerful force, to be added to problems of implementing fiscal policy, the growth of conventional debt and Ricardian equivalence effects, impelling governments towards a more conservative fiscal policy (see Box 15.3). No wonder fiscal consolidation has become the guiding rule in the conduct of fiscal policy in recent years.

---

10 A.J. Auerbach, J. Gokhale and L. Kotlikoff, 'Generational accounting: A meaningful way to evaluate fiscal policy', *Journal of Economic Perspectives* (Winter 1994).

Box 15.3

Can fiscal contraction be expansionary?

Policy-makers are often reluctant to cut government deficits because of the fear that withdrawing fiscal stimulus might lower aggregate demand and cause unemployment. This fear is rooted in the standard Keynesian analysis, according to which increases in government expenditures are transmitted through a fiscal multiplier into increases in aggregate demand. The standard analysis also suggests that the effects of a fiscal contraction would be broadly symmetric to those of a fiscal expansion.

This assessment of the effects of reductions in budget deficits may not apply to countries with very large budgetary imbalances combined with high debt ratios. In such economies, a fiscal contraction may *increase* economic activity in both the short and the longer run. Attempts to explain this paradoxical outcome focus on the central role played by *expectations* about future policy actions and interest rates.

Suppose that a heavily indebted government with a large budget deficit makes a firm commitment to significantly reduce its budget deficit. Provided financial market participants regard the policy measures as fully credible, long-term interest rates are likely to fall quickly. A credible policy will be seen as evidence of the government's commitment to price stability and to its own financial integrity. Hence, the risk premium in long-term interest rates will decline.

A reduction in long-term interest rates will have expansionary effects on both demand and supply. By lowering the cost of capital, it will increase investment. The debt-servicing burdens of households, firms and the public sector will be eased, stimulating consumption and investment. Diminished uncertainty about the sustainability of the budgetary situation will boost confidence of investors and consumers. These expansionary effects might well outweigh the traditional negative short-term impulse from fiscal consolidation.

Empirical identification of expansionary fiscal contraction is difficult, since account must be taken of other factors which might have been responsible for the economic growth. There is, however, evidence of a negative fiscal multiplier from the experiences of the 1983–86 Danish stabilisation programme and the 1987–89 Irish stabilisation. In both cases, the fiscal imbalances before the intensification of consolidation efforts were clearly unsustainable and risk premia in interest rates were extremely high. Following the adoption of front-loaded fiscal consolidation programmes, which relied heavily on expenditure reductions, both countries rapidly experienced an improvement in economic performance, with stronger growth and declining unemployment. The coexistence of robust growth during periods of fiscal contraction in a number of developing and transition countries also suggests the possibility of a negative fiscal multiplier. At least for some countries, the 'macroeconomic model' used by market participants appears to be consistent with the existence of a negative multiplier.

Governments need to exploit these market sentiments in a constructive way. For countries with large fiscal imbalances and high levels of public debt, the economic outlook can be strengthened, even in the relatively near term, by the adoption of strong deficit reduction measures. The credibility of such a fiscal adjustment programme would be enhanced by front-loaded action to achieve the necessary degree of medium-term fiscal consolidation.

Box 15.3 continued

The precise way in which fiscal adjustment is implemented seems to be important. Fiscal contraction by spending cuts is effective, whereas taxation increases can have a depressing effect on growth. This is because an increase in taxation raises the cost structure of the economy, worsens its competitiveness and can be read by the market as a signal of postponed adjustment.

Sources: For a theoretical derivation of the proposition that a fiscal deficit can have a contractionary effect, see Alan Sutherland 'Fiscal crises and aggregate demand: can high public debt reverse the effects of fiscal policy?' *Journal of Public Economics*, 65 (1997). Frank Barry and Michael Devereux, 'The macroeconomics of government budget cuts: Can fiscal contractions be expansionary?', in William Robson and William Scarth (eds), *Deficit Reduction: What Pain, What Gain?* (Toronto: C.D. Howe Institute, 1994), provides a useful survey of the literature. Ireland's experience is described in Dermot McAleese, 'Ireland's economic recovery', *The Irish Banking Review* (Summer 1990), updated in 'The Celtic Tiger: Origins and Prospects', *Policy Options Politiques*, July/August 2000.

15.4 Fiscal policy in Europe

The Treaty of the European Union 1992 (or Maastricht Treaty) laid down a number of rules governing the conduct of fiscal policy. These rules were intended to apply both in the run-up to economic and monetary union (EMU), and after EMU was established. They throw interesting light on the close links which European policy-makers believe to exist between fiscal policy and price stability. Underlying the Maastricht criteria was the conviction that the new European currency would be accepted only if price stability within the euro area was assured, and that this would be achieved only if member states' borrowing and debt were strictly limited.

Before being admitted to the monetary union, member states had to comply with two fiscal conditions: (a) the budget deficit : GDP ratio must not exceed 3 per cent; and (b) the ratio of government debt to GDP must not exceed 60 per cent (Table 15.7). Under the Treaty, the Commission has to make the initial evaluation of a member state's position, but member states took a collective view on the admissibility of candidates. To judge from the data in Table 15.7, some flexibility in interpretation of the debt : GDP rule was applied in determining eligibility for EMU in 1998. Two participating states, Belgium and Italy, had debt ratios exceeding 100 per cent.

A number of supporting provisions were added to the original fiscal clauses under the Stability and Growth Pact (1997). First, central banks were forbidden to provide overdrafts to governments or to purchase government securities directly in support of budget deficits. Second, the Commission and other member states were precluded from rescuing a member state which defaults on its debt (the 'no bail-out' clause). Linked with this was the provision that governments cannot even have privileged access to financial institutions (such as concessionary interest rate or loan privileges).

Table 15.7 Maastricht fiscal targets v actual levels

	Borrowing target: 3% of GDP Borrowing 1999		Debt target: 60% of GDP Debt Ratio 1999		Pass or fail	
	1996	1999	1996	1999	1996	1999
Austria	−5.1	−2.0	72.4	64.0	F	F
Belgium	−3.4	−0.9	132.2	110.0	F	F
Denmark	−1.0	+3.0	71.0	49.3	F	P
Finland	−3.0	+2.3	62.5	42.6	F	P
France	−4.2	−1.8	56.1	58.2	F	P
Germany	−3.9	−1.1	61.5	60.7	F	F
Greece	−7.9	−1.6	111.8	103.7	F	F
Ireland	−2.6	+2.0	81.3	45.2	F	P
Italy	−6.8	−1.9	124.5	110.8	F	F
Luxembourg	1.5	+2.4	6.2	5.8	P	P
Netherlands	−3.5	+0.5	79.4	58.7	F	P
Portugal	−4.5	−2.0	72.2	57.0	F	P
Spain	−4.7	−1.1	67.8	62.3	F	F
Sweden	−4.5	+1.9	80.8	61.3	F	F
UK	−3.8	+1.2	55.5	42.4	F	P
EU(15)	−4.2	−0.6	72.0	67.6		

Note: General government net lending (+) or borrowing (−) as a percentage of GDP; general government gross debt as a percentage of GDP. P and F indicates pass or fail to satisfy the Maastricht Treaty fiscal criteria. Definitions of debt and deficits differ from those of OECD used in previous tables.

Source: Economic Forecasts (Spring 2000) *European Economy*.

The obligation to avoid 'excessive government deficits' is an essential element in the strategy to ensure price stability. But, once in the single currency system, what is to stop a member state breaking out of these disciplines? The sanctions proposed to deal with such eventualities are outlined in Box 15.4.

'Market' restraints can be expected to reinforce the institutional restraints, operating mainly through the interest rate. But the disciplinary weight of this constraint has yet to be ascertained. Although budget deficits and the long-term interest rate are positively correlated, the sensitivity of bond yields to the level of a member state's borrowing and debt may be much weaker in a single currency than in a multi-currency Europe. For example, only a weak relationship between the debt ratio and interest rates has been found in a study of state finances in the US.[11] Here, the main disciplinary mechanisms seem to originate in budgetary rules and legislation. While up to the late 1970s the US federal government gave large grants-in-aid to the states, with the aim of creating a level playing field in basic economic infrastructure, since then the system has evolved into one of

---

11 B. Eichengreen, 'One money for Europe? Lessons for the US currency union', *Economic Policy* (April 1990).

Box 15.4

Fiscal discipline in the EMU

Once member states have joined the EMU, the Maastricht conditions must continue to be met and the Treaty lays down conditions to ensure this is so. The Stability and Growth Pact (1997) elaborated on these fiscal rules. Additional measures are specified in instances where governments run 'excessive' budget deficits. These measures are:

- The member state at fault will have to publish additional information, to be specified by the Council, before issuing further bonds and securities.
- The European Investment Bank will be asked to consider its lending policies towards that state.
- The member state may be required to make a non-interest bearing deposit with the Community until the excessive deficit has, in the view of the Council, been corrected.
- The Commission may impose fines.
- Member states will not be allowed to vote on their case during the process of review.

A number of steps must be completed before the Council can decide that an excessive deficit exists:

1. Failure to meet criteria must be determined by a Commission report which takes account of 'all relevant factors'.
2. The Commission report is sent to the Council which undertakes an assessment as to whether a failure does indeed exist.
3. The Council makes recommendations and implements sanctions.

Source: Treaty of the European Union, art. 104; Stability and Growth Pact.

'competitive federalism',[12] whereby states are expected to finance an increasing proportion of their own activities. An interesting feature of the system is that, while most US states impose a balanced-budget provision or public debt limitation, the initiatives for such fiscal restraint seem to have been locally generated. Many states use tax/expenditure legislation, or line-item veto authority by state governors, to control the budget. These measures oblige states to increase taxes, or to reduce spending, if budget deficits are excessive. Interest rates do not appear to be the main disciplinary mechanism. The imperative of remaining cost competitive *vis-à-vis* other states obliges state governments to focus their spending carefully. 'Fiscal mercantilism' is a phrase sometimes used to describe the use of fiscal instruments (special grants and tax concessions) to

---

12 The key change occurred in 1978. This was the year of Proposition 13 in California, which initiated a tax revolt that swept across the US. The proposition, passed by referendum, cut back property taxes, limited future increases to 2 per cent per year and dictated that state tax increases must pass both houses of the California state legislature with a two-thirds majority. The architects of this proposal reshaped the role played by the public sector in California.

attract economic activity from one area to another. A classic example is the migration of many corporations to New Jersey in order to escape high taxes in New York City.

The Maastricht criteria and the Stability and Growth Pact were designed to force EU member states to maintain fiscal balance. But balance may be brought about by any number of different combinations of spending and taxation. Business lobbies are pushing hard to ensure that low deficits will be achieved at low levels of taxation and spending. Between 1990 and 1996, government spending as a percentage of GDP rose from 48 per cent to 50 per cent in the EU-15. A fall in the government spending ratio took place in only three of the 15 member states: Belgium, Ireland and the Netherlands. Since then, the arguments of the 'smaller government' lobby have gained more acceptance. Some decline in the spending : GDP ratio has occurred, although automatic stabilisers have contributed to the decline also.

Thus, many governments in Europe have become converted to the belief that the public sector's share of GDP is excessively high. There is general support for curbing the growth of public spending, seeking more efficient ways of managing public services and privatising activities which are not essential for government to manage. New ideas have also been advanced regarding the distribution of taxes. As we saw in Chapter 9, proposals have been made to intensify environmental taxation and reduce taxes on labour. *Fiscal reform* has joined *fiscal balance* as an issue commanding the attention of European governments.

Finally, it is worth noting that fiscal activism has not been altogether ruled out by EU rules. The Stability and Growth Pact states that:

> Each member will commit itself to aim for a medium term budgetary position of close to balance or surplus. This will allow the automatic stabilisers to work, where appropriate, over the whole business cycle without breaching the 3 per cent reference value for the deficit.

Thus a country with a 2 per cent budget surplus could, if necessity arose, inject a fiscal stimulus of 5 percentage points of GDP without breaching the maximum deficit. Some view this as providing reassuring scope for the use of fiscal tuning. Others worry that the euro area members will find the constraints burdensome and inappropriate in the event of a major economic crisis, a worry that will be accentuated by the addition of new, economically weaker members to the euro area. Pressures on fiscal balance arising from the pensions cost of Europe's ageing population will also remain an ongoing concern for European policymakers.

15.5 Conclusions

The most significant factor affecting the conduct of fiscal policy in recent times has been the need to control public sector debt. Heavily-indebted countries were paying what is known as the *debt penalty* – their governments were borrowing in order to stand still. As the interest burden grows, two consequences can be observed. First, any stimulatory effect of a public sector deficit diminishes, sometimes even to the point where a deficit actually causes an economic contraction. Second, over time the deficit becomes a source of structural distortion, through rising taxes and lower investment. *The deficit, originally intended as a solution to the problem of low growth and unemployment, becomes part of the problem itself.*

As interest payments on debt increase, governments are forced to focus on the *primary budget balance*, i.e. the budget balance net of interest payments. Countries with fiscal problems and significant levels of outstanding debt – for example, Greece, Italy and Belgium – find that, in order to stabilise the debt, they must run large primary surpluses. A high, and rising, debt : GDP ratio arouses fears that a government may be tempted to 'inflate' its way out of the debt problem, thereby alleviating the real burden of its fixed interest debt. No matter how vigorously an indebted government may protest its intention not to resort to such an expedient, the financial markets will remain nervous and will demand an interest rate premium to compensate for the risk. This risk premium has adverse implications for investment which, in turn, exacerbates the deficit problem.

High debt : GDP ratios have led to a decoupling between financial markets and the markets for real goods and services. Financial markets have become more volatile. Fiscal policy has become more constrained than previously by the sometimes fickle judgement of financial markets. The liberalisation of the financial sector has further constrained the ability of countries to run expansionary fiscal policies. Fiscal policy has now to be conducted more carefully than hitherto, particularly by countries with already high borrowing. Furthermore, EMU fiscal rules have stipulated quite specific constraints on existing and prospective member states of the euro area.

Better control of budget deficits will, it is hoped, lead to greater efficiency in government spending and a more enterprise-friendly tax system. A lower deficit means that the government is borrowing less from the pool of national savings. These savings can therefore be redeployed to finance private sector investment which, so it is argued, will yield greater productivity per worker than public sector spending. Professor Alan Blinder, in a presentation to President-elect Clinton in 1993, predicted that a deficit reduction programme would result in lower interest rates, more business confidence and *a 1 per cent increase in the US's standard of living after four years.*[13] Projections of this type rest on the assumption that, in the long run, resources released by a cutback in government will be absorbed by the private sector. In the *short run*, deficit reduction (and structural readjustment) might lead to losses of output and jobs, just as the Keynesian model would predict. But *as the debt level increases, the potential contractionary effect of fiscal cutbacks diminishes.* A key factor is the reaction of the financial markets. If they believe the deficit reduction programme will be adhered to, they will respond by buying more bonds, thus driving down long-term interest rates. The resultant

---

13 This perspective, according to one source, was advanced strongly by Professors Blinder and Summers, saying that the contractionary impact of deficit reduction might not be as great as predicted. See Bob Woodward, *The Agenda: Inside the Clinton White House* (New York: Simon & Schuster, 1994), pp. 83–6.

relief to mortgage holders and businesses generates more investment and consumer spending.

How much more spending? A new feature of the debate on this question is the growing awareness of the importance of *private* debt as well as *public* debt in influencing expenditure by the private sector. The huge increase in household debt : disposable income ratios has had a profound effect through the 1990s on consumer demand in the UK, Japan, the US and the Scandinavian countries. It has enhanced the impact of real wealth effects on private sector spending. Thus, the effects of changes in interest rates may prove to be a more potent force nowadays than in the past. A decline in interest rates has psychological, political and economic dimensions. Theories of expansionary fiscal contraction draw on all these aspects. They imply that deficit reduction of sufficient magnitude and of the right quality could even be 'costless'. Some European governments, for example, have been able to cut their deficits without detriment to economic growth.

Fiscal policy, however, still has a role to play in stabilising the economy. Automatic stabilisers continue to perform a valuable function, and will continue to do so as long as government remains a key player in the economy. In addition, structural changes in the budget may also be required to deal with *severe* downturns or upturns. Instead of 'fine-tuning' aggregate demand, fiscal policy may have to settle for the more modest objective of 'coarse-tuning', that is, responding only to prospective major deviations from potential output.[14] Singapore, for example, cushioned the fallout from the regional currency crisis by deliberate fiscal stimulus in 1998. This involved engineering a budget deficit for the first time in a decade. A balanced budget is not, in all circumstances, a sign of good economic management.[15]

The need for such intervention may be prompted by external disturbances or domestic shocks such as a collapse in asset prices or a sudden shift in investment demand. The scope for fiscal policy being effective will, however, depend on international responses. A small country, in particular, may find a proposed fiscal expansion, through, say, a tax cut, being frustrated by leakages through imports (consumers may spend a large part of their additional disposable income on imported cars or foreign holidays) or by capital outflows (if bond holders and investors lose confidence in the government). Increasingly, fiscal policy will have to be implemented on a coordinated basis if it is to be effective. Single country fiscal initiatives are likely to be frustrated, as the failure of President Mitterrand's efforts to spend France out of the early 1980s recession demonstrated. The open-economy dimensions of fiscal policy are discussed further in Part III.

The accumulation of public debt and the growing sophistication of markets have made demand management policy more problematic and less effective. This is a fact of life, deserving neither praise nor condemnation. It is not necessarily a

---

14 A. Lindbeck *et al.*, *Turning Sweden Around* (Cambridge, MA: MIT Press, 1994).
15 G. Nicoletti, 'A cross-country analysis of private consumption, inflation and the debt neutrality hypothesis', *OECD Economic Studies*, No. 11 (Paris: OECD, 1988).

'good' development for the world economy. The belief that counter-cyclical policy did work, and could be applied, kept business confidence and investment high for many decades. 'Thinking made it so' – the belief that the economy would never be allowed to slide into depression ensured that depressions were avoided. We have referred on more than one occasion to the sustained growth of the postwar economy and the much reduced amplitude of business fluctuations during this period. Fiscal policy objectives have been radically revised because of a fear of the financial collapse of heavily indebted countries, and also because of a widespread belief that the marginal productivity of public sector spending has declined. This latter belief has fuelled the movement towards 'smaller government' and to a comprehensive review of the economic role of government in the field of micro- as well as macroeconomic policy.

✔ Summary

1. The approach suggested by counter-cyclical, or Keynesian, fiscal policy is fiscal stimulus when the economy is operating below full employment, and fiscal contraction when the economy is at full employment. This theory transformed not only the way economists thought about fiscal policy, but also the way fiscal policy was conducted in industrial economies. Counter-cyclical policy focused on the policy mix between fiscal and monetary policy, ways of identifying how much extra aggregate demand was needed and the size of the fiscal injection needed to shift aggregate demand to the required degree.

2. The unsound financial position of many industrial countries has forced governments to reassess the role of fiscal policy. This change in perspective on fiscal activism can be explained under six main headings: (a) knowledge gaps and time-lags, where the amount of necessary accurate information available to authorities often fell short of their requirements; (b) political considerations, which distorted the extent and timing of fiscal action; (c) inefficiencies of the public sector, which have led to public opinion becoming more critical of budget deficits than in the past; (d) links between aggregate demand and inflation, proposed by the Lucas critique; and (e) evidence accumulated in the 1970s that expansionary fiscal policy did little to raise the real level of output in the medium term, but instead stoked up inflationary pressures, and finally (f) the adverse impact of rising public debt on interest rates and investment.

3. The escalation of public sector debt led to a radical review by economists of the theoretical interactions between debt, deficits and private sector spending. Out of this review emerged the development of the concept of Ricardian equivalence. It has also stimulated fresh investigation into the issue of the sustainability of public debt. The appropriate definition of a country's indebtedness has also received attention, since formal calculations of public debt exclude unfunded state pension liabilities. Research on generational

accounting attempts to broaden the coverage of calculation to include all taxes and transfers, not just pension liabilities.

4. The Maastricht Treaty laid down a number of rules governing the conduct of fiscal policy which were intended to apply both to existing and aspiring members of the euro. Before being admitted to the monetary union, member states had to comply with two fiscal conditions: (a) the budget deficit : GDP ratio must not exceed 3 per cent; and (b) the ratio of government debt to GDP must not exceed 60 per cent. There is general support for curbing the growth in public spending, seeking more efficient ways of managing public services and privatising activities which are not essential for government to manage. Fiscal reform has joined fiscal balance as an issue commanding the attention of European governments.

5. Fiscal policy still has a role to play in steadying the economy and, in particular, in preventing major downturns and booms. Instead of fiscal fine-tuning, however, we shall have to be satisfied with coarse-tuning policies, applied with circumspection.

Questions for discussion

1. Business often supports the objective of fiscal rectitude in the belief that it will lead to lower taxes. Explain how these two phenomena are linked.

2. A lobby group suggests a constitutional amendment to the effect that government budgets must be balanced, arguing that allowing politicians discretionary power leads to large deficits and escalating debt. Analyse this proposal.

3. The government plans a reduction in income taxes, to be financed by borrowing, with the aim of increasing demand to stimulate the economy. Discuss this policy proposal. In your reply, comment on the perspective of Ricardian equivalence proponents on such a proposal.

4. Discuss the ways in which a persistent budget deficit could lead to inflation.

5. Explain why, and how, a country's public debt, if it exceeds a certain threshold level, might lead to a contractionary budget having a stimulating effect on aggregate demand (expansionary fiscal contraction).

Exercises

1. Assume the following situation occurred in an economy:

   Unemployment rises and output falls dramatically, consumption and investment fall, and interest rates decline. The money supply declines and prices actually fall. Furthermore, the stock market crashes.

   Propose remedies for this situation.

2. The 1996 Annual Economic Report of the European Commission stated that (in reference to the French economy):

    fiscal consolidation is a necessary condition for a stable macroeconomic environment conducive to growth and employment. It should enable an easing of monetary policy, compatible with the monetary stability objective, which should offset the adverse effect on economic activity of budgetary restraint. (p. 24)

    Explain each step of this argument by answering the following questions:

    (a) What is a stable macroeconomic environment?
    (b) What is meant by fiscal consolidation?
    (c) Why is (b) necessary for (a)?
    (d) Through what mechanisms would (a) be conducive to growth and employment?
    (e) Revise your understanding of the terms 'an easing of monetary policy' and 'monetary stability' (see Chapter 13).
    (f) What evidence would you wish to consult in order to be satisfied that monetary policy could be 'eased' without endangering 'the monetary stability objective'?

3. Would an average, well-run business agree to limit itself to a zero borrowing target over the business cycle? Why do some business lobbies urge governments to constrain government spending according to this rule? Is this a sensible rule for governments to adopt?

4. A country has a debt ratio of 130 per cent of GDP, it pays 10 per cent interest on this debt and its nominal growth rate is 7 per cent. What primary balance (as per cent of GNP) should it be targeting if it wants to stabilise the debt ratio? You are told that its total deficit is currently running at 9 per cent of GDP. Does this country have a fiscal problem?

    Another country has a debt ratio of 40 per cent, it pays 7 per cent interest and its nominal GDP is growing at 6 per cent annually. Its present total budget deficit : GNP ratio is 1.7 per cent. Is this country's debt ratio growing or declining?

    Do these figures approximate the position in any of the countries which are listed in the tables to this chapter?

5. New Zealand's Fiscal Responsibility Act 1994 requires the government to identify and publish its fiscal objectives. The New Zealand government has specified prudent levels of public debt to be below 30 per cent of GDP in the short run and below 20 per cent in the longer term.

    Are these targets high or low by international standards?

    Would you recommend other governments to follow New Zealand's example?

📖 Further reading

A useful assessment of fiscal policies for the euro area is provided in OECD *Economic Outlook* (December 1998), 'Challenges for monetary and fiscal policies in the euro area'. The implications of population ageing are addressed in ECB *Monthly Bulletin* (July 2000). A business-oriented view of government spending and debt is lucidly articulated in the UNICE Competitiveness Report, *Making Europe More Competitive: Towards world class performance* (Brussels, June 1994). The Ricardian equivalence concept was introduced into the modern fiscal debate in 1974. Its author, R.J. Barro, summarises the argument and subsequent criticisms in 'The Ricardian approach to budget deficits', *Journal of Economic Perspectives* (Spring 1989). The classic statement of the Lucas critique appears in R.E. Lucas, 'Expectations and the neutrality of money', *Journal of Economic Theory* (April 1972).

Appendix 15.1: The sustainability of debt

Let D = Total Nominal Debt, Y = Nominal GDP and k = Debt : GDP ratio.

Then:

$$k = D/Y \tag{1}$$

Differentiating (1) we obtain:

$$\frac{dk}{dt} = \frac{\frac{dD}{dt} \cdot Y - \frac{dY}{dt} \cdot D}{Y^2} \tag{2}$$

The growth rate of the debt, dD/dt, is by definition,

$$\frac{dD}{dt} = B + iD \tag{3}$$

where B = primary deficit (i.e. the budget deficit *less* interest payments on outstanding debt); and iD = interest payments on debt.

By inserting (3) into (2), the growth of the Debt : GDP ratio, dk/dt, may therefore be written as:

$$\frac{dk}{dt} = \frac{(B + iD)Y - \frac{dY}{dt} \cdot D}{Y^2}$$

$$= \frac{(B + iD)Y}{Y^2} - \frac{\frac{dY}{dt} \cdot D}{Y^2}$$

$$= \frac{B + iD}{Y} - \frac{\frac{dY}{dt}}{Y} \cdot \frac{D}{Y}$$

$$= \frac{B}{Y} + i \cdot \frac{D}{Y} - g \cdot \frac{D}{Y}$$

$$= b + i.k - g.k$$

$$\frac{dk}{dt} = b + (i - g)k \tag{4}$$

where: $b = B/Y$ = ratio of primary deficit to GDP; and $g = (dY/dt)/Y$ = growth rate of nominal GDP.

The condition for $dk/dt = 0$, that is for a stabilisation in the Debt : GDP ratio, is:

$$b = (i - g)k \tag{5}$$

If the nominal interest rate exceeds the nominal GDP growth rate, i.e. $i > g$, the stability condition indicates that there must be a primary surplus (b must be positive). If the growth rate exceeds the interest rate, a primary deficit is consistent with a stable debt ratio provided it docs not exceed $(i - g)k$.

Consider the case of a country with a current debt : GDP ratio (k) of 60 per cent, running a primary deficit/GDP (b) of 1.5 per cent, paying an interest rate of 6 per cent on debt and with a nominal growth rate of 4 per cent. In this situation its debt : GDP ratio will grow this year at the rate of 2.76 per cent.

$$\begin{aligned}
\frac{dk}{dt} &= b + (i - g)k \\
&= 0.015 + (1.06 - 1.04)(0.60) \\
&= 0.0276
\end{aligned}$$

To stabilise the debt ratio, the primary deficit and/or the initial debt : GDP ratio must be reduced. To find by how much, we set the above equation (4) equal to zero. Suppose a debt : GDP ratio of 60 per cent is agreed, then the formula indicates that it will be necessary to convert the primary deficit of 1.5 per cent into a primary surplus of 1.2 per cent ($b = 0.012$):

$$\begin{aligned}
\frac{dk}{dt} &= b + (i - g)k = 0 \\
0 &= b + (1.06 - 1.04)0.60 \\
b &= -0.012
\end{aligned}$$

Interest rates on government bonds have often been higher than nominal growth rates. For instance, the average annual long-term interest rate in the US for 1994 was 7.1 per cent while the growth rate was 6.2 per cent. In the case of the UK the corresponding figures were 8.2 per cent and 5.9 per cent and for Germany 6.9 per cent and 5.1 per cent. Since all these countries had an outstanding debt ratio, the condition for stabilisation required a primary surplus. By the end of the century the situation had changed radically; nominal GDP exceeded long-term interest rates in both the US and the UK.

Government budget constraint

$$(G - T) + iD = \frac{dD}{dt} + \frac{dM}{dt}$$

$$= \text{change in debt} + \text{change in money supply}$$

where G = government spending less interest on debt
T = net taxation
iD = interest on debt.

Since Maastricht regulations forbid monetary financing of the debt, $dM/dt = 0$, then

$$(G - T) + iD = \frac{dD}{dt} = B + iD$$

Hence the derivation of equation (3) above.

Chapter 16

BUSINESS FLUCTUATIONS AND FORECASTING

The inevitability of the business cycle, as it used to be called, I take for granted. Good times bring into existence: first, incompetent business executives; second, wrongful government policies; and, third, speculators. Working together, they ensure the eventual bust.

> J. K. Galbraith, 'Challenges of the new millennium', *Finance and Development* (December 1999), p. 5.

It is not enough to assert that since there have always been business cycles there always will be business cycles. Understanding what causes business cycles and how these causes have changed suggests that business cycles will not be as important in the future as they were in the past.

> S. Weber, 'The end of the business cycle', *Foreign Affairs* (July 1997), p. 67.

Introduction

Fluctuations in economic growth are an endemic feature of industrial economies. Periods of above-average growth tend to be succeeded by periods of below-average growth. Occasionally, the level of economic activity declines even in absolute terms. These economy-wide trends are mirrored across a wide range of industries. However, macroeconomic cycles must be distinguished from cycles which are particular to individual industries. The latter can sometimes be entirely independent of the former. Some industries are in long-run decline (steel, coal), while others (personal computers, mobile telephones) are enjoying a sustained boom, even during economic recessions.

From a business perspective, the timing of these upturns in economic activity can have a crucial bearing on product prices and corporate profits. A takeover deal, or an investment in a new market, which might be profitable if completed at the start of an economic upturn, could prove disastrous if succeeded by an economic downturn. Property and construction are particularly prone to cyclical fluctuations, but so is the demand for many consumer goods which are dependent on discretionary spending, such as fashion clothing and household durables. Business fluctuations have a major impact on the profits of the banking sector. Non-performing loans and the number of business failures tend to move in unison with the state of health of the economy. The instability of the market system, therefore, is a matter of profound practical importance.

For this reason, companies put considerable resources into predicting the course of the cycle and estimating the implications of the cycle for their sales and costs. The most widely read, and eagerly sought, economic articles among the business community tend to be those containing economic forecasts and projections. These are prepared by international organisations such as the World Bank, International Monetary Fund, OECD and the European Commission, and also by national research institutes, banks and stockbrokers. Some large corporations prepare their own projections. The demand for these forecasts fluctuates in line with the cycle itself, as many economic forecasters have had occasion to discover. When profits decline, the providers of macroeconomic forecasts and statistics tend to be among the first casualties!

In this chapter we use the terms *fluctuations* and *cycles* interchangeably. 'Cycle' implies the existence of regular fluctuations of equal size and timespan. Postwar empirical analysis suggests that economic fluctuations are, in fact, quite irregular. To be sure, there are peaks and troughs in GNP, but the time-lapse between them, and the size of the gap between peak and trough, varies markedly from case to case. The term 'fluctuations' gives a more accurate impression of the phenomenon.

The severity of economic fluctuations has moderated significantly since the inter-war period. There has been no repeat of the Great Depression (August 1929 to March 1933), which involved a 53 per cent fall in US industrial production and a 32 per cent decline in non-farm employment.[1] Yet two severe recessions occurred in the 1970s, the second of which lasted into the early 1980s, and another downturn was recorded in the early 1990s. From a systemic viewpoint, these postwar fluctuations have been relatively limited in severity. However, although mild in a macro-sense, they have had serious implications for many firms and have spelled disaster for others.

The reasons for a more stable performance of the industrialised economies have been much analysed. One explanation focuses on the growing share of sectors such as health and education in economic activity as a nation becomes more prosperous. Demand for such activities is more stable than for others. Another, not unrelated, explanation attributes a strong stabilising role to government spending, which, until the 1990s, had also been increasing its share in national output. Public sector spending is much less dependent on the performance of the economy than private sector spending. Demand management policies (in the 'coarse-tuning' sense described in our chapter on fiscal policy) have also played an important part in saving the economy from a really major depression.

Chapter outline

This chapter analyses the topic of business fluctuations in five steps:

1. The size, duration and incidence of these fluctuations. We focus on the larger economies, because many smaller economies experience upturns and downturns in a passive sense, buoyed up or sucked down mostly by the changing fortunes of their larger trading partners.

---

1 V. Zarnovitz, 'Theory and history behind business cycles: Are the 1990s the onset of a golden age?', *Journal of Economic Perspectives* (Spring 1999).

2. The causes of these fluctuations and the reasons for their diminished amplitude. This raises the question of whether, in today's more open and market-driven economy, we can continue to assume that the amplitude of the cycle will remain subdued.

3. The effects of business fluctuations. Obviously, they matter to individual firms. Do they still matter if all firms are taken together? In other words, is overall economic growth adversely affected by business fluctuations?

4. Predicting economic fluctuations and the accuracy of economic forecasts.

5. The link between macroeconomic forecasts and company projections.

16.1 Business fluctuations – the facts

Business cycles refer to fluctuations in aggregate economic activity that are widely diffused throughout the economy and have identifiable 'peaks' and 'troughs'. Recovery and expansion is followed by downturn and contraction. Identifying the precise contours of a particular business cycle, and defining its turning point and peak, can be a complex statistical exercise, but such complications are not considered here. Cyclical analysis can be performed on a large range of variables, but most macro-studies focus on industrial production, GDP and investment. In part, this choice is dictated by data availability – volume indices for services (which account for a much larger proportion of GDP than industry) are highly unreliable. Traditionally, industrial production has been regarded as a key source of instability in an industrial economy and manufacturing is a leading sector in generating cycles. Most modern studies focus on *growth cycles*, i.e. deviations from trend growth of the aggregate variable chosen for investigation, whereas formerly analysis focused on the *'classical'* cycle, i.e. changes in the absolute value of the aggregate variable.

The salient features of business fluctuations can be traced with the assistance of Figure 16.1. This tracks GDP growth rates for a selection of major industrial countries during the period 1961–2000:

1. The infrequent incidence of negative growth rates is striking – over the 40-year period, only four such instances were recorded in the US, two in Japan, three in Germany and three in the UK.[2]

2. There are significant fluctuations around the average (and trend) growth rates for each of the countries. Each growth cycle tends to have a different amplitude and different periodicity than the others. The sequence of change from boom to contraction is *recurrent, but not periodic*.

3. No compelling evidence has been found to confirm the existence of systematic long-run cycles such as the Kondratieff 40–50-year cycle or the Juglar 10-year cycle. Yet the search for regularities in the data continues.

---

2 Most cyclical analysis uses quarterly data which provide a greater degree of variation than the annual data, but suggest the same qualitative conclusions.

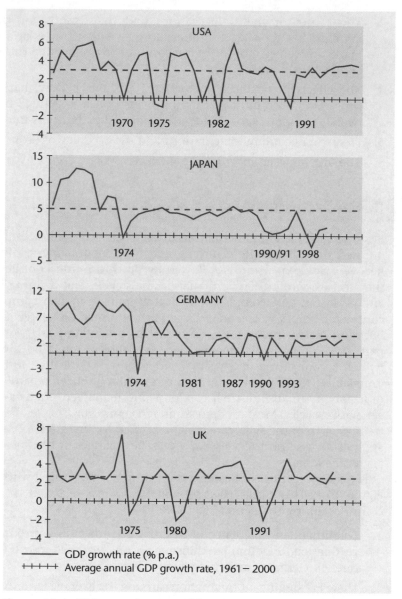

Figure 16.1 GDP growth rates of four major economies, 1961–2000

4. Sustained periods of prosperity and fast growth are followed sooner or later by a relative (or absolute) downturn. As the period of boom conditions lengthens, the probability of a slowdown increases. After a number of years' recession, the probability of economic recovery increases.[3]

---

3 While booms are usually associated with inflation and depressions with deflation, the correlation between inflation and economic activity through moderate cyclical fluctuations is much less clear. For example, during the stagflation of the 1970s, depressed growth went hand in hand with high inflation.

5. Even fast-growing economies experience growth cycles. The dynamic Asian countries, which enjoyed an average annual growth rate of 8 per cent for three decades up to the mid-1990s, recorded a standard deviation in their GDP growth of 2.3 percentage points (Table 16.3). This was higher in absolute terms than the industrial countries' 1.8 percentage points, but considerably lower relative to trend growth (Box 16.1).

6. Industrial economies stay on average approximately three times longer in the expansion phase of the cycle than in recession. Expansions lasted 51 months, compared with 15 months for recession (Table 16.1). Downturns tend to be shorter, but also more abrupt than upturns. Data for industrial countries show that the average cumulative loss of production due to recessions amounted to 11.7 per cent of industrial production, compared with a corresponding average gain of 25 per cent due to expansions.

7. There appears to be a strong degree of synchronisation of cycles among individual industrial countries, but cycles in the European economies, taken as a group, are not generally synchronised with those in North America and

Box 16.1

Business cycles in the dynamic Asian economies (DAEs)

Although the DAEs were able to sustain impressive rates of growth, they also experienced the business cycle fluctuations characteristic of industrial countries. During the period 1967–96, there were only four years of negative growth rates in the individual DAEs. But 'growth recessions' – defined as periods in which an economy continues to grow at a rate that is substantially below its long-run trend – were more common. Nineteen cyclical downturns, in which actual GDP fell more than 1 per cent below its long-run trend, were identified (Table 16.3). At cyclical troughs, GDP was on average about 4.5 per cent below trend. This is a larger output gap than the 3 per cent average estimated during downturns in the major developed countries over the past 20 years. But since their average growth rate is about three times higher than that of the major industrial countries, DAEs appear to have been less severely affected by business cycle downturns. This successful run was shattered by the downturn of 1997–98. However, by the year 2000, all except Indonesia had resumed their upward track.

In the past, cyclical trends in the DAEs were linked to developments in the industrial countries. Most of the DAEs experienced downturns in the mid-1970s, for instance. In recent years, the link between business cycles in the DAEs and the OECD area has become weaker. The correlation coefficient between growth rates in the OECD area and in the DAEs was 0.94 between 1971 and 1981. During the following decade, it fell to 0.46. As the DAEs have grown rapidly, domestic developments have played a larger role in determining business cycle trends. In addition, the influence of China on Hong Kong and Taiwan has increased as a result of economic integration in southern China.

Table 16.1 Business cycle characteristics

	Recessions		Expansions	
	Total change In output	Duration in months	Total change In output	Duration in months
US	−8.672	15	22.512	46
Canada	−9.195	14	20.330	35
Japan	−10.095	13	28.878	56
Germany	−11.373	24	33.708	77
France	−7.862	11	12.350	42
UK	−9.810	14	18.445	45
Italy	−13.742	15	35.491	63
Spain	−16.529	13	26.535	90
Belgium	−11.417	14	17.323	39
Netherlands	−9.247	20	15.408	30
Ireland	−10.641	15	39.219	53
Luxembourg	−21.821	16	30.362	39
Average	−11.7003	15	25.046	51

Notes: Total output change equals the average monthly decline (rise) in industrial production, multiplied by the average duration of contractions (expansions). Changes are expressed in terms of logarithms, while 'duration' refers to months. All figures are averages over completed recessions or contractions.

Source: M.J. Artis, Z. Kontolemis and D. Osborn, 'Classical Business Cycles for G7 and European Countries', *Journal of Business* (April 1997).

Japan.[4] Apart from the UK, business fluctuations follow a broadly similar path between European countries. With the increasing intensity of intra-European trade and capital mobility, cyclical trends are rapidly transmitted from one economy to the other.

The less synchronised are fluctuations in the major economies, the more stable the global economic system. If the US economy is heading towards its peak at a time when the EU is descending towards its trough, the EU will find it easier to reallocate resources, which have been made redundant by poor domestic market conditions, to the production of exports for the American market. This stabilises EU economic activity. Simultaneously, the booming US economy will benefit from the higher rate of growth in imports from Europe. These imports will divert US domestic spending from its over-stretched domestic sector and will help to restrain price increases. The outcome is mutually advantageous: less unemployment in Europe and less inflation in America. The amplitude of the fluctuation in both areas is moderated.

---

4 M.J. Artis, Z.G. Kontolemis and D.R. Osborn, 'Classical business cycles for G7 and European countries', Centre for European Policy Research Discussion Paper No. 1137 (March 1995). The 'stubbornly asynchronous' nature of UK and euro area business fluctuation is analysed in M.J. Artis and W. Zhang, 'Further evidence on the International Business Cycle and the ERM: is there a European Business Cycle?', *Oxford Economic Papers*, 1999.

Box 16.2

How changes in domestic activity affect economic variables

Pro-cyclical variables: (+) *in economic activity lead to* (+) *in these variables*:

industrial output, investment, commodity prices, business profits, labour productivity, imports, private sector credit, property prices.

Counter-cyclical variables: (+) *in economic activity in domestic economy lead to* (−) *in these variables*:

unemployment rate, number of lay-offs, bankruptcies, foreign trade balance, short-term inventories, non-performance loans.

Acyclical variables: (+/−) *in the domestic economic activity have a zero or near-zero effect on these variables:*

health services, staple foods, exports, primary education.

Economic variables respond in different ways to each stage of the cycle (Box 16.2). Some respond *pro-cyclically*, i.e. they increase (fall) as output increases (contracts), others respond *counter-cyclically*, i.e. they fall (increase) as aggregate output increases (declines). Some economic variables are *acyclical* – their values are relatively unaffected by fluctuations in aggregate economic variables.[5]

Sectoral responses to recessions and booms tend to be diverse. This is one strong motivation for firms to diversify sales and production into different sectors of the market. The lower the degree of synchronisation of fluctuations in economic activity at sectoral and international levels, the greater the potential gains from sectoral and geographical diversification.

While empirical studies confirm that business cycles are less prevalent and of lower amplitude than they were prior to the Second World War, these cycles have still caused significant losses of output. They add to the uncertainty of business and cause many to lose their jobs.

So much for the facts about economic fluctuations. We now consider the causes of these fluctuations and the reasons why their amplitude has become less extreme.

---

5 David K. Backus and Patrick J. Kehoe, 'International evidence on the historical properties of business cycles', *American Economic Review* (September 1992).

16.2 What causes fluctuations?

Causes of economic instability

Business cycles are caused by a mixture of factors. Some theories of the business cycle focus on the *intrinsic instability of the free market*. Other theories focus on the role of *random external shocks* such as the Iraqi invasion of Kuwait (1990) and the Kobe earthquake (1995). *Policy-induced shocks* have been identified as another cause of cycles. Shifts in monetary and fiscal policy, for example, can sometimes turn out to be pro-cyclical, an eventuality which becomes more likely when government fiscal decisions are influenced by the approach of elections.[6] At several junctures during the past four decades, *banking and financial crises* have brought booms to an untimely end; South-east Asia, Brazil and Russia all suffered in this way during the 1990s.

Keynesian economics attributes cycles to shifts in aggregate demand, caused primarily by the highly volatile behaviour of investment. Taken together with the assumption of pervasive nominal price rigidities, shifts in investment demand could impact on the *volume* of aggregate demand instead of on *prices*. Suppose that investment expands because of a more upbeat assessment of future economic prospects. This will be magnified, through the multiplier, into a much larger increase in sales throughout the economy. The resultant rise in aggregate demand will give a further reinforcing stimulus to investment. Firms will find that their inventories have fallen. New stocks will be ordered to keep up with extra sales. This very act, of course, adds another stimulus to aggregate demand, justifies the expectations of the original investors and makes them even more bullish. Optimistic expectations become self-fulfilling. The economy enters a boom. This continues until eventually the market begins to believe that capacity growth has been reached. Then investors become more cautious and demand for additions to inventories begins to subside. Resources employed in producing the annual additions to firms' inventories and capital stock might have to be 'let go'. A downward spiral is set in motion, fuelled by the same forces that drove the economy upwards during the boom. This process of cumulative and circular causation has been formalised in a simple but revealing way in the multiplier–accelerator model (see Box 16.3).

Real business cycle theory explains cyclical shocks in terms of spurts and starts in technological advance. An improvement in technology leads to a rise in productivity, a higher real wage and a correspondingly greater willingness to work. Hoteliers and restaurant workers in Mediterranean countries, for example, work long hours during the tourist season when the productivity of work is high, and take leisure time during winter when productivity is low. Cycles, in this view, are generated by rational economic agents and 'real' factors. We do not require nominal rigidities or money illusion to explain their existence. Random factors such as wars and natural disasters can have effects similar to the technology shocks analysed in real business cycle theory.

---

6 The term political cycle was introduced by the Polish economist Michael Kalecki, 'Political aspects to full employment', *Political Quarterly* (October 1943).

Box 16.3

The multiplier–accelerator model

The investment accelerator idea was for a long time the leading theory behind the explanation of cycles. The British economist Sir John Hicks wrote: 'the main cause of fluctuations is to be found in the effect of changes in output (or income) on investment.' Although several important developments have occurred in the theory of business fluctuations during the last three decades, many economists believe that the accelerator principle of investment remains an important explanation of the business cycle.

Consider a simple model where output is determined as follows:

$$Y = C + 1 \tag{16.1}$$

Consumption is a function of income alone, but with a one-period lag; thus, $C = aY_{-1}$. Investment (I) is a function of the change in income, also with a one-period lag, and an exogenous level I_0, determined by 'animal spirits'.

$$I = b(Y_{-1} - Y_{-2}) + I_0 \tag{16.2}$$

Combining (16.1) and (16.2), we have

$$Y = (a + b)Y_{-1} - bY_{-2} + I_0 \tag{16.3}$$

Output is a function of its lagged levels in the two periods. Given plausible parameters, a cyclical behaviour following a rise in I_0 can be generated by this model.

Sources: J.D. Sachs and F. Larraín, *Macroeconomics in the Global Economy* (Hemel Hempstead: Harvester Wheatsheaf, 1993), chapter 17; J.R. Hicks, *A Constitution to the Theory of the Trade Cycle* (Oxford: Oxford University Press, 1950).

Policy induced shocks seem a rather unlikely cause of business fluctuations. The task of policy would seem to be to moderate fluctuations not to cause them. Unfortunately, experience shows practice to be at variance with precept in this respect. Both monetary and fiscal policies have often been found to function in a surprisingly pro-cyclical way. Sometimes this is intentional (the political business cycle); at other times, the pro-cyclicality arises because of implementation and other lags.

Banking and financial crises attracted global attention during the 1990s, though this type of crisis seems to have long been an intrinsic feature of the market system. During the Asian boom, banks lent too much to dubious building and other speculative projects in domestic currency on the basis of funds borrowed in dollars at what appeared relatively low dollar interest rates. All went well as long as confidence in the sustainability of the building boom lasted. Once confidence began to falter, however, the bubble burst. The financial sector's balance sheet began to look dodgy; dollar loans to the banks were recalled; and bank depositors began to take fright. Falling output, high interest rates and depreciating exchange rates added to the disarray and sense of panic. Serious damage was inflicted on the

Asian economies through this process. (In Korea, capital flows reversed from inflows of $5 billion per quarter in the first half of 1997 to an outflow of $20 billion in November, while the won's exchange rate was cut in half.) Worse, through a process of contagion, economies with relatively sound banking and financial systems also suffered speculative attacks (the *contagion effect* for these countries is then similar to an external random shock). These types of crises indicate the presence of systemic flaws in the market system akin to the market failures discussed in Part I. Thus rational behaviour on the part of the individual lender to one of these countries (anxious to get money back quickly), once it is replicated by all lenders, leads to an irrational outcome (an unnecessary and unwarranted recession in the whole economy). And just as in the case of individuals standing up in a football stadium to get a better view or panic exit from a theatre, each individual's doing the 'rational' thing leads to a sub-optimal collective outcome.

These theories of business fluctuations have developed from experience of different historical cycles. In analysing any particular situation, we must use the theory that seems most appropriate in the circumstances.

Why has the amplitude of the cycle diminished?[7]

Reference has already been made to the small number of negative annual growth rates in postwar experience. The downturns are steeper and longer-lasting for industrial production than for GDP, but even there the incidence has been mild, especially by comparison with the inter-war period of 1919–39. Why have downswings in the cycle become shallower and expansions become longer? For example, the expansion in the US economy from 1991 to 2000 has been the longest ever in peacetime.

First, the shift in composition of output from the industrial sector to the tertiary sector has made total GDP less volatile. The purchase of new durable goods, such as cars and washing machines, can be easily deferred or advanced, but services have to be produced and consumed simultaneously and are less easy to postpone. Demand for services such as education, basic health needs and counselling is highly income-elastic in the long term, but can be relatively insensitive to short-term reductions in GDP. Once a certain level of health provision and education is established, it proves extremely resistant to downward adjustment. A ratchet effect appears to operate. Of course, not all services are stable in this sense – tourism, theatre and real estate services are highly cyclical.

---

7 We take this reduction in the severity of cycles as an established fact. It has been repeatedly affirmed by empirical researchers. But inevitably, every empirical generalisation in economics seems to invite challenge sooner or later. It has been claimed that the contrast between postwar and prewar cyclical behaviour is not as self-evident as it might appear if postwar indexes of economic activity were calculated on the same basis as prewar indexes. Research on this subject continues but, at the end of the day, the generalisation is likely to be qualified rather than refuted. Zarnovitz, for example, finds that the coefficient of variation (a statistical measure of dispersion) of America's real GDP for the period 1946–83 was one-half that of 1875–1918 and only one-third that of 1919–45: Victor Zarnovitz, *Business Cycles: Theory, history, indicators and forecasting* (Chicago and London: University of Chicago Press, 1992).

Second, the rising share of government spending in GDP has added an element of stability to the economy. Government spending, including that of publicly owned corporations, is much less sensitive to cyclical conditions than the private sector. This, in part, reflects the nature of the services provided by government (health, social welfare, education, interest on public debt), as well as the lesser degree of discipline exerted by market forces on state-owned corporations, which makes their investment decisions less sensitive to fluctuations in profits.

Third, automatic fiscal stabilisers tend to moderate the effect of private sector volatility. Economic booms are choked off by higher leakages to the public sector via growth in tax revenues and reductions in the social welfare bill, while budget deficits buttress private sector spending during the downturns.

Fourth, policy activism has played a role in averting major crises. As we have already seen, a more critical view is now being taken of activism than was previously the case. Consider, for example, an early, optimistic assessment of policy activism by Arthur F. Burns, a distinguished business cycles scholar and former chairman of the Federal Reserve Board:

> The general expectation of the postwar period has been that the government would move with some vigour to check any recession that developed, and that its monetary, fiscal and regulatory actions would contribute to that objective. By and large, this confidence has been justified by events. Not only has monetary policy in the main been shaped with a view to promoting stable prosperity, but fiscal policy – which previously had been handicapped by the convention of normally balanced budgets – has lately also been guided by the state of the economy.[8]

In retrospect, we have seen that the record of demand management has been more mixed than the above quotation would suggest. *Yet the ability of governments to take action in the event of a major disruption of demand, say, following a stock market crash, or of an unjustified and contagious bout of inflationary expansion, is an important stabilising influence on the economy.* It is a point on which economists of all shades of opinion would agree.

Confidence that the government would set a 'floor' below which the real economy will not fall and a 'ceiling' beyond which real growth will be discouraged helped to ensure that fluctuations stayed within manageable bounds. The readiness of governments to intervene in order to avert a financial crisis strengthens investors' confidence. Closer supervision of the financial system can also help to avert crises – although disaster has been only narrowly averted in Japan and even in the better regulated US during the past decade.

16.3   Business fluctuations and growth

Instability in a country's growth path seems to be negatively related to the trend rate of growth. For example, on the basis of the performance of the US economy over the past 100 years, Zarnovitz finds that *periods of high instability have been*

---

8 Arthur F. Burns, *The Business Cycle in a Changing World* (New York and London: Columbia University Press, 1958), p. 49.

associated with lower average economic growth. 'Growth was generally higher when stability was greater. Instability of aggregate demand and of the price level impedes growth,'[9] he concluded. One reason for this finding may be that sustained growth creates a climate which is conducive to innovation, adjustment and structural change which, in turn, tends to create faster growth. Schumpeter's process of 'creative destruction' may be replicated more effectively in an economy which grows faster but experiences smaller oscillations than in a free market *laissez-faire* economy, characterised by textbook boom and slump. Fast-growing economies provide a friendly environment for innovation, new competition and reallocation of resources. Steady growth does not dispense with the need for adjustment. But it makes adjustment easier and less traumatic.

The combined effect of a decline in the relative size of the government sector, cautious use of anti-cyclical policies and increased openness of the world economy may lead to greater instability in the future. The long-run implications for the stability of the economy of the shift in spending from the public sector to the private sector remain uncertain.[10] In some countries, such as the US, rectification of the public sector's finances has been accompanied by what appears to be an excessive amount of dissaving in parts of the private sector. There are continuing concerns voiced by central bankers – such as Federal Reserve Chairman, Alan Greenspan and others – that the 'new economy' is spurring imbalances that at some point will abruptly adjust, bringing the economic expansion, its euphoria and wealth creation to an abrupt halt.

Whatever the future holds, the objective of policy is clear: to try to extend the expansionary phase of the economy, to moderate its excesses and to avoid the recessions that have in the past brought business cycles to completion.

16.4 Forecasting the business cycle

The business cycle has altered in character. The amplitude of cycles, in particular, has diminished in recent decades. Yet there has been no corresponding diminution in the demand for forecasts of variables such as GDP, interest rates, inflation and exchange rates. How are these eagerly sought and read forecasts formulated? How accurate are they? How do firms use macro-forecasts and why are they important?

---

9 V. Zarnovitz, *Business Cycles: Theory, history, indicators and forecasting* (Chicago: University of Chicago Press, 1992), p. 230.

10 Writing in 1969, the economic historian Angus Maddison concluded that: 'government policy has obviously added greatly to the buoyancy of the economy and has been one of the main causes of rapid economic growth'. Economists nowadays describe the effects of government intervention in less glowing terms: Angus Maddison, 'Comment', in Martin Bronfenbrenner (ed.), *Is the Business Cycle Obsolete?* (New York: John Wiley, 1969), p. 500.

How are forecasts made?

In preparing a forecast of a variable, a forecaster's first step is to examine carefully the behaviour of that variable in the past. There are many different ways in which this can be done.

First, econometric and mathematical models are used. These models can vary from small ad hoc models to models with literally hundreds of variables and equations. Consumption, investment, exports, imports, prices, wages and productivity will all figure in such models. Some technical assumptions will have to be made – about commodity prices, exchange rates, fiscal policy, and so on. One powerful advantage of a macroeconometric model is that it helps to ensure consistency of the overall forecast (especially important where several countries' performance is involved). It can also be used to test alternative policy assumptions and to identify major sensitive points of the overall projections. These models are voracious consumers of, and are crucially dependent on, good quality, up-to-date data.

Second, judgement has to be applied in interpreting the results of the model. The model results need to be assessed by sectoral specialists and country experts. A good team of economists can be helpful at this stage. For instance, the Federal Reserve's track record in forecasting inflation and growth was consistently better than the consensus views of private sector forecasts – one possible explanation for which might be the expertise of the Bank's sizeable research staff (as C. Romer and D. Romer argued in the June 2000 issue of the *American Economic Review*).

These macroeconomic forecasts are often at work behind the scenes in the production of forecasts of specific variables of interest to business, such as inflation, nominal interest rates and exchange rates. In such instances, macro forecasts will often be complemented by less formal techniques such as 'eyeballing' of past trends (Chartism) and application of rules of thumb and key historical ratios. Often, in practice, it is not just the variable itself that is closely scrutinised but how that variable has behaved *in conjunction with a selection of other variables*.

Are forecasts accurate?

Do forecasters get it right, on average? We know that it is impossible for any forecaster to be correct all the time, but how often do they come close to the actual outcome?

In an attempt to answer this question, Professor John Kay reported the results of a review of the record of 34 individual forecasters and forecasting organisations in the UK in the period since 1987.[11] He found that forecasters tend to cluster around a consensus – and that this consensus will more than likely be wrong. He found that all the forecasts for GDP growth in 1993 and 1994 were substantially below the actual outcome, while all the forecasts were above the actual outcome

---

11 John Kay, 'Cracks in the crystal ball', *Financial Times* (29 September 1995).

Table 16.2 Forecasting errors for growth and inflation

| | | Growth | | | | | Inflation | | |
| | | Actual | Errors | | | | Actual | Errors | |
			OECD	Random				OECD	Random
US	(1987–92)	2.0	1.3	1.8	US	(1987–92)	3.6	0.5	0.7
Japan	(1987–92)	4.4	1.3	1.8	Japan	(1987–92)	1.2	0.6	1.0
Germany	(1987–92)	3.1	1.4	1.3	Germany	(1987–92)	3.1	0.4	0.9
France	(1987–92)	2.5	0.9	0.9	France	(1987–92)	2.9	0.6	1.0
Italy	(1987–92)	2.5	1.1	0.7	Italy	(1987–92)	6.2	1.5	1.5
UK	(1987–92)	1.5	1.9	1.7	UK	(1987–92)	6.1	0.7	1.1
Canada	(1987–92)	2.0	1.8	1.9	Canada	(1987–92)	3.3	1.5	1.5
G7	(1974–82)	2.7	2.2	3.5	G7	(1974–82)	10.2	3.0	4.2
G7	(1982–91)	2.9	1.3	1.9	G7	(1982–91)	4.3	1.0	1.5
G7	(1987–92)	2.6	1.4	1.5	G7	(1987–92)	3.8	0.9	1.1

Note: Actual refers to the level of output growth or inflation recorded in the economy or group of economies in question. OECD and Random refer to the Root Mean Square Error of forecasts of growth/inflation made by the OECD Model and a Random Walk Model respectively.

Source: Computed from *OECD Economic Outlook* (June 1993).

in 1991 and 1992. The consensus forecast, he went on, 'failed to predict any of the important developments in the [UK] economy over the past seven years – the strength and resilience of the 1980s consumer boom, the depth and persistence of the 1990s recession, or the dramatic and continuing decline in inflation since 1991'.

This type of forecasting record is not peculiar to the UK. Reviews of the forecasting record of many international think-tanks reveal similar results. A study by the OECD, for example, in 1993 quantified its degree of success in prediction by means of *the root mean square error technique*. This involves finding the difference between the forecast value of a variable and the actual outcome. This difference, or 'error', is then squared in order to standardise positive and negative mistakes.[12] These squared errors are then averaged, and the square root is taken of this figure. The result is the root mean square error (RMSE) of a forecast. The larger the RMSE, the less accurate the forecast.

In Table 16.2, the RMSE of OECD forecasts since 1974 for seven major market economies are considered. For the sake of comparison, the performance of the sophisticated OECD techniques is contrasted with that of a simple naive 'random walk' technique, whereby the forecasted value of a variable next year is assumed to be the same as its actual value this year.

---

12 Suppose the forecast for output growth is 4 per cent and growth of 2 per cent actually occurs. This error of −2 is then squared. The squared error of the forecast is 4. If, on the other hand, the forecast value is 6 per cent, the square error would also be 4. Had the gap between forecasts been 3 per cent instead of 2 per cent, then the square error would have been 9. Thus, the square error of a forecast does not discriminate between positive and negative errors, and also penalises larger forecast errors.

Four conclusions can be drawn from these tables. First, random walk models tend to perform as well as, if not better than, the OECD model when predicting GDP growth in Germany, France, Italy and the UK. Second, conventional forecasting techniques are more successful at predicting inflation than at predicting growth. The inflation forecasts clearly outperform random walk methods. Third, the overall record of forecasts with regard to *total* OECD countries' inflation and growth has been consistently better than the random walk method since 1974. Fourth, the RMSE of the forecasts has declined since 1974 for both output and growth. However, since the accuracy of random walk measures has also improved, an open verdict must be recorded as to how much of this improvement has been due to improved technique and how much to a decline in the year-to-year variability of the macroeconomic variables themselves.

Instead of RMSE, one could use the mean error and the mean absolute error. One could also examine how an organisation's forecasts compare with others in terms of these efficiency indicators and the degree to which forecast errors are persistent. A comprehensive analysis of European Commission forecasts published in 1999 reveals a similar pattern of results to the OECD study.[13]

No matter how interpreted, the impression is that many key economic forecasts have proved disappointingly inaccurate. One basic problem has to do with the reliance of forecasts on past data. First, *while the past may seem like a good yardstick for predicting the future, it will fail to take account of random shocks* (internal or external) on the economy. These shocks are, by definition, unpredictable through systematic analysis, yet they happen all the time and can have a major impact on the forecast variables. For example, the Kobe earthquake had a major impact on the Japanese economy, initially most acutely reflected in the performance of the Nikkei, Japan's most closely followed equity index. Yet forecasters, using historical data to forecast Japanese GDP growth or the future values for the Nikkei, could not possibly have accounted for such a random event. Similarly, in the UK, most forecasters using pre-1992 trends to predict growth, interest rates or exchange rates could not have predicted the precise timing of sterling's exit from the ERM in November 1992, and so probably would have got the 1993 forecasts wrong.

Second, *the use of historical data assumes that the factors which have driven each of the previous cycles are the same ones driving the present cycle. Factors which were present in past cycles may no longer be relevant in determining this business cycle.* 'New economy' factors not present in earlier cycles may be crucially important in interpreting the current cycle. Also, the roles of asset prices, household debt, computer-led productivity increases and globalisation were not nearly as prominent in earlier cycles. Forecasts based on earlier cycles will be generally off the mark, because they failed to take this into account. Even if it is the case that cycles look the same, different factors may be driving each.

---

13 F. Keereman, 'The track record of the Commission's forecasts', *Economic Paper No. 137*, European Commission (October 1999).

Table 16.3 Growth in the dynamic Asian economies and the seven largest OECD countries since 1965

	Average rate of growth[a]	Standard deviations
OECD Major Seven[b]	2.7	1.8
DAEs (1965–92)	8.0	2.3
Korea	8.2	2.3
Taiwan	8.4	1.2
Hong Kong	7.2	2.9
Singapore	8.4	2.0
Thailand	7.4	2.1
Malaysia	6.8	0.7

Notes: (a) For the Major Seven, the average growth rate shown is for the period 1970 to 1990. For the DAEs the growth rate was estimated over the period 1965 to 1992, except for Hong Kong and Malaysia, for which the period begins in 1966 and 1970, respectively. (b) For the seven largest countries, these estimates are based on a sample of 21 cyclical downturns. In the case of the DAEs, 19 cyclical downturns have been identified.

Source: OECD, *Economic Outlook* (June 1993).

Third, *past relationships between key economic variables may change over time.* For example, analysis of historical experience showed that if house prices have risen less than average incomes for a period, they will rise faster in the next period; and, when the ratio of prices to incomes becomes too high, they rise less quickly. But this relationship was observed in a period when house prices consistently rose, so that the price people would pay for a house was often limited only by what they could borrow. The past relationship may not persist in an era of lower inflation and in the wake of a traumatic period when many householders become locked in a negative equity position. Forecasts based on historical data will not reflect such structural changes.

Fourth, *official forecasts are prone to over-optimism.* Cambridge economist Wynn Godley noted that the UK Treasury had never forecast a recession. Some would reply that the forecasting exercise prevents recessions by alerting authorities to the need for remedial action, but there is an undoubted element of 'cycle denial' at work also. Buyer beware!

The above analysis explains why forecasters so often seem to err in the same direction. Their forecasts are all based on the same faulty foundation of a given set of past data and estimated behavioural relationships.

Does it matter if forecasters get it wrong? Ultimately, the answer to this question will depend on the uses to which the forecast is put. In the case of the Kobe earthquake, forecasts of the Japanese economy were seriously affected. The accompanying fall in the Nikkei index led ultimately to the collapse of Baring Brothers merchant bank – because one of its traders was speculating heavily on the value of the Nikkei and made a spectacular mistake. So if forecasts are being used in this way, accuracy is important. The accuracy of forecasts may also matter at a political level, in so far as they may influence the timing of an election and the nature of political promises and programmes. But Mr Greenspan's spectacularly wrong forecast about the US stock market in his 'irrational exuberance' speech at the end of 1996 seems to have caused no harm either to the economy, to his reputation or – still less – to the stock market, which continued its rise from 6400 in December 1996 to nearly double that three years later.

Economics is not very good at answering questions about what will happen; it is much better at answering the question: *if* something happens (be it faster growth, higher interest rates or an exchange rate depreciation), what will be the consequences for the economy? Caution must therefore be used when utilising economic forecasts. Fortunately for the economics profession, such sage advice will not stop forecasters forecasting or commentators commentating on them, or businesses demanding them. Nature abhors a vacuum. In this instance, however, it is useful to be aware that what replaces the vacuum can sometimes be as empty as the vacuum itself.

16.5 Macro-forecasts and the firm

A firm might have many reasons for using economic forecasts. If it was considering an investment, interest rate forecasts could help it decide how, and when, to borrow. If forecasts for interest rates show that interest rates in six months' time will be lower, the firm may defer taking out the loan until credit becomes cheaper. Likewise, if forecasts point to higher interest rates in the future, it may decide to take the loan out now as credit is cheaper, or even may decide not to take the loan out at all if the repayments would be too high in the future. Similarly, firms with foreign transactions will regularly consult exchange rate forecasts for guidance. An exporting firm would surely be interested in the likely future direction of the relevant currency in projecting income and payment flows for the company. Firms are not interested exclusively in macroeconomic forecasts, such as those on economic growth, interest rates and exchange rates, but also in integrating these forecasts into its own sales and costs projections for the company. This integration can proceed on a *top-down* or a *bottom-up* basis. Top-down forecasts begin with macroeconomic projections and work out the implications of these projections for the firm (Box 16.4).

Top-down methods are relevant only to a large firm or to projections for an entire industry. For a small firm, its future sales path will be determined primarily by micro-factors within its own control, rather than by macro-trends. In all cases, market share projections based on *top-down* techniques should be compared with *bottom-up* forecasts based on projections of sales managers, opinion surveys of regional sales offices and extrapolation of past sales, which take account of specific factors relevant to each element in the company's product range.

Box 16.4

Top-down forecast of demand for personal computers

1. Forecast growth of GNP and other macroeconomic indicators, such as disposable income, that are closely related to PC sales.
2. Prepare PC industry forecast in volume and value terms, drawing on aggregate forecasts.
3. Regionalise forecasts and break down by product category.
4. Make use of external information regarding the competitive environment (domestic v foreign costs; changes in exchange rates; new entrants to industry) and supplement this information with analysis of consumer preferences and company capacity. Develop market share projections for the company.
5. Review company sales forecast disaggregated by region and product line.
6. Develop market share projections and compare with *bottom-up* forecasts based on opinion surveys of regional sales offices and other micro-projections.

Source: Dale G. Bails and Larry C. Peppers, *Business Fluctuations: Forecasting techniques and applications* (New Jersey: Prentice Hall, 2nd edn, 1993).

16.6 Conclusions

Comparison of growth rates over the past 40 years highlighted the size, duration and incidence of business cycles and fluctuations. The exercise revealed a low incidence of negative growth rates, but significant fluctuations around average and trend growth rates for the major industrial countries. There is no compelling evidence of the existence of systematic long-run cycles. Sustained periods of prosperity and fast growth, however, tend to be succeeded sooner or later by a relative or absolute downturn.

In industrial economies, downturns have been greatly moderated in the postwar period. These economies have stayed on average approximately three times longer in the expansion phase of the cycle than in the recession phase. There is a strong degree of synchronisation of cycles among European economies, but little between the different continents. This may have helped to moderate world fluctuations.

Business fluctuations occur in an erratic fashion. Their characteristics change over time. One important development has been that the amplitude of business cycles has diminished. In particular, downswings in cycles have become shallower and expansions have become longer. The increasing share of government spending in GDP and the shift from the industrial to the tertiary sector have made national output behave in a less volatile way. Policy measures have also helped to avert major crises, though their effectiveness in moderating smaller fluctuations is dubious.

Studies of the relationship between business fluctuations and growth suggest that higher instability is associated with lower average economic growth. However, opinion is divided as to what exactly causes this instability. For example, some theories attribute cycles to random external shocks, others to internal shocks, still others to policy-induced shocks. Real business cycle theorists emphasise the role of discrete shifts in technology such as the current information and biotechnology boom. Others focus on inherent tendencies towards self-fulfilling over-optimism and over-pessimism in a market system.

Economic forecasters try to extrapolate from what has happened in the past in order to make predictions about the future. There are various methods used to obtain these forecasts. Highly complex mathematical and statistical models are often used by such organisations as the World Bank and the OECD. But using such sophisticated methods does not prevent forecasters from getting it wrong. In fact, no matter how much information forecasters have at hand, they will never be right all the time.

It is wrong, therefore, for business to expect great precision from forecasts. The forecast is only a means of attempting to reduce uncertainty; it cannot eliminate that uncertainty. Forecasts can be useful as sources of information and for teasing out issues of interest to the firm.

✔ Summary

1. Business cycles refer to fluctuations in aggregate economic activity that are widely diffused throughout the economy and have identifiable peaks and troughs. Most modern studies focus on growth cycles, that is, deviations from trend growth of the aggregate variable under investigation. Economic variables respond in different ways to each stage of the cycle. Some respond pro-cyclically, some respond counter-cyclically, while some are acyclical. Empirical studies indicate that business cycles are less prevalent and of lower amplitude than they were prior to the Second World War. However, these cycles have still caused significant losses of output and add to the uncertainty of business.

2. Business cycles are caused by a mixture of factors. Some theories of the business cycles focus on the intrinsic instability of the free market, others focus on the role of random external shocks. Policy-induced shocks have also been identified as another cause of business cycles. Each theory of the cause of business fluctuations has some plausibility and relevance to some historical cycles. In analysing any particular situation, we must use the theory most appropriate in the circumstances. Many factors have contributed to the diminished amplitude of cycles in the postwar period: for example, the shift in composition of output from the industrial sector to the tertiary sector, the rising share of government expenditure in GDP and – but more debatably – policy activism.

3. Instability in a country's growth path seems to be negatively related to the trend rate of growth. One reason for this finding may be that sustained

growth creates a climate which is conducive to innovation, adjustment and structural change, which in turn tends to create faster growth.

4. Despite the diminished amplitude of cycles, forecasts for variables such as GDP, interest rates and inflation are still in great demand. There are many ways in which these forecasts can be developed. Usually, the past behaviour of the variable, and other related variables, is used to develop forecasts. However, the picture will always be incomplete, which explains why no forecaster can predict the future with perfect accuracy. In practice, historical data are not always a reliable guide to future behaviour. Relationships between key variables may change over time, factors driving cycles can change over time, and there will always be unpredictable random shocks. Thus, caution must be exercised when using economic forecasts.

5. Firms frequently make use of economic forecasts. For investors, interest rate forecasts are of crucial concern, while foreign exchange forecasts can be used by exporting firms with large foreign exchange risk exposure. Macroeconomic forecasts are often integrated into the firms' own sales and cost projections which can proceed on a top-down or a bottom-up basis.

? Questions for discussion

1. Why do economic cycles (or business fluctuations) occur? What are the implications of these fluctuations for business?

2. Would you expect government intervention to increase, or to diminish, the amplitude of business cycles?

3. It is often assumed that business cycles have little effect on the long-run growth of the economy. In other words, the business cycle represents transitory deviations around a given trend growth rate.

   Do you agree? If this statement were true, why should economists be concerned with business cycles?

4. Evaluate the usefulness of economic forecasts to business, especially in the light of their indifferent prediction record.

☞ Exercises

1. Show how you would present a macroeconomic forecast of the economy (choose between the US, German, French or UK economies) to other business people. What use, if any, could a firm make of such a forecast?

2. A stockbroking firm provides your business with a quarterly review containing forecasts of GNP growth for one, two and three years ahead. You are asked to evaluate the forecasting record of this firm. How would you propose doing this?

📖 Further reading

An overview of business cycles is available in V. Zarnovitz, *Business Cycles: Theory, history, indicators and forecasting* (Chicago: University of Chicago Press, 1992). See also K. Mayhew and J. Muellbauer, 'Business cycles', *Oxford Review of Economic Policy* Vol. 13 (3), 1997. A useful description of forecasting techniques is outlined in D.G. Bails and L.C. Peppers, *Business Fluctuations: Forecasting techniques and applications* (New Jersey: Prentice Hall International, 2nd edn, 1993). Theoretical aspects of business cycles are explained in F.E. Kydland, *Business Cycles Theory* (Aldershot: Edward Elgar, 1995), and M.P. Niemira and P.A. Klein, *Forecasting Financial and Economic Cycles* (New York: John Wiley, 1994).

Part III

THE GLOBAL ECONOMY

Introduction to Part III

This part assesses how the world macro-environment impacts on business. It examines the benefits – and challenges – to the global economy arising from the growth in foreign trade, capital flows, foreign investment and migration. It also discusses the exchange rate regime that is most suitable to the needs of countries adjusting to the more liberal and open system. Excessive exchange rate volatility adds to problems of adjustment and generates large costs for business. Excessive rigidity can cause similar problems. The search continues for ways of avoiding balance of payments and exchange rate turmoil.

Think global, act local.   As the world economy becomes more open, even small firms have to take this rule seriously. The domestic market is no longer the secure base it once was, and foreign markets are no longer as difficult to penetrate or as remote. The globalisation of the economy brings opportunities and threats to firms. There is hardly any country nowadays that is not concerned with its international competitiveness. National policies have become *more outward-looking*, as evidenced by the implemention of the Uruguay Round, the relaxation of controls on capital mobility, the globally more benign stance towards foreign investment and the establishment of the World Trade Organisation in 1995. The consolidation of Europe's 1992 single market programme marks another watershed in the move towards a liberal world trade system.

The first two chapters of Part III explore the economic implications of the globalisation of markets. By this we mean the reduction of tariff and non-tariff barriers on merchandise goods, the extension of an open trade regime to the services sector, the opening of world capital markets and the decline in barriers to the exchange of knowledge and technology. This is regarded as a strongly positive development for world economic growth and employment. But there could be serious short-term adjustment costs which domestic policy needs to address. Fear of such adjustment costs underlies the resistance to immigration in host countries. We discuss how the world economy has become more integrated, what gains can be expected to follow the growth in trade and what conditions are necessary in order to ensure that these gains will be realised.

Next we discuss the balance of payments, exchange rates and the world monetary system. If trade is important for welfare, it is important that the world payments system functions smoothly. Misaligned exchange rates, balance of payments crises and foreign exchange turmoil impose heavy costs on business. Companies spend heavily trying to find ways of limiting their exposure to foreign currency risks. There has been active debate over the optimal exchange rate system for an individual country or group of countries. Europe has been deeply embroiled in that debate, first under the European Monetary System and then with the creation of the single currency and a European Central Bank.

This part is designed to provide the reader with an understanding of the main ideas underlying the consensus for freer trade, liberalisation of factor movements and a multilaterally agreed world trade order governed by rules. We draw extensively on analysis and concepts of Parts I and II. For example, the gains from trade are analysed with the aid of concepts such as economies of scale and the economic gains from competition, which were introduced in Chapters 3–7, while the analysis of balance of payments and exchange rates has close ties with the macroeconomic chapters on monetary and fiscal policy.

Chapter 17

FOREIGN TRADE: PATTERNS AND POLICY

Introduction

A world-wide consensus in favour of free trade took hold of economic opinion in the 1990s. Notwithstanding the occasional setback, such as the failed Seattle trade summit of 1999, the consensus has remained firm. Political considerations played a key part in the development of this consensus, motivated by the desire to avoid trade wars and to promote faster growth. Business has supported free trade through its representative organisations, though the reaction 'on the ground' depends greatly on whether the particular enterprise is export- or home market-oriented. Export industries tend to be enthusiastic proponents of the merits of trade liberalisation. To them, freer trade means easier access to foreign markets, profitable investment opportunities and a greater spread of fixed costs. Import-competing firms in 'sensitive' sectors of the economy tend to see things differently. To them freer trade means the erosion of domestic market shares and the danger of job losses. The views of the pro-trade group have clearly prevailed.

There is growing evidence that trade liberalisation brings benefits to those countries ready to grasp the opportunities of global markets. The resultant gains outweigh the losses caused by adjustment to freer trade. Efforts to close the domestic market to foreign competition have proved both unavailing and counter-productive. Free trade versus protection is no longer the main issue in international trade. The conditions under which liberalised trade is conducted – the maintenance of 'level playing fields' and fair trading rules – have become the major subject of debate.

Economics concludes that foreign trade brings major benefits, but the reasoning behind this conclusion sometimes appears counter-intuitive, or just wrong. What many businesses might consider a 'bad' thing – cheaper imports, pressure on domestic market shares and job losses in industries which compete with imports – appear in economic models as a 'good' thing: an expression of the gains which accrue to society from trade. According to the economist's view, a country sells exports only in order to enjoy more consumption of imports. Higher exports are not a gain in the true sense. They imply that goods produced at home are being enjoyed by someone else. *They are beneficial to a country only to the extent that they enable its citizens to consume more imports* – now, or sometime in the future. Hence the notion that a country with a trade surplus (i.e. which exports more than it imports) benefits more from international trade than a country with a trade deficit is based upon a complete misunderstanding of the gains from trade.

Different perspectives on foreign trade can translate into different approaches to trade policy. It is important to understand the institutional background, the assumptions and the evidence on which discussion of global trade issues is now based.

Chapter outline

This chapter provides an analytical overview of trade issues under five headings:

1. An overview of trends in global trade patterns and institutions.
2. Analysis of how nations benefit from foreign trade.
3. Empirical estimates of the gains from trade.
4. Trade policy, protection and new trade issues.
5. Determinants of competitiveness in the global market.

17.1 Trends in global trade

The global trade environment has changed in three major ways in recent decades. International trade has grown rapidly in value and volume, the composition of trade has altered significantly, and trade flows have been extensively liberalised.

Growth in trade

The total value of world exports of goods and services is close to US$7000 billion. Among the few statistical regularities in modern economies is the tendency for growth in trade volume consistently to exceed growth in output. For example, between 1973 and 1999, world trade increased by 4.5 per cent annually compared with an annual growth in world output of 2.7 per cent (Table 17.1). During the 1990s, trade grew by nearly 6 per cent annually, more than twice as fast as world output. Economic growth in the EU (2 per cent p.a.) has been below the world average, but its trade continues to expand at more than double this rate.

A feature of the world trade system is that *successful exporters tend also to be fast-growing importers*. With only one exception (Korea), each of the top ten leading exporters is included among the top ten leading importers (Table 17.2). The export performance of Asian countries has been matched by an equally dramatic increase in imports into Asia. Exports from the EU to Asia have risen more than six-fold between 1980 and 1993, while the share of developing Asian countries in EU exports jumped from 7 per cent to nearly 20 per cent in the same period – overtaking, in the process, the 18 per cent share held by the US.[1]

---

1 Statistics taken from Commission of the European Communities, 'Towards a new Asian strategy', Brussels 1994 (COM94 314).

Table 17.1(a) World merchandise trade and gross domestic product, 1900–99 (average annual percentage change in volume)

	1900–13	1913–50	1950–73	1973–99
Merchandise trade	4.3	0.6	8.2	4.5
Gross domestic product	2.5	2.0	5.1	2.8

Source: World Trade Organisation, *Regionalism and the World Trading System* (Geneva, April 1995); *International Trade Statistics* (1995); own estimates.

Table 17.1(b) Value of world exports, 1999 (US$ billion)

World merchandise exports	5460
Commercial services	1340
Total	6800

Source: WTO and own estimates.

Table 17.2 Leading exporters and importers in merchandise trade in 1999

	Exporters				Importers		
Rank	Country	$US bn	% share	Rank	Country	$US bn	% share
1	US	695.0	12.4	1	US	1059.9	18.0
2	Germany	540.5	9.6	2	Germany	472.6	8.0
3	Japan	419.4	7.5	3	UK	320.7	5.5
4	France	299.0	5.3	4	Japan	310.7	5.3
5	UK	268.4	4.8	5	France	286.1	4.9
6	Canada	238.4	4.2	6	Canada	220.2	3.7
7	Italy	230.8	4.1	7	Italy	216.0	3.7
8	Netherlands	204.1	3.6	8	Netherlands	188.9	3.2
9	China	194.9	3.5	9	Hong Kong	181.7	3.1
10	Belgium–Luxembourg	184.1	3.3	10	Belgium–Luxembourg	169.4	2.9
11	Hong Kong	174.8	3.1	11	China	165.7	2.9
12	Korea	144.2	2.6	12	Mexico	148.2	2.5

Source: WTO, press release, 6 April 2000.

Foreign trade has become more important for virtually all countries, even for large countries such as the US, but trade ratios differ markedly between countries. A rough measure of the rising importance of trade is the ratio of exports and imports to GDP. Between 1990 and 2000, the export : GDP ratio of low income countries doubled from 12 to 24 per cent. Middle income countries also registered a steep rise in the export : GDP ratio from 22 to 28 per cent. The range of variation in trade ratios is striking, from 5 per cent in Rwanda to 153 per cent in Singapore (Table 17.3). At any one time, however, small countries tend to have a higher trade ratio than large countries, assuming comparable levels of economic

Table 17.3 How important is trade?

Country	Exports of goods & services as a % of GDP (1998)
The least trade-dependent nations	
Rwanda	5
Brazil	7
Albania	9
Uganda	10
Argentina	10
India	11
Peru	12
Iran	13
Bangladesh	14
Major industrial economies (G7 nations)	
US	12
Japan	11
Germany	27
France	27
UK	29
Italy	27
Canada	41
The world's most trade-dependent nations	
Singapore	153
Hong Kong	125
Malaysia	114
Ireland	80
Estonia	80
Belgium	73
Netherlands	76

Source: World Development Indicators, The World Bank (2000).

development. The top five trade-oriented countries, with export : GDP ratios in the range 73 per cent to 185 per cent, are small countries. Ironically, while small countries trade more proportionately than large countries, small firms tend to be less trade-oriented than large firms. In most countries, a small minority of large firms account for the predominant share of total exports.

Composition of trade

About 80 per cent of total trade consists of merchandise trade and 20 per cent of commercial services. Most of this trade is between developed countries – they trade much more with each other than with developing countries.

The product composition of trade is changing rapidly. Trade in food and primary commodities has declined relative to manufacturing. Manufactured goods dominate world trade, accounting for 72 per cent of merchandise flows. In recent decades, the share of *high-tech trade*, which includes pharmaceuticals, chemicals, precision engineering and electronics, has risen steeply. Office and telecom equipment, for example, has increased its share of world trade from 5 per cent in the early 1980s to 13 per cent in the late 1990s – slightly higher than the share of agricultural products. Trade in commercial services, such as transport, tourism and financial services, accounts for about 20 per cent of total trade. Services trade can be especially important for countries that rely heavily on tourism – for example Egypt (64 per cent of total exports) and Greece (63 per cent). Advances in technology and deregulation have opened up large sections of the service industry to international competition. Income from foreign investment has increased in tandem with the globalisation of financial markets.

A large part of trade consists of *intra-industry trade*, defined as the exchange of broadly similar goods. Intra-industry trade has risen rapidly in the past three decades and now accounts for more than half of all trade in manufactures between the industrial countries.[2] A recent study, based on an analysis of over 2000 different manufactured goods, shows that 64 per cent of trade between EU countries in 1992 was intra-industry in character.[3] Many practical examples of intra-industry trade can be given. The UK exported US$130 billion worth of machinery and transport equipment in 1997, but it also in the same year imported US$135 billion worth of these products. Germany is the second largest exporter *and* importer of automotive products in the world. The causes of intra-industry trade, and its implications for structural adjustment and the gains from trade, have been the subject of much study.

A high proportion of foreign trade consists of trade between different branches of the same company. This is called *intra-firm trade* (IFT). A multinational, for example, might buy components for a machine from subsidiaries in one country, assemble it in another country and export it to a subsidiary in a third country. Intra-firm trade has been estimated to comprise over one-third of US merchandise trade.[4] An estimated 26 per cent of trade in Japanese electrical machinery and 23 per cent of its transport equipment trade consists of intra-firm transactions. IFT tends to be particularly prevalent in R&D-intensive and human capital-intensive industries such as machinery, pharmaceuticals and telecommunications. Large firms are particularly active in intra-firm trade. Multinational companies often undertake their own marketing, service/repair and wholesale/distribution operations in foreign markets as a way of maintaining competitive advantage while limiting exposure to outsiders. Intra-firm trade allows multinationals to profit from different national taxation systems. A free trade environment allows a company to carry out R&D in one country (where research subsidies and R&D tax concessions are favourable), manufacture in another (where taxes on manufacturing are low), and export the finished product and R&D services to third countries.[5]

2 *OECD Jobs Study* (Paris, 1994), p. 84.

3 M. Brülhart and R. Elliot, 'A survey of intra-industry trade in the European Union', in M. Brülhart and R. Hine, *Intra-industry Trade and Adjustment: The European Experience* (London: Macmillan, 1998).

4 OECD, *Intra-Firm Trade* (Paris, 1993).

5 H. Grubert and J. Mutti, 'Taxes, tariffs and transfer pricing in multinational corporate decision making', *Review of Economics and Statistics* (May 1991), pp. 285–93. These authors found that differing tax systems were an important determinant of industrial location. See Chapter 18 for discussion.

Another form of trade is countertrade, whereby payment for one set of goods is effected by means of another set. The most common type of countertrade is *bilateral barter*, but there are more complex forms such as *offset* (where a certain proportion of a purchase from one country is offset by corresponding sales to them) and *buy-back trade* (where a firm investing in one country undertakes to purchase part of the output of the investment). Countertrade was prevalent in developing countries and in former socialist countries up to recently. By 1990, it was estimated to have accounted for up to 10 per cent of world trade and 20 per cent of developing countries' trade.[6] With the reform of the economic regime in these countries since then, countertrade has diminished in relative importance.

Trade regimes

Foreign trade has become easier to transact. Tariff barriers have fallen drastically and so have transport and communication costs. Quotas and other forms of quantitative restrictions are used in some sectors but do not constitute a significant barrier in most. Despite ongoing concern about non-tariff barriers, the general momentum has been in favour of freer exchange. But this has not happened by chance. Trade liberalisation has been given institutional force through a series of regional and multilateral trade agreements negotiated during the past five decades. And these agreements, in turn, have been founded on a growing conviction of the economic benefits of free trade.

The General Agreement on Tariffs and Trade (GATT) was founded in 1947. It established two core principles for the conduct of trade policy. First, a *non-discrimination* ('most favoured nation') clause stipulates that any trade concession extended to one member applies to all other members. Second, *national treatment* requires that the same treatment as regards taxes/subsidies should be given to foreign goods once they have entered the country as to domestic goods. Through a succession of trade rounds, GATT succeeded in putting these important principles into effect. Initially attention was focused on achieving deep reciprocal cuts in tariffs on manufactured goods. Later attention shifted to the control of non-tariff barriers to trade such as voluntary export restraints and other forms of quantitative restraints. The Uruguay Round extended the coverage of the Agreement to trade in services and agricultural products. New procedures for handling trade disputes were worked out and the remit of the organisation was extended through the establishment of the World Trade Organisation (WTO) (Box 17.1).

In addition to the multilateral agreements, numerous free trade area agreements, common markets and economic unions have been negotiated. The European Union (EU) is without doubt the most conspicuous and successful of these regional trade agreements. Another is the North American Free Trade Agreement (NAFTA), ratified in 1993 by the US, Mexico and Canada and with an expanding list of applicants. As well as trade liberalisation, NAFTA involves the

---

6 W. Brown and J. Hogendorn, *International Economics: Theory and context* (Reading, MA: Addison-Wesley, 1994), pp. 356–9.

Box 17.1

The World Trade Organisation (WTO)

On 1 January 1995, the World Trade Organisation (WTO) was established with headquarters in Geneva. The WTO provides the contractual framework within which governments undertake to implement legislation and regulations for foreign trade. It is a platform for collective trade debate, negotiation and adjudication among member countries.

Out of a potential 155 members, 136 had joined by early 2000. The remainder, including China and Russia, were still in process of negotiation. Over three-quarters of WTO members are developing countries and countries in economic transition.

The WTO has been assigned the following responsibilities:

■ to put into effect and oversee the provisions of the Uruguay Round (such as tariff reductions, services trade rules and trade-related investment programmes);
■ to implement the plurilateral agreements, such as those on civil aircraft, government procurement, trade in dairy products and meat;
■ to act as a forum for trade negotiations and settlement of disputes;
■ to conduct periodic trade policy reviews of member states.

The main anti-discriminatory provisions of the GATT (the WTO's predecessor) are contained in a revised format in the WTO Agreement, notably the 'most-favoured nation' (MFN) clause and the principle of 'national treatment'.

WTO is basically a system of rules dedicated to *open, fair and undistorted competition*. The WTO agreement on agriculture is designed to provide increased fairness in farm trade. That on intellectual property will improve conditions of competition where ideas and inventions are involved, and the GATS (General Agreement on Trade in Services) will do the same thing for trade in services. The plurilateral agreement on government procurement will extend competition rules to purchases by thousands of government/public sector entities in many countries.

WTO is committed to ensuring better environmental protection and to promoting sustainable development. Linkages between trade policies, environmental policies and sustainable development are to be given priority. International competition policy is also high on the agenda.

The position of developing countries in the WTO is a subject of concern. In the past, their interests have been taken into account by means of escape clauses. However, many are now 'graduating' to developed status; and transition periods are running out. Despite their numerical majority, many developing countries complain about the imbalance in bargaining power between them and the developed countries. Another complaint is that key decisions are taken 'behind doors' by the principal trading partners (the 'Quad' comprising the US, the EU, Japan and Canada). The WTO has promised to give top priority to resolving this issue.

Many applicant countries, especially socialist countries, have a high level of trade-distorting intervention through their economies. Their trading partners worry about how 'fair' trade would be in such circumstances. These controls will have to be substantially scaled down prior to membership. In the case of China, major problems have arisen in agreeing a mode of compliance with the intellectual property accord and with the WTO rules on subsidies.

Source: World Trade Organisation (www.wto.org).

removal of capital restrictions and many non-tariff trade barriers. Free trade areas, however, unlike common markets and economic unions, do not commit their members to a common external trade policy. Many other regional trade organisations exist throughout all five continents, including ASEAN (Association of South East Asian Nations), LAFTA (Latin America Free Trade Agreement), MERCOSUR and APEC (Asia-Pacific Economic Community) to mention just a few. Those with a taste for them will find a bountiful selection of acronyms from which to choose.

17.2 Explaining the gains from international trade

'Trade will very powerfully contribute to increase the mass of commodities and therefore the sum of enjoyments.' This is how David Ricardo, the originator of the theory of comparative advantage, described the gains from trade in 1817. Not only does trade bring material advantage, he argued, but it brings people together, forges common links and helps the cause of peace. 'Perfectly free commerce', he asserted, 'binds together by one common tie of interest and intercourse the universal society of nations throughout the civilised world.'[7] Although the wording sounds anachronistic, the same sentiments are expressed regularly by politicians and opinion leaders.

Gains from trade

1. *Traditional gains*
   - Comparative advantage
   - Variety of products

2. *Modern extensions*
   - Competition and contestability
   - Economies of scale and scope
   - Innovation and R&D
   - Product and quality improvement

The gains from trade in one sense are easy to understand. Foreign trade results in cheaper prices and a wider range of goods available to the consumer. Freedom of trade means that buyers for department stores and retail chains can search the world for cheaper sources of supply. They do so for their own profit, and customers benefit as a result. The search for reliable and better quality automobiles led to the growth of Japanese exports to Europe and the US, thereby

---

7 D. Ricardo, *Principles of Political Economy and Taxation* (1817). Ricardo's views have been echoed by the Nobel prize-winner Milton Friedman, who argued that 'free trade would foster peace and harmony among nations' and, even more ambitiously, that 'the century from Waterloo to the First World War offers a striking example of the beneficial effects of free trade on relations among nations. As a result [of free trade] it was one of the most peaceful in human history among Western nations' (M. and R. Friedman, *Free to Choose: A personal statement*, Harmondsworth: Penguin Books, 1990).

adding to what Ricardo called the 'enjoyments' of millions of car owners in Europe and America. But, as already remarked, there are losers as well as gainers from trade, and protection-seeking business lobbies exist everywhere. In order to assess the balance of advantage, we must analyse the four components of the gains from trade:

- *comparative advantage* gains, arising from efficient allocation of a country's resources;
- gains from *enhanced competition and contestability* of markets;
- gains from *exploiting economies of scale*;
- gains from the *stimulus to innovation, access to knowledge and R&D, and thereby to economic growth*.

Comparative advantage

> By means of glasses, hotbeds and hotwalls, very good grapes can be raised in Scotland, and very good wine too can be made of them at about thirty times the expense for which at least equally good wine can be bought from foreign countries. Would it be a reasonable law to prohibit the importation of all foreign wines, merely to encourage the making of claret and burgundy in Scotland? (Adam Smith, *Wealth of Nations*, Volume 1 (1776), p. 480)

The essence of comparative advantage is the idea that nations, like individuals, should concentrate on what they are best at producing. If one person is an accomplished musician and another a computer wizard, it is more efficient to allow each person to specialise in one field rather than have each of them produce their own music as well as their own computer programs individually. The musician would 'export' music to the computer specialist and the latter, in exchange for these music imports, would 'export' computer services. This seems a mutually advantageous way of trading. In this way the musician and the computer wizard will end up with more goods than if they try making both goods individually. As with individuals, so with nations.

The theory of comparative advantage goes one important step further. It shows that even if one nation is, in an absolute sense, more efficient than another in all activities, trade could be mutually beneficial. The essence of the theory can be illustrated by an arithmetical example:

Suppose there are two countries, England and Portugal, each producing two commodities, wine and clothing. Assume that perfect competition prevails in all markets and that there are constant returns to scale, zero transport costs and only one factor of production: labour. Add the further assumption that labour is always fully employed; if displaced in one industry, it can move costlessly to another. In our example, a worker in England can produce 3 units of wine in the wine industry, or 3 units of clothing in the clothing industry. A worker in Portugal can produce either 6 units of wine or 4 units of clothing. Note that the Portuguese worker is more productive in absolute terms in both industries. (This assumption was not as 'unrealistic' when made by Ricardo in the early nineteenth century as it would appear now.)

Unit of output per person at work

	Portugal	England
Wine	6	3
Clothing	4	3

In a state of autarky (i.e. a situation of zero international trade), one unit of clothing will exchange for 1.5 units of wine within Portugal. In England a unit of clothing will exchange for one unit of wine. Clothing is more expensive in Portugal than in England. By the same reasoning, wine is cheaper in Portugal than in England.

Suppose England takes two workers out of the wine industry and assigns them to work in the clothing industry. This means that wine production falls by 6 units and clothing production increases by 6 units. The 6 units of clothing are exported to Portugal. Given that, in Portugal, 1 unit of clothing exchanges for 1.5 units of wine, the exporters of the 6 units of English clothing return with 9 units of wine. Result: *England has gained 3 units of wine: Portugal is left exactly as well off as before.* (see Box 17.2) One can adjust this example to illustrate a case where Portugal gains and England is left as well off as before. Or, the more likely case, where both countries gain.

Box 17.2

Comparative advantage in action

Using the figures in the text for labour productivity and assuming a price of one unit of clothing per 1.5 units of wine.

England
Two workers reallocated from wine to cloth implies:

   −6W + 6C

Cloth is exported to Portugal in exchange for wine:

   −6C + 9W

Net result: −6W + 9W = +3W

Portugal
Exports 9W in exchange for 6C from England:

   −9W + 6C

To produce 9W it must give up 6C in domestic product:

   +9W −6C

Net result: 0

The above example is capable of extension and modification in many ways. But its essential features convey what is now seen as the core message of international trade theory:

- A country can have an absolute disadvantage in all goods and yet gain from trade with the more efficient partner.

- The gain is realised through imports – they enable England to consume wine more cheaply and Portugal to consume clothing more cheaply. Exports are in a sense 'bad' (one is giving away to foreigners goods which one would like to consume at home) and imports are 'good' (they add to consumption). Exports are useful solely as a means of obtaining imports.

- The total gain from trade may be unevenly shared. In the above numerical example, England gets all the gain, Portugal none. It all depends on the clothing : wine price ratio, which in turn will be determined by world demand and supply. Countries benefit most from trade by obtaining high prices for their exports and paying the lowest possible prices for their imports.

- Trade involves mutual gains. It is not a zero-sum game, whereby gains to one country mean losses to another. Not only is it possible for both countries to gain, it is the most likely outcome in practice since only at the extremes of the possible price range will one country acquire all the gain.

The gains from trade can also be illustrated by means of the production frontier curve, introduced in Chapter 2. Units of wine are drawn on the vertical axis and units of clothing on the horizontal axis (Figure 17.1). We look at England's production frontier. Under autarky, consumption possibilities for England are limited to that production frontier. With the introduction of trade, the range of consumption possibilities for England is expanded. The new range can be represented by curve FF. England could shift production from A to P, exporting PR of clothing in exchange for RB of wine to reach a new consumption point B. Point B is clearly a superior consumption point to A. More of each good can be consumed at that point. England has benefited from trade.

Behind these net gains are losses to factors of production. These do not emerge clearly from the Ricardian analysis, though in a broader context one could see that free trade was good news for England's clothing industry and bad news for producers in the English wine industry. Modern trade theorists have developed more complex diagrams and mathematical models to analyse these issues.

Competition and contestability

The comparative advantage gains are derived on the assumption of perfect competition. However, when a country's domestic market is shielded from foreign competitors, competitive forces are likely to be weak. Domestic producers have an incentive to collude, safe in the knowledge that the home market will not be attacked from abroad. Small countries with strong protectionist regimes are particularly prone to monopoly influences, since in many industries the domestic market will be small in relation to the minimum efficient size of the firm.

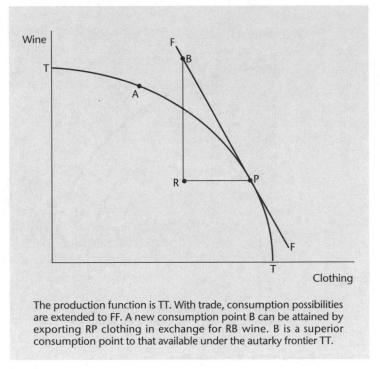

The production function is TT. With trade, consumption possibilities are extended to FF. A new consumption point B can be attained by exporting RP clothing in exchange for RB wine. B is a superior consumption point to that available under the autarky frontier TT.

Figure 17.1 How trade allows more consumption

In such circumstances, the liberalisation of trade can give a sharp boost to competition in the domestic market. As the market becomes more contestable, domestic producers have to fight hard to stay in business. The reductions in general inefficiencies and in 'managerial slack' under this process are referred to as the 'X-efficiency' gains. Increased competition in the manufacturing sector and exposure to world class competition was considered as a major source of X-efficiency gains for the economies of the EU member states. Today, the same processes are observed in services such as banking, insurance and transport, where radical improvements in efficiency have been recorded in response to external competitive pressures following trade liberalisation.

X-efficiency gains can be depicted as a general outward shift of the production frontier (from TT to T^1T^1). This does not imply that all industries gain equally – in some industries the intensity of competition among domestic producers may have been higher under protection, and the potential efficiency gains from the trade lower, than in others. The essence of the gain arises because, through elimination of waste and better utilisation, the same stock of productive factors can produce more output. This concept is given expression in Figure 17.2.

The competitive effects of free trade are not fully captured by the above static analysis. This is because competition leads to second- and third-round benefits – indeed, to an ongoing process of continuous improvement and innovation. In a

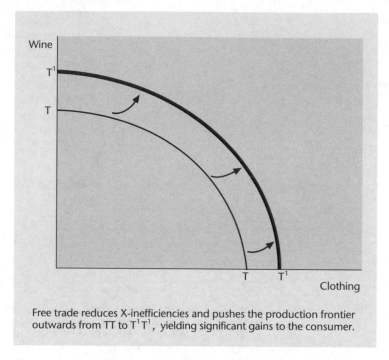

Free trade reduces X-inefficiencies and pushes the production frontier outwards from TT to T^1T^1, yielding significant gains to the consumer.

Figure 17.2 X-efficiencies and free trade

globally competitive market, a firm cannot afford to stand still. It must engage in renewal and re-evaluation. This is hard work for the firm, but redounds to the benefit of the consumer. Competition confers 'dynamic' gains on the trading country in addition to the 'static' gains of Ricardian comparative advantage. Once considered relevant only to smaller countries, nowadays larger countries include the stimulative effects of more competition as a major source of gain.

Economies of scale and scope

'The division of labour is limited by the size of the market.' Adam Smith's dictum provides the key to the third source of gain from foreign trade. While the 'competition' gains described above are derived from the opening of *domestic* markets to foreign competition, scale economies arise as a result of the opening of *foreign* markets to domestic producers. Widening the extent of the market makes it possible for domestic producers to specialise on narrower product ranges (horizontal specialisation) and to integrate the output process (vertical specialisation). Specialisation leads to lower unit costs and, by so doing, makes it possible for domestic firms to compete in foreign markets (now assumed to be untrammelled by trade restrictions). Franchisers can export their services to foreign countries, reduce unit cost and make more profit; car manufacturers, by selling to foreign markets, can attain viable production levels.

Many small firms are able to trade globally on the basis of an extremely specialised product range. This is economies of scale in action. The exploitation of the potential economies of scale does not require huge plants. A single factory in Ireland, employing just over 200 people, provides sufficient soft drink concentrate to supply over 17 per cent of the global consumption of Coca-Cola products. One Nordic firm, Nokia, supplies 27 per cent of the world market for mobile telecommunications equipment, much of it produced in Scandinavia.[8] Sweden accounts for some 40 per cent of the world paperboard market; Swiss-manufactured watches comprise one-third of world exports of watches; and Italy accounts for over half of world exports of precious metal jewellery.[9] By extending the size of the market, foreign trade gives small producers the opportunity to exploit economies of scale. For small countries, exports provide a means of escape from the limitations of their small size.

By exposing domestic firms to competition and forcing them to improve efficiency, free trade has the effect in some countries of stimulating mergers and acquisitions. This can lead to an increase in industry concentration ratios. It would obviously be wrong, however, to interpret this as evidence of a diminution of competitive pressure. 'Rationalisation' of industries is a normal part of the adjustment process, to be expected rather than resisted by the authorities. Nevertheless, it is a rather paradoxical outcome, which needs to be monitored by the competition authorities.

Growth effects

Trade has been described as the 'handmaiden of growth'. It encourages economic growth by bringing about changes in attitudes and motivation favourable to industrialisation, by acting as a conduit for technological change, and by encouraging innovation and investment. People learn, and are influenced by, foreign commercial contacts. To survive against foreign competition, firms must invest in R&D and innovate. Imports also incorporate technical improvements; hence the positive causal link from imports to economic growth. This fourth source of gain derives, but is distinct, from the first three. It is a case of the whole effect of trade being greater than the sum of its parts. This broader canvas has been encapsulated in *The Economist* (20 April 1991):

> Liberal trade: is it a good thing or not? This is less a matter of doctrine – though the answer is exceptionally well-grounded in economic theory – as of coincidence that the expansion of global trade since 1945 went hand in hand with unprecedented economic growth. Or that the nearly closed economies of Eastern Europe and the Soviet Union failed on every measure. Or that the most protected economies in the third world (India and Argentina, for instance) squandered their potential, while neighbours (such as Thailand and Chile) embraced trade and thrived. Or that, in otherwise fairly open economies, the most protected industries are the most backward (steel in America, farming in Japan, computing in Europe).

---

8 *The Economist* (9 October 1994); *Business Week* (17 July 2000).
9 Michael E. Porter, *The Competitive Advantage of Nations* (London: Macmillan, 1990).

Evidence of a positive association between export growth and economic performance has been accumulating at a rapid rate. The World Bank has been to the forefront of research on this topic and it has been a consistent and vocal advocate of outward-looking policies. Openness produces better results because it involves working *with* rather than *against* the market. In the case of developing countries, the World Bank pointed out that not only did protection deny developing countries the benefits of trade, but it led to destructive side-effects such as the substitution of capital for labour (a perverse effect given the abundant labour supply in these countries) and 'rent-seeking'.[10] Worse, as a result of their deliberate isolation from the world economy, the countries of the former Soviet bloc found themselves a generation behind in much industrial technology.

The experience of countries that have isolated themselves from international commerce alerts us to another benefit of trade, which has been emphasised in the business literature. Manufactured exports provide a powerful incentive to technological upgrading in imperfect world technology markets. The exposure of a firm's products to a demanding and sophisticated market forces management to improve product quality. Because firms that export have greater access to best-practice technology, there are benefits to the enterprises and spillovers to the rest of the economy which are not reflected in market prices. These information-related externalities are an important source of productivity growth. Both cross-country evidence and more detailed studies at the industry level in Japan, Korea and Taiwan confirm the correlation between exports and rapid productivity growth.[11] Countries such as Hungary and the former Czechoslovakia, which exported manufactures to the Soviet Union, found virtually no quality control necessary and, as a result, they had no need to engage in the continuous innovation on which long-term economic success so much depends.[12] When the market to the East collapsed, firms in those countries had great difficulty in competing against Western goods of a much higher quality.

---

10 *Rent-seeking* in this context refers to the diversion of entrepreneurial effort to socially unproductive activities such as lobbying for protection or for a government subsidy against foreign competition. In other circumstances this effort would be directed to innovation or tighter cost control. We have already encountered this concept in our analysis of monopoly (Chapter 6). It was originally applied to trade protection in an article by Anne Krueger in the 1970s and it has been extended into a theory of the more cumbersomely titled *directly unproductive profit-seeking* by J. Bhagwati.

11 See World Bank Policy Research Report, *The East Asia Miracle: Economic growth and public policy* (Oxford: Oxford University Press, 1993), p. 23.

12 An interesting exponent of this view is the Hungarian economist, Janos Kornai:

The most important long-term drawback of Hungary's export ties with the Comecon countries is the low levels of quality standards in these markets. ... It is relatively easy to sell products in these markets that would be unacceptable in hard-currency markets. This is one more reason for the need to coolly but resolutely shift Hungary's sphere of interest to markets that insist on better-quality goods. (J. Kornai, *The Road to a Free Economy*, New York: Norton, 1990)

Selling to higher-quality markets is also the fourth part of Michael Porter's diamond of comparative advantage (see below).

17.3 Quantifying the gains from trade

Some critics argue that the expansion of trade, much of it intra-industry trade in similar goods and services, yields at best trivial gains which come at a heavy cost to the physical and social environment. Empirical measurement of the gains from trade contradicts this view. Trade brings gains which are far from trivial. They can be measured in several ways. First, trade gains can be measured by reference to countries that have changed from complete isolation to free trade, or vice versa.

The gains from trade relative to a position of autarky (or complete isolation from trade) have rarely been estimated. Virtually no country closes its borders to trade completely. Japan's position pre-1850 might qualify as an exception. During the period 1850–74, after trade was liberalised, prices of import-substitutes fell to one-third of their autarky level. According to one estimate, Japanese GDP increased by as much as 65 per cent as a result of opening its market.[13] Studies of the effects of economic sanctions and blockades (such as those once applied to South Africa or Libya) show similar effects. The economy of Southern Rhodesia (as Zimbabwe was previously called), where sanctions were at least partially enforced, was estimated to have suffered a 13 per cent loss as a result of restricted trading opportunities.[14] The standard of living of small countries in particular would be seriously undermined if possibilities of international trade were to disappear. Imagine a country such as Belgium having to manufacture all its own machinery, its own cars and trucks, its own computers and aircraft. The cost of producing them domestically would obviously be prohibitive.

Rather than studying the effects of moving from one polar extreme (no trade) to the other (free trade), most estimates of the gains from trade quantify the benefits of *incremental* movements towards freer trade. Two trade liberalisation initiatives have been intensively studied: Europe's single market programme and the Uruguay Round.

The single market programme involved the removal of non-tariff barriers on trade between member states and the opening of the hitherto protected services industries to foreign competition. Frontier controls were abolished, fiscal regimes made more compatible, and public procurement contracts opened to tender and publicised more transparently. The total gain to the member states from the programme was estimated to be between 4.5 and 6 per cent of GDP, equivalent to about 200 billion ECUs in 1992 values.[15] The composition of these estimated gains is especially revealing. Some were straightforward efficiency gains, derived from comparative advantage considerations, but the largest sources of gain related to economies of scale and intensified competition within the European market.

---

13 J.B. Huber, *Journal of Political Economy* (May/June 1971).

14 G. Hufbauer, *Economic Sanctions Reconsidered – Supplemental case studies* (Washington, DC: Institute of International Economics, 1993). Ironically, in view of his many past criticisms of the unequal nature of the global trade system and its alleged tendency to harm developing countries, Fidel Castro in August 1994 blamed the disastrous condition of the Cuban economy on its lack of access to this trade system (as a result of US trade sanctions).

15 'The economics of 1992', *European Economy* (March 1988).

Box 17.3

The Uruguay Round

Market access should boost world income by an extra US$510 billion annually.

By the time market access commitments are fully implemented in 2005, the reduction of international trade barriers following the Uruguay Round agreement will result in an increase in world income of US$510 billion annually. This WTO estimate may underestimate the impact because it is based on only *one* aspect of the Round, namely *liberalisation of trade in goods*. It ignores the beneficial impact of other aspects concerning, for example, strengthened trade rules, procedures and institutions; market access commitments; and rules for trade in services.

Highlights from the *ex ante* studies of the Round include:

- Estimated annual income gains:

	$bn
US	122
EU	164
Japan	27
Developing economies	116
China	19
Chinese Taipei	10
Other	52
Total	510

- Agreement to reduce tariffs on industrial goods by 40 per cent, with the proportion of industrial products entering the developed country market with zero duties more than doubling from 20 to 44 per cent.
- Reforms in agriculture involving a 36 per cent reduction in export subsidies, and a decline of 18 per cent in domestic support to agricultural producers.
- Strengthening the rules, procedures and institutions governing subsidies, technical barriers and discriminatory internal taxes, thus helping countries to anticipate and defuse potential trade conflicts.
- Recent research, reported in Laird (2000), indicates that a 40 per cent reduction in barriers to trade in services could produce welfare gains of as much as $332 billion in 2005.

Sources: The Results of the Uruguay Round of Multilateral Trade Negotiations. Market Access for Goods and Services: Overview of the results (Geneva: GATT Secretariat, November 1994); Sam Laird, 'Dolphins, mad cows and butterflies – the multilateral trading system in the 21st century', CREDIT research paper, University of Nottingham, no. 00/16, November 2000.

Similar methodologies were applied to estimating the economic effects of the Uruguay Round. Up to the time the agreement was signed, estimates of the gains were in the range from US$212 billion to US$274 billion (in 1992 dollars), equivalent to only 1 per cent of world GDP in 1992. Subsequent estimates raised this amount to US$510 billion, based on a 'new' and more 'realistic' world economic model (see Box 17.3). A large proportion of these gains derived from the reduction of agricultural protection. This explains why the EU emerges with a gain of US$164 billion, or one-third of the total. Industrial countries see the liberalisation of agriculture as a 'concession' but, for reasons explained earlier, these quantification exercises show them to be major beneficiaries of the process; they are expected to obtain over 70 per cent of the estimated gains of the Round. A complete liberalisation of trade would, following this logic, provide even more gains than those obtained from the partial liberalisation of the Uruguay Round. Partick Messerlin, for instance, estimates that the total cost to the EU of its remaining external trade barriers is equivalent to around 7 per cent of GDP, or US$600 million.[16]

These figures must all be taken with a large grain of salt. They are based on a diverse range of methodologies, including computer simulations, assumed price elasticity values, business opinion surveys and arbitrary assumptions. This much is readily admitted by their progenitors. Yet it is often asserted that the estimates are likely to underestimate the true gains, because certain dynamic benefits have defied quantification.[17] But this point can be argued both ways. If labour adjustment were to prove slow and unemployment to escalate they could just as easily overestimate the gains. Also the estimated gains may be low because trade in manufactured goods has already been substantially liberalised in Europe and the developed world. Like macroeconomic forecasts, they are not flawless predictors, simply the best available, and have to be treated with caution. Unlike the macro-forecasts, however, estimates of the gains from trade can never be shown to be wrong. Because they involve comparison between actual ex-post trade flows and hypothetical trade flows (as they would have been had the Uruguay Round been unsuccessful or the EU's single market programme never occurred), the estimates cannot be confronted with what actually happened.[18] The manner in which these estimates are commonly presented often gives a misleading impression of precision and authority.

A third way of estimating the effects of free trade is by comparative analysis. Countries which choose outward-looking trade regimes can be compared with countries opting for inward-looking or protectionist trade regimes. One study

16 Patrick Messerlin, *Measuring the Costs of Protection in Europe* (Washington, DC: Institute for International Economics, 2000).

17 International Monetary Fund, 'The Uruguay Round: Results and implications', *IMF World Economic Outlook* (Washington, DC, August 1994).

18 The achievement of the Uruguay Round has been described by an analogy with riding a bicycle. If the bicycle stops, the cyclist falls. Had the Uruguay Round failed, the *status quo ante* may not have been maintained. The whole system might have been overwhelmed by protectionist pressures. The Uruguay Round agreement was, therefore, more important than estimates based on the assumption of the *status quo* being maintained would indicate.

Table 17.4 Developing countries: trade orientation and economic performance

	1974–85	1986–92
Strongly outward-oriented		
Real GDP growth	8.0	7.5
Real per capita GDP growth	6.1	5.9
Total factor productivity	2.6	3.8
Moderately outward-oriented		
Real GDP growth	4.3	4.8
Real per capita GDP growth	2.2	2.5
Total factor productivity	0.9	2.4
Moderately inward-oriented		
Real GDP growth	4.4	2.4
Real per capita GDP growth	1.8	−0.1
Total factor productivity	1.3	0.3
Strongly inward-oriented		
Real GDP growth	2.3	2.5
Real per capita GDP growth	−0.3	−0.1
Total factor productivity	−0.4	0.3
All developing countries		
Real GDP growth	4.1	3.8
Real per capita GDP growth	1.7	1.5
Total factor productivity	0.8	1.4

Notes: Annual percentage change unless otherwise noted.
Developing countries are classified into four categories according to the orientation of their trade strategy during the past two decades: (1) strongly outward-oriented, where trade controls are either non-existent or very low; (2) moderately outward-oriented, where the average rate of effective protection for the home market is relatively low and the range of effective protection rates relatively narrow; (3) moderately inward-oriented, where the overall incentive structure favours production for the domestic market; and (4) strongly inward-oriented, where the overall incentive structure strongly favours production for the domestic market.

Source: IMF, *World Economic Outlook* (May 1993), p. 76.

divides developing countries into four categories ranging from strongly outward-oriented to strongly inward-oriented and finds that the outward-looking groups have clearly outperformed the inward-looking groups. Growth in total GDP, in GDP per person, in total factor productivity (which measures the efficiency of both capital and labour inputs) and other indices all testify to the benefits of outward-looking strategies (Table 17.4). Work on this subject continues. The World Bank published a multi-country, 7-volume, 3000-page study of the effects of trade liberalisation in 1991. Its central finding is a ringing confirmation of previous studies: 'liberalisation clearly tends to accelerate economic growth'.[19] While differences in economic performance happen for many reasons other than

---

19 D. Papageorgiou, M. Michaely and A. Choksi, *Liberalising Foreign Trade* (Washington, DC: World Bank, 1991), p. 85. However, see D. Greenaway, 'Liberalising foreign trade through rose-tinted glasses', *Economic Journal* (January 1993) for a warning about the validity of some of the evidence.

choice of trade policy, the results are nevertheless consistent with a highly positive view of the benefits of trade. More recent research adds another twist to this story. Because growth helps to alleviate poverty, and trade helps growth, trade can play an important part in alleviating poverty. A WTO secretariat study published in June 2000 found that developing countries that are most open to trade are catching up fastest with living standards of the developed countries. For example, thirty years ago South Korea was as poor as Ghana. Today, as a result of trade-led growth, it is as rich as Portugal. In summary, globalisation is good for growth and growth is good for the poor.

17.4 Trade policy and protection

When imported goods are in direct competition with a firm's domestic sales, free trade poses the threat of falling prices, employment cutbacks and lower profits. The firm's existence may be placed in jeopardy and it lobbies for protection.[20]

Arguments in favour of protection have a long history. Although an ardent advocate of free trade, Adam Smith identified four cases where protection was justified (see Box 17.4). These exceptions are still considered valid. First, there is obvious justification for protecting *strategic defence industries*. The export of technically advanced products to hostile nations is often prohibited. Second, if a domestically produced good is subject to a tax, imported goods should be taxed by the same amount, if necessary by imposition of a tariff. (This is an early and rudimentary form of the *level playing field argument*.) Third, *countervailing duties on imports* could legitimately be used in order to discourage the arbitrary use of protection by others, and to encourage them to abide by international trade rules. Fourth, the case for *transitional protection* is widely accepted as a way of moderating the painful adjustment costs of freer trade. These, and other possible justifications for protection, have absorbed a great deal of research effort over the years.

Modern analysis, however, goes well beyond this. It focuses on sources of distortions in the system and on the *optimal form of intervention* to remedy them. Four sources of possible distortion are of particular importance in trade analysis:

1. unemployment and the capacity of an economy to adjust,
2. foreign monopoly power,
3. failure of prices to signal future changes in comparative advantage,
4. neglect of environmental effects.

---

20 Economists have tended to take a jaundiced view of such lobbying, as evidenced in the conclusion of a 1903 manifesto signed by a number of distinguished British economists: 'protection brings in its train the loss of purity in politics, unfair advantage to those who wield the powers of jobbery and corruption, unjust distribution of wealth and the growth of sinister interests' (quoted in J. Bhagwati, *Protectionism*, p. 31).

> ### Box 17.4
>
> ## Adam Smith's argument for protection
>
> Smith is usually viewed as an early champion of free trade. His masterpiece, *The Wealth of Nations*, contains a blistering attack on the protectionist philosophy of the mercantilist school. Yet Smith, as an intelligent and practical person, envisaged exceptional cases in which protection could be justified:
>
> 1. *Defence of the country* – Protection of defence industries such as shipping could be justified on non-economic grounds.
> 2. *Level playing field* – If a country imposes a tax on domestic producers it should levy a similar tax on imported substitutes.
> 3. *Retaliation* – A retaliatory tax might be a useful deterrent to protectionist practices by other countries. Smith instanced the case of the French who *have been particularly forward to favour their own manufactures by restraining the importation of such foreign goods as could come into competition with them.*
> 4. *Transitional protection* – 'When particular manufacturers have been so far extended as to employ a great multitude of hands, humanity may require that the freedom of trade should be restored only by slow gradations and with a good deal of reserve and circumspection' (Adam Smith, *Wealth of Nations*, Bk IV (1776), pp. 488–91). Free trade agreements normally have transition periods designed to allow time for adjustment by the affected employees. This may not only be justifiable for reasons of 'humanity': it may also make good economic sense.

Unemployment and the capacity to adjust

An implicit assumption of trade theory is that resources are fully employed. This means that labour and other factors of production 'released' from import-competing industries are redeployed elsewhere in the economy. In terms of our earlier example, workers in England's wine industry displaced by Portuguese imports move to the clothing industry where their output has a higher value. This reallocation is an integral element in reaping the gains from trade.

Suppose, however, that those who lost their jobs in the wine industry were not successfully redeployed. Then, instead of moving from A to P in Figure 17.3, the economy's production point moves to P*. This point lies below the production frontier, reflecting the fact that people are unemployed. Trade will take place at P*, but clearly the gains from trade will be reduced and may even be completely negated by this failure to reallocate. This problem is real and immediate to those affected. To argue that resources will be reallocated in the long run may be valid but can sound complacent. Referring to the communication gap between economists and the public on the merits of free trade (Box 17.5), Alan Blinder criticised the economics profession for *speaking in a long-run equilibrium dialect to*

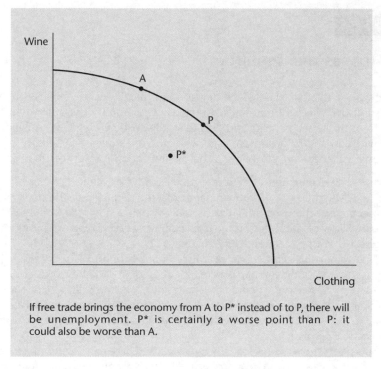

If free trade brings the economy from A to P* instead of to P, there will be unemployment. P* is certainly a worse point than P: it could also be worse than A.

Figure 17.3 Free trade and unemployment

people who live in a short-run disequilibrium world. No wonder what we say sounds Greek to them [21]

Yet labour displaced in import-competing industries does generally succeed in finding alternative employment in the long run. Even over the past twenty years, there have been massive reallocations of the workforce. In German manufacturing, for example, between 1972 and 1991, employment fell by 35 per cent in the steel industry, by 55 per cent in clothing and textiles, and by 41 per cent in beverages. During the same period, there was a rise of 8 per cent in employment in the food-processing industry, 9 per cent in the chemical industry, 33 per cent in office and computing machinery, and 54 per cent in automobile manufacture. Similar patterns are evident in other countries. Large numbers of jobs have disappeared in household domestic service as maids and butlers have been replaced by washing machines and vacuum cleaners. The millions of jobs 'lost' have to a large extent been compensated by jobs found in 'new' industries, such as computers and electronics and commercial service activities. Too much focus on the short run can lead to the neglect of the powerful productivity gains obtained by such reallocation.

Studies of the income profile of workers displaced by import competition show a wide variation in experience across sectors. The scale of adjustment depends on

21 A. Blinder, *Macroeconomics under Debate* (Hemel Hempstead: Harvest Wheatsheaf, 1989), pp. 152–3.

Box 17.5

Job losses and imports

Economists are often accused of having their heads in the clouds when it comes to discussing the effects of free trade. Critics say with some justification that trade theorists tend to overplay the benefits and downplay the costs. Professor Alan Blinder responds to this charge in the following passage, which demonstrates his capacity to see the trade adjustment process in a clear light rather than through rose-tinted glasses:

> Virtually all economists support free trade; but a frustrating number of non-economists do not. Members of our fraternity are constantly amazed at the depth and strength of protectionist sentiment, which we view as evidence of either rent-seeking behaviour or low intelligence. Doubtless, some protectionists qualify under both rubrics. But I want to suggest that there is more to the matter.
>
> One reason for economists' near-unanimous support of free trade is our use of the long-run, full-employment framework for policy evaluation. In our world, workers displaced by foreign competition move into industries in which our country has a comparative advantage. That can only raise productivity; so both GNP and social welfare should rise. How, except as viewed through the distorting lenses of a special pleader, could that be bad?
>
> But people unencumbered by advanced degrees in economics see trade policy differently. They live in real space and time, where unemployment truly exists and workers displaced by foreign competition often move into unemployment rather than into new jobs. So they reason that our GNP will fall if our markets are opened to free trade. How, except in the strange world of the economic theorist, could that be good?
>
> The two world-views generate different predictions. Which is right? Consider a concrete example. Korean firms learn how to make television sets efficiently and want to export them to the US. The TV industry and its workers petition Congress for a strict quota to 'save jobs'. Economists scoff at the idea. According to standard trade theory, the US can only gain by opening its borders to Korean TVs. A quota cannot save jobs; it can only trap labour in an industry in which the United States has no comparative advantage.
>
> Though over-simplified and missing many of the qualifications that a good trade theorist would want, this conclusion probably characterises the typical economist's view of the matter. And it is also probably the right view in the long run. It might even be right for the short run, if the unemployment rate were 4 percent. But suppose Korea learns how to make TVs when the US unemployment rate was 10 percent. Who can honestly assure a displaced factory worker that she will quickly find a new job at a wage close to her present one, as she would in the world envisioned by Ricardian comparative advantage? Isn't it more likely that she will suffer a spell of joblessness, perhaps a lengthy one? Aren't these short-run costs relevant to any social decision?
>
> I anticipate your response and I agree with it: the appropriate solution is not to erect trade barriers but to pursue a vigorous full employment policy so that displaced workers will be quickly re-employed. This is precisely my point. Conditions of full employment are necessary to validate standard propositions in trade theory. High unemployment calls

Box 17.5 continued

many of these propositions into question. Both the positive predictions of trade theory and its normative prescriptions may be wrong. For example, when unemployment results from a rigid real wage, free trade may reduce both employment and welfare. Furthermore, if unemployment were eradicated by abolishing the wage floor, patterns of trade might reverse. Those who are wary of free trade may have a valid point in the presence of unemployment, as even Adam Smith realised. At the very least, trade adjustment assistance should perhaps become a more integral part of the advocacy of free trade.

Now, I am not trying to argue for protectionism. Though we may all be dead in the long run, someone will be alive. And a nation that protects one senile industry after another winds up looking like a nursing home for state capitalism. Economists correctly seek to avoid this outcome. Besides, the mere existence of unemployment does not in itself imply that protection is better than free trade.

I am arguing, however, that trade theorists could do their job better if they paid more attention to the short run. At a minimum, it would narrow the communication gap between economists and the public. We insist on speaking in a long-run equilibrium dialect to people who live in a short-run disequilibrium world. No wonder what we say sounds like Greek to them.

The phenomenon of unemployment, of course, is not unknown to trade theorists; and some interesting work has been done. But ask yourself what fraction of the enormous trade theory literature deals with unemployment: 10 percent? 5 percent? Can that be an optimal allocation of resources?

Source: Alan S. Blinder, *Macroeconomics under Debate* (Hemel Hempstead: Harvester Wheatsheaf, 1989); (first published in *American Economic Review*, May 1988).

the countries between which trade is being liberalised. If closer integration is taking place between countries with similar income per capita and structure, intra-industry trade is likely to dominate the outcome. Firms will produce a more specialised range of output, but whole industries will not be put out of business, and comparatively little inter-industry labour adjustment may be necessary. Where trade liberalisation takes place between rich and poor countries (e.g. North–South trade), adjustment is likely to be more painful. Those with sector-specific skills lose income. The beneficiaries are those with the skills and the adaptability to fit into new employment patterns. These are usually younger and better-educated employees. Prospects for successful labour market adjustment are enhanced by factors such as:

- fast economic growth,
- flexibility of wages and openness to new entrants,
- prompt availability of retraining and re-skilling programmes for displaced employees,
- the length of time available for adjustment.

Conditions of full employment are not satisfied in the labour markets of many countries around the world, especially in Europe. This warns against any over-optimistic assessment of the adjustment capacity of a modern economy. A surge in imports may exacerbate unemployment and government intervention may well be justified to assist adjustment. *But it does not follow that import restrictions are the optimal form of intervention.* To the extent that unemployment is the fault of domestic policies rather than trade policies, the problem should be dealt with directly at source rather than indirectly through trade measures.

A more general interpretation of the unemployment argument is that *trade provides benefits only if prices reflect social opportunity costs*. When large numbers are unemployed, the wage obviously fails to reflect social cost, since the alternative to being at work in an import-competing industry is very likely being idle.

Monopoly power

One of the oldest arguments for protection (the optimum tariff argument) states that, if a country is exposed to monopoly exploitation by importers, it can improve its welfare by (a) placing a countervailing tariff on imports, or (b) subsidising the import-competing industry. Here less trade means more welfare. (By the same reasoning, a country with unexploited *monopsony* power should impose an export tax, as OPEC producers have done.)

Take, for example, the subsidisation of Airbus Industrie, a government-backed consortium of companies from France, Britain, Germany and Spain. The market for civilian aircraft had for a long time been dominated by Boeing and McDonnell-Douglas (now merged). Airbus was set up to develop an alternative European source of supply. Subsidies played a big part in the growth of Airbus. Since its establishment in 1970, an estimated US$28 billion has been sunk into the consortium by the European taxpayer (some of that sum has been repaid from profits on the A320). In return, Airbus has become a major player in the civilian aircraft market. By 1994, its share of global production of civilian aircraft had surpassed 50 per cent.[22] To determine the success of Airbus in economic terms is more complex. Cost-benefit studies show that (a) Airbus and its employees gained, (b) profits in the US civilian aircraft industry fell, (c) the European consumer benefited from lower airfares, and (d) the European taxpayer had to finance subsidies. The net impact of these forces on European welfare is still being debated. A good case can be made that the reduction in fares and the indirect labour market and innovation spillover effects following the establishment of Airbus compensated for the cost of the subsidies from the European taxpayer. On balance, Airbus would qualify as a case of successful intervention.[23]

---

22 'How Airbus soared past its American rival', *Sunday Times* (16 April 1995).
23 See L. Tyson, *Who's Bashing Whom? Trade conflict in high technology industries* (Washington, DC: Institute for International Economics, 1992). But see G. Klepper, 'Entry into the market for large transport aircraft', *European Economic Review*, No. 4 (1990) for a contrary viewpoint.

The justification for such intervention, of course, was not just to offset US monopoly power. In addition to this optimum tariff consideration, there were many externalities through positive spillover effects from domestic industry or from the development of indigenous technical and human capital.

Changes in comparative advantage

In our example, comparative advantage leads Portugal to specialise in wine and England to specialise in clothing. From the viewpoint of the theory, it does not matter which country exports which good. Yet, in practice, countries do worry about this – and with reason. Britain's industrial growth drew sustenance from its comparative advantage in clothing. The factory system developed, and with it the opportunity to exploit economies of scale and technological progress; income was distributed from landowners to industrialists, who had a high propensity to reinvest; real wages were reduced by lower food prices; and a self-sustaining cycle of industrial advance was generated. The same benign process would have been less likely had England happened to find its comparative advantage emerging in food (wine) rather than manufacturing (clothing). Hence, the industry in which a country specialises initially may have a powerful influence on its future development. In certain circumstances, government intervention may be necessary in order to ensure that a long-term view is taken of a country's comparative advantage.

Japan is often considered an outstanding example of a country where government took deliberate measures to assist and guide the evolution of comparative advantage. Opinions differ as to the effectiveness and efficiency of such intervention. But the approach taken by the Japanese authorities was described approvingly as follows:

> The Ministry of International Trade and Industry (MITI) decided to establish in Japan industries which required intensive employment of capital and technology, industries that in consideration of comparative cost of production should be the most inappropriate for Japan, industries such as steel, oil refining, petrochemicals, automobiles, electronics, computers. From a short-run, static viewpoint, encouragement of such industries would seem to conflict with economic rationalism. But from a long-range point of view, these are precisely the industries where income elasticity of demand is high, technological progress is rapid, and labour productivity rises fast. (OECD, *Industrial Policy of Japan* (Paris, 1972))

The same ideas lie behind the Cecchini Report's lapidary comment that 'comparative advantage is no longer seen as divine inheritance'.[24] 'Nor', it adds, are 'market structures and rivals' behaviour set in tablets of stone'. Concern with dynamic comparative advantage continues to motivate governments to make strategic interventions, particularly in the high-tech sector. The league tables of world market share in high-tech products are monitored carefully. Indeed the perceived loss of market share in these products was one of the factors which pushed the European Commission to propose the formation of the 1992 single

---

24 P. Cecchini, *The European Challenge 1992* (Aldershot: Wildwood House, 1988), p. 85.

market programme. Protection of these industries at a national level had not succeeded, for all the reasons outlined earlier: insufficient scope for economies of scale serving national markets, suppression of competition behind import restrictions, specialisation patterns out of line with comparative advantage. To develop these sectors, a large domestic market was needed, an open market of 360 million people instead of national markets of 3 to 60 million. In addition, efforts had to be made to ensure that the educational and R&D infrastructure was in place from which comparative advantage could develop. Finally, anti-dumping and competition rules were needed in order to allow European and third country suppliers to compete on a level playing field. The reasons for the Commission's intervention are similar to those of MITI in Japan. *Strategic trade theory*, as it is now known, draws on both externality theory and on dynamic considerations from industrial organisation to provide a framework for analysing these issues.

Environment protection[25]

Firms in countries with strict environmental standards worry about the impact of those standards on their competitiveness in world markets (the 'eco-dumping' problem). At the same time, governments and firms in countries with less strict standards express concern about new barriers being erected against their exports. The treatment of exports from countries which use child labour, deny freedom to trade unions, and ignore animal health and welfare rules is becoming the focus of more disputes. These are difficult issues to resolve.

The principle of non-discrimination ordains that a country cannot discriminate against imports merely because the exporting country has environmental policies different from its own. In the absence of this principle, any country could unilaterally apply trade restrictions not just for the purpose of enforcing its own laws in its jurisdiction but to impose its standards on others. In such circumstances the scope for abuse would be great. It would work against the main objective of the multilateral trade system – to provide stable and predictable market access through agreed rules. For this reason, the US was ruled out of order in 1991 by a GATT tribunal for placing an embargo on imports of tuna products from Mexico because Mexico's tuna fishing regulations did not satisfy the US's dolphin protection standards.

Another principle is that governments are free to agree multilaterally on any set of environmental restrictions they like. Trade in the products of endangered animals is outlawed by multilateral agreement. Discrimination is allowed against imports produced by prison labour. If sufficient support could be found, the rules could be extended to cover child labour and other labour market conditions. The important point is that intervention must not be unilateral.

---

25 For a discussion of these issues in the EU context, see M. Brülhart and D. McAleese, 'External trade policy', in A. El-Agraa, *The European Union: Economics and Politics*, (Harlow: Financial Times Prentice Hall, 2000).

WTO rules also allow governments to protect their *own* environment from damage arising from domestic production or from the consumption of domestically produced *or* imported products. It is when one country's environmental problem is due to production or consumption activities in *another* that application of the rules becomes complicated. One constraint is that countries are prohibited from making market access dependent on changes in the domestic policies or practices of the exporting country. Countries are allowed to impose restrictions on imports which might endanger the health or safety of its citizens (sanitary and phytosanitary measures), but subject to the requirement that the measures do not arbitrarily discriminate between countries where the same conditions prevail and that they are not a disguised restriction on international trade.

Different national systems, whether in environmental, health, social or fiscal matters, can have a significant impact on trade flows. For individual firms this can have important implications. It is tempting to seek protection to 'compensate' for such differences and thereby create 'fair' trading conditions. The difficulty is that firms in other countries will have no difficulty in finding instances where your system hurts them and use this to justify restrictions on your exports. Hence some internationally agreed compromise is essential.

The above discussion shows that the case for liberal trade is open to challenge and must be kept regularly updated and revised. As a long-run strategy, however, the case remains strong. In any event the decline in transport costs, the information revolution and the increased ease of communication have also contributed to making international trade barriers much less enforceable than in the past. Faced with this fact, business has little choice but to adjust. In a sense, acceptance of the case for free trade between nations is the logical extension of the case for free trade within national boundaries. But this argument implies that internationally accepted 'rules of the game' must be put in place analogous to those enforced in domestic trade. The WTO is addressing this issue and has reinforced procedures to deal with government subsidies, patents and intellectual property issues, dispute settlement and dumping. An agreed international code of fair trade practices is vital if the world trading system is to gain acceptance and confidence among nations of widely different income levels and aspirations.

17.5 What determines comparative advantage?

Which industries and firms will prosper in a global trading system? Given the rapid pace of technological change and the propensity of comparative advantage to change over time, this question must be addressed by firms and governments. Ultimately, it is individual firms which exploit and develop comparative advantage. They know the market better than any civil servant or economist. Yet sometimes comparative advantage can be changed as a result of government intervention.

Following Ricardo, we say that a country will export goods and services in which its comparative advantage is greatest. A country with abundant capital will export goods and services which are intensive in human and physical capital (US); a resource-rich country will export resource-intensive goods (Argentina, Kuwait, Australia); and labour-abundant countries will export labour-intensive goods (Bangladesh, China). This approach does not imply that a country's comparative advantage remains fixed in any one category indefinitely. A country can progress from one stage to another, in accordance with what is called the Stages Theory of Comparative Advantage.[26] For example, Japan specialised in the export of low-cost, labour-intensive goods before advancing to the export of human capital-intensive goods.

The world's fastest growing industries are heavily reliant on human capital. As Professor Thurow noted:

> Consider what are commonly believed to be the seven key industries of the next few decades – microelectronics, biotechnology, the new materials industries, civilian aviation, telecommunications, robots *plus* software. All are brainpower industries. Each could be located anywhere on the face of the globe. Where they will be located depends upon who can organise the brain power to capture them. In the century ahead comparative advantage will be man-made.[27]

Ideally we need a theory of the determinants of trade which is more strongly rooted in an analysis of firms. An industry's export performance is only as good as the export performance of its firms. Usually only a minority of firms engage in exporting. Looked at this way, the issue becomes one of determining what factors explain the successful performance of this select group.

Michael Porter, author of the best-seller *The Competitive Advantage of Nations*, has identified four major determinants of national competitive advantage. The so-called Porter Diamond (Figure 17.4) consists of:

1. *Factor endowments* – countries with abundant supplies of a factor relative to another will export goods intensive in that factor.

2. *Demand conditions* – a country which has a sophisticated domestic market will export better quality goods with higher income elasticities.

3. *Firm strategy and rivalry* – vibrant domestic industries need strong competition and rivalry in the domestic market to keep them fit and lean for exporting.

4. *Related and supporting industries* – countries with industrial clusters gain economies of scale and can build on this to consolidate comparative advantage.

Each of these concepts has been discussed in general terms already. Porter skilfully puts empirical content into these abstractions and relates them to the behaviour of individual firms and industries.

---

26 B. Balassa, *Comparative Advantage, Trade Policy and Economic Development* (New York: New York University Press, 1989).

27 L. Thurow, *Head to Head: The coming economic battle among Japan, Europe and America* (London: Nicholas Brealey Publishing, 1993), p. 45.

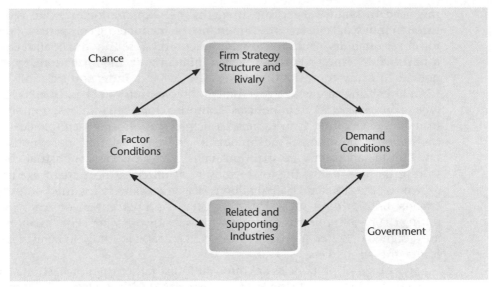

Figure 17.4 Porter's diamond

Source: adapted with the permission of The Free Press, a Division of Simon & Schuster, Inc., from *The Competitive Advantage of Nations* by Michael E. Porter © 1990, 1998

In addition to these four determinants, Porter considers two further forces determining the evolution of comparative advantage: *chance* and *government policy*.

Recent theories of economic geography show how comparative advantage of a nation may be determined by trivial and random events. Once an industry takes off, cumulative learning processes and increasing returns to scale reinforce its comparative advantage. The industry becomes 'locked in' to its original location. According to the originator of this theory, Brian Arthur, insignificant circumstances become magnified by positive feedbacks to tip the system towards the actual outcome we observe.[28] The small events of history become important. Chance, in other words, plays a vital role in determining the comparative advantage of nations, and a lucky accident can get an industry started in a particular location. Arthur instances Silicon Valley in California, and Krugman lists similar examples in his work on trade and economic geography.[29] This line of thought has given new impetus to the case for intervention and to the search for the 'right' industrial policy.

Porter also assigns an important role to government policy. He rejects protectionism as a policy option but advocates a proactive approach to building up comparative advantage. In line with current thinking, he stresses the importance of participation in global markets, but he adds an important clause *through continuous upgrading*, and sees no future for isolationist policies. He stresses

---

28 B. Arthur, 'Competing technologies, increasing returns and lock-in by historical events', *Economic Journal* (March 1989), p. 127.

29 P. Krugman, *Geography and Trade* (Cambridge, MA: MIT Press, 1991).

the need to build on existing strengths, i.e. exploitation of scale economies through industrial clusters, the importance of encouraging competition, the need for macro-stability, and the establishment of a sound fiscal and economic infrastructure. Porter's ideas have been influential in the formation of industrial policies in many countries (including New Zealand, India and Ireland).

An interesting case where government intervention can be justified is in *export-promotion policies*. These policies comprise loan guarantees, export credit insurance, marketing grants, subsidised information and technological advice, trade fairs, mobilisation of the diplomatic service to push national exports, and so on. Considerable sums are spent on such policies by some industrial countries. During the mid-1990s, the total exposure of official export credit agencies had grown to an estimated US$380 billion. Heavy losses were incurred on exports to Nigeria, Brazil, the ex-Soviet Union and Iraq. As a percentage of exports covered during the period, this was equivalent to a subsidy of 19 per cent.[30] Export credits are designed to help national exporters gain an early foothold in countries seen as future growth markets.

Export-promotion policies are interventionist rather than protectionist and, as such, are less prone to the types of flaw associated with the latter. They were used actively by the Japanese and by other successful Asian exporters. Much interest is being shown in them by China, and also by European countries in transition which are anxious not to repeat past mistakes on protection, yet eager to find ways of breaking into difficult and expensive export markets.[31] Indeed, this topic is of considerable interest to the developed world also, as it grapples with the problems of analysing the barriers facing many peripheral countries and small and medium-sized enterprises (SMEs) in their attempts to take full advantage of the global market in the post-Uruguay Round era. Having won the intellectual case as regards telling governments what *not to do* in trade matters, there is room for further economic research on the topic of what governments *should* do in order to exploit comparative advantage more effectively.

Low costs, high quality and *continuous innovation* are the vital ingredients for success in the global marketplace. Industries characterised by product differentiation and oligopoly power are a common feature of the world trade system and for them the need to upgrade quality is particularly pressing. Instances include automobiles, aircraft, computers and telecom equipment. Competitive advantage in these cases is nurtured by a variety of forces: standard comparative costs, oligopolistic rivalry, government intervention and even corporate inertia (the firm's own history and corporate characteristics).[32] If the share of intra-industry trade were taken as an indicator of the extent of imperfectly competitive or oligopolistic influence in international trade, the proportionate share of trade influenced by the above considerations may well be as high as 40 per cent.

---

30 M.G. Kuhn *et al.*, 'Officially supported credits: Recent developments and prospects' (Washington, DC: IMF, March 1995). 'Export credits: Giving arms a hand', *The Economist* (5 November 1994).

31 A. MacBean (ed.) *Trade and Transition: Trade Promotion in Transitional Economies* (London: Frank Cass, 2000).

32 D.B. Yoffie, *Beyond Free Trade: Firms, governments and global competition* (Cambridge, MA: Harvard Business School Press, 1993).

Conclusions

An increasingly high proportion of the world's output is being traded internationally. The composition of the world's merchandise trade flows continues to move from primary goods towards manufactured goods. Within manufacturing, high-tech industries are the most dynamic element. Trade in services has also begun to take off. In addition to traditional service activities such as tourism, new activities are entering the global market: hitherto protected activities such as banking and insurance and technology-led activities such as software and information processing. Three factors – income growth, improvements in transport and communications, and trade liberalisation – have been critical determinants of these developments.

The globalisation of markets has had a profound effect on the modern business environment. Firms are being driven to become more efficient and dynamic in order to survive. Global competition is bringing many benefits to the consumer in terms of cheaper and better quality goods and services. Trade has helped to bring faster growth to many countries. But there is also a downside. The relentless search for improved efficiency has imposed a heavy burden of adjustment on import-competing industries and on the people who are dependent on them for a living. To minimise this burden is a major challenge to policy.

One way to ease the adjustment burden is to liberalise by forming regional trade agreements with similarly structured economies. Another option is to arrange generous transition periods designed to give firms time to restructure. Direct and indirect protection of sensitive sectors has also been resorted to. Agriculture, steel, clothing and textiles are the most common examples. Protected pockets of economic activity exist even in the most sophisticated economies. For example, the Japanese market is protected by numerous opaque non-tariff barriers which make exporting to Japan problematical and expensive.[33] It is important that protection should be designed so as to ease, not prevent, adjustment. Protective measures should be transparent and of limited duration.

A growing weight of evidence suggests that it is better to participate in international specialisation than to resist it. But because protectionism is rejected does not mean that unqualified *laissez-faire* must be embraced. First, protection is only one of many possible forms of state intervention. Even in a liberal global system, governments and industry have to consider ways of promoting competitive advantage. This exercise will entail taking a longer-term view of a nation's competitive position than free enterprise alone might adopt. Government assistance should aim to ensure that people and firms are encouraged to make full use of the opportunities of the external economy. Second, the gains from trade will be realised only if resources can be kept fully

---

33 Empirical studies suggest that the main cost of protection falls on the country imposing it, in particular on its consumers, not on the countries whose exporters are denied access. Japanese protection, according to one estimate, has cost consumers an amount equal to 3.8 per cent of Japanese GDP; the overall national loss is 0.6 per cent of Japanese national income. (Studies for other countries reach qualitatively similar conclusions.)

employed. Large-scale unemployment not only undermines popular support for free trade, it also undermines some of the reasoning and the theoretical assumptions upon which the case in its favour is based. Free trade, therefore, requires the existence of a price system which functions well and which has appropriate levels of government intervention to cope with externalities and income distribution. To some extent, the exposure to foreign trade will help this condition to be fulfilled. For example, trade contributes to keeping domestic markets competitive and flexible. Nevertheless, one can safely say that, far from *laissez-faire* being a condition for obtaining the gains from trade, the case for free trade is consolidated by a certain degree of state intervention. This point has been made in a different way by Peter Drucker:

> The world economy has become too important for a country not to have a world-economy policy. Managed trade is a delusion of grandeur. Outright protectionism can only do harm, but simply trying to thwart protectionism is not enough. What is needed is a deliberate and active – indeed, aggressive – policy that gives the demands, opportunities and dynamics of the external economy priority over domestic policy demands and problems.[34]

The specifics of this 'aggressive' policy have to be worked out on a country-by-country basis. As markets become more competitive, and production and marketing become more globalised, a new generation of trade issues is coming to the fore. Market access has been subjected to new scrutiny and the concept of the level playing field is seen to involve much more than the absence of trade barriers.[35] National competition policy, intellectual property investment incentives, labour standards and environment regulation are areas of policy which impact strongly on trade flows. Free trade disposes of one set of trade barriers, only to move the searchlight to new, indirect, and hitherto ignored, barriers. There is continuing need to adapt the architecture of the world trading system. Countries which assign priority to micro-efficiency and macro-stability, and constrain government intervention within tight parameters, will be best placed to take advantage of this evolving system.

---

34 P. Drucker, 'Trade lessons from the world economy', *Foreign Affairs* (January/February 1994), p. 108.
35 OECD, *New Dimensions of Market Access in a Globalising World Economy* (Paris, February 1995); J. Bhagwati and R. Hudec, Fair Trade and Harmonisation (Cambridge, Mass.: MIT Press, 1996).

Summary

1. Trade continues to grow rapidly, much faster than world output. Manufactured trade is expanding fastest, much of it consisting of exchange of similar goods called intra-industry trade. Trade in services was boosted by technological advance and by deregulation, but it is as yet poorly documented.

2. A landmark development in the world trade regime was the completion of the Uruguay Round and the establishment of the World Trade Organisation (WTO) in 1995.

3. Motivating the global trend towards freer trade was the belief that trade yields significant economic benefits. Economic theory explains these benefits as deriving from greater efficiency in the allocation of given resources (the law of comparative advantage), and also from so-called dynamic factors such as better scope for exploiting economies of scale, more intense competition, stimulus to the adoption and gestation of technological advance and a resultant upgrading of product quality.

4. But there are downsides to an open trade environment, notably for those who lose their jobs, or the value of their share capital, in import-competing industries. Also, trade fulfils its potential and delivers gains to society only if the domestic price system is functioning smoothly and reflecting domestic social costs and benefits. These caveats to the free trade case are important for many transition and developing countries.

5. Comparative advantage changes over time. Not only this, but the profile of national comparative advantage can be altered by economic policy. Comparative advantage nowadays is *made*, not *given*. Government policy can play a role in determining it, through long term investment in human capital and physical infrastructure. Government policy can also play a role through the provision of incentives. Governments, and economists, continue to search for ways of improving the efficiency of their national industries and to build on, and consolidate, their competitive advantage.

6. The world trade system faces new challenges in developing a consistent and acceptable approach towards environment-related trade issues and towards global competition rules to ensure that trade is both free and 'fair'. The dispute settlement procedures of the WTO will be tested in coming years.

? Questions for discussion

1. According to official estimates, world income will increase by over $500 billion following implementation of the Uruguay Round. What, in your view, are the main sources of these gains? Why have so many countries, both developed and developing, participated in this major movement towards global free trade?

2. What is comparative advantage and what determines it? Can a comparative advantage be developed through judicious use of economic policies?

3. Why do smaller countries trade more as a percentage of GNP than large countries? Does this help or hinder their efforts to improve living standards?

4. The WTO's Trade Policy Review Board has on occasion expressed concern about the vulnerability of some developing economies arising from their heavy export reliance on a limited number of products and markets. Explain why such concentration might be a problem. What measures would you suggest to help a country achieve greater export diversification?

5. Adjustment to freer trade can involve heavy economic costs to the people affected, arising from financial and employment losses in import-competing industries. What measures should the government take in order to minimise these adjustment costs?

6. Is there a case for the government using subsidies to encourage the development of domestic industries by helping them win export markets? Is this fair play, or is it a form of hidden protectionism?

Exercises

1. Suppose that in Sweden 1 unit of labour can produce 10 units of timber and 10 units of steel, whereas in the UK 1 unit of labour can produce 8 units of steel and 6 units of timber. In what product does the UK have a comparative advantage? In what product does Sweden have a comparative advantage? Would your answer be different if 1 unit of Swedish labour could produce 14 units of steel instead of 10?

2. Examine EU–Japan trade figures in recent years. In every year since 1958 (with the exception of 1961) the main European countries have experienced deficits on merchandise trade with Japan. Comment on the extent and structure of the trade imbalance. Compare this imbalance with EU trade balances with other countries and regions. In the light of your empirical findings, should Europe's merchandise trade deficit with Japan be a cause for concern? (For relevant data, see World Trade Organisation, *International Trade: Trends and statistics*, or Eurostat trade figures.)

3. Japanese car imports into Europe have been restrained by voluntary export quotas. Use a demand and supply diagram to show the effect of this quota on the price of Japanese cars in Europe. One research study found that the effect of the quota was to raise the price of the average Japanese car to the EU consumer by 12 per cent. It also found that the price of competing European cars rose by 7 per cent. How would you explain this?

4. Analyse the following assessment of the effects of protection. Can it be reconciled with the theory of the gains from trade outlined in this chapter?

> The Japanese were undoubtedly greatly helped by the building up of immense protective walls about them. Foreign car makers had dominated the Japanese market, and indeed had local plants until the 1930's when the militarists shut them out. Those doors were not opened again until the Japanese manufacturers were firmly established and becoming exporting powers themselves. Indeed, right until the 1990's there were complaints from foreign car makers – and from foreign

manufacturers in other areas – that Japanese bureaucrats typically twist, bend and extend the rules, via administrative guidance or inspections or any other excuse, effectively to shut foreigners out of the market. Thus, in the case of cars, small suppliers to the Japanese market not only faced stringent safety rules different from those in their home country, but also had to pay for lengthy inspections of each individual car to make sure that it met the peculiar and usually highly particular rules and regulations of the Japanese market, all of this adding expensive cost and time to selling to Japan. (Kevin Rafferty, *Inside Japan's Power Houses: The culture, mystique and future of Japan's greatest corporations* (London: Weidenfeld & Nicolson, 1995), p. 13)

5. Sometimes protection is justified on the grounds that it is good for all industries. One favourite ploy is to list all the domestic goods and services purchased by the protected industry and to compute all the extra jobs thereby 'created' as a benefit of protection. What is wrong with this approach?

6. Consider the following statement by Adam Smith. How would you explain continuing high levels of protection of the wine industry in many countries? Make the case for and against complete liberalisation of the industry.

    By means of glasses, hotbeds and hotwalls, very good grapes can be raised in Scotland, and very good wine too can be made of them at about thirty times the expense for which at least equally good wine can be bought from foreign countries. Would it be a reasonable law to prohibit the importation of all foreign wines, merely to encourage the making of claret and burgundy in Scotland? (Adam Smith, *Wealth of Nations*, Volume 1 (1776), p. 480)

7. What are the three most important export industries in your country? Examine their export performance during the past decade. What factors explain your country's comparative advantage in these industries? Is Porter's Diamond useful in this exercise?

Further reading

There are several good textbooks on international economics for readers wishing to delve more deeply. Examples include: L.A. Winters, *International Economics* (London: Allen & Unwin, 4th edn, 1991) and B. Sodersten and G. Reed, *International Economics* (London: Macmillan, 3rd edn, 1994). An influential, business-oriented interpretation of global trade which relates economic theory to strategic firm behaviour is Michael Porter's *The Competitive Advantage of Nations* (London: Macmillan, 1990). J. Bhagwati, 'Free trade: Old and new challenges', *Economic Journal* (March 1994) presents an assessment by one of the world's foremost thinkers on these matters. The impact of globalisation and trade on living standards is top of the research agenda as we enter the 21st century. See D. Ben-David and Alan Winters, 'Trade, Income Disparity and Poverty', WTO Special Study no. 5 (June 2000) for a strong conclusion that open economies are performing better than the less open economies.

Chapter 18

CAPITAL FLOWS AND FOREIGN INVESTMENT

A major feature of the world economy over the past decades has been the growing integration of national economies. International trade in goods and services grew faster than gross domestic product, links between national financial markets strengthened, more people moved across borders, foreign direct investment (FDI) expanded rapidly, and so did the activity of transnational corporations (TNCs). (United Nations, *World Investment Report 1993: Transnational Corporations and Integrated International Production* (New York: UN, 1993), p. 113)

Introduction

In Chapter 17, we analysed the gains from foreign trade in the context of an economy where capital, labour and other factors of production are mobile *within* nations, but immobile *between* nations. Factors of production were assumed to be able to move costlessly between industries within the same country, but they could not move abroad. Trade theory shows how, in such circumstances, foreign trade can act as a partial substitute for international factor mobility. Capital-rich countries can achieve higher returns for their relatively abundant capital by exporting capital-intensive goods. Likewise, populous countries achieve higher-paid employment and more prosperity by exporting labour-intensive goods and services. The output of labour is exported rather than labour itself.

In this chapter account is taken of the growing international mobility of factors of production. Flows of international capital are growing in volume and variety. This mobility takes many forms – mutual fund investment, lending by banks to governments, and speculative flows by hedge funds and derivatives traders. Alongside this, firms have become globalised. Few leading companies nowadays are located exclusively in their home country. Foreign investment has become an essential element in firms' investment and production strategies and is undertaken, not just by huge multinationals in the conventional sense, but also by medium-sized companies in both industrial and developing countries. This globalisation involves movements of financial and physical capital across countries, as well as the mobility of cooperant factors such as know-how and technical skills. International labour mobility has grown too, although not to the same extent as capital mobility. We discuss this in Chapter 19.

Chapter 17 showed how foreign trade can contribute to growth. Can the same be said of the international exchange of capital and labour? Does factor mobility confer benefits on both the receiving country (the host country) and the sending country (the home country), or is it a zero-sum game? Does it help the process of economic development? What are the gains from such mobility and how are they measured? Should economic policy-makers remove obstacles to inward and outward movement of productive factors, or does the process of integration make such obstacles redundant?

Chapter outline

1. Recent trends in level and composition of capital flows.

2. Analysis of capital flows in a simple, general framework. This analysis shows how capital flows can potentially add to the welfare of both host and home countries. The basic analysis is extended to cover the effects of capital mobility on tax revenues.

3. Extension of the framework to analyse the extent and motivation of one important type of capital flow: foreign direct investment. The multinational firm has been the leading force behind direct investment flows. Its activities involve the transfer between countries of a 'package' of productive factors: capital, technology and skilled management talent.

4. The economic effects of foreign investment. Most research has focused on the effects on the host country, but donor countries can also gain. Witness the rush to invest in China and the complaints from some governments of being barred from investing in Japan. Policies for maximising the potential benefits from inward investment are outlined. Through outward processing, export platforms, and strategic replacement of exports by affiliate production in domestic markets, multinationals exert a strong influence on world production and trade patterns.

18.1 Capital flows

The past three decades have witnessed major changes in the level and composition of capital flows, both among industrial countries and between industrial and developing countries. The 1990s has been described as 'the decade of equity finance' reflecting the huge increase in foreign direct investment and international equity flows during the decade. This has contrasted with earlier decades where the dominant form of international capital movement was portfolio debt finance, involving both government and private sectors. The world capital market has now become more integrated than at any time since the pre-1914 heyday of the gold standard. There are several striking indicators of this enhanced level of integration.

- The stock of international bank lending, which includes both cross-border lending, domestic lending and lending denominated in foreign currency, has risen to around half the value of industrial countries' GDP.

- The rising share of government bonds held by foreigners. According to the Bank of International Settlements, the average proportion of industrial countries' government debt held by non-residents has risen to 25 per cent. In 1997, 38 per cent of US debt was held by non-residents.[1]
- Private sector issuers of bonds and securities have recourse more frequently to the international markets. Often these transactions are linked to mergers and acquisitions activity. Net issues of international bonds exceeded $1,100 billion in 1999.[2]

As capital markets have become more integrated, there has been a proliferation of different types of mobile investment funds designed for the private investor. An individual, with even as modest a sum as £5000 sterling, can choose from a welter of attractive and exotic investment funds, each with its own risk and geographical profile. There are funds specialising in the Far East, North America, Europe and the 'emerging' economies of Asia and Latin America.

Both supply and demand factors have contributed to the increase in capital mobility. On the supply side, there has been a huge increase in the amount of investible funds in industrial countries, representing the effects of higher incomes, an ageing population profile and a tendency to replace or enhance public sector pension schemes (often financed out of current tax revenue) with privately funded schemes. On the demand side, the growing pressure on fund managers to produce better returns has led them to search further afield for foreign investment opportunities in order to achieve both higher average returns and a more diversified portfolio. The performance of fund managers is being monitored ever more closely and regularly. Competition between them is intense. In addition, both supply and demand conditions have been affected by two further developments: (1) the gradual removal of government-imposed barriers to capital mobility, and (2) the development of information technology.

The path to capital market integration has, however, not been entirely smooth. Nowhere was this more evident than in the emerging economies during the late 1990s. Up to then, private capital had flowed in generous amounts into the rapidly growing and profitable markets of the Asian tigers and countries in transition. By the mid-1990s, East Asia was the recipient of over US$100 billion of private capital annually. Transition economies absorbed a further US$45 billion out of a total flow to emerging economies that peaked at US$214 billion in 1996 (Figure 18.1). Following the 1997 currency crisis in Thailand, capital inflows quickly converted into capital outflows as foreign lenders to these countries ran for cover. In the space of two years, the five most exposed Asian economies (Thailand, Korea, Indonesia, Malaysia and the Philippines) suffered a dramatic reversal from net private capital inflows of US$63 billion in 1996 to a net outflow of US$30 billion in 1998. The reverberations of the shock were felt throughout the developing world and, for a while, capital market disintegration

---

1 Bank of International Settlements, *Annual Report* Basel (June 2000); US Treasury Department, *Treasury Bulletin*.
2 Data from IMF *World Economic Outlook* (October 1999).

rather than integration was the main theme of debate. Since 1998, as Figure 18.1 shows, there has been a recovery of sorts. By the year 2000, net private capital flows to all emerging economies had reached $119 billion, and the scale of the net outflow from Asian emerging countries had diminished significantly. During this time, however, capital flows between different parts of the developed world had been relatively unaffected by the crisis and continued their upward trajectory.

Governments still try to persuade their citizens to keep their savings at home through various tax devices and through limits on the deployment of pension fund assets, but these measures have become less pervasive in recent years. When average returns on capital and their variances differ systematically between countries, investors will want to hold a portion of their total assets abroad, and it has become increasingly difficult to prevent them doing so.

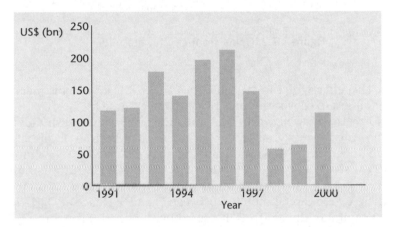

Figure 18.1 Emerging market economies: net private capital flows

18.2 Basic model

Imagine a world divided into two areas, the North and the South. Capital earns a low rate of return in the North where it is relatively abundant and a high rate of return in the South where it is relatively scarce. Initially, there is zero capital mobility between the two areas. Now assume restrictions on capital mobility are eliminated. Capital will be expected to move from the North towards the South, where returns are higher. These flows will continue until the rate of return is equalised in the two areas. Economic welfare is increased by such mobility because capital is deployed where it is most productive. In a sense, the argument is a re-run of the theory of comparative advantage.

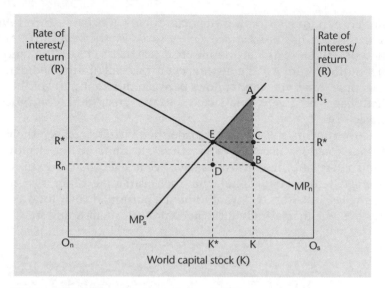

Figure 18.2 Gains from capital mobility

The effects of capital mobility can be illustrated by means of Figure 18.2. Assume a fixed world supply of capital, measured by the distance O_nO_S. The richer North is endowed with O_nK, and the poorer South with O_SK of capital. Curves showing the marginal product of capital at each level of capital stock in each area are drawn as the downward-sloping lines, MP_n and MP_S. As more capital is added to the stock, its marginal productivity declines. (The information required to draw these curves is derived from the production functions for each country.) Initially there is zero capital mobility between N and S. Hence at O_nK, the marginal return on capital in the North is measured by the vertical distance O_nR_n. For the South, with capital stock O_SK, the marginal product is the vertical distance O_SR_S. The marginal product of capital is lower in the capital-abundant North than in the capital-scarce South.

Suppose restrictions on capital mobility are removed. Capital now flows from North to South in response to the higher rate of return in the South. As capital flows into the South, its marginal product declines. At the same time, the marginal product in the North rises. Eventually equilibrium is reached, at the point E (K^*,R^*). Capital no longer has an incentive to migrate. Returns are equalised in both areas.

The global economic gains from this redeployment of the world's capital stock are represented by the triangular area ABE. It represents the difference between what the redeployed capital produced in the South and what it had been able to produce in the North. Thus at K, the marginal product of one unit of capital was KB in the North. By shifting to the South the same unit of capital produced an output of KA. With respect to that unit, the gain from mobility was AB. Similar gains accrue, at a declining rate, as a result of each unit movement of capital until we reach K^*. At this point the value of the marginal product in each region is the same. The gain from the exchange of capital, represented by the triangle ABE, is a gain of economic efficiency, analogous to the gains from trade (Chapter 17) and to the welfare gain of moving from monopoly to competition (Chapter 6).

The distribution of the gain between the two areas and between capital owners (capitalists) and the rest of the population (workers) can also be worked out from Figure 18.2.

The South attracts capital K*K, for which it pays interest of OR* per unit, amounting in total to K*KCE. The sum of the marginal products of K*K, however, equals K*KAE. Hence the net gain to the South is ACE. From the North's point of view, it has exported K*K capital for which K*KCE has been received from the South. Had this capital stayed in the North, it could have produced only K*KBE. Hence the North gains BCE. Thus *both areas gain from capital mobility*. Like trade, a mutually beneficial exchange is being transacted, not a zero-sum game.

This win-win outcome at an aggregate level, however, masks the existence of losers and gainers within regions. Capitalists in the South lose – the return on their capital has fallen by AR_SR*C. The effect of capital mobility has been to make their capital less scarce. By contrast, capitalists in the North clearly gain. The capital they deploy at home now earns a return of $R*EK*O_n$ instead of R_nDK*O_n, while their exported capital earns ECBD more than it was earning at home. Hence, the total gain to northern capital owners amounts to R_nBCR*. There are corresponding losses and gains for non-capital factors of production (for convenience often described simply as labour) in each region. Thus, labour in the South gains relative to capital – workers there become more productive as a result of the capital inflows – while workers in the North lose relative to northern capital – capital per worker declines as a result of the North's capital outflows.

Capital mobility and taxes

Because each region is better off as a consequence of capital mobility, it is possible for the government in each region to compensate the losers while still leaving some of the population better off than before. The theory does not assert that compensation *will* happen, only that it *could* happen, given political commitment to this objective and an appropriate tax regime.

Paradoxically, redistribution through taxation, although strictly speaking required in order to make a cast-iron case for capital mobility, is made more difficult by the international mobility of capital itself. As many governments are learning, the scope for taxation of capital has become increasingly circumscribed. Capital mobility, by redistributing income, creates a case for public intervention if compensation of the losers is considered desirable. But it also makes the policies needed to effect such transfers more difficult to implement.

Suppose the equilibrium rate of return was OR_0 and that capital was immobile internationally (Figure 18.3). Suppose further that the government decided to levy a tax, equal to RT, on capital earnings. If capital were immobile, a tax on capital equal to RT would be an effective way of transferring income from capital owners to others. The capital stock could be considered fixed at OK_0, hence the

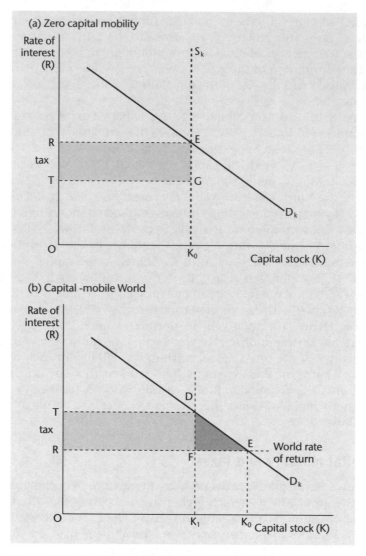

Figure 18.3 Taxing capital in a capital-mobile world

vertical supply curve K_0S_k. The interest rate charged to borrowers cannot exceed OR because at any higher rate, supply exceeds demand and the rate of return will fall. The incidence of the tax falls entirely on capital and there is a transfer of REGT from capitalists to the government. In the long run, domestic savings might be affected by the tax. But even if the supply curve were not completely vertical, the sensitivity of savings to the net of tax return is likely to be low.

By contrast, when capital is mobile, foreign and domestic investment funds compete actively for the same capital. Any gap between domestic and foreign interest rates will be immediately competed away. If domestic interest rates were higher than the foreign interest rate, capital would flow into the country, driving down the domestic rate. In other words, the supply curve of capital becomes horizontal instead of vertical. The equilibrium rate of interest, OR, is set by international supply and demand.

In these circumstances, suppose a tax of RT were imposed. Capital would leave the country until the *net return*, that is OT less tax RT, equalled the 'ruling' rate attainable elsewhere, OR. The objective of the tax has been frustrated. True, tax revenue RTDF has been collected. But, capitalists have not lost income. All that has happened is that the price of capital to domestic borrowers has been raised – the tax has been fully 'passed on'. The portion of capital staying in the region continues to earn the higher gross return while capital which has left the country earns the world rate of return. The outflow of capital has led to a loss of national welfare of DFE, representing the distortionary effect of the tax.

The above example reaffirms two significant lessons which are already familiar to the reader. First, the revenue collected from a tax tells us little about the incidence of the tax (i.e. who is truly paying it). Second, the incidence of a tax must be calculated before reaching a conclusion about its economic effects. In a world of increasing tax-consciousness and greater capital mobility, the possibility of avoiding tax through relocation must be kept in mind by the authorities.

Extensions and qualifications

Capital outflows from Europe played a critical part in the development of the economies of North America, South America and Australasia. This century has seen the vital contribution of US capital to the recovery of postwar Europe and, later, the beneficial effects of capital assistance to Korea and the NICs. The EU's Structural Funds programme involves significant flows of capital from the prosperous core of Europe to the peripheral regions. Capital inflows, if utilised properly, offer a welcome opportunity to build up infrastructure and to tackle bottlenecks to development in a capital-scarce economy – much as is envisaged in a more formalised and abstract way in the basic model. Such inflows offer not just a higher rate of return to the providers of capital but also the opportunity of spreading risks.

One indirect spillover effect of global capital mobility is to improve the macro-management of an economy. A mobile capital stock obliges governments to manage their finances carefully. There is no longer a large captive pool of domestic savings which remains impervious to the conduct of domestic policy. Finance ministers have to frame their budgets and control government finances in a way that will not frighten capital markets. Capital markets take a dim view of spendthrift policies. If these policies persist, domestic and foreign investors will move their assets to safer havens. Domestic interest rates will rise, the government will be blamed and there will be a negative political fall-out. Capital flows, therefore, act as an external and impersonal discipline on macroeconomic policy.

Although capital mobility has increased, the vast bulk of the world's capital still remains more attached to its domestic market than to foreign markets. Only 11 per cent of the EU's pension fund assets are invested outside the EU; the corresponding figure for US pension funds is 8 per cent. Domestic savings also supplied most of the capital requirements of the developing Asian countries even at their peak performance. Less than 1 percentage point of their 33 per cent investment : GDP ratio was provided by foreign capital (Table 18.1). For all developing countries, the domestic savings/GDP ratio was 26 per cent during the period 1993–2000, to which figure capital flows from the rest of the world added only 2 extra percentage points. The US savings ratio, low by international standards at 16 per cent, was raised just a further 1.6 percentage points by net external financing.[3] Latin America is heavily dependent on foreign resources, yet its net foreign borrowing averages only 3 per cent of GDP. Interestingly, the originator of comparative costs might not have been surprised by this. Ricardo took the view that feelings of *fancied or real insecurity ... check the emigration of capital* and *induce most men of property to be satisfied with a low rate of profit in their own country, rather than seek a more advantageous employment for their wealth in foreign nations.*[4]

Another feature of capital mobility is the preponderance of two-way exchange between industrial countries rather than the unidirectional movement analysed in the basic model. Total direct foreign investment outflows from the industrial countries amounted to $590 billion in 1998, whilst inflows in the same year came to $461 billion. Western Europe exported $400 billion of capital and imported $236 billion. This pattern parallels the intra-industry trade ratios noted in chapter 17 and can be explained in a similar way. One obvious factor is product differentiation. Investments in different locations have different characteristics in terms of yields and risks and therefore investors view international diversification as an important vehicle for risk spreading. Investment funds managers like to have a diversified portfolio and modern telecommunications technology is making this cheaper and easier to achieve. The investment boom in the 'emerging markets' during the 1990s owes much to this search for new ways of diversifying risk.

While it is possible to finesse the gains from capital mobility, account should also be taken of certain adverse effects associated with it which are not incorporated in the basic model:

1. *International capital flows can be very volatile.* What flows in can just as easily flow out. In former times, a larger proportion of capital inflows were 'rooted' in the host country, taking the form of direct investment in enterprises, property, and infrastructure. The comparatively illiquid nature of these investments meant that the foreign investor was in for the long haul. Nowadays capital flows are invested in much more liquid forms – government bonds and equities, which are easily realised and carry no loyalty or longer-term commitment.

---

3 Net capital inflows closely resemble the balance of payments current account deficit or surplus but exclude unrequited transfers and factor income.
4 D. Ricardo, 'Principles of political economy and taxation', in P. Sraffa, *The Works and Correspondence of David Ricardo*, Vol. 1, (Cambridge: Cambridge University Press, 1953), pp. 136–7.

Table 18.1 Savings, investments and lending, 1993–2000 (% GDP)

	Investment	Savings	Net borrowing from rest of world
Developed Countries			
US	18.0	16.4	1.6
EU	19.7	20.5	−0.8*
Japan	28.0	30.1	−2.1*
Developing Countries	27.8	26.2	1.6
of which:			
Africa	20.1	16.3	3.8
Asia	32.7	32.8	−0.1*
Middle East & Europe	22.0	20.6	1.4
Latin America	21.5	18.4	3.1

* If savings exceed investment, the country is a net lender to the outside world.

Source: IMF, World Economic Report (October 1999)).

2. *Capital inflows can cause unsustainable inflationary pressures.* Foreign investors can cause unsustainable property and equity booms. They also cause problems through increasing the supply of high-powered money. This creates difficulties for the monetary authorities in the host country, particularly if that country is trying to establish an anti-inflation reputation.

3. *Capital flows can lead to short-term misalignments of the exchange rate.* These lead to distorted price incentives and inefficient trade and investment decisions. Hence many countries continue to impose restraints on these flows. Because of its restrictions on short-term capital inflows, Chile was spared much of the disruption that Asian countries suffered during the currency crisis of the 1990s.

4. *Capital mobility can weaken a country's tax base by forcing governments to offer excessive enticements to investors.* Tax competition among governments over which offers the lowest tax can be sub-optimal.

18.3 Foreign direct investment and multinationals

Foreign direct investment (FDI) involves the acquisition of a controlling interest in a domestic enterprise by foreign capital owners. It differs from simple capital movements in that a mix of productive factors, such as technical know-how, marketing, managerial and financial expertise, is transferred alongside financial capital. Often the financial transfer is the least significant element in the package.

The main agent of FDI is the multinational enterprise (MNE).[5] Examples of FDI include: the establishment of a subsidiary plant in a foreign country; the takeover

---

5 Foreign investment is undertaken not just by huge multinational enterprises, but also by many medium-sized enterprises.

of a domestic firm by a foreign corporation; creating a joint venture with a domestic firm (as part of a privatisation programme); a licensing agreement with a domestic company to manufacture a brand owned by a foreign company. FDI by its nature tends to involve a stronger and more long-term commitment than portfolio capital movements. While fund managers respond to short-term profit opportunities, direct investment responds to longer-term assessments of prospective returns. These assessments take account of the future economic growth of host countries, taxation policy, trade and currency regimes, labour costs, environmental regulations and political stability – in short, the entire gamut of variables that influence the business climate.

FDI has the potential to play a major direct role in a country's development. Because it involves a package of productive inputs, some of which are in very short supply in the host country, governments have devised elaborate schemes for attracting such investment, comprising tax incentives, capital grants and labour training programmes. But FDI also has its critics, and the multinationals have been a subject of controversy for many years. Some argue that FDI inhibits development, or that branch plants contribute less to the national economy than appears.

Trends in FDI

There are two ways of measuring FDI. One way is to focus on the *stock* of capital at a particular date. Each country has an inward stock representing capital owned by foreigners in the economy and an outward stock representing capital owned by the country's nationals in foreign countries. An alternative approach is to study annual *flows* of inward and outward investment. FDI flows fluctuate a good deal more than the stock indices; even the direction of the net flow can change from year to year. A large mergers and acquisitions deal, for example, can exert a disproportionate impact on the annual flow data. Nevertheless, capital flow data can highlight changes in investment patterns which capital stock indices will be much slower to reveal.

Using investment position as a criterion, the world's major outward investors are the US, EU and Japan (Table 18.2). The rapid growth in the world outward stock is also evident from this table. Within the EU, the UK, followed by Germany, France and the Netherlands, are the largest outward investors. The value of the stock of capital invested abroad amounted to about $3964 billion in 1998. This represents a build-up of assets going back many years. Stocks of gross outward direct investment amount to 49 per cent of GDP in the Netherlands, 31 per cent in the UK and 12 per cent in Germany (Table 18.3). A 10 per cent return on this investment could translate into a significant fraction of annual income in these countries.

Developed countries with a large outward capital stock also tend to have a large inward capital stock.[6] Thus, the US has an outward stock of $1022 billion and an inward stock of $811 billion, while in the EU the two are about equal. Japan is a

---

6 The figures for outward (inward) FDI stock positions for the four major European investors in 1997 were: UK $413 billion ($274 billion), France $226 billion ($174 billion), Germany $326 billion ($137 billion), Netherlands $213 billion ($128 billion), UN, *World Investment Report* (1998).

Table 18.2 Inward and outward stock of foreign-owned capital (US$bn)

	1980	1990	1998
European Union*			
Inward	143	406	1303
Outward	153	477	1175
United States			
Inward	83	395	811
Outward	202	435	1022
Japan			
Inward	3	10	36
Outward	20	201	310
Latin America and the Caribbean			
Inward	48	116	431
Outward	3	13	45
East, South and South-East Asia			
Inward	32	146	610
Outward	2	38	329
of which			
China			
Inward	n/a	14	262
Outward	n/a	3	23
India			
Inward	1	2	14
Outward	0	0.03	0.7

Note:
* Excluding intra EU FDI stock (estimated).
n/a: not available.
These statistics are based on balance of payments figures and sometimes differ from statistics compiled directly by national authorities.

Source: United Nations, *World Investment Report*, 1991, 1999 (1999 figures are author's own estimates).

Table 18.3 Stocks of FDI (% GDP)

	Outward		Inward	
	1973	1996	1973	1996
US	7.7	10.4	1.6	8.3
UK	9.1	30.7	13.9	20.5
Japan	2.5	5.6	0.4	0.7
Germany (W)	3.4	12.4	3.8	5.9
Netherlands	25.8	49.1	n.a.	30.4
Developing countries	0.6	4.9	5.4	15.6

Source: Computed from J.H. Dunning, *The Globalisation of Business* (London: Routledge, 1993) and *World Investment Report* (United Nations, various years).

clear exception to this rule (as is Germany to some extent also). Japan's outward stock is high, having grown very rapidly in the 1980s, but its inward stock is abnormally low. In absolute terms, its net inward capital position amounted to only a fraction of that of the UK. The rapid growth of Japan's outward investment seems to follow logically from its strong export performance and its sustained series of balance of payments surpluses since the early 1980s. Less easily explained, in economic terms at least, is the minimal growth of Japan's inward investment. Historically, the Japanese have preferred to license foreign technology in the belief that this was a better way of developing indigenous expertise. This approach was implemented by imposing government restrictions and institutional barriers on inward investment in Japan (see Box 18.1).

Table 18.2 shows that developing countries are, as one would expect, net recipients of foreign capital. China has become a major actor in the field with a foreign capital stock of US$262 billion. Annual foreign direct investment flows into China reached $45 billion in the late 1990s. China has now become the third largest recipient of foreign direct investment in the world, behind only the US and UK.

As we would expect, industrial countries tend to be significant net outward investors. By the late 1990s, gross outward flows from industrial countries amounted to 91.6 per cent of total outflows of $650 billion (Table 18.4). The flow figures, however, show only part of the picture. They exclude capital mobilised by borrowings and equity partners in the host country. The United Nations estimates that the total flow of capital associated with global investment could be three times the flows recorded in Table 18.4.

Table 18.4 Regional distribution of FDI inflows and outflows (percentage)

	Inflows		Outflows	
	1995	*1998*	*1995*	*1998*
Developed countries	63.4	71.5	85.3	91.6
of which:				
US	17.9	30.0	25.7	20.5
Japan	–	0.5	6.3	3.7
EU	35.1	35.7	44.7	59.5
Other	10.4	5.3	8.6	7.9
Developing countries	32.3	25.8	14.5	8.1
of which:				
Asia	20.7	13.2	12.3	5.6
Latin America	10.0	11.1	2.1	2.4
Developing Europe	0.1	0.2	–	–
Other	1.5	1.3	0.1	0.1
Rest of world	4.3	2.7	0.2	0.3
Total	100	100	100	100

Note: Total FDI inflows for 1998 amounted to US$649 billion.

Source: UNCTAD, *World Investment Report* (1999).

Box 18.1

Why is inward foreign direct investment to Japan so low?

Japan receives a remarkably low volume of inward investment relative to its economic size and influence. At the end of 1998, the stock of capital accumulated by Japanese residents abroad (outward stock) exceeded the capital of foreigners in Japan (inward stock) by a factor of 9. Most other industrial countries have ratios of between 1 and 2 (Table 18.1). Investment flow data reveal a similar picture. Japan absorbed only 0.5 per cent of total FDI inflows in 1998, while accounting for 3.7 per cent of outflows. Is this low share a function of market forces, or does it represent the effects of formal and informal barriers to inward investment?

Historically, the Japanese government has placed a high priority on promoting indigenous technical and managerial strengths. It pursued this objective by encouraging Japanese firms to license foreign technology. As recently as 1987–91, the value of Japan's technological imports (defined as payments of royalties and licence fees to foreign owners of patents, copyrights and other non-financial intangible assets) was nearly ten times greater than inflows of FDI. The value of these technological imports was two or three times that of other major developed countries, such as France, Germany, the UK and the US.

Direct manufacturing investment by foreigners in Japan was discouraged. Until 1990, the Foreign Exchange and Foreign Trade Council Law enabled the government to restrict inward FDI, on the grounds that the investment might adversely affect similar domestic business activities or the smooth performance of the Japanese economy. Foreign firms faced special difficulties in merger and acquisition activities because of Japan's institutional framework. An inward investor had to contend with the large share of corporate stock owned by financial companies and *Keiretsu* firms (large conglomerates), the lifetime employment and seniority system, and the complex, multi-layered distribution networks. Preferential group trade practices decrease the transparency of business transactions and discriminate against the prospective foreign investor. Furthermore, hostile takeovers were institutionally difficult since, up to 1990, prior notification was required. Thus, targeted companies had time to prepare their defences.

Finally, the strength of the yen and high property and stock market prices have also deterred foreign investors. The importance of this factor can, however, be disputed. The strong yen has not prevented foreign investors from continuing to complain about lack of access to the Japanese market.

Japan is not the only country to adopt a guarded position regarding foreign investment. Switzerland and Norway have also closed off, explicitly or implicitly, easy access to their domestic markets by outside investors, particularly in cases where foreigners seek to purchase existing assets such as equity in domestic firms, natural resources or residential property. All three countries also happen to have built up strong industrial sectors.

Japan's favourable approach to outward investment contrasts with its restrictive policy towards inward investment. A European Commission report argued that: 'the benefits for the economy of its FDI and other activities have helped Japan become one of the world's most powerful economies.'[1] Japan's inward investment policies have been liberalised in recent years.

Box 18.1 continued

However, the implementation process has been slow and the economy's slow growth during the past decade has deterred investors.

Japan's policy towards foreign investment raises the question of who benefits from FDI. Pressure for change is coming from outside Japan, from potential investors in the US and Europe, which suggests that gains accrue to them from establishing a presence in the Japanese market. This pressure has undoubtedly had an impact, since the inward stock of foreign-owned capital has more than doubled in dollar terms since 1992. But if the theory of this chapter is correct, and gains from FDI are mutual, Japan should lose from a restrictive policy in investment, as it has from its trade restrictions.

Note: 1. European Commission, 'Trade and Investment', Discussion Paper (Brussels, December 1994), p. 16.

Sources: United Nations, *World Investment Report* (New York, 1993); R.Z. Lawrence, 'Why is foreign investment in Japan so low?', *Transnational Corporations* (December 1992); OECD, *The Performance of Foreign Affiliates in OECD Countries* (Paris, 1994).

The flow figures also confirm the level of Japan's outward FDI. Poor returns on outward FDI, exacerbated by the rise in the value of the yen relative to other major currencies in the mid-1990s, accentuated the preference for investing at home rather than abroad. According to balance of payments statistics, total investment earnings on Japan's stock of outward capital amounted to only around 3 per cent.

Inward investment to Asian developing countries rose from an annual average of $14 billion in 1985–90 to an estimated $90 billion in 1996, the peak level prior to the currency crisis of 1997–98. The integration of China into the global economy has led to a huge upsurge in foreign investment, tempered only by the regionally selective and cautious approach of the Chinese authorities. The liberalisation of trade and investment rules, privatisation programmes and stabilisation measures have also led to large inflows of foreign direct investment into Eastern Europe and Latin America throughout most of the 1990s.

Underlying these statistics, and perhaps representing the greatest change, is the transformation in policy towards FDI in most potential host countries. Controls over the foreign ownership of domestic assets have been progressively liberalised and in many cases abolished altogether. Numerous countries now welcome foreign investment, which had until recently viewed it with suspicion and worried about the loss of autonomy implied by the increased reliance on foreign investment. Most European governments are no longer concerned, as they were in the 1950s and 1960s, about the takeover of their domestic industry by American multinationals, but now actively seek ways of encouraging investment regardless of nationality. The British government sees no infringement in its sovereignty in offering generous incentives to Japanese and Korean investors, and is pleased to have captured the leading share of inward investment from the Far East into the EU.

Increased flows of direct investment have been especially prominent in the services sector. Outward FDI has been growing at 15 per cent for tertiary industries, compared with 10 per cent for secondary industries, and 6 per cent for primary industries. The services sector represents nearly one-half of total inward capital stocks.[7] Examples include banking and insurance, airlines and tourism, distribution and telecommunications. New markets for services have opened up in cellular phones, satellite-based television, data communication and long-distance networks, which provide attractive opportunities for multinationals to exploit their competitive technological advantages and spread development costs. India, in particular Bangalore, has, for example, a thriving software industry to which virtually all the major US software producers have contributed by direct investment. Growth in services FDI is expected to continue, because of the fast underlying growth of such high income-elastic activities, trade liberalisation, and the tremendous scope for exploiting cheap production capabilities abroad for many high-value service functions.

Why invest abroad?

Most large firms have some international involvement, and the extent of such involvement is continuously increasing. It has been estimated that 30–40 per cent of the sales of the leading industrial companies are produced outside their national boundaries. Their combined sales exceed the value of global trade.[8] The globalisation of production and markets by MNEs has been helped by three major influences: growth in world trade, capital market integration and technological advance, including innovation in managerial structures and techniques.

A business can 'go international' in many ways:

- it can export from the home country,
- license a foreign business to produce the good or service,
- or engage in production abroad.

Only when it chooses the last step does it enter the statistics for FDI. At this point a further decision has to be taken regarding the mode of control over its foreign production. For instance, the MNE could decide to start by building a new factory from scratch, i.e. a 'green-field' operation. Alternatively, it could organise a takeover of an indigenous company, or it could arrange a joint venture or a merger with a local company.

An enterprise chooses the direct investment path because it expects a higher return from exploiting its advantages itself than from selling its know-how to an indigenous company. The latter has the advantage of greater familiarity with local customs, culture and business environment but there are offsetting problems with a firm selling its know-how. To make it profitable for a firm to engage in production abroad, Dunning has set out three sets of conditions which must be satisfied (see also Box 18.2).

---

7 United Nations, *World Investment Report* (New York: UN, 1998), p. 62; European Commission, 'Trade and investment', *Discussion Paper* (Brussels, December 1994), p. 6.

8 J.H. Dunning, *The Globalization of Business* (London: Routledge, 1993), p. 107.

> ## Box 18.2
>
> # The ownership, location, internalisation (OLI) paradigm
>
> ### Ownership advantages
>
> *(a) Intangible assets*: Proprietary knowledge, technology, trademarks, product management, marketing, R&D, stock of firm-specific human capital.
>
> *(b) Economies of size*:
> - Economies of scale and scope, at plant and enterprise level,
> - Better access to product markets,
> - Product or process diversification,
> - Cheaper input supplies or exclusive access to inputs.
>
> ### Location advantages
>
> *(a) Labour costs and other inputs.*
>
> *(b) Availability of skilled labour*
>
> *(c) Market size, growth of market*
>
> *(d) Government*:
> - Access to world markets,
> - Low tax regime,
> - Environmental regulation and planning procedures,
> - Political stability.
>
> *(e) Other costs*:
> - Transport and communication costs,
> - Infrastructure (commercial, legal, transportation),
> - Psychic distance (language, culture, business, customs).
>
> ### Internalisation advantages
>
> *(a) 'Failures' in markets for final goods and inputs*:
> - Buyer uncertainty about nature and value of final output,
> - Avoid costs of enforcing property rights,
> - Control supplies and conditions of sale for inputs.
>
> *(b) Monopoly power*:
> - Control market outlets,
> - Engage in anti-competitive practices such as cross-subsidisation and predatory pricing,
> - Ability to avoid or exploit government intervention.
>
> *(c) Product differentiation*:
> - Need to protect quality of product.
>
> *Source*: J.H. Dunning, *Explaining International Production* (London: Unwin Hyman, 1988); J.H. Dunning and D. Greenaway, 'Trade and foreign direct investment', *European Economy*, No. 52 (1993).

Ownership advantages

The firm must possess some special monopoly advantage – such as proprietary knowledge, a trade mark or brand name, a patent, access to cheaper inputs, access to customers, or economies of scale and scope – which cannot be replicated by other firms. If this condition is not satisfied, an indigenous company could start up independently and produce an equivalent good locally. FDI would not exist. Ownership advantages comprise all the competitive advantages of a firm.

Location advantages

To explain why an investor sets up abroad or in one host country rather than another, the chosen host country has to offer some special location advantages (as compared with the cost of exporting from the home country, for instance). The list of significant locational variables includes: labour costs (defined in the broadest sense to include the industrial relations climate as well as direct labour costs), the availability of skilled labour, transport and communication costs, R&D capability, the size of the domestic market, access to the domestic and other markets, government incentives and taxation policy, and cultural similarity. Assigning precise weights to these variables is a crucial concern to any industrial promotion authority. Studies of the determinants of the Japanese FDI tend to find that the most influential factors in the host country are corporate tax rates, trade union activity and R&D capability. Regional labour costs, unemployment and transport infrastructure are also important in determining which particular country in a geographical region is chosen as a location for the investment.

Internalisation advantages

Lastly, there must be some source of 'market failure', which impedes the sale of these ownership advantages to a local bidder. These internalisation advantages often arise in knowledge-intensive industries. Take, for example, the case of a drug company which discovers a new formula for treating a disease. To understand and evaluate the product – in short, *to be able to make a well-informed bid* – the buyer must know how useful the drug is and how much it would cost to produce. However, by divulging such information to every prospective buyer, the firm is undermining its own commercial advantage, and soon it would find that its specialised knowledge is no longer exclusive enough to qualify as an ownership advantage. The only solution to this market 'failure' is for the firm to set up a subsidiary to manufacture the drug abroad under the direct control of the parent company.[9]

Often a firm can avail of economies of scale or scope or reputation *only by producing the good itself*. Automobile companies for this reason usually insist on ownership of foreign production facilities rather than licensing others to produce on their behalf. By selling production rights, the firm would inevitably lose some degree of control and endanger its reputation. People buy a Mercedes because it is

---

9 There is considerable evidence of a strong link between technology and outward investment: countries and sectors with the greater propensity to generate know-how prove to be the most significant sources of outward FDI (J.A. Cantwell, *Technological Innovation and the Multinational Corporation*, Oxford: Basil Blackwell, 1989).

made by Mercedes. Their attitude might change if they were told that it was made by a local manufacturer *for* Mercedes. Another reason for internalisation might be the weakness of the legal system in host countries. If know-how is franchised or licensed, a fraudulent foreign partner could be difficult to prosecute and, hence, the MNE might feel safer retaining complete control over the foreign operation itself.

In many cases, the choice between licensing and direct provision can be finely balanced. If the particular advantage can be 'de-bundled', licensing and franchising are likely to become more attractive. The possibility of de-bundling a brand name from its production may explain why franchising is common in the international retail trade. The parent firm may have an ownership advantage (such as ownership of a brand name – McDonalds, for instance, or Coca-Cola) but, since this can be sold on to local businesses at a realistic price, there is no internalisation advantage relative to the local franchisee.[10]

The logic behind internalisation advantages draws on the transaction cost approach (discussed in Chapter 5). Whenever transactions such as establishing a relevant price through licences can be organised and carried out more cheaply within the firm than through the market, they will be internalised and undertaken by the firm itself. The multinational corporation faced with imperfections in input markets, such as patented technical knowledge and human capital, will attempt to internalise these markets within its organisation so as to maximise profits.

Dunning's carefully composed scheme indicates that all three elements are necessary for a direct foreign investment decision to be profitable. The company must *own* something valuable which cannot be costlessly replicated. Market failure must dictate that this advantage should be *internalised* rather than be sold for others to exploit. And the host country must present a *locational* advantage to the company to induce it to set up business abroad in preference to supplying from a home base.

18.4 Effects of foreign investment

Direct investment embodies 'a package of potential growth-enhancing attributes, including technology, managerial and technological know-how, and access to international markets'.[11]

Most countries welcome *inward* investment, even those which formerly regarded it with mistrust. Virtually all recent legislation on foreign investment has been intended to liberalise the regime applied to FDI. A majority of

---

10 However, there is no clear-cut boundary between FDI and franchising/licensing; rather, a continuum of degrees of control and ownership. Furthermore, control can be confined to a number of different organisational areas and does not necessarily relate positively to the size of the stake held by the parent. Modern practice is for MNEs to leave their subsidiaries considerable operational leeway, even if they are majority-owned by the parent. A subsidiary of AAB in Indonesia, owned 100 per cent by AAB International, might be more independent than the local McDonalds, even though the latter is tied to its parent only through a franchise agreement.

11 United Nations, *op. cit.*

governments also believe that *outward* investment benefits their economies. But there is some residual ambivalence about this. Host countries continue to worry about the long-term consequences of foreign investment on the domestically-owned sector of the economy, and are concerned with the fiscal costs of attracting the multinationals. Within home countries too, there is concern that the internationalisation of production will mean the 'export' of jobs.

At the level of the firm, there is less ambiguity. The majority of firms regard freedom to establish abroad as an important facility which allows them to exploit their competitive advantages. Apart from the internalisation factors outlined above, there is the practical matter that, as firms get bigger, they start to outgrow the domestic market. As their domestic market share approaches saturation point, further expansion could cause trouble with competitors, or suppliers, or might be blocked by monopoly legislation. Going international is a means of diversifying the firm's operations, and of keeping in touch with new markets and new ideas in a direct way.

A business strategy of globalisation works to the firm's advantage but does it also contribute to the national economy? The answer is generally yes. The static gains from foreign investment are the same as those from capital mobility outlined in Figure 18.1. Through foreign investment, capital and its associated resources are deployed where their productivity is highest. This brings mutual benefits to both home country and host country parties. But, in addition to these static gains, there are important dynamic gains which are specific to direct investment flows and which therefore require separate analysis. A European Commission report describes FDI *as a dynamic process which raises total wealth to the advantage of all those involved.*[12] This dynamic process has motivated countries as diverse as Singapore, Poland, Portugal and Ireland, and regions as diverse as Scotland and North Carolina, to rely heavily on inward investment for economic development.

Foreign investment is sought for many reasons, some more substantive in economic terms than others.

Multinationals generate externalities. FDI involves the import of productive factors such as marketing know-how, training facilities and technological expertise. Multinationals, for example, account for some 80 per cent of private R&D spending in the world and, directly and indirectly, for a similar proportion of world trade.[13] The host country benefits from the spillover effects of these activities. The head office of the multinational, of course, charges its subsidiaries for inputs of productive factors supplied by the parent so the mere fact that know-how is passed on does not constitute proof of net gain to the host country. A gain to the host country occurs only when the price charged (the private cost) is less than the social benefit (the full economic benefit from the operation). Spillovers and externalities arising from the multinational's activities reflect the potential dynamic gains from foreign investment. Typical spillovers include labour training, upgrading the production skills and motivation of local component

---

12 European Commission, *op. cit.*, p. 14.
13 Dunning, *op. cit.*, p. 287.

suppliers, stimulus to competition, development of managerial skills and of knowledge about foreign markets and other types of demonstration effects.[14]

Multinationals create more jobs. Or, in the case of a takeover of an ailing domestic firm, they 'save' jobs which would otherwise be lost. This argument seems reasonable, but in economic terms it is badly articulated. Just because an activity 'creates' jobs is not an automatic indication of its merits. If the activity did not exist, jobs might be created elsewhere in the economy. Furthermore, the new activity might be responsible for the displacement of existing jobs in other sectors of the economy. The relevant comparison is between what is produced with foreign investment versus what would have been produced in its absence. If, in the absence of foreign investment, labour would have remained unemployed, questions must be asked about the labour market. If the host country's unemployment originates in labour market inflexibility, it would be better to tackle this problem at source (through the type of labour market policies described in Chapter 13) rather than by attacking the symptoms.

Foreign investment generates tax revenues. Foreign subsidiaries pay corporation (profits) tax to the host government and their workers pay income tax and indirect tax on their spending. The sum of all these taxes can amount to a sizeable contribution to the exchequer, which can, so the argument goes, be offset against any grants or incentives paid to the foreign firm. Exercises of this type win high marks in popular debate but they suffer the defect of neglecting the alternatives forgone. Thus, alternative domestic activities to those of the foreign firm would also have generated tax revenues. It is the net addition to tax revenues by comparison with this hypothetical alternative, not the gross tax revenues, against which the cost of fiscal investment incentives should be offset. Another qualification to keep in mind is that tax revenues can be artificially boosted by 'transfer-pricing' activity (see Box 18.3). In this instance, one exchequer's gain is another's loss and, from a global point of view, the position could be suboptimal.

Foreign investment generates foreign exchange. The initial investment may take the form of loans from the parent company or from a foreign bank. Once the subsidiary is in operation it may generate exports or displace imports. Against this, one would have to deduct outgoings of dividends and loan repayments. If the net result is a positive contribution to the balance of payments, this seems like a reason for supporting the project. However, this argument too is deficient. First, it ignores the foreign exchange earnings and outgoings if the resources had been used in an alternative way. Second, even if the foreign investor makes a positive net contribution to foreign exchange earnings relative to, say, alternative investments, this is not the only economic criterion on which to judge the desirability of foreign investment. As in the 'create jobs' argument, there may be more efficient ways of achieving foreign exchange balance. If shortage of foreign

---

14 See, for example, T. Ozawa, 'Foreign direct investment and economic development', *Transnational Corporations* (February 1992); J. Cantwell, 'Foreign multinationals and industrial development in Africa', in P. Buckley and J. Clegg (eds), *Multinational Enterprises in Less Developed Countries* (London: Macmillan, 1991); and S. Young, N. Hood and E. Peters, 'Multinational enterprises and regional economic development', *Regional Studies*, Vol. 28, No. 7 (1994).

Box 18.3

Transfer pricing

Transfer pricing is an accounting practice used by multinational enterprises to limit their overall tax burden. It arises because of the existence of different national tax regimes. Profits earned in a high-tax country are 'transferred' for tax purposes to a low-tax country. To reduce its overall corporation profits tax burden, a multinational can arrange for its subsidiary in a low-tax country to be undercharged (or overpaid) for goods and services purchased from (sold to) another subsidiary located in a higher tax jurisdiction. In this manner, profits in the subsidiary in the low-tax country are artificially inflated, while profits reported for the operation in the high-tax country are reduced.

For example, suppose that a US multinational company has a plant in Ireland, which produces an intermediate product for export to another subsidiary of the same multinational located in a high-tax country, say Germany. The Irish subsidiary pays corporation profits tax at 10 per cent; the German subsidiary pays 30 per cent. If the two tax rates were identical, the Irish plant would sell the components to the German plant for £10 million at an arm's length price of £20 per unit. However, with different tax rates, the multinational has an incentive to inflate this price. Suppose it charged £40 per unit instead of £20; the Irish subsidiary would be paid £20 million instead of £10 million. The amount of profit reported in Ireland would increase by £10 million; profits attributed to Germany would fall by the same amount.

Assume that, in the initial situation, the subsidiary in each country earned £5 million profits. Total tax paid would amount to £2 million (£1.5 million in Germany and £0.5 million in Ireland). Now, after the higher transfer price, £10 million profits are transferred to low-tax Ireland. Tax is paid in Ireland at 10 per cent and the tax bill on its £15m profits amounts to £1.5 million. Results: (a) the company's overall tax bill is reduced to £1.5 million, not counting the write-off in respect of losses of its German subsidiary; (b) the Irish government gains an extra £1 million in tax revenue; and (c) the German authorities are less happy – they lose £1.5 million of tax revenue.

Effect of transfer pricing on profits and taxes

	Without transfer pricing	With transfer pricing
Per unit price	£20	£40
Sales revenue	£10m	£20m
Profits – German operation	£5m	–£5m
Profits – Irish operation	£5m	£15m
Total tax payable	£2m (£1.5m+£0.5m)	£1.5m (£0m+£1.5m)

Transfer pricing is a touchy subject. Multinationals rightly point out that there is a limit to the amount of transfer pricing that can be done. Tax authorities are alert to the possibility of profit-switching from one jurisdiction to another, and will if necessary 'see through' such transactions if they are made too blatant. However, this leaves plenty of scope for discretion and for honest disagreement as to the 'true' costs of goods and services supplied from one part of a multinational to another.

Box 18.3 continued

Proposals for a system of unitary taxation have been recommended, whereby a multinational would pay a single tax on all its sales, such revenue to be assessed by some proportional formula. Hence, if 60 per cent of a firm's sales revenue was earned in the US, the authorities would assume that 60 per cent of its global profits originated there also, and levy tax accordingly. The idea does not seem to have taken off. Yet the problem will not go away, and there is continuing pressure within the EU, for example, to proceed to greater harmonisation of corporate tax rates as the only really effective mechanism for dealing with the problem.

exchange is a problem, adjusting the exchange rate may be a better policy than offering incentives to foreign investors.

To assess the net gains from foreign investment, therefore, a fully fledged cost–benefit analysis is needed. The benefits from FDI should be compared with costs such as capital and training grants, tax incentives, rent allowances, interest rate subsidies and other forms of implicit or explicit assistance. Theory helps us to ask the right questions in carrying out such an exercise and to avoid major conceptual errors in the definition of benefits and costs, but in the end there is no substitute for detailed assessment of each project under alternative scenarios. Such assessments inevitably prove controversial – different assumptions about the hypothetical or counterfactual situation can yield different results.

Empirical studies are plagued by the problem of trying to assess the counterfactual, i.e. the difference between the actual impact of MNEs and the situation that would have prevailed in their absence. Recent research emphasises that FDI is an important vehicle for the transfer of technology and that it can generate significant productivity growth in host countries, provided that they have the necessary skills to utilise that technology.[15]

Increasingly, attention is being focused on the contribution of MNEs to developing the innovatory capabilities of host countries and on ways in which governments can maximise this contribution. To maximise the potential spillovers, the host country needs to develop:

1. *An integrated policy approach*, whereby efforts to attract FDI are complemented by stable macroeconomic policies and by supportive microeconomic policies on linkages, industrial clusters, education and R&D, rather than being pursued in isolation. Higher level of educational attainment in the host country enhance the positive spillovers of high tech inward FDI by raising the host country's absorptive capacity. Competition policy needs special attention if multinationals are being given incentives to produce for the domestic market. Multinationals can cause losses to the host country if they are allowed to operate in a monopoly environment. Repatriated monopoly

---

15 E. Borzenstein, J. De Gregorio and J. Lee, 'How does foreign direct investment affect economic growth?', *Journal of International Economics*, 4, 1998.

Box 18.4

Incentives and foreign direct investment

Foreign investors are strongly influenced by investment incentives. Although they often express reservations about projects whose potential profitability relies solely on host country incentives, once a company has narrowed its choice of sites, incentives *do* count. Studies on foreign investment incentive criteria have found that, although incentives are a secondary consideration in corporate strategic planning, an attractive incentive package can influence the final decision on where to invest.

Unlike other factors affecting FDI, incentives have the advantage of being under the direct control of governments. Many developing countries and regions offer extremely generous incentive 'packages'. However, an incentive competition between governments is costly and can generate inefficient investments, with disappointing results for the 'victor'. If it goes too far, the 'winning' country obtains no net benefit – all of the 'rent' goes to the foreign investor. European countries bidding for foreign investment are similar to the prisoners in the prisoners' dilemma case outlined in chapter 7. If all refused to offer incentives, foreign investors would invest in Europe anyway, attracted by the need for market access. But in the absence of cooperation, each country will compete against the other.

In the automobile industry, for example, regions of the US have found that the scale of incentives required to induce FDI lies between $120 million and $325 million per plant, well in excess of the financial capacities of many developing countries. The UK government has provided grants amounting to more than £20,000 per job created to greenfield Japanese and Korean subsidiaries.

Reducing incentives requires cooperation among governments. Efforts to date have focused on the regional level. In particular, the OECD has long sought closer harmonisation of investment policies among its members. The EU has placed a ceiling on total incentive packages, while allowing for some regional variation. Under WTO rules, financial subsidies that distort trade have to be curbed.

International harmonisation of incentives is difficult to achieve. The main problem is that of ensuring transparency. Incentives come in all sorts of guises and national and regional authorities are adept at concealing exactly how much has been provided. Also, there is disagreement about how the incentives to the investor, such as tax breaks or training grants, should be measured. The value of an incentives package may depend on a firm's tax situation, for example, and some training may be more firm-specific than others. But the diminishing effectiveness of the incentives as their use widens, their tendency to distort trade flows and the danger of an incentives war are factors encouraging the authorities to put a concerted effort into controlling their level.

Source: United Nations Conference on Trade and Development, *Incentives and Foreign Direct Investment* (New York: United Nations, 1996); United Nations, *World Investment Report* (New York: United Nations, various years).

profits, earned through sales on the home market, involve a direct loss to the nationals of the country, and not just in redistribution of income. The most efficient way to handle the difficulty is to bid away monopoly profits by opening the market to foreign competition. Direct controls are unlikely to be the answer to this problem. Guidelines for multinational were adopted by governments of the 29 members of the OECD in June 2000 that address these issues.

2. *Targeted incentives*. Promotion agencies must target the industrial and service sectors most concordant with the country's evolving comparative advantage, and calibrate the incentive package to achieve the desired mix of foreign investors. This last task is made all the more necessary by the intense competition for investment projects among different countries and regions. Countries compete for projects and those offering below the 'market' level of incentives will lose projects. Going above the ruling incentive level can prove expensive. There has been an escalation of incentive levels – particularly within Europe – as countries seek to alleviate their unemployment problems through inward investment. There is a real danger that excessive competition for FDI among governments will raise incentives to an uneconomic level. Good project cost–benefit analysis should help to avoid this danger. Also governments should think of providing attractions other than financial incentives – a pleasant environment, reduction of hassle and specialised services.

3. *After-care policies*. The authorities should keep in touch with the foreign firms, discuss their plans and prepare the groundwork for expansion, extension of linkages with the local economy and structural change. Included here is the need to upgrade continuously the economic and physical infrastructure in order to maintain the attractiveness of the host country for international business. The foreign subsidiaries themselves should also be encouraged to invest and upgrade. The 'branch-plant' or 'screwdriver industry' syndrome can lead to an over-dependent and poor-quality productive base. Subsidiaries of this type should be encouraged to upgrade.

4. *Support for indigenous industry*. The search for foreign investment projects must not lead to a neglect of indigenous firms. An innovative and competitive economy needs plenty of small and medium-sized enterprises (SMEs); the externalities of the multinationals are mostly delivered through the agency of these firms.

Foreign investment continues to engender feelings of disquiet and suspicion. Looked at objectively, there are indeed circumstances in which multinationals can impose costs on an economy. These costs are, however, avoidable, and the consensus among economists is that the potential benefits significantly outweigh the potential losses.

18.5 | Conclusions

This chapter has discussed the role of mobile capital, focusing on the extent to which this mobility might contribute to higher living standards in host and home countries. We started with a simple analysis and gradually introduced more realistic conditions. We concluded that openness to exchange of productive factors has the potential to provide important net static and dynamic gains to the world economy. But theory also warns that not everyone gains, and we should not be surprised if national and sectoral interests are differently affected.

Capital and labour mobility are to some extent interrelated. The point is often made, in the context of discussion of underdeveloped regions, that one can choose between *bringing capital to people, or people to capital.*

One way to bring capital to people is through foreign investment. Foreign direct investment brings the technical and marketing know-how (human capital) which host countries need if they are to convert the opportunities of the free market into real achievements. Another form of capital inflow is portfolio capital that enables the host country to invest more rapidly and to upgrade its labour force. Convergence is then achieved not by a process of levelling up the poorer countries and levelling down the richer ones to a single average, but primarily by raising the performance of the poorer countries to the high standards of the richer countries. Finally, the ability to invest abroad provides one other gain that is becoming increasingly important: spreading risk through portfolio diversification.[16]

Capital flows and liberalisation of trade and capital movements go hand in hand. Some foreign investment, such as outward processing, is directly trade motivated. Here access to the host country markets and access from the host country to third markets is essential. A liberal approach to capital and foreign exchange is also necessary to reassure the foreign company that it will be able to repatriate its profits and liquidate its investment as and when necessary.

✔ Summary

1. International trade in factors of production generates economic gains in much the same way as international trade in goods and services. Both parties to the transaction can benefit. It is a positive-sum game.

2. Capital has become increasingly mobile internationally. This applies to both portfolio flows and direct investment. Transaction costs of moving capital have been reduced as a result of information technology and the removal of official restrictions. The supply of funds has increased as a result of greater prosperity and the growth of the pensions industry. Demand for international investment has been stimulated by intense competition among fund managers for high returns and diversified portfolios.

16 P. Lane, 'Trade and economic convergence: The Credit Channel', *Oxford Economic Papers* (forthcoming).

3. The gains from capital mobility derive from the allocation of capital to sectors and locations where its productivity is highest. Two indirect effects of capital mobility are that domestic capital has become harder to tax. High taxes lead to capital flight. Also capital mobility places constraints on governments' fiscal policy. There are potential downsides: speculative inflows and outflows of capital can be destabilising, can lead to exchange rate misalignments and can erode a country's tax base.

4. Foreign direct investment is a special form of capital mobility in that it involves a 'package' of factors – know-how and skilled management alongside capital. Firms produce abroad in response to ownership advantages, locational incentives and internalisation economies (the OLI theory). In addition to standard economic gains, multinationals bring to the host country what the United Nations describes as 'a package of potential growth-enhancing attributes'.

? Questions for discussion

1. 'The international mobility of capital, both in the form of portfolio capital and direct foreign investment, can make a significant positive contribution to economic welfare.' Evaluate this statement. Examine some of the problems associated with enhanced capital mobility.

2. 'The international mobility of factors of production can contribute significantly to the reduction in international differences in income and wealth.' Discuss in the context of portfolio capital mobility.

3. Explain the contribution made by multinational enterprises to (a) a host country, and (b) a home country of your choice. Is it possible for you to conclude that both host and home country benefited from investment by multinationals?

☞ Exercises

1. A foreign firm is proposing to set up a new 'greenfield' plant to manufacture auto parts in your country. List the economic benefits which you would expect to be generated by the plant, then draw up a list of likely costs.

2. What is the difference between 'direct' investment and 'portfolio' investment? Are the economic effects of the two types of investment likely to differ?

3. Outline the main 'locational' advantages of your country for a foreign investor. How can/should this be improved?

Further reading

Most international economics textbooks contain a chapter or two on the economics of factor mobility between countries. P. Lindert, *International Economics* (Homewood, Ill: Irwin, 9th edn, 1991) is particularly useful. A leading authority on direct investment and multinationals, Professor John Dunning, *The Globalization of Business* (London: Routledge, 1993) provides a flavour of where the debate is at on this topic. Another good source is P.J. Buckley, *Foreign Direct Investment and Multinational Enterprise* (Basingstoke: Macmillan, 1995). John Stopford, 'Multinational corporations', *Foreign Poilcy* (Winter 1998–99) provides a readable, pointed overview of multinationals from the perspective of strategic management. Today's multinationals, he argues, bear little resemblance to their forebears as they reinvent themselves to adapt to new competitors and new organisational structures, including strategic alliances.

Chapter 19

LABOUR MIGRATION

Introduction

Because of its humanitarian and cultural dimension, labour migration is a sensitive and controversial topic. Yet, in economic terms, it can be visualised as another example of international exchange of a factor of production leading to mutual gains. Professor John Kenneth Galbraith, no starry-eyed admirer of the free-market system, describes migration as *a process that helps those who go, the place they go to and those they leave behind.*[1]

This chapter considers only voluntary migration induced by economic circumstances. We exclude forced migration from totalitarian regimes or war zones. Economic analysis, drawing on the same framework used to analyse capital movements, provides important insights into the consequences of migration for each of the parties concerned. However, many aspects of the migration process are ignored in the simple model. When they are taken into account, the net balance of advantage and disadvantage becomes more complex to assess, and it becomes easier to appreciate the ambivalence of both host countries to immigration and of sending countries to emigration. Business is often caught in the middle: it has to cope with a welter of immigration laws and regulations on the one hand, and on the other, with the necessity of competing with firms that employ illegal immigrants.

Most countries tend to encourage migration *within* their national boundaries – domestic labour mobility is generally regarded as a good thing – but they display less enthusiasm for mobility between nations.[2] Thus, the EU encourages labour mobility between member states through reciprocal recognition of educational and professional qualifications, anti-discrimination rules and equality of social welfare treatment. But strict limits are applied to applications by non-EU citizens for admission to the EU labour market. Many other host countries, such as Australia, Switzerland and the US, place restrictions on the number of immigrants.[3]

---

1 J.K. Galbraith, *The Nature of Mass Poverty* (Cambridge, MA: Harvard University Press, 1979).
2 This is not to deny that regional policy is active in these countries, and that after a point internal migratory flows can also be seen as a problem.
3 During the mid-1990s, there was a limit of 150,000 visas in Australia and 700,000 in the US.

Chapter outline

This chapter examines the economics of migration in the following steps:

1. Recent trends in migration.
2. Standard model showing how migration can tield gains to home country, to host country and the migrants themselves.
3. Extension of model to include wider considerations of an economic, social and political nature.

19.1 Recent trends

Three trends are evident in the pattern of migration in recent years.

- The number of people migrating has increased. Over 100 million people reside outside the country of their citizenship today compared with 80 million in the late 1980s.[4] Two-thirds of these are economic migrants, one third refugees.
- Migration has become more globalised. African emigrants move to Europe, Asians migrate to the Middle East and Australia, and Europeans migrate to North America.
- Emigration patterns have been influenced by the regionalisation of the world economy, as evidenced by migratory flows from East to West Europe, from Thailand and the Philippines to Japan, and from South and Central America to North America.
- Migration is not just a developed country problem; developing countries (South Africa, Pakistan, Argentina) attract 60 per cent of all migrants.
- Although the number of immigrants has increased in absolute numbers, their share of total population is still relatively modest. Between 1960 and 1990 immigrants in the UK increased their share of total population by 2 percentage points.[5] The total share of immigrants is below 5 per cent in most countries and exceeds 10 per cent in only four. However these figures, being derived from official sources, omit unrecorded or illegal migration. In some countries this may imply a significant underestimation of the scale of migration. The number of illegal immigrants smuggled into Europe has been estimated at 400,000 per year and at 200,000 per year into the US.

During the past two decades the share of foreigners in total population rose rapidly in several European countries (see Table 19.1). Foreign residents increased by 3 million in Germany since 1980, by 1 million in Italy and by over 400,000 in the UK and Switzerland. Absolute numbers of foreign residents are greatest in Germany, France and the UK. Austria has experienced the greatest increase in

---

4 S. Stanton Russell and M.S. Teitelbaum, 'International migration and international trade', *World Bank Discussion Paper*, No. 160 (1994); D. Papademetriou, 'Migration', *Foreign Policy* (Winter 1997–98).
5 B. Bell, 'The performance of immigrants in the UK: Evidence from the GHS', *Economic Journal* (March 1997).

Table 19.1 Foreign population resident in main host European countries

	1980	1998
	Thousands (% of total population)	
Switzerland	893	1341
	(14.1)	(19)
Belgium	879	903
	(8.9)	(8.9)
Germany	4453	7366
	(7.2)	(9.0)
France	3582	3597
	(6.3)	(6.3)
Austria	282	733
	(3.7)	(9.1)
Netherlands	521	678
	(3.7)	(4.4)
UK	1601	2207
	(2.8)	(3.8)
Italy	299	1250
	(0.5)	(2.1)

Source: J.-P. Garson, 'International migration: Facts, figures, policies', OECD Observer (June/July 1992); OECD, International Labour Migration (Paris, 1999).

foreign residents in percentage terms, up from 4 per cent to 9 per cent of the population, most of this increase occurring during the 1990s. Not surprisingly, given the scale and speed of change, the issue of immigration has aroused much controversy in that country. The most cosmopolitan country in Europe is Luxembourg (not shown in Table 19.1); over one-third of its population and over a half of its workforce is foreign-born. Most (89 per cent) of Luxembourg's migrants are well-paid EU civil servants and bankers from adjacent countrries who are easily assimilated and cause minimal friction.

Countries such as Australia, Canada and the US have traditionally given succour and opportunity to immigrants. US immigration amounts to 9 per cent of the population, up from 6 per cent a decade ago (Table 19.2). This is a very significant rate of increase. Although the overall percentage of foreign-born population is higher in Australia (21 per cent) and Canada (17 per cent), this percentage has been fairly consistent over the past decade.

In the early postwar years immigrants into Europe were welcomed as a source of much-needed labour, willing to undertake work that nationals shunned. Latterly, too, the contribution of skilled foreigners to the development of key economic sectors has become recognised. More than one-third of those employed in Silicon Valley are foreign born, many providing essential services in lower paid sectors but many others at the cutting edge of the new industries. Nevertheless, there are also strong undercurrents of unease and resistance to large-scale inflows of immigrants. In Europe the high unemployment rate has no doubt contributed to this change in attitude, while in the US concern about ethnic and linguistic mix and assimilative capacity have been central to the debate.

Table 19.2 Foreign-born population and labour force

	Foreign-born population				Foreign-born labour force			
	Thousands		% of total population		Thousands		% of total labour force	
	1986	1996	1986	1996	1986	1996	1986	1996
Australia	3247	3908	20.8	21.1	1901	2239	25.4	24.6
Canada	3908	4971	15.4	17.4	2359	2681	18.5	18.5
United States	14080	24600	6.2	9.3	7077	14300	6.7	10.8

Source: OECD, *International Labour Migration* (Paris, 1999).

Migration patterns must be evaluated in the context of world population trends. Between 2000 and 2025, the world's population is expected to increase from 6 billion to 8 billion. During this period, and notwithstanding the immigration levels observed to date, the number of people in Europe is projected to decline marginally from 582 to 580 million. This forms a stark contrast with the increase in population of North Africa from 170 to 249 million and in Asia from 3.6 to 4.9 billion. The populations of the US, Canada and Australia are expected to increase by over 20 per cent over the next 25 years – an increase that is largely related to their higher rates of immigration.

19.2 Effects of migration – the basic model

We begin with the model used earlier to analyse capital flows. World labour supply, assumed to be fixed, is depicted on the horizontal axis and wage per hour on the vertical axis (Figure 19.1). The world is divided into two regions, the North and the South. Each region has a fixed stock of capital (shorthand for all productive factors other than labour). Within each region there are two sets of individuals: workers and employers. Employers own the nation's stock of capital and land. Initially, there is no mobility between North and South. The North has a labour stock of $O_N L$. Because of the North's superior infrastructure, level of human capital investment and technology, labour productivity is relatively high in the North and wage is $O_N W_N$. By contrast, labour productivity is relatively low in the South. Labour supply of $O_S L$ earns a wage equal to $O_S W_S$.

The existence of this wage differential provides a powerful incentive to migrate from the South to the North. As migration proceeds, the wage gap narrows. Eventually, a new equilibrium is reached at L^*. At that point, wages are equalised and nobody has any incentive to migrate. Complete convergence has been achieved. The wage level falls in the North, and it rises in the South. The equilibrium wage lies between the initial North and South level.

The effects of migration can be worked out as follows:

- Southern workers who remain at home obtain a rise in pay to $O_S W^*$ and gain $W^* E R W_S$ in increased wages.

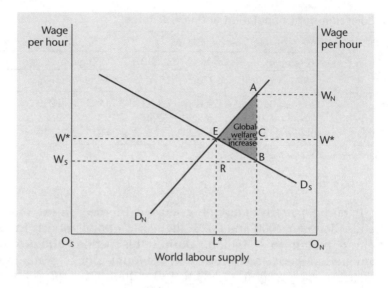

Figure 19.1 Labour migration in the basic model

- Workers in the North experience a pay decline of W_NW^* and lose W^*CAW_N as a result.
- Migrating Southern workers, who were initially earning O_SW_S, now earn OW^*, a gain of ECBR.
- Employers in the South do badly. They have to pay an extra W^*ERW_S to their employees and they also lose profits of EBR because of the reduction in output.
- Employers in the North make additional profits of W^*CAW_N as a result of the fall in the wage level. In addition, they earn a profit of ACE on the output produced by the immigrants.
- Global welfare increases by the triangle ABE, of which CEA accrues to the North, and CEB to the South (including therein the higher income received by the South's emigrants).

The profile of the effects of migration parallels that of the effect of capital mobility. There are gainers and losers in each country, but by appropriate income redistribution the gainers could compensate the losers. Because of this, freedom to migrate, according to this model, is welfare-enhancing. The world as a whole gains because people go to the country where their marginal productivity is highest.

Although the model is based on many simplifying assumptions, it yields some remarkably realistic predictions. First, it predicts that workers and employers in the North are likely to adopt different positions regarding immigration. Trade union representatives are likely to advocate restrictions, while employers would be expected to adopt a more permissive approach. Immigration for them means lower labour costs. Second, the model predicts some ambivalence in the home region. Workers remaining in the South benefit in so far as their real wage increases, but owners of other productive factors tend to lose as higher labour costs eat into profits. The South's GNP will fall. The emigrants themselves are of course better-off, but they will no longer be around to vote in the home country elections.[6]

Making the model more realistic

Wages are not everything

There are psychic and economic costs associated with migration. Also potential migrants will have to weight the northern wage OW_N by the probability of their getting a job at that wage. When the North's unemployment rate is high, this probability will be less than unity. Potential emigrants will also care about the quality of life, which is often thought to be superior in one's native country, due to proximity to friends and relatives and a familiar lifestyle. Hence, migration will continue to a point where the *expected value* of the pay in the North (i.e. the wage rate multiplied by the probability of getting a job at that wage) equals the expected value of pay in the South, after taking account of the psychic advantages of being employed at home:

$$W_n(1-\phi U_n) = W_s(1-\phi U_s)f$$

where: W = wages
  U = the unemployment rate
  ϕ = a parameter by which the unemployment rate is weighted
  f = the non-pecuniary advantage of staying in the South for the marginal migrant.
  Subscripts n and s refer to North and South.

This equation shows how the unadjusted North–South wage gap can give a misleading impression of the intensity of the incentive to migrate. For example, suppose the non-pecuniary advantages of staying at home (f) was valued at 1.5, i.e. 50 per cent of Ws, and that the rate of unemployment was the same in the two areas. The incentive to migrate would disappear when wages in the South had risen to two-thirds of the level in the North.

Time dimension

Migrants respond not just to *current* pay differences but to the expected profile of earnings over time. The migration decision can be conceptualised as depending on the balance between, on one side, a stream of benefits over time (higher real income, job security, better promotion prospects) and, on the other, a stream of costs (absence from home, psychic disutility of migrant status) and a significant upfront cost (removal expense, travel expenses, uncertainty). This 'human capital' approach emphasises that migration is an investment decision, involving

---

6 For all that, there are few instances of countries trying to restrict emigration, whereas controls on immigration are the norm. This may be due to governments assigning higher weights to the incomes of (native) workers relative to other income groups.

a fixed irrecoverable cost (of movement) and an uncertain future stream of returns.[7] Four important implications follow from this approach.

- Since young people have a longer period in which to write off initial costs than older people (the duration of the investment is longer), young people are more likely to migrate than older people.
- More clever and dynamic persons have a greater prospect of future promotion and advancement in the host country, and hence have a greater incentive to migrate than those less talented.
- Two-way flows can be expected, younger workers emigrating, older workers returning and also among highly skilled and highly specialised individuals.
- As incomes equalise, less migration will take place. This explains the fall-off in migration for the Iberian countries to northern Europe. By the same token, greater income divergence encourages migration. This crude economic imperative underlies the continuing flows from North Africa and eastern Turkey to the EU.

19.3 Migration, public finances and jobs

Migration has many spillover effects on the economy. Sometimes migrants prove to be more educated, innovative and enterprising than the norm. If so, they may bring positive externalities to the host country, and their departure involves negative externalities for the sending countries. India and Morocco, for example, complain that their electronics graduates are being lost to Europe and North America. Sending countries such as Mexico argue that they lose further in so far as they have to provide pre- and post-retirement social services to these migrants, many of whom return to Mexico late in life.

Market-size effects can be another source of externalities. Immigration to the US, Canada and Russia in the nineteenth century was essential to the development of the immense natural resources of these areas. Productivity increased with numbers up to a critical minimum point, such that the social benefit of an individual immigrant exceeded the individual earnings. If, on the other hand, immigration leads to the development of congested suburbs and shanty-towns, the externalities become negative. The argument that migration promotes cultural diversity is also double-edged. Such diversity can, of course, be an advantage, but it can also become a source of serious social friction, especially if the migrants are of markedly different race, language and religion to the majority and are slow to integrate.

---

7 In formal terms, the present value of staying at home (PV) can be represented as:

$$PV = \sum_{t=0}^{n} \frac{w_t - f_t}{(1 + r)^t}$$

where: w_t = the real income difference at time t, adjusted for unemployment
$\quad\quad\ \ $ f = the financial/psychic cost of migration at time t
$\quad\quad\ \ $ t = the time in years
$\quad\quad\ \ $ n = the duration of the investment horizon
$\quad\quad\ \ $ r = the rate of discount.

Two other important externalities relate, first, to public finances and, second, to the job displacement and wage effects of migration.

Public finance effects

There are good reasons for believing that immigration would have a positive impact on public finances in the host country. People tend to migrate at an age when they are unlikely to draw heavily on the education and health facilities of the host country. Also, the cost of certain indivisible public expenditure, defence being a classic example, can be spread over a larger working population, to the advantage of all. If migration policy is applied selectively, giving preference to the better-educated, this will further improve the probability of fiscal gains by reducing the likelihood of unemployment, and maximising the probability that the immigrant will be a net contributor to the public finances.

On the other hand, however (and on complex issues there nearly always is another hand), where migrants are mainly unskilled, as is predominantly the case with South–North migration, the net impact on the public finances is less clear. Unskilled migrants are likely to have more difficulty finding work in the host country. For instance, the unemployment rates of foreign workers in Belgium, France, Germany and Sweden have been between 50 and 100 per cent higher than for nationals (see Chapter 14), although by no means all migrants to these countries are unskilled. A serious fiscal burden falls on the host country if people move solely in order to avail of its better standard of social services (Box 19.1).

The net impact on the host country's public finances thus depends upon the motivation, skills and circumstances of the migrant – all of which are likely to change over time. For example, European experience shows that although many migrants arrive on their own, intending to return home, the majority of migrants who stay eventually send for their families.

For the sending country, emigration can reduce the burden of public goods provision. However, this gain must be balanced against the loss of potential future tax revenue from the emigrants. The lifecycle patterns of migration and of the consumption of public goods mean the sending country is more likely to suffer a net fiscal loss. People tend to migrate in early adulthood. This means that emigrants tend to be concentrated in the age-group that has just received public schooling at taxpayers' expense, yet the migrants will not be around to pay taxes from their adult earnings. Also, the more skilled the migrants and the more income they could earn, the greater the future income forgone in the sending country.

> Once migration has become an established option for educated people, more people will want to become educated. Higher education will attract as many people as can get an adequate yield on their education by staying at home plus the extra number flowing abroad. This can be major public expenditure with no offset in future tax yields. (Richard Layard, *East–West Migration* (Cambridge, MA: MIT Press, 1992), p. 39)

A 'brain-drain' tax has been proposed to deal with this problem. Emigrants would pay an extra education-related tax in the 'North' that would be passed back

Box 19.1

Migrants and government finances

The economic theory of migration, like the theory of trade outlined in Chapter 17, stresses the potential for mutual gains from migration. This emphasis tends to favour a liberal approach to immigration policy. But clearly, in view of the widespread restrictions on immigration, the arguments in favour of free movement of labour have proven less persuasive than arguments for free trade in goods.

One reason for this is that the model treats 'labour' as if migrants and natives consisted of homogeneous units of labour. But in reality labour is highly differentiated. When account is taken of different segments of the labour market, one sees that migration can have significant income distribution effects. This on its own would not make immigration a distinctive problem – trade also has potentially strong effects on income distribution. The real contrast arises from the dynamic and spillover effects. In the case of trade, they are generally accepted as positive, but the dynamic and spillover effects of migration are much less clear. They are certainly more ambiguous and controversial than the dynamic effects of trade.

The impact of migration on government finances is an example of one such spillover effect. A theme of this chapter is the contrasting fiscal impact of skilled and unskilled migrants. Educated migrants bring with them a stock of human capital, much of it paid for by the government of the sending country. They are likely to find work quickly and to pay taxes in excess of their drawings on government sources. An immigrant with less than a high school education, by contrast, is likely to cause a net drain on public finances. They are likely to have a larger sized family, have weak language skills and poorer job prospects. Largely because of the preponderance of low skilled immigrants, foreign-born residents of the US have a 35 per cent higher probability of receiving public assistance than native-born Americans. By 1998, almost a quarter of immigrant households were receiving some type of assistance, as compared to 15 per cent of native households.

From time to time, efforts are made to quantify the fiscal effects of migration. One way of doing so is to compare the stream of taxes paid by an average immigrant over his or her lifetime in the host country and subtract from it the stream of government assistance absorbed. The OECD presents the following estimates of the net present value:

Education level of immigrant	Net present value of contribution to US government finances (US$)
Below high school	−89,000
At high school	−31,000
Above high school	105,000
Average all groups	−3,000

These estimates confirm that (a) better educated migrants are hugely advantageous to the host country and (b) less educated immigrants tend to be net recpients of state assistance. The estimates further implied that the US public purse was $15 billion to $20 billion worse off in 1996 as a result of immigration.

The general gist of these findings mirrors the experience of most host countries. When immigrants are skilled and motivated, they can make a significantly positive contribution to the economy. A particularly striking example is Israel, which received inflows of 700 thousand immigrants from the former Soviet Union during the four years 1989–92 against a population level of 4 million, without detriment to GNP per person. These immigrants helped spearhead Israel's successful 'new economy' sector, reflected in rapid overall expansion of the economy during the 1990s. Host countries have learnt from experience and immigration restrictions have been framed accordingly. Many host countries use a points system weighted towards the better-educated immigrants who will provide the most economic benefit to the host country.

Two points, however, should be noted in qualification of the above. First, if the estimates were extended to later generations of immigrants (the majority of whom will advance up the fiscal ladder to become net contributors) the net fiscal effect changes radically. Then even unskilled immigrants can be shown to have a positive fiscal impact. Second, while economic cost-benefit is important, humanitarian and political considerations are also important in determining policy towards immigrants.

Sources: *OECD Economic Surveys United States* (Paris: OECD, 1997); *The Economist* (29 November 1997); George Borjas, *Heaven's Door: Immigration Policy and the American Economy* (Princeton: Princeton University Press, 1999).

to the governments in the 'South'. The control and supervision needed in order to implement such a proposal would, however, be extremely costly. Other variations of the 'brain-drain' tax have been proposed, but none has yet been implemented.[8]

Migration, wages and job displacement

Many efforts have been made to quantify the areas of loss and gain indicated in Figure 19.1. The estimates, however, tend to be subject to large margins of error. Furthermore, generalisation is difficult, given the distinctive characteristics of migration in different parts of the world. In a comparatively inflexible labour market, such as Europe's, immigration may increase the unemployment rate of unskilled native workers. In the flexible US labour market, immigration is unlikely to cause unemployment but can have a depressing effect on unskilled wage levels. Underlying these hypotheses is the fear that, in a completely open labour market, industrial wages would tend towards some global average level. While this would appeal to the poorer countries, better-off countries worry about the possibility of a decline from their present levels to a world average wage of about $2000 per annum.

---

8 Numerous efforts have been made to quantify the economic value of the brain-drain transfer from South to North. Estimates suggest that it may exceed by many times the total value of all official development assistance in the opposite direction. According to a 1994 OECD report, 'the most skilled talented and motivated people represent a wholly disproportionate share of those who migrate from the less-developed countries ... this haemorrhaging does much to widen the gaps between regions' (OECD, *Migration and Development: New Partnerships for co-operation, Paris*, 1994, pp. 142 and 150).

Take, for example, the case of the US. Immigration into the US during the 1980s consisted preponderantly of low-skilled and poorly educated people. As a result, the supply of unskilled workers increased. The fraction of the US labour force that had completed less than high school education rose significantly. Towards the end of the decade, the proportion of less educated workers was 7 per cent higher than it would have been if, in each skill group, the ratio of immigrants to natives had been the same as it had been in 1980. Having estimated that the relative wages of the less educated fall by over 3 per cent with each 1 per cent rise in their relative numbers, one study concluded that immigration between 1980 and 1988 cut the relative wages of less educated Americans by 21 per cent. Although there is continuing controversy about the reliability of such estimates, more recent studies confirm that the fears of some threatened groups about the effects of immigration are not unfounded.[9] Of course, the native lower-paid workers could be compensated out of the extra output generated by the immigrants. A practical way of implementing such compensation would be through an improved education system for the children of the lower paid, thus leaving them less vulnerable to competition. But will compensation actually be provided? The real incomes of the lower paid in industrial countries have continued to stagnate. It is scarcely accidental that this happened to coincide with significant levels of immigration, though changing technology and freer trade must also be factored in to provide a complete explanation.

Austria is an interesting case study, of a small country which has accommodated a large population of new migrants, many from Eastern Europe in particular, since the late 1980s.[10] The share of migrants in the labour force rose from 5 per cent in 1987 to 10 per cent in 1997. Yet, the unemployment rate of Austrians remained relatively low by European standards (4 per cent). This has been explained by reference to two factors: first, migrants proved to be efficient job-seekers; and second, they competed for a different segment of the labour market to the national workforce. Natives and immigrants were not in direct competition. The study does not claim that no displacement occurred. Immigration may have made it more difficult for the unemployed and other groups to enter the workforce. Nevertheless, the absence of visible detrimental effects on the group that would have been expected to be most adversely affected is significant.

---

9 L.F. Katz and K.M. Murphy, 'Changes in relative wages, 1963–1987: Supply and demand factors', *Quarterly Journal of Economics* (February 1992). For recent literature see: W. Cline, *Trade and Income Distribution* (Washington, DC: Institute for international economics, 1997) and *OECD economic surveys – United States* (November 1997) which analyses the immigration issue in relation to the US experience.

10 R. Winter-Ebmer and J. Zweimüller, 'Do immigrants displace native workers? The Austrian experience', *CEPR Discussion Paper*, No. 991 (July 1994).

19.4 Conclusions

Migration involves people moving from areas where labour productivity is low to where it is high. The economic motivation for such migration is obviously very strong. Unskilled workers receive nearly ten times more in the North than in the South, and skilled workers six times as much.[11] While those with specialised skills are welcome in most countries, there is a potential conflict of interest between host and sending countries arising from the former's preference for the skilled, well-educated migrant – precisely the type of person the sending country wants to keep at home and whose externalities could make a major difference to its development. Efforts to adjust the free market to take account of such externalities have had little success. The more skilled remain heavily represented in migration flows from developing to developed countries. Lower transportation costs, more information and a rising stock of migrants abroad are making migration more attractive to an increasing number of people in low-income countries, despite restrictions in the host countries.

As explained in Chapter 18, an alternative to migration is to bring capital to people through foreign investment. Foreign investment, combined with a liberal trade policy, acts as a substitute for migration. This line of thinking is neatly encapsulated in Layard's comment that:

> A free trade pact that ensures Eastern European countries access to Western European markets is the best single migration policy that could be put in place. (Layard, *op. cit.*, p. 51)

The potential of trade to act as a substitute for factor mobility has long been recognised in international trade theory. The theory shows that income differences between countries can be reduced through trade, even when factors of production are completely immobile between countries. The theory has been influential in persuading Western Europe of the importance of trade liberalisation with Central and Eastern Europe as an alternative to the prospect of 'catastrophic' immigration. Such considerations also carried weight among decision-makers in the US, and led them to embrace the idea of NAFTA as a vehicle for ensuring more rapid growth in Mexico and, consequently, reducing the volume of migration. This connection underlies a comment in *Business Week* following the 1995 Mexican peso crisis:

> Reviving Mexican prosperity is more politically important than ever at home because of smouldering US resentment about the influx of new immigrants into key states such as California and Texas.[12]

Within the EU, freer access for goods and services to the single market is rightly seen as a means of easing the problems of the less developed regions and lessening the need for migration.

---

11 A. Wood, *North–South Trade, Employment and Inequality: Changing futures in a skill-driven world* (Oxford: Oxford University Press, 1994).
12 *Business Week* (16 January 1995).

✔ Summary

1. Labour has become increasingly mobile internationally and the labour market has become significantly more 'globalised'. Demand and supply factors have both contributed to this. Advancing technology, strong economic performance and low population growth means that current and prospective remuneration levels in the North have remained high both in absolute terms and relative to the South. On the supply side, rapid population growth combined with poor economic performance in many parts of the developing world provides a growing stream of young people eager to seek their fortune in more promising labour markets. Cheaper transport costs, and easier communication through television and the web means that people are better informed of job opportunities and comparative economic conditions than ever before. The transactions costs of moving from one labour market to another have been dramatically reduced.

2. Some countries have been significantly affected by labour migration. In Europe, Austria, Germany and Italy have experienced large inflows of migrants. The ongoing prosperity and openness of the US and Australian economies have also acted as powerful magnets for immigrants. Supplier ('home') countries such as Mexico, Morocco, Turkey, India and eastern Europe have also experienced problems. Partly because of the nature of immigration restrictions, they find they are losing skilled people, rich in human capital that a developing country badly needs.

3. The gains from labour mobility derive from the reallocation of workers from locations where their productivity is relatively low to countries where their productivity is higher. The predominant direction of flow is from poorer to richer countries, as economic theory would predict. The gains from this movement are realised through higher global productivity.

4. In assessing the costs and benefits of migration, account must be taken of fiscal effects and externalities as well as the standard productivity effects. Also the implications of immigration for particular segments of the host country's labour market must be faced up to. Migration has potentially important consequences for the real wages of unskilled workers in host countries, but so far it has proved difficult to disentangle this effect from other more powerful influences such as technology and education.

❓ Questions for discussion

1. 'The value of migration as a means for enhancing economic efficiency is well known. However, at some point, it can become socially disruptive and inefficient, notably where local regimes perform so poorly that mass emigration occurs.' ('One market, one money', *European Economy*, October 1990, p. 27)

   Do you find the efficiency arguments for migration convincing? What criteria would you use in deciding the point at which migration becomes disruptive?

2. Of the EU's 370 million citizens, only about 5 million live outside their country of birth, and only 3.1 million work outside it in another EU state (*The Economist*, 27 February 1996). Give economic reasons for this low degree of labour mobility.

3. Free trade between the EU and its European and North African neighbours is often considered as a superior alternative (economically speaking) to mass migration. Explain the reasoning behind this belief.

4. 'If a truly global market for labour ever appears, it will be for highly skilled workers only.' What economic grounds could be used to justify this prediction?

☞ Exercises

1. Suppose a country's unskilled workforce increases by 10 per cent as a result of immigration. Trace out the effects on (a) unskilled employees, (b) capital owners, (c) skilled professionals, and (d) government finances, in the host country and the home country. (Use a diagram such as Figure 18.3 to illustrate your answer.)

   Would your answer change if you were told that there had been high unemployment in the host country at the time of the migration?

2. Suppose the marginal product of labour curve in the sending country shifts upwards and outwards from the origin. What effect will this have on the incentive to emigrate? What factors could cause the curve to shift in this way?

   Explain why free trade has been proposed, in the context of both NAFTA and EU trade relations with eastern Europe, as contributing to a reduction in international inequalities and an easing of the migration problem.

3. There has been much concern about the migration of skilled staff in technological R&D in central and eastern European countries to the West. During the period 1989 to 1993, for instance, around 70 per cent of Hungarian researchers left domestic research agencies and facilities, many of them attracted by better opportunities in western Europe and America (*ACE Quarterly Phare*, Brussels: EC, Summary 1995, p. 17). Analyse the economic costs and benefits of such migration.

4. Outline the main fiscal effects of migration from the perspective of home country and the host country respectively.

5. Reference is frequently made to the growth in the services sector in developed economies and the increasing share of employment in services in total employment. What impact does this structural change in northern economies have on immigration?

6. In the context of the standard model in this chapter, why are countries more likely to impose stronger restrictions on immigration than on emigration?

📖 Further reading

R. King, *Mass Migration in Europe: The legacy and the future* (London: Belhaven Press, 1993) offers a geographer's perspective on these matters. Julian L. Simon, *The Economic Consequences of Immigration* (Oxford: Basil Blackwell, 1989) and Richard Layard, *East–West Migration* (Cambridge, MA: MIT Press, 1992) consider the economics of movements between countries. George Borjas's *Heaven's Door: Immigration policy and the American Economy* (Princeton: Princeton University Press, 1999) is a provocative, controversial and astringent book that assesses the overall effects of immigration on America. For a concise, readable overview of immigration (including the linkage between the ageing of Europe's population and future demand for young immigrants), see J. Coppel, J-C. Dumont and I. Visco, 'Trends in Immigration and Economic Consequences', OECD Economic Department Working Paper, No. 284, Paris 2001.

Chapter 20

THE BALANCE OF PAYMENTS: WHAT IT IS AND WHY IT MATTERS

Introduction

This chapter provides a bridge between the analysis of 'real' international transactions and the exchange rate.[1] International trade in goods, services and factors of production can, as we have seen, bring major economic benefits. But, for these benefits to be realised, there must be an efficient payments mechanism. The balance of payments, the exchange rate and the exchange rate regime are three different but interrelated aspects of the financing of international transactions. The analysis of these issues has been motivated by the belief that the international system will work properly only if (a) business has easy and reliable access to foreign exchange, and (b) there is a relatively stable relationship between domestic and international prices.

The balance of payments is an important statement of account. It shows, on one side, all sources of supply (inflows) of foreign exchange, such as receipts from exports of goods, and services and capital inflows and, on the other side, all the sources of demand (outflows) for foreign exchange, such as payments for imports of goods, and services and capital outflows.

A company contemplating an investment or a new marketing drive in a foreign country usually seeks information on that country's balance of payments position as part of its overall economic assessment of the market. This chapter explains why. It shows how the balance of payments statement should be interpreted, and outlines the uses and pitfalls of balance of payments analysis for business.

We begin by analysing the *current* account of the balance of payments. References in common speech to 'the US deficit' or 'the Japanese surplus' or a country's 'balance of payments constraint' are short-hand for the balance of payments on current account. A country with a deficit, say, in this sense buys more from foreigners than it sells. That is, for current transactions demand for foreign exchange exceeds supply. To make ends meet, the country must obtain more foreign exchange, either by borrowing abroad or by selling its foreign assets. As long as there are sufficient foreign currency reserves, or willing lenders, the deterioration in the country's *capital* position creates no problems. Over time, however, as reserves decline and net foreign debt rises, two things are likely to happen. First, the country may have to offer higher interest rates in order to

---

1 The exchange rate is defined as the price of foreign currency in terms of domestic currency. It is the price that brings into equilibrium the demand and supply of various 'real' flows, such as the trade in goods, services and foreign investment. (See Chapter 21.)

persuade foreigners (and its own capitalists) to hold more of its debt. Second, its exchange rate may come under pressure. Each of these outcomes could have adverse implications for anyone doing business in those countries. The choice of policies for dealing with this situation can affect economic growth and the general business climate. Moreover, since a deficit in one country implies a corresponding surplus in others, surplus countries cannot remain aloof from the deficit countries' problems.

Sometimes too much can be read into the balance of payments statement. A common misperception is that the existence of a deficit or surplus reflects the balance of advantage from trade between countries. Deficit countries in particular often accuse surplus countries of hogging the benefits of trade at the deficit countries' expense. This is another manifestation of the mercantilist fallacy that one country is doing another a favour by consuming its goods and services. Another common fallacy is the belief that a balance of payments surplus is a sign of economic strength, while a deficit is a sign of weakness. There is no logical reason for this supposed association. In any given year, some industrial countries will have surpluses and others deficits. And not all poor countries have balance of payments deficits.

Chapter outline

This chapter analyses the balance of payments in three steps:

1. Analysis of the balance of payments and its sub-components.
2. The concept of *balance of payments equilibrium* and the criteria for deciding at what stage a country has a balance of payments disequilibrium (or 'problem').
3. Policies for restoring balance of payments equilibrium.

20.1 What is the balance of payments?

The balance of payments is a statement of all transactions between residents of the home country and the outside world during a specified period of time. These transactions are grouped under two key headings: current items and capital items. The balance of payments statement is compiled using the double entry book-keeping method familiar to students of accountancy (Table 20.1).

The current account

The current account is a record of cross-border transactions in goods, services, factor income and transfers within a certain period of time. Annual, quarterly and even monthly balance of payments figures are published. Transactions involving an inflow of foreign currency are entered with a positive sign; outflows with a negative sign.

The current account has four major components. The first is the merchandise trade balance, often called the balance of visible trade or just *the balance of trade*.

Table 20.1 Balance of payments statement

Current Account
Goods trade
Services
Trading and investment income
Current unilateral transfers
Balance on current account

Capital Account
Foreign direct investment
Portfolio capital
Basic balance
Short-term capital
Change in official reserves
Net errors and omissions

The trade balance measures the difference between the value of current exports of merchandise goods and the value of imports over the same period. This is a widely publicised part of the balance of payments. Traditionally, merchandise trade has dominated other components of the current account in value. Also trade data tend to be more reliable and up-to-date than other balance of payments statistics.

Services trade consists of tourism, transport, cross-border banking and insurance, and new activities such as telemarketing and software. Because services are intangible and difficult to trace, data on this trade are unreliable. Services are often delivered at their point of production and not shipped across country borders. Thus, a Japanese tourist paying to be shown around the Acropolis is said to *import* a service from Greece to Japan (without having to take the Greek tourist guide home to Kyoto). At other times, the service is delivered to the consumer. A Tokyo business consultant who travels to Sydney to advise on sales prospects in Japan is exporting a service from Japan to Australia.

The third component of the current account is the *balance of trading and investment income* (also known as factor income). It includes interest payments on foreign debt, dividends and royalties on foreign direct investment, and income flows between residents and non-residents in relationship to stocks, bonds or patents. Salaries earned abroad by domestic residents or by foreigners working in the domestic country are also included. The earnings of a British student from a summer job in a New York restaurant enters as an import of foreign factor services in the US's current account.[2] The repatriated profits of a Nissan plant in the UK

---

2 Note, however, that the earnings of a British student who took up permanent residence in the US would no longer appear in the balance of payments. Salaries only enter the balance of payments when paid to seasonal, border and other short-term (less than a year) workers, whose main residence is outside the host country. An interesting case are embassies. Due to their status as part of the territory of their home country, the salary paid to a Japanese gardener employed by the US embassy in Tokyo enters the Japanese balance of payments as a factor export and appears with a positive sign in the balance of factor income. If, however, this same gardener were running a landscaping business and serving the US embassy as one of several clients, the activity would count as a Japanese *services* export. This example indicates that in many cases allocating individual transactions to balance of payments categories can be somewhat arbitrary.

Table 20.2 Current balance of payments as a percentage of GDP

	1980	1990	2000	$ billion
US	0.1	−1.6	−4.5	−419.4
Japan	−1.0	1.2	2.6	102.4
Germany	−1.7	3.3	0	3.4
Italy	−2.2	−1.6	1.6	10.1
UK	1.2	−3.5	−1.8	−22.1
Norway	1.7	3.3	14.2	10.6
Portugal	−3.7	−0.3	−10.3	−10.2

Source: IMF; OECD.

are recorded with a positive sign in Japan's balance of services, since they involve a receipt of foreign exchange in return for the services of Japanese capital and entrepreneurship, and as a negative item in the UK's balance of payments. Developed countries tend to have positive net earnings from 'trading and investment income', because richer countries invest, or have invested in the past, more in poorer countries than the latter can afford to invest in the rich.

The fourth component is *unilateral transfers*, often referred to as the balance of international transfers. These transactions consist of unrequited payments such as foreign aid, or remittances to family members abroad. Government aid to a developing country enters the balance of payments with a negative sign for the donor and a positive sign for the recipient.

The *current account balance* is the sum of the four components: trade, services, factor incomes and unilateral transfers.[3] Among developed countries, the current account balance in year 2000 ranged from a surplus of 14 per cent of GDP in Norway, to a deficit of over 10 per cent in Portugal. Most developing countries and countries in transition tend to run current account deficits while the industrial countries as a group tend to have current account surpluses. The US stands out as a conspicuous exception to this rule, with a deficit of 4.2 per cent of GDP ($419 billion) (Table 20.2).

Since, by definition, one country's surplus is another's deficit, the global sum of countries' current accounts should in principle be zero. In fact, the sum of the world's current accounts added up to −$230 billion in 2000. This vast sum is a veritable 'black hole', a measure of our statistical ignorance. It reflects factors such as goods in transit (which appear as an export for the sending country but have not yet been recorded as imports by the recipient), smuggling, drug transactions, and straightforward errors in statistical compilation.

---

3 The current account balance corresponds to the value of $(x − m)$ in the national income equation in Chapter 11.

Capital account

Current account transactions account for only a small proportion of the total value of international transactions. As capital has become more mobile and investment more globalised, the capital side of the balance of payments has grown in importance. Hence considerably more attention is now being devoted to this section of the balance of payments than formerly.

We divide the capital account into four components: foreign direct investment, portfolio investment, short-term capital flows and change in official reserves.

Direct investment refers to transactions where the investor acquires 'a significant degree of influence on the management of a foreign enterprise' (*IMF Balance of Payments Manual*, 1993, p. 86). Transactions such as the establishment of a new plant in the US by a Japanese car manufacturer or the takeover of an American corporation by a British company are classified as direct investment. Note, however, that only the amount of funds actually transferred from one country to another in respect of the transaction appears in the balance of payments. In many cases this will be a small fraction of the total cost of the plant or the takeover. Suppose, for example, that the total cost of the Japanese plant in the US was $200 million. Assume that the plant is incorporated as a separate company in the US, and will therefore qualify as a resident for balance of payments purposes. Funds borrowed from American banks by the subsidiary to finance the investment do not appear in the balance of payments. Only the amount lent to the subsidiary from outside the US is recorded.

Portfolio investment refers to transactions in instruments of more than one year to maturity. It includes the acquisition of foreign bonds and financial securities, and investment in a minority (less than 10 per cent) stake in foreign firms. Portfolio transactions include transactions both by governments and by the private sector. Consider, for example, the acquisition of US government bonds by a Japanese bank. This would be recorded as a capital outflow in the Japanese balance of payments and a capital inflow in the US balance of payments.

Short-term capital refers to investment in instruments maturing in less than one year. It includes huge volumes of inter-bank transactions as well as transactions undertaken to hedge against foreign exchange risk. Speculative capital movements mostly take the form of short-term capital. The rationale behind the distinction is that short-term capital is expected to be generally more mobile, less 'rooted', easier and less costly to liquidate, than long-term capital. It also tends to be the most sensitive element in the capital account to changes in interest rates. Analysis of movements of short-term capital provides valuable insights into how current account imbalances are being financed or into how vulnerable a country may be to foreign exchange speculators.

Official reserves are held by monetary authorities, usually the central bank. They take the form of foreign exchange, balances with the International Monetary Fund and gold. About 15 per cent of world reserves are held in gold (Table 20.3). Gold has some attractions as an international reserve, but it suffers one major

Table 20.3 Official holdings of reserve assets, all countries

	end-1999 US$ (bn)	(%)
Foreign exchange	1746	81
US dollars	1344	
Pound sterling	68	
Japanese yen	89	
Others	245	
Gold	300	14
Fund-related assets	122	5
Total reserves	2168	100

Source: *Bank of International Settlements Annual Report*, 2000; IMF.

disadvantage – it yields no income. Hence the only return from holding it is the prospect of capital appreciation. Foreign exchange by contrast, being held in the form of short-tem government bills, does yield an income. Some 80 per cent of the world's reserves is held as 'foreign exchange'. The bulk of these reserves is invested in high-quality, liquid, short-term government securities; only a small fraction is held as actual foreign currency notes. Dollar reserves amounted to over $1344 billion out of total foreign exchange reserves of $1746 billion. The dominance of the dollar contrasts with the pound sterling, once the world's most sought-after reserve currency after gold, which now accounts for only 3 per cent of world official reserves. The Japanese yen also remains little used as a reserve currency. A major question for the future is whether the euro (which constitutes the bulk of 'other' foreign exchange reserves) will gain world-wide acceptance.

Sometimes a distinction is made between *autonomous* and *accommodating* transactions in the balance of payments. Autonomous items refer to all current transactions plus long-term capital transactions. These respond to 'real' long-term competitiveness factors. Accommodating items consist of movements in reserves and short-term capital, and are seen as reacting passively to prior movements in autonomous items.

To illustrate the distinction, consider the example of a country which increases its demand for imports. This leads to an increase in the demand for foreign exchange. If the exchange rate is fixed, this increased demand could be financed by a drawdown of the central bank's foreign reserves. The change in official reserves is a passive transaction: it accommodates the increase in demand for imports, not vice versa. If the central bank was concerned about the depletion of its reserves, it could engineer a rise in the short-term interest rate. This would attract short-term capital inflows. Again, such inflows would be defined as accommodating transactions. However, short-term capital and a large part of portfolio capital investment move in an accommodating sense – as the direct consequence of the balance in autonomous transactions. As capital markets have become more liquid, the dividing line between accommodating and autonomous transactions has become less distinct.

Two further points may be noted. First, *different transactions in the balance of payments statement are often closely related*. For example, the establishment in the UK of a new plant by a Japanese automobile company might entail the following sequence of transactions:

- *Direct investment* inflows related to total capital costs.
- An *increase in imports* of machinery and intermediate goods as the factory is constructed.
- When the plant starts operation, an *increase in UK exports* as the subsidiary starts selling to the continental European market.
- *Trading and investment* outflow as profits are repatriated to Japan.

All these transactions are interrelated. Balance of payments analysis requires careful attention to these intertemporal connections between one section of the statement and another.

Second, since the balance of payments is drawn up on double-entry principles, the sum of the two sides of the statement must, in principle, add up to zero. In this sense, *the balance of payments always balances*, i.e. it can never be in deficit or surplus. However, because transactions in the balance sheet are measured and reported through different channels, they hardly ever match in reality. This explains the need for a balancing item (errors and omissions), appended to avoid an 'imbalance of payments' – which is a conceptual impossibility.

The balance of payments and the indebtedness of nations

The current account can be compared to a household's current budget. If outgoings (imports) exceed earnings (exports), the resultant deficit has to be financed either by borrowing or by selling assets. Similarly, a country's current external deficit can be covered either by obtaining loans from non-residents, be it through public or private lenders, or by sale of assets to foreign investors.[4] The reverse applies in the case of a current account surplus: it can be used to give loans to non-residents, to pay back previous loans, or to buy assets abroad.

Whether a household is a net creditor or a net debtor depends on its past financial record. If it has been living beyond its means for a prolonged period, a household's debt can grow bigger than the value of its assets, thus turning the household into a net debtor. A thrifty family, on the other hand, which consistently spends less than it earns, can build up wealth in assets and credit. The same applies to countries' economic relations with the rest of the world. The sum of a country's foreign assets less the sum of its liabilities towards non-residents at any point in time is called the *international investment position*. The international investment position is a *stock* concept. It provides a snapshot picture of the situation at one particular moment in time, while the balance of payments provides a record of transaction *flows of funds* over a period of time.

---

4 Each of these forms of financing a current account deficit appears on the credit side of the capital account, which again illustrates why these two sides of the balance of payments should balance out.

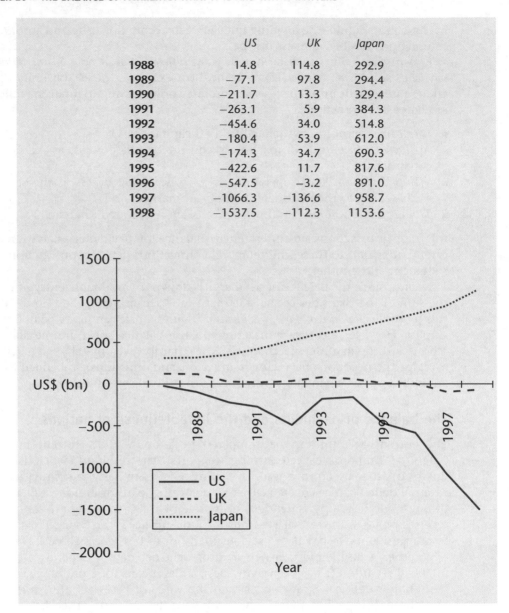

	US	UK	Japan
1988	14.8	114.8	292.9
1989	−77.1	97.8	294.4
1990	−211.7	13.3	329.4
1991	−263.1	5.9	384.3
1992	−454.6	34.0	514.8
1993	−180.4	53.9	612.0
1994	−174.3	34.7	690.3
1995	−422.6	11.7	817.6
1996	−547.5	−3.2	891.0
1997	−1066.3	−136.6	958.7
1998	−1537.5	−112.3	1153.6

Figure 20.1 International investment positions 1988–98 ($US bn)

The change in the international investment position between the beginning and the end of a period is equal by definition to the current account balance over that period. As a result, the international investment position is approximately equal to the cumulated sum of all past balances of the current account. (Valuation changes reflecting changes in exchange rates and asset prices can enter the equation in any one period, hence 'approximately'.)

The international investment positions of the US, UK and Japan are charted in Figure 20.1. Japan is a major world creditor; and both the UK and the US have switched from being creditors to debtors within the past decade. This diversity of pattern is common among developed countries. Some such as Australia, Canada and New Zealand (not shown in Figure 20.1) have been sustained net debtors, utilising their access to the global capital market to build up their economies.

The big story of the 1990s was the way a succession of deficits from the 1980s onwards reduced the US's net foreign wealth so that it changed from being a net creditor to the world's largest debtor. By the end of 1998, the net external debt of the US reached $1538 billion. That is a large sum in absolute terms but it is still less than 10 per cent of US GDP. Also the net balance is the balance between the $6 trillion that foreigners have invested in the US and $5 trillion that Americans have invested abroad. Generally the returns on Americans' foreign assets exceed the return foreigners have obtained from their US investments. This differential rate of return needs to be kept in mind in assessing the economic significance of the net international investment position. In contrast with the US, Japan is a major world creditor. Its net investment position has continued to grow and by end 1998 it had become a net lender to the tune of $1153 billion. But because much of this investment was in low yielding foreign bonds, Japan has obtained a modest return on its foreign investments. Thus, a country like the US appears to have done well by borrowing cheap portfolio capital from foreigners and then investing this money in direct investment projects abroad.

Some developing countries such as Kuwait, Singapore, Venezuela and Saudi Arabia have adopted a deliberate policy of allocating part of their revenues to direct foreign investment projects. This policy has enabled them to build up strong creditor positions. But these are exceptional cases. Most developing countries are net creditors, some such as India mildly so (less than 20 per cent of GDP), others with more deep indebtment ranging from Mexico and Morocco (over 40 per cent of GDP) to Sri Lanka, Jamaica and Côte d'Ivoire (over 60 per cent of GDP).[5] Not surprisingly, countries that are more open and trade-oriented tend to have larger gross flows of direct investment and portfolio equity invstment.

20.2 Balance of payments problems

Definition of a problem

'The balance of payments always balances.' True, but why then do countries have a balance of payments problem? When speaking of such a problem attention has tended to focus on imbalances in the *current account*, with some allowance being made for any long-term capital flows which have implications for the current account. (The concept of *basic balance*, incorporating current account and

---

5 P. Lane and G. M. Milesi-Ferretti, 'The external wealth of nations', IMF Working Paper WP/99/115 (August 1999).

Table 20.4 How growth cutbacks 'improve' the current balance of payments

Mexico 1993–96	1993	1994	1995	1996
Real GNP	2.0	4.5	−6.2	5.1
Current a/c balance (as a % of GDP)	−5.8	−7.1	−0.5	−0.7
Korea 1996–99	**1996**	**1997**	**1998**	**1999**
Real GNP	6.7	5.0	−6.7	10.7
Current a/c balance (as % of GDP)	−4.4	−1.5	12.8	6.1

Source: OECD, Economic Outlook (June 2000).

autonomous capital transactions, addresses this qualification.) Bearing this in mind,

> A country can be said to have a balance of payments problem when the current account deficit and the accumulated international investment position have reached a level where continuance of the deficit is no longer judged sustainable.

Some features of this definition have to be clarified. First, the *time dimension* needs to be specified, since a transitory deficit (as a result of a strike, earthquake or a bad harvest) presents fewer problems than one that is expected to persist. Second, the *size* of the deficit must be considered in relation both to the country's GNP and to its outstanding debt position. Third, the *method of financing* of the deficit has to be examined. A deficit financed by an inflow of foreign equity is less a cause of concern than one financed by foreign purchases of government bonds. In the case of equity finance, if the investment turns out to be unprofitable the liability automatically disappears. In the case of government borrowing, the liability remains, regardless of how wisely or unwisely the borrowed money was spent. The maturity of the borrowed funds would also have to be analysed. Long-term inter-governmental borrowing is obviously a more stable source of finance than short-term private capital invested for speculative reasons. Fourth, *free trade conditions* must be stipulated. A current account balance can always be sustained by tariffs, or quotas or other administrative measures. Since the purpose of the international payments system is to facilitate trade not to inhibit it, this situation could not be deemed an equilibrium one. Finally, a deficit can always be reduced by lower economic growth. A slowdown in economic activity has an immediate negative impact on import demand and as a result improves the current account. Mexico's deficit fell from 7 per cent to 0.5 per cent of GDP following the economic collapse of 1994–95 and a similar outcome accompanied Korea's downturn in 1997–98. In the latter case, a deficit of 1.5 per cent in 1997 was followed by a surplus of 12.8 per cent in 1998 (Table 20.4). Hence, in *evaluating a country's current account, one must have regard to the growth rate*.

Even with these elaborations, there remains the thorny question of how to judge whether a current account position is *sustainable*. The host country for the investment might have one view of the matter – while the foreign investors, concerned about the security and liquidity of their investment, can have another. There are also questions of political sustainability. Is one country gaining too much economic influence over another through the capital position built up as a result of sustained current account imbalances? Neither theory nor experience suggests a definitive threshold level for a current account deficit that will make it unsustainable and trigger a strong investor reaction. We know that the trigger point will depend on the characteristics of the economy in question, including its exchange rate policy and degree of openness, its saving and investment record, the health of its financial system and the structure of capital flows financing the deficit. Judgement, as well as careful statistical review, is necessary in adjudicating the issue of sustainability.

Why does the current account balance matter?

An unsustainable current account imbalance matters for a number of different reasons. Each type of imbalance, deficit and surplus, creates its own set of problems. However, a deficit tends to result in more immediate and pressing problems than a surplus. Let us begin by considering the type of problem likely to confront a chronic deficit country.

A country with a current account deficit is absorbing more goods and services from foreigners than it is earning from export of goods and services to them. In this limited sense, a deficit signifies that a country is 'living beyond its means'. Suppose, however, that the deficit is being used to purchase capital equipment which will enhance the country's future earning capacity. In that case, running a deficit might make good economic sense. The deficit should then be financed by long-term capital inflows through the public or private sectors. When the time comes for the accumulated debt to be serviced and repaid, spending will have to fall below the value of domestic production. If productive capacity has been added to, this can be achieved without any deterioration in living standards.

Ascertaining the use to which a deficit is put is obviously difficult. One must rely on a counterfactual model which would indicate the composition of GDP, in terms of investment, private consumption and government spending, as it would have been had the deficit been lower. Different macro-models often come up with radically different answers to this question. The reactions to the UK and the US deficits of the 1980s illustrate the distinct ways in which a deficit can be interpreted. To one school of thought they were indicative of the economy's strength, to another a sign of a chronic lack of competitiveness.

Critics of US policy have been concerned about the potentially adverse effects of the deficits on the US economy. Writing at the end of the 1980s, Paul Krugman described the deficit as involving 'a gradual mortgaging of future US income to foreigners'. The deficit in his view gives rise to

> one definite cost and some vaguer risks: the definite cost is, by definition, that you owe people money. From now on, the United States will be obliged to deliver a stream of interest payments to foreign bondholders, rents to foreign landowners, and dividends to foreign stockholders. Our payments to foreigners are a direct drain on our resources, and the longer the trade deficits continue, the larger this drain will become.[6]

---

6 Paul Krugman, *The Age of Diminished Expectations* (Cambridge, MA: MIT Press, 1994), p. 48.

> ### Box 20.1
>
> ## How to interpret a current account deficit
>
> Nigel Lawson, Britain's former Chancellor of the Exchequer, attributed Britain's current account balance of payments deficit in the late 1980s to the strength of the economy. The prospect of attractive rates of return led to capital inflow, higher investment and, in turn, more imports and a current account deficit.
>
> > Some see a current account deficit as a sign of economic weakness: 'Britain in the red' as the newspapers are wont to put it. But, of course, a current account deficit is manifestly not at all like a company running at a loss. A better analogy is with a profitable company raising money overseas – either borrowing, or reducing its holdings of overseas assets, or attracting new equity. A company with greater investment opportunities than it could finance from retained profits would look for additional funds from outside. A country in a similar position will draw on the savings of the world, particularly in today's global market. (Special lecture to the Institute of Economic Affairs, London, 21 July 1988)
>
> In hindsight this turned out to be an unduly complacent view of what was to become a series of UK current account deficits amounting to a cumulative total of £100 billion between 1988 and 1991. Eventually restrictive monetary and fiscal policies had to be introduced which led to lower growth and higher unemployment.
>
> This case illustrates the point that identifying a balance of payments problem is a matter of judgement. It is possible to make an incorrect judgement, and unfortunately the penalty for doing so can be severe.

A decade later, the US deficit has grown even larger, the investment position has worsened even more and economists continue to express misgivings. Their concerns are based on the type of issues outlined in Chapter 14 in the discussion of the sustainability of government debt. Many would agree with Dr Catherine Mann's view that the US current account trajectory as at 1999 would be sustainable for only another three years.[7]

The economic costs of running an unsustainable current account deficit are three-fold.

First, the greater the reliance on foreign creditors, the greater is the country's exposure to the volatility of international capital markets. This can have a number of adverse effects. Highly indebted countries generally have to pay higher rates of interest for further credits. Worse still, if there is a loss of confidence on the part of creditors, the supply of capital can dry up regardless of the interest rate on offer. Such a collapse of creditor confidence led to successive economic crises in heavily indebted developing countries right through the 1990s (Mexico, Indonesia, Brazil, among many others).

---

7 C. L. Mann, *Is the US Trade Deficit Sustainable?* (Washington DC: Institute for International Economics, 1999).

Second, the loss of confidence scenario can lead to excessively large devaluations of the exchange rate, which involves both loss of real income and inflationary repercussions that only add to the problems of the deficit country. These were important considerations in Turkey's balance of payments crisis of 1993–94. Fear of such an overreaction in investment sentiment motivates current concern about the US deficit. An excessive depreciation of the dollar (25 per cent has been mentioned) would disrupt financial markets and have adverse knock-on effects on investment and consumption in the US and throughout the world.

Third, the more a country's international investment position moves into the red, the more ownership over its economic assets moves into the hands of foreigners. From a strictly economic point of view, this should not matter. The country is simply trading off future consumption in favour of present consumption, just as one would do by mortgaging one's house in order to splurge on a long vacation. But foreign ownership of domestic assets, with its overtones of a loss of national economic sovereignty, can be a politically sensitive issue.

Deficits can create special problems for developing countries with weak access to global capital markets. For this reason, countries such as India and Brazil have to pay far more attention to the current account of the balance of payments than the UK or Portugal. With globalisation of capital markets, the balance of payments has virtually disappeared from the policy agenda in many industrial countries. But, even for these countries, access to the global capital market can be fickle, capable of being turned on and off quickly. In other words, the international debt *position* of the country continues to be crucial, even if the current account *in any one year* has diminished in significance (Box 20.2).

The example of Korea is instructive in this respect. Korea borrowed heavily abroad. The big push to build up steel, chemicals and automobile industries in the 1970s, and light industry in the 1960s, was accompanied by large government-induced inflows of foreign capital. At one stage Korea's external debt : GNP ratio reached 50 per cent, giving it 4th place in the world debt league. However, its balance of payments deficits, and the resultant foreign debt, reflected high domestic investment ratios. In this way, Korea managed to maintain its growth, develop a strong export sector and enhance its creditworthiness, right up to the mid-1990s. Around that time, it fell into the trap of other Asian tigers; borrowing short abroad in order to finance domestic long-term projects of dubious economic viability. The resultant currency crisis proved costly in economic terms.

By definition, one country's surplus is simply another country's (or group of countries') deficit. Any country, whether in overall deficit or surplus, will have bilateral surpluses with some countries and bilateral deficits with others. The US has a large trade surplus with Brazil (export : import ratio 1.57), and a large deficit with Japan (export : import ratio 0.46). Its overall export : import ratio is 0.72, indicating a net deficit. Similarly Japan, with an overall export : import ratio of 1.38, has ratios of 1.77 with the US but a ratio of 0.27 with the Middle East.[8]

Countries with large deficits tend to blame surplus countries for their problems, particularly if the latter are large and conspicuous. In the US, protectionist lobbies

---

8 IMF, *Direction of Trade Statistics Quarterly* (December 1999).

Box 20.2

A tale of 3 deficits: the US deficit, Third World debt forgiveness and deficits in Euroland

Three contrasting balance of payments issues face the global economy at the turn of the century. One concerns the sustainability of the US current account deficit. The second concerns the sustainability of developing countries' external debt. The third issue is whether balance of payments deficits continue to have economic significance for member states of the newly formed euro area.

US deficit

Is the US current account deficit sustainable? The current account deficit amounted to over 4 per cent of GNP in 2000. US net international indebtedness reached $2,000 billion in 2000, nearly 20 per cent of GDP. Although there is currently no lack of eager lenders (foreigners investing in the US earned handsome returns during the 1990s), those taking a longer view fear that the balance of payments position will not remain sustainable for much longer.

Sustainability is ensured if the path of the current account is consistent with intertemporal solvency – in simpler words, if the economy will be able to meet the future cost of servicing its external debt. To do this, it must have the capability of changing from being a deficit country to having a current account surplus.

In assessing sustainability, the composition of foreign assets and liabilities is as important as the level of debt. Thus 90 per cent of US liabilities are denominated in dollars not foreign currency. And equity liabilities leave a borrower less exposed in case of an economic downturn than fixed interest liabilities. These factors tend to diminish the vulnerability of the US economy.

But a current account deficit rising to 5 per cent of GDP is not sustainable over the long term. Sooner or later, global investors will switch off US assets. Perhaps they will move to the euro area instead. If this happens too quickly there could be a collapse in US asset values. To avoid a crisis, one or all of the following will be needed:

- a rise in the US household saving rate (it fell from 8 per cent in 1990 to 1 per cent a decade later).
- faster growth in rest of world to boost US exports.
- devaluation of the US dollar.

The difficulty with the first proposal is that 80 per cent of the income of US residents is spent on goods and services produced at home. As a result, the main impact of the rise in US saving will be a fall in demand for US goods and services. Similarly, only a fraction of an increase in expenditure in the rest of the world (ROW) will be spent on US products. Dollar devaluation (expenditure switching) may therefore have to figure prominently in any programme to reduce the deficit.

Developing countries' debt

At the other end of the spectrum to the US are the world's 40 heavily indebted poor countries (HIPC). These countries include some of the world's poorest nations. Their per capita income has declined from $400 in 1980 to $300 in 1998. Their problems have less to

Box 20.2 continued

do with present current account deficits than with the accumulation of past deficits. They have an acute external debt problem. Their average external debt is 117 per cent of GDP and debt service takes up 5 per cent of GDP. HIPCs on average allocate slightly more budgetary resources to debt service than to education and healthcare taken together. Because their debt is so high, foreign lenders have switched off and thus HIPCs are unable to run larger current account deficits. Here we speak of the *sustainability of debt* rather than the *sustainability of deficits*.

Debts are defined as non-sustainable if the ratio of debt to exports exceeds 150 per cent and debt/government revenue exceeds 250 per cent. The basis of the definition is pragmatic – any country with debt of this magnitude is unlikely to be able to ever repay the loan.

An HIPC initiative was launched in 1996 with the objective of bringing these countries' debt burden to sustainable levels, through write-offs and special terms. Under revised terms agreed in 1999, forgiveness of half HIPC external debt has been provided for, amounting to nearly $50 billion. A key issue is how to forgive debt without giving better managed countries a signal to behave less responsibly and qualify for write-offs too. The creditors have tackled this by making forgiveness contingent upon satisfactory policy performance. This is a reasonable approach, but not without its drawbacks. Countries such as Nicaragua, with an external debt/GDP ratio of 295 per cent and receiving net aid of $117 per person, receives HIPC debt relief while a similarly poor country such as India, with a debt/GDP of 20 per cent, gets only $2 net per capita aid, and no debt relief.

Deficits in Euroland

Current account imbalances have for a long time been a policy concern of European countries. But they have not been a pressing concern for regions *within* these countries, for most of which the balance of payments position is not even recorded. Will the current accounts of the member states of the euro area become likewise irrelevant, now that the euro has become the single currency for all?

In one sense the answer is yes. Already there is a marked reduction in interest in the balance of payments of individual member states. Balance of payments policy, as such, is no longer a feature of national economic policy. Only the overall deficit or surplus of the euro area affects the value of the euro. The balance of payments position of the UK may have some implications for sterling, but the current account of France does not feature in the world currency markets' assessment of the euro.

However, this is not the same as saying that the balance of payments doesn't matter. In economic terms, movements in a euro country's current account will continue to have an important impact on the level of domestic aggregate demand. Also, the profile of its foreign assets and liabilities affects the stability of its national income in face of business fluctuations. Thus the GNP of a country suffering a negative domestic shock will be stabilised by foreign earnings if it has a positive net foreign asset position, and destabilised if it has net external debt.

Source: For US, C. Mann 'Is the US Current Account Deficit Sustainable?' *Finance and Development* (March 2000) and P. Krugman, *The Age of Diminished Expectations* (MIT Press, Cambridge, MA, 1990); for HIPCs IMF *World Economic Outlook* (May 2000 pp. 137–48) and World Bank Economic Indicators 2000.

used the deficit as a justification for deflecting the Government trade policy. Trading partners are put under pressure to import more from the deficit countries. They are also likely to be subjected to 'voluntary' restraints on their exports. They will be encouraged to invest more in the deficit country to relieve its BOP situation (while at the same time, and inconsistently, this very increase in investment may arouse nationalistic unease). Often such investment abroad may turn out to be unprofitable. This could happen because of exchange rate losses, as the surplus itself leads to a strengthening of the currency *vis-à-vis* the borrower.[9] More prosaically, there is also the possibility that investment decisions taken under pressure to placate the deficit countries may end up being poorly advised.

While surplus countries may have problems, the most pressing difficulties are likely to be felt by the deficit country. In every year between 1982 and 2000, the Japanese have recorded a large current account surplus and the Americans an even larger deficit. The US deficits have surely been more problematic than Japan's surpluses.[10]

Can countries go bankrupt?

What happens if a country keeps running current account deficits over a prolonged period of time? If deficits are run for too long, liabilities may become a multiple of assets. Creditors might lose confidence in the ability of the country to honour its debts. When this occurs to a private firm, it is declared bankrupt and its remaining assets are liquidated and distributed among the creditors. But what happens to a country which loses the confidence of its creditors and thus becomes insolvent?

First, countries cannot be dissolved and their assets carved up among their lenders as in the case of private firms. There is no international authority through which debt enforcement can be imposed in a legally binding way. International law on this matter consists mostly of informal agreements, the adoption of which is ultimately left to the discretion of the sovereign signatories. Indeed, it is precisely the notion of national sovereignty that is protected most of all by international law. Hence, were the government of a creditor country to send out its army in order to liquidate its insolvent debtor abroad, the international community would be likely to weigh the infringement of national sovereignty as a more serious offence than the debtor's non-compliance with its contractual duties.

Second, the real problem is that even a temporary default destroys the reputation of the borrowing governments. They find it increasingly difficult and expensive to obtain credit. Exactly the same happens if they are perceived to be accumulating excessive foreign debt. In order to assess debtor profiles and to determine interest premia, international banks carry out regular analyses of

---

9 Of course, this will be a paper loss in terms of the surplus country's currency. Whether it also involves an economic loss is less certain since the revaluation effectively means an improved terms of trade.

10 It was precisely for this reason that Keynes proposed that the international community should impose an annual tax on balance of payments surpluses. The aim was to ensure greater symmetry in pressure to adjust as between deficit and surplus countries. The suggestion was never implemented.

Box 20.3

Balance of payments, country indebtedness and country risk ratings

A country's foreign indebtedness (private and public sector) is by definition related to the sum of its past balances on the current account. A highly indebted country has acquired its debt through running large deficits at some time in the past. As the current account worsens, foreign indebtedness increases and country risk ratings might be expected to increase.

Country credit ratings are compiled regularly by international banks and by financial service companies. Banker judgements, as represented by country credit ratings, are published regularly in *Institutional Investor*, a monthly financial journal read primarily by market professionals. The published risk rating for a country is derived by averaging approximately 100 individual bank ratings of that country.

A study by Somerville and Taffler represents bankers' country credit assessment by a linear model. It tries to identify the variables which are believed to exercise the most influence on bankers' assessment of country risk. The authors find that the *Institutional Investor* country rating is determined by the following variables:

Variable	Impact on country credit status
Public sector external debt/exports (%)	Negative
Investment/GDP (%)	Positive
Import cover (number of months' imports covered by reserves)	Positive
Real total debt (US$m constant prices)	Positive

The first three variables influence country ratings just as one would expect. Thus, countries that have accumulated large amounts of public external debt (i.e. government foreign debt) relative to exports tend to have higher country risk profiles. By contrast, those with high investment ratios and high reserves tend to have lower risk profiles. This means that bankers look not so much at the current account deficit in any one year (a variable not found to be significant), but at the accumulation of deficits over time by the government sector. They take solace from the fact that investment ratios are high and that reserves are sufficient to cover a reasonable proportion of imports. This model is consistent with the view that a current account imbalance must be interpreted in a broad context. According to the Somerville–Taffler view, long-term balance of payments variables do have an impact on country risk.

The reason for the positive sign on the level of real debt is difficult to explain. Perhaps, as the authors suggest, it indicates that larger economies have larger debt in absolute terms. For this reason there are more bankers who are familiar with these countries' problems. And bankers tend to feel more comfortable about lending to those countries whose economies they feel they know well. This may well be yet another example of the triumph of hope over rational assessment.

Box 20.3 continued

Comparing *Institutional Investor* ratings with actual outcomes, bankers appear to be poor forecasters of debt-servicing difficulties among less-developed countries. But so is the equation used to represent their forecasts. Hence the shortcomings of banker judgement are of a fundamental and systematic nature (Somerville and Taffler, 1994).

Alternative country ratings, prepared by the Economist Intelligence Unit (EIU), are published regularly by *The Economist*. These are drawn from EIU's own estimations, based on economic and political factors. Country ratings of *Institutional Investor* and the EIU, issued before the Mexican crisis of late 1994, suggested no imminent vulnerability of the Mexican economy or currency. Yet in retrospect we know that the worsening balance of payments current account, the shortened maturity of government external debt and the pessimistic assessments of the Mexican government's ability and willingness to deal with its economic and political problems all played a role in the stampede out of the Mexican peso in late December 1994. Recent crises have included South East Asia, beginning in Thailand in mid-1997; the Russian default of August 1998; and Brazil 1998–99. In none of these cases did the *Institutional Investor* ratings show a significant dip ahead of the onset of the crisis.

Sources: R.A. Somerville and R.J. Taffler, 'The reliability of banker judgement in LDC credit risk assessment', City University Business School, Working Paper Series 94/4, 1994; R.A. Somerville and R.J. Taffler, 'LDC credit risk forecasting and banker judgement', *Journal of Business Finance and Accounting* (forthcoming). J. Calverley, *Country Risk Analysis* (London: Butterworth, 2nd edn, 1990).

'country risk'. These profiles are constructed around various economic, social and political indicators in which the current balance of payments, the level of debt, in absolute terms and relative to GDP, and export performance carry a prominent weight (see Box 20.3). It is in the interest of every debtor country not to be rated as a risky borrower.

Third, the stage could eventually be reached when credit lines were closed and a country could find it impossible to borrow. In that event, foreign suppliers demand foreign exchange guarantees and payment in advance. The supply of imports declines, factories are left idle for want of spare parts and key raw materials, transport becomes difficult because of oil and petrol shortages. Eventually the 'problem' is solved, but in a manner that accentuates difficulties elsewhere – by cutting back growth, restricting trade and devaluing the exchange rate.

Finally, political factors also play a role. A debt crisis involves rather humiliating overtures to international organisations and creditor governments, which reflect badly on the domestic government's competence. Sometimes the 'sting' can be taken out of this action by blaming the situation on the incompetence of previous governments and/or the recklessness of multinational bank lenders. This was the basis of the 'debt-forgiveness' package – the effective 50 per cent write-off of foreign borrowings of the world's poorest and most heavily-indebted countries agreed in 1999.

From a growth perspective, the objective should be to maintain a sound credit rating. This will ensure that the costs of borrowing are kept to the minimum. Also it ensures that, in the event of unforeseen emergencies, a country can borrow abroad without the disruption of its investment plans which might otherwise be necessary. This can only be achieved if a sustainable current balance is maintained over time. Long-run current account deficits must therefore be matched by levels of profitable investment which will repay directly or indirectly the costs of financing them.

20.3 How to correct a balance of payments imbalance

Current account deficits and surpluses can each cause serious friction. Suppose some countries are running a series of chronic deficits and others apparently endless surpluses. What can be done to restore the situation to a more sustainable state? We begin by considering the effects of automatic adjustment mechanisms and then proceed to discuss policy options. Analysis of policy options, in turn, presupposes certain assumptions about the *cause* of the balance of payments problem which policy is attempting to address.

Automatic adjustment mechanisms

Automatic adjustment mechanisms refer to the processes whereby *ex ante* imbalances between the supply and demand for foreign exchange are brought into *ex post* equilibrium. Starting from a position of initial current account balance, consider the effects of, say, a fall in the value of manufactured exports caused by an exogenous decline in foreign demand. Two factors are immediately set into operation which tend to reduce the deficit thereby created.

- The fall in demand for exports automatically creates a decrease in the demand for imports required as inputs for their production.
- The fall in aggregate demand generated by the decline in exports further reduces the demand for imports.

Note, however, that the adjustment mechanism is still only a partial one. The initial deficit is reduced but not eliminated. Consequently, other mechanisms must come into play in order to restore equilibrium.

One such mechanism is incorporated in the monetary approach to the balance of payments. According to this approach, the current account deficit results in a decline in deposits held in domestic banks. The balance of payments deficit, in other words, reduces the domestic money supply and, at constant prices, the value of real balances. If it is accepted that households maintain a given relation between their cash balances and levels of expenditure, a further fall in income and imports must occur in order to preserve monetary equilibrium.

There are a number of ways by which this adjustment can occur. Reduced cash balances mean less spending (the real balance effect). Also, the decline in money lends to a rise in interest rates. This causes investment to fall, leading again to a fall in imports. Financial intermediaries can also be introduced into the analysis. The adjustment process might be viewed as leading from reduced reserves in the banking system, to increases in the interest rate on overdrafts, to reduced borrowing and spending. The decrease in aggregate demand, by whatever process it comes about, must continue until full equilibrium is restored.

The automatic adjustment mechanism described above stresses the link between the current account deficit, the deterioration in the liquidity position of individuals and/or domestic banks, and the translation of the latter into a reduced level of advances and, eventually, lower aggregate demand. While relatively simple in theory, in practice the process may take a long time to work through the system. When private capital is internationally mobile, it may be that a very small increase in domestic interest rates will attract private capital inflows which offset the current account deficit and thus ease the liquidity constraint.[11] Official policy could also encroach upon the automatic adjustment mechanism by 'sterilising' the monetary effects of balance of payments disequilibrium. For example, the central bank might offset the liquidity-reducing effects of the deficit by short-term measures designed to increase domestic liquidity. Alternatively, the government might borrow abroad in order to restore the liquidity loss.

The automatic adjustment process can also operate on the supply side. Suppose we are in a world of classical full employment. To eliminate the deficit then requires more than just switching demand from imports to exports. Resources must be released from production of 'non-traded' goods and reallocated to the production of both exports and import-competing ('traded') goods. In an economy where prices are flexible, this adjustment is achieved by a change in the price of traded relative to the price of non-traded goods and services.

Thus, returning to our example of a downward shift in the demand for a country's exports, factors released in the export industry seek employment elsewhere in the economy. This will lead to a fall in the domestic price of non-traded services (taxis, restaurants, accounting and professional services, etc.). Prices in the traded sector will be much slower to fall because, at a fixed exchange rate, they will be largely determined by international market conditions. Hence the *profitability* of the traded sector will increase and resources will be drawn into it. *Domestic production of importable and exportable goods will increase relative to the production of non-traded goods and services*. The nearer an economy is operating to 'classical' conditions, the more relevant this type of adjustment will be to the process of equilibrium.

A strong automatic adjustment mechanism is particularly evident in a small open economy. Changes in the demand for exports translate into changes in the demand for imports. A shift in the demand for imports will have implications for the money supply and the level of aggregate demand, and so on. The process of adjustment may be delayed by institutional rigidities and *ad hoc* government interventions. A key issue is whether adjustment is effected through changes in

---

11 However, private capital will continue to flow only if it is convinced that the underlying balance of payments position is secure.

real variables such as the level of employment and the growth rate or by means of changes in relative prices. Economic policy aims to ensure that the process of adjustment is carried through with minimum loss in terms of output and efficiency, and with maximum use of the price mechanism. In practice this means not waiting until reserves and foreign borrowing capacity are exhausted before taking action. Our next task is to analyse the type of action to be taken, which would give firms and individuals an opportunity to make structural changes in good time, before a crisis point is reached.

Balance of payments policies

Balance of payments policies are concerned with maintaining balance of payments equilibrium. Effectively this means keeping the deficit or surplus at a sustainable level. As an extreme example, suppose a country with a current account deficit reaches a stage where reserves and borrowing capacity are depleted. As we have seen, in such circumstances, the country does not go bankrupt. However, it will find it progressively more difficult to secure essential imports. What policy instruments are available to the government to remedy the situation? For illustrative purposes, we consider the case of a country with an unsustainable deficit.

If the deficit country is operating at full employment and production is by definition at full capacity, *expenditure reduction* policies would be one way of resolving the deficit problem. Reductions in the real level of economic activity brought about by, say, restrictive fiscal policies will decrease the level of import demand. If the propensity to import is high, this policy can be highly effective in restoring balance of payments equilibrium.

Recall that the total income of a country is defined as:

$$Y = C + I + G + X - M$$

where C is private domestic consumption, I is domestic investment, G is government consumption, and $X - M$ represents exports less imports.[12]

Income can also be defined as:

$$Y = C + S + T$$

where S is savings and T is taxes. In equilibrium the two definitions are identical.

$$C + I + G + (X - M) = C + S + T.$$

Hence,

$$(I - S) + (G - T) = (M - X)$$

that is, excess investment over savings + government budget deficit = balance of payments deficit.

---

12 For simplicity, we assume zero unilateral transfers and net factor income.

The balance of payments deficit has a counterpart in (a) the budget deficit and (b) the excess of investment over savings. Assuming full employment, it follows that one solution to the deficit is to cut spending. This can be done by some combination of measures such as:

- increasing domestic savings,
- reducing investment,
- restrictive fiscal policies.

Expenditure switching policies, by contrast, focus on the redeployment of resources. There are three standard methods of expenditure switching:

- commercial policy,
- improved competitiveness, and
- exchange rate changes.

(1) *Commercial policy* comprises price and non-price measures designed to restrict imports and stimulate exports, e.g. tariffs, quotas, export subsidies. Besides being a source of friction with a country's trading partners, commercial restrictions are rarely an efficient way of rectifying a balance of payments problem. But in a crisis they may be the only practicable way of dealing with it. Hence the existence of a specific WTO provision for imposing temporary trade restrictions in cases of exceptional balance of payments difficulties. India used this clause to justify quantitative import restrictions during the 1990s. Note that these trade restraints will be effective only if there are unutilised resources available to satisfy the demand which is diverted from imports to domestic goods. If this assumption is not valid, diverted demand will meet a fixed domestic supply, domestic prices will rise, and the initial competitive advantage accruing to domestic suppliers through import barriers (or export subsidies) will be eroded.

What is needed to resolve the deficit problem is a way of altering the composition of output. In effect, we have to incentivise resources to move to the traded sector from the non-traded sector. The next two policies address this objective.

(2)   *Cost competitiveness* can be defined in a broad sense to include price and non-price factors such as product quality, reliability of supply and back-up market services. Improving a nation's competitiveness involves a wide range of measures such as restraints on domestic costs and incomes, improvements in infrastructure, correcting bottlenecks in the supply of skilled labour, establishing an orderly industrial relations system and so on. A country's long-run competitive position can also be influenced by its policy towards research and development and its success in product innovation and technology. Countries with balance of payments deficits often consider themselves to be suffering from lack of *competitiveness*. Their exports and import-competing industries are unable to 'hack it' in a globalised economy. The lack of dynamism in the traded sector is perceived as holding back economic growth. Expansion of the economy is frustrated by balance of payments crises, as imports demand outstrips export revenues. The solution is to improve competitiveness.

(3) *Exchange rate changes* involve a *combination of expenditure switching and expenditure reduction*. The objective is to reduce domestic spending, to maintain output at a high level, and to reallocate output towards the traded sector, all at the same time.

Depreciation of the exchange rate makes imports more expensive and improves the price competitiveness of exports. For a large country, a depreciation can be far more effective than an expenditure reducing policy as a means of cutting a current account (see Box 20.4).[13] The reason is that expenditure reduction policies, achieved through, say, a cut in government spending or a rise in taxation, cuts spending on imports (as the policy intends), but it also cuts spending on domestic goods (an unwanted and potentially unemployment-creating side-effect in the short run). Expenditure switching, therefore, is needed to pick up the incipient slack in demand for domestically produced goods by stimulating exports and import-competing activities. Devaluation offers the necessary incentives for this and, in addition, provides an inducement to suppliers to shift to traded from non-traded production.

The effectiveness of a devaluation, however, is subject to certain practical and institutional constraints, which are particularly relevant to smaller countries. First, a devaluation raises exporters' costs by raising the price of imported imports, an effect which is more pronounced in a small trade-dependent country. Second, the favourable competitive effects often come into play only in the medium to longer term. Third, depreciation of the exchange rate can lead to domestic inflation, compensatory income claims and the beginning of a wage–price spiral.

For all that, there are many instances of successful devaluations. Sometimes such devaluations are forced upon the deficit country by capital speculation. Devaluations can also help to insulate a country against competitive disadvantages arising as a result of devaluations in the currencies of its trading partners. Sometimes they are made in order to bring about what is hoped will be a once-for-all correction in a country's cost structure. Given the right circumstances, a devaluation can play a constructive part in rectifying a balance of payments deficit crisis. A detailed analysis of exchange rates will be provided in Chapter 21.

While this analysis has focused on policy measures to correct a deficit, the same framework can be applied to analyse measures for correcting a surplus. Thus,

---

13 According to the basic macroeconomic equations, the current account balance (in this context mostly referred to as net exports) results from a mismatch between domestic savings and investment. If residents save more than they invest, or, in other words, they have a surplus of output to be sent abroad, net exports are positive. Conversely, a country turns into a net importer if its residents do not save as much as they invest, which means also that they consume and invest more than they produce. Total spending by domestic residents, i.e. the sum of consumption and investment, is called absorption. Thus, if absorption exceeds production, the current account is in deficit. These fundamental relationships underline the importance of the balance between savings and investment for the determination of the external balance.

Box 20.4

Expenditure switching and the US deficit

'The United States has a current account deficit because it spends more than it earns.' This view of the cause of the deficit has interesting policy implications. One is that total spending might have to be curtailed. The second is that the cut in spending must as far as possible be concentrated on imports. To achieve such a reorientation requires therefore a mixture of expenditure reduction and expenditure switching. A policy which aims merely to cut US demand will not lead to the right *kind* of demand cut. Krugman explains the analysis with the aid of a simple arithmetical example.

He starts with the observation that, despite the increasing openness of the US economy over the past forty years, most of the income of US residents is spent on goods and services produced at home. As a result, the main impact of a reduction in US expenditure will be a fall in demand for US goods and services. Similarly, only a fraction of an increase in expenditure in the rest of the world (ROW) will be spent on US products.

To see the problem this causes, consider the example illustrated in the table below. Suppose the US reduces its spending by $100 billion, while the ROW simultaneously increases its demand by the same amount. Unfortunately, this does not translate smoothly into a $100 billion reduction in the trade deficit. At least $80 billion of the reduction in US spending is likely to represent a fall in demand for domestically produced goods and services, with only $20 billion representing a fall in demand for imports. Meanwhile, no more than $10 billion of the rise in spending in the ROW is likely to be spent on US goods, with $90 billion being spent on ROW products. The outcome is a net reduction in demand for US products of $70 billion, and an equal increase in demand for ROW products. Instead of a smooth reduction in the US trade deficit, we get a combination of recession in the US and inflation abroad. To make the adjustment work, some way has to be found to switch $70 billion in spending from ROW to US products. The easiest way to do this is to lower the foreign exchange value of the dollar, which makes US goods cheaper to ROW residents and ROW goods dearer to US residents.

The lesson of this example is that devaluing the dollar can be an effective element in a deficit-reduction policy package.

	Total demand	Demand for US products	Demand for ROW products
US	−100	−80	−20
ROW	+100	+10	+90
Total	0	−70	+70

Source: P. Krugman, *The Age of Diminished Expectations* (Cambridge, MA: MIT Press, 1994).

surplus countries are urged to liberalise commercial policy by dismantling non-tariff barriers on imports. For them, expenditure-expanding programmes are appropriate, provided this can be effected without giving rise to inflation. Measures can be taken to reduce the propensity to save by reducing taxes, making house purchases more attractive and reducing the length of the working week (so that people have more inducement to spend).

In the last analysis, surplus countries too are under pressure to realign their currency. Surpluses, like deficits, can often be difficult to correct. A government with a surplus can hardly be expected to instruct its producers to become less competitive. Self-interest, in fact, will lead its firms to redouble their efforts to increase competitiveness in the face of revaluation or stiffening competition from foreigners. This makes good sense for the individual corporation. But it frustrates the global system's capacity to deal effectively with a troublesome imbalance.

20.4 Conclusions

The structure of the balance of payments in developed countries has been undergoing profound change. Deregulation and liberalisation have led to rapid growth in services trade. The proliferation of multinationals has fuelled the growth of royalty and dividend payments and international marketing and consultancy services. Most significant, however, has been the quantum leap in capital account transactions, as technology makes it easier to transfer capital and relaxation of exchange controls legalises such transfers.

Defining a sustainable balance of payments position has, as a consequence, become more problematic. Capital flows have made it possible to contemplate a much longer period of deficits or surpluses on the current account. Eventually, however, sustained imbalances cause friction even in a capital-mobile world. In that event, the same ease of capital mobility that for long made it unnecessary to implement corrective action, can precipitate the need for it in moments of difficulty. There is, unfortunately, no ready formula for determining whether a particular country has, or is likely to have, a balance of payments problem. Balance of payments analysis involves good judgement, as well as good economics.

Balance of payments problems remain a serious constraint on development in many countries. This is particularly the case for developing countries with restricted access to world capital markets and with relatively fixed exchange rate regimes. Developed countries, however, can also be affected. The problem of huge OPEC surpluses dominated discussion in the 1970s. Balance of payments policy in the 1980s and the 1990s has been preoccupied by the twin problems of the Japanese surplus and the US deficit. For decades, the UK government has wrestled with the problem of 'stop-go' policies. Each expansion of the economy was brought to an end by a balance of payments deficit, caused by import demand outstripping export capacity.

In the present environment, the main themes of debate focus on automatic balance of payments adjustment mechanisms, optimal levels of foreign borrowing, the changing composition of external assets and liabilities, and interdependence between one country's balance of payments deficit and other countries' surpluses. In a world still heavily dominated by the triad of the EU, Japan and the US, the development of a cooperative rather than a confrontational approach is important not only for the triad itself, but also for developing countries. The latter rely more than the richer countries on access to world markets in order to earn the foreign currency needed to achieve faster growth and to service their external debt.

Remedies for a balance of payments problem may be found in a number of possible measures: trade policy, aggregate demand (absorption) policy, improved competitiveness and changes in the exchange rate. Much balance of payments analysis has, in fact, been conducted in the context of an implicitly assumed fixed or quasi-fixed exchange rate regime. Once flexible exchange rates are introduced, the balance of payments problem evaporates – at *some* price, demand and supply of foreign exchange will be equilibrated. But in solving the balance of payments problem this way, the danger of creating another is accentuated. That danger is inflation. To understand this requires an analysis of the function and role of the exchange rate. This will constitute the theme of the next two chapters.

 ## Summary

1. The balance of payments consists of current transactions and capital transactions. Current transactions include trade in goods, services trade, trading and investment income and unilateral transfers. Capital transactions refer to net stock changes in portfolio capital, foreign direct investment, short-term capital and official reserves.

2. The balance of payments on current account is an important economic variable. It represents the difference between current outflows and inflows of foreign exchange. The current account balance impacts on the level of aggregate demand and on the level of a country's international indebtedness. For example, a succession of current account deficits since the 1980s has reduced the US's net foreign wealth to the point where the US has been transformed from being a major creditor country to being the world's largest debtor country.

3. A current balance of payments deficit means that a country is spending more foreign exchange than it is currently earning. In some cases, running a deficit is a perfectly defensible, even a desirable, strategy. For example, a rapidly growing economy may run a deficit, and in so doing draw on external capital, to support its investment programme. But a deficit incurred to finance extra consumption will sooner or later be judged unsustainable by the world

markets. Corrective action will then have to be taken. A country running a persistent surplus could also be considered in a disequilibrium position, not least because of the objections of its trading partners. There is, however, no simple rule-book to guide us in deciding when a country has a balance of payments problem or when its balance of payments is in disequilibrium. Balance of payments analysis requires judgement.

4. There are automatic adjustment mechanisms which tend to restore balance of payments equilibrium. Surplus countries can find that the resultant rise in liquidity attracts growing import demand. By contrast, a decline in demand for a country's exports dampens that country's demand for imports. A change in the current account has other automatic repercussions on the domestic price level and the country's international competitiveness. But automatic income and price adjustment mechanisms are rarely sufficient to ensure equilibrium. Policy action may also be required.

5. Expenditure changing and expenditure switching policies are mechanisms for speeding up the adjustment process. Deficit countries can ease their balance of payments by curbing net government spending or encouraging saving; and surplus countries can stimulate import demand and reduce the surplus through expansionary budget policies, subject to the caveats about the effectiveness of such policies mentioned in our discussion of fiscal policy (Chapter 15). Expenditure switching policies refer to price incentives designed to induce a switch in spending between traded and non-traded goods and services. Three such policies are: commercial policy, domestic competitiveness measures and exchange rate changes.

6. In a world of freely floating exchange rates, balance of payments problems as such are unlikely to surface. Impending deficits or surpluses, if not matched by offsetting capital flows, will bring about exchange rate fluctuations which will neutralise the threatened imbalance. Exchange rate fluctuations may, however, raise difficulties for the authorities no less acute than the balance of payments difficulties experienced by countries with a fixed exchange rate regime.

? Questions for discussion

1. Under what circumstances could a country simultaneously have a balance of trade surplus and a current account deficit?

2. How would you explain the rapid growth in capital account transactions relative to merchandise trade transactions in recent years?

3. What, if anything, does the fact that a country has a current account surplus tell us about the strength of that economy?

4. How would you define a balance of payments disequilibrium? Discuss some of the economic forces which tend automatically to restore the balance of payments to equilibrium.

5. What problems, if any, is a country which runs a persistent current account balance of payments deficit likely to encounter? Contrast them with the problems of a country with a persistent surplus.

6. Should a tax be imposed on countries running a persistent balance of payments surplus, on the grounds that such surpluses are deflationary and a danger to the world trading system?

☞ Exercises

1. Honey and Moon from Korea spend a working holiday in Britain. During their visit, they affect all four major components of the current account of the UK's balance of payments. What transactions could they have made?

2. Classify the following transactions in the UK balance of payments:

   (a) British Airways purchases a jet from Airbus for £60 million, and receives a three-year credit from a French bank to finance the transaction.
   (b) A US tourist travels to Britain and spends £1000 financed by dollar travellers' cheques.
   (c) Mercedes Benz sells €4 million of its cars to a UK distributor, allowing 90 days' trade credit until payment is due.
   (d) Herr Schmidt in Bonn sends his grandson in London €4000 for his university fees.
   (e) A resident in Phoenix, Arizona, receives a £10,000 dividend from British Telecom plc which is deposited in a local bank.

   Specify a balancing capital account transaction in each instance.

3. Consider any country with a balance of payments deficit on current account. Reviewing the economic record of the country, should the authorities take steps to reduce this deficit? If so, how should this be done?

4. Review recent trends in the current account balance of payments of any major industrial country. What would be the likely effect on the current account balance: (a) faster economic growth in the economy of its trading partners; (b) faster growth in its own economy; and (c) rapid inflation relative to its trading partners?

5. Does it make sense for a developing country to run a current balance of payments surplus? In your answer, give examples of developing countries that have surpluses.

Further reading

Two major world balance of payments problems – the US deficit and the Japanese surplus – are dissected in a readable and enlightening way in Paul Krugman, *The Age of Diminished Expectations* (Cambridge, MA: MIT Press, 1994). Catherine Mann's *Is the US Trade Deficit Sustainable?* (Washington DC: Institute for International Economics, 1999) brings the discussion up to date. The IMF's *World Economic Outlook*, published twice yearly, contains information on the balance of payments and foreign position of the main countries and regions and commentary on these problems. The IMF's *Balance of Payments Statistics Yearbook* provides a wealth of detail on national balance of payments statistics. Any reader interested in the minutiae of balance of payments methodology should consult the IMF, *Balance of Payments Manual* (1993).

Chapter 21

COPING WITH EXCHANGE RATES

Introduction

> Every one pfennig rise in the dollar adds $20 million to our profits. (Helmut Werner, Mercedes Benz CEO, *Business Week*, 29 April 1996)

Exchange rate variations can cause major headaches for firms, especially those with a diversified sales pattern. Bilateral rates between the major currencies are subject to violent and unpredictable swings. Even in the course of a relatively quiet year currency swings in the range of 10–20 per cent would not be uncommon. Given that profit margins in most industries lie in the range of 3–10 per cent of sales, a firm's profits can quickly be eroded by unexpected shifts in exchange rates. There are ways of avoiding or minimising exchange rate risk, but they are not costless. Attempts to forecast exchange rate changes are also unlikely to be effective in protecting profits (for reasons to be explained). This chapter outlines the causes of exchange rate volatility and analyses how business can cope with it. In Chapter 22, the various ways by which government can alleviate exchange rate problems are analysed.

Business and government have conflicting perspectives on the exchange rate. At one extreme, exchange rate changes can mean the difference between prosperity and closedown for the low margin exporter, or the domestic manufacturer competing with low cost imports. At the other, to the government a 'strong' exchange rate regime connotes lower inflation, lower interest rates and high political prestige, free from the fear of the potential inflationary consequences of devaluation. To the consumer, a strong currency means lower prices for imported goods.

Although a weak currency helps the traded sector in the short run, it could have adverse repercussions on the long-run competitive position. Michael Porter articulated the danger in this way:

> The expectation of a lower exchange rate leads firms towards a dependence on price competition in price-sensitive segments and industries. Automation and other forms of innovation that improve productivity, and the shift to higher order competitive advantages are retarded. Thus a balance needs to be struck. *Currency pressures need to be strong enough to promote upgrading but not so great as to run ahead of factor quality and other preconditions for upgrading to succeed.* (M. Porter, *The Competitive Advantage of Nations*, London: Macmillan, 1990, p. 642)

Finding the golden mean between exerting pressure to improve quality and destroying the cost base of a nation's industry can be a difficult task. Strong, prosperous economies do indeed tend to have strong exchange rates, but it does not follow that strong exchange rates have made them prosperous. Arguably, a slightly undervalued currency provides a greater inducement to growth than an overvalued one. This factor certainly helped Germany's and Japan's postwar economic success.

Chapter outline

The chapter proceeds as follows:

1. The foreign exchange market and the effects of changes in the exchange rate on business behaviour.
2. Exchange rate theory. This involves analysis of purchasing power parity and other economic 'fundamentals' in influencing exchange rates.
3. Reasons for exchange rate volatility and the implications of this volatility for business.
4. Methods by which business can cope with exchange rate fluctuations. These include use of the forward market, options and other hedging devices.

21.1 How exchange rates work

Foreign exchange markets

The foreign exchange (forex) market is the world's largest financial market. Currencies are traded in financial centres around the world, connected by communications systems that allow nearly instantaneous transmission of price information and trade instructions. Total net turnover amounts to almost $1700 billion per day. The most active market is London ($600 billion per day), followed by New York and Tokyo. The annual turnover of these centres increased by 26 per cent between 1995 and 1998 (Bank of International Settlement estimate), and since then this rapid growth shows no sign of abating.

The *spot* foreign exchange market refers to the market for foreign exchange deliverable on the day the contract is made. The market operates by means of communications on computer screens and telephones by four categories of participants: dealers/traders (predominantly large international banks), brokers, institutions (mutual funds, pension funds, insurance companies) and central banks. In addition to the spot market, there is the *forward* market and *futures* market, and a market for *swaps* and *options* (derivatives). Spot transactions dominate trading, accounting for half of total turnover. Information on spot rates is available in daily newspapers; usually in the form of data on *closing rates* and on the day's *spread* or *trading range*, the latter indicating the range between the highest and lowest bid during the day. A major development in the market in recent years has been the surge in swaps and derivatives transactions, as banks and their customers have become increasingly anxious to hedge their foreign exchange positions. These sophisticated instruments will be analysed later in the chapter. Further details of the forex market are provided in Appendix 21.1.

The exchange rate is defined here as *the price of foreign currency in terms of domestic currency*. It is the amount of domestic currency needed to buy one unit of foreign currency – just as the price of apples is the amount of domestic currency needed to buy an apple. Thus, it cost a US citizen $1.99 to buy a pound sterling in 1991; five years later, it cost only $1.53. Looked at from the UK perspective, a dollar cost 50p in 1991 as compared with 65p in 1996. During this period, the dollar had become more expensive and sterling cheaper. On this bilateral basis, we say that the dollar has *appreciated* and sterling has *depreciated*. The percentage depreciation/appreciation lies between 22 and 28 per cent, depending on the base from which the calculation is worked out.

During the 1990s, the pound sterling altered in value relative to other currencies as well as the dollar. The pound depreciated by 15 per cent relative to the Deutschmark and by 34 per cent relative to the yen. It appreciated by 13 per cent relative to the Italian lira. To obtain an impression of the trend in sterling's overall value, one must take an average of these diverse bilateral depreciations and appreciations. For this purpose, a weighted average is used, the weights being related to the proportion of total UK trade with each country concerned. Often trade weights are modified by other *ad hoc* adjustments to take account of the degree of price-sensitivity of trade with certain countries, the currency in which trade is denominated and other factors. The resultant trade-weighted index is called the *nominal effective exchange rate* (EER) (see Box 21.1). Estimates of the EER of four leading currencies are shown in Figure 21.1. During the period 1990–95,

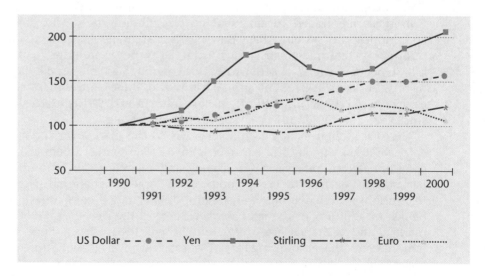

Figure 21.1 Nominal effective exchange rates (EERs)

Source: OECD, *Economic Outlook* (December 2000). A synthetic euro value has been computed for period prior to 1999.

the EER of the yen soared by 90 per cent, to fall back to near its original level in 1998. It rose by 24 per cent between 1998 and 2001. Sterling's EER fell by 10 per cent during 1990–95 and rose by 20 per cent from 1995 to 2000. Thus EERs fluctuate less than bilateral rates, but are still fairly volatile.

Impact of exchange rate on firms

Imagine the case of a UK exporter selling to the US. From the point of view of the UK firm, what matters is the sterling value of the firm's export sales, but for the US consumer all that matters is the dollar price of the UK goods. The sterling/dollar exchange rate is of no relevance to the consumer's decision to buy the good. In setting price, therefore, the seller must take account of the degree of competition from competing dollar-priced goods. Suppose 100 units were sold at a price of $1.50 per unit, yielding total revenue of $150. The UK exporter converts this into sterling at the current exchange rate, assumed here to be 50p per dollar. Sales revenues in sterling of £75 can now be compared to the sterling costs of producing the exports (see Box 21.2). In the illustrative examples, profits earned amount to £5, yielding a profit/sales ratio of 7 per cent.

Consider now the effect of a sterling depreciation, from 50p to 64p per dollar. At the same dollar price of the good (i.e. $1.50 per unit), dollar sales revenue remains constant. But the sterling value of these sales rises from £75 to £96. The UK firm's export profits increase to £26, a more than five-fold increase. The 28 per cent depreciation has generated a quintupling of profits. This *magnification effect* of depreciation on profit margins is a key factor in understanding why depreciation gives a strong incentive to higher exports.

A similar incentive effect applies to a domestic UK firm competing against goods imported from the US. The sterling depreciation makes the UK market *less* attractive to US exporters for exactly the same reason that it made the US market *more* attractive to UK exporters. This eases the pressure on UK import-competing firms from foreign competition. Some scope for raising sterling price may be exploitable. UK firms will have the opportunity of charging higher prices *and* expanding sales on the UK market.

Three major qualifications are needed in order to bring the example closer to reality:

1. The sterling depreciation is unlikely to leave the UK firms' cost structure unaffected. The sterling price of their imported raw materials and intermediate inputs will rise as a result of the depreciation. Hence, some of their competitive advantage will be eroded.
2. Employees may demand compensation for the price increases caused by the devaluation. This is especially likely to happen if prices of necessities such as food are affected.
3. The appreciation of the dollar may force US producers to upgrade as a means of preserving market share. Japanese firms, for example, responded to the stronger yen by vigorous productivity and quality improvements which more often than not over-compensated for the currency appreciation. This is

Box 21.1

The exchange rate – basic definitions

Nominal exchange rate

The exchange rate is usually defined as the price of a unit of foreign currency in terms of domestic currency. It is the amount of domestic currency needed to buy one unit of foreign currency. For example, on 19 July 2000, the price of one US dollar was 1.08 euros. A British firm had to pay 67p sterling and a Japanese firm 109 yen. These rates are *bilateral* rates.

Exchange rates change over time. Over the year to July 2000, the yen had appreciated by 12 per cent relative to the dollar, while the euro had depreciated by 10 per cent relative to the dollar.

Nominal effective exchange rate (EER)

Bilateral exchange rates do not all rise or fall in unison *vis-à-vis* any particular currency. As we have seen above, in any period the dollar might become weaker against the Japanese yen but appreciate against the euro. If we want to comment on the overall weakness or strength of a currency, some way must be found of summarising the diverse pattern of depreciation and appreciation. The nominal effective exchange rate (EER) is designed to do precisely this.

The nominal EER is defined as *the exchange rate of the domestic currency vis-à-vis other currencies weighted by their share in the country's trade*. It is a weighted average of the value of one currency's bilateral exchange rates with a group of other currencies. Two issues have to be decided: (a) how many currencies to include in the index, and (b) the weight to be given to each currency.

Ideally all currencies should be included but, for reasons of practicality, the number of currencies in the EER 'basket' is usually limited to those that are of major importance to the country concerned.

To determine the weights to attach to each bilateral exchange rate, the simplest approach is to consider weightings based on the amount of trade between countries. Hence in the construction of an EER index for the US more weight would be given to Canada than to the UK or Germany, since Canada is the major trading partner of the US. An alternative weighting system would take account of total payments rather than just merchandise trade. In some instances more complex formulas can be employed, which incorporate information on third country effects and the price sensitivity of different types of trade.

Real effective exchange rates (REERs)

Real effective exchange rates (REERs) are used to assess the competitive position of a country relative to its competitors or sometimes to make inferences about how close actual exchange rates are to their long run equilibrium level.

Suppose a country's nominal EER had devalued by 10 per cent but, during the same period, its domestic inflation was 10 per cent while its trading partners had zero inflation. Clearly there has been no devaluation in real terms. Any competitive advantage secured by the 10 per cent nominal devaluation has been counteracted by the 10 per cent increase in

Box 21.1 continued

domestic prices relative to foreign prices. The real effective exchange rate (REER) takes account of price level changes between trading partners by adjusting the nominal EER by the ratio of foreign to domestic inflation.

The IMF's *International Financial Statistics* contains REERs based on a nominal EER index for 18 industrial countries and weights computed from its *Multilateral Exchange Rate Model* (MERM). The Bank of England, The Federal Reserve and J.P. Morgan also publish trade-weighted nominal and real effective exchange indices.

Box 21.2

How changes in the exchange rate affect profits

	(A) Exchange rate $1 = £0.50	(B) Exchange rate $1 = £0.64
Sales in US market	100 units @ $1.50 per unit = $150	100 units $1.50 per unit = $150
US sales converted to sterling	£75	£96
Costs	£70	£70
Profit	£5	£26

Result. Depreciation of sterling makes exports to the US market more profitable. It creates a strong incentive to increase export volume. This could be done by reducing the dollar price or by additional spending on marketing/distribution. Either way, sales of British exports expand. This will lead to more jobs in the firm itself and to greater demand for intermediate goods from other British firms.

precisely the spur which Porter sees as the advantageous side of strengthening the currency.

The combined effect of these negative factors could, in certain circumstances, offset the positive effects of sterling's depreciation on the UK's cost-competitiveness.

Taking all firms together

The arithmetical illustration above can easily be translated into the familiar demand and supply framework. Instead of confining the analysis to one firm, the various demand and supply responses of all firms can be added together by lateral

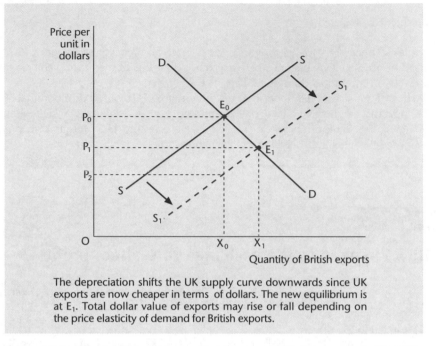

The depreciation shifts the UK supply curve downwards since UK exports are now cheaper in terms of dollars. The new equilibrium is at E_1. Total dollar value of exports may rise or fall depending on the price elasticity of demand for British exports.

Figure 21.2 Effect of sterling depreciation on British exports to the US

summation. The UK export supply curve will be the sum of individual firms' responses to the sterling equivalent of the dollar price ($P_\$ \times ER$) while the US consumer's demand for UK exports is determined by the dollar price ($P_\$$). This situation is depicted in Figure 21.2.

A depreciation of sterling shifts the supply curve of UK goods outwards. This reflects the fact that, for each given dollar price, sterling profits rise as a result of the devaluation, and therefore more will be supplied. The depreciation has no impact on the US demand curve. The new equilibrium is at E_1. At E_1, the dollar price has fallen and the quantity exported has risen, as one would expect. An opposite effect applies to US exporters to the UK (Figure 21.3). Their supply curve moves inwards to the left. This happens because the dollar equivalent of the sterling price at E_0 has fallen as a result of the devaluation. The new equilibrium occurs at E_1. At this point, the sterling price is higher than its E_0 level but the dollar price is lower – bad news for the US exporter, but good news for the UK firms competing against imports. Exploiting the fact that import quantities have fallen from OM_0 to OM_1, import-competing firms are able to sell more at a higher sterling price.

Hence, a depreciation of sterling will, other things being equal, lead to:

- an increase in volume of UK exports,
- a reduction in the volume of UK imports,
- a fall in the dollar price and a rise in the sterling price of UK exports, and
- a rise in the sterling price and a fall in the dollar price of UK imports.

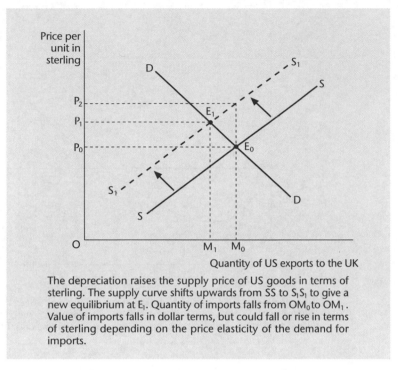

The depreciation raises the supply price of US goods in terms of sterling. The supply curve shifts upwards from SS to S_1S_1 to give a new equilibrium at E_1. Quantity of imports falls from OM_0 to OM_1. Value of imports falls in dollar terms, but could fall or rise in terms of sterling depending on the price elasticity of the demand for imports.

Figure 21.3 Effect of sterling depreciation on US exports to the UK

All the above effects are favourable to the traded sector of the UK economy. This explains why domestic industry usually prefers a devaluation to an appreciation of the national currency.

Effects on trade balance and the J-curve

So far, we have analysed the effects of devaluation on the volume of trade. The next step is to study the combined (net) effect on the value of exports and imports. Suppose the depreciation was caused by concern over the UK's current balance of payments deficit. Will a depreciation cause the gap between the value of imports and exports to narrow? The normal expectation is that it will. However, the ultimate impact depends on the price elasticities of demand in the two markets. If the export and import demand elasticities are low, then the possibility of a depreciation worsening the trade balance cannot be ruled out. In the immediate aftermath of a devaluation, the trade balance often does tend to worsen, taking a period of a year or more to improve. This rather counter-intuitive phenomenon of a negative short-term effect followed by a positive longer-term effect on the current account balance of payments is called the *J-curve effect* (Figure 21.4).

The J-curve effect can be illustrated by an extreme case. Suppose that the demand for imports into the UK had zero price elasticity of demand in the short run. In Figure 21.3, the curve DD would be vertical. A 10 per cent depreciation

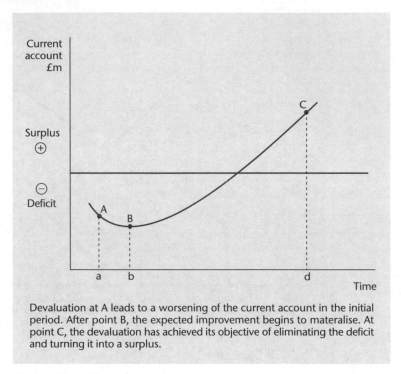

Devaluation at A leads to a worsening of the current account in the initial period. After point B, the expected improvement begins to materalise. At point C, the devaluation has achieved its objective of eliminating the deficit and turning it into a surplus.

Figure 21.4 The *J*-curve

shifts the supply curve of US products up by 10 per cent. Despite the rise in price, the quantity sold remains unchanged. Hence, the sterling value of imports increases by the same percentage as the depreciation. Suppose now that, in the US, the demand curve for imports from the UK was also price inelastic. Then DD in Figure 21.2 would be vertical. The depreciation shifts the supply curve of UK exports to the right. Since the demand curve is vertical, the dollar price falls by the amount of the depreciation and export revenue in dollars falls by the devaluation percentage. In sterling terms, export receipts remain unchanged. Hence, if the elasticities of demand for exports and imports are each zero, the effect of depreciation of 10 per cent in sterling terms would be:

- a rise in value of imports of 10 per cent in sterling terms,
- no change in export receipts in sterling terms, and hence
- a worsening of the current account.

The J-curve effect will be observed whenever prices adjust faster than volumes to exchange rate changes. The J-curve does not relate just to devaluations: exactly the same line of reasoning might be applied to explain why an appreciation could, in the short run, lead to an improvement in the trade balance.[1]

The J-curve effect is an intriguing possibility, but it must not blind us to the fact that, in general, one can expect a depreciation to have a positive impact, and an

---

1 A. Rose and J. Yellen, 'Is there a J-curve?', *Journal of Monetary Economics* (July 1989).

appreciation to have a negative impact, on the trade balance. A strengthening currency will, over time, tend to erode export sales and profits. Profits may be further reduced by rules which require a firm in an appreciating currency to write down holdings of foreign assets denominated in the depreciated currencies.

21.2 Exchange rate theory

Exchange rate movements affect both the individual firm and the economy. Realignments of the exchange rate can be of positive benefit to an economy and can assist the process of adjustment to changes in a country's competitive position, to sectoral imbalances, or to a variety of demand and supply 'shocks'. However, excessive exchange rate volatility can have detrimental effects. It can lead to:

- disruption of domestic anti-inflation programmes,
- systemic instability, whereby changes in one country's currency cause problems for other countries,
- misalignments over periods of time leading to sub-optimal investment and marketing decisions, and
- transaction and hedging costs.

We need to understand, therefore, both how to define an equilibrium exchange rate and how to explain why large fluctuations from this level are frequently observed.

Purchasing power parity (PPP)

Purchasing power parity (PPP) links movements in exchange rates to differences between the price level in the domestic country and that of its major trading partners. PPP theory draws its inspiration from the *Law of One Price*. According to this law, if two goods are identical, they will sell at the same price. Otherwise it will pay someone to buy where it is cheaper and sell where it is dearer. *Arbitrage* is the process which ensures that the existence of any price differential between one country and another is exploited in order to make a riskless profit. Extended to all goods this becomes the theory of *absolute* PPP. Its central postulate is that the general level of prices, when converted to a common currency, will be the same in every country. If this were not so, arbitrageurs would have profitable incentives to trade, until the differential disappeared. From this, absolute PPP deduces that the *exchange rate will be such that the general level of prices will be the same in every country*.

$$P_d = ER \times P_f$$

The Law of One Price, however, applies only in a rather unreal world of zero transport costs, absence of trade barriers, perfect competition and no possibility of market segmentation. If these conditions are not satisfied, price differentials will not be arbitraged out of existence.

A weaker version of PPP, *relative* PPP, states that:[2]

---

2 L.S. Copeland, *Exchange Rates and International Finance* (Wokingham: Addison-Wesley, 1989).

changes in the exchange rate are determined by the difference between relative domestic inflation rates in different countries.

$$\%\Delta ER = \%\Delta P_d - \%\Delta P_f$$

where: ER = exchange rate (units of domestic currency per unit of foreign currency)

P_d = domestic price level

P_f = foreign price level

$\%\Delta$ = change as per cent of starting level

Proponents of this theory argue that, if the domestic inflation rate exceeds the foreign rate, exports and import-competing activities in the domestic currency will become price-uncompetitive. As a result, exports will fall, imports will increase and the current account balance will worsen. Furthermore, inward foreign direct investment will be discouraged by the high price of domestic assets and, for the same reason, outward direct investment will be encouraged. Foreign assets will become a more attractive buy; domestic assets will appear overpriced. Balance of payments pressures will eventually lead to pressures on the exchange rate. Hence, the negative relationship between relative inflation and a country's exchange rate. An alternative formulation of this principle is that *prices in different countries tend to change at the same rate over time, after correction for changes in the exchange rate.*[3]

Relative PPP is easy to understand in the context of goods which are easily traded between two countries. But the links between prices, the balance of payments and exchange rates operate more slowly and problematically in the case of *non-traded goods and services*, such as housing, medical services, education and government administration.[4] Suppose house prices were rising faster in the UK than in the US. Since houses cannot be physically exchanged between the two countries, the rise in UK house prices will not affect the UK's balance of payments: UK imports and exports will not be *directly* affected. There could, of course, be *indirect* effects; the higher cost of housing could generate demands for compensatory pay rises, which would impact on manufacturer's costs – but these indirect effects will take time to work through. Hence, the exchange rates are likely to respond more to prices of traded goods than to the overall price index.[5]

In an open trading environment, PPP would be expected to hold at a bilateral level, and it is usually tested on this basis. Where PPP is calculated with more than one trading partner, each with a different inflation rate, a formula needs to be found for applying it at a multilateral level. Foreign inflation is then defined as the *trade-weighted average* of trading partners' inflation, and the corresponding exchange rate is the *effective exchange rate* (EER).

---

3 This illustrates an important point: relative PPP can serve both as a theory of inflation and as a theory of exchange rate determination. The former aspect has a decisive bearing on a country's choice of an exchange rate regime, as will be seen in Chapter 22.

4 The 'price' of non-marketed public sector output is defined as the cost of producing it which in practice is often tied to the remuneration of its providers.

5 Even this can involve minor statistical complications if the basket of goods consumed differs between countries and relative goods' prices are changing.

Balance of payments and monetary approaches

An alternative to PPP as an explanation of the equilibrium exchange rate is the *balance of payments approach*. This theory focuses more directly on the link between the trade/current account balance, modified to take account of long-term capital flows, and movement in exchange rates. According to this view, a country with a persistent deficit is likely to devalue and a country with a persistent surplus is likely to revalue. This approach differs from, but is consistent with, PPP theory. PPP states that if country A has higher inflation than country B, A's currency will have to depreciate because it will run into a deficit if it fails to devalue. The balance of payments approach incorporates this PPP view, but allows for the possibility that exchange rates are affected by 'real' factors, as well as relative inflation rates. Examples of these factors (or economic *fundamentals*) are:

- changes in the growth rate,
- changes in the composition of aggregate demand,
- equity and bond market performance,
- size of budget deficits and public debt, and
- governance and political stability.

Each of these factors can have major implications for the balance of payments, and hence for a country's exchange rate.[6]

Probing deeper one might ask why countries have current account deficits and/ or different inflation rates. The *monetary approach to the balance of payments* emphasises the role of money supply growth rates in the home country relative to foreign countries. Recall that more money supply implies lower interest rates and cheaper credit. If money supply rises faster than real income, pressure builds up on domestic prices which makes exports less competitive and imports more competitive. The real balance effect, generated by the rise in money supply relative to prices, further increases import demand. A depreciation of the exchange rate is necessary in order to restore the balance of payments to equilibrium (see Chapter 20). Hence, the chain of causation proceeds from increases in money supply to a current account deficit, to exchange rate depreciation.[7] By the same reasoning, a restrictive monetary policy reduces money supply, raises interest rates, diminishes import demand and improves the current account. Although the theory is plausible, empirical tests of the monetary theory have not been successful in explaining exchange rate variations (Box 21.3). Nevertheless, more comprehensive asset-based theories have developed from it which have been helpful in explaining short-run oscillations in exchange rate.

Empirical analysis of PPP

Empirical studies have shown that absolute PPP does not work. Given the strict assumptions needed for the theory to be valid this is not surprising. Readers

---

6 This is not to say that PPP theory ignores such economic fundamentals, since all of these factors affect inflation, and hence PPP.

7 In theory, balance of payments adjustment can also occur via interest rates.

Box 21.3

The monetary approach to the balance of payments

The monetary approach to the balance of payments can formally be summarised as follows:
Begin with the standard relative PPP equation:

$$e = p - p^* \tag{1}$$

where: e = the exchange rate (% change)
  p = the domestic inflation rate (% change)
  p^* = foreign inflation rate (% change)

(all variables are expressed in log form indicating annual percentage change; * denotes foreign).

According to the classical monetary theory, inflation is determined by the excess of money supply growth (m) over growth in money demand. The latter is determined by growth in income (y) and the level of interest (i), multiplied by their respective elasticities of demand, k and h:

$$p \; = m - k.y - h.i \tag{2}$$

$$p* = m^* - k.y^* - h.i^* \tag{3}$$

Putting these three equations together we obtain:

$$e \; = p - p^* = (m - m^*) - k(y - y^*) - h(i - i^*) \tag{4}$$

Coefficients k and h are assumed to be the same in each country.

Equations such as (4) have been estimated, using e as the dependent variable, with mixed and generally weak results. One obvious explanation for this is that deviations of actual exchange rates from their PPP-ordained level are common. Another is that potentially crucial variables, such as exchange rate expectations based on an assessment of the economic fundamentals, have been excluded. Third, there are long and variable lags between changes in money supply and changes in prices. For these reasons, it is not surprising that econometric studies have given only weak support to the monetary approach to the balance of payments. Nonetheless, the monetary approach marks the beginning of a new theoretical perspective, an asset approach to determining the exchange rate, which has proved fruitful in explaining the volatile behaviour of current markets.

Source: R. Dornbusch, Foreword in J. Bhandari and B. Putnam, *Economic Interdependence and Flexible Exchange Rates* (Cambridge, MA: MIT Press, 1983).

Table 21.1 Purchasing power parities and actual exchange rates per US dollar

	Actual exchange rate				PPP			
	1985	1990	1995	1999	1985	1990	1995	1999
US	1.00	1.00	1.00	1.00	1.00	1.00	1.00	1.00
Japan	237	144	94	114	222	195	170	161
UK	0.77	0.56	0.63	0.61	0.57	0.60	0.65	0.66
Euro area	n.a.	n.a.	n.a.	0.93	n.a.	n.a.	0.93	0.94

Source: OECD, Main Economic Indicators (Paris, various editions); OECD, OECD Economic Outlook (Paris, various editions).

familiar with *The Economist*'s Big Mac index will appreciate the shortcomings of the Law of One Price as applied to the price of hamburgers.[8] Comprehensive price comparisons, covering 2500 consumer goods and services, 250 types of machinery and equipment and 30 occupations in the public sector, tell a similar story. Actual exchange rates diverge considerably from what one would 'expect' on the basis of PPP.

Empirical PPP estimates nevertheless have many practical uses. They are widely used for comparing living standards between countries (as we have seen in Chapter 2). For example, the European Commission uses income comparisons based on PPP rather than current exchange rates in analysing regional convergence trends. *Eurostat* publishes data on the cost of living in the 15 capitals of the EU.[9] PPP figures are also used to calculate cost of living allowances for staff working overseas. Imagine the case of an executive about to be posted to Tokyo in 1999. The executive's current US salary is $50,000 p.a. How much yen would be required to provide a standard of living in Tokyo equivalent to that provided by a salary of $50,000 in the US? At the 1999 market rate of exchange (114 yen to the dollar), the answer would be 5.7 million. Consulting PPP data, however, we find a very different answer. As Table 21.1 shows, the PPP rate was 161 yen per dollar. Hence on this basis the executive would need 8 million yen in order to have maintained the US standard of living. Clearly there is room for negotiation!

Discrepancies between the PPP and the actual exchange rate are common. In 1985, when the dollar was strong, the PPP rate was 222 yen to the dollar, but at that time the actual exchange rate, at 237 yen to the dollar, was *higher* than the PPP rate. (In terms of our example, the firm should have paid the executive fewer yen than the market rate translation.) In a world of fluctuating currencies, market exchange rates can be a poor indicator of international comparisons of costs of living.

---

8 In 1986 *The Economist* launched a Big Mac index. The idea was that McDonalds went to great pains to ensure consistent quality no matter where the Big Mac was sold. Hence, the Law of One Price would suggest that the domestic price in each country multiplied by the dollar exchange rate should equal the US price ($2.36 in 1996). Needless to say no such correspondence is found. The local price of a hamburger depends on non-traded inputs such as rents and labour, and both taxes and other degrees of competition differ between countries. For these and many other reasons, the Law of One Price and, by extension, PPP do not hold.

9 Eurostat, *Cost-of-Living Comparisons in the European Union* (Luxembourg).

Relative PPP indices, although more plausible theoretically than the absolute indices, have yielded mixed results in analysing and forecasting exchange rates. A study of exchange rate change in major currencies published in the early 1980s referred to the 'collapse' of PPP.[10] Later studies indicate equally unfavourable results when applied to the experience of the dollar, yen and Deutschmark. Relative PPP fared better when tested against the experience of smaller European countries. This probably reflects the fact that closer trade ties, lower transport costs and policy convergence provided a more favourable environment for arbitrage, which is the key mechanism driving the PPP model. Also, PPP performs better when tested against the weighted average EER rather than against bilateral rates.

PPP tends to perform poorly when large structural shocks occur, such as the oil price increases in the 1970s, a rapid increase in unemployment or a deterioration in a country's fiscal position. In these circumstances the market's perception of the economy – its capacity to adhere to a low inflation regime, its commitment to finance its debts, etc. – undergoes significant change. Actual or anticipated political instability also impacts severely on the exchange rate. (These events may not necessarily affect the *present* current account balance, but they could have important implications for the *future* balance.) It is the anticipation of future difficulties which motivates capital flows and moves the exchange rate. Furthermore, PPP is not useful in the very short term, which is the trader's perspective. Most dealers regard it as at best a proximate indicator of the future exchange rate with a wide +/− 25 per cent of plausible variation for the exchange rate over the medium term.

Yet for all its limitations, PPP analysis provides essential input to understanding exchange rate trends:

- It works well in the long run, especially in conditions of very large differences in inflation.

- It provides a guide to the general trend in exchange rates, in particular where the main changes underlying the trend are of monetary origin.

- In a quasi-fixed exchange rate system, inflation differences give a useful indicator of pressure for currency realignment.

- For the conduct of macroeconomic policy, it is an important reminder that the exchange rate and the price level cannot be divorced from each other. Policies which affect the trend of domestic (relative to foreign) prices are likely to affect the exchange rate.

PPP is an important benchmark for the analysis of movements in the exchange rate, particularly in the medium to long run and as a gauge of international price competitiveness. But there is still the problem of explaining divergence from PPP. In a floating exchange rate system, short-term currency volatility tends to overpower everything else, including PPP. Why is this so?

---

10 J. Frenkel, 'The collapse of PPPs during the 1970s', *European Economic Review* (May 1981).

21.3 Capital flows and exchange rate volatility

Knowledge of a country's economic 'fundamentals' – its inflation rate, balance of payments, growth rate, and so on – is a necessary input for understanding of exchange rate movements. But it is not sufficient. To understand the reasons for exchange rate volatility, we must study the determinants of international capital flows. These flows, not sudden changes in economic fundamentals, are responsible for most of the turbulence observed in the foreign exchange markets.

The growing volume of capital movements has forced a rethink of traditional exchange rate theory. The PPP and balance of payments approaches concentrate on the equilibrating role of the exchange rate in balancing *flows* of foreign exchange. The modern approach emphasises the role of the exchange rate in bringing supply and demand of domestic and foreign *assets* into equilibrium. The assets in question consist of cash, bills and bonds of varying maturity and equities held in different currencies. Investment in these assets is highly mobile, and moves to wherever the expected return is greatest. The expected return is determined by: (a) the difference between the present interest rate at home and abroad, and (b) expected future changes in exchange rates, interest rates, probability of repayment, etc. Thus, expectations about the future play a key role in determining the present deployment of assets. Any change in these expectations will call forth portfolio adjustment by domestic and foreign investors. During periods dominated by unexpected events ('news'), asset prices will be subject to frequent and substantial change. Hence, the exchange rate will exhibit a high degree of volatility. Since, by definition, 'news' cannot be predicted on the basis of past information, *by and large fluctuations of exchange rates associated with 'news' will be equally unpredictable*. Also, if 'news' of a significant nature occurs often, exchange rate fluctuations will be not only unpredictable, but also very large.

Of course, current account transactions are also, to some extent, influenced by expectations. The decision to enter an export market or to expand capacity is based not just on present prices and costs, but also on the expected evolution of the price-cost matrix into the future. These predictions are formed under the same conditions of uncertainty as apply to capital transactions. The crucial distinction, however, concerns the *different speed of response between asset and goods prices*. As expectations change in response to unexpected events ('news' and 'shocks'), owners of capital can take lightning decisions on how to allocate their assets. Flows of goods and services are much slower to change. Companies must have regard to market share; they are loath to abandon certain markets, as they expect that exchange rate changes will be compensated by offsetting changes in domestic costs. Price stability for certain products can be an important attribute in itself, and price changes are costly to implement. It takes time to enter and to exit a market. For these reasons, the prices of most goods and services are less responsive than asset prices to changes in expectations. Short-run asset movements, therefore, will tend to dominate current account transactions, and the exchange rate may frequently change in response to expectations, even if relative product prices do not change. This explains why breaches of the PPP rule are common in the short run.

Interest rate parity

There are two main determinants of international portfolio capital movements: (a) the difference between interest rates at home and abroad, and (b) expectations about future exchange rates. Suppose, for example, that the rate of interest is 10 per cent in the UK and 5 per cent in Japan. Assuming capital between these countries is free to move, the question arises as to why fund managers do not immediately reallocate capital from Japan, where it is earning only 5 per cent per annum, to the UK, where it could earn 10 per cent per annum. Rational investors must have some reason for permitting this apparent anomaly to continue. According to the theory of interest rate parity, the reason is that the yen is expected to appreciate relative to sterling. This expected appreciation compensates exactly for the interest forgone by keeping money in Japan. The equilibrium condition is:

domestic interest rate *less* foreign interest rate = expected change in exchange rate.

This relationship is known as the *Uncovered Interest Rate Parity* (UIP).[11]

What determines exchange rate expectations? Obviously, they are much influenced by systematic changes in economic fundamentals such as persistently high balance of payments deficits, inflation, money supply growth or government budget deficits. One way to quantify the effects of these different influences would be to regress the interest rate differential on a selection of 'fundamentals'. Empirical analysis, however, repeatedly yields disappointing results in such cases. Economic fundamentals do play a role, but that role is difficult to quantify, and accounts for only part of total exchange rate variation.

One problem might be that we are using the wrong dependent variable. If the interest parity condition does not hold, interest rate differences may not be a good proxy for the market's (unobservable) exchange rate expectations. An alternative approach is to use the *forward exchange rate* as a proxy for exchange rate expectations. The forward exchange rate represents the rate at which, say, dollars can be traded for pounds today, deliverable at a specific date in the *future*. If that rate were, in any one transaction, considered too high, entrepreneurs would enter the market in the expectation of making a profit. In so doing, the market price will shift in a direction closer to their expectations. Hence, the forward rate for each time-period in the future represents the market's best guess of what the future spot rate will be. It closely resembles the currency forecasts regularly compiled by financial journals.

The *Covered Interest Rate Parity* (IRP) theory states that there will be a close tie between the forward exchange rate and differences in the interest rates; otherwise opportunities for riskless profit arise by arbitraging between the spot and forward market.

---

11 It is also called the International Fisher Equation, after Irving Fisher, the originator of the idea that the nominal interest rate is divisible into a real rate and a premium due to expected inflation or, in this case, currency depreciation.

Table 21.2 An example of the forward market

	Interest rate	Interest difference
Pound sterling	6.5%	–
Yen	0.4%	−6.1%
US dollar	7.0%	+0.5%

	Spot	1-year forward	% change
Yen	164.1	154.5	+6.0
US dollar	1.498	1.507	−0.6

A practical example may illustrate this point. On 31 July 2000, one-year international interest rates were as reported in Table 21.2.[12] Sterling interest rates were 0.5 percentage points lower than the dollar and 6 percentage points higher than the yen. Focusing on the sterling–yen relationship, recall that the explanation why fund managers do not move capital to the UK is that they expect sterling to fall relative to the yen. We now check if this is true, on the assumption that the forward rate is a measure of exchange rate expectations. The theory predicts that as the market expects sterling to depreciate relative to the yen – and that the amount of the expected depreciation should be just about the same as the difference in interest rates (6 per cent) – the yen should be selling at 6 per cent premium relative to sterling.

The data indicate that this presumption is approximately correct. The spot rate was 164 yen per pound. The yen was trading in the forward market at 154, a 6 per cent premium. This signalled the market's belief that the yen would appreciate relative to sterling over the year.

The next step is to ask a much researched question: how well does the forward exchange rate track future movements in the spot exchange rate? The answer can be found by comparing the forward market rate at time t for delivery at time $(t + 1)$, f_t^{t+1}, with the future spot rate, S_{t+1}. The results indicate that the forward rate tracks the future spot rate very poorly. This means that, even if it were possible to explain the forward rate by exchange rate fundamentals, we would still be unable to explain actual movements in the spot rate. (In the specific example of Table 21.2, readers will be able to check market expectations against the outcome in July 2001.) Interestingly, however, the results also show that the forward rate is an *unbiased* predictor of the future rate (see Box 21.4). This suggests that there is no systematic source of bias in the forward rate's predictions of the future.[13] But, regardless of the bias of the forecasts, the variance of the forecasts and of the subsequent spot exchange rates is extremely high. This is because exchange rates are affected by shocks which are intrinsically unpredictable.

---

12 International money rates are the interest rates which deposits in each currency would attract on the international market (i.e. free of any distortions from domestic authorities).

13 If bias did exist, that would be a challenge to find the missing systematic factors. Note, incidentally, that interest rate parity is not expected to hold exactly. Central bank intervention and transactions costs alone will prevent complete parity being realised.

Attempts to relate exchange rate 'overshooting', defined as excessive volatility in relation to its long-run equilibrium value, to changes in economic fundamentals indicate that exchange rates are far more volatile than the underlying fundamentals. The fundamentals do sometimes change rapidly and unexpectedly, and 'shocks' and 'news' undoubtedly contribute to volatility. But the 'news' component in any situation is difficult to estimate, and no combination of 'news' or 'shock' variables has yet been able to explain comprehensively the volatility of exchange rates.[14] Since informational surprises about fundamentals do not explain exchange rate changes, the search for an explanation has extended in two directions.

'Bubbles' and *'bandwagons'* refer to the possibility that investors behave irrationally. Prices are chased upwards for no well-based reason, the upward spiral is fuelled by the bandwagon effect or herd instinct – both features of many speculative markets. Famous examples of bubbles in the seventeenth and eighteenth centuries include the Mississippi Land Scheme in Paris in 1719–20, the related South Sea Bubble in London during the same period, the Dutch Tulip Bubble in 1636, and the Railway Mania in England in 1846–7. In each case frenetic and apparently irrational price surges were followed by a massive price collapse (hence the bubble analogy). Bubbles are not exclusively a phenomenon of the remote past. The property booms of the 1980s in the UK and the US had similar characteristics. Bubbles and bandwagons also affect currency markets. Much forex dealing defies rational explanation. Investors move in because everyone else is doing so. One irreverent insider described the market as 'a disparate group of highly-paid people with a common economic purpose but with the collective intelligence of a baby trout'.[15] But all investors in bubbles are not necessarily irrational. It may make good sense to invest in a bubble, provided the investor knows when to sell out! Although it was common knowledge that the dollar was overvalued in the mid-1980s, it was not rational for any one trader to sell dollars, nor for any fund committee to order its manager to sell its dollar holdings. The reason was that participants did not know the precise time at which the trend reversal would take place. The time-horizon of the investor is a critical variable – many traders and investors take a very short-run view.[16]

Technical analysis, or chartism, is widely used by foreign exchange traders.[17] Basically, it involves the use of graphical representations of past price fluctuations

---

14 Often what matters is not the change in the economic fundamental, but whether it is higher or lower than 'expected' by market.

15 M. Baker, *A Fool and his Money* (London: Orion, 1995). Inevitably, there are different views as to whether exchange markets fluctuate more than underlying fundamentals; empirical tests have been inconclusive (see R. Meese, 'Testing for bubbles in the foreign exchange markets: A case of sparkling rates', *Journal of Political Economy*, April 1986). There are, however, such things as 'rational stochastic speculative bubbles'!

16 Another example of apparently irrational behaviour is the *peso problem*. From April 1954 to August 1976, the spot peso exchange rate was fixed at 0.08 dollars per peso. Despite the spot rate being constant during this period of over 20 years, futures and forward contracts sold at a discount. This reflected the small probability of a large, discrete shift in the value of one or more of the 'fundamentals' which would force a devaluation of the exchange rate. Up to 1976 it appeared that the forward rate was an inefficient (biased) estimator; after, the market was seen to be right.

17 Chartism was originated around the late 1800s by Charles Dow. He formulated a basic theory of trading which is a forerunner of modern technical analysis and produced a number of rules for forecasting, all connected with the identification of trends in prices.

Box 21.4

Are foreign exchange markets efficient?

The foreign exchange market is efficient if it fully and correctly utilises all available information in forecasting exchange rates. If the market uses the best possible forecast of future exchange rates, then no superior forecast exists, and there can be no sustained advantage to speculation. Formally:

Market efficiency implies that:

$$f_{t+1}^t = E_t[S_{t+1}] + P_t + u_{t+1}$$

where: f_{t+1}^t = forward (*t*+1) market price at time *t*

$E_t[S_{t+1}]$ = a mathematical expectation conditional on the information set available at time *t*

S = the spot rate

P = the market risk premium

u = a random variable.

The *efficient market hypothesis* states that: u_t is a random variable with mean zero (white noise). In other words:

the gap between the forward rate and the spot rate actually ruling when the forward contract matures is the sum of two components: a completely random expectational error and a risk premium.

The forward rate is an unbiased predictor of the spot rate provided the investors are risk-neutral, implying *P* is constant, i.e. actual change in spot rate = the expected future rate plus or minus a random error.

The forward rate, however, often fails to detect key turning points. The rule-of-thumb hypothesis that *S* follows a random walk, i.e.

$$S_t = S_{t-1} + u_t$$

has been found to slightly outperform a number of different models (Meese and Rogoff, 1983).

Is u_t random? Most studies suggest that it is, but there is also some evidence that currency markets have become less efficient in the last decade, contrary to what one would expect. One way to test for this is to examine expectations, as found, say, in the *Eurocurrency Investors Review* and other summaries of exchange rate forecasts, to see if they are 'rational'. If they are, the difference between $E[S_{t+1}]$ and S_{t+1} should be the random variable u_t.

The problem with this test is that there is a wide divergence of forecasts, they can change rapidly and they are difficult to summarise. The median forecast rate was chosen by Frankel and Froot (1987). Their survey revealed a persistent bias in respondents' expectations, particularly in the mid-1980s. But, unless we can identify an alternative which will consistently outperform the models used for such forecasts, knowing that the forecasts are biased may be of little practical use. The authors ruefully concluded that: 'there is nothing in our results to suggest that it is easy to make money speculating in the foreign exchange markets' (p. 295).

Sources: R. Meese and K. Rogoff, 'Empirical exchange rate models of the seventies: Do they fit out of sample?', *Journal of International Economics* (1983); J.A. Frankel and K.A. Froot, 'Using survey data to test standard propositions regarding exchange rate expectations', *American Economic Review* (1987).

for forecasting purposes. Foreign exchange traders use technical analysis for general guidance. The key to successful technical analysis is the accurate and consistent determination of current trend. The aim is not to explain but to identify trends from careful examination of past data, including analysis of moving averages, past peaks and troughs. Exchange rates are often strongly influenced by support and resistance points, that is, specific rates which are hard to breach, because at that rate the market tends to consider the exchange rate too low or too high. Resistance and support points tend to congregate around whole numbers or those with a special resonance. The reasons for this resistance have to do with market sentiment rather than with meticulous examination of fundamentals. Likewise, a falling currency will often receive support from the market after a certain level of decline has been reported. Experience shows that support and resistance points are subject to change once the market is given sufficient time to adjust to a new set of parities.

Chartism has an exotic jargon of its own: *head and shoulders, reverse head and shoulders, double bottom, flags* and *pennants*. For all this, chartists have had mixed results in forecasting exchange rates. Some individual chartists have scored very highly, but the variance is high and there is a low degree of consensus among the various forecasters. Like the theories based on economic fundamentals, chartism cannot be ignored – but neither can it be relied upon.[18]

The coexistence in the foreign exchange market of chartists and 'fundamentalists', the former relying on technical analysis and the latter relying on analysis of economic fundamentals, can give rise to considerable instability of its own. Some experiments have been made to apply chaos theory to explain exchange rate gyrations.[19] Work in this area is still in its infancy.

A point of practical importance is whether exchange rate volatility 'washes out' over time. The evidence suggests that it does not. A comparison of returns to different currency portfolio shows sustained differences in the average annual return between different currencies. In an illustrative example (see Table 21.3) we see that the highest average annual return accrued to a holder of yen and French francs (12 per cent p.a.), and the lowest to a holder of Deutschmarks (10 per cent p.a.) during the period from the late 1970s to the early 1990s. The variance is highest in the case of the dollar, yen and sterling. Over a long period, a difference of even one percentage point matters a great deal. Hence, although often a frustrating exercise, the reward for getting exchange rate forecasts right is sufficiently high to justify continuing investment into finding a better predictive model. The persistence of different long-run rates of return, after correcting for variance, reinforces the view that exchange rate volatility can lead to *exchange rate*

---

18 M. Taylor and H. Allen, 'Chart analysis and the foreign exchange market', *The Bank of England Quarterly Bulletin* (November 1989).

19 Systems that exhibit sensitivity to the initial conditions and that show a seeming randomness or irregularity in their trajectory are called *chaotic systems*. The outcome of a chaotic system can be predicted (it is by definition a deterministic process), but for a relatively short time only. The overall long-term evolution of the system in a general sense can also be predicted. For an application of this approach to exchange rates, see P. De Grauwe, H. Dewachter and M. Embrechts, *Exchange Rate Theory: Chaotic models of foreign exchange markets* (Oxford: Blackwell, 1993).

Table 21.3 Historical rates of return, 1979–92

Selected individual currency portfolios						
Period	*US dollar*	*Japanese yen*	*Deutschmark*	*Pound sterling*	*French franc*	*Dutch guilder*
(a) Annual average return	11.81	12.67	10.24	12.04	12.18	10.59
(b) Standard deviation	31.33	25.56	8.73	19.06	7.81	8.07
(c) Risk : return ratio	2.65	2.02	0.85	1.58	0.64	0.76

Sources: Computed from IMF, *International Financial Statistics*.

misalignments, sustained over fairly long periods. Exchange rate misalignments cannot be predicted in advance, they cannot be cheaply covered against, and they can add significantly to the difficulties of a company trading on international markets.

21.4 Strategies for coping with exchange rate risk

Faced with continuing uncertainty in exchange rates, the first priority of most companies is to protect themselves against the risks of unexpected exchange rate changes. Managers frequently assert that they are in business to trade and manufacture, not to speculate in foreign currency.[20] A wide range of instruments can be used to close off exchange risks. However, the more volatile the exchange rates (hence risk), the more resources have to be spent in order to hedge this risk.[21]

Using the forward market

The forward and futures markets offer a number of instruments to companies wishing to reduce their exposure to exchange rate risk.

A foreign exchange *forward contract* is an over-the-counter (OTC) transaction between a bank and its customer (a company wishing to minimise exchange rate risk), whereby the bank agrees to buy or sell a specified amount of currency at an agreed rate for delivery at a specified future date. This is a highly flexible instrument which can be tailored to individual companies' requirements – forward contracts are flexible on the principal amount, on start and expiration dates, and they can be written in all major currencies. The foreign exchange will be transacted at the agreed forward contract rate irrespective of any exchange rate movements over the lifetime of the contract. In this way, the forward contract eliminates exchange rate risk for the company.

---

20 J. Roberts, *$1,000 Billion a Day: Inside the foreign exchange markets* (London: HarperCollins, 1995); also M. Goldstein *et al.*, *International Capital Markets: Part 1. Exchange rate movements and international capital flows* (Washington, DC: IMF, 1993).
21 Stable exchange rates would thus benefit all firms in the long run (except for banks).

Returning to the Table 21.2 example of the forward market on 31 July 2000, note that the yen was trading at a premium *vis-à-vis* the pound sterling, i.e. the forward rate for delivery in one year's time was 154.5 yen per pound sterling, compared with the spot rate of 164 per pound. By contrast, the US dollar was trading at a *discount*, i.e. the forward rate for delivery of dollars in twelve months was 1.51 dollars per pound, compared with a spot rate of 1.49 per pound.

The forward market enables companies to close-off any risk of loss from movements in the exchange rate. The downside of the transaction is that it also closes off the possibility of gain. Thus, suppose the yen were to appreciate more than the forward rate indicates; an exporter to Japan would have done better by converting yen at the time of sale (one year later) into the domestic currency. An exporter to the US who had believed that the dollar would depreciate by less than the forward rate would also have made money. Often firms worry about the danger of losing advantage to competitors which are less risk-averse and more ready to gamble on their instincts about future exchange rate developments.

Forward transactions cover the firm's exchange risk by transferring the risk to the bank supplying the forward contract. Consider a UK bank which agrees to sell euros three months forward to a domestic company at a rate of 60p per euro. The forward contract eliminates exchange rate risk for the company, but it places the bank in an exposed position. If the euro appreciates, the bank will lose money. Prudence dictates that the bank should take action to limit its exposure. To do this, it will engage in offsetting transactions in the wholesale market. A German bank which had offered forward contracts to its domestic customer in the opposite direction of the UK bank, for example, would be an ideal partner in such a deal. A *swap* could be arranged on the wholesale market which matched each currency exchange with a reverse exchange on a forward basis. Many forward contracts are written as part of a swap. Since the forward rate is agreed for both contracts, there is no exchange risk for the participants. Swaps are flexible and are used to hedge against specific foreign exchange (forex) risk and maturity exposures; they can also move exposure forward or back in time.[22] Thus, behind every retail transaction, there is usually a large set of associated wholesale transactions. The value of the latter greatly exceeds the value of retail foreign exchange transactions.

A foreign exchange *futures contract* is similar to a forward contract in that it secures a fixed exchange rate for receipt or payment at a future date. Unlike forward contracts, futures contracts are traded on the open market. To enhance marketability, they are standardised with regard to expiration dates and currencies. They cannot be tailored to a company's individual needs in the way a forward contract can. For this reason, futures contracts are used primarily by forex traders rather than by individual firms seeking to cover risk. Most futures contracts are 'closed out' before they mature (i.e. sold back to the bank or to another company).

---

22 Banks in this situation reduce one set of risks but add another. This risk, called *counterparty risk*, concerns the possibility that the contracts entered into by the bank will not be honoured.

Options and hedges

Forward and futures contracts offer protection against forex risk to a company which has a definite commitment to make or receive a future payment in foreign currency. Options are resorted to in cases where future payments or receipts are uncertain.

Consider a company which is tendering for a foreign contract to be carried out at some future date. The company has to base its quotation on some estimated future rate for foreign currency. The company could sell its anticipated foreign currency income forward in order to cover its revenue side, but failure to secure the contract would leave it in a highly exposed position.

To avoid this risk, the company can enter into an *options contract* with the bank, securing a fixed rate for a fixed fee. A foreign currency options contract gives the company the right to buy (call option) or sell (put option) a specified amount of foreign currency *on* or *before* a specified expiration date at a fixed *strike* price. Unlike the forward or futures contract, the company is not obliged to exercise the option unless it chooses to do so. Options are written on either US or European exercise terms. Under US terms the option can be exercised at any time prior to maturity; under European terms it can be exercised only upon maturity. Corporate treasurers rely almost exclusively on over-the-counter options (OTCs), while large institutional investors rely more on traded options. Option contracts have been on the market since the early 1980s, and have become increasingly popular in recent years.

The company in our example would buy a *put* option from the bank. This confers a right, but not an obligation, to sell the foreign currency at the predetermined rate. The company could then be in a position to tender for the foreign contract without fear of exchange rate risk. If the contract is not awarded, the company merely lets the currency option lapse – or, if it pays to do so, it will sell the option on at a profit. If the tender is successful, the company will hold on to its forward option until the payment date under the contract. Currency options are an ideal instrument for managing the downside risk arising from exchange rate movements, while leaving open the upside potential for profits. The most an options purchaser can lose is the fee paid for the contract, while potential gains depend on the spread between the contract exchange rate and the spot rate.[23] An illustrative example of the possible outcomes is given in Box 21.5.

The above instruments may be used by companies to *hedge* risks associated with exchange rate changes.

> Hedging refers to the process whereby a company offsets an existing exposure in a given currency by taking an opposite position in that currency with the same or similar risk.

Given the wide array of foreign exchange instruments available and the explosion in derivatives trading, there are many possible hedging strategies: forward contracts, futures, swaps, options, forward swaps and even swap-options. Trade in currency options alone is doubling every three years and new instruments are being regularly devised. An example is the foreign exchange swaps involving the

---

23 Hence options contracts offer significant opportunity for speculative gain.

Box 21.5

A foreign currency options contract

A British company is tendering for a German contract and it enters into a *put* option, giving it the right to sell €160,000 on or before a date one year from now at a strike euro/sterling price of €1.60 per pound sterling. The cost of the option is a 3 per cent premium or fee on the capital value, i.e. €4800 or £3000.

1. **Where the tender is successful and the € depreciates to 1.80**
    (a) Company receives €160,000 as a result of the contract.
    (b) Exercises its put option and receives £ at €1.60 per pound   = £100,000
    (c) Market value of €160,000 at spot rate of 1.80   = £88,888
    (d) Profit from exercising option   = £11,112
    (e) Cost of option   = £3,000
    (f) Net profit   = £8,112

    Note that this is a *notional* profit. Had the company not taken out the options contract, it would have received only £88,888 instead of £100,000, a difference of £11,112. From this saving, we must deduct the cost of the option, £3000. Thus the net gain from having the option is £8112.

2. **Where the tender is successful and the euro appreciates to 1.40**
    (a) Company receives €160,000 as a result of the contract.
    (b) Does not exercise option, but pays cost of option, i.e. £3000.

    In the case of an appreciation of the euro, the company is better-off to let the option lapse. Under the options contract, the company would have received £100,000 for the €160,000, but by selling the euro on the spot market it could obtain £114,286. Although the £3000 premium must automatically be paid, the gain from selling at the new spot rate of 1.40 compensates for this. Thus the company makes a net gain of £11286.

3. **Where the tender is unsuccessful and the euro depreciates to 1.80**
    (a) Company does not receive contract.
    (b) Cost of purchasing €160,000 at spot rate of 1.80   = £88,888
    (c) Exercises profit option and sells euro at 1.60 per pound   = £100,000+
    (d) Profit from exercising option   = £11,112+
    (e) Cost of option   = £3,000−
    (f) Net profit   = £8,112

    The contract is not awarded but the company can sell the €160,000 at the more favourable rate of 1.60 as agreed in the options contract. This allows the company to make an actual profit of £8112.

4. **Where the tender is unsuccessful and the euro appreciates to 2.25**
    This case is similar to case (2), except for the fact that the company fails to secure the contract. It lets the option lapse.

Box 21.6

Example of a swap

Interest rates payable on five-year loan (% p.a.)

	US$	UK£
Firm A	8	10
Firm B	10	11

Assume five-year borrowing rates for Firm A and B in two currencies as above. Firm A can obtain loans at a cheaper rate in both currencies (in terms of Chapter 17, it has *absolute* advantage in both markets), but it can borrow *comparatively* cheaper in dollars relative to Firm B. We suppose further that Firm A wants to borrow sterling and Firm B wants to borrow in dollars for their respective trade and investment transactions.

An arrangement is now made by an intermediary bank as follows:

A borrows dollars @ 8 per cent.
A lends dollars to B @ 8.5 per cent which is currency that B wants to borrow.
B borrows sterling @ 11 per cent.
B lends sterling to A @ 9.5 per cent.
Firm A is satisfied because it now receives sterling at a cheaper rate than it would have paid had it borrowed on its own account.
Firm B obtains a dollar loan at 8.5 per cent, a saving of 1.5 per cent. If it lends sterling at 9.5 per cent, it breaks even. At any rate between 9.5 and 10 per cent, B makes a profit, as does A.

As a result of the swap, both firms are better off than they would be borrowing directly in the foreign currency on their own account. This is another example of mutual gains from trade based on comparative advantage. It gives an opening to banks arranging swaps for profitable arbitrage.

exchange of the principal and interest payments backed by a loan in one currency for the principal and interest payments on a loan in a second currency. Swaps allow firms to lower their cost of foreign exchange management in situations where the firm is better known and has easier credit terms in one market than another. They are often used to provide long-term financing in foreign markets where the forward market might not be developed (Box 21.6).

Internal methods of managing exposure

In addition to the use of market instruments, a firm might also choose to control currency risk through internal mechanisms of exposure management. These include netting, matching, leading and lagging, pricing policy and asset/liability management. These methods may not always be available to the firm – their use is restricted in some countries. For instance, in a country with no proper forex market and strict foreign exchange controls, it will be essential to develop internal methods of hedging.

Two or more companies which trade with each other might engage in a *netting* agreement, whereby they cancel out amounts payable and receivable, leaving only the difference to be settled. Similarly, it makes sense for an individual company to *match* its outflows and inflows in a given currency, using US dollar receipts to make US dollar payments, for example. Both these methods substantially reduce reliance on the foreign exchange markets.

Leading and lagging are techniques whereby a company advances or delays foreign currency payments when a devaluation or revaluation of the domestic currency is expected, in the hope of reducing the amount of domestic currency needed to settle its debts.

In situations where a devaluation of the domestic currency is expected, a company can cover its exposure by *invoicing in foreign currency* instead of in the domestic currency.

Geographical diversification of sales and purchases: firms can diminish risk by spreading it. This is the basic argument for diversifying exports and imports.

Asset and liability management strategy may be deployed to ensure that assets and liabilities are as far as possible matched in the same currency. Suppose a Japanese car manufacturer decides to establish a new plant in the US. The total cost of constructing the plant is $200 million. If the Japanese investors choose to finance the new plant by borrowing yen from a Japanese bank, they take on a large exposure to the dollar, all the more so if account is taken of value of future flow of dollar sales. If the dollar depreciates *vis-à-vis* the yen, the yen value of the company's US asset will fall, while the loan outstanding remains unchanged. The company can hedge this risk by borrowing the $200 million in dollars from a US bank. The company's dollar loan would be exactly matched by its asset of $200 million and its exchange rate exposure would be closed off in respect of that transaction.

Company exchange rate exposures

The unpredictable and volatile nature of international currency markets explains why exposure management is such an important area of policy for any company engaged in international trade. However, many companies still do not hedge exchange rate risk. Some, especially small firms, are deterred by the costs. Others might consider the risk of exposure worth accepting. The forward rate is as likely to be above, as it is to fall below, the future spot rate (by definition since it is an 'unbiased estimator'); thus a company which chooses not to hedge exchange rate risk leaves open the possibility of making large short-run gains. This, however, is a dangerous strategy. Spectacular losses, as well as gains, have been made on forex dealings; one short-run loss on a very large receipt or payment could be enough to drive the company out of business.

Alternatively, a company may actively seek such short-run gains by using the available instruments for speculative purposes. Large multinationals nowadays tend to have their own treasury departments which undertake the trading and cover functions that banks used to carry out for them. The treasury departments are often tempted, and sometimes encouraged by their Board of Directors, to try to earn profits by running a *net trading position* (accepting a net exposure) in different currencies. While the range of instruments available to companies to hedge their risks has expanded, these new instruments are equally useful for speculative purposes. Speculative activity is not confined to the banks and other financial institutions. The turmoil on international currency markets in recent years has increased the potential for short-run profit, and all types of companies have begun to participate in the market. As global competition intensifies, companies may be encouraged to use the foreign exchange markets for profit as well as for protection. This is especially likely where a company's competitors are engaged in speculative activity. The line between hedging and speculation is no longer as clear as it was.

Four much publicised examples of this activity are:

1. In early 1994, Metallgesellschaft, the German metals, mining and engineering group, incurred losses of more than DM 2 billion through futures contracts on oil (sometimes used as a currency hedge). A similar fate befell Ashanti Goldfields, an African gold mining firm, in 1999.

2. Quantum Fund, a hedge fund associated with George Soros, allegedly made profits of $1 billion out of sterling's fall from the exchange rate mechanism of the EMS in September 1992. The fund lost equally spectacular sums in the late 1990s.

3. Proctor and Gamble lost heavily in 1994 from a series of complex interest rate swaps.

4. The most spectacular case of all was the collapse in 1995 of one of Britain's oldest and most prestigious merchant banks, Barings Bank, as a result of unauthorised activities of an employee in Japanese stock market futures and options markets.

21.5 Conclusions

When the fixed exchange rate system was abandoned in 1973, a US dollar was worth ¥ 270. By mid 2000, it was worth just over ¥ 100. The pound sterling, which was worth US$4.80 in the mid-1950s, had fallen in value to US$1.50. These long-term trends have been accompanied by large variations in exchange rates over shorter (1–3-year) timespans. Exchange rate uncertainty is an important source of potential gain and loss to any business engaging in trade outside its national borders. As markets become more international, fewer firms can afford to ignore these issues.

Economic theory has no fully satisfactory explanation of exchange rate variations, but it can provide useful guidance. Relative inflation rates have certainly played a part in accounting for the historical strength of the Deutschmark and the yen relative to the dollar and sterling. These and other fundamentals, such as productivity growth, budget deficits and domestic investment rates, also go some way to explaining movements in the exchange rate. But we are still far short of having a theory which could provide a reliable basis for forecasting exchange rates. A survey on the literature by two long-standing experts concluded that:

> Exchange rates are moved largely by factors other than the basic, observable, macroeconomic fundamentals. Econometrically, most of the action is in the error term.[24]

The relative weights to be attached to the 'fundamentals' keep changing. Interest rates are seen as the crucial factor in some circumstances; in others it can be political stability, or inflation, or the budget deficit, and so on. The relationships are both unstable and dynamic. This conclusion amounts to a clear warning as to the inadequacy of the simple demand and supply diagram with which we began our discussion. This depicts a unique well-defined equilibrium exchange rate. If no such equilibrium exists (if we are in fact talking of a situation of a multiplicity of unstable equilibrium points), it might be better to think of equilibrium as a wide range of possible outcomes rather than a single equilibrium point. Taking a broader view might also bring us closer to the market where calculations based on purchasing power parity and suchlike are seen as providing *bounds* (of, say, plus or minus 25 per cent) within which 'the equilibrium' can be found. This approach is unsatisfactory and far short of the ideal, but may contain more intellectual honesty than chasing the will-o'-the-wisp of a unique correct value for the exchange rate – a value which time is bound to prove incorrect.

The foreign exchange market has become more similar to the stock market, the oscillations of which also continue to defy rational explanation. So much so that many market participants have become sceptical about the usefulness of economic models in exchange rate prediction and have turned instead to technical (chartist) analysis as a tool for forecasting. Some researchers are experimenting with the idea that the interaction of fundamentals and chartists in the foreign exchange market introduces a significant number of non-linearities to make chaotic motion in exchange rates possible (chaos theory).[25]

The reason why exchange rate changes are notoriously difficult both to explain and to predict can be boiled down to one major factor. Capital flows, not trade, make exchange rates change. Almost $1700 billion passes through the foreign exchange market per day: compared with which, world exports of $6000 billion per year fades into insignificance. Capital responds to exchange rate expectations and these are subject to seemingly irrational impulses and bandwagons. In the case of exchange rates, prediction is even more difficult than explanation.

---

24 J. Frankel and R. Dornbusch, 'The flexible exchange rate system: Experience and alternatives', in S. Borner (ed.), *International Finance and Trade* (London: Macmillan, 1988). A less restrained view of the fundamentals approach is contained in the laconic comment of a forex trader and friend of the author's: 'That's the theory. It sounds great. It doesn't work.'

25 Many would dismiss forecasts based on chartist analysis or chaos theory as mere guesswork. Perhaps the emergence of these forecasts is more a result of human dislike of the unknown than evidence of their superior performance.

Economic and political fundamentals change in a way which even the most savvy prophets cannot foresee.[26] Even if it were possible to obtain good forecasts of the fundamentals, exchange rate forecasts generated by the 'fundamentalist' model would, as we have seen, still be subject to large error. The precise impact of changes in each of the fundamentals on the exchange rate can be difficult to determine. Hence, the cynical advice: *in exchange rate forecasts, specify the level or the date, but never both.*

Exchange rates are highly volatile – much more so than domestic prices. This underlines the need for sound corporate strategy for dealing with foreign exchange risk. Various methods of coping with foreign exchange risk have been explained. Foreign exchange cover is needed not only for current transactions, but also to cover translation exposure in firms with assets and liabilities located in different countries and currency zones.[27] The provision of this cover can be costly, but the penalty for not having it may prove even more expensive. Large corporate treasurers have departed from the past practice of leaving forex management to their banks and are now managing it themselves to a much greater extent than before. For smaller companies, some elementary knowledge of hedging options and exchange rate risk is needed to ensure that they have an adequate level of protection for their business. But 'adequate' is not the same as 'complete'. Even the best practice techniques usually give only partial cover, as the quotation from the chief executive of Mercedes Benz at the start of this chapter exemplifies.

The present world exchange rate system has been characterised by misalignments and periodic currency crises. This is a source of worry for the smooth functioning of the international monetary system. Currency instability in the 1980s and early 1990s gave renewed impetus to the drive for a common currency in Europe. The wild oscillations in the exchange rates of emerging economies and the associated lasting damage done to countries such as Indonesia – has fuelled concern about the global financial system ('architecture'). The role of the IMF, in particular, is being re-examined Governments have progressed from concern about the *level* of the national exchange rate to concern about choosing the right exchange rate *regime* within which that level is determined. Exchange rate regimes are the subject of the next chapter.

---

26 One small set of people who might out-perform a random-walk model are market movers, such as central banks or fund managers, who have access to such enormous resources that their predictions can be self-fulfilling.

27 Also known as 'accounting exposure', translation exposure is that exposure which arises when a multinational company's foreign currency-denominated balances and transactions are consolidated into the group financial statements, denominated in the currency of the parent company. Exchange rate fluctuations may result in substantial translation losses or gains.

✔ Summary

1. Exchange rate movements can have a significant impact on a firm's bottom line. The net long-term impact depends on the extent of the 'pass-through' from exchange rate changes to the domestic price level and domestic costs and to the underlying price elasticities of demand.

2. There is no single, comprehensive theory of the exchange rate capable of explaining the violent swings in market exchange rates. Relative purchasing power parity (PPP) states that if prices in two countries change at a different rate, the exchange rate will appreciate or depreciate so as to preserve price, or purchasing power, parity between the two countries. PPP theories focus on relative inflation rates as the determinant of exchange rate behaviour. Other theories emphasise the balance of payments, different rates of money supply growth and portfolio asset effects.

3. Exchange rates remain difficult to predict, partly because economic 'fundamentals' change unpredictably and sometimes violently, partly because of irrational elements in foreign exchange markets such as bubbles and bandwagons and market 'sentiment'. The value of forex transactions on the market vastly exceeds the value of global trade in goods and services.

4. To cope with this volatility, business must understand its degree of exchange rate exposure and apply risk-reducing measures as appropriate. Use can be made of the forward market, swaps and options and other types of hedging instruments available on the market. Also there are *internal* mechanisms for reducing exposure such as netting, leads and lags, matching assets and liabilities. But there is no costless way of offsetting exchange rate risk, and each firm must carefully balance the benefits of risk reduction against the cost of the instruments to achieve it.

5. Because exchange rate volatility imposes costs on the trading sector, and through it on the economy, governments have begun to explore alternatives to a floating exchange rate regime such as currency area agreements or, in the limit, abolishing different national currencies and replacing them with a common currency as in Europe's euro.

❓ Questions for discussion

1. Purchasing power parity states that countries with high inflation rates tend to have depreciating currencies. Can you explain why?

2. Why should the discovery of a natural resource, say oil, be expected to lead to a strengthening of a country's currency?

    What effect would you expect such an appreciation to have on the oil-producing country's:

(a) manufacturing sector
(b) exporters
(c) consumers?

3. Why do large differences in interest rates continue to prevail between countries notwithstanding the increasing international mobility of capital which must tend to reduce them? (Consider, in your discussion, the contrast between, say, 10-year government bond yields in Japan and the US, 1.6 per cent versus 6.6 per cent respectively in mid-2000.)

4. Why are exchange rates volatile? What can government do to try to reduce such volatility? Does government action sometimes cause volatility?

5. Foreign exchange risk is a major concern for multinationals. Is exchange rate exposure a problem just for multinationals or could a firm with a wholly domestic market orientation also be affected?

6. Explain why firms with highly price-elastic demand for their product (price-takers) are more likely to be affected by currency fluctuations than those with low price-elasticity of demand (price-makers).

7. It has been said that 'good currency risk management and good business management are synonymous'. Do you agree? Discuss the main market instruments which a firm can purchase in order to reduce its foreign exchange exposure.

8. A company can also deal with the exposure problem through internal exposure management. What does this entail?

☞ Exercises

1. Suppose the one-year interest rate on British pound deposits is 8 per cent, the dollar interest rate is 6 per cent, and the current $/£ spot rate is $1.50.

    (a) What do you expect the spot rate to be in one year?
    (b) Suppose both the US and UK implement new policies that lead to an expected future spot rate of $2. Suppose further that the dollar interest rate rises to 7 per cent. What spot rate would be consistent with these two changes?

2. 'Overly strong currencies cut first into profits and then into market share, fewer jobs, financial instability and social unrest.' Comments of this nature were often made during 1995, as the Japanese yen soared and the Japanese economic growth declined.
    What indicators would you use to determine whether a currency is 'overly strong'? Explain the effects mentioned above (loss of profits, market share, etc.). Use data on Japan or on the economy of any other currency which you think might be overvalued to illustrate your answer.

3. A British company has to make a US$1 million payment in three months' time. It has a sterling balance of £550,000 available now and requires advice on whether to invest this amount in sterling or in dollars.

Given that:

the US deposit rate is 5 per cent p.a.
the sterling deposit rate is 8 per cent p.a.
the spot dollar exchange rate is £0.55
the three-month forward rate is £0.60.

(a) Where should the company invest for better return over the next three months?
(b) Assuming that interest rates and the spot exchange rate remain as above, what forward rate would make the firm indifferent between the two currencies?
(c) Assuming that the US interest rate and the spot and forward rates remain as above, where would you invest if the sterling deposit rate were to rise to 14 per cent p.a.?
(d) With the originally stated spot and forward rates and the same dollar deposit rate, what is the equilibrium sterling deposit rate?

Further reading

For a review of trends and theories see Richard Meese, 'Currency fluctuations in the post-Bretton Woods era', *Journal of Economic Perspectives* (Winter 1990). Robert Hutchinson, *Corporate Finance: Principles of investment, financing and valuations* (London: Stanley Thornes, 1995) provides a clear and incisive account of options and futures. Adrian Buckley, *Multinational Finance* (London: Phillip Allen, 1986) is very helpful on the subject of foreign currency exposure and techniques of exposure management. John Roberts, *$1000 Billion a Day: Inside the foreign exchange markets* (London: HarperCollins, 1995) is a breezy and highly informative insider's account of the dealing room. An accessible and comprehensive assessment of the ongoing literature on the topic is provided in Ken Rogoff, 'The purchasing power parity puzzle', *Journal of Economic Literature* (June 1996).

Appendix 21.1: The global foreign exchange market

The global foreign exchange market is the world's largest financial market. It is not a physical location; rather it comprises numerous financial centres around the world, connected via the telephone and other telecom devices which allow almost instantaneous transmission of information. The progressive liberalisation of cross-border capital flows, together with improvements in trading and settlement practices and the rapid advance of technology have resulted in an unprecedented expansion of foreign exchange trading over the past decade. Three broad categories of foreign exchange instruments are traded: contracts for spot delivery, forwards and swaps, and other derivatives. The most significant development in the market in recent years has been the expansion in trade in derivatives, notably interest rate options and futures (Table 21.A1). A *derivative* is an off-balance sheet agreement which defines certain financial rights and obligations which are contractually linked to interest rates, exchange rates or other market prices.

The foreign exchange market has expanded rapidly. Net daily turnover more than doubled during the 1990s. London remains the most active participant in the market, followed by New York and Tokyo.

Table 21.A1 **The expansion of financial derivatives markets**

	(US$ billion)			
Instruments	1986	1990	1995	1999
Exchange-traded instruments	583	2,292	9,185	14,035
Interest rate options and futures	526	2,054	8,605	12,179
Currency options and futures	49	72	81	130
Stock index options and futures	18	166	499	1,726
Over-the-counter instruments	500	3,451	17,990	88,201

Source: Bank for International Settlements Annual Report, 1995 and 1996; Bank for International Quarterly Review (June 2000).

Foreign exchange transactions are organised at wholesale (or interbank) or retail market level. There are four groups of participants: dealers (traders), brokers, customers (mainly institutional investors) and central banks. The wholesale market consists of dealers' trade both with other dealers and with non-dealing banks. Retail market transactions involve the banks and their customers. However, the rapid market developments of recent years have made the distinction between the two increasingly blurred; many larger retail customers have gained access to the wholesale market through improved communications with the dealing banks. Wholesale market activity dominates the foreign exchange market.

Dealers

The dominance of the wholesale market reflects dealers' position-taking activity. A position is simply a market commitment. For example, a dealer who buys a futures contract takes a long position; a dealer who sells a futures contract takes a short position. Dealers buy and sell foreign exchange on their own account and may take open positions in a currency. They are employed by banks and other financial institutions which need to have a continuing presence in the foreign exchange market. These are dominated by the forty or fifty large dealing banks which actually make markets. Market makers are dealers who stand ready to buy and sell assets at any time, thus satisfying the public's demand to trade immediately. Dealers can make enormous profits for the banks which employ them, but they can also make enormous losses. For this reason, most banks have internal controls, limiting the size of dealers' open positions. The limits on open positions, especially overnight positions, mean that banks try to offset the exposures that result from retail trades, either by finding another customer with exactly the reverse requirement or by trading on the wholesale market. If another bank is willing to undertake the reverse transaction, a 1:1 ratio between wholesale and retail orders is generated. If not, up to four or five wholesale market transactions may be needed to cover the risk associated with a forward, swaps or derivative contract. However, these internal controls are not as effective in some banks as in others, and some dealers may retain highly exposed positions. This can result in financial disaster, as the much-publicised collapse of Barings Bank in February 1995 demonstrated. A dealer operating from the Singapore branch of the bank built up a large exposure which involved Barings in losses well in excess of the bank's equity capital. Barings was sold to a Dutch bank, ING, for a nominal sum of £1.

Brokers

Brokers match orders to buy and sell currencies for a fee. However, unlike dealers, they cannot take positions themselves. Brokers keep a 'limit book' containing information on the public bid and ask prices of the dealers they (the brokers) have contacted, and match incoming demands for, or supplies of, foreign currency with the dealer currently offering the best price. To offer their clients the best prices, brokers must obtain the best possible information by remaining in frequent contact with the dealers. As the volume of transactions increases, this becomes increasingly difficult. Therefore, many of the larger banks have dispensed altogether with brokers; instead they maintain close relationships with the dealers themselves in order to have access to timely quotes.

Customers

Customers include non-financial companies and those financial institutions which do not maintain a constant presence in the market as dealers. Customers may enter the foreign exchange market to buy foreign exchange for imports and to sell foreign exchange received for exports. They may also use the forward, swaps and derivatives markets to hedge foreign currency exposure arising from foreign trade and investment. In addition, they may enter the market for speculative purposes.

The main players in the foreign exchange market have been the large dealing banks. These traditional players have been joined by a new set of players: institutional investors, such as pension funds, insurance companies, investment funds and bank trust departments.

Of these, pension funds are the largest players, followed by insurance companies. They are investing increasing proportions of their assets abroad in order to improve yield and reduce risk. Investment funds have also grown rapidly. Total assets managed by the world's 500 largest money managers amounted to $33.6 trillion in 1999.

Central bank

Central banks enter the market to satisfy the needs of their governments and to influence the exchange rate. The role of central banks becomes especially significant in times of extreme currency turmoil. A central bank might then intervene in the foreign exchange market directly, or else indirectly through interest rate policy, to relieve pressure for devaluation. The power of a modern central bank, however, has been much eroded in recent years by the twelvefold increase in the derivatives market since 1990 and by the associated growth of hedge funds and institutional investors in the forex market.

Chapter 22

EXCHANGE RATE REGIMES AND THE EURO

Introduction

In a free market, price is determined by the forces of supply and demand. As demand and supply conditions change, price fluctuates upwards and downwards. Normally such fluctuations would be seen as an expected feature of the market system, certainly not as evidence of a malfunction in the system which requires correction. We saw in Chapter 3 the danger of government attempts to suppress such flexibility. Black markets, queues and bureaucratic distortions are the unwanted and costly side-effects of such intervention.

The foreign exchange market is an unusual market. In one sense it has all the attributes of a perfectly competitive market (large numbers of buyers and sellers, full information, flexibility) from which the benefits of the free-market system might be expected to flow. The market price is flexible and volatile. To some this is by no means an unwelcome feature. Currency traders thrive when the market is unstable, since it is from hedging and speculative transactions that they derive their income. Others, notably those with a heavy involvement in real international transactions, are affected less benignly. To them, currency volatility can be costly and often threatening. They support official efforts to intervene in the market. Why should market forces be welcomed in one context but treated with suspicion in another?

Part of the answer lies in the volatile nature of the market. As we have seen, the foreign exchange market is unusually prone to destabilisation through 'overshooting' and 'undershooting' the equilibrium exchange rate. The 'herd instinct', described as 'a self-organising process of infection among traders', can lead to prices which deviate from fundamental values.[1] This volatility, in turn, can have strongly adverse repercussions on the economy, particularly in situations where there is rigidity in domestic prices and costs. Examples of such adverse effects include:

- large speculation-fed devaluation can disrupt domestic stabilisation and anti-inflation policy;
- competitive devaluations by a country's trading partners can damage trade relations;

---

1 See T. Lux, 'Herd behaviour, bubbles and crashes', *Economic Journal* (July 1995).

- currency turmoil in one part of the world can spread to other countries without apparent reason, involving a headlong rush into 'safe' currencies and out of non-core currencies, with consequent unwarranted revaluations and devaluations;
- long-term planning and investment decisions can be distorted by sustained currency misalignments.

This chapter analyses the case for government intervention in the foreign exchange market. The starting-point is that both the exchange rate *level* and the exchange rate *regime* are important for an economy. An exchange rate level which is too high creates problems for exporters; an exchange rate which is too low can lead to high costs of imported inputs and inflation.[2] An exchange rate regime which is too rigid can lock business into an unsustainable cost disadvantage: a regime which is too flexible generates uncertainty. Most businesses take the view that they have enough uncertainty to deal with as a result of global competition and open markets without having to cope with the extra expense and hassle of volatile exchange rates. Ideally the global exchange rate system should provide (a) a *level* of the exchange rate which leaves industry in a reasonably competitive state *vis-à-vis* foreign competitors, and (b) an exchange rate *regime* to ensure that this level is sustained. As we have seen, the free market has not been able to deliver either of these requirements.

The question posed in this chapter is whether governments, through intervention in the forex market and/or through selection of a different exchange rate regime, can create a more efficient outcome in transacting international business than a wholly free forex market.

Free market imperfections are not automatically corrected by state intervention. History suggests that this is particularly true of state manipulation of exchange rates. Many countries have suffered from ill-advised and politically motivated initiatives affecting their exchange rate. For example, the British economy suffered serious damage as a result of Churchill's insistence on a return to the gold standard in 1925 at an overvalued rate. The delayed devaluation of 1967 by the Wilson government also caused problems. Many economists have contended that the overvalued exchange rate in the early 1980s inflicted lasting injury on large sectors of UK industry and contributed to the 17 per cent decline in manufacturing jobs in the five years 1979–84. The adherence of the UK and Italy to what many believed was an overvalued rate *vis-à-vis* the Deutschmark led to the European currency crisis of 1992–93.[3]

Exchange rate reform concerns choosing the best system for maintaining a competitive exchange rate, while at the same time maintaining price stability.

---

2 'Yen's rise catastrophic, says Japanese business leaders' – *Financial Times* headline (20 April 1995) goes on to report the warning of the Japan Automobile Manufacturers' Association that the strong yen (80 yen per dollar) would affect employment levels. The Japanese government was urged to take action 'to calm currency markets'. (Of course, this pressure must be seen in context. Exports comprise only 9 per cent of Japan's GDP as compared with shares of three and four times that in most European countries.)

3 E. Roll, *Where Did We Go Wrong? From the gold standard to Europe* (London: Faber, 1995).

The choice of regime is an active item on the agenda of many countries, not only in Europe where the debate on participation in the euro gathers pace, but also in Latin America and among transition economies.

The exchange rate regime which is 'best' for an individual country is rarely self-evident, nor will adherence to it always be politically expedient. Much depends on the economy's stage of economic development, its trade patterns and the degree of economic integration with neighbouring countries. The well-being of an economy can be affected for good or ill by decisions on the exchange rate. While free-floating exchange rates lead to costly volatility, attempts to control the exchange rate, if based on mistaken analysis, can also inflict heavy costs on business.

Chapter outline

This chapter analyses what governments can and should do to set parameters on exchange rate movements in the following steps:

1. Description of the global exchange rate system. Today's world is characterised primarily by a floating system, but there are different types of floating regimes, and some countries have chosen to peg their exchange rate to another currency or group of currencies.

2. Assessment of the experience of the *floating currencies*.

3. The tools of intervention and the effectiveness of proposed measures to achieve greater exchange rate stability.

4. Economic and Monetary Union (EMU) and the introduction of the euro. For the 12 countries of the euro area, this has involved the abandonment of something close to a free float in favour of the extreme rigidity of a single currency.

22.1 The global exchange rate system

Under the Bretton Woods system, which lasted from 1946 to 1973, industrial countries' exchange rates were tied to the US dollar, and through it to gold, at 'fixed' parities. The exchange rate could be adjusted, but adjustments were infrequent and reluctant.[4] Since 1973, the major currencies have operated under a floating regime, while smaller countries have adopted a range of fixed and flexible options. The present global exchange rate system has the following features (Figure 22.1).

1. The world's three major currencies, the US dollar, the yen and the euro, are 'independently floating'. By this we mean that the authorities have not committed themselves to maintaining a particular value of their currency either *vis-à-vis* each other or *vis-à-vis* any other exchange rate index. At the

---

4 A brief history of the origins of the present system is provided in Appendix 22.1.

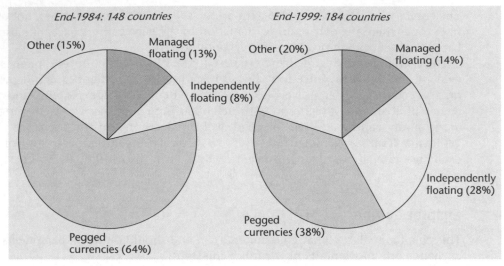

Figure 22.1 **Exchange rate arrangements, % of currencies**

same time, they do intervene in the forex market, and the exchange rate is considered an important factor in the economy.

2. A growing number of countries have adopted a flexible exchange rate regime. Within this group, which includes more than half of all currencies, a distinction is made between currencies which are 'independently floating' and those which are 'managed floating'. Exchange rates in the latter group are allowed to float, but only within certain limits. By the end of the 1990s, nearly one-third of all national currencies were independently floating and a further 14 per cent were managed floaters. Large developing countries such as India and Iran, small developed countries such as Norway and New Zealand, and many other small and medium-sized developing countries have converted to an independently floating system. However, the dividing line between independent and managed floaters is often blurred.

3. Some currencies are linked at a fixed rate ('pegged') to another currency or basket of currencies. Within the fixed-rate category, there are different types of arrangements. Some countries have pegged to a single currency: Argentina, Barbados, Ecuador and Panama to the US dollar, Estonia and Bulgaria to the euro, Lesotho to the South African rand. Others have adopted a composite peg or are tied to the SDR.[5] For example, Morocco's dirham is linked to the euro and the dollar. The degree of fixity of a currency link can itself be quite variable. Some countries choose a relatively fixed band of variation within which their currency can fluctuate, but others adjust the band regularly ('crawling bands'). Chile, Colombia, Israel and Poland are examples of crawling band currencies.

4. Although countries with pegged currencies are numerous, their combined economic weight in world trade is modest. They are mostly small open

5 SDR, or *standard drawing right*, is a notional unit of currency based on the world's major currencies.

Table 22.1 Exchange rate regimes and country characteristics

Country	Population (millions)	Openness (exports/GDP)	Currency	Exchange rate arrangement
Armenia	3.7	18.9	Dram	Managed float
Azerbeijan	7.6	24.5	Manat	Managed float
Belarus	10.2	62.0	Belarussian Rouble	Managed float
Bulgaria	8.3	45.2	Lev	Currency board
Czech Republic	10.3	60.0	Koruna	Managed float
Estonia	1.5	79.8	Kroon	Currency board (fixed to DM/Euro)
Georgia	5.3	14.0	Lari	Floating
Hungary	10.1	49.8	Forint	Pre-announced crawling peg
Kazakhstan	15.0	30.6	Tenge	Managed float
Kyrgyz Rep.	4.8	35.3	Som	Managed float
Latvia	2.4	47.7	Lats	Fixed to SDR
Lithuania	3.7	47.2	Litai	Currency board (fixed to DM/Euro)
Moldova	4.3	46.5	Leu	Floating
Poland	38.7	25.7	Zloty	Floating
Russia	146.7	31.7	Rouble	Managed float
Slovenia	2.0	56.7	Tolar	Managed float
Tajikstan	6.1	n.a.	Tajik	Managed float
Turkmenistan	4.8	n.a.	Manat	Fixed
Ukraine	50.1	39.8	Hryvnia	Managed float
Uzbekistan	24.0	22.2	Som	Managed float

Source: European Bank for Reconstruction and Development (EBRD), *Transition Report 1999* (London 1999), updated by author to June 2000; Openness figures are taken from The World Bank web page: www.worldbank.org

economies, for which a pegged system has important advantages which would not apply to a larger country.

5. Countries have been moving towards more extreme exchange rate regimes. Increased capital mobility makes a floating regime more viable; but it also makes a strong commitment to exchange rate fixity more attractive, under the umbrella of sustainable monetary and fiscal policies.

The diversity of options available within the world exchange rate system is reflected in the regimes chosen by countries of the former Soviet Union (Table 22.1). At one extreme are Russia, the Ukraine and Poland with flexible exchange rates. At the other are countries like Bulgaria and the Baltic states, which have adopted a peg to other currencies. Generally the trend has been towards more flexible exchange rate regimes in these countries.

Many countries are dissatisfied with their exchange rate regime, but each is dissatisfied for different reasons. The major industrial countries worry about the destabilising effects of large exchange rate fluctuations on national prestige, competitiveness and inflation. Developing countries have still different concerns. Many feel vulnerable to speculative attack and seek security by attaching their national currencies to *exchange rate anchors*.

22.2 Floating exchange rates

> There are no major difficulties to prevent the prompt establishment by countries of a system of exchange rates freely determined in open markets, primarily by private transactions, and the simultaneous abandonment of direct controls over exchange transactions. A move in this direction is the fundamental prerequisite for the economic integration of the free world through multilateral trade.[6]

Milton Friedman's advocacy of flexible exchange rates in 1956 rested on the proposition that a system of freely floating exchange rates was 'the fundamental prerequisite' for achieving free trade. Ironically, many economists now regard floating rates as a danger to free trade. To understand why we need to understand both the theory itself and how the system has worked out in practice.

Floating exchange rates – in theory

Any economy is vulnerable to shocks – to 'real' shocks, such as changes in composition of demand and supply, and to 'monetary' shocks, such as the creation of excessive money supply, or foreign capital outflows. Suppose a shock leads to an outward shift in the country's demand for foreign exchange (from D_0D_0 to D_1D_1 in Figure 22.2). If the exchange rate is fixed at E_0, an excess demand equal to Q_0Q_1 will develop. This excess demand can be dealt with by:

1. central bank intervention, supplying Q_0Q_1 of foreign currency in each period;
2. import controls or similar trade interventions designed to bring the demand for foreign exchange back to D_0D_0;
3. improvement in cost competitiveness, resulting in a fall in the demand for imports. The demand curve will shift backwards from D_1D_1 towards D_0D_0;
4. cutbacks in domestic spending, leading to a lower domestic demand for imports and traded goods.

If the exchange rate were flexible instead of fixed, a fifth possibility would be:

5. a depreciation in the exchange rate, leading to a new equilibrium at OE^*, with value of foreign exchange transactions OQ^*.

The case for flexible exchange rates is that option 5 is more efficient than any of options 1–4. With respect to option 1, it is clear that central bank intervention can last only for a limited period. The case against option 2 is that the exchange rate system exists to facilitate trade, not to hinder or restrict it. To save the system by restricting the benefits of trade is to subvert its *raison d'être*. The objections to adjustment options 3 and 4 need more careful analysis. Reductions in spending will, of course, bring about equilibrium. As national spending falls, so does demand for imports. Simultaneously, there is a decline in demand for domestically produced goods, thereby releasing resources to produce more

---

6 M. Friedman, 'The case for flexible exchange rates', in *Essays in Positive Economics* (Chicago: University of Chicago Press, 1953), p. 173.

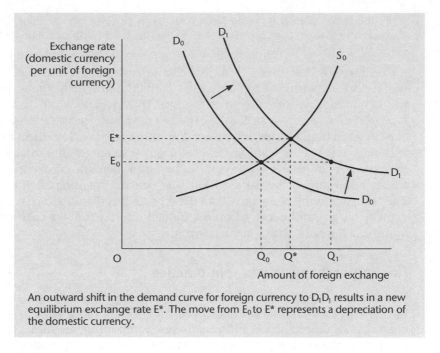

An outward shift in the demand curve for foreign currency to D_1D_1 results in a new equilibrium exchange rate E*. The move from E_0 to E* represents a depreciation of the domestic currency.

Figure 22.2 Changes in the exchange rate and payments imbalances

exports. Hence lower spending is associated with a lower demand for foreign exchange and a greater supply. This process is further strengthened by a fall in the domestic price level. The income and spending effects are then reinforced by a competitive effect. Domestic prices fall relative to foreign prices. Exports and import-competing industries become more competitive, at each given exchange rate. S_0S_0 will shift outwards, and D_1D_1 will shift inwards. A new equilibrium will be established at the unchanged exchange rate E_0, somewhere between Q_0 and Q_1. In an economy with perfectly flexible prices, a fall in domestic prices has exactly the same effect on the forex market as a devaluation of the same percentage.

If domestic prices are flexible downwards, the adjustment can take place with minimal real effects on economic activity. However, if domestic prices are inflexible, the entire burden of adjustment falls on real income. The fall in aggregate spending (demand) will lead to increased unemployment and lower output rather than lower domestic prices. In such circumstances a devaluation of the exchange rate is a more efficient way of restoring equilibrium. In a memorable analogy, Friedman likened the argument for flexible exchange rates to the argument for daylight saving time. Why, he asked, do we change the clock in summer when exactly the same result could be achieved by having each individual change routine? The reason is that:

> it is much simpler to change the clock that guides all than to oblige each individual separately to change his patterns of reaction to the clock, even though all want to do so.

By the same token it is far simpler to allow one price to change, namely, the price of foreign exchange, than to rely upon changes in the multitude of prices that together constitute the internal price structure.[7]

Contrary to what many think, speculators are not seen as a problem in this theoretical framework. Suppose traders correctly anticipate the outward shift in the demand curve for foreign exchange. They will have an incentive to buy foreign currency now, wait for the expected devaluation, and then sell the foreign currency at a higher price in terms of domestic currency. The effect of their action will be to raise the spot price of foreign exchange in anticipation of the forthcoming imbalance between supply and demand. This gives producers advance warning of the depreciation, and spreads out the period of adjustment. The adjustment, by being anticipated, becomes less disruptive. The exchange rate depreciates gradually, instead of in a sudden discrete fall. Speculation performs a useful *stabilising* function in such instances.

Floating exchange rates – in practice

Flexible exchange rates, therefore, have many cogent arguments in their favour, not only in theory but also in practice. Under the floating system, countries have been able to adjust their economies to new competitive realities, global trade has risen faster than world production, GATT rounds of trade liberalisation have been concluded, and the system has been able to cope with the huge increase in capital transactions.

One practical advantage of a floating system is the *increased autonomy* it gives to governments in the conduct of their monetary policies. This is seen as a major advantage by the industrial powers. Their monetary authorities are committed to price stability. Once this is achieved, the precise value of the currency can be decided by the market. Some small countries also have found this an appealing argument. New Zealand and Switzerland are among the many countries that have operated successfully under a free floating system (Box 22.1), while several transition countries such as Poland and Slovenia have also opted for flexible rates.[8]

Another advantage of floating is that it places a *low foreign reserves requirement* on the country. For some poorer countries this may be a decisive consideration. They may lack the resources to finance a peg even if they wanted to. In the case of Poland and Slovenia, for example, the scarcity of foreign reserves was a prime factor in their decision to adopt flexible exchange rates.

This is the positive side of the story. The negative side comes to the fore whenever the forex markets are in turmoil. At such times, countries find their currencies shifting by large discrete amounts – with severe impacts on the real economy – for seemingly inexplicable reasons. Criticism of volatility in the real exchange rate focuses on three points:

---

7 Ibid.
8 T.D. Willett and F. Al-Marhubi, 'Currency policies for inflation control in the formerly centrally planned economies', *World Economy* (November 1994).

Box 22.1

How small industrial countries choose an exchange rate regime

The choice of exchange rate regime is never straightforward, particularly for a small industrial country. A number of factors determine the suitability of a regime: the degree of trade openness, the geographical composition of trade, the sensitivity of industry to price fluctuations, the inflation record of the country in question and of its trading partners, and the degree of autonomy of its monetary authorities. This analysis focuses on the experience of four small industrial countries in their choice of exchange rate regime.

Austria

A small open economy in the centre of Europe, Austria has close trading links with one dominant trading partner, Germany, which accounts for about 40 per cent of Austrian exports. Given this, the 'overriding objective' of Austria's exchange rate policy between 1979 and 1998 has been to peg the schilling to the Deutschmark. (Prior to 1979, the schilling was pegged to a trade-weighted basket of currencies.) By pegging the schilling to a low-inflation anchor, it was hoped that Austrian inflation would converge to the low German level. In addition, the harmful effects of schilling/Deutschmark exchange rate fluctuations on Austrian trade and tourism would be eliminated. This was felt to outweigh the drawback that the 60 per cent of Austria's trade with countries other than Germany was left exposed to exchange rate fluctuations. The schilling remained stable *vis-à-vis* the Deutschmark and as a result, inflation also remained low. The Deutschmark peg was widely viewed as a success and was considered to have made an important contribution to Austria's strong economic performance. The decision to participate in the euro was seen as a continuation of this successful formula

Australia and New Zealand

On the other side of the world are two small open economies which have chosen a radically different exchange rate policy. Both the Australian dollar and the New Zealand dollar have been allowed to float since the mid-1980s. Unlike Austria, Australia and New Zealand have a wide diversity of trading partners. Europe and Japan are the main markets for primary commodities, the US for manufactures. In addition, the two countries trade significantly with each other. Their main trading partners have a mixed record on inflation. Thus, no single obvious choice of anchor currency presents itself. This may explain why the Australian and New Zealand authorities have tried almost every conceivable exchange rate regime in the recent past. Both currencies were pegged to the pound sterling until 1971; then to the US dollar, until 1973 in the case of the Australian dollar, and until 1974 in the case of the New Zealand dollar. Next they tried pegging their currencies to a trade-weighted basket of several trading partners. After experiments, the Australian authorities finally decided to float the dollar in 1984. The New Zealand authorities followed suit in 1986.

Both Australia and New Zealand have discovered that a floating regime has many advantages. It has eliminated the costly delays in realignments associated with the previous fixed or quasi-fixed regimes, and both countries had achieved a low rate of inflation and a

Box 22.1 continued

stable effective exchange rate by the early 1990s. Tight monetary policy in the form of higher interest rates was necessary to ensure this stability. The resurgence of inflation associated with a 15 per cent depreciation of the dollar necessitated a return to higher interest rates to ensure the sustainability of the float. Concern about higher inflation arising from the weakness of the New Zealand dollar prompted an increase in New Zealand interest rates. Indeed, permanently higher interest rates might be viewed as the *premium* which has to be paid for adopting a floating regime. However, while the New Zealand authorities have adopted a *clean* float, meaning no intervention by the monetary authorities in the foreign exchange market, the Australian authorities maintain a limited role for foreign exchange market intervention, alongside a tight monetary policy.

Switzerland

Another economy which has opted for a floating regime is Switzerland. It adopted this regime in 1973. The obvious similarities between the Swiss and Austrian economies – both are small, open, economies, with strong German trade links – have caused many to question their fundamentally different exchange rate policies. Why have the Swiss authorities allowed the Swiss franc to float rather than pegging it to the Deutschmark and the euro?

The answer seems to be that the Swiss found that the floating regime works well for their economy. Given that, they see no reason to change. Swiss inflation has never been significantly higher than the German level, and the Swiss authorities are confident in their ability to maintain a stable currency through appropriate monetary policy, i.e. high interest rates when needed. (On two occasions, however – in 1978 and again in 1987, the Swiss National Bank departed from its strict monetary policy temporarily and intervened to reverse the appreciation of the franc.) The autonomy of the Swiss National Bank – the Swiss government is prevented by law from intervening in the realm of monetary policy – and the credibility of its monetary policy have been critical to the success of the float.

Conclusion

Since the demise of the Bretton Woods system in 1973, small countries have had a wide variety of exchange rate regimes from which to choose. The choice is not clear-cut, and many countries have experimented with a variety of regimes. Pegging requires the subordination of monetary policy to the maintenance of the exchange rate parity. A country with a good independent inflation record, such as Switzerland, might be better off not having its hands tied, while for a country with a poorer track record than its dominant trading partner, pegging might help by reducing the interest rate premium (because of enhanced credibility) and by ensuring that the monetary authorities will follow a stable course (important in young and fragile democracies).

Sources: OECD, *Economic Surveys: Australia, Austria, New Zealand, Switzerland* (various editions); *Osterreichische Nationalbank Annual Report*; *Reserve Bank of New Zealand Bulletin*; *Reserve Bank of Australia Bulletin*; *Schweizerische Nationalbank Annual Report* (various editions).

- Volatility inhibits trade and investment.
- Destabilising speculation exacerbates the problem.
- Domestic stabilisation measures can be undermined.

Cost of volatility

That volatile exchange rates deter international business by raising transaction costs and causing uncertainty seems a highly plausible assertion. Yet it has proven surprisingly difficult to make an accurate assessment of the effects of currency fluctuations on trade.[9] This may imply that the adverse effects of currency volatility on trade are smaller than is commonly believed. World trade has expanded faster than world GDP during the period of both fixed and floating exchange rates which suggests that any trade-suppression effects of exchange rate variation have been overwhelmed by pro-trade influences. As we saw in Chapter 17, the ratio of the growth of trade to the growth of GDP has remained high right into the 2000s. EU countries have also experienced a continuing rise in the ratio of trade to GDP notwithstanding their different exchange rate regimes. Doubtless the currency turmoil of the 1990s involved a significant economic cost in terms of lost output and investment. One side might argue that this exemplifies the damage caused by exchange rate volatility. But the opposite case could also be made: that the damage was caused by insufficient flexibility, i.e. by government efforts to resist an exchange rate adjustment which was warranted by economic fundamentals.

Another argument is that volatility leads to currency misalignments and that this also impacts adversely on trade performance. There is little doubt that such misalignments occur and that they have an adverse impact on business confidence and trade performance in individual countries. The global impact of the misalignments tends to be harder to identify for two reasons. First, the adverse effect on one country of being overvalued has a counterpart advantageous effect on others because by definition they are undervalued. Second, misalignments can happen under fixed exchange rate systems as well as floating systems.

Destabilising speculation

The second objection relates to the causes of currency volatility. Again there is a common belief that exchange rate fluctuations are 'excessive' and that much of this can be attributed to speculators. Supporting evidence focuses on the fact that forex traders pay limited attention to fundamentals, and chartists none at all. Irrational and speculative forces, fuelled by the fear of being out of step with others in the market, are features of a floating exchange rate system.[10]

---

9 M.C. Thursby and J.G. Thursby, 'The uncertainty effects of floating exchange rates: Empirical evidence on international trade flows', in S.W. Arndt, R.J. Sweeney and T.D. Willett (eds), *Exchange Rates, Trade and the US Economy* (Cambridge, MA: Ballinger Publishing Company, 1985). The effects of exchange rate volatility on trade are notoriously difficult to detect. The empirical evidence is limited and 'inconclusive'. See *International Trade Policies: The Uruguay Round and Beyond* (Washington, DC: IMF, 1994).

10 Note that forex market participants have an interest in encouraging currency fluctuations. The more volatility, the greater are trading volumes and sales of hedging instruments and, hence, the greater are banks' incomes from trading commissions and margins (regardless of speculation on their own account).

Speculation, far from acting as Friedman's textbook stabiliser, may well be exacerbating the volatility of the market. The chairman of Sony expressed a widely held business view on this point:

> In 1973 the experts claimed that exchange rate fluctuations serve to adjust automatically the differences in industrial competitive power among countries. Now I am tempted to ask whether the experts were right in claiming this. What was not anticipated in 1973 was that the freely fluctuating rates would spawn speculation and money trading. The resulting rates did not necessarily reflect competitive power of the fundamentals of national economies. (Akio Morita, Chairman: Sony Corporation, 'How to renew the global economic framework', *International Economic Insights*, Washington, DC, March/April 1993, p. 25)

Domestic stability

Governments do not like to appear ineffective, yet that is how they are often perceived in times of currency turmoil. Even the might of the combined intervention of the US and Japanese authorities, for example, proved unavailing against the bearish sentiment towards the dollar in March–April 1995. The headline of the *Financial Times* (4 April 1995) – 'Dollar hits record low as Japan and US fail to halt slide' – sums it up (see Figure 22.3). Official intervention in the forex market can involve the authorities in huge financial losses. Small countries

Dollar hits record low as Japan and US fail to halt slide

By Philip Gawlth in London and George Graham in Washington

Intensive efforts by US and Japanese officials to halt the dollar's recent decline yesterday failed to prevent the currency falling to a record low against the yen.

Repeated bouts of dollar-buying by the Federal Reserve and the Bank of Japan failed to boost the currency. Efforts to talk up the dollar by Mr Robert Rubin, the US Treasury secretary, and Mr Masayoshi Takemura, the Japanese finance minister, also had negligible impact.

At lunchtime in New York, the dollar was trading at DM1.3737 and Y86.28, having earlier touched a new low of Y86.00. Traders estimated that the Fed and the Bank of Japan together bought $2bn to $3bn. There was no evidence of any support for the dollar from European central banks.

Stories such as the above were typical of the period from end-March to early April 1995 (and many periods before and since) when official intervention was overwhelmed by private capital flows, in this instance reflecting adverse market sentiment towards the dollar.

Figure 22.3 *Financial Times*, 4 April 1995

feel even more vulnerable. Their efforts to stabilise the economy can be undermined by a change in market sentiment. Those most affected are countries with a poor record of consistency in the past, with a really acute inflation problem, or with exposure to large international capital flows inwards and outwards. The problem of *contagion*, arising from these global capital movements, dominated the exchange rate literature during the late 1990s.

22.3 Search for stability

The problem of currency instability can be approached in a number of ways. We shall consider two approaches here. First, a country could choose an anchor currency or group of currencies, and pre-commit to some range of variation around that anchor. Second, the country could continue to float its currency, while deploying special measures to reduce exchange rate variability.

Tying to an anchor currency

For this approach to be effective, the anchor currency has to have certain features. *First*, it should be the currency of a stable, low-inflation country. In this way, the anchor will serve the dual role of providing exchange rate stability as well as controlling domestic inflation. *Second*, the proposed relationship with the anchor must be specified clearly: single currency, fixed parity, fixed but infrequently adjusted parity, fixed but frequently adjusted parity (crawling peg), or floating within narrowly defined fluctuation margins. *Third*, domestic monetary and fiscal policies must be consistent with the exchange rate policy. *Fourth*, the authorities must be able to defend the arrangement, through appropriate intervention mechanisms. There must also be the political will to implement the measures needed to maintain the arrangement.

In practice the last requirement often proves difficult to satisfy. Political will falters when the adjustment costs imposed on an economy by its choice of anchor prove too much to bear. Realisation of this difficulty has led to renewed investigation into the conditions needed to ensure that adjustment costs are kept to the minimum. The *theory of optimum currency areas* emphasises the importance of the following additional factors.

Trade and investment links

A substantial share of the country's trade and foreign investment flows should be conducted with or in terms of the anchor currency. Thus a currency link between Estonia and the euro makes sense; one between Estonia and the yen would not.

Proneness to asymmetric shocks

Difficulties arise when a shock affects one part of a fixed-exchange area but not another. Suppose that aggregate demand shifts from one part of a fixed-peg area (declining area) to another part (the booming area). If exchange rates are fixed, the declining area is likely to experience a recession and unemployment, while the booming area will be threatened with inflation. These problems are not going to be easy to solve. Hence, to avoid them, economies forming a fixed exchange rate area should be reasonably similar in regard to economic structure and policy.

Labour mobility

If asymmetric shocks arise but labour moves freely within the area, then the declining area will experience emigration, not unemployment, while immigration will relieve the over-heating problem in the booming area. Thus, extensive labour mobility within the US makes adjustment to asymmetric shocks much easier there than in, say, an area like Europe where labour mobility is comparatively limited.

Wage and price flexibility

If wages and prices are flexible, a declining economy need not experience emigration. The declining area would experience a decline in prices and costs, relative to the booming area. This would boost demand for the declining area's exports and keep its output at full employment level.[11]

Counter-cyclical fiscal transfers

Adjustment is easier if mechanisms exist whereby the booming region automatically transfers resources to the declining region. In a single currency area, this is done by federal or central authority transfers. Some rudimentary transfers of this nature were provided as part of the European integration programme to strengthen the sustainability of the euro.

Credibility of link

The degree of wage and price flexibility is not to be regarded as something given and unalterable. It can be influenced by institutions such as the exchange rate regime. When everybody knows that the exchange rate is fixed (or abolished, through a single currency), then the adverse effects of holding out for higher than equilibrium pay will be anticipated. This anticipation will lead to more flexibility than would otherwise be the case. If there is a pegged arrangement, the government has a major task in persuading its citizens that the peg will not be altered lightly. The more persuasive it is, the less painful the adjustment to shocks. One advantage in a country 'tying its hands', through a binding and irreversible commitment with regard to the exchange rate, is that its credibility will be enhanced.[12]

The choice of an anchor requires careful economic analysis. The precise type of link between the anchor currency and the national currency also needs serious attention. Some countries use the anchor in a rather casual way (such as frequently adjusted pegs or crawling pegs); others tie themselves to the anchor more tightly.

---

11 This is, of course, the standard classical adjustment mechanism described in chapters 11 and 14.
12 G.S. Tavlas, 'The new theory of optimum currency areas', *World Economy* (November 1993); P. de Grauwe, *The Economics of Monetary Integration* (Oxford: Oxford University Press, 2nd edn, 1994).

Measures to influence the exchange rate

A pegged system is one where limits are set on the range of variation of the exchange rate. At any time, the authorities may be called upon to intervene in order to ensure that the market exchange rate stays within the permitted range of variation. For example, a currency might come under pressure because of speculative capital outflows. In order to forestall a depreciation of the currency, a variety of measures could be used. We consider the five main instruments: open market intervention, interest rates, impediments to short-term capital movements ('sand in the wheels'), policy coordination, and ministerial government statements.

The first line of defence is *direct intervention* in the forex market. The central bank could sell foreign exchange reserves.[13] In some instances, such intervention may 'see off' the doubters and reassure the market as to the authorities' determination to defend the currency. It may be no coincidence that both Singapore and Taiwan, two countries with large forex reserves, were least affected by the East Asian crisis in the late 1990s. But there are limits to this policy:

- Official reserves are finite, and the capacity of government to borrow from the private sector and international agencies may be small in relation to total potential capital flows.
- Even coordinated intervention by several central banks can be ineffective (as the EMS crisis of 1992–93 and the dollar fall of Spring 1995 illustrated). The Bundesbank reportedly spent DM 92 billion in support-purchases of EMS currencies during August and September 1992 – to no avail (*Monthly Report of the Deutsche Bundesbank*, January 1993).
- Intervention may have undesirable side-effects on money supply and interest rates.

A second line of defence is the *interest rate*. By changing the rate at which banks can borrow from the central bank, interest rates throughout the economy can be raised. This rewards those who keep their money in domestic currency and, in theory, makes it more expensive for the speculator to sell domestic currency. Yet, interest rate policy, like direct intervention, has limitations:

- A rise in interest rates affects all borrowers not just the speculators. The corporate sector may as a result be exposed to a double blow – higher interest on borrowings and weaker consumer demand – which may not be consistent with the requirements of domestic economic balance. (At this stage the business sector becomes torn between support for currency stability and opposition to the measures necessary to achieve it.)
- Higher interest rates are particularly unwelcome in countries with high debt : GDP ratios and high budget deficits.
- Higher interest rates give markets 'a taste of blood' and can add to market nervousness. Overnight and interbank interest rates sometimes reach astronomical heights as expectations of devaluation gather strength. In

---

13 The author is indebted to Dominic Burke whose M.Litt thesis for Trinity College addressed this issue.

September 1992, the Swedish Riksbank's marginal lending rate rose to 500 per cent and the 1-month interbank rate was 70 per cent. Yet speculators were not deterred. To understand why, consider the following case. Suppose a non-resident speculator borrowed kronor from a Swedish bank at 70 per cent, converted the kronor into US dollars and deposited the dollars at 6 per cent interest. This seems very unprofitable since devaluation at an annualised rate of approximately 64 per cent would be required to break even. But if a devaluation of 5 per cent were to take place within a week after borrowing, the annualised equivalent would be over 250 per cent, leaving a tidy profit to the speculator.[14] Hence, if the market is convinced that depreciation is imminent, even the highest interest rates may not be effective.

In most circumstances, high interest rates motivated solely by the need to defend the currency are difficult to sustain.

A third line of defence is termed *throwing sand in the wheels* of the forex market.[15] Included here are measures such as the direct controls on capital movements, taxation of gains on currency speculation, limits on open positions held by the banking system, enforcement of high capital reserve requirements against such open positions and restrictions on foreign participation in the domestic capital market.[16] While these measures are popular with the electorate (the currency speculator has few admirers), two factors restrict their long-term usefulness:

- The increased mobility of capital and the wide range of instruments for speculation have made the identification of speculative transactions increasingly difficult.
- Capital controls are a two-edged sword. They penalise *bona fide* long-term investors as well as speculators. Genuine investors, once bitten, will be twice shy. The country imposing the controls will pay a penalty in terms of higher long-term interest rates. In many countries, this is a decisive argument against arbitrary imposition of capital controls.

A fourth possibility is *enhanced international coordination of economic policy*. Governments could agree *target exchange rate zones* within which their currencies would be allowed to fluctuate and could further undertake to coordinate their domestic economic policies so that these zones proved viable. If one currency was thought to be *depreciating* too much, the *appreciating* currency's government could respond by (a) reducing interest rates, and (b) taking other measures to expand

14 Developments in the derivatives markets may also have weakened the power of the interest rate defence. For some hedging strategies, a rise in the spread between domestic and foreign interest rates mandates a forward or spot sale of the domestic currency. Thus, raising the interest rate could have a perverse effect: inducing sales instead of purchases (Goldstein *et al.*, *International Capital Markets, Part I: Exchange Rate Management and International Capital Flows* (Washington, DC: IMF, 1993), p. 17).

15 B. Eichengreen, J. Tobin and C. Wyplosz, 'Two cases for sand in the wheels of international finance', *Economic Journal* (January 1995).

16 Often called the Tobin tax proposal after Nobel prize-winner James Tobin, who recommended the imposition of a tax on forex transactions in order 'to throw sand in the wheels of our excessively efficient international money market'. See J. Tobin, 'A proposal for international monetary reform', *Eastern Economic Journal* (Winter 1978) (reprinted in J. Tobin, *Essays in Economics*, Cambridge, MA: MIT Press, 1982).

aggregate demand. Countries can and do cooperate – via meetings of the major economic powers, the IMF and the Bank of International Settlements. Within the European Union, there are regular meetings of finance and monetary officials. But national interests take precedence over international priorities. If an economy was at full capacity, the authorities would be unlikely to stimulate demand merely to assist its neighbour with the depreciating currency.

Finally, *ministerial and government statements* on exchange rate policy can, on occasion, have a calming effect on the market. Unfortunately, they can also exacerbate the situation. Ministers do not always adhere to the carefully-prepared script of their central bank and finance officials. Sometimes politicians in supposedly cooperating countries make contradictory statements. Repeated assurances by a government that it will not devalue can inflame suspicions that this is precisely what is being considered. Rhetoric without supporting action can be equally unproductive, since then it only serves to highlight a country's lack of resolve and possible disagreements within the government. A classic example of confused signals was the US Treasury Secretary's reported affirmation that 'a strong dollar is vital to US economic interests', just at the time when the dollar's nominal effective exchange rate had fallen by 11 per cent over the previous year.[17] As Germany's former finance minister, Theo Waigel, remarked: 'it is an illusion to believe that government and central banks can go against the markets for any length of time'.[18] Exchange rate expectations are not subject to the whim of governments or monetary authorities. Neither intervention nor interest rate policy nor public statements will ultimately be successful unless there is real economic convergence with the countries to which one's currency is being linked. However, there are three useful lessons for governments facing speculative attacks on their currency:

- First, defence of an exchange rate position will work only if that position has a high degree of credibility. The target must not be over-ambitious, and it must be consistent with economic fundamentals and macroeconomic policies.[19]
- Second, the authorities must carefully decide which instrument or combination of instruments to use and how much reliance to place in each one.
- Third, if a strategic retreat has to be made, the authorities should retreat to a defensible position. If a devaluation proves necessary, the amount of devaluation should be sufficient to convince the market that the traded sector can 'live' comfortably with the new rate, and yet not by such a large amount as to create fears of an inflationary spiral. To be sure, this is not an easy task. (See Box 22.2 on the 1994–95 Mexican peso crisis.)

---

17 Reported in *The Financial Times* (30 March 1995).
18 Reported in *The Financial Times* (6 April 1995).
19 This point was forcefully made in the conclusion of the *Deutsche Bundesbank Annual Report 1992*: 'Exchange rate expectations cannot be controlled in the long run contrary to the fundamentals by intervening in the market.' Neither intervention nor interest rate policy nor public statements, it goes on to say, will ultimately be successful unless there is real economic convergence with the countries to which one's currency is being linked.

Box 22.2

The Mexican peso crisis, 1994–95

In the five years to the end of 1994, the Mexican government had built up a reputation for cautious economic management. Monetary and fiscal discipline was allied to control of wages and prices with the objective of reducing inflation to OECD levels, balancing the budget and creating sustained growth. By 1994, the strategy appeared to have been successful. Inflation had fallen from 27 per cent in 1990 to 7 per cent in 1994, and was forecast to fall to 4 per cent in 1995. Massive deficits had been eliminated and replaced by balanced budgets. Economic growth averaged 3.5 per cent per annum from 1989 to 1992, although there was a sharp reduction in 1993 to 0.7 per cent (Table 22.2).

Table 22.1 Mexico – economic statistics

	1990	1991	1992	1993	1994	1995	1996
Exchange Rate Ps : $	2.81	3.02	3.09	3.15	3.44	6.50	7.50
GDP growth	4.5%	3.6%	2.8%	0.7%	4.5%	−6.2%	5.1%
Consumer prices	26.7%	22.7%	15.5%	9.8%	7.0%	35.0%	34.4%
Trade (deficit) $bn	(0.9)	(7.3)	(15.9)	(13.6)	(18.5)	+7.0	+6.5
BoP current a/c $bn	(7.5)	(14.6)	(24.4)	(23.4)	(24.7)	(1.6)	(2.3)
External debt $bn	104.3	116.6	117.6	130.2	139.0	174.0	175.0

Note: Parentheses means deficit.
Sources: IMF, The Economist, OECD.

In January 1994, Mexico acceded to NAFTA as a full member, joining the US and Canada. Together with membership of the OECD, this appeared to set the seal of international approval on the success of its development strategy.

The exchange rate anchor

The anchor of monetary and fiscal policy for six years had been the establishment of a stable relationship between the Mexican peso and the US dollar by the Salinas government. Since November 1991 the peso had been permitted to depreciate by a maximum of Ps0.0004 per day against the US dollar. By setting a definite limit on the amount of depreciation, this regime encouraged business to abandon its traditional preoccupations with devaluations and inflation hedges, and to concentrate instead on 'real' business. In return for a stable peso, labour and business agreed to low wage and price increases. The stable exchange rate with the dollar enhanced the attractiveness of Mexico to foreign (mainly US) investors. Large inflows of direct investment and portfolio investment occurred.

Against these successes there were some negative developments, the importance of which is particularly clear in hindsight. First, the current account showed a worrying trend. The deficit had increased each year from a level of $4bn in 1989 to $23.4bn in 1993. As 1994 progressed, the projected deficit rose to $29bn or 8 per cent of GDP. Its causes could be traced to a consumer boom, and ominously it was financed primarily by short-term external debt.

Box 22.2 continued

A second negative factor was that the political background in Mexico during 1994 became volatile. There were two assassinations of major political figures, one of whom was the ruling party's presidential candidate, and the Chiapas peasant revolt continued to simmer. Foreign investors were becoming uneasy and, as a result, the foreign reserves had fallen from $30 billion to $6 billion over the year.

To correct the current account deficit, some devaluation was judged necessary. It was hoped that if the extent of the devaluation could be limited to a modest amount, the trade balance would improve and confidence could be restored, without fatal damage to the low-inflation objective. Accordingly, on 20 December 1994, only 19 days after he had been sworn into office, Finance Minister Jaime Serra announced an immediate 12.7 per cent devaluation of the peso and the continuation of the crawling devaluation of Ps0.0004 per day.

Aftermath of devaluation

The devaluation worked out disastrously wrong. Instead of reassuring markets that the realignment was a one-off adjustment, it aroused fears of further and deeper devaluations. The peso proved impossible to support at the new level. By March 1995, it traded at over 7 pesos to the dollar, as compared with 3.5 at the outbreak of the crisis in December. Domestic short-term interest rates rose to 42 per cent by January 1995 and the stock market (ZPC) index, which in the past had been buttressed by massive inflows of money from foreign pension, investment and mutual funds, dropped 23 per cent. US investors saw a massive decline in the dollar value of their investment in Mexico and were thus deterred from further investment. Real wages for Mexican workers fell precipitously in dollar terms.

Causes of the crisis

One view is that the economic 'fundamentals' made a devaluation necessary and desirable. The relevant fundamentals would include:

- the 28 per cent rise in the real effective exchange rate between 1990 and 1993, continued into 1994;
- the weakening of fiscal and monetary policy associated with the 1994 election campaign, leading to a surge in imports; and
- the build-up of short-term Mexican debt held by foreigners, mainly US mutual funds.[1] There was a significant bunching of maturities around the end of 1994.

The Mexican case illustrates the problem of *excessive reliance on the exchange rate anchor strategy* to fight inflation. It resulted in an overvalued exchange rate and an unsustainable current account deficit financed by short-term capital inflows. What happened was therefore in accord with theoretical expectations. The proposed devaluation went wrong because it was too small and delayed too long. It got out of control because of the absence of appropriate 'flanking policies', i.e. carefully worked-out fiscal and monetary policy measures to ensure its effectiveness.[2] Pegged exchange rate regimes, some argued, are inherently crisis-prone in countries like Mexico.

▶

Box 22.2 continued

An alternative interpretation acknowledges the overvaluation of the peso but argues that the market overreacted. It sees the Mexican case as illustrating the power of speculative capital movements to disrupt stabilisation programmes. (Mexican competitiveness could have been restored by any number of possible combinations of domestic inflation and devaluation (the *multiple equilibria problem*). Thus a 60 per cent devaluation followed by a 50 per cent inflation yields the same improvement in competitiveness as a 20 per cent devaluation followed by a 10 per cent inflation. On this view, market panic resulted in an excessive devaluation (overshooting). This forced a much weaker peso – and by extension a much higher inflation rate – than was objectively warranted by fundamentals. Strong 'contagion effects' were evident in other South American and Asian markets, engendered by these same irrational market movements.

Conclusion

Whichever view is correct – and there are other interpretations in addition to the above – the crisis constituted a serious setback for Mexico. Mexican inflation rose from 7 per cent in 1994 to 35 per cent in 1995. Investor confidence in Mexico was dealt a severe blow, and GDP suffered. Another effect of the devaluation was the severe impact of increased import and financing costs on the many foreign companies which had decided to establish in Mexico following the NAFTA Agreement. The depreciation of the peso has damaged trade, as theory would lead one to expect, and it could have created difficulties for NAFTA – such wild exchange rate fluctuations are not conducive to a healthy growth of trade and factor exchange. Fears were voiced that the painfully built-up consensus in favour of competition, macro-stability and openness would also be undermined. Certainly it was affected and inflation was not reduced again to single figures until 2000. However, Mexican governments have continued their commitment to a reformist, outward-looking strategy.

Notes:
1. There was a major difference between importing capital from US banks during the 1970s and importing capital from mutual and other investment funds in the 1990s. Banks lend mostly against specific projects with a long-term view, whereas fund managers regard the whole world as an investment opportunity, and their horizon is dictated by the need to publish daily asset prices. An adverse movement in fund prices can lead to large-scale redemptions – and early retirement for the fund manager!
2. An emergency economic plan designed to stabilise the economy was launched in January 1995, followed by an austerity plan in March 1995. An international rescue package was agreed in February by the US and the IMF comprising $20 billion from the US Treasury and $17.5 billion from the IMF, with possible additional funding from other sources. This was designed: (a) to pay for the increased cost of debt servicing and imports, and (b) to repay, or to allow for the rescheduling of, debt. The second element in the strategy included measures to cut public spending and the pact on wages and prices, which the government had agreed with the unions and business organisations. Implicit in this package was a large decline in real earnings per worker.

Sources: R. Dornbusch and A. Weber, 'Mexico: Stabilisation, reform and no growth', *Brookings Papers on Economic Activity* (1994), pp. 253–316. IMF, 'Factors behind the financial crisis in Mexico', *World Economic Outlook* (May 1995); B. Eichengreen, 'The morning after: The Mexican peso in the aftermath of the 1994 currency crisis', NBER Working Paper 6516 (Cambridge, Mass.: National Bureau of Economic Research 1998).

Business is affected by currency instability, by the level of the exchange rate, the nature of the exchange rate regime and the methods of defending it. Business organisations need to understand all three aspects of exchange rate policy; and also to appreciate the sometimes unwelcome implications of such policy for interest rates.

22.4 Establishing a single currency – the euro

The difficulty of defending a pegged system and of preventing exchange rate volatility have prompted some member states of the EU to implement a radical alternative. Rather than floating their currencies, in January 1999 these 11 countries adopted the most irrevocably fixed regime of all – a single currency.

The road to the single currency began in 1970 with the Werner Report (see Box 22.3). This report proposed the establishment of an economic and monetary union (EMU) in three stages over a ten-year period. The European Council accepted the proposal in 1972. Howver, soon afterwards came the oil crisis and the deep recession of the 1970s. Policy divergencies within the European Community widened and the entire EMU project had to be placed in abeyance.

Nevertheless, concern about the adverse effects of exchange rate volatility on the process of European integration remained. Following a Franco-German initiative, the European Monetary System came into operation in March 1979. Key operational features of the EMS were:

- fixed bands around central exchange rates,
- provision for realignment,
- intervention backed by cooperative financial arrangements,
- creation of a monetary unit, the ECU.

The EMS operated fairly successfully for 12 years. Exchange rate variability was reduced and inflation rates converged to those of low-inflation members, notably Germany.[20] Yet the system encountered a number of difficulties. *First* there were problems within the system itself. Infrequent realignments during the latter years of the system gave rise to misaligned parities, which the market considered unsustainable. *Second*, with the liberalisation of capital controls, the volume of speculative capital flows was greatly increased. Too often, narrow exchange rate bands meant the speculators enjoyed one-way options. *Third*, there was a large asymmetric shock to the system – the reunification of Germany in 1990. This necessitated a huge increase in German public borrowing. To keep inflation in check the Bundesbank raised interest rates. In order to prevent their currencies depreciating against the Deutschmark, the other EMS participants had to follow suit. Thus an unwelcome hike in interest rates was forced of Germany's neighbours at a time of deep recession and high unemployment.

---

20 Lower inflation was achieved in the lifetime of the ERM, but lower inflation was also attained by countries outside the ERM. For this reason, empirical studies on the inflationary consequences of the ERM are generally inconclusive. See M.J. Artis and M.P. Taylor, 'The achievements of the European Monetary System', *Economic and Social Review* (January 1989).

Box 22.3

Background to EMU

1970 **Werner Report** recommends implementation of economic and monetary union with single currency

1972 All member states (including three new members, UK, Denmark and Ireland) agree to EMU by 1980. Oil crisis later that year effectively derails programme

1979 European Monetary System (EMS) introduced.

1989 **Delors Report** proposes a three-stage move to EMU

1991 **Treaty of European Union (Maastricht Treaty)** agreed setting down detailed framework for EMU (enters into force 1993)

1992 Exchange rate crisis: UK and Italy withdraw from EMS

1993 EMS exchange rate bands widened to 15%

1997 Stability and Growth Pact introduces regulations to strengthen budgetary discipline and clarifies excessive deficit procedure

1998 Member states eligible for participation in EMU decided by reference to four criteria of sustainable convergence (the Maastricht criteria) and central bank independence

1999 EMU begins: European Central Bank starts operations, euro introduced. Three member states (UK, Sweden and Denmark) do not participate

2002 Euro notes and coins to enter circulation and become legal tender in euro area. All monetary transactions to be through euro

Considerations such as the above confirmed that the EMS was an interim measure rather than a long-term solution to problems of excessive exchange rate volatility. At a political level there was a growing conviction that, in order to complete the single market, a single European currency was essential. Jacques Delors, President of the European Commission, reverted to the idea that EMU was the way forward. The Delors Report,[21] published in 1989, proposed a three-stage move towards EMU. The European Council endorsed the programme, out of which emerged the treaty of the European Union (the Maastricht Treaty) in 1992. To qualify for participation in the euro, a member state had to satisfy the following *convergence criteria*:

- *price stability*: the rate of inflation could not exceed the average rates of inflation of the three member states with the lowest inflation rate by more than 1.5 per cent,

- *interest rates*: long-term interest rates could not exceed by more than 2 per cent the average interest rates of the three member states woth the lowest interest rates,

- *government debt*: public debt could exceed 60 per cent of GDP only if the trend was declining towards this level,

21 J. Delors, *Report on Economic and Monetary Union*, Report to European Council by Committee Chaired by J. Delors (Brussels: European Commission, 1989).

- *budget deficit*: national budget deficits had to be close to or below 3 per cent of GNP,
- *exchange rate stability*: a national currency could not have devalued within the two previous years and must have remained within the margin of fluctuation.

Soon after the Maastricht Treaty was signed the EMS began to come under strain. This developed into a fully-fledged currency crisis and in September 1992 the UK and Italy withdrew from the exchange rate arrangement. There were further exchange rate adjustments and eventually it was agreed to widen the band to ± 15 per cent in 1993. The new version of the EMS is very close to a floating rate system.

Pro-EMU governments inferred from these events that only complete fixity in a single currency would permanently solve the exchange problem. With this in mind and in order to complete the provisions of the Maastricht Treaty, the Stability and Growth Pact was adopted at a sustainable level. Multilateral supervision, fines on excessive deficits and annual submission of stability reports were approved to guarantee this discipline.

In May 1998, the European Council defined the list of countries eligible for participation in the single currency, based on their satisfying the five convergence criteria and also having independent central banks. The same year also saw the establishment of the European Central Bank and the appointment of its executive committee. The final stage of monetary union began in 1999 when the euro became a currency in its own right and exchange rates between participating countries were irrevocably fixed. Four EU countries (Denmark, Greece, Sweden and the United Kingdom) did not proceed to this stage, leaving a total of eleven countries in the EMU. However, subsequently Greece applied successfully for membership and the euro area expanded to 12 countries on 1 January 2001.

The concluding phase of EMU will take place in 2002 when the euro will enter circulation and national notes and coins will cease to be legal tender.

The case for EMU

Economic and monetary union promises several types of efficiency gains.[22] First, a single currency eliminates the *transaction costs* of exchanging one EU currency into another. The European Commission estimated transaction costs at about one-half per cent of GDP (ECU13 to 19 billion per year) for the EU as a whole.[23] Transaction costs were estimated to be particularly high (about 1% of GDP) for small, open member states. Savings on transaction costs were expected to be higher for small and medium-sized enterprises than for large, multinational companies. According to European Commission estimates, transaction costs

---

22 For a comprehensive assessment of the benefits and costs of EMU, see P. de Grauwe, *The Economics of Monetary Integration* (Oxford: Oxford University Press, 2nd edn, 1994). See also J. Vinals, 'Building a monetary union in Europe', in T. Balino and C. Cotarelli, *Frameworks for Monetary Stability* (Washington, DC: IMF, 1994).

23 See European Commission, *European Economy No. 44: One Market, One Money – An Evaluation of the Potential Benefits and Costs of Forming an Economic and Monetary Union* (Brussels, October 1990).

amount to 15% of profits for the average company, but up to twice this level for smaller companies. Ultimately, the euro should make cross-border payments almost as simple as domestic payments.

Second, EMU has eliminated *exchange rate uncertainty* within the euro area. Exchange rate movements add to a company's uncertainty about its future revenue and discourage trade. By eliminating the need for hedging mechanisms on intra-EU transactions, monetary union entails savings on hedging costs as well as on transaction costs. Because exchange rates are fixed, interest rates must also converge and the resultant decline in money market and bond rates was an important consideration for the more inflation-prone and weaker member states. (However, large divergences in bank lending rates still continue because of different regulatory and tax systems.) More generally, the reduction in uncertainty – not only exchange rate uncertainty but also uncertainty about monetary and fiscal policy – was seen as encouraging investment, and thereby GDP growth.

A third efficiency gain arises from the increased *transparency in prices*. A single currency makes it easier to compare prices in different European markets. The increased comparability of prices will strengthen competition and hence increase efficiency. The transparency effect might also help to enhance awareness of costs in other EU countries and bring about greater consistency in labour cost developments in the euro area.

Fourth, the euro will *enhance the role of the EU in the international monetary system*. The new currency has already begun to compete with the dollar and the yen as a major international currency and reserve asset. Member states are able to economise on their holdings of external reserves, and as non-members add to their euro holdings, seigniorage gains will accrue to the euro area as a whole. In addition, EMU will allow the EU to speak with a single, more influential voice in international monetary discussions. (Member states will no longer be represented by their individual central banks, but by the ECB.) This will assist cooperation between the European Union, the United States and Japan, and over time perhaps even bring about more stable exchange rates internationally and a more balanced tri-polar monetary regime.

These various effects of the euro were expected to deepen the process of trade and investment integration. More important, many argued that the absence of a single currency, and the continuance of exchange rate turbulence, could frustrate and even endanger the integration process. A strong and controversial version of the above arguments asserted that a single market without the euro would not be sustainable – for economic and political reasons.

Drawbacks of the euro

Critics of the euro animadvert the *loss of autonomy in economic policy* for member states which follows its implementation. EMU precludes the option of using the exchange rate as an instrument of economic adjustment at national level. This loss of the exchange rate option involves a definite cost. In addition, member states surrender control over monetary policy to a new and untried institution. There are fears that the Bundesbank's successful low-inflation record will not be

Box 22.4

Economics of Euro: europtimists versus eurosceptics

The euro project continues to provide fertile ground for controversy. At one end of the spectrum, supporters of EMU stress the following for advantages:

1. *Transaction costs*: A single currency eliminates all the costs arising to firms and individuals through conversions from one member currency into another.
2. *Exchange rate uncertainty*: Exchange rate uncertainty and costs of hedging are avoided. As a result, interest rates in weaker economies will converge towards the (lower) level of the stronger economies.
3. *Transparency of prices*: As goods and services are priced in the same currency, the pro-competitive effects of the Single Market are strengthened. The euro also makes employers and employees more conscious of the necessary wage and price discipline.
4. *External benefits*: The euro will lead to a more balanced distribution of international reserve assets, a small amount of seigniorage will be generated, and the ECB will become a more powerful actor than national central banks.

Eurosceptics focus on the downsides of EMU:

1. *Loss of exchange rate autonomy*: the exchange rate can help to insulate a country from external inflationary pressure and to protect its competitiveness.
2. *Inappropriate monetary policy*: a single currency means a single monetary policy and a single interest rate for all participating states. This 'one-size fits all' policy could prove damaging in case of asymmetric shocks and unsynchronised business fluctuations.
3. *Enlargement of membership*: inclusion of weaker economies such as Greece and the transition economies will result in a dilution of the ECB's committment to price stability and/or the collapse of the system.
4. *Stability and Growth Pact fiscal targets too restrictive*: member states have widely divergent needs and their fiscal constraints need to determined accordingly.

After its second year of operation, the general consensus was that the euro and the ECB made a solid start. True, the euro proved to be weaker than expected. The US$/euro exchange rate fell from 1.12 in early 1999 to 0.85 in May 2000; the EER (both nominal and real) fell by around 15 per cent. However, despite this, inflation stayed around 2 per cent, unemployment fell and growth recovered. A good result but clearly not overwhelming. To improve matters, the authorities must focus on structural reforms designed to enhance flexibility and hence diminish the incidence and potential damage of asymmetric shocks. Meanwhile, of the non-participating countries, Denmark remains sceptical (a report of the Economic Council in mid 2000 concluded that the purely economic costs and benefits for Denmark of EMU membership were *small and uncertain*), the UK economy is doing fine and the electorate is unlikely in the short run to see merit in changing to the euro, and Sweden continues to be wary. In a contrasting vein, Greece happily joined the euro area in 2001.

Sources: OECD, *EMU One Year On* (Paris 2000); *Report of Economic Council on Danish Economy*, Spring 2000. (www.dors.dk)

replicated by the European Central Bank. Some governments simply dislike the idea of losing autonomy over monetary policy, regardless of how well the new ECB might work. There is also concern that *the fiscal targets could prove to be contractionary and divisive*, especially in the light of the pressures that Europe's ageing population will place on government spending.

Three questions hang over the economic impact of EMU. The first concerns the nature of the economic shocks affecting different member states. If these are highly asymmetric, i.e. affect different states to a markedly different degree, some adjustment mechanism must be found to restore balance. In the absence of exchange rate adjustment, the burden falls on wage and domestic cost flexibility. The second question, therefore, concerns the extent to which markets in Europe will be capable of evolving more flexible structures. A third issue relates to the capacity of tax and transfer mechanisms within the EU to prevent politically unacceptable gaps in living standards opening up between member states. While the scale of transfers required has been debated in Europe for many years, the present degree of fiscal integration is extremely modest. These queries raise doubts as to whether the proposed monetary union satisfies the criteria for a successful *optimum currency area*, given that:

- labour mobility is limited, by cultural and linguistic barriers,
- wages and prices are comparatively inflexible,
- fiscal transfers are as yet very small – less than 2 per cent of total GDP (by contrast, the tax-transfer system in the US offsets roughly 40 per cent of region-specific income shocks),
- the share of intra-EU trade in the total trade of member states is quite low (just over 50 per cent in the UK and Germany).

Structural funds go some way towards redressing the regional imbalances arising from asymmetric shocks, but after EMU the burden of adjustment will mostly fall on domestic prices and wages or, failing that, on output and employment levels. Thus, enhanced policy initiatives will be needed to increase flexibility and competitiveness, supplemented with a larger pool of structural funds, if the euro is to work smoothly.

Significant potential benefits could follow from the euro, and likewise significant economic costs. The EU at present falls short of an optimum currency area. In the event of further enlargement of the EU, this shortfall is likely to become even more acute. Hence, the balance between benefits and costs will differ between member states. The potential growth-boosting effects of a monetary union have probably been oversold by its proponents – as de Grauwe rightly warns, 'we should not expect too much additional economic growth from a monetary union'. But it must be remembered that there is a strong political motivation to EMU and in the final analysis political considerations carry more weight than the economic calculus. Viewed in this context, it should be a cause of neither surprise nor censure that the Danes narrowly voted against EMU membership in September 2000.

22.5 Conclusions

This chapter began with a description of the world's exchange rate arrangements. Most major currencies operate a policy of independent floating *vis-à-vis* each other. While some smaller countries adhere to managed or pegged systems, a significant number have floating currencies. But few countries are genuine 'free floaters' in the sense of being insouciant about the value of their currencies. Many try to exercise some influence over the degree of exchange rate flexibility.

Governments are concerned by the disruptive effects of excessive volatility on trade and investment, the damage caused to their economies by resulting exchange rate misalignments, and the possibility of their domestic stabilisation policies being weakened by freak sporadic and irrational changes in market sentiment. These adverse effects are particularly likely to affect smaller countries.

Business shares this concern. Of course, as we saw in Chapter 21, companies can protect themselves against short-term volatility by currency hedging transactions and by internal exposure management. But these measures are neither costless nor comprehensive. Even the best forward cover cannot insulate a firm from the effects of sustained misalignment of its currency. Such misalignments create serious problems for business. Profit calculations are thrown into disarray and investment decisions undermined. An overvalued exchange rate could enable foreign competition to establish a bridgehead in the domestic market from which it will not easily be dislodged, even when eventually the misalignment is corrected. For all these reasons, business considers exchange rate variations as an unpleasant fact of life, which they would rather not have to cope with.

What can be done to improve the situation? One way is to ensure that governments choose an appropriate exchange rate regime. If an anchor-currency regime is chosen, there are many criteria in addition to trade patterns to bear in mind. Labour mobility, price and wage flexibility and the nature of economic shocks are also important. The anchor itself must be stable. In particular, the credibility of a country's choice of the anchor currency must be established by supporting fiscal policies. We saw that anchor currencies are widely used, particularly by smaller countries.

Another response to the volatility problem was the development of quasi-fixed systems such as the EMS. After the turmoil of 1992, however, it became clear that the system would have to be made more flexible by widening the band of variation or else it had to be replaced by some more radical form of fixity. Out of this has emerged Europe's single currency, the euro. The gains from the euro include the reduction in foreign exchange transaction costs and in exchange rate uncertainty. Supporters claim that eliminating these will contribute to positive business expectations and to increased trade, investment and growth. In addition, an autonomous ECB is likely to have greater success in achieving lower inflation for participating countries with a higher than average inflation record. A single currency will also allow the EU to play an enhanced role in the global economy and contribute to the evolution of a more stable international monetary system.

One method of assessing the implications of a single currency is to study the experience of a group of states which already have a single currency in place, such as the US. The question could be asked whether individual states like California or New England would be better off if they had their own currencies than with the dollar? The absence of active canvassing on their part for a separate currency suggests that they would not. But this observation is not a conclusive case for a single currency. Perhaps there are economic losses but the political benefits of belonging to a Union outweigh them. Besides, the preconditions for making a single currency work are nearer to being satisfied within the US than in Europe: English is the common language, labour is highly mobile between states, and the fiscal system is fully integrated. Opponents of the single currency also point out that the growth experience of Europe, despite its myriad of currencies, has been in no way inferior to that of the US. Notwithstanding the large weight of the US in Canada's trade, the Canadian economy has prospered under a floating exchange rate, independent of the dollar. Alas, there are no easy answers to this complex issue.

Many countries continue to opt for floating regimes, and, if anything, opinion outside of Europe has nowadays come to take a more optimistic view of their operational viability. To make a floating regime work, however, consistent macro policies must be maintained. These can be supplemented by policies directed towards stabilising the exchange rate. The usefulness of forex intervention, interest rate changes, capital and regulatory controls, macroeconomic coordination and official exhortations were considered in turn. Each has a potential part to play, but we emphasised the need to ensure that the exchange rate target (be it a specific rate or a currency band) was credible. Defensive measures will not be effective if the target is perceived to be unsustainable by the market. A sustained assault on a currency is difficult to resist. In some instances, trying to resist may well be harmful to national development.

We conclude that exchange rate instability will remain a feature of the global system. It is likely that the system will evolve towards a tripolar structure around the dollar, the euro and the yen, with strong commitments within regional currency areas but loose commitment between them. Some smaller countries will try to limit their exposure to speculative attack by pegging their currencies to an appropriate anchor and, above all, by paying attention to the conduct of macro-economic policies. As a result of enhanced capital mobility and freer trade, fund managers, corporations and individuals will seek maximum returns and will have to take on foreign currency exposures. Speculators will continue to operate, despite the best efforts of governments to 'throw sand in the wheels'. Whatever the merits of a single currency within Europe, it is unrealistic to expect any similar development on a global scale. Lack of political solidarity and economic convergence will be the dominant barrier to any such development.

✔ Summary

1. There is continuing debate about the type of global exchange rate system best suited to the needs of an increasingly integrated world economy. Some argue that there should be greater fixity in exchange rates between countries.

Others believe that the present system of independent floating among the major currencies is, though far from ideal, the best available.

2. The major currencies float more or less freely against each other. But side-by-side with this flexibility, a large number of countries are seeking more stable arrangements. Many small countries in particular have pegged their currencies to anchor currencies such as the euro and the $US. Others have adopted composite pegs whereby their exchange rate is tied to a weighted average of the currencies of their trading partners. The larger countries, however, are adhering to flexible rates. A remarkable exception to this rule is monetary union in Europe, whereby powerful national currencies such as the franc and the Deutschmark have submerged their identities in a single European currency.

3. A floating exchange rate system has many advantages: smooth adjustment, greater domestic policy autonomy and less need for international reserves. But it has one major downside – exchange rate volatility. This volatility is exacerbated by speculation and may be costly to business (though the expected negative correlation between volatility and trade volumes has proven hard to ascertain statistically) and makes governments uncomfortable.

4. The search for stability has rekindled interest in the theory of optimum currency areas, that is, in the economic characteristics of an ideal fixed exchange rate or common currency area. Among the criteria to be considered are share of trade with the area, vulnerability to shocks, price flexibility and factor mobility.

5. Attention has also been focused on the policies available to the authorities to restrain excessive fluctuations in the exchange rate. These policies comprise direct intervention by the monetary authorities in the exchange market, altering domestic interest rates, imposing taxes on financial transactions ('throwing sand in the wheels'), public statements, and policy coordination in defence of target exchange zones. None of these expedients offers a definitive 'solution' to the volatility problem. Exchange rate expectations cannot be controlled by intervening in the market contrary to the long-run fundamentals.

6. Economic and Monetary Union (EMU) represents a major initiative by the European governments to impose stability on thier monetary systems. Opinions are still divided as to which constitutes the greater danger to European trade: too much currency flexibility leading to disruption of normal trade relations or too much rigidity which will weaken the capacity of member state economies to adjust to external and internal 'shocks'. There are potential gains from the euro, ranging through reduced transaction costs, greater transparency and ease of trading. But nobody can be sure of the imponderable costs which this dramatic and historic initiative might yet impose.

? Questions for discussion

1. Discuss the advantages of the system of independently floating exchange rates. Does the choice of a floating regime indicate that the authorities do not care about the level of the exchange rate?

2. Why are some European politicians willing to surrender control of monetary policy and face stringent budgetary rules in return for monetary unification?

3. What criteria would need to be satisfied for the countries of the EU to constitute an optimal currency area? Does the EU at present satisfy these criteria, in your view?

4. Discuss the economic advantages and disadvantages to the UK of participation in EMU.

5. What is an 'anchor' currency? Why should a country wish to 'anchor' its currency to another?

6. Evaluate the measures available to the authorities to moderate currency variation in a floating exchange rate regime.

☞ Exercises

1. The forex market is not the only market to exhibit volatility. Think of the stock market or the housing market. Why should governments intervene to stabilise prices in one but not in the other? What is so special about the exchange rate?

2. Examine the current exchange rate regime of one developed and one developing country. In each case, list (a) the advantages and (b) the disadvantages of the present regime.

3. In January 1994, the currencies of the French franc zone in Africa devalued by 50 per cent relative to the franc. This was followed by a rise in their inflation rate from 0.5 per cent per year in 1990–93 to 33 per cent in 1994. GNP, which had been falling in real terms by 1 per cent annually in 1990–93, rose by 1.5 per cent in 1994. What happened to the real exchange rate of the devaluing countries? In your view, are these observations consistent with the predictions of PPP theory?

4. Can a country have a strong currency and a competitive currency at the same time?

📖 Further reading

A challenging overview of exchange rate developments and theory is provided in M. Obstfeld, *International Currency Experience: New lessons and lessons relearned*. The *Brookings Papers on Economic Activity*, No. 1 (1995), p. 135. A more recent review is M. Mussa *et al.*, 'Exchange Rate Regimes in an increasingly integrated world economy', IMF Occasional Paper, No. 193 (Washington DC, August 2000). See OECD, *EMU: One year on* (Paris, 2000) for an assessment of the euro.

The literature on EMU ranges from the upbeat *One Market, One Money*, published by the European Commission in *European Economy* (October 1990) to the sharply critical analysis of Bernard Connolly, *The Rotten Heart of Europe* (London: Faber & Faber, 1995). P. de Grauwe, *The Economics of Monetary*

Integration (Oxford: Oxford University Press, 4th edn, 2000), provides a well-balanced, analytical assessment of costs, benefits and transition problems. *The National Institute Economic Review* has published an ongoing commentary on EMU, which provides objective insight into the UK perspective on this issue. For a detailed analysis of anchor currencies and the potential of the euro to fulfil this role, see P. Honohan and P. Lane, 'Pegging to the dollar and the euro', *International Finance* (Autumn 1999) and R.N. Cooper, 'Key currencies after the euro', *The World Economy* (January 1999).

Appendix 22.1: Exchange rate regimes – a brief history

International trade requires an efficient system of international payment. At one time, trade was settled via direct barter. When some commodities, particularly metals, became generally acceptable as a means of payment throughout the world, barter was replaced by the monetary system. This appendix looks at the evolution of the monetary system from the first gold standard to the present global exchange rate system.[24]

The gold standard

Gold has been used as a means of payment for domestic and international trade since ancient times. However, until the 1870s, gold and silver coexisted as the main monetary metals. These circulated alongside bank notes, which were backed by gold or silver. Gradually, the bimetallic standard began to disappear, as gold coins drove silver coins from circulation. The UK was the first country to adopt a gold standard when, in 1819, the Bank of England was legally required to exchange currency for gold on demand. During the 1870s, most European countries, Japan and the US moved towards the gold standard, and by 1879 the gold standard had evolved from a domestic standard to an international monetary system. The UK, with its highly developed financial institutions and its dominant role in international trade, became the centre of the international financial system built on the gold standard.

The system was based on four main principles:

1. The gold standard was a *fixed* exchange rate regime. Each country set a fixed price for gold in terms of its currency, at which it stood ready to buy or sell. The relative gold values of any two currencies gave their mint parity exchange rate.
2. At that price, gold was *convertible* into currency and currency into gold.
3. Exports and imports of gold were allowed to flow freely from one country to another. This facilitated the development of highly integrated goods and capital markets.
4. Central banks were obliged to back the issue of money notes with gold reserves. This rule imposed monetary restraint by limiting the authorities' ability to print money. Thus the gold standard promoted price stability.

---

24 For a comprehensive historical analysis of the international monetary system, see H.G. Grubel, *The International Monetary System* (Harmondsworth: Penguin Books, 4th edn, 1984).

The system also provided an automatic adjustment mechanism, through which balance of payments disequilibria would be eliminated. This process is known as Hume's *price-specie-flow* mechanism. Gold flowed out of a country running a trade deficit (excess imports had to be paid for) and flowed into a country with a trade surplus. Thus, a trade deficit implied a shrinking money supply, and a trade surplus an expanding money supply. The declining money supply in the deficit country placed downward pressure on prices, increasing competitiveness in international markets and eliminating the trade deficit. Likewise, the gold inflow as a result of the trade surplus increased the domestic money supply and led to inflation. The rising price of domestic goods reduced competitiveness, eliminating the surplus. Thus, trade balance was restored. Capital movements could also play a role in the adjustment process. The decline in money supply in the deficit country would place upward pressure on interest rates, leading to a capital inflow which offset the initial gold outflow. Similarly, capital outflows associated with lower interest rates in the surplus country offset the initial gold inflow. Provided capital was sufficiently interest-sensitive, the two countries could continue to run a current account imbalance.

The inter-war period

With the outbreak of the First World War, many countries suspended the convertibility of their currency into gold. The system of fixed exchange rates was replaced by a floating rate system. As governments financed their military build-up through monetary expansion, inflation accelerated. Inflation was higher in Europe than in the US. US trade expanded rapidly, and the dollar was increasingly used to finance international transactions. After the war, the European countries continued to float their currencies, and most depreciated rapidly relative to the dollar. The pound sterling fell to a low of $3.40 per pound in 1920. The depreciation of sterling and fear of consequent inflation caused the UK Chancellor of the Exchequer, Winston Churchill, to seek a return to the gold standard in 1925 at the pre-war parity of $4.86.[25] Most other currencies had followed by 1927.

However, the system proved impossible to sustain for a variety of reasons. First, many countries continued to restrict inter-country gold flows in order to alleviate their balance of payments problems. New controls on inflows and outflows of gold seriously limited the effectiveness of the automatic adjustment mechanism. Adjustment problems were further exacerbated by the downward inflexibility of domestic prices. In addition, many central banks no longer retained the bulk of their reserves in gold but kept them in currencies convertible to gold. Thus the gold standard was effectively transformed into a *gold exchange standard*. Second, the Great Depression of 1929 led to a collapse of banking systems around the world, and confidence in the convertibility of currencies collapsed.

The UK abandoned convertibility in 1931, and other countries followed suit. The world monetary system disintegrated into currency blocs, of which the

---

25 See J.M. Keynes, 'The economic consequences of Mr. Churchill', *Essays in Persuasion* (New York: Norton, 1931).

sterling area (the UK and most of the Commonwealth) and the US dollar bloc were the most important. Some currencies floated freely. The depression worsened, reserve levels were eroded and there was a rise in protectionism. International trade and finance effectively collapsed. The resultant economic lessons were so severe that the prevention of such a situation became the primary aim of postwar policy-makers.

The Bretton Woods system

In July 1944, representatives of 44 countries met in Bretton Woods, New Hampshire, with the objective of re-establishing a workable monetary system. The negotiations culminated in the establishment of the International Monetary Fund (IMF), which was intended to police a system of exchange rates known as the Bretton Woods system. The Bretton Woods system worked on a gold exchange standard, whereby countries had fixed exchange rates against the US dollar, and the price of the dollar was fixed in terms of gold (at $35 per ounce).

Like the gold standard, the Bretton Woods system was based on the principles of *fixed exchange rates* and *convertibility*. Convertibility is a term which may be used in two different contexts: convertibility into gold and convertibility into other currencies. Only the US maintained gold convertibility during the Bretton Woods era, but the agreement specified that member countries' currencies would be convertible into other members' currencies at fixed rates. The US and Canadian dollars became convertible in 1945, but it took another decade before convertibility was restored to most of the war-torn European countries. The Bretton Woods system only became fully operational in the late 1950s. The early convertibility of the US dollar, combined with its anchor position in the Bretton Woods system and its rising economic and political power during the inter-war period, made it the key global currency of the postwar period. Most European countries were willing to accept US dollars in payment for goods and services.

As far as fixity of exchange rates was concerned, the par values of any two currencies expressed in terms of US dollars (or gold) gave their official exchange rate or parity. For example, in 1946, the pound sterling was valued at 3.6 g of fine gold or $4.03. The French franc was valued at 0.75 g of fine gold or $0.84. Thus the official pound sterling/French franc exchange rate was £1:FF 4.8. Exchange rate fluctuations were limited to a narrow band (+/− 1 per cent) around this official exchange rate. Monetary authorities were obligated to intervene in the foreign exchange market to ensure that the exchange rate stayed within this band.

Provision was made for realignment in cases of 'fundamental disequilibrium', defined by reference to chronic and persistent balance of payments difficulties. Realignments of less than 10 per cent were left to the country's own initiative; those of 10 per cent or more were subject to the approval of the IMF. Thus the Bretton Woods system did not irrevocably fix exchange rates; rather it was an *adjustable peg* system. An inherent weakness in the system was that much-needed adjustments were often delayed, with resultant bouts of heavy currency speculation and depletion of a country's reserves in the run-up to a devaluation. In addition, while deficit countries were forced to devalue, surplus countries played little or no role in the adjustment process. (This was known as the asymmetry problem.)

The breakdown of the Bretton Woods system

The Bretton Woods system depended critically on confidence in its anchor currency – the US dollar. In the late 1960s, US public expenditure arising from the war in Vietnam and new domestic social programmes led to growing balance of payments and budget deficits. The US current account, for long in surplus, recorded a deficit in 1969. Two years later, a trade deficit of $2.7 billion appeared for the first time this century. US inflation rose, leaving the dollar more and more overvalued relative to other currencies (particularly the strong Deutschmark and yen) and pushing up the prices of all goods except gold (its price being fixed at $35 per ounce). By the mid-1960s, the growth in dollar reserves held abroad and the steady depletion of US gold reserves began to undermine international confidence that the US could sustain sales of gold for dollars.[26] At the same time, the dominance of the dollar was being challenged by the resurgence of the European economies and Japan. The parities established under the Bretton Woods system (including the price of gold) had become seriously out of line with reality.

International tension increased. As early as 1965, the French President de Gaulle protested about the ability of the US to finance its expenditure through seigniorage (i.e. the power to finance its budget deficit by printing dollars – a *'privilège exorbitant'* available only to the US by virtue of the dollar–gold link), and France began an elaborate programme of building up its gold reserves by swapping dollars for gold. In 1968, a two-tier gold market was created, with official transactions between central banks still at $35 per ounce, and private market transactions at a substantially higher price as determined by supply and demand. However, the speculative run on the dollar soon became unsustainable. The system finally broke down when President Nixon was forced to sever the gold–dollar link in 1971. Later that year, there was an attempt to return to fixed exchange rates known as the Smithsonian Agreement, which increased the dollar price of gold and set new parities for other currencies in terms of the dollar. This arrangement was effectively abandoned in 1973.

The floating rate era

After the demise of the Bretton Woods system, most countries adopted floating exchange rates. Although this was viewed as a temporary measure at the time, the international monetary system has been characterised by floating to a more or less managed degree by most of the major currencies ever since. This 'non-system' of managed floating is neither universal nor stable. While most industrial countries allow their currency to float, other currencies are pegged to an anchor currency or a basket of currencies. Still others, notably the euro countries, have attempted to

---

26 See R. Triffin, *Gold and the Dollar Crisis: The future of convertibility* (New Haven, CT: Yale University Press, 1957).

create their own monetary sub-systems. Many countries have experimented with a number of different variants of a managed float since the demise of Bretton Woods. However, it is worthwhile remembering that the current non-system has remained in place for almost as long as the Bretton Woods system which preceded it. Its durability is primarily a result of its flexibility. Each country can choose that regime which best suits its individual circumstances.

Although most central banks still hold some gold reserves, gold transactions have been largely discontinued. SDRs play a minor role, and the IMF retains a surveillance role, whereby it monitors the performance of individual countries and provides them with advice. However, there is no international body with effective control over exchange rates. The US dollar remains the most widely used international currency; but the euro may in time prove a sturdy competitor.

The post-Bretton Woods period has seen an explosion in foreign exchange market activity, brought about by the removal of capital controls, technological advance and the increased internationalisation of business activity. It has also been characterised by considerable volatility in foreign exchange markets. This has caused discomfort, and prompted calls for reform of the system, particularly in the aftermath of the periodic currency crises of the 1990s. But there is no consensus about what sort of reforms are needed. Some argue for restrictions on capital flows; others want fewer restrictions but better surveillance of governments' domestic policies and more focused assistance from international bodies such as the IMF and the World Bank. At the time of writing, the latter policy approach appears much the more promising. Scepticism about the suitability of a universal fixed exchange rate regime to the modern global economy prevails.

INDEX